COMPETITIVE EMPLOYMENT ISSUES AND STRATEGIES

COMPETITIVE EMPLOYMENT ISSUES AND STRATEGIES

Edited by

Frank R. Rusch, Ph.D.
Professor of Special Education
College of Education
University of Illinois at Urbana-Champaign

·P·A·U·L·H·
BROOKES
PUBLISHING C?

Baltimore • London

Paul H. Brookes Publishing Co.
Post Office Box 10624
Baltimore, Maryland 21285

Copyright © 1986 by Paul H. Brookes Publishing Co., Inc.
All rights reserved.

Typeset by Brushwood Graphics Studio, Baltimore, Maryland.
Manufactured in the United States of America by
The Maple Press Company, York, Pennsylvania.

Library of Congress Cataloging-in-Publication Data
Competitive employment issues and strategies.

  Bibliography: p.
  Includes index.
  1. Handicapped—Employment—United States—Addresses, essays,
lectures. 2. Vocational rehabilitation—United States—Addresses, essays, lectures.
I. Rusch, Frank R.
HD7256.U5C4655 1986   362'.0425   85-30929
ISBN 0-933716-59-1 (hc.)

Contents

Contributors

Martin Agran, Ph.D.
Department of Special Education
Utah State University
Logan, UT 84322-6500

Paul E. Bates, Ph.D.
Department of Special Education
Southern Illinois University
Carbondale, IL 62901

G. Thomas Bellamy, Ph.D.
Specialized Training Program
Center on Human Development
College of Education
University of Oregon
Eugene, OR 97403

Wendy K. Berg, M.S.
Division of Developmental Disabilities
Department of Pediatrics
University Hospital School
251 Hospital School
University of Iowa
Iowa City, IA 52242

Philip E. Bourbeau, Ph.D.
Follow Through Project
Division of Teacher Education
College of Education
University of Oregon
Eugene, OR 97403

Janis Chadsey-Rusch, Ph.D.
Secondary Transition Intervention Effectiveness
    Institute
College of Education
University of Illinois
Champaign, IL 61820

John P. Dineen, M.A.
CDMRC, WJ-10
University of Washington
Seattle, WA 98195

Denetta L. Dowler, M.A.
Rehabilitation Research and Training Center
806 Allen Hall
P.O. Box 6122
West Virginia University
Morgantown, WV 26506

Robert W. Flexer, Ph.D.
College of Education
Department of Special Education
Kent State University
Kent, Ohio 44242

Laurie H. Ford, M.S.
CDMRC, WJ-10
University of Washington
Seattle, WA 98195

John L. Gifford, Ph.D.
Secondary Transition Intervention Effectiveness
    Institute
College of Education
University of Illinois
and Developmental Services Center
Champaign, IL 61820

Sue Hamre-Nietupski, Ph.D.
Department of Special Education
University of Northern Iowa
Cedar Falls, IA 50614

Robert H. Horner, Ph.D.
Division of Special Education and Rehabilitation
Room 135, College of Education
University of Oregon
Eugene, OR 97403

Cheryl Hanley-Maxwell, Ph.D.
Department of Special Education
College of Education
University of Illinois
Champaign, IL 61820

Orv C. Karan, Ph.D.
Research and Training Center on Community
    Integration for the Mentally Retarded
Harry A. Waisman Center on Mental Retardation
    and Human Development
1500 Highland Avenue
University of Wisconsin
Madison, WI 53705-2280

Catherine Berger Knight, Ph.D.
Research and Training Center on Community
    Integration for the Mentally Retarded
Harry A.Waisman Center on Mental Retardation
    and Human Development
1500 Highland Avenue
University of Wisconsin
Madison, WI 53705-2280

Thomas R. Lagomarcino, M.Ed.
Department of Special Education
College of Education
University of Illinois
Champaign, IL 61820

David M. Mank, Ph.D.
Specialized Training Program
Center on Human Development
College of Education
University of Oregon
Eugene, OR 97403

James E. Martin, Ph.D.
Department of Special Education
School of Education
Austin Bluff Parkway
University of Colorado
Colorado Springs, CO 80907

Johnny L. Matson, Ph.D.
Department of Psychology
Louisiana State University
Baton Rouge, LA 70803

Dennis E. Mithaug, Ph.D.
Dean and Professor of Special Education
School of Education
University of Colorado
P.O. Box 7150
Colorado Springs, CO 80933-7150

James W. Moss, Ph.D.
CDMRC, WJ-10
University of Washington
Seattle, WA 98195

John Nietupski, Ph.D.
Department of Special Education
University of Northern Iowa
Cedar Falls, IA 50614

Ernest L. Pancsofar, Ph.D.
Department of Special Education
Bowling Green State University
Bowling Green, OH 43404

Adelle Renzaglia, Ph.D.
Department of Special Education
College of Education
University of Illinois
Champaign, IL 61820

Larry E. Rhodes, Ph.D.
Specialized Training Program
Center on Human Development
College of Education
University of Oregon
Eugene, OR 97403

Frank R. Rusch, Ph.D.
Director
Secondary Transition Intervention Effectiveness
    Institute
College of Education
University of Illinois
Champaign, IL 61820

Michael S. Shafer, M.S.
Research Associate
Rehabilitation Research and Training Center
1314 West Main Street
Virginia Commonwealth University
Richmond, VA 23284-0001

Robert L. Schalock, Ph.D.
Hastings College and Mid-Nebraska Mental
    Retardation Services
2727 West 2nd Street
Box 1146
Hastings, NE 68901

Richard P. Schutz, Ph.D.
Secondary Transition Intervention Effectiveness
    Institute
College of Education
University of Illinois
Champaign, IL 61820

Susan Stainback, Ed.D.
Department of Special Education
University of Northern Iowa
Cedar Falls, IA 50614

William Stainback, Ed.D.
Department of Special Education
University of Northern Iowa
Cedar Falls, IA 50614

R. Timm Vogelsberg, Ph.D.
Temple University, RA #949
Developmental Disabilities Center
13th and Columbia
Philadelphia, PA 19122

David P. Wacker, Ph.D.
Division of Developmental Disabilities
Department of Pediatrics
University Hospital School
251 Hospital School
University of Iowa
Iowa City, IA 52242

Richard T. Walls, Ph.D.
Rehabilitation Research and Training Center
806 Allen Hall
P.O. Box 6122
West Virginia University
Morgantown, WV 26506

Paul Wehman, Ph.D.
Director, Rehabilitation Research and Training
  Center
Virginia Commonwealth University
Richmond, VA 23284-0001

David M. White, Ph.D.
Institute for Child Behavior and Development
51 Gerty Drive
University of Illinois
Champaign, IL 61820

Richard J. Zawlocki, M.A.
Rehabilitation Research and Training Center
806 Allen Hall
P.O. Box 6122
West Virginia University
Morgantown, WV 26506

Foreword

GROWTH, IN PROGRAM design and in service provision, is the concept behind this book. *Competitive Employment Issues and Strategies* describes programs designed to produce growth of the individual with disabilities. It also chronicles the tremendous growth in the provision of services to adults, youth, and children with disabilities that has occurred during the past 26 years. Growth has not been easy for either the individuals or the service agencies involved.

I have been involved with special education and vocational rehabilitation since 1959. Much of what is considered state-of-the-art in the provision of services today evolved during that period, and my involvement allows me the opportunity to reflect on what I have observed and experienced: Much has changed; yet much has stayed the same.

When I entered the field of special education, persons with sensory disabilities, with physical disabilities, and with mental retardation were the primary groups served by both special education and vocational rehabilitation. Of persons with mental retardation, only those who were labeled "educable" were considered eligible for programs designed to keep them within the mainstream of society. "Trainable" and "custodial" retarded persons were relegated to classes in church basements, sheltered workshops, and residential institutions. At the time, many "educable" retarded persons were also served in residential institutions. The sights and sounds of the large institutions serving in excess of 2,500 persons remain with me today.

When I entered graduate school at the University of Wisconsin–Madison, my classmates and I enrolled in a variety of courses focused on "the mentally retarded." I will never forget our instruction and discussions about those children and youth who were considered to be "trainable" or "custodial" retarded. The common belief system was that these groups were incapable of learning and were better off in sheltered settings. We were also taught that the parents of "educable" students were made uncomfortable by the sight of "trainable" students in the same school where their educable children were enrolled. The presence of the "trainables" made the parents of "educables" reluctant to place their children in special education. Therefore, the practice of educating "trainables" in church basements or other isolated settings was considered to be appropriate, both administratively and programmatically.

Fortunately, times have changed. Only recently, however, has the pace of change accelerated. Research focused on the competitive employment of persons with disabilities was a new frontier in the mid-1960s, and development and implementation of this important concept have taken time. The Vocational Rehabilitation Administration had begun to fund Rehabilitation Research and Training Centers in Mental Retardation, and my colleagues and I at the University of Oregon (where I had moved upon completion of my graduate work) were successful in competing for the third center. One of the early pioneers on the frontier of competitive employment was a young assistant professor, James Crosson.

Crosson was among the first to demonstrate that persons with severe mental retardation could be taught useful vocational skills by employing the principles of applied behavior analysis. Almost simultaneously, another young assistant professor, Marc Gold, was demonstrating the same. From the work of these young men, as well as from that of Nate Azrin, Don Baer, and others, interest in improving the provision of employment-focused training for persons with severe disabilities emerged as a major national effort.

Research Centers at the Universities of Oregon, Washington, Kansas, Wisconsin, Illinois, and Virginia Commonwealth produced increasing amounts of data as well as program recommendations relevant to providing employment training to a variety of persons with disabilities. Simultaneously, principles of applied behavior analysis were refined and expanded, the civil rights movement culminated in pivotal court cases and federal legislation, large custodial residential institutions were viewed for what they were, and the normalization principle was eloquently promulgated by Wolf Wolfensberger and Burton Blatt. Most recently, there has been an increased interest, at the federal level, in supporting research and demonstration projects designed to facilitate the transition of youth with disabilities from school to the world of work. And so growth continues, now at a brisker pace.

Yet, several factors still stand in the way of further progress. Conflicting service agency jurisdictions impede a coordinated effort to assist persons with disabilities, federal regulations encourage dependence rather than independence, the supply of appropriately prepared habilitation specialists is inadequate to meet employment demands, and there are still people who believe that persons with severe disabilities cannot benefit from systematic programs of instruction.

Of ongoing frustration, too, are the many professionals who declare that a given program won't work. Not having seen, with their own eyes, programs in other areas of the country that are successful, these professionals assert that their program and knowledge is best and that other work about which they hear cannot be the same. Such an attitude reflects a parochialism that hinders growth, not only professionally within the human services but for the individual clients as well.

This book provides both the advocates and the nay sayers with a comprehensive review of issues, program models, and instructional strategies relevant to preparing persons with disabilities for competitive employment. The first section of the text presents an interesting introduction to the full topic of competitive employment and particularly to the new concept of *supported work;* it also describes successful models for implementing competitive employment training programs. The second section of the text focuses on methods used to train persons with disabilities for competitive employment. Chapters emphasize assessing work behavior, establishing effective community-based training stations, coordinating service delivery, generalizing and maintaining work behavior, observationally reporting work behavior, analyzing work behavior, identifying potential jobs, developing curricula, and providing for social validation. Each of these chapters not only offers useful guidance but also expands the horizons of future possibilities. The third section focuses on issues related to competitive employment of persons with disabilities. Each of the issues is clearly presented and thoughtfully analyzed.

As I study the changes in program design and delivery that have occurred over the past 26 years, I am pleased by the growth that has taken place. This text is a milestone in reflecting that growth. Yet, the text also underscores that, while significant gains have been made, there is much more ground to cover, and many, many promises to keep.

Herbert J. Prehm, Ph.D.
Assistant Executive Director
The Council for Exceptional Children

Preface

THIS VOLUME IS about employment; its contributors are acknowledged authorities on employment, not only in the United States but also internationally. It has been developed to provide a forum for review of the research in the human services fields that are related to employment services for individuals with handicaps. Such a forum should serve to publicize a data base by which to structure and, eventually, deliver "best practices." Employment "best practices" have advanced so dramatically over the past decade that a text such as this is needed for several reasons. Foremost among these is that, in the field of competitive employment, sufficient progress toward the goal of providing solutions to problems for employees with handicaps (for example, working with co-workers to maintain employment) now enables the *approach to competitive employment* to be distinguished from other approaches to vocational training and employment (see Chapter 1). *Competitive Employment Issues and Strategies* contains an extensive, highly reliable body of behavioral research data that supports an array of effective technological solutions to employment-related problems.

Contributors to this volume have been involved in applied research for a number of years and have attempted to identify ways to improve employment services for adolescents and adults with handicaps. Consequently, they recognize the sociopolitical issues that must be confronted in order to change traditional ideals and services so that equal employment opportunity and participation among persons with disabilities can be fully realized.

Throughout this text, terms such as *persons with disabilities, persons with handicaps,* or *persons with mental retardation* are used. The text embraces all individuals with disabilities, handicaps, mental retardation, severe handicaps/disabilities, or other conditions who are distinguished by their absence in the workplace. The vast majority of persons with disabilities are either underemployed or unemployed, and individuals with severe disabilities are virtually excluded from active participation in community living. Therefore, existing employment-oriented services must be restructured to encompass the goals of persons with disabilities to achieve full participation in communities, and to earn a wage in integrated settings that produce goods and services valued by society.

As the title reflects, the primary emphasis of this text is on issues and strategies in competitive employment. The issues presented are not unique to one disability group, but apply to all persons with disabilities. Similarly, the strategies outlined in the 11 chapters constituting Section II have proven effective with persons demonstrating diverse disabilities. The most significant contribution of this text is its focus upon strategies for creating service options that should be universally accessible to anyone who wishes to be meaningfully employed.

Three broad options are available to persons with disabilities who are making the transition from school to work, or from unemployment/underemployment to competitive employment. These include: 1) no special services, 2) time-limited services, and 3) ongoing services (Will, 1984). Typically, the person who requires *no special services* relies upon his or her own resources to obtain employment, or upon services that are generally available to everyone, such as trade schools and community colleges. As the term implies, *time-limited services* refer to services that are offered temporarily for short periods of time to persons with disabilities, such as services provided by state vocational rehabilitation programs. The third service option is geared toward individuals who require *ongoing support* for the duration of their employment.

A distinction must be made between competitive employment and supported employment. *Competitive employment* refers to integrated work that results in minimum wage or better. While also referring to integrated work, *supported employment* may result in less than a minimum wage, a minimum wage, or more than a minimum wage. The most distinguishing feature between these two employment outcomes is the type of services each requires. The latter assumes that ongoing services are needed for the duration of the employment period, whereas competitive employment assumes that only time-limited services are required to maintain the target employee on the job. This does not preclude providing services throughout the individual's employment. *Time-limited* refers to services offered for discontinuous periods of time versus services offered continuously, as with ongoing services and in supported employment. As implied by its title, this volume focuses on issues and strategies that relate to *competitive employment* for persons who will require time-limited services.

The strategies presented here relate to a new competitive employment model referred to as *supported work,* and must be distinguished from those discussed in Chapter 1 and elsewhere, which have sought a similar outcome, that is, employment. The supported work model is based on the assumption that employment-training programs teach actual job skills, such as how to complete assigned tasks, as well as the social skills needed to interact with co-workers on the job. Furthermore, supported work assumes that job-placement services result in long-term adjustment. Adoption of the proposed model is complicated by numerous obstacles, the most significant of which include continued reliance upon rigidly sequenced curriculum objectives, focusing upon the "world of work" instead of survival skills, and traditional training toward arbitrarily established performance criteria rather than the standards of the work place.

The supported work model incorporates well-planned, systematic processes that lead to competitive employment. Thus, it is based on a community-referenced curriculum that targets skills and behaviors that have been identified by examining *actual* employment settings as opposed to being dictated by convenience, donation of arbitrary equipment, or stereotypic views of what persons with disabilities "should" do. In keeping with this approach, training takes place in actual, not simulated, work settings. By its emphasis on actual community needs, the supported work model challenges traditional training approaches and current administrative guidelines and practices that reduce or prevent meaningful employment of persons with disabilities.

This text is intended for advanced undergraduate and graduate students, researchers, service providers, and others interested in improving employment opportunities and enhancing quality of life for persons with handicaps.

Section I of this volume introduces the concept of competitive employment. Existing obstacles to the adoption of this approach are discussed in Chapter 1. Chapter 1 also describes several models that have developed over the past two decades to alleviate and reduce these obstacles. Chapters 2 through 6 present five model programs that exemplify the supported work model.

Each of these five model-program chapters introduces a different approach to achieving competitive employment. At the same time, however, they share certain features that underlie the supported work model. Paul Wehman's program is university-based and field-based; that is, he has replicated the Virginia Commonwealth University program throughout the state of Virginia. Similarly, Timm Vogelsberg has developed competitive employment opportunities for individuals with handicaps in Vermont. Paul Bates, in turn, has designed public school programs that prepare students for competitive employment in southern Illinois. In Chapter 5, Tom Lagomarcino provides an overview of the efforts of the University of Illinois and a local rehabilitation agency (Developmental Services Center) to develop a supported work program that is administered by the rehabilitation facility. Finally, Chapter 6 presents a university-based, supported work program focused entirely on the food-services industry.

Sections II and III focus upon supported work methodology and issues related to competitive employment. These two sections are introduced by Drs. Robert Horner and John Gifford on pages 89–91 and 235–239, respectively. Section II provides the reader with state-of-the-art practices that result in achievement of more meaningful employment outcomes for persons with disabilities. Section III introduces contemporary issues related to competitive employment.

REFERENCES

Will, M. (1984, June). Bridges from school to working life. *Interchange*, 2–6.

Acknowledgments

THE INDIVIDUALS WHO have contributed to this text deserve special tribute. Their willingness to share knowledge and experience in the area of competitive employment has resulted in a unique volume.

In addition, several individuals who have created opportunities for service providers to develop programs that foster independence among persons with disabilities deserve mention. John Stern, Lee Valenta, and Susie Hubbard deserve much credit for installing competitive employment services throughout the state of Washington. They were very supportive of early competitive employment research and development efforts. Several people in the state of Illinois deserve similar recognition. Carl Suter, Susan Suter, and Bill Murphy have asked important and timely questions related to why social service agencies should continue to waste millions of dollars supporting a statewide delivery system that fosters total dependence. Their collective leadership toward developing new services in Illinois has resulted in consumers and providers challenging the status quo. I am particularly pleased that many people have had the opportunity to work with these leaders.

Not to be overlooked is the Office of Special Education and Rehabilitative Services. Assistant Secretary Madeleine Will and her staff have provided a clearer understanding of why competitive employment is important to persons with disabilities.

Finally, I am indebted to Elton, Eric, Silas, Nancy, Jim, and the countless others who have so willingly allowed me to study short periods of their lives to reach a better understanding of employment.

COMPETITIVE
EMPLOYMENT
ISSUES AND STRATEGIES

SECTION I

COMPETITIVE EMPLOYMENT PROGRAMS

Introduction

Frank R. Rusch

ONE OF THE primary outcomes of education is preparation for adulthood. With adulthood come certain responsibilities and roles that we are all expected to assume. One of these roles is the role of "contributor to society," which can be fulfilled in various ways, including finding and maintaining employment. In addition to its benefit to society, employment is also important to the individual. Through employment we derive monetary rewards that can be used to purchase desired goods and services; employment also provides intangible rewards, such as the opportunity to interact with others, development of self-worth, and a chance to contribute to society (Turkel, 1972). Employment is tantamount to our daily lives because it structures our individual adjustment. Indeed, our residential and recreational opportunities are influenced by our employment status.

Madeleine Will (1984), Assistant Secretary of the Office of Special Education and Rehabilitative Services, has suggested that employment is critical to the lives of most Americans, regardless of whether their work is specialized (e.g., banking, computer science, medicine), entry level (e.g., maid services, janitorial services, food services), or supported (e.g., work crews, enclaves). Will's statement has important implications for persons with handicaps because these individuals are likely to be employed in entry-level or supported employment positions. Unfortunately, prevailing educational and adult services to persons with handicaps have resulted in few employment opportunities for them in this country.

Recently, the United States Commission on Civil Rights (1983) reported that between 50% and 80% of all persons with disabilities are unemployed. These data suggest that a disproportionately large number of disabled persons do not obtain meaningful jobs. Several follow-up studies conducted in Vermont (Hasazi, Preskill, Gordon, & Collins, 1982), Virginia (Wehman, Kregel, & Zoller, 1984), and Colorado (Mithaug & Horiuchi, 1983) reflect similar figures. For example, Wehman et al. (1984) indicated that less than 12% of all severely disabled individuals were employed in Virginia and that all of them were underemployed. Based on these findings it appears that, in spite of considerable recent attention upon elementary and secondary education, meaningful employment outcomes for graduating students who are disabled have not resulted.

Few studies provide longitudinal data on postschool employment of students who are disabled. Mithaug, Horiuchi, and Fanning (1985) reported the results of a statewide follow-up study of special education students in Colorado who graduated from high school in 1978 and 1979. The findings reflected personal interview responses from 234 former students classified as physically disabled, behaviorally disordered, mentally retarded, and learning disabled. The major results of the study suggested that while the participants appeared to have made positive adjustments to their communities with nearly 70% working at least part-time and contributing to their own support, most of the graduates' earnings were at marginal levels, with annual incomes showing little improvement over those reported in follow-up studies conducted decades ago.

Several million individuals in this country, who are currently not given the opportunity to engage in meaningful employment, possess the potential to live and work in the community, if provided with the necessary education. These individuals have been the focus of attention by special educators, vocational educators, and vocational rehabilitation personnel during the past several decades. Unfortunately, those individuals who are mentally retarded, physically disabled, and/or otherwise considered severely disabled have not successfully made the transition to the community. Most of them either work in sheltered settings, are underemployed, or are unemployed and live with family, relatives, friends, or alone, without any hope of participating in their community in the manner in which most nondisabled persons participate.

Overwhelming data suggest that rehabilitation agencies and high schools, the primary vehicles for vocational services to individuals with handicaps, have been ineffective in preparing these students for competitive employment. Bellamy, Sheehan, Horner, and Boles (1980) reported that over 100,000 severely disabled adults are served in rehabilitation day programs that typically lack vocational training and placement opportunities. The average annual earnings of these participants, as estimated by the Department of Labor for work activity centers, is $160 per year (U.S. Department of Labor, 1979).

We are at a crucial point in the education of persons with disabilities. It is time to implement current best practices in order to prepare persons who are handicapped for community integration, particularly if integration includes employment. To date, with a few exceptions, educational best practices related to employment for persons who are severely disabled have not attained a level of universal adoption that results in meaningful outcomes, that is, employment.

All persons with handicaps should be prepared for employment while they are young—between the ages of 13 and 21. This employment preparation must begin in the schools. Furthermore, not only must preparation for employment begin in the schools, school and rehabilitation personnel must assume a leadership role to enhance the meaningful transition of these persons from school to work.

COMPETITIVE EMPLOYMENT PROGRAMS

Recently, the employment situation for persons with handicaps has improved due, primarily, to the development of competitive employment programs (CEPs). These CEPs share the following components:

1. The community is first *surveyed* to identify possible job placements and their associated social and vocational survival skills.
2. *Community-based (nonsheltered) training sites* are established within actual community work settings whereby potential employees (students) are taught to perform the skills necessary for actual employment.
3. Once the individual is trained in the community work setting (i.e., the nonsheltered training site), he or she is *placed into a targeted job*.
4. *Training and long-term follow-up of decreasing intensity* is provided to facilitate maintenance of acquired skills, in addition to training skills unique to the new employment site.

The CEPs that share these common components have been developed as part of high school and rehabilitation programs, and recently have been referred to as the supported work model of competitive employment. The term *supported work* stresses our emerging interest in "supporting" the employment of persons who are handicapped, rather than *placing* these persons into employment and *hoping* that they make the transition. By addressing the transition from school to work or rehabilitation facility to competitive employment, the supported work model offers the advocacy and coordination necessary to provide employment training and, ultimately, community placement and adjustment. The model is relatively new, and the best practices facilitating handicapped individuals' participation in society are still being identified. The purpose of this text is to present to the reader a compilation of information related to the supported work model that will result in large-scale change in the practices being used by special educators, vocational educators, and rehabilitation personnel to support the transition of youth and adults into meaningful employment.

WHY COMPETITIVE EMPLOYMENT?

Compared to sheltered employment, competitive employment offers numerous advantages to persons who are handicapped. Most often, competitive employment involves placement in community-integrated settings in which the employee receives at least minimum wage, interacts with nonhandicapped co-workers, produces valued goods or services, and has opportunities for increased earnings and responsibilities. Sheltered employment, on the other hand, usually entails employment in segregated centers where the employee receives an average hourly wage of 43¢ (U.S. Department of Labor, 1979), has little if any contact with nonhandicapped co-workers, and produces goods of questionable societal and personal value.

The bias underlying this book is the goal of preparing all persons with handicaps for integrated employment. Although the merits of any one training option over another can be argued, we take the position that competitive employment is a more viable option for handicapped persons than ever realized. Recent progress in application of developing behavioral technology has been so encouraging that we need to change our placement goals. No longer do we need to consider exclusively the long-term day care or extended sheltered

employment options for any group of persons. Instead, we are increasingly demonstrating the *employability* of mildly, moderately, and severely handicapped persons, as well as other persons with disabilities. This is the most significant of the employment trends discussed earlier. *Competitive employment,* as the term is used in the remaining chapters of this book, is defined as follows.

DEFINITION

Competitive employment is work that produces valued goods or services at a minimum wage or more, and in a setting that includes non-handicapped workers and provides opportunities for advancement.

Producing Valued Goods or Services

Sheltered workshops typically pay less than minimum wage for work that has little or no social or personal value. Regrettably, these conditions often persist for the lifespan of the workshop "client." If, on the other hand, the purpose of employment is to make money and provide a valued community service, the accomplishments of the employee need to be stressed. In competitive employment, where employees work for the profit or benefit of the employer, competence and contribution are reinforced.

Minimum Wage or More

Most youths entering the job market expect to be working for a minimum wage, or more. By contrast, working for *any* wage is rarely a primary goal for persons who are handicapped. As indicated in a 1979 U.S. Department of Labor study,

> The typical client in the workshop in 1976 was a white, 25-year-old, mentally retarded male who had never married, and who lived in a dependent type living arrangement or group home residence operated by the workshop, or with parents. He worked about 2 hours a week at subcontract work in a work activities center as his first employment experience. His monthly earnings of about $31 were supplemented by public assistance [Supplemental Security Income of $147]. (p. 14)

In the United States, few major public or private efforts have been made to prepare persons with mental retardation, and other persons who are handicapped, for nonsheltered competitive employment. Thus, in spite of a few exemplary research and demonstrations projects, the number of adults who are handicapped and are currently participating in the American work force is low.

Nonhandicapped Co-workers

As we attempt to competitively employ persons with handicaps, we must consider society's values. In the work place nonhandicapped co-workers provide a measure of what should be taught (i.e., survival skills) and how well we should teach them (i.e., determining the range of acceptability). For example, to assure that they remain competitively employed, employees must be taught to perform tasks within tolerable, preestablished industrial norms. Competitive employment focuses on teaching potential employees to work within the boundaries of acceptable work performance while performing valued services, as well as teaching co-workers the value of employees who can be taught to contribute to the overall employment gains of the employer in ways that may depart from traditional values.

Opportunities for Advancement

Performance during competitive employment is often used by employers as a basis for advancing employees. For example, a competent, probationary employee might be advanced to nonprobationary status; a helper may be promoted to laborer; an employee might receive adjusted, incremental pay increases; or a successful employee might have his or her position redesigned to better reflect working conditions.

SUMMARY

Competitive employment is the normal and expected career path for persons who are nonhandicapped. The opportunity to go to work every day and to be part of a work force produces profitable personal and societal outcomes. Although competitive employment may not be a suitable option for everybody, it should be available so that all persons can, to the greatest extent possible, enjoy and engage in work that may result in individual or societal gains. The ability of educators to change their own attitudes and expectations, as well as those of other educators, parents, and employers, remains the major roadblock to competitive employment.

REFERENCES

Bellamy, G. T., Sheehan, M. R., Horner, R. H., & Boles, S. M. (1980). Community programs of severely handicapped adults: An analysis of vocational opportunities. *JASH Review, 5*(4), 307–324.

Hasazi, S., Preskill, H., Gordon, L., & Collins, C. (1982). *Factors associated with the employment status of handicapped youth.* Paper presented at meeting of the American Educational Research Association, New York.

Mithaug, D., & Horiuchi, C. (1983). *Colorado statewide followup survey of special education students.* Denver: Colorado State Department of Education.

Mithaug, D. E., Horiuchi, C. N., & Fanning, P. (1985). A report on the Colorado statewide followup study of special education graduates. *Exceptional Children, 51*(5), 397–404.

Turkel, S. (1972). *Working.* New York: Pantheon.

U.S. Commission on Civil Rights. (1983, September). *Accommodating the spectrum of disabilities.* Washington, DC: U.S. Commission on Civil Rights.

U.S. Department of Labor. (1979, March). *Study of handicapped clients in sheltered workshops* (Vol. II). Washington, DC: U.S. Department of Labor.

Wehman, P., Kregel, J., & Zoller, K. (1984). *A follow-up of mentally retarded graduates' vocational and independent living skills in Virginia.* Manuscript in preparation.

Will, M. (1984, March/April). Bridges from school to working life. *Programs for the Handicapped,* p. 2.

Chapter 1

Obstacles to Competitive Employment and Traditional Program Options for Overcoming Them

Frank R. Rusch, Dennis E. Mithaug, and Robert W. Flexer

EVIDENCE FROM A variety of studies suggests that many persons with handicaps—even severe handicaps—are achieving some degree of independence by earning an income. Yet, the handicapped population continues to be underrepresented in the competitive employment sector. Attainment of full employment potential is hampered by obstacles from a variety of sources, ranging from population characteristics and types of services provided to the state of the economy. Historically, three disciplines (i.e., education, medicine, and psychology) have sought to reduce certain obstacles' influence on employment by developing model programs. The approach taken by these disciplines in developing such models has been influenced by their unique philosophy of treatment, the professional roles for which model originators were educated, and the direct service context for which a given model was designed.

The purpose of this chapter is: 1) to identify and describe existing obstacles to competitive employment and 2) to provide an overview of four well-known program models' provisions for overcoming such obstacles.

OBSTACLES TO COMPETITIVE EMPLOYMENT

Obstacles contributing to underemployment or unemployment of persons with handicaps include: 1) specific employee skill and behavior deficits, 2) deficient assessment and training procedures, 3) disregard for social validation of work goals and procedures, 4) lack of a systematic approach to service delivery, 5) inadequate personnel preparation, and 6) economic and policy considerations deterring efforts to promote competitive employment.

Specific Employee Skill and Behavior Deficits

Persons with handicaps often display behaviors and response deficits that conflict with employer expectations and employment norms. For example, they may have difficulty learning certain jobs, meeting performance and productivity standards, or adapting to varying demands across work settings. Such problems usually involve additional cost for the employer in terms of time or lack of efficiency, hence, they are potential obstacles to com-

petitive employment. In their examination of
the reasons why persons who are labeled mentally retarded lose their jobs, Greenspan and
Shoultz (1981) distinguished between *social*
and *nonsocial* factors. Included in the social
category were behaviors such as aggressiveness, stealing, emotional outbursts, verbal
abuse, and lack of social awareness (e.g.,
repeating oneself, excessive inquisitiveness).
In addition, being perceived as different from
nonhandicapped peers in appearance (i.e.,
clothing selection, grooming, cosmetic use)
also reduced acceptance and increased the likelihood of job termination. *Nonsocial* reasons
were represented by inadequate productivity,
lack of spontaneous initiation of appropriate
tasks, deficits in maintenance and generalization of acquired skills, lack of a work ethic, and
health problems.

Productivity has repeatedly been identified
in the employment literature as a factor associated with job success (Brickey, Browning, &
Campbell, 1982; Hill & Wehman, 1979;
Kochany & Keller, 1981; Schalock & Harper,
1978; Sowers, Thompson, & Connis, 1979).
For example, Brickey et al. (1982) found that
the reason most often cited for job failure was
slow performance; out of 29 responses given
by employers for terminations, the greatest
number (12) was for slow performance in completing tasks. When examining the reasons for
dismissal of workers who are handicapped,
Rusch, Martin, Lagomarcino, and White (1983)
found that termination resulted primarily from
inadequate productivity. Hill and Wehman's
(1979) survey of supervisors and co-workers
revealed that two major problems presented by
employees with handicaps included: 1) slow
work performance and 2) inability to change
routine. Similarly, Kochany and Keller (1981)
suggested that insufficient work speed and
failure to change tasks constitute problem areas
for this group of employees.

In contrast to the findings of Brickey et al.
(1982) and Rusch et al. (1983), Greenspan and
Shoultz (1981) reported that out of 30 workers,
17 lost their jobs because of lack of social
skills. Of the 17 workers fired for social reasons, five lost their jobs primarily because of

temperament (i.e., emotional disturbances),
three for character-related reasons (i.e., anti-
social or irresponsible behavior), and nine for
lack of social awareness (i.e., failure to understand the subtle norms of the work place).
Assessment of the evidence concerning causes
of terminations suggests that lack of productivity and various social factors constitute important obstacles to continued competitive employment for workers who are disabled.

Deficient Assessment and Training Procedures

One of the most difficult problems facing employment trainers relates to a lack of information about what skills and behaviors to train.
We assume that each client has unique needs
and abilities and try to develop his or her
program accordingly. In these efforts, we look
to the available assessment instruments to provide us with the appropriate directions. Unfortunately, the instruments frequently used to
identify client needs tell us little about employment prerequisites. For example, the assessment tools that are based on the psychological measurement approach are of little
value in identifying adult training needs (Menchetti, Rusch, & Owens, 1983). Furthermore,
motor-measurement and work-sample approaches to assessment overlook the need to
consider other behaviors that are equally predictive of success (e.g., interpersonal skills,
grooming). In addition, long-term employment objectives expressed as *work readiness*
tend to impede the development of adaptive
work skills because they are so vaguely
defined.

As a result, the dominance of psychological
testing must be replaced with community-
referenced assessment procedures that identify
socially valid criteria for survival and then
assess the client on these criteria. Examples of
this type of assessment tool include the *Prevocational Assessment and Curriculum Guide*
(Mithaug, Mar, & Stewart, 1978) and the *Vocational Assessment and Curriculum Guide*
(Rusch, Schutz, Mithaug, Stewart, & Mar,
1982), both of which are based on items derived from employer expectations.

The failure of employees to demonstrate appropriate production and social skills may be attributed in part to deficiencies in employment training procedures. Transition to competitive employment is often hindered by training personnel who lack knowledge of what skills should be trained, how best to train such skills, and how most effectively to structure programs to facilitate placement in competitive settings (Gold, 1975; Pomerantz & Marholin, 1977; Rusch, 1983). Training for competitive employment is conducted primarily in sheltered workshops, where the typical training method—supervision accompanied by vague instructions and occasional prompts to stay on task—encourages dependence upon sheltered placement and emphasizes working on overly simplified tasks, rather than developing longitudinal employment objectives (Gold, 1973, 1975; Martin, 1980). Specifically, in addition to nonfunctional assessment tools (Menchetti et al., 1984), vocational training procedures have suffered from vague training of attitudes rather than specific work skills, and a lack of explicit maintenance and generalization training (Rusch & Mithaug, 1980).

Finally, one of the greatest impediments to successful competitive employment is insufficient training focusing on generalization of newly acquired skills across tasks, settings, persons, and time. To date, behavioral research has paid little attention to this problem, focusing instead almost exclusively upon changing behavior in treatment settings (Gardner, 1971; Koegel & Rincover, 1977; McNamara & McDonough, 1972; Rusch, Schutz, & Heal, 1983). Taken together, inappropriate test instruments, lack of specificity in training objectives, and failure to train for results beyond the immediate setting exemplify a pattern of training procedures that has frustrated, rather than facilitated, the goal of competitive employment.

Disregard for Social Validation of Work Goals and Procedures

Inadequate training procedures contribute considerably to the employee skill deficits identified earlier. Yet, lack of a socially validated curriculum may hinder job success even more. *Social validation* refers to methodology that considers the social treatment context in evaluating community expectations and satisfaction (Wolf, 1978). As such, social validation combines the basic needs of target individuals and the expectations of employers, co-workers, family members, advocates, and other significant persons in developing curriculum and intervention priorities. A disregard for social validation of work goals and performance can result in workers being perceived as successful by community trainers while being terminated from their jobs by employers who perceive them otherwise. (The reader is referred to Chapter 15 for a discussion of social validation.)

Few training programs gather normative data on nonhandicapped co-worker behavior. Yet, such data may provide social validation for the *focus of treatment* (i.e., whether a given behavior is critical to successful placement) and for the *intervention effect* (i.e., the acceptable performance level for that behavior) (Rusch, Chadsey-Rusch, White, & Gifford, 1985). Until perspectives other than just those of change agents (e.g., placement coordinators) are considered, many employees will be trained according to curricula with goals that do not match the realities of the work place.

Two procedures have been used to evaluate the social validity of focus of treatment and intervention effect: social comparison and subjective evaluation. *Social comparison* involves comparing a target employee's behavior before and after training with similar behavior of successful co-workers (i.e., co-workers whose performance meets the employer expectations). Based on this model, social validation is demonstrated when, after training, the target behavior is at least as valued as the corresponding behavior of the valued co-worker. Using *subjective evaluation,* the target behavior is evaluated by experts or significant others with whom the employee has contact (e.g., supervisors, co-workers) in order to verify that change resulting from training is perceived as important.

Successful competitive employment requires that trained employees display a variety of valued behaviors not only in the work place but also outside the job, for example, in such areas as mobility, domestic ability, self-care, money and time management, and telephone use (i.e., survival skills). Gross behavioral deficits or excesses, including bizarre or self-destructive behavior must also be eliminated in order for persons with disabilities to gain access to integrated settings. However, behavior and behavior problems vary across individuals as do reactions of others in various settings. Behavior and the uniqueness of persons as they interact with their environments require a highly parochial view in employment training. Social validation of treatment focus has obvious importance for competitive employment by using problem identification as a way of removing obstacles to successful employment.

Social validation of intervention programs is important to the successful integration of persons with handicaps into our communities. Subjective evaluations and social comparisons are necessary for incorporating all community members as collaborators in behavior change leading to employment integration. Not only can their opinions be referenced with respect to shared interests and expectations, but sometimes significant others can be involved directly in behavior-change efforts. (The reader is referred to Chapter 16 for a discussion of co-workers' roles.)

Lack of Systematic Approach to Service Delivery

Even if training practices resulted in successful worker placement, a major obstacle remains: the lack of a systemic approach to service delivery. As Magrab and Elder (1979) stated:

> The service delivery system . . . in the United States is really a series of fragmented service delivery systems in the area of community and social services, education, vocational rehabilitation, and health delivery. Each of these systems was developed independently in response to needs within each of these areas over the past decades. (p. x)

Reasons for the current fragmented and duplicative service structure, as cited by Schalock (1983), include: 1) overlapping legislation and

lack of a clear national policy, 2) multiple funding sources without financial coordination, 3) multiple planning bodies and inadequate control and responsibility, and 4) competition among service providers for resources. A similar list of problems has been enumerated in relation to services for adult day and work programs (Bellamy, Sheehan, Horner, & Boles, 1980). Although federal and state agencies responsible for support and direction of government services have attempted to improve current practices, many problems remain to be solved, for example, discontinued service as a result of the mismatch between the goals of public schools and those of adult service programs.

Uncoordinated efforts between and within the major components of the service system are also reflective of the inconsistent nature of vocational education programs. Among the major impediments to attainment of successful competitive placements of individuals, Phelps and Thornton (1979) identified not only a lack of interagency cooperation, but also the failure of service agencies to involve employers, labor organizations, and business and industry organizations in the vocational training process. Without the cooperation of local businesses and industry in assessment, placement, and on-site training, the success of vocational training programs is seriously jeopardized.

The lack of a systematic service delivery approach probably produces the greatest harm to individual trainees. For persons with significant habilitative needs who will require services over extended periods of time, total habilitation planning is necessary for positive outcomes. Therefore, services must be provided in numerous settings, and interactions among and between residential, employment, and leisure and recreational environments are essential. To achieve these goals, multiple agencies must work in synchrony. Yet, such cooperation for the benefit of the person who is handicapped is difficult in the absence of effective case management models. Failure to practice systemic case management planning can result in cross-system interference; for example, psychotropic medication administered in residential settings can adversely affect employment competencies (Agran & Martin, 1982). In working toward the enhancement and competence of those whom they are charged to serve, local service providers may have to fight interagency rivalry and differences in service philosophy and delivery. (The reader is referred to Chapter 9 for a discussion of interagency collaboration.)

Inadequate Personnel Preparation

Another employment obstacle is inadequate personnel preparation programs. Special vocational curricula, as well as programs focusing upon adult needs, are underrepresented in university and other training programs. Recruitment, training, and professionalization problems related to staffing of adult vocational programs are illustrated by the lack of specifically trained staff in these agencies as well as the need for training perceived by persons currently filling staff roles (Vogelsberg, Williams, & Friedl, 1980). Universities are lagging behind in preparing professionals for adult service staff roles. Historically, programs training personnel who staff adult and vocational programs have represented one discipline, such as special education, to the exclusion of vocational education or vocational rehabilitation. To date, inservice efforts by universities and agencies to instill cross-disciplinary training have met with little success (Phelps & Thornton, 1979).

Future personnel preparation efforts must focus on training *integrators of service;* that is, effective professionals cannot confine themselves to their own instructional program role, agency, and discipline (Sailor & Guess, 1983). Obtaining adequate services for consumers who are disabled (i.e., ensuring that all parts of the system work for the benefit of the consumer in order to increase his or her participation in community and work life) requires stamina and aggressiveness. Therefore, professionals being trained for this difficult role must be provided with a sound philosophical base in addition to advocacy skills. Existing service delivery obstacles will remain until personnel preparation programs incorporate best practices in training

endeavors, providing a broadened perspective of the full support network available. (The reader is referred to Chapter 22 for a more thorough discussion of personnel preparation issues.)

Economic and Policy Considerations Deterring Competitive Employment

A final area that impinges upon competitive placement success relates to economic and policy considerations. For example, a depressed economy that reduces the number of available jobs increases competition between handicapped and nonhandicapped workers, usually to the disadvantage of the former group of employees. Another economic obstacle is the real or imagined fear that competitive employment for handicapped individuals will result in ineligibility for public support funds (Wysocki & Wysocki, 1979). In many instances, it is in the individual's best financial interest to remain dependent upon public welfare. Paradoxically, funding for community-based residential facilities, including attendant care, medical services, and funds for personal needs, continues to be available only to individuals who have been labeled *inconsequential producers*. Thus, if inconsequential producers prove themselves capable of productive work by demonstrating social or vocational competence, they become ineligible for Title XX and, consequently, Title XIX funds of the Social Security Act (PL 92-323). (The reader is referred to Chapter 23 for an indepth treatment of these issues.)

Such disincentives for competitive employment at the individual level are often matched by disincentives at the program level. Funding to service agencies is often based on the number of participants in a program rather than qualitative changes in the population served (Pomerantz & Marholin, 1977). Furthermore, entitlement programs (e.g., Title XIX, Title XX) are founded on the assumption that individuals with handicaps cannot benefit from traditional services or even extended sheltered employment opportunities offered in sheltered workshop programs, hence the development of work activity programs. Rules and regulations governing work activity programs require that, to be eligible for income maintenance (SSI), individuals must be incapable of productive employment. Inability to work also entitles these individuals to the Title XIX Medicaid program. In short, by being unresponsive to best employment training practices, policy often prevents employers and prospective employees from benefiting from the most effective habilitation programs.

Summary

The preceding section discusses several obstacles that separately and collectively dramatically influence our ability to serve the employment needs of individuals with handicaps. Historically, each of these obstacles has influenced efforts of distinct disciplines toward meeting employment needs. The following section gives an overview of the contribution of each of these disciplines to the development of well-known models designed to prepare persons with handicaps for maximum employment.

PROGRAM MODELS

Four models for employment preparation are currently used to serve the needs of persons with handicaps: 1) special education work experience, 2) vocational education, 3) career education, and 4) vocational rehabilitation. To facilitate an understanding of the relationships among program models, the models are discussed in terms of their philosophical, professional, and direct service roots. Final sections address the potential shortcomings in overcoming competitive employment obstacles.

Contributions to Model Development

A distinct philosophy guides each model's goals, objectives, and program structures. Although the source of specific philosophies is often difficult to determine, educational, psychological, medical, and training orientations comprise some of the major influences on current employment models. In many cases, these orientations have not only had a direct impact on the models, but have exerted indirect

influence through the professional preparation of program staff and the context in which program services are delivered.

Program philsophy based on an educational orientation emphasizes curriculum, instructional techniques, and classroom management, whereas the psychological approach stresses mental testing, developmental progressions, and behavior modification (Kauffman & Hallahan, 1981; Wolfensberger, 1972). The medical orientation, in turn, is characterized by its conceptualization of treatment as a means of curing a sickness. Consequently, medical interventions are applied to the passively ill person to cure identifiable pathologies whereupon the individual is no longer sick (Wolfensberger, 1972). Finally, the focus of the training model is similar to that of the educational model except that its objectives tend to be narrower, more specific, and more practical (Landy & Trumbo, 1980).

The specific discipline in which model originators are trained and the direct context in which services are provided further mold specific program models. For example, special education preparation has been influenced by the mental testing and developmental progression approaches contributed by psychology as well as curriculum and instructional techniques derived from general education. In addition, special education training includes a data-based approach attributable to an emphasis on research and innovative best practices espoused by early departments of special education (Lilly, 1979).

In contrast to special education, professional preparation in rehabilitation services and vocational education has been influenced more by the day-to-day realities of placing individuals in jobs and considering placement from the employer's viewpoint. This contrast is reflected in variations in underlying philosophies. Historically, rehabilitation services have primarily focused on fusing the medical model with a training approach. For example, short-term services are provided to overcome handicaps to employment, and methods of placement rely on available industry-based training approaches used with nonhandicapped employees. Vocational education, in turn, has been influenced by the educational orientation of providing general preparation and adaptation competencies while taking into account the job skills that need to be trained for the targeted employment situation. Consequently, standardized, industry-based curricula are coupled with stringent entrance and exit criteria to ensure homogeneous outputs.

The development of the four employment training models (work experience, vocational education, career education, and vocational rehabilitation) can be traced to the disciplines of education, psychology, and medicine, which, in turn, influence preparation of vocational professionals. Work experience is the result of efforts by special educators to improve the job opportunities of special education students. The vocational education model emanated from the secondary school's attempts to provide job-related training for non-handicapped students planning to enter the labor force directly upon graduation from school. Career education, as applied to programming for handicapped students, reflects the combined efforts of special education, regular education, and vocational education. Finally, the rehabilitation model represents the approach used by counselors whose original focus was to rehabilitate disabled workers previously employed in competitive industry.

Special Education Work Experience

The major structure for the special education work experience model has been the work-study program that combines the efforts of special education and rehabilitation services. Within this administrative arrangement, counting teacher salary as state matching for federal rehabilitation funds is justified through role reassignment, whereby the teacher/coordinator conducts a work experience program. Fiscally, the match generates additional case service dollars for the high school handicapped population. The curriculum combines part-time instruction by the school and work placements of varying length in which the primary emphasis is on learning how to work through exposure rather than instruction.

The work experience program originated from model projects of the 1950s and 1960s, which demonstrated that mentally retarded students receiving work experiences during their school years were more likely to find employment after school than those completing a predominantly academic course of study. In the last decades, work experience programs have developed to include several common components, for example: 1) classroom simulations in which students perform craft assembly activities and learn such prevocational skills as punctuality and attendance; 2) in-school work experiences during which students work from 1 to 3 hours a day in a job within the school setting; 3) vocational assessment conducted in the school district's evaluation center to determine students' work adjustment, manual dexterity, and vocational aptitudes and interests; 4) off-campus work experiences in which students spend half-days or less on academic work and job-related academics and the other half-days to learn on-the-job behaviors and general employability skills; 5) full-day work experiences that are extensions of the half-workday and under the supervision of the teacher, work-study coordinator, and/or the vocational rehabilitation counselor; and 6) postschool job placements that may or may not involve school personnel (Johnson, 1980). Johnson (1980) summarized the advantages and disadvantages of the special education work experience programs:

Advantages
1. Students are provided with exposure to work settings.
2. Work experience programs may allow students to encounter success (sometimes for the first time) in school-related activities.
3. These programs are often highly motivating to students.
4. Work experience programs frequently involve cooperation among several agencies including primarily vocational rehabilitation.
5. Teachers, work-study coordinators, and rehabilitation counselors who are familiar with the students' learning needs provide support and encouragement. This support includes personal/emotional support, counseling, and advocacy for the students.

Disadvantages

1. Because special educators have not generally had either training or experience in a given vocational area, they may not have knowledge of or access to the variety of work settings a vocational educator has (Alley & Deshler, 1979).

2. Emphasis is on general employability skills which may or may not transfer to work settings. This is a particular problem for mentally retarded students who frequently do not learn efficiently through inference and implication and who often demonstrate inefficient transfer skills (Robinson & Robinson, 1975).

3. Jobs selected for students are typically those which the work-study coordinator, teacher, or rehabilitation counselor can "get" rather than jobs directly related to individual student aspirations. A specific training plan is usually not developed.

4. Available jobs are typically those for which little training is required and may be categorized as unskilled or low level semi-skilled. Jobs encountered by handicapped students are typically dead end, of low remunerative value, and may lead to future underemployment, job dissatisfaction, and/or disruptive behavior caused by boredom. (Gold, 1973, p. 19)

According to Halpern (1974), it has been difficult in many work-study programs to shift the instructional emphasis in the school from academic subjects, despite the opinion of participating teachers that employment survival skill training is more important. Moreover, since the curriculum in most programs is not guided by specific regulations, implementation of the work experience component is often inconsistent. Nevertheless, the work-study model has been of benefit primarily to students with mild handicaps by allowing them to practice work support behaviors in multiple work environments, and by providing contact with nonhandicapped persons and locally available work (Bellamy, Rose, Wilson, & Clarke, 1982). Although it is hoped that realistic job experience will enhance employability, the short-term emphasis on rehabilitation and the lack of specificity from a standard industry training approach cannot ensure that needed employment skills are taught, or deal with the logistics of out-of-school work placements. Results from the Colorado statewide follow-up

study of special education students graduating from school in 1978 and 1979 confirmed this view (i.e., that work-study programs are less than helpful) (Mithaug, Horiuchi, & Fanning, 1985). For example, most (72%) of the 234 respondents indicated that work-study teachers were not helpful in preparing them for the future. Items related to vocational education teachers received similar responses, with 61% of the respondents indicating that they were not helpful. By contrast, the efforts of special education teachers received positive responses, with 72% of the participants indicating that they were helpful (Mithaug et al., 1985).

Vocational Education

Vocational education programs, typically available for regular education students in the secondary grades, are also available to special education students on a selective basis. The purpose of vocational education courses is to provide students with the worker attitudes, skills, and behaviors that are important for entry into a specific industry in the community. Vocational education enhances worker productivity while meeting the labor market demands of business and industry. Since the 1960s federal and state legislation has authorized set-aside funds earmarked for the vocational education of handicapped and disadvantaged students.

Vocational education programs offer courses that train students for specific occupational roles such as carpenter, secretary, motel manager, data processor, dental assistant, farmer, cook, or electronics technician, or clusters of closely related occupations such as a secretarial cluster that includes receptionist, typist, general secretary, and officer manager. The particular program of study within a school reflects the local and state labor market supply and demand. The program structure usually consists of a *laboratory class* in which students perform tasks similar to those in a given occupational cluster, and a *related class* in which students learn safety procedures and pertinent concepts and theories concerning the work they are performing (Johnson, 1980).

Vocational education programs offer special education students opportunities to learn valuable skills that will help them secure employment after school. The recent follow-up data provided by Mithaug and his colleagues illustrate the value provided by these programs (Mithaug et al., 1985). As presently structured, vocational education offers a number of programs, as summarized in a review by Johnson (1980):

Advantages

1. Vocational education provides training for [students] in occupational areas for which there is demand in the labor market, as well as assistance in securing employment upon program departure or completion.
2. It assists students in developing specific skills in a work or work-like environment designed to facilitate skill transfer to the work place.
3. It provides relevant and motivating hands-on learning experiences.
4. It prepares students to perform tasks that are relevant to their occupational choice and that are required for successful employment, under the supervision and instruction of an individual experienced in the occupation for which the student is preparing.
5. It provides [students] with leadership development training through participation in regular vocational youth organizations. The emphasis here is on participation of handicapped students, regardless of program placement, in regular youth organizations rather than in separate organizations that exclude nonhandicapped students.
6. It prepares students for occupations that are challenging and remunerative and may enable many handicapped individuals to break the cycles of unemployment and underemployment they frequently experience.

Disadvantages

1. Vocational instructors may feel uncomfortable or negative about working with handicapped students.
2. Vocational instructors may not know how to modify their programs, when necessary, to meet the needs of handicapped students.
3. Technological and industrial changes may make some specific occupations obsolete in the future.
4. General employability skills may receive insufficient emphasis. This is especially critical for youngsters who need highly structured activities through which to acquire these skills.

5. Some programs may not be sufficiently flexible in time or content to accommodate students who cannot master all the occupationally relevant tasks within traditional course or curricula time frames. (p. 20)

This evaluation reflects advocacy of vocational education for all special education students. Access to vocational education by persons who are severely handicapped has yet to be established. Nevertheless, vocational education offers opportunities for this population that should be considered seriously.

Career Education

Career education became a national priority for refocusing educational programming in the early 1970s, and was advocated by Sydney Marland, former U.S. Commissioner of Education, to infuse meaning into the learning experiences of all students, including those with handicaps. As a result, the following steps were taken:

1. The U.S. Office of Career Education was established in 1974.
2. The Career Education Implementation Incentive Act of 1977 (PL 95-207) was passed, which provided federal funds for infusing career education into the school curricula.
3. The Council for Exceptional Children organized a Division on Career Development in 1976.

Today, the concepts, if not the practices, of career education provide important insights into the way in which instructional programming that incorporates career education concepts can improve educational outcomes at all grade levels. The important characteristics of career education include:

A purposeful sequence of planned educational activities that assist individuals in their career development

The process of systematically coordinating all school, family, and community components to facilitate each individual's potential for economic, social, and personal fulfillment

The development of activities and experiences that focus on productive work activity—both paid and unpaid—as a way of life

The assisting of students in learning the important knowledge, skills, and attitudes they need for the various life roles and settings comprising their lives

A process of career awareness, exploration, and skills development at all levels and ages

A system adopted by all educators, with meaningful input and involvement from family, agencies, business and industry, and other community resources

A total educational concept, not a specific course or instructional program, for application to K–12 and beyond as needed

An educational approach that focuses on the self-development as well as the career development of individuals (Brolin, 1982, p. 27)

Implementation of career education programs in the school may take several forms, typically involving several phases. One sequence includes a career awareness phase for early elementary students, a career orientation phase for upper-elementary students, a career exploration phase for junior high and middle school students, and a career preparation phase for high school students and adults. Because both career education and vocational education occur in the public schools, the two terms are frequently used interchangeably. However, Brolin and Kokaska (1979) pointed to significant differences between the two types of programming (see Table 1).

The work of Brolin (1976) represents one of the most impressive efforts to translate career education concepts into a curriculum for use with handicapped students. Brolin listed 21 major competencies he considered to be most important for mildly mentally retarded students to acquire before leaving secondary programs. Although this competency-based career education model is a significant step toward useful implementation of important concepts, more work in this area is needed. For example, the Brolin curriculum consists of 400 instructional objectives with no guidelines for determining which to train. Also, the validity of the original list of competencies has not been determined. Although Brolin indicated that the list includes skills that are most important, we do not know the methods used to validate their importance. Finally, users of the curriculum need to know how to relate community placement demands and student deficits with the recommended objectives in the curriculum (Mithaug, 1981).

Rehabilitation

Since the approach used in vocational rehabilitation is well documented elsewhere (Bitter, 1979; Brolin, 1976), it will not be repeated here. The major phases of this model include

Table 1. Differences between career education and vocational education programs

Career education	Vocational education
Focuses on both paid and unpaid work (e.g., volunteer, leisure and recreation, homemaking)	Focuses on paid work (although unpaid work is referred to in the Vocational Education Amendments)
Emphasizes general career skills	Emphasizes occupational preparation
Promotes cognitive, affective, and psychomotor skill development	Promotes psychomotor skills for entry into occupational society
Meets the needs of the learners	Meets needs of labor market
Is a system-wide effort, not specific courses or an instructional program	Is defined in terms of courses and is an instructional program
Is taught by all educators	Is generally taught by vocational educators
Focuses on all instruction programs at all levels of education	Focuses on the secondary and postsecondary levels
Involves family, agencies, and business/industry	Involves primarily business/industry

From Brolin and Kokaska (1979, p. 102).

intake, vocational evaluation, vocational training, job placement, and follow-up. Rehabilitation evaluations are extensive, involving medical, psychological, sociocultural, vocational, and educational evaluations. Furthermore, in cases where the results do not indicate definitive vocational potential, the approach allows for an extended evaluation of up to 18 months. During the vocational evaluation the client undergoes: 1) work evaluation during which he or she responds to vocational aptitude tests, interest tests, work and job samples, and situational assessments; and 2) a work-adjustment phase, which is usually most important for persons with mental retardation who frequently have not been exposed to a wide range of work experiences or prevocational skills that reflect a capacity for employment. This is usually the rationale for employing an extended evaluation. By the end of this period the counselor makes a decision regarding the applicant's eligibility or ineligibility for rehabilitation services.

Work adjustment in a controlled environment utilizes production on real tasks, similar to light production tasks in industrial settings, to develop work habits and attitudes expected in community employment (Bitter, 1979). Work is generally simple and repetitious—of the bench-assembly variety—such as assembling small appliances, sorting, packaging, or collating paper.

When adults are referred to a sheltered employment setting, they typically undergo a work evaluation over a 90- to 120-day period. Based upon the results of this assessment, which usually has a psychological trait orientation, trainees are placed in one of three programs: work activity, extended sheltered employment, or transitional employment. Candidates whose production rate is 25% of that of nonhandicapped workers qualify for work activity programs. Extended sheltered employment is available for individuals whose production rate exceeds the 25% limit, but are believed to be incapable of attaining the skill levels required in community jobs. Finally, transitional employment, the process of training skills needed for competitive employment and placing the

trainees in community jobs, is available to those individuals who demonstrate the highest vocational potential.

The work-adjustment phase, which occurs during extended sheltered employment, is designed to prepare individuals for competitive employment by enhancing their employability. In a setting that simulates the daily performance demands of a competitive work setting, employees are expected to acquire those work support behaviors that are required in any job. Behavior modification and counseling methods are utilized to improve skill deficits. By performing only work that happens to be available in environments that may be dissimilar to competitive settings, employees may not become properly prepared for the on-the-job training strategy necessary when a placement occurs. In transitional programs, a small percentage of persons are placed in competitive employment; many are work ready at placement, and the short-term rehabilitation perspective, which focuses on general attitudes and habits (psychological traits), is insufficient to improve significant skill deficits often associated with handicaps. Transitional programs have not been successful.

Following an extensive vocational evaluation according to the rehabilitation model, the client begins a program sequence that usually involves personal adjustment training, prevocational training, compensatory skill training, and vocational training. The latter involves the development of specific job skills. The final steps of this model, job placement and follow-up, present major problems especially for trainees with handicaps. Job placement is viewed as a selective process in which the best available job opportunity is matched as closely as possible to the client's skills and needs. Once the placement is made, minimal counselor contact is expected, and the employee is assumed to be able to function independently. Moreover, any subsequent adaptation occurs on the part of the employee as he or she adjusts to the new environment.

Most of the analysis related to the job-person match is done during the planning stage prior to placement. This approach is illustrated in the

Minnesota Theory of Work Adjustment, which is mostly reflected in the rehabilitation model through psychological trait analysis, short-term training, and medical perspectives. From this process-and-outcome view of vocational rehabilitation, the adjusted employee is characterized by personal satisfaction, acceptable performance, and job maintenance. In short, the Theory of Work Adjustment describes the worker and the work setting from a matching perspective. Degree of correspondence between worker and work setting can be described in terms of: 1) how well the person fulfills the requirements of the work (ability to do the job) and 2) how well the work environment fulfills the client's needs and expectations (reinforcement system to meet his or her needs). According to this theory, both the client and the potential work environments must be assessed to secure a proper match during placement. To avoid mismatch, training and counseling are used to guide the process.

According to this approach and other selective placement models, the standard on-the-job training strategy of industry is used after placement to assist the employee in the initial adjustment period. As described by Evans and Herr (1978),

> On-the-job training usually is a distinctly informal process. A brief job demonstration by a first-line supervisor or by a worker selected by the supervisor, followed by a period of trial-and-error learning, with occasional help from supervisors or from nearby workers characterizes the great majority of such training. If the performance is satisfactory, the on-the-job training may be terminated, and checks on quality and quantity of performance then will be handled as they are for any other worker. (p. 250)

Several difficulties are encountered when using on-the-job training with students who are handicapped. First, current employees, who serve as instructors, can easily deny new employees success by deliberately failing to train or by mistraining. Second, the lack of systematic work procedures may result in methods of training that are contradictory across employees and of insufficient intensity or duration for some employees who are handicapped. On-the-job training, however, offers the advantage of training on real work that predicts the actual work domain while training costs are kept to a minimum.

Model Provisions for Overcoming Obstacles

Table 2 illustrates the provisions offered by each of the four employment training models for overcoming or reducing obstacles to competitive employment. The vocational education and vocational rehabilitation models provide for overcoming worker skill deficits, vocational education by training students in specific occupations (e.g., carpentry, office management, home economics), and vocational rehabilitation by including a work-adjustment phase during which adults are taught to perform tasks that reflect aspects of job requirements (e.g., they might be taught to assemble electronic switches or package component parts, or other light industrial tasks). All four models fail to provide the assessment or training needed to meet the expectation of specific work assignments.

The career education model, the vocational education model, and the vocational rehabilitation model provide in part for social validation of the work goals and performance criteria set by employers. Career education models, as proposed by Brolin (1976), for example, include competencies believed essential for life-long adjustment to changing roles and settings. In addition, career education considers the expectations of parents and significant others in the development of employment goals. By incorporating school, family, service agencies, and business and industry in a partnership, the career education curriculum helps provide for a systemic approach to employment training. These statements must be interpreted cautiously, however, as there is no data base to demonstrate that in practice career education programs achieve these goals.

To a lesser extent, the work experience and vocational education models have developed links among entities in the traditional support network. That is, work experience has brought the schools and vocational rehabilitation services together in a joint venture, while the voca-

Table 2. Model provisions for overcoming obstacles to competitive employment

Obstacle	Special education work experience	Vocational education	Career education	Vocational rehabilitation
1. Skill and behavioral deficits	No	Yes	No	Yes
2. Deficient assessment and training procedures	No	No	No	No
3. Disregard for social validation	No	Yes	Yes	Yes
4. Lack of systematic approach	Yes	Yes	Yes	No
5. Inadequate staff training	No	No	No	No
6. Economic and policy deterrents	No	No	No	No

tional education model has fostered a closer relationship between educational services and business and industry. Therefore, in terms of systematic service delivery, all models except vocational rehabilitation achieve some level of distinction.

Two final obstacles—deficiencies in staff training, and economic and policy deterrents to competitive employment—are not addressed in any employment training model. Development of competency-based personnel preparation programs that provide rigorous training in behavioral analysis techniques in conjunction with field-based practica sites have not emerged (e.g., Mori, Rusch, & Fair, 1983). In terms of policy, no model has taken steps toward positively influencing personnel to plan, instruct, coordinate, and advocate for services necessary for persons with handicaps to secure and maintain competitive employment. In contrast, traditional preparation approaches hope that a placement is successful if the worker remains on the job for short periods after placement—as in the vocational rehabilitation model. In addition, no model attempts to teach staff to recognize the supportive networks that are a necessary part of a professional's repertoire.

Summary

This section overviews four approaches developed over the past two decades to better serve persons with handicaps. Although the models have enjoyed some success, no one model sufficiently addresses all the complex prob-

lems (obstacles) that *impinge* on competitive employment of persons with handicaps.

GENERAL SUMMARY

To overcome or minimize the obstacles to competitive employment discussed in this chapter, an exemplary employment training model must include components of several of the models. Such a model should: 1) identify the skills and behaviors that are critical to successful, long-term employment; and 2) teach prospective employees these skills and behaviors. Furthermore, its assessment and training elements should focus upon matching the trainee to the job and teaching the employee to not only acquire certain skills but to maintain acquired skills at a level that is acceptable to co-workers and supervisors on the job. This social validation component is important for ensuring that persons placed in competitive employment remain employed for periods well beyond traditional periods of successful adjustment—2 months or less. Long-term employment will result in numerous changes and challenges to the target employee and his or her place in society.

The challenges facing prospective employees who are handicapped are numerous and complex. Indeed, these challenges pose lifelong consideration for coordination of services. Consequently, new personnel are needed who are well equipped to understand and alleviate the varied obstacles to competitive employment. Existing personnel must learn about new service delivery models and better teaching methods that challenge outdated, status quo approaches. Additionally, new models and methods will only be as successful as a professional's understanding of existing and emerging issues. The following chapters provide a complete overview of emerging competitive employment service de-

livery models, methods, and issues that challenge the status quo. Today, the challenges of competitive employment for all persons are made to all professions providing employment training to students and adults, including special education, vocational education, and vocational rehabilitation.

REFERENCES

Agran, M., & Martin, J. E. (1982). Use of psychotropic drugs by mentally retarded adults in community programs. *Journal of The Association for the Severely Handicapped, 7,* 54–59.

Alley, G. R., & Deshler, D. (1979). *Teaching the learning disabled adolescent: Strategies and methods.* Denver: Love Publishing.

Bellamy, G. T., Rose, H., Wilson, D. J.,& Clarke, J. Y. (1982). Strategies for vocational preparation. In B. Wilcox & G. T. Bellamy, *Design of high school programs for severely handicapped students* (pp. 139–152). Baltimore: Paul H. Brookes.

Bellamy, G. T., Sheehan, M. R., Horner, R. H., & Boles, S. M. (1980). Community programs for severely handicapped adults: An analysis of vocational opportunities. *Journal of The Association for the Severely Handicapped, 5,* 307–324.

Bitter, J. A. (1979). *Introduction to rehabilitation.* St. Louis: C. V. Mosby.

Brickey, M., Browning, L., & Campbell, K. (1982). Vocational histories of sheltered workshop employees placed in projects with industry and competitive jobs. *Mental Retardation, 20,* 52–57.

Brolin, D. E. (1976). *Vocational preparation of retarded citizens.* Columbus, OH: Charles E. Merrill.

Brolin, D. E. (1982). *Vocational preparation of persons with handicaps* (2nd ed.). Columbus, OH: Charles E. Merrill.

Brolin, D. E., & Kokaska, C. J. (1979). *Career education for handicapped children and youth.* Columbus, OH: Charles E. Merrill.

Evans, R. N., & Herr, E. L. (1978). *Foundations of vocational education* (2nd ed.). Columbus, OH: Charles E. Merrill.

Gardner, W. I. (1971). *Behavior modification in mental retardation.* Chicago: Aldine/Atherton.

Gold, M. W. (1973). Research on the vocational habilitation of the retarded: The present, the future. In N. R. Ellis (Ed.), *International review of research in mental retardation* (Vol. 12, pp. 97–147). New York: Academic Press.

Gold, M. W. (1975). Vocational training. In J. Wortis (Ed.), *Mental retardation and developmental disabilities: An annual review* (Vol. 7, pp. 254–264). New York: Brunner/Mazel.

Greenspan, S., & Shoultz, B. (1981). Why mentally retarded adults lose their jobs: Social competence as a factor in work adjustment. *Applied Research in Mental Retardation, 2,* 23–28.

Halpern, A. (1974). Work-study programs for the mentally

retarded: An overview. In P. L. Browning (Ed.), *Mental retardation: Rehabilitation and counseling* (pp. 120–137). Springfield, IL: Charles C Thomas.

Hill, M., & Wehman, P. (1979). Employer and non-handicapped coworker perceptions of moderately and severely retarded workers. *Journal of Contemporary Business, 8,* 107–112.

Johnson, C. M. (1980). *Preparing handicapped students for work: Alternative for secondary programming.* Reston, VA: Council for Exceptional Children.

Kauffman, J. M., & Hallahan, D. P. (Eds.). (1981). *Handbook of special education.* Englewood Cliffs, NJ: Prentice-Hall.

Kochany, L., & Keller, J. (1981). An analysis and evaluation of the failures of severely disabled individuals in competitive employment. In P. Wehman, *Competitive employment: New horizons for severely disabled individuals* (pp. 181–198). Baltimore: Paul H. Brookes.

Koegel, R. L., & Rincover, A. (1977). Research on the difference between generalization and maintenance in extra-therapy responding. *Journal of Applied Behavior Analysis, 10,* 1–12.

Landy, F. J., & Trumbo, D. A. (1980). *Psychology of work behavior.* Homewood, IL: The Dorsey Press.

Lilly, M. S. (1979). *Children with exceptional needs: A survey of special education.* New York: Holt, Rinehart & Winston.

Magrab, P. R., & Elder, J. O. (1979). *Planning for services to handicapped persons: Community, education, health.* Baltimore: Paul H. Brookes.

Martin, J. E. (1980). Work productivity and the developmentally disabled. In J. A. Leach (Ed.), *Productivity in the workforce: A search for perspectives* (pp. 81–85). Champaign, IL: University of Illinois, Office of Vocational Education Research, Department of Vocational and Technical Education, College of Education.

McNamara, J. R., & McDonough, T. S. (1972). Some methodological considerations in the design and implementation of behavior therapy research. *Behavior Therapy, 3,* 361–379.

Menchetti, B. M., Rusch, F. R., & Owens, D. (1983). Vocational training. In J. L. Matson & S. E. Breuning (Eds.), *Assessing the mentally retarded* (pp. 247–284). New York: Grune & Stratton.

Mithaug, D. E. (1981). *Prevocational training for retarded students.* Springfield, IL: Charles C Thomas.

Mithaug, D. E., Horiuchi, C. N., & Fanning, P. (1985). A report on the Colorado statewide followup study of special education graduates. *Exceptional Children, 51*(5), 397–404.

Mithaug, D. E., Mar, D. K., & Stewart, J. E. (1978). *Prevocational assessment and curriculum guide*. Seattle, WA: Exceptional Education.

Mori, A. A., Rusch, F. R., & Fair, G. W. (1983). *Guidelines and best practices: Special populations—moderately/severely handicapped*. University of Illinois (Personnel Development Series). Urbana-Champaign, IL: Leadership Training Institute—Vocational and Special Education.

Phelps, L. A., & Thornton, L. J. (1979). *Vocational education and handicapped learners: Perceptions and inservice needs of state leadership personnel*. Urbana, IL: University of Illinois, College of Education.

Pomerantz, D., & Marholin, D. (1977). Vocational habilitation: A time for a change. In E. Sontag, J. Smith, & N. Certo (Eds.), *Educational programing for the severely and profoundly handicapped* (pp. 129–141). Reston, VA: Council for Exceptional Children, Division on Mental Retardation.

Robinson, H. B., & Robinson, N. M. (1975). *The mentally retarded child*. New York: McGraw-Hill.

Rusch, F. R. (1983). Competitive vocational training. In M. E. Snell (Ed.), *Systematic instruction of the moderately and severely handicapped* (2nd ed.) (pp. 503–523). Columbus, OH: Charles E. Merrill.

Rusch, F. R., Chadsey-Rusch, J., White, D. M., & Gifford, J. L. (1985). Programs for severely mentally retarded adults: Perspectives and methodologies. In D. Bricker & J. Filler (Eds.), *The severely mentally retarded: From research to practice* (pp. 119–140). Reston, VA: Council for Exceptional Children.

Rusch, F. R., Martin, J. E., Lagomarcino, T., & White, D. W. (1983). *Why mentally retarded workers lose their jobs: A comparison between mentally retarded and their nonhandicapped co-workers*. Unpublished manuscript.

Rusch, F. R., & Mithaug, D. E. (1980). *Vocational training for mentally retarded adults: A behavior analytic approach*. Champaign, IL: Research Press.

Rusch, F. R., Schutz, R. P., & Heal, L. W. (1983). Vocational training and placement. In J. L. Matson & J. A. Mulick (Eds.), *Handbook of mental retardation* (pp. 455–466). New York: Pergamon Press.

Rusch, F. R., Schutz, R. P., Mithaug, D. E., Stewart, J. E., & Mar, D. (1982). *Vocational assessment and curriculum guide*. Seattle, WA: Exceptional Education.

Sailor, W., & Guess, D. (1983). *Severely handicapped students: An instructional design*. Boston: Houghton Mifflin Co.

Schalock, R. L. (1983). *Services for developmentally disabled adults: Development, implementation, and evaluation*. Baltimore: University Park Press.

Schalock, R. L., & Harper, R. S. (1978). Placement from community-based MR programs: How well do clients do? *American Journal of Mental Deficiency, 83*, 240–247.

Sowers, J., Thompson, L. E., & Connis, R. T. (1979). The food service vocational training program. In G. T. Bellamy, G. O'Connor, & O. C. Karan (Eds.), *Vocational rehabilitation of severely handicapped persons* (pp. 181–205). Baltimore: University Park Press.

Vogelsberg, R. T., Williams, W., & Friedl, M. (1980). Facilitating systems change for the severely handicapped: Secondary and adult services. *Journal of The Association for the Severely Handicapped, 5*, 73–85.

Wolf, M. M. (1978). Social validity: The case for subjective measurement or how applied behavior analysis is finding its heart. *Journal of Applied Behavior Analysis, 11*, 203–214.

Wolfensberger, W. (1972). *Normalization: The principle of normalization in human services*. Toronto: National Institute on Mental Retardation.

Wysocki, J., & Wysocki, P. (1979). An employee's guide to employment disability. *Journal of Contemporary Business, 8*, 59–66.

Chapter 2

Competitive Employment in Virginia

Paul Wehman

INCREASING EVIDENCE SUGGESTS that persons with mental retardation can work competitively in nonsheltered employment provided appropriate support systems are available (Brickey, Browning, & Campbell, 1982; Brickey & Campbell, 1981; Kraus & MacEachron, 1982; Revell, Arnold, Taylor, & Saitz-Blotner, 1982; Sowers, Thompson, & Connis, 1979; Wehman et al., 1982). However, to date, placement options have usually been limited to: 1) sheltered workshop or adult activity centers, 2) competitive employment without job-site training and follow-up, and 3) refusal of services because of a perceived limited potential for gainful employment.

In the past it was considered highly unlikely that individuals diagnosed and classified as moderately or severely mentally retarded could work competitively. However, as suggested by the community-based vocational training model introduced in Chapter 1, many of these individuals are able to gain and retain employment.

In the state of Virginia and elsewhere across the country, several programs focusing upon competitive employment for clients with mental retardation have been established. To highlight the need for support during all phases of such competitive employment (i.e., training, placement, and follow-up), we have chosen to use the term *supported work model* (Wehman & Kregel, 1985). A supported work model provides for direct training at the job site. Daily training and advocacy is given by professional staff until the student successfully demonstrates independence. At that time, staff members begin systematically to reduce their time at the job site. The components and cost effectiveness of a supported work model have been described earlier (cf. Hill & Wehman, 1983; Revell & Arnold, 1984; Wehman, 1981; Wehman & Kregel, 1985). Program elements include: 1) job placement, 2) job-site training, 3) ongoing assessment, and 4) job retention. Table 1 provides a checklist of the types of activities that make up this model.

In a supported work arrangement, staff essentially provide assistance to help students not only gain employment but also learn the skills required at the job site, adjust to the work environment, and, ultimately, retain the job. The supported work model provides a highly individualized approach to job placement and retention. Employment is not wage subsidized; that is, employers immediately hire the students with their own funds, thus being able to access the Targeted Job Tax Credit program. Counselors may purchase services from rehabilitation facilities and other day programs

I am indebted to the following persons for their help with this chapter: Grant Revell, Janet Hill, Mark Hill, Connie Britt, Pam Pendleton, Valerie Brooke, Wendy Wood, and Sherrill Moon. Also, I am most appreciative of the federal support given to the Rehabilitation Research and Training Center by the National Institute of Handicapped Research, U.S. Department of Education, Grant No. G028301124 and the Research Projects Branch of Special Education Programs for Grant G008430106.

Table 1. Checklist of activities for supported work model of competitive employment

What is involved in helping the student get a job?
    Structuring efforts to find a job for student and matching student strengths to job needs
    Communicating with employers on behalf of student
    Planning transportation and/or travel training
    Emphasizing parents' involvement in identifying appropriate job for student
    Communicating with social security representatives
What is involved in teaching the student a job?
    Providing behavioral skill training aimed at improving student work performance
    Providing necessary social skill training at job site
    Working with employers/co-workers in helping student
    Helping student and co-workers adjust to each other
What is involved in monitoring the student's job progress?
    Getting regular written feedback from employer on student's progress
    Utilizing behavioral data on student's work speed, proficiency, need for staff assistance, etc.
    Implementing periodic student and/or parent satisfaction questionnaires
What is involved in helping the student keep a job?
    Implementing planned efforts to reduce staff intervention at job site
    Providing follow-up to employer through phone calls and/or visits to job site as needed
    Communicating to employer if and when staff accessibility is needed
    Helping student relocate or find new job if necessary

that offer supported work services. While supported work may involve placement in more sheltered settings like work stations in industry or sheltered enclaves, this chapter focuses on competitive employment. The purpose of this chapter is to describe how a supported work approach to competitive employment has been successful for individuals with mental retardation in Virginia, specifically at the Virginia Commonwealth University Rehabilitation Research and Training Center. This highly successful model must be integrated into rehabilitation services nationwide.

RATIONALE FOR SUPPORTED WORK MODEL

The supported work model of employment services emphasizes placement in and maintenance of long-term competitive employment. Traditionally, vocational rehabilitation counselors serving individuals with mental retardation have depended heavily on the services offered by sheltered workshops. While workshops can provide some of the services needed by persons with severe disabilities—nationally, many workshops are moving toward developing industrial work environments—the training and employment services offered by many sheltered workshops continue to be significantly limited. As documented in a number of studies and reports (Perlman, 1978; U.S. Commission on Civil Rights, 1983; U.S. Department of Labor, 1979) these limitations include:

1. The vast majority of persons with mental retardation who are trained in sheltered workshops do not move to competitive jobs.
2. The average earnings generated through sheltered work programs leave participants financially dependent on government, community, and family income supplements. Also, sheltered work programs offer minimal benefits, usually only vacation and sick leave.
3. Participation in a sheltered work program usually requires reliance on public subsidy to the facility for long-term placements. As a result, the participant is dependent on the community for both subsidized work and subsidized income, as well as numerous public relief benefits. This community dependence creates the perception that the individual with mental retardation is minimally productive.

Many workshop programs depend heavily on labor-intensive benchwork contracts to generate income and work opportunities. Work behaviors and trade-related skills learned from assembly and disassembly activities performed in a sedentary work environment, for example, do not transfer well to industrial jobs identified as being within the potential abilities of persons with mental retardation who are currently in workshops. Therefore, traditional workshop programming in nonindustrial settings neither prepares its clientele for competitive employment by offering industrially related experiences, nor provides an opportunity for persons remaining in the sheltered work environment to move beyond substantial public subsidy.

Without access to a supported work model, vocational rehabilitation counselors face significant difficulties when attempting to place persons with moderate and severe mental retardation outside sheltered workshops. Thus, the supported work approach recognizes that the vocational rehabilitation counselor is primarily a coordinator of services. A student who requires 40–80 hours of one-to-one job-site follow-up after placement presents the counselor or work experience coordinator with a dilemma that is usually resolved by considering the individual too severely handicapped for competitive employment. Hence, the result is often case closure or workshop placement.

Counselors who attempt to provide services using the state agency vocational rehabilitation program model are familiar with the term "not feasible for employment services." Some persons do encounter vocational handicaps specifically related to their disability that are too severe and limiting to allow for their return or movement into competitive employment. However, the results of the supported work model of employment for persons with mental retardation clearly proves that many persons, who were refused services because of the severity of their handicap, have successfully retained competitive-level employment (Wehman et al., 1982). In Virginia, such individuals' lack of feasibility for services was a product of the limitations of the service options made available to them by the vocational rehabilitation program, *not* solely a function of their own handicaps. By offering persons with mental retardation intensive evaluation, orientation, training, and follow-up services at in-

dustrially based job sites, many can become and remain productive, financially independent, and fully integrated in their community.

CHARACTERISTICS OF PARTICIPATING CLIENTS AND SETTINGS

Since the fall of 1978, 145 persons with mental retardation have been placed into part- and full-time competitive employment through the efforts of university-based, federal grant–supported staff and local agency staff in the Richmond, Norfolk, and Virginia Beach areas. Referrals of persons with mental retardation who require special placement and job-site training assistance have come from rehabilitation counselors, adult day programs, special education programs, and parents. Participants have been selected from a referral list on the basis of variables such as parental and agency support, client interest in having a job, presence of job near home, travel availability, etc. The present abilities of individuals were viewed as a minor selection factor since the placement-training model is designed to ameliorate skill deficits. Finally, the main focus was on individuals who traditionally have been excluded from competitive employment services or who have typically been considered "unemployable" by rehabilitative services. *Competitive employment* is defined, in part, as working for at least a minimum wage.

Table 2 summarizes the variables that are highly descriptive of the population (i.e., age, race, sex, Supplemental Social Security Income status prior to employment, measured intelligence or estimate, records not available, and nature of living arrangements). Most program participants had limited academic skills and few, if any, independent travel skills.

As illustrated in Table 2, 68% of the subjects were men and 32% were women with a median measured intelligence of 48 and a median age of 28. Over 90% had no independent travel skills before employment. The majority of participants lived in their natural home (72%),

Table 2.   Client profile

Age range: 17 to 61 (median age: 28)	Program participation at placement date
Sex	Sheltered workshop: 36%
Male: 68%	Public school: 18%
Female: 32%	Adult activity center: 27%
Race	Home and no day program: 19%
Black: 35%	
White: 65%	

Residence	At placement	Current or at most recent separation
Natural home	72%	69%
Group home	19%	8%
Supervised apartment	6%	11%
Living independently	3%	12%

36% were placed in sheltered workshops, 27% in adult activity centers, and 18% in public schools. Nineteen percent were at home without a program. All individuals were receiving social security income before placement into competitive employment.

RESULTS OF KEY OUTCOME MEASURES RELATED TO COMPETITIVE EMPLOYMENT

The effectiveness of vocational programs for persons with mental retardation may be measured in several ways. However, if the focus is exclusively on an outcome of competitive employment that provides *unsubsidized* wages for clients, the number of meaningful measures decreases considerably. Hill (1984) provides detailed quantitative analyses of the relationships between different outcome and predictor variables. In this discussion, however, it is our intent only to present descriptive summary data in order to verify the effectiveness of our employment efforts.

As illustrated in Table 3, a total of 206 placements were made with over 100 employers primarily representing service occupations such as custodial work, hotel and restaurant, and hospitals. Most placements earned entry-level minimum wage. One hundred and forty-five clients have been placed in 206 possible jobs. At this point 71 individuals are still working.

To date, the mean length of competitive employment for our clients is 15.5 months. To be meaningful this figure must be compared with data on *nonhandicapped* individuals who are working in similar positions. A study by the National Hotel and Restaurant Association (P. Nelon, personal communication, 1983) indicates that over 2,300 individuals in comparable entry-level positions retained their jobs for less than 5 months. Our clients, who either lost their jobs, resigned, or otherwise needed different placements were replaced into new jobs much more quickly and with far less staff time required for training and follow-along.

Over $900,000 has been earned by 145 clients, with client taxes amounting to $126,634. The mean number of staff hours spent with each client was 177, including: 1) point of initial placement, 2) intensive job-site training, and 3) ongoing follow-up services. Figure 1 graphically presents the total number of clients placed to date and those who are still working successfully.

CHARACTERISTICS OF SUPPORTED WORK MODEL

In order to accomplish our placement retention goals, we have successfully used a supported model of employment services (Kraus & MacEachron, 1982; Revell, Wehman, & Arnold, 1984; Wehman & Kregel, 1985). Using this model, professional staff provide individualized and intensive assistance to the client through: 1) job placement, 2) job-site training and advocacy, 3) ongoing assessment, and 4) follow-along and transition. The key components summarized in Table 1 are presented in more detail in the following discussion.

Table 3. Results of key employment outcome measures

Number of clients placed (October 1978–December 1983)	145
(Total number of placements =	206)
Number of clients currently working	71
Median measured intelligence	48
Mean length of time clients stayed in positions before changing job or stopping	15.5 months
Mean length of time *nonhandicapped* co-workers or idential industries[a]	5 months
Cumulative client wages earned	$928,882
Cumulative client taxes contributed	$213,642
Mean staff hours per client	177
Mean cost per client	$4,277
(Mean cost per placement)	$3,010

[a]Based on National Hotel and Restaurant Association Survey of 2,300 nonhandicapped workers in food service industry.

Key Assumption Underlying Use of Supported Work Model

The success of any job placement is influenced by several assumptions including:

1. The community labor market has been screened or assessed for the types of jobs that appear likely to have vacancies or turnover, and that appear to be within the capacity of the student(s) to be placed.
2. A preemployment vocational program, ideally beginning at an early age in school, has provided at least a limited degree of training for students. This training will provide competency in some of the vocational skills that may be required in the target types of jobs (Rusch, Schutz, & Agran, 1982; Wehman, 1983).
3. An evaluation of student adaptive behaviors, parent/caregiver attitudes, transportation possibilities, etc., has been undertaken with such data available to staff working within the supported work model (Phelps & McCarty, 1984; Rusch & Mithaug, 1980).

The degree to which these assumptions can be met will influence how well the placement meets student and employer needs. If any of the above assumptions are not met, placement is

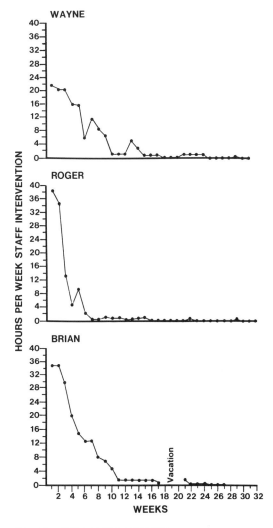

Figure 1. Fading of intervention time.

not precluded. However, the placement and retention process is slowed down, resulting in greater expense for staff to implement job-site training. Furthermore, fulfillment of the assumptions should facilitate transition into adult programs that might provide placement or follow-along if placement is already made.

Program Component 1: Job Placement

The placement of the student in a job appropriate to his or her abilities is the first major component of the supported work model. The job placement process involves more than simply finding a job for a student. Major aspects of the process include:

Matching job needs to student abilities or
potential

Facilitating employer communication with the
student

Facilitating parent or caregiver communication

Establishing travel arrangements or providing
travel training

Analyzing the job environment to verify all
potential obstacles

Several key points need to be highlighted
about job placement within the supported work
model. First, effective placement is predicted
on an accurate analysis of work environment
requirements. This process has been variously
referred to as *ecological analysis* (Wehman,
1981), *top-down curriculum* (Brown et al.,
1979), or *job analysis* (Rusch & Mithaug,
1980; Schutz & Rusch, 1982; Vandergoot &
Worral, 1979). The critical factor is that adequate detail be provided in terms of job requirements, characteristics of the work environment, and other features that may influence
job retention. These details, in turn, will facilitate the job match, that is, pairing job requirements with student abilities.

Second, job placement can take place with
students who do not possess all the necessary
work or social skill competencies for immediate job success. The strength of the supported
work model is that the person making the
placement knows that job-site help will be
available once the placement occurs. This is a
significant departure from traditional placement approaches that require the students to be
"job ready."

Third, travel, social security, job interview,
and other nonwork-related factors are handled
in the job placement process. Within a more
traditional placement framework, the student
or caregiver often handles most of these concerns if a job is made available. However, job
placement of moderately and severely mentally
retarded youth would be impossible or highly
unlikely without this type of support.

Job placement is frequently carried out not
by a placement specialist, but by a job coordinator or work experience specialist, who
handles not only placement but all aspects of
the supported work process. While this approach offers the benefits of continuity across
all model components, it suffers from the disadvantage of leaving less time for the job
coordinator to concentrate on job identification. Our experiences have shown, however,
that informal job contacts are valuable and that
jobs arise from good relations between job
coordinators and employers.

Program Component 2:
Job-Site Training and Advocacy

As noted earlier, on-the-job training is not a
new concept. However, most currently used
models do not contain active involvement early
in the placement of a trained professional staff
person. Rather, employers are usually seen as
the "trainers," and brief and infrequent follow-
up checks or visits after the placement sub-
stitute for specific training. In short, such models omit a major step—skill training and
adjustment to the work environment.

Our placement experiences, as well as
communication with others who use a supported work approach, strongly indicate that
job-site training and advocacy is an essential
feature of the supported work model. This
program componenet involves two major processes: 1) behavioral training of skills, and
2) advocacy on behalf of the student at the job
site. Among the few investigations of application of behavioral training to vocational
skills in nonsheltered or competitive work environments, Rusch has clearly been the leader
with studies related to acquisition of selected
work skills (Schutz, Jostes, Rusch, & Lamson,
1980), time telling (Sowers, Rusch, Connis, &
Cummings, 1980), time on-task on job (Rusch,
Weithers, Menchetti, & Schutz, 1980), as well
as selected communication training (Karlan &
Rusch, 1982). The technology of behavioral
training needs to be extended to nonsheltered
work environments with individuals who here-
tofore have been considered poor candidates
for competitive employment. Applications of
reinforcement principles, manipulations of
antecedent stimulus conditions, and use of
co-workers as peer trainers are all areas that
require closer investigation.

Student advocacy or promotion is the other principal feature of component 2. In some cases, workers who are handicapped will need less focus on training with more time spent on orientation to the new job site. Such orientation might involve the following types of activities on the part of the job coordinator: identifying restroom facilities; locating cafeteria and/or vending machines; working out communication problems between student and co-workers; communicating with parents/caregivers about how the job is going; and counseling students on improving general work behaviors (getting to work on time, appropriate appearance, etc.).

Program Component 3:
Ongoing Assessment

A major feature that differentiates the supported work from more traditional job placement approaches is ongoing assessment or monitoring of student performance. Typically, a rehabilitation counselor will place a client and then possibly check with employers later to see how things are working out. This type of "assessment" is insufficient, especially with severely handicapped youth who may have quit or been terminated by the time such checks are made (Brolin, 1982).

Once a placement is made, there is a need to immediately gauge the employer's perceptions of the handicapped student's performance using two major performance indicators: supervisor evaluation data and performance data. Although quantifiable data are the most desirable, in some instances verbal feedback to an on-site staff person may be sufficient. The amount of assessment data collected is related to variables such as the student's ability level, amount of staff available for data collection, and, above all, the specific need for data to evaluate a certain problem.

Program Component 4:
Follow-Along and Transition

Although follow-up is consistently being referred to within the rehabilitation system, it is unclear how much follow-up is required to assure clients' job retention. For example, such variables as the nature of the follow-up in terms of frequency of employer contact, communication with clients, and re-placement into an alternative job influence the quality of placement.

In one of the few papers that address the issue of follow-up quality, Hill, Cleveland, Pendleton, and Wehman (1982) listed regular on-site visits to employers, phone calls, periodic review of supervisor evaluation, client progress reports, and parent evaluations as ways in which to promote retention. Ultimately, this component of the supported work model may be the most critical since handicapped workers are often immediately at risk of losing their jobs in competitive environments unless some type of retention plan is devised.

Many of the clients reported on in this chapter have received and continue to receive follow-up services as needed. Figure 2 shows the amount of time initially spent with three clients and the gradual fading of follow-up. These graphs are representative of many of our individual placements. Although a number of intensive days are necessary at first, on-site staff time usually drops off sharply. Maintenance of the placed individuals in their jobs is viewed as a critical aspect of their habilitation.

IMPLICATIONS OF
MODEL AND RESULTS

A major strength of the results reported in this chapter is that they span a longer time period than many earlier reports on job placement of persons with mental retardation. As reflected by our results, a substantial emphasis has been placed upon maintaining individuals in jobs, not only placing them into employment. Another distinguishing feature of our model is the avoidance of subsidized wage arrangements.

Results of our program indicate that many more persons with mental retardation could be working competitively than already are. Consequently, social security income and other transfer payments may not be necessary for many of the current recipients if they were given appropriate training and support. Furthermore, our data raise some serious questions about the viability of long-term sheltered

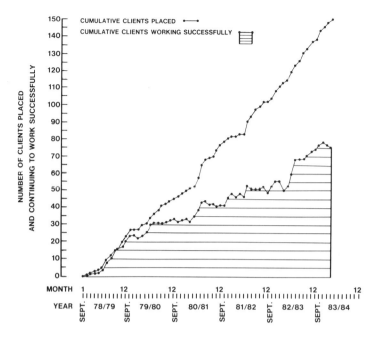

Figure 2.   Cumulative success ratio of competitively employed clients.

workshop employment and adult activity center placement for persons who are able to benefit from the economic and social benefits of competitive employment.

Programs such as the supported work model described here have not yet become a significant part of the educational and community service system for persons with mental retardation. Typically, service delivery practices lag behind research and demonstration efforts by a number of years. However, the necessary changes and modifications of community and educational services may be speeded up based on the following recommendations:

1. Many more demonstrations showing the competitive employment potential of persons with retardation are necessary. Due to the current lack of model programs to be emulated, states are unable to make large-scale conversions for segregated adult centers into integrated nonsheltered employment programs.

2. A financial incentive system for sheltered workshops and other adult day programs is necessary to provide placement and job retention follow-along services. Most day programs do not receive funds contingent on helping people become competitively employed and maintain employment. While large amounts of work-adjustment dollars flow into rehabilitation facilities, no specific competitive employment outcomes are attached.

3. Training rehabilitation counselors must place greater demands on local (workshop) vendors for job placement and job retention of referral clients. Counselors must request more employment services for their clients from local service programs and should refuse to pay for services that are beneath the potential of mentally retarded clients.

4. More funding and leadership is needed by rehabilitation and developmental disability agencies for nonsheltered and competitive employment-oriented programs. These two areas need to work more closely together toward the more unified purpose of paid competitive employment for persons with mental retardation.

5. Greater leadership at the state and federal

levels is required to encourage liaison between schools and adult service agencies for meaningful vocational transition.

6. At the school level, vocational and special education personnel must place much more emphasis on job placement reflecting nonsubsidized wages. Schools must get more involved in community-based employment training and placement.

These recommendations are not inclusive. For example, they address the significant training needs and improvement required in rehabilitation counseling and special education preservice programs in order to implement the model described here. However, following the above recommendations will begin to make the current service system more responsive to the competitive employment potential of persons with mental retardation. Vocational programs such as the supported work model must become more integrated into the overall service delivery system. To achieve this goal, new sources of funding become imperative—the focus of the next section.

FUNDING OPTIONS FOR SUPPORTED WORK

Vocational rehabilitation and school administrators attempting to incorporate the supported work model into their service system are faced with difficult issues such as zero-growth budgets, substantial cutbacks in alternative funding sources, hiring freezes, and employee layoffs. However, current applications of the supported work model point to funding and personnel options that potentially provide a means for supporting alternative service methodologies in spite of the above limitations.

Federal and State Vocational Rehabilitation Funding

Counselors serving severely disabled, mentally retarded individuals are dependent at present on purchase-of-service arrangements with community adjustment and training service vendors. Frequently, a costly work-adjustment

and training service vendors. Frequently, a costly work-adjustment program for a client results in placement in either a subsidized sheltered employment slot or on a waiting list for sheltered employment. Instead, monies currently directed toward purchase-of-service for noncompetitively oriented programs could be redirected toward staffing of competitively oriented service methodologies. By placing limits on purchased adjustment services, defined by objective progress reports and movement toward specified behavior targets, the average client preplacement could be shortened and dollars made available for alternative services.

Fee-for-Service Arrangements

The use of industrial enclaves and client orientation in preparation for competitive employment represents a growing trend in progressive sheltered workshop programming. Workshops that adopt an industrial orientation can become a provider of supported work job placement and follow-up services. State vocational rehabilitation agencies should encourage community service vendors to provide supported work services and incorporate the cost of the service into a fee-for-service agreement.

Job Training Partnership Act

As of November 1983, programs utilizing variations of the supported work model are operating in 4 of the 14 Service Delivery Authorities in Virginia. These programs provide employment services to persons with handicaps and are funded wholly or in part through monies made available by the Job Training Partnership Act (JTPA). The programs are supervised by the state vocational rehabilitation agency and provide intensive job-site training and extended follow-up. JTPA funds are primarily used to support costs for training and employment staff as well as such client-related expenses as assessment, wage subsidies for on-the-job training, and transportation. The authority given through the JTPA program to the local community to determine needed services allow a great deal of flexibility in devising a supported work program that complements available services. Furthermore, the JTPA program encourages joint programming among the state vocational rehabilitation program, community mental retardation services, other public programs providing services for persons with disabilities, and private vendors of services such as sheltered workshops. Thus, the JTPA program offers an excellent opportunity to expand available service methodologies, such as the supported work model, which emphasize retention of competitive manpower in industry.

Projects With Industry

As mentioned, the supported work model utilizes *industrially based* assessment and orientation services, adjustment and skill training at the job site, and intense follow-up after employment; thus it is consistent with the federal Projects With Industry (PWI) model. Formal or informal applications of the supported work models utilize business advisory groups, a primary feature of PWI programs. As state vocational rehabilitation agencies prepare for possible direct participation in the federal Projects With Industry program, the supported work model represents a viable service option appropriate to PWI funding.

The funding options listed above are not mutually exclusive. To derive maximum benefit from available funds, state vocational rehabilitation and department of education agencies having difficulty in effectively providing for the employment service needs of persons with mental retardation must review:

1. Current case service patterns and the impact on competitive placements resulting from these expenditures
2. Current agency staffing patterns, particularly among full-service counselors who have traditionally depended on a now shrinking case service budget to serve clients, and who spend a small percentage of their time on job placement and job retention services
3. Supplementary funding available through

JTPA, PWI, and other federal, state, and private resources that are oriented specifically to employment services for persons with handicaps.
4. The opportunity for cooperative programming, both with other public agencies and with the private sector.

Redirection of existing resources and utlization of supplementary funding and programming options provide vocational rehabilitation administrators with the means to implement applications of the supported work model.

SUMMARY

If persons with mental retardation and other severe handicaps are to become less dependent on social security disability income and other forms of government transfer payments, competitive employment placements are essential. The Rehabilitation Research and Training Center at Virginia Commonwealth University is investigating numerous research issues related to this issue. A special focus of this center will be the supported work model (i.e., how it works, its cost effectiveness, and optimal ways to train staff in the model).

Federal and state vocational rehabilitation agencies must effectively assist persons with mental retardation and other severe disabilities in retaining competitive employment if these agencies are to retain or reestablish their credibility as viable employment service organizations. Applications of the supported work model have demonstrated its effectiveness in assisting persons with moderate and severe mental retardation to retain competitive employment. Both as providers and users of vocational rehabilitation services, state vocational rehabilitation agencies are responsible for the employment of persons with disabilities. Consequently, these public agencies must take the lead in integrating the supported work model into their own service programs and into other viable community resources, including sheltered workshops.

REFERENCES

Brickey, M., Browning, L., & Campbell, K. (1982). Vocational histories of sheltered workshop employees placed in projects with industrial and competitive jobs. *Mental Retardation, 20,* 52–57.

Brickey, M., & Campbell, L. (1981). Fast food employment for moderately and mildly retarded adults. *Mental Retardation, 19,* 113–116.

Brolin, D. E. (1982). *Vocational preparation of persons with handicaps* (2nd ed.). Columbus, OH: Charles E. Merrill.

Brown, L., Branston-McClean, M. G., Baumgart, D., Vincent, L., Falvey, M., & Schroeder, J. (1979). Using the characteristics of current and subsequent least restrictive environments in the development of curricular content for severely handicapped students. *AAESPH Review, 4,* 407–424.

Hill, J. (1984). *Longitudinal tracking and analysis of competitively employed mentally retarded workers.* Paper presented at Washington State Job Placement Conference, Seattle.

Hill, M., Cleveland, P., Pendelton, P., & Wehman, P. (1982). *Strategies in the follow-up of moderately and severely handicapped competitively employed workers.* Unpublished manuscript, Virginia Commonwealth University, Rehabilitation Research and Training Center, Richmond.

Hill, M., & Wehman, P. (1983). Cost benefit analysis of placing moderately and severely handicapped individuals into competitive employment. *Journal of The Association for the Severely Handicapped, 8,* 30–39.

Karlan, G., & Rusch, F. R. (1982). Analyzing the relationship between acknowledgment and compliance in a non-sheltered work setting. *Education and Training of Mental Deficiency, 86,* 650–653.

Kraus, M., & MacEachron, A. (1982). Competitive employment training for mentally retarded adults: The supported work model. *American Journal of Mental Deficiency, 86,* 650–653.

Perlman, L. G. (1978). *Job Placement Study.* National Industries for the Severely Handicapped, Washington, DC.

Phelps, L. A., & McCarty, T. (1984) Career education for handicapped individuals: Student assessment practices. *Career Development for Exceptional Individuals, 6,* 30–38.

Revell, G., & Arnold, S. (1984). The role of the rehabilitation counselor in providing job oriented services to severely handicapped mentally retarded persons. *Journal of Applied Rehabilitation Counseling, 15*(1), 22–27.

Revell, G., Arnold, S., Taylor, B., & Saitz-Blotner, S. (1982). Project transition: Competitive employment services for the severely handicapped mentally retarded. *Journal of Rehabilitation, 48*(1), 31–35.

Revell, G., Wehman, P., & Arnold, S. (1984). Supported work model of employment for mentally retarded persons: Implications of rehabilitative services. *Journal of Rehabilitation.*

Rusch, F. R., & Mithaug, D. E. (1980). *Vocational training for mentally retarded adults: A behavior analytic approach.* Champaign, IL: Research Press.

Rusch, F. R., Schutz, R. P., and Agran, M. (1982). Validating entry-level survival skills for service occupations: Implication for curriculum development. *Journal of The Association for the Severely Handicapped, 7,* 32–41.

Rusch, F. R., Weithers, J. A., Menchetti, B. M., & Schutz, R. P. (1980). Social validation of a program to reduce topic repetition in a non-sheltered setting. *Education and Training of the Mentally Retarded, 15,* 208–215.

Schutz, R. P., Jostes, K. F., Rusch, F. R., & Lamson, D. S. (1980). Acquisition, transfer, and social validation of two vocational skills in competitive employment setting. *Education and Training of the Mentally Retarded, 15,* 306–311.

Schutz, R. P., & Rusch, F. R. (1982). Competitive employment: Toward employment integration for mentally retarded persons. In. K. Lynch, W. Kiernan, & T. J. Stark (Eds.), *Prevocational and vocational education for special needs youth: A blueprint for the 1980's* (pp. 133–159). Baltimore: Paul H. Brookes.

Sowers, J. A., Rusch, F. R., Connis, R. T., & Cummings, L. E. (1980). Teaching mentally retarded adults to time-manage in a vocational setting. *Journal of Applied Behavior Analysis, 13,* 119–128.

Sowers, J., Thompson, L. E., & Connis, R. T. (1979). The food service vocational training program: A model for training and placement of the mentally retarded. In G. T. Bellamy, G. O'Connor, & O. C. Karan (Eds.), *Vocational rehabilitation of severely handicapped persons.* (pp. 181–205). Baltimore: University Park Press.

U. S. Commission on Civil Rights. (1983, September). *Accommodating the spectrum of individualized abilities.* Washington, DC: U.S. Commission on Civil Rights.

U.S. Department of Labor. (1979, March). Study of handicapped clients in sheltered workshops (vol. II). Washington, DC: U.S. Department of Labor.

Vandergoot, D., & Worral, J. D. (Eds). (1979). *Placement in rehabilitation: A career development perspective.* Baltimore: University Park Press.

Wehman, P. (1981). *Competitive employment: New horizons for severely disabled individuals.* Baltimore: Paul H. Brookes.

Wehman, P. (1983). Toward the employability of severely handicapped individuals after three years. *Journal of The Association for the Severely Handicapped, 7,* 5–16.

Wehman, P., Hill, M., Goodall, P., Cleveland, P., Brooks, V., & Pentecost, J. H. (1982). Job placement and follow-up of moderately and severely handicapped individuals after three years. *Journal of The Association for the Severely Handicapped, 7,* 5–16.

Wehman, P., & Kregel, J. (1985). A supported work approach to competitive employment of persons with moderate and severe handicaps. *Journal of The Association for Persons with Severe Handicaps, 10*(1), 3–9.

Chapter 3

Competitive Employment in Vermont

R. Timm Vogelsberg

SINCE 1979 THE development of model employment training programs has greatly increased the number of vocational options available to individuals with mental retardation in Vermont. To obtain funding for the first small demonstration program, the concept of competitive employment for individuals with mental retardation had to be recognized and accepted at the state level. Thus, as a result of local, regional, and statewide efforts, four competitive employment programs are currently in operation with two additional programs expected to begin services in 1985. In this chapter, the development, history, service design, and location, as well as the successes and failures of the three oldest programs, are delineated. In addition, program data covering a 5-year, 3-year, and 1-year period at three different geographic locations are detailed.

In the late 1960s, the right of individuals with severe handicaps to integration into community settings began to gain acceptance primarily as a result of deinstitutionalization, the Education for All Handicapped Children Act (Public Law 94-142), the Rehabilitation Act of 1973 (Public Law 93-112), model projects, and various professional publications. From an initial focus on functional living and self-care skills, increased attention was directed to expected adult environments. Thus, many of the previously accepted limitations of individuals with handicaps were dissolved with expanded application of behavioral technology to assist in the development of complex skills.

As a result of such changes, individuals considered severely handicapped developed the abilities to:

1. Work at a normal rate (Bellamy, Horner, & Inman, 1979).
2. Learn the skills necessary to hold a competitive position (Goodall, Wehman, & Cleveland, 1983; Rusch & Mithaug, 1980; Vogelsberg, 1984; Vogelsberg, Ashe, & Williams, 1986; Wehman, 1981; Wehman & Hill, 1979).
3. Move independently about the community crossing complex intersections and using public transportation (Certo, Schwartz, & Brown, 1975; Sowers, Rusch, & Hudson, 1979; Vogelsberg & Rusch, 1979).
4. Engage in recreation activities (Wehman, 1979).
5. Interact in a socially appropriate fashion

This chapter would not have been possible without the cooperation and support of the Vermont Department of Mental Health, Division of Vocational Rehabilitation, Agency of Human Services, and the Federal Department of Education, Office of Special Education and Rehabilitative Services.

Individuals who deserve recognition for their support and assistance are numerous and must include at least: Wes Williams, Bill Ashe, Wayne Fox, Sr. Elizabeth Candon, Richard Surles, Ron Melzer, Dave Burrus, Richard Hill, Roger Strauss, Mike Moeykens, Rich Hutchins, Tim Flynn, Dave Boyer, Patty Morgan, Debby Patterson, Robyn Schenck, Peggy Spaulding, Bob Phillips, Kathie Goodblood, Rich Wheeler, Susan Brody Hasazi, David Pitonyak, George Collier, Bill Sugarman, and Ellen Berrings.

(Schutz, Williams, Iverson, & Duncan, 1984).

6. Learn family life and sex education skills (Hamre-Nietupski, Ford, & Williams, 1977).

7. Compose menus, develop shopping lists, and purchase groceries (Nietupski, Certo, Pumpian, & Belmore, 1976).

Gradually, increased integration of public school programs underscored the service discrepancies between quality public school service and existing adult services. Thus, many progressive professionals recognized that the development of quality services at the public school level was inadequate to guarantee long-term maximization of the skills of an individual who was severely handicapped. Frequently, after years of high quality and intensive educational services, a student with severe handicaps would "graduate" to a fragmented and uncooperative adult service system. If he or she received any services at all, they were likely to be in the form of a day program, work activity program, or sheltered workshop.

The problems inherent in the present adult service system have been repeatedly delineated (Appleby, 1978; Greenleigh Associates, 1975; Stanfield, 1976; Vogelsberg, Williams, & Friedl, 1980; Whitehead, 1977) and are not expanded upon in this chapter. Among these problems, perhaps the most far-reaching is the inability of present community programs to provide the necessary support for individuals with severe handicaps to enter the competitive employment market (Bellamy, Sheehan, Horner, & Boles, 1980).

DEVELOPMENT OF
VOCATIONAL SERVICE

Based on the necessity to expand vocational opportunities for individuals with severe handicaps, a series of activities were begun in 1979 to address the need and to conceptualize a long-term plan for development. Briefly, these activities consisted of:

1. Funding of statewide surveys of adult facilities, public school service providers, and adult service providers to compare Vermont services to national services (Vogelsberg et al., 1980)

2. Development of a comprehensive review of the literature of adult service models to assist in the conceptualization of a state model (Vogelsberg, Williams, & Friedl, 1980)

3. Forming a State Task Force on Mental Retardation and Vocational Rehabilitation to provide a report to the Secretary of Human Services on a comprehensive vocational service model (Hill et al., 1980)

4. Preparation of a comprehensive vocational services operational plan for implementation (Vogelsberg, Williams, & Fox, 1981)

5. Funding the first competitive employment program in Central Vermont (Vogelsberg, Williams, & Ashe, 1981)

The first program was funded in 1980 through a Division of Vocational Rehabilitation Establishment Grant with matching Department of Mental Health funds. Once this program (Project Transition) had been in operation for 1 year, it developed a sufficient data base and service design to assist in securing federal funds from the Department of Education, Office of Special Education and Rehabilitative Services. As a result, the second program (Project Transition II) was initiated as a special project in 1981. Since then a third (Project Transition III) and fourth program (Project Transition IV) have been started with more programs expected in the near future.

DESCRIPTION OF EMPLOYMENT
TRAINING PROGRAMS

Funding

After the establishment grant funding period expired, a service fee was developed and implemented for the first regional program. A similar fee-for-service arrangement is likely to be adopted by the other regional programs once their establishment grant funds expire. The only exception is the program in Burlington, Project Transition II, which recently received federal funds to develop a Postsecondary Training and Employment program at a local college (Trinity College). The goal of this project is to become a tuition-based postsecondary/college program that will lead to competitive employment placements for students.

Administrative Issues

The first competitive employment program, located in a regional mental health center, was funded with some skepticism from both regional and local service providers. To guarantee that the center would be capable of providing community employment placements in addition to its numerous responsibilities and objectives for the individuals it was already serving, certain administrative guidelines were developed. These guidelines included the establishment of:

1. Separate budgets for the special program
2. Cooperative interagency agreements between multiple agencies
3. Separate staff responsibilities that precluded any training or instruction within the adult day program (Model program staff could provide instruction only in community settings.)
4. Separate advisory and support boards
5. Guarantee of qualified consultation
6. Consistent monthly descriptive data concerning the program and its progress
7. Specific placement and disability expectations
8. Staff development and training
9. Quarterly and annual written reports to funding agencies

Although the guidelines forced a separation between the existing day program and the new vocational program, they were necessary to ensure the success of the model program. Due to its multiple needs and a difficult staff-to-trainee ratio (approximately 1:15), the day program would readily have utilized any additional resources to continue traditional day activities. After the program had operated successfully for a number of years, the original guidelines were no longer as strictly followed.

Service Design

Each program follows an on-the-job training approach that consists of: 1) identification of a position, 2) analysis of the position, 3) evaluation of potential workers, 4) matching of workers and available positions, 5) placement of workers on a job with an on-the-job trainer, 6) intensive instruction for a 2- to 6-month period with gradual fading of the trainer, and 7) long-term follow-up services to guarantee maintenance of the position.

A training component preceding actual placement was not utilized in the present model primarily because available service occupations typically included many unique responsibilities as well as dissimilar equipment and settings. In addition, program developers hoped that the placement activities would generate additional training activities in existing programs to support the newly designed placement efforts.

Each program includes a training coordinator, a job developer, an on-the-job trainer, and secretarial and technical support. Approximately one individual per month is placed into a competitive position, and referrals are accepted from multiple agencies and individual families. Trainees pass through four distinct program phases to reach the goal of a competitive placement: 1) referral, 2) job development and evaluation, 3) on-the-job training and placement, and 4) follow-up. Each phase is described below.

Referral Potential workers are referred from public schools, work activity centers, sheltered workshops, Vocational Rehabilitation Offices, Department of Mental Health offices, and parents or guardians. Once an individual is referred, permission for release of records and potential evaluation is required from the referring agency and parents. Since referring agencies have different expectations and requirements, separate written interagency agreements have been established. All trainees who are going to be placed into competitive employment become *clients* of the Division of Vocational Rehabilitation.

In addition to being classified as *mentally retarded* and *severely disabled,* referred individuals also have to be termed *unemployable* according to traditional Vocational Rehabilitation criteria. Hence potential clients who can acquire employment through less intensive instruction or traditional programs are referred elsewhere. As part of these efforts, identification of the need to develop less intensive models to facilitate employment is an ongoing program activity.

Job Development and Evaluation   Evaluation of referrals and development of appropriate placements occur concurrently. The former is concerned with an accurate description of a trainee's skill strengths and deficits, while the latter focuses on the identification and analysis of potential positions within the community.

Evaluation   During the evaluation phase previous records are examined and pertinent data are recorded in a comprehensive case management system (Vogelsberg, Spaulding, Patterson, Schenck, & Phillips, 1984). Demographic data are also collected and verified along with previous psychological and medical information. For specific training purposes two evaluation instruments are utilized: *The Vocational Assessment and Curriculum Guide* (VACG) (Rusch, Schutz, Mithaug, Stewart, & Mar, 1982) and a locally developed instrument, the *Individual Skill Inventory*. The VACG, which is administered first, provides a series of curriculum objectives that can be forwarded to referring agencies should a decision be made to wait for placement. The *Individual Skill Inventory,* in turn, is utilized to identify specific client skills and deficits, and match these to identical areas incorporated in a job skill inventory for a specific position in the community.

As with many service programs, applicants for service outnumber available resources. Thus a waiting list for placement has been developed containing evaluation information for future placements. Although a complex system was developed to identify the best candidate for each position by matching the results of job skill inventories with individual skill inventories (Vogelsberg et al., 1986), decisions are usually made based upon transportation, agency and parent support, and perceived interest in a given position.

Original expectations to perform a job sample of identified positions, assist trainees with the interview process, try out the job, and then make a placement decision turned out to be too idealistic and rarely implemented. Instead, employers usually require that positions be filled as quickly as possible. It is not unusual for an on-the-job trainer to work a position for a few days while a worker is identified and prepared for the position.

Job Development   Two different forms of job development are utilized with each program: generic and specific. *Generic job development* refers to the process of improving employer receptivity of workers with handicaps through local presentations, newspaper articles, attendance by program staff at Chamber of Commerce meetings, and calling upper-level regional managers of various businesses. In some instances a regional manager has asked a local store manager to assist project staff in identifying a suitable position. Once a position is identified, the development process becomes job specific. Although it is uncertain how many generic contracts or presentations directly effect the number of positions secured, specific feedback from employers and identification of positions by upper-level management reflect that it is a functional and necessary activity.

Specific job development consists of the program job developer making phone contacts, setting up meetings with employers, explaining the program, promising that follow-up and training will be available, and eventually securing a position. Once a position is identified, an initial job analysis form is filled out and the on-the-job trainer comes on the job to prepare a job skill inventory modeled after that developed by Belmore and Brown (1976). Depending upon the complexity of a given position, the on-the-job trainer frequently works the position to guarantee that all components are accurately identified. For one position within a large electronics plant, the on-the-job trainer had to enter a 2-week training program prior to initiating training.

Employers are given a number of assurances prior to their commitment to provide a position. For example, they are promised that the job will be completed to their satisfaction each day and that at the end of a 2-week job tryout period, they can decide not to continue to work with the program. These guarantees mean that during the initial training stages, the on-the-job trainer is frequently responsible both for training and performing some components of a job. Furthermore, they allow the programs to avoid utilizing salary subsidies, instead concentrating on Targeted Job Tax Credit as the main incentive for employers. Out of 91 placements, no employer has ever decided at the end of the 2-week tryout period not to accept a worker; however, the option to be able to make that decision is reassuring.

For positions on which complete descriptions of job requirements or expected performance standards are not available, the job developer and the on-the-job trainer establish a description and standard for the employer to review, revise, and eventually approve.

On-the-Job Training and Placement The description of the job requirements and standards are utilized in the first stages of the on-the-job training. This stage, the *job tryout,* consists of a 2-week period during which workers receive limited instructional assistance to complete position requirements. At the end of the 2 weeks, the trainer, worker, and supervisor meet to identify priority training objectives. This meeting also serves to: 1) assist the trainer to identify what is most important to the employer; 2) provide some interaction between the employer, trainer, and worker; and 3) obtain an initial evaluation of progress.

Following the meeting, specific high priority training objectives are identified and intensive instruction is begun. Frequently, trainees have difficulty punching a time clock or orienting to the location—these were seldom priority objectives, however. Rather, priority objectives usually consist of specific job responsibilities such as correctly bagging groceries, interacting with customers, or labeling store items. As each worker becomes more independent in various aspects of the position, the trainer gradually fades out of the job site. As part of this process, the trainer often initiates a position, moves to another position to work with a different trainee, and then returns

to the first position. Each trainer's schedule is determined on a weekly basis to allow sufficient flexibility to accomodate position changes, retraining, and new positions.

Concurrent with training of specific job skills, multiple community survival skills are also taught. To achieve this goal, cooperative training from other agencies is sought to assist trainees in getting to and from work, dressing appropriately, preparing meals as necessary, and managing money once they begin to receive pay checks. When successful, this approach means that the program assists in monitoring and developing other programs. When other responsibilities prevent cooperating agencies from providing instruction, the job trainer is responsible for assuring that all necessary skills for successful employment are present. On occasion, this means that the job trainer becomes responsible for many additional skill areas, not traditionally considered vocational. If a given skill is necessary for continued employment, instruction is provided. Once a trainee demonstrates 95% of the work routine independently and receives observation and training for less than 20% of the position, he or she enters the follow-up phase of the program.

Follow-Up During this phase the trainee receives ongoing observation and training, as necessary, including gradual fading of the trainer, increased employer supervision, and ongoing evaluation on at least a monthly basis. Evaluation forms filled out by employers, parents, trainers, and the worker are discussed in monthly meetings to assure that any concerns or discrepancies are identified and resolved. During such meetings, concerns other than those of a strictly vocational nature are identified. Also individualized program plans (IPP), individualized education programs (IEP), individualized written rehabilitation programs (IWRP), or other group planning meetings are attended to assure that comprehensive services are provided as necessary.

If at any time a trainee requires more than 20% of the position requirements for observation or training, he or she is placed into a retraining phase and provided with intensive instruction until he or she is capable of returning to the follow-up phase. If job requirements are expanded or revised, a trainer frequently has to return to the position to assure a smooth transition and a satisfied employer.

Parental Support and Consent Specific activities involving parents and guardians occur throughout the four program phases. These contacts, which are essential for entry into a position and continued support for a given position, consist of four separate activities: 1) initial vocational inventory, 2) introduction to the program, 3) job placement, and 4) follow-up (Vogelsberg et al., 1984).

During the initial vocational inventory, expectations and desires for the worker's adult life are outlined. In addition, program staff and parents and guardians discuss ideal positions, concerns about issues in the community (transportation, benefits, physical limitations, and attitudes), interest in providing parental consent for release of records, and other program-related matters.

If parental consent for placement is granted, a program staff member (usually the training coordinator) visits the parents, provides them with detailed information about potential positions in the community, and explains specific areas of concern. At these meetings, the benefits and the effect of employment on benefits are carefully examined. At the completion of such a meeting, parents have the option to allow their son or daughter to be evaluated for placement or be contacted in the future after they have had time to consider the possibility of a community position for their son or daughter. Parents who are not interested in placement receive information about and referrals to other adult service agencies as well as a listing of parents who have been involved with the program whom they might want to contact.

If, on the other hand, parents agree to work further with the program, an evaluation is conducted and the potential worker's file becomes active. Once an appropriate position is identified, parents are contacted again, provided with detailed information about the position, and asked for their approval of the placement. As mentioned, placement decisions are frequently based on the amount of support available from the parent, the cooperating agency, and available transportation options, rather than a pure trainee-job match. If these three variables are not present, a decision is frequently made to wait for another position while a stronger support system is developed.

After placement, parents receive continual information about their son's or daughter's successes and failures on the job. Long-term support related to appropriate dress, scheduling, and transportation is frequently necessary, and it is not unusual during the initial months of a position for transportation to be provided by parents or subsidized by Vocational Rehabilitation. Once the worker enters the follow-up phase, monthly contacts are initiated with parents, employers, and workers. In some instances, trainees have become so independent in other survival skills as a result of placement in competitive community jobs that they were eventually able to move to more independent living arrangements. A few workers have been assisted to make the move from their natural home into a group home or supervised apartment setting or from a group home into a supervised apartment.

Parental support or lack thereof is a major variable in the long-term success or failure of a placement. When the service system is unavailable to assist, parents frequently become responsible for new activities with their son or daughter. In one instance, a parent expressed interest in becoming a job trainer to assure an appropriate community employment opportunity for her son.

RESULTS

Descriptive data are collected for each employment training program in four major areas: 1) demographic data, 2) training and follow-up, 3) employment, and 4) financial. The data are collected monthly from each program and compiled into a quarterly summary. Since new positions are developed, lost, or changed each month based upon employment (and sometimes worker) situations, the data series are fluid and constantly changing. The information in Table 1 about three employment training programs—site, location, and months in operation—is presented in an attempt to simplify a developing complex system.

Demographic Data

A total of 91 placements have been secured for 73 different workers. Eighteen individuals have lost positions and have been provided with training and placement services in a second employment site. Table 2 presents descriptive data concerning the 91 placements. Although IQ scores have not proven to be effective indicators of success or failure on the job, they do provide an indication of the workers' level of handicap. Level of handicap (degree of mental retardation) has been a constant source of discussion during advisory board meetings. One agency, for example, was concerned only with numbers of placements, while a second was more interested in level of handicap as a demonstration of competence. The majority of placed individuals are classified as either mildy or moderately mentally retarded. A small number of individuals considered severely mentally retarded have also been successfully placed. Once stronger educational and residential support services have been developed, it is anticipated that this population will become a higher placement priority.

Most workers who have received community job placements reside in their natural homes. Not only can natural home settings provide extra support when necessary, but the varied hours required by many community placements cannot always be accomodated by adult service residential settings.

Training and Follow-Up Information

These data include information about the referral source, prior work history, job titles, range of training hours, follow-up hours, and additional services paid for by the Division of Vocational Rehabilitation. The programs were developed to provide services to any individual considered severely disabled and mentally retarded. Thus, although typically located within (or associated with) regional mental health organizations, programs accepted referrals, performed evaluations, and made placements from multiple sources.

Of the 73 workers placed, 28 had some prior paid work history. Job titles for placements vary widely (see Table 3). Although placements tend to be in kitchen and custodial positions due to availability and the receptivity of employers in these fields, a number of positions of higher complexity and salary have been developed. For example, a training enclave established in a large electronics assembly plant resulted in four electronic assembler positions. The electronics enclave is the most complex position developed and varies from the other placements by having a 3- to 6-month training period prior to placement. Once a worker met criterion, he or she was eligible to become a temporary employee at the plant and (if everything went well) eventually a full-time permanent employee. A worker in one of the four available positions has been promoted and is a full-time employee who has learned to make multiple adjustments to new assembly boards independently.

Table 1. Site, location, and time in operation for three employment training programs

Program	Months in operation	Number of placements	Location
Transition I	56	49	Central State Barre, Vermont
Transition II	36	30	Northwest State Burlington, Vermont
Transition III	9	12	Southeast State White River Junction, Vermont

Table 2. Demographic information

Number of placements	Number of workers	Range of ages	Men	Women	Range of IQ's	Residential settings	Previous program training
Project Transition I: 4/1/80–11/1/84 (56 months)							
49 13 Placed twice (26%)	36	17–53 $\overline{X}=28$ MDN = 24	18	18	45–79 $\overline{X}=61$ MDN = 62	24 Natural home 10 Supervised apartment 2 Group home	18 High school 5 Work experience 4 None 3 Institution 3 Day program 3 Competitive work
Project Transition II: 11/1/81–11/1/84 (36 months)							
30 5 Placed twice (17%) 5 in Electronics enclave	25	19–49 $\overline{X}=23$ MDN = 23	12	13	10–73 $\overline{X}=55$ MDN = 59	13 Natural home (12-Parents) (1-Husband) 5 Supervised apartment 5 Group home 1 ICF/MR 1 Community care home	9 Sheltered workshop 8 High school 5 Work experience 1 Day program
Project Transition III: 3/1/84–11/30/84 (9 months)							
12	12	18–50 $\overline{X}=32$ MDN = 32	8	4	56–73 $\overline{X}=66$ MDN = 67	10 Natural home (7-Parents) (3-Wife) 2 Community care home	4 High school 4 Activity center 2 CETA positions 1 Odd jobs 1 Competitive work

42

Table 3. Training and follow-up information

Placement referral source	Prior work history	Job titles	Range of training hours	Range of follow-up hours	Vocational rehabilitation services
		Project Transition I: 4/1/80–11/1/84 (56 months)			
12 Day program	13 Competitive work	21 Kitchen work	3–327	3–180	24 None
11 Vocational rehabilitation	11 Work experience	6 Custodial	$\overline{X}=50$	$\overline{X}=62$	13 Clothing/shoes
6 Public school	6 None	3 Courtesy clerks			10 Transportation
4 Mental health	4 Day program	3 Stock clerks	MDN = 56	$\overline{X}=40$	3 Medical assistance
2 Personal	2 High school	2 Wood sorters			2 Watch/clock
1 Social rehab. services		2 Lacquer dippers			2 Equipment
		2 Chamber persons			1 Tutor assistance
		2 Pants pressers			
		1 Laundry assistance			
		1 Asst. cook			
		1 Book binder			
		1 Sock turner			
		1 Newspaper tying			
		1 Desk clerk			
		1 Loom cleaner			
		(55% Kitchen/custodial)			
		Project Transition II: 11/1/81–11/1/84 (36 months)			
10 Public school	9 High school	13 Custodial	12–995	1–169	16 Follow-up assistance
6 Sheltered work	7 Competitive work	6 Kitchen work	$\overline{X}=234$	$\overline{X}=34$	10 None
5 Vocational rehabilitation	5 Sheltered work	4 Electronic assembly			4 Clothing (shoes)
4 Day program	4 None		MDN = 157	MDN = 12	4 Transportation
		1 Stock clerk			2 Supportive family counseling
		1 Courtesy clerk	Enclave		
		1 Shield cleaner			2 Tutor assistance
		1 Washout person	412–995		5 Enclave work incentive allowances
		(34% Kitchen/custodial)	$\overline{X}=735$		
		Project Transition III: 3/1/84–11/30/84 (9 months)			
8 Mental health	8 Competitive work	3 House persons	6–143	0–35	11 None
2 High school	3 Vocational training program	2 Day porters	$\overline{X}=56$	$\overline{X}=9$	1 Clothing
2 Vocational rehabilitation	1 Volunteer	2 Housekeepers			
		1 Laundry aide	MDN = 49	MDN = 2	
		1 Customer service			
		1 Linen presser			
		1 Janitor			
		1 Floor porter			
		(83% Custodial)			

43

The average number of training hours per placement has varied widely depending upon the complexity of the position and the worker's level of handicap. One program has developed more complex positions and worked with more severely handicapped individuals as reflected in the average number of training hours—234. The other two programs show an average of 50 hours of training per position. Each program is expected to develop one new position a month (12 placements per year), and as the quality of public school and adult service programs improves, programs should be able to expand both the type of position and degree of handicap that can be accomodated.

Employment

Twenty-six of the 91 positions are full time with full benefits; the remaining positions are part time, the average number of hours worked per month being approximately 100. Absenteeism and tardiness have been minimal; some workers have been found to come to work too early or on days they were not scheduled to work. Table 4 provides the data summary for employment information. Accurate success rates are difficult to measure because of the multiple evaluation systems utilized by different agencies. The Division of Vocational Rehabilitation (VR) in the state of Vermont considers individuals successfully employed if they have been on the job for a 3-month period. To assure comparability of program data, this measure is reported along with the long-term success program placements. The Barre program has an 82% success rate after 3 months on the job, or a 66% success rate over the 56 months the program has been in operation. Similar figures apply to the Burlington program (88% for 3 months and 64% for 36 months) and the White River Junction Program (83% for 3 months and 83% for 9 months). Reasons for loss of positions have been varied and similar to other results of reports about position losses (Kochany & Keller, 1980; LaGreca, Stone, & Bell, 1982). The reasons for position losses are equally divided between employer and employment changes and worker adjustment difficulties.

Financial Information

According to the Whitehead study (1977), individuals with mental retardation in sheltered settings earned an average *annual* salary of $417. In comparison, the average *monthly* salary of the individuals placed in the programs described here is $365, $400, and $275, respectively. No position has been accepted at less than minimum wage, and one position demands an hourly wage of $9.58. Many of the workers were not accepted in sheltered settings and had been in work activity and day programs prior to being placed by the employment training programs. Total salaries earned by workers over the 56-, 36-, and 9-month periods of the programs are $325,945 (Table 5). Each placement costs a program approximately $7,000, while the annual costs for a day program in Vermont are $5,000. On a yearly basis, therefore, it is less expensive to the service system to maintain individuals in a day program. However, the yearly costs for the day program are continual, whereas placement costs are a one-time-only expenditure for 65% of those individuals placed. The difficulty with the present cost-benefit analysis, which demonstrates that over time the placement programs save money, is that state service agencies operate on a yearly budget and are still responsible for the extra costs each year for placement activities. Careful analysis of costs per placement, savings to Social Security, and savings to the social service system is being prepared for future publication.

PROGRAM REPLICATION

Administrative Issues

The first competitive employment program in Vermont, initiated 5 years ago, has been replicated three times in three different locations. Each program has taken a similar approach and has encountered similar difficulties—mostly those typically met with in other forms of adult services. Continued efforts must aim at improving the quality of services by serving more severely handicapped individuals in more complex positions.

Table 4. Employment information

Employers	Range of hours worked per month	Range of days absent	Range of times tardy	Percent job status
Project Transition I: 4/1/80–11/1/84 (56 months)				
18 Restaurants	16–172	0–22	0–11	24 Presently employed
8 Manufacturing				12 Terminated due to trainee
5 Nursing homes	$\overline{X}=106$	$\overline{X}=3$	$\overline{X}=1$	9 Terminated due to employer or
3 Custodial services				employment changes
3 Department stores	MDN = 112			2 Laid off
3 Motel/hotels				1 Terminated due to parents
2 Private clubs	14 Full Time			1 Terminated due to medical difficulties
2 Grocery stores	(28%)			
2 Dry cleaners				
1 Auto supply				
1 Distributor				82% Success by VR 3-month standard
1 University				66% Success after 56 months
				61% Success for second placements
Project Transition II: 11/1/81–11/1/84 (36 months)				
5 Saga Foods	8–180	0–24	0–6	6 Presently employed
4 Digital Electronics				5 Terminated due to trainee
3 Carburs Restaurant	$\overline{X}=100$	$\overline{X}=2$	$\overline{X}=1$	1 Laid off
3 Grocery stores				1 Terminated due to employer or
2 Sears dept. store	MDN = 81			employment changes
2 Howard Johnsons				1 Moved out of state
1 Coca-Cola	10 Full Time			1 Took a better position
1 Chittenden Bank	(30%)			
1 Jacques Store				
1 Zayres				88% Success by VR 3-month standard
1 Ramada Inn				64% Success after 36 months
1 Shell Craft				40% Success for second placements
1 General Electric				
1 Millibride Wire				
1 Sweetwaters Restaurant				
1 Sirloin Saloon				
1 New England Rustics				
Project Transition III: 3/1/84–11/30/84 (9 months)				
4 Sheraton North Country Inn	16–146	0–6	0–3	10 Presently employed
				2 Terminated due to trainee
4 P & C Grocery	$\overline{X}=72$	$\overline{X}=1$	$\overline{X}=1$	
1 Hanover Terrace				
1 South Royalton House	MDN = 78			83% Success by VR 3-month standard
1 Hartland Township	2 Full Time			83% Success after 9 months
1 Skunk Hollow Inn	(16%)			

Location As new programs developed, program location became an issue, and the new programs are located outside the regional mental health offices. This allows for better program separation and guarantees both autonomy and better coordination between funding agencies. In addition, locating a community-based employment training program in a traditional business location, while adding only marginally to expenses, improved the expectation of the program becoming a small, efficient self-contained business rather than another program within a large regional service setting.

Funding The programs were developed through a Vermont Division of Vocational Rehabilitation Establishment Grant with matching funds from the Vermont Department of Mental Health. As mentioned, the program

Table 5. Financial information

Type of employer assistance	Fringe benefits	Range of pay per hour	Range of monthly salaries	Range of preemployment benefits	Range of postemployment benefits
Project Transition I: 4/1/80–11/1/84 (56 months)					
21 None 21 TJTC 5 CETA 3 NARC-OJT	43 Vacations 12 Insurance 10 Sick Days	$3.10^a–6.05 $\overline{X}$ = $3.49 MDN = $3.35	$54–660 $\overline{X}$ = $364 MDN = $336	SSI 18 Recipients $3–436 $\overline{X}$ = $271	SSI 17 Recipients $2–385 $\overline{X}$ = $174
59% Initiated benefits		9 Raises (25%) 1 Promotion	Total salaries = $199,316	SSDB 14 Recipients $81–789 $\overline{X}$ = $361	SSDB 13 Recipients $81–878 $\overline{X}$ = $383^b
Project Transition II: 11/1/81–11/1/84 (36 months)					
18 TJTC 11 None 1 Public school	12 Insurance 10 Vacations 4 Sick days	$3.35–9.58 $\overline{X}$ = $4.05 MDN = $3.35	$27–1540 $\overline{X}$ = $400 MDN = $300	SSI 18 Recipients $25–468 $\overline{X}$ = $312	SSI 16 Recipients $1–458 $\overline{X}$ = $237
63% Initiated benefits		5 Raises (16%) 1 Promotion	Total salaries = $116,575	SSDB 7 Recipients $157–319 $\overline{X}$ = $257	SSDB 7 Recipients $157–319 $\overline{X}$ = $258^b
Project Transition III: 3/1/84–11/30/84 (9 months)					
7 TJTC 4 None 3 NARC-OJT	12 Vacations 4 Sick days 0 Insurance	$3.35–4.30 $\overline{X}$ = $3.61 MDN = $3.61	$144–546 $\overline{X}$ = $275 MDN = $275	SSI 5 Recipients $167–478 $\overline{X}$ = $292	SSI 5 Recipients $167–478 $\overline{X}$ = $274
75% Initiated benefits		2 Raises (16%)	Total salaries = $10,054	SSDB 0 Recipients	SSDB 0 Recipients

^{a}Minimum wage, 1980. ^{b}Cost of living increase.

46

that has now gone beyond the establishment grant time period has established a fee-for-services schedule whereby reimbursement is received for each individual placed. These funds are presently available and other innovative approaches to funding similar programs are being investigated. The tuition-based postsecondary model mentioned earlier is an example of a possible future base for similar programs. Small local colleges appear to be natural and ideal locations for training and employment services for individuals with handicaps who leave secondary public school services.

Cooperative Agreements Throughout the program development, written cooperative agreements with multiple agencies have been necessary to guarantee success of the programs (Vogelsberg et al., 1981). Consequently, fears related to competition for limited positions, duplication of services, or increased fragmentation of services as a result of entry of a new program into an area have been reduced or eliminated through careful analysis of existing services, written agreements on referral, placement, support, funding, and cross-agency advisory boards.

One of the first rules developed for cooperative agreements was that each agency involved in assisting a worker to become employed would be recognized and given credit for assistance. Although this stipulation has frequently meant that multiple agencies each counted the same placement, it was necessary in order to maintain cooperative relationships.

Training and Salaries of Program Personnel The ideal training program would include well-paid professionals at the Master's level with preservice training specifically preparing them for their current position. Unfortunately, only few personnel preparation programs graduate individuals for this type of program, and the budget that can usually be developed through state funds is limited. Therefore, the programs in Vermont have typically hired bachelor's degree special education or psychology graduates and provided them with technical assistance and training to run the program. While this may not be the preferred

approach, it has proven effective. It appears that the on-the-job training positions are destined to be entry-level high-turnover jobs. Few professionals are interested in the continual schedule variations necessary due to the limited availability of community positions. Furthermore, in a number of placements, the "handicapped" worker made more money than the on-the-job trainer.

Program Evaluation

Level of Handicap Although the programs were developed to provide community placements for individuals classified as *severely handicapped,* discussions have continued between funding sources about the acceptable level of handicap. At present, attempts are being made to direct services towards more severely handicapped workers. As the existing, traditional service system begins to develop improved placement services for less handicapped individuals, intensive training programs such as those described here should become more available to workers with severe handicaps.

Types of Positions Most workers are placed in janitorial and kitchen jobs. These positions, which are high turnover and easily acquired, are the most available and least difficult to develop. However, the newly established programs were not meant to provide just janitorial or kitchen service positions. A continual evaluation of positions acquired and job development efforts, therefore, is necessary to move away from these traditional employment options. In contrast, if kitchen and janitorial services are the main type of positions developed, a training program in these fields would be appropriate and more cost effective. An ideal system, however, would consist of multiple employment training sites prior to entry into adult service support.

Wages Many of the placed workers enter their first paid position in the community, whereas the average individual in society tends to have held a number of jobs in varying locations and at varying wages prior to settling into a long-term position. The programs are not able to move a competent worker into a higher paying or higher quality position. Again, an ideal service system would have provided training and employment in a series of positions of gradually increasing quality based upon the individual worker's acquisition capabilities rather than the availability of services.

Number of Placements The difficulty inherent in defining the level of handicap makes it difficult to measure the number of placements expected or the level of handicap of each placement. Thus, the traditional expectation that the more severely handicapped the individual, the more difficult the placement, is not always true. For example, capable individuals who have learned the job requirements quickly have abused their newly acquired finances and independence. As a result, they have frequently required more follow-up observation to maintain a position than the worker who lives in a group home and is classified as severely mentally retarded. The average placement figure for each program has been one placement per month (12 placements annually). Through ongoing technical assistance, attempts are made to assure a variety of both full- and part-time positions.

CONCLUSION

Once the first competitive employment program, developed in Vermont 5 years ago, proved to offer individuals who are mentally retarded an alternative to sheltered employment or day activities, many parents, professionals, and advocates began to assist in the establishment of future programs.

The current four programs of this type are initial demonstrations of improved vocational alternatives for individuals with severe handicaps. However, before the quality of comprehensive services for individuals with significant handicaps can be improved, a number of issues must be resolved, including: 1) acceptance of community-based instruction at the public school level, 2) expansion of vocational education programs, and 3) initiation of multiple supportive options in the community. Given these favorable changes, employment training programs may be able to direct their services to long-term follow-up and development of better positions for those individuals already working in the community.

During the 1970s, individuals with mental retardation gradually became accepted in competitive and supported employment. If dedicated professionals continue these efforts, the quality of services for individuals with significant handicaps will continue to expand and improve in the 1980s. Improved services will assist individuals in increasing their personal independence and result in more satisfying and cost-effective outcomes. The necessary technology and resources are available. Review and revision of existing systems, improved community acceptance, and continued advocacy are necessary to maintain the present momentum.

REFERENCES

Appleby, J. A. (1978). *Training programs and placement services*. Salt Lake City, UT: Olympic Publishing Co.

Bellamy, G. T., Horner, R. H., & Inman, D. P. (1979). *Vocational habilitation of severely retarded adults: A direct service technology*. Baltimore: University Park Press.

Bellamy, G. T., Sheehan, M. R., Horner, R. H., & Boles, S. M. (1980). Community programs for severely handicapped adults: An analysis. *Journal of The Association for the Severely Handicapped, 5*, 307–324.

Belmore, K., & Brown, L. (1976). A job skill inventory strategy for use in public school vocational training programs for severely handicapped potential workers. In L. Brown, N. Certo, K. Belmore, & T. Crowner (Eds.), *Madison's alternative for zero exclusion: Papers and programs related to public school services for secondary age severely handicapped students* (Vol. VI, Part 1, pp. 143–218). Madison, WI: Madison Metropolitan School District.

Certo, N., Schwartz, R., & Brown, L. (1975). Community transportation: Teaching severely handicapped students to ride a public bus system. In L. Brown, T. Crowner, W. Williams, & R. York (Eds.), *Madison's alternative for zero exclusion: A book of readings* (Vol. V, pp. 147–232). Madison, WI: Madison Metropolitan Public Schools.

Cuvo, A. J., & Davis, P. K. (1983). Behavior therapy and community living skills. In M. Hersen, R. M. Eisler, & P. M. Miller (Eds.), *Progress in behavior modification* (pp. 125–172). New York: Academic Press.

Goodall, P. A., Wehman, P., & Cleveland, P. (1983). Job placement for mentally retarded individuals. *Education and Training of the Mentally Retarded, 4,* 271–278.

Greenleigh Associates (1975). *The role of the sheltered workshop in the rehabilitation of the severely handicapped.* New York: Report to the Department of Health, Education, and Welfare, Rehabilitation Services Administration.

Hamre-Nietupski, S., Ford, A., & Williams, W. (1977). Implementation of selected sex education and social skills programs with severely handicapped students. *Education and Training of the Mentally Retarded, 12,* 364–372.

Hill, R., Lagor, R., Moore, T., Hanzl, Z., Burrus, D., Williams, W., & Vogelsberg, R. T. (1980). Report to the Secretary of Human Services on mental retardation and vocational rehabilitation. *Center for Developmental Disabilities Monograph Series, 1,* 1–35.

Kochany, L., & Keller, J. (1980). An analysis and evaluation of the failures of severely disabled individuals in competitive employment. In P. Wehman & M. Hill (Eds.), *Vocational training and placement of severely disabled persons: Project Employability* (Vol. 2, pp. 47–72). Richmond, VA: Virginia Commonwealth University.

LaGreca, A. M., Stone, W. L., & Bell, C. R. (1982). Assessing the problematic interpersonal skills of mentally retarded individuals in a vocational setting. *Applied Research in Mental Retardation, 3,* 37–53.

Nietupski, J., Certo, N. Pumpian, I., & Belmore, K. (1976). Supermarket shopping: Teaching severely handicapped students to generate a shopping list and make purchases functionally linked with meal preparation. In L. Brown, N. Certo, K. Belmore, & T. Crowner (Eds.), *Madison's alternative for zero exclusion: Papers and programs related to public school services for secondary age severely handicapped students* (Vol. VI, Part 1, pp. 220–270). Madison, WI: Madison Metropolitan Public Schools.

Novak, A. R., & Heal, L. W. (1980). *Integration of developmentally disabled individuals into the community.* Baltimore: Paul H. Brookes.

Rudrud, E. H., Ziarnik, J. P., Bernstein, G. S., & Ferrara, J. M. (1984). *Proactive vocational habilitation.* Baltimore: Paul H. Brookes.

Rusch, F. R., & Mithaug, D. E. (1980). *Vocational training for mentally retarded adults: A behavior analytic approach.* Champaign, IL: Research Press.

Rusch, F. R., Schutz, R. P., & Heal, L. W. (1983). Vocational training and placement. In J. L. Matson & J. A. Mulick (Eds.), *Handbook of mental retardation* (pp. 455–466). New York: Pergamon Press.

Rusch, F. R., Schutz, R. P., Mithaug, D. E., Stewart, J. E., & Mar, D. K. (1982). *VACG: The vocational assessment and curriculum guide.* Seattle, WA: Exceptional Education.

Schutz, R. P., Vogelsberg, R. T., & Rusch, F. R. (1980). A behavioral approach to integrating individuals into the community. In A. Novak & L. Heal (Eds.), *Integration of the developmentally disabled into the community* (pp. 107–120). Baltimore: Paul H. Brookes.

Schutz, R. P., Williams, W., Iverson, G. S., & Duncan, D. (1984). Social integration of severely handicapped students. In N. Certo, N. Haring, & R. York (Eds.), *Public school integration of severely handicapped students: Rational issues and progressive alternatives* (pp. 15–42). Baltimore: Paul H. Brookes.

Sowers, J., Rusch, F. R., & Hudson, C. (1979). Training a severely retarded young adult to ride the city bus to and from work. *AAESPH Review, 4* 15–23.

Stanfield, J. S. (1976). Graduation: What happens to the retarded child when he grows up? In R. M. Anderson & J. G. Greer (Eds.), *Educating the severely and profoundly retarded* (pp. 403–412). Baltimore: University Park Press.

Vogelsberg, R. T. (1984). Competitive employment programs for individuals with mental retardation in rural areas. In P. Wehman (Ed.), *Proceedings from the national symposium on employment of citizens with mental retardation.* Richmond, VA: Virginia Commonwealth University.

Vogelsberg, R. T., Ashe, W., & Williams, W. (1986). Community based service delivery in rural Vermont: Issues and recommendations. In R. Horner, L. M. Voeltz, & B. Fredericks (Eds.), *Education of learners with severe handicaps: Exemplary service strategies* (pp. 29–59). Baltimore: Paul H. Brookes.

Vogelsberg, R. T., & Rusch, F. R. (1979). Training severely handicapped students to cross partially controlled intersections. *AAESPH Review, 4,* 264–273.

Vogelsberg, R. T., Spaulding, P., Patterson, D., Schenck, R., & Phillips, R. (1984). Project Transition: Competitive employment case management system. *Center for Developmental Disabilities Monograph Series, 4,* 1–127.

Vogelsberg, R. T., Williams, W., & Ashe, W. (1981). Improving vocational services through interagency cooperation. In C. L. Hansen (Ed.), *Severely handicapped persons in the community* (pp. 169–201). Seattle, WA: Program Development Assistance System.

Vogelsberg, R. T., Williams, W. W., & Fox, W. L. (1981). Comprehensive vocational services operational plan. *Center for Development Disabilities Monograph Series, 2,* 1–43.

Vogelsberg, R. T., Williams, W., & Friedl, M. (1980). Facilitating systems change for the severely handicapped: Secondary and adult services. *Journal of The Association for the Severely Handicapped, 5,* 73–85.

Wehman, P. (1979). *Recreational programming for developmentally disabled persons.* Baltimore: Paul H. Brookes.

Wehman, P. (1981). *Competitive employment: New horizons for severely disabled individuals.* Baltimore: Paul H. Brookes.

Wehman, P., & Hill, J. W. (1979). *Vocational training and placement of severely disabled persons: Project Employability* (Vol. I). Richmond, VA: Virginia Commonwealth University.

Whitehead, C. W. (1977). *Sheltered workshop study: A nationwide report on sheltered workshops and their employment of handicapped individuals.* Washington, DC: U.S. Department of Labor.

Wilcox, B., & Bellamy, G. T. (1982). *Design of high school programs for severely handicapped students.* Baltimore: Paul H. Brookes.

Chapter 4

Competitive Employment in Southern Illinois

A Transitional Service Delivery Model for Enhancing Competitive Employment Outcomes for Public School Students

Paul E. Bates

RESEARCH STUDIES, PANELS of experts, and commissions all agree that there is a lack of correspondence between the demands of high school and those of the postschool world, whereby secondary education generally fails to establish the requisite skills for successfully making the transition from school to the working world (Wilcox & Bellamy, 1982). The inadequacy of secondary special education for persons with mental retardation was well documented by Stanfield (1976). Results of this follow-up study of public school graduates showed that: 1) no graduates were self-supporting, 2) 94% were living with their families, 3) only 10% left their neighborhood to travel in the community at large, and 4) for those not involved in adult day programs, watching television constituted their major activity. Unfortunately, the postschool status of persons with mental retardation as well as persons with other handicaps does not appear to have changed drastically in the past decade.

The usual postschool condition—unemployment or underemployment and minimal participation in community life—points to an urgent need to examine the appropriateness of public school programs, while demonstrating the effectiveness of alternative education models. A major objective of the Education for All

Handicapped Children Act (PL 94-142) was to ensure an appropriate education for all handicapped persons to enable them to obtain their maximum degree of self-sufficiency. Since holding a job and living independently are often the measures by which adult life is evaluated, public school programs must be geared toward facilitating these outcomes. According to PL 94-142, Section 504 of the Rehabilitation Act, and the Education Amendments of 1976 (PL 94-482), vocational training and related independent living programs must be developed for all persons with handicaps.

In attempting to comply with these mandates, educators have experienced difficulty in developing appropriate employment training programs for students with handicaps, including those classified as severely handicapped. In the absence of progressive leadership and programmatic guidelines, younger students have not received employment experiences, whereas the vocational preparation of older students has been restricted primarily to benchwork tasks traditionally associated with sheltered workshop employment (e.g., bagging golf tees). Vocational trade classes and community work experiences are denied most students who experience severe handicaps because of their perceived lack of potential and need for assistance and support. It is not surprising, therefore, that these students have failed to succeed in competitive employment.

Results of recent research have demonstrated that persons who are moderately and severely handicapped are capable of acquiring and maintaining competitive employment (Rusch, 1983; Wehman, 1981). Much of this research has been gathered on postschool-age individuals. If the potential for greater community integration and participation of students with similar handicaps is to be realized, a model for delivery of employment services in the public schools is needed.

The number of students with handicaps who are being educated in public school settings has increased tremendously. Additionally, expansion of personnel preparation programs has resulted in a large number of teachers capable of working with this population. Nevertheless, guidelines regarding the components of an appropriate education have emerged only recently (Bates, Renzaglia, & Wehman, 1981; Wilcox & Bellamy, 1982). Common to these guidelines is an emphasis on curriculum and instructional activities that promote fuller participation in community life by persons with handicaps. That is, the goal is to enable all students to live and work as independently as possible in their home communities.

Project EARN (Employment and Rehabilitation = Normalization) (see Figure 1) is an educational service delivery model that incorporates many recently developed guidelines into a longitudinal training and competitive employment training program in the public schools for students who are handicapped. The model was adapted from Mithaug and Haring's (1977) program for rehabilitation and placement of handicapped adults by: 1) extending vocational training recommendations to elementary- and intermediate-age students, 2) operationalizing the transition planning process, and 3) focusing on competitive employment as the primary outcome measure.

The programmatic aspects of Project EARN have been implemented through short-term demonstration grants from state agencies and consultative arrangements with public schools.

Implementation of the model relies upon the use of behavioral technology for extended assessment and training activities throughout a student's public school experience and beyond. In this chapter, each of Project EARN's components is described along with supporting evidence regarding the value of the model for persons who are severely handicapped. Results of program demonstrations conducted under the auspices of Project EARN are also presented. Finally, several issues impacting on the success of public school vocational training efforts are discussed.

PROJECT EARN COMPONENTS

Assess Job Availability

Since most students who are handicapped are likely to remain in their home communities after public school graduation, their communities represent the primary source of potential employment. Consequently, school personnel should assess local availability of jobs to ensure that school-based efforts conform to postschool requirements. Assessment of local job availability often includes developing a list of employment situations where former students have succeeded, a tally of the frequency of specific help-wanted ads in local newspapers, a listing of employment openings from local job services, discussions with area rehabilitation counselors, telephone or written surveys of employers, discussions with business and service clubs, and personal contacts with employers. Assessment activities may also include investigations of vocational education class offerings in area high schools. Based on available information, relevant career and vocational training experiences are then developed.

By assessing the community first rather than the student apart from the community, Project EARN departs from traditional practices. While persons who are handicapped have succeeded in a variety of career areas, persons who are severely handicapped are most often placed in entry-level service occupations such as food services and janitorial/housekeeping services (Martin, Rusch, Tines, Brulle, & White, in

---

COMMITMENT TO PHILOSOPHY OF ZERO EXCLUSION,
INTEGRATION, AND NORMALIZATION

ASSESS LOCAL COMMUNITY FOR JOB AVAILABILITY

IDENTIFY REQUISITE SKILLS FOR EMPLOYMENT
(Community-Referenced Curriculum Development)

ASSESS STUDENTS' VOCATIONAL PREFERENCES AND
PERFORMANCE ON REQUISITE SKILLS

DEVELOP TRANSITION PLANS AS PART OF STUDENTS' IEPs

IMPLEMENT LONGITUDINAL VOCATIONAL EDUCATION

| Career | School-Based | Related Skills | Community-Based |
| Awareness/Exploration | Vocational Training | Instruction | Vocational Training |

PLACE STUDENTS IN COMPETITIVE EMPLOYMENT

PROVIDE FOLLOW-UP SUPPORT

EVALUATE PROGRAM EFFECTIVENESS

Figure 1. Project EARN: A service delivery model for longitudinal vocational training of moderately and severely handicapped persons in the public schools.

press; Wehman & Hill, 1982). This should not be interpreted as a justification for not expanding employment efforts into industrial, technological, and other areas; however, it does suggest that public school programs should assure training experiences in occupations that traditionally represent employment outcomes for students who are handicapped.

After identifying food services as likely employment outcomes, Pancsofar, Bates, and Bronkema (1981) conducted a telephone survey of 50 restaurant managers in southern Illinois to identify employment possibilities for persons who were moderately and severely handicapped. The managers were approached in two ways: 1) by a person who identified himself as a professional representing mentally retarded high school students, and 2) by a person identifying himself as a college student looking for work. Seven (14%) of the managers reported job openings to the professional, whereas 17 (34%) listed vacancies when approached by the college student. This difference is disturbing and suggests the need for better public relations with employers. In two of the restaurant settings, follow-up contacts resulted in competitive placements within 2 months of the initial survey.

Identify Requisite Skills for Employment

Once jobs available in the community have been identified, the next step consists of conducting a detailed assessment of the specific skills required to succeed in a *variety* of employment situations. One example of a direct observation strategy for identifying requisite skills in competitive employment is the *Job Skill Inventory* (Belmore & Brown, 1978), which consists of three major components. First, general information regarding the work and social requirements of the job is described. Second, specific work skills are task analyzed on the basis of direct observations of persons currently employed in the specific job. Third, supportive skills and other pertinent information that might influence job success are identified. Often such supportive skills (e.g., social-interpersonal, independent living, and transportation) are most critical for long-term job retention. For example, the social-interpersonal competencies required to get along with co-workers and supervisors (e.g., giving and receiving praise, accepting criticism and negative feedback, asking for assistance, and engaging in small talk) are essential for success in community employment.

A detailed assessment of specific job skills allows for the development of a community-referenced curriculum from which longitudinal vocational training experiences can be developed. Table 1 provides examples of basic vocational competencies for janitorial, food service, and laundry employment, identified through an analysis of several job skill inventories. These competencies are divided into three levels of difficulty or complexity. In establishing priorities for a public school vocational program, these levels could correspond to elementary, intermediate, and secondary behavioral objectives.

These specific vocational competencies become functional skills when a student must perform them as part of a vocational routine or sequence. For all community work experiences and community job placements identified in Project EARN, skill sequences are developed to identify the order in which all job tasks must be performed. A sample skill sequence for the job of animal caretaker at a university research laboratory is presented in Table 2.

In addition to specific vocational competencies identified through community assessment activities, *general* work behaviors have also been targeted through observation of realistic employment settings. Such general work habits include behaviors related to arrival at the job, work performance, break time, departure, and use of work-produced income. Specific competencies associated with these basic work habits are listed in Table 3.

Assess Students' Vocational Preferences and Performance on Requisite Skills

Traditionally, comprehensive vocational evaluations have included psychological assessments, work sample evaluations, situational

Table 1. Basic service industry competencies

Level	Janitorial	Food service	Laundry
I	Emptying wastebaskets Dusting tables Refilling towel dispensers Disposing of trash Cleaning ashtrays Dusting shelves	Rinsing platters Changing dishwater Sorting silverware Wiping tables Scraping dishes	Folding sheets Folding towels Hanging clothes on a line Folding clothes

II	Cleaning mirrors
	Cleaning sinks
	Cleaning urinals
	Sweeping floors
	Waxing and polishing tables
	Wet mopping floors;
	    solution preparation
	Spot cleaning walls
	Washing painted walls
	Waxing paneling
		Matching and sorting
		    (knives, forks, & spoons)
		Setting tables
		Cleaning up spills
		Polishing silverware
			Drying clothes
			Washing clothes by hand
			Sorting clothes
			Pressing laundry with a
			    clothes presser
			Hanging/bagging clothes

III	Waxing floors Cleaning windows Cleaning toilets Damp mopping floors Replacing toilet paper Vacuuming Using floor buffer String mopping floors Spot cleaning carpets Cleaning & polishing furniture Cleaning vinyl and/or leather furniture Sealing floors Stripping floors	Washing dishes Drying dishes Bussing restaurant tables Operating a dishwasher Unloading a dishwasher	Washing clothes (washing machine) Pressing laundry with an iron Marking/tagging clothes Bundling/tying/labeling laundry

Table 2. Task sequence for animal caretaker position

1. Change clothes
2. Prepare water bottles
3. Obtain clean cages
4. Transport bottles and cages to Room 51E
5. Obtain rack of breeder cages
6. Push sawdust can in position for bedding replacement (Mon. & Thurs.)
7. Push food can in position
8. Fill clean cage with two scoops of bedding (Mon. & Thurs.)
9. Transfer ID tag from dirty cage to clean cage
10. Transfer rats by tail to clean cage
11. Fill feed tray
12. Put clean water bottle in cage
13. Return cage to shelf
14. Repeat until all cages have been cleaned
15. Clean counter tops
16. Sweep floor
17. Mop floor
18. Transport dirty cages to cage cleaning room
19. Proceed to Room 29 and repeat procedure
20. Use washing machine to clean cages
21. Change clothes

assessments, and on-the-job tryouts. Unfortunately, most of these efforts have been directed toward collecting a limited behavioral sample in a limited time period for the purpose of identifying characteristics that can be used to predict future performance. Such assessment practices have been labeled *static* because the student's existing characteristics are considered separate from the student's abilities when

Table 3. Basic work habits

1. *Arrival behaviors*
   Arrive on time (daily)
   Check in
   Go to work area
   Begin work independently
2. *Work behaviors*
   Work independently
   Work persistently
   Work at an acceptable rate
   Request assistance when needed
3. *Break Time behaviors*
   Go to break on time
   Engage in appropriate social behavior
   Return to work on time
4. *Departure behaviors*
   Stop working at an appropriate time
   Organize work materials
   Check-out from work
5. *Money-related behaviors*
   Work for money
   Exchange money for tangible items
   Save money

provided training (Gold, 1980; Menchetti, Rusch, & Owens, 1983).

As an alternative to these practices, *dynamic* assessment techniques emphasizing direct observation of behavior in different jobs and under varying supervision conditions for extended periods of time have been recommended (Bates & Pancsofar, 1985). These assessments involve repeated measurements of specific behaviors related to employment success (e.g., quality of performance, attending to task, productivity, punctuality, compliance to supervision, co-worker social interaction, etc.).

Figure 2 provides an example of an assessment of a Project EARN student who was employed as a dishwasher in a small restaurant. Daily performance was recorded under conditions involving one-to-one supervision, corrective feedback, and intermittent social reinforcement. This information was used to decide when to withdraw supervision and reduce reinforcement.

Student preference is an important consideration in the vocational assessment process. Also, parents' willingness to support employment options and employer evaluation of the student's suitability for particular careers are important. If a student has had limited vocational training experiences in community-based sites, Project EARN encourages long-term job rotation whereby the student is exposed to multiple community employment experiences. By increasing the breadth of a person's experience in community employ ment, more information is available from which a viable career placement can be selected.

Develop Transition Plans as Part of Students' Individualized Education Programs

According to Brown et al. (1981), transition plans should be developed and revised continually throughout a student's public school experience. This recommendation has been operationalized to include a Transition Plan to which representatives from various educational programs in the school district, com-

Teacher Jan S.   Student Sara N.

Environment Walgreens

Program Changing dishwasher

April

	Dates 20	* 21	* 22	* 23	* 24	*
1. Press on-switch	+ +	− + + −	+ + + +	+ + + +	+ + + + +	+
2. Turn lever to open	− −	− − − −	− − − −	− − − −	− − − − −	−
3. Watch drain until water stops	− +	− + − +	− + − −	+ − + −	+ + + + +	+
4. Turn drain lever to shut position	− −	− − − −	− − − −	− − − −	− − − − −	−
5. Open door of dishwasher	− +	− + + +	+ + + +	+ + + +	+ + + + +	+
6. Inspect strainer for debris	− −	− − − −	− − − −	− − − −	− − − − −	−
7. Remove strainer trays	+ +	+ + + +	+ + + +	+ + + +	+ + + + +	+
8. Rinse debris in sink	− +	− − + −	− + − −	+ − + −	+ + + + +	+
9. Replace strainer plates	− −	− − − −	− − − −	− − − −	− − − − −	−
10. Close washer door	+ +	+ + + +	+ + + +	+ + + +	+ + + + +	+
11. Turn hot water faucet clockwise	− −	− − − −	− − − −	− − − −	− − − − −	−
12. Watch drain until water flows	− +	+ − + +	− + + +	+ + + +	+ + + + +	+
13. Turn hot water faucet counterclockwise	− −	− − − −	− − − −	− − − −	− − − − −	−
14. Open dishwasher door	+ +	+ + + +	+ + + +	+ + + +	+ + + + +	+
15. Press off-switch	− −	− + + +	+ + + −	+ + + −	+ + + + +	+
Steps independent	4 8	6 6 6 7	8 7 7 8	5 8 8 9	5 9 9 9 9	9

Figure 2.   Task-analytic assessment for changing dishwater.

munity agencies, and employers provide input annually.

The transition planning process has particular relevance to students who are in their last years of public education. After these individuals have participated in a series of vocational training experiences, a final Transition Plan is formalized to ensure smooth transition into the adult work world. A number of significant persons in the students' lives (e.g., vocational educator, special teacher, parent, potential employer, vocational rehabilitation counselor) as well as a variety of service agencies (e.g., group home director, rehabilitation counselor, and local social security representative) are consulted when developing this final Transition Plan.

According to McDonnell, Wilcox, Boles, and Bellamy (1983), "Transition is easily conceptualized as a bridge. Like a bridge, transition is only as strong as the foundation on either side (the quality of school preparation on one side and the quality of adult service opportunities on the other) and the construction of the span itself [the planning process]" (p. 2). During a student's public school experience, such planning should include increasingly greater involvement in vocational training activities. Finally, at the conclusion of public school eligibility, transition planning should identify behavioral objectives that assure continuity from school to postschool community employment.

Implement Longitudinal Vocational Training

Career Awareness and Exploration Students should participate in career awareness and vocational exploration experiences from a young age, with increasing involvement in this curriculum area as they become older. Such longitudinal training activities result in greater awareness by both students and their families of career opportunities and needed vocational competencies. Many behaviors associated with entry-level service careers are practiced by students within the home setting. Specific behaviors associated with service occupations that overlap with household responsibilities

include janitorial/housekeeping, laundry, and food services. In Table 4, a listing of household chores associated with these career areas is provided. Corresponding household responsibilities can be made simple for younger students and progressively more difficult as students grow older and become more skilled.

School-Based Vocational Training School-based training should involve students in vocational activities that are as similar as possible to potentially available community employment. Such experiences may include simulated industrial and technological work stations and vocational training in food service and janitorial occupations. In addition to ensuring the relevance of the vocations involved in a training program, the environmental conditions of a school-based training program should resemble closely the conditions experienced in community employment situations, including: 1) specific time for work to begin, 2) typical length of work periods, 3) established break times, 4) realistic supervisor-worker ratio, 5) typical number of supervisor contacts, and 6) set time for the work period to end.

Related Skills Instruction Independent living skills are essential to successful employment. Students should be taught appropriate pedestrian and transportation skills to increase their mobility in the community as well as needed budgeting, banking, shopping, meal planning and preparation, housekeeping, recreational, and social-interpersonal skills. In addition, students should learn how to use their free time by becoming aware of leisure opportunities, and participating in a socially appropriate manner. Emphasis needs to be placed on training social-interpersonal skills that are essential to relating to people on the job and in the community. For example, Pancsofar, Bates, Krissberg, and Bronkema (1982) reported a successful intervention involving a young woman who exhibited noncompliance and verbal aggression toward her supervisor in a community restaurant. In this study, a token reinforcement system for compliance successfully established appropriate social responses and work behaviors to supervisor instructions. In addition, the number of

Table 4.   Vocational entry-level behaviors associated with household chores

Janitorial/Housekeeping skills

Bathroom cleaning	General home cleaning
Clean bathtub/shower	Empty trash
Clean sink	Dust
Clean mirror	Vacuum
Clean toilet	Sweep
Clean floor	Mop
Restock towels	Wax floors
Empty trash	Clean windows
Bedroom responsibilities	Yardcare responsibilities
Change bedding	Pick up yard
Make beds	Store materials
Pick up floors	Weed
Clean surfaces/dust	Cut grass

Food service

Plan meals	Store items
Prepare salads	Wash glasses, dishes, silverware
Assist cook	Rinse/dry
Set table	Sort
Serve food	Store in cabinets
Dispose of trash	
Clear table	

Laundry skills

Place dirty clothes in laundry	Set dryer
Collect clothes baskets	Activate dryer
Sort clothing	Unload dryer
Load washer	Fold clothing
Measure detergent	Stack clothing
Set wash cycle	Press clothing
Activate machine	Hang clothing
Unload washer	Store clothing
Load dryer	

supervisor instructions declined over the course of the study since the woman's increased compliance enabled her to benefit from instruction and perform more effectively.

Community-Based Vocational Training Although a school-based vocational training program can help students acquire useful skills, it cannot be assumed that students will use these skills in actual employment settings. If the goal is to promote competitive employment, educators must conduct instruction in those settings where these skills are required. Therefore, as indicated throughout this text, community-based training sites must be established with community employers in occupations that represent potential employment opportunities (e.g., food service, janitorial, industrial/technological). In the elementary and intermediate years, students' community-based vocational training may consist of volunteer work for area churches, senior citizen centers, public parks, and public service organ-

izations. At age 16, students should begin to rotate through a series of 12- to 18-week paid or unpaid community work experiences in jobs that represent available employment in the community. In most cases, continuous supervision and training by school staff is necessary. Full implementation of this component of Project EARN requires flexible staff roles and scheduling, and individually determined insurance coverage.

A summary of recommendations for vocational preparation is presented in Table 5. These recommendations reflect a commitment to the provision of longitudinal career awareness opportunities, school-based vocational training, related skills instruction, and community-based vocational training. Success in community employment is measured by dollars earned and by a reduction in dollars spent to sustain nonemployment outcomes, integration with nonhandicapped persons, and consumer satisfaction.

Table 5. Program recommendations for longitudinal Vocational training in public school settings

Elementary program (ages 6–12)
  Establish value of work
  Associate productivity and reinforcement
  Increase daily time (15 min.–1 hour)
  Develop household responsibilities
Intermediate program (ages 13–15)
  Increase daily vocational time (1–2 hours)
  Increase breadth of vocational experiences
  Delay incentives
  Promote independence
  Integrate vocational with other curriculum areas
    (social, mobility, money management, leisure,
    and self-help)
Secondary program (ages 16–21)
  Increase time (2–8 hours)
  Community training rotation
  Postschool transition planning
  Reduce supervision
  Delay work incentives

Place Students in Competitive Employment

Once a job has been selected and a student is placed, training is initiated to ensure success. As with the community-based vocational training experiences, an on-the-job teacher is available to provide instruction and supervision. This support is necessary to establish a student's adherence to the job routine, continuous attention to a task, competitive production, and work quality. When the student meets the employer's performance expectations, involvement is withdrawn systematically, with primary responsibility being transferred to the employing supervisor.

In addition to a systematic decrease in the amount of school-provided assistance, the number of hours worked per day by the student is typically increased. During the student's final semester in the public school, he or she attains full- or part-time employee status. A summary of student placement data from 1 school year and an extended summer program is presented in Table 6.

Provide Follow-Up Support

After a student is employed and school personnel begin to withdraw their involvement, a systematic plan is formulated to ensure extended follow-up services, including less frequent direct observations, supervisor evaluations, and co-worker interviews. Such follow-up activities serve as a means of early identification of problems, thus allowing school staff to intervene and prevent potential terminations. One useful method for collecting information on student performance in community employment has been employer/supervisor evaluations. The frequency and quality of employer/supervisor evaluative feedback are extremely important components in competitive employment.

Weekly or monthly employer evaluations are recommended for extended community work experiences (e.g., 3–6 months). The frequency and specificity of such evaluations should contribute toward individual program modifications and overall curriculum development. When used in combination with direct observations of student performance, the subjective evaluations by employers and supervisors provide sensitive information for individual program adjustments that increase the likelihood of a successful placement.

A supervisor's evaluation form (see sample in Figure 3) should be summarized as part of the cumulative record of a student's performance in a given employment situation. This type of subjective report can be used in conjunction with objective performance records for individual program planning (White & Rusch, 1983).

Since follow-up should continue beyond graduation, postschool agency personnel such as vocational placement specialists, rehabilitation counselors, and adult services social workers should be involved. Their role in the follow-up process is particularly crucial to long-term maintenance of employment by representing services available to trainees beyond the age of 21. Follow-up activities should be specified in the student's Transition Plan.

Evaluate Program Effectiveness

The ultimate success of a school-based competitive employment program is determined by the long-term employment success achieved by program graduates. Follow-up questionnaires should be used at regular intervals to identify occupations in which graduates have suc-

Table 6. Summary of student involvement in Project EARN for 1 school year

Client	Age	Classification	Employment history	Months in EARN	Dollars earned			Job classification
					Unsubsidized	DORS	CETA	
R.B.	19-4	Mod. MR	None	3	770			Dishwasher
L.N.	18-8	Mod. MR	None	11	2,605			Dishwasher
B.L.	19-9	Mod. MR	School janitor assistant (9 mo.)	11	770	550	950	Groundskeeper
T.H.	20-8	Mod. MR	None	2		180		Janitor
R.S.	18-2	Mod. MR	Sheltered workshop	1			100	Dishwasher
V.M.	19-2	Mod. MR	None	4			400	Dishwasher
L.S.	18-4	Mod. MR	None	3			375	Janitor
T.R.	19-3	Mod. MR	None	8	900			Dishwasher
R.M.	19-8	Mod. MR	None	4		180	500	Janitor
J.N.	19-0	Sev. MR	None	5		250	500	Busperson
V.W.	21-8	Mod. MR	None	4			680	Dishwasher
D.M.	21-2	Mod. MR	Sheltered workshop	4			750	Janitor
P.B.	20-6	Sev. MR	Sheltered workshop	4			580	Laundry asst.
P.S.	22-6	Autistic	Goodwill	8	2,550			Busperson
Subtotals:					7,595	1,160	4,835	

Grand total dollars earned = $13,590.00

Source: Bates and Pancsofar (1983).

Trainee/Employee name: _____ Placement date: _____
Job title: _____ Current date: _____
Job site: _____ Job coach: _____

Please evaluate the employee on each of the statements below by using the following scoring system:

KEY

A = Excellent   D = Needs improvement
B = Above average   F = Possible reason for dismissal
C = Average   NA = Not applicable

1. The employee:
   a. Arrives and leaves on time _____
   b. Maintains good attendance _____
   c. Calls off work appropriately _____
   d. Takes meals and breaks appropriately _____
   e. Maintains a good appearance _____
   f. Works at a constant rate without reminders _____
   g. Initiates work on his or her own _____
   h. Is a dependable worker _____
   i. Has mastered all aspects of the job _____
   j. Works at an acceptable speed _____
   k. Gets along with co-workers _____
   l. Follows instruction from supervisor _____

2. What specific job skills need to be better performed?
   _____
   _____
   _____

   What specific social skills need to be better performed?
   _____
   _____
   _____

3. In order for the employee to follow directions regarding the job, the supervisor:
   a. Can just give *verbal* instructions
   b. Has to give many *gestures* as well as verbal instructions
   c. Has to show the employee exactly what to do before he or she knows what is expected

4. The employee is: a. a good worker _____ b. an average worker _____ c. a below-average worker _____

5. School staff is present: a. too often _____ b. too little according to the employee's needs _____ c. an appropriate amount of time _____

6. Does the school staff in any way interfere with your supervision or plans for the employee?
   a. no _____ b. yes _____ (If yes, please briefly describe)
   _____
   _____

   Other comments:
   _____
   _____
   _____

Figure 3.   Supervisor evaluation form. (From Wehman, P., & Hill, M. (1982). *Vocational training and placement for the severely disabled* (Vol. 4). Richmond, VA: School of Education, Virginia Commonwealth University. Adapted by permission.)

ceeded and problems that have interfered with successful employment. Program evaluation data from supervisors provide information from which the effectiveness of a vocational curriculum can be judged. For example, Davis, Bates, and Cuvo (1983) asked co-workers and supervisors 13 questions regarding appropriateness of placement, acceptability of the training methods, and program success. Responses from these co-workers and supervisors provided social validation data in support of Project EARN.

SUMMARY

At present, graduates of public school programs serving students with handicaps are not likely to be competitively employed. Indeed, Stanfield's (1976) observation regarding the status of persons with mental retardation has been reconfirmed by DeFazio and Flexer (1983) in their description of the employment outlook for adults:

> The typical mentally retarded adult has significant habilitative needs, but he/she has few if any options as to where work is performed or services are received. Usually, he/she is assigned to work in degrading, segregated, and inefficiently organized work settings that are isolated physically, philosophically, and technologically from the normal work world of nonhandicapped persons. The employees of these facilities characteristic-

ally perform borrowed, unchallenging, frivolous work of marginal habilitative or social valued community work settings. Typically, work is performed with cast-off and often inappropriate equipment and supplies, at artificially imposed, substandard rate and under conditions that most nonhandicapped workers would reject as being dehumanizing. (p. 157)

The competitive employment model described in this chapter is designed to enhance postschool employment of persons with handicaps. Although many persons have succeeded in competitive employment as a result of implementation of this model, several problems must be addressed before the goal of competitive employment for all handicapped persons can be realized. Project EARN is one of many public school demonstration programs that have shown that students, provided appropriate educational opportunities, can succeed in competitive employment (Bates & Pancsofar, 1983; Brown et al., 1983; Clarke, Greenwood, Abramowitz, & Bellamy, 1980; Maurer, Bates, Hamre-Nietupski, Nietupski, & Teas, 1981; Maurer, Teas, & Bates, 1980). The model described here requires a strong commitment by parents, teachers, and administrators to the philosophy of zero exclusion, integration, and normalization. Such a commitment will lead to localized adaptations of the Project EARN model that best serve consumers of public education services.

REFERENCES

Bates, P., & Pancsofar, E. (1981). Longitudinal vocational training for severely handicapped students in the public schools. In R. York, W. K. Schofield, D. J. Doader, D. L. Ryndak, & B. Reguly (Eds.), *Proceedings from the 1981 Illinois Statewide Institute for Educators of the Severely and Profoundly Handicapped* (pp. 105–122). Springfield, IL: Department of Specialized Educational Services, Illinois Board of Education.

Bates, P., & Pancsofar, E. (1983). Project EARN (Employment and Rehabilitation = Normalization): A competitive employment training program for severely disabled youth in the public schools. *British Journal of Mental Subnormality, 29 (57),* 97–103.

Bates, P., & Pancsofar, E. (1985). Assessment of vocational skills. In A. F. Rotatori & R. Fox (Eds.), *Assessment for regular and special education teachers: A case study approach.* Austin, TX: Pro-Ed.

Bates, P., Renzaglia, A., & Wehman, P. (1981). Characteristics of an appropriate education for severely handi-

capped students. *Education and Training of the Mentally Retarded, 16,* 142–149.

Bellamy, G. T., Horner, R. H., & Inman, D. P. (1979). *Vocational habilitation of severely retarded adults: A direct service technology.* Baltimore: University Park Press.

Belmore, K., & Brown, L. (1978). A job skill inventory strategy designed for severely handicapped potential workers. In N. G. Haring & D. D. Bricker (Eds.), *Teaching the severely handicapped* (Vol. 3, pp. 223–262). Columbus, OH: Special Press.

Brown, L., Ford, A., Nisbet, J., Shiraga, B., Vandeventer, P., Sweet, M., & Loomis, R. (1983). *Teaching severely handicapped youth to perform meaningful work in nonsheltered vocational environments.* Unpublished manuscript.

Brown, L., Pumpian, I., Baumgart, D., VanDeventer, P., Ford, A., Nisbet, J., Schroeder, J., & Gruenewald, L. (1981). Longitudinal transition plans in programs for severely handicapped students. *Exceptional Children, 47,* 624–631.

Clarke, J. Y., Greenwood, L. M., Abramowitz, D. B., & Bellamy, G. T. (1980). Summer jobs for vocational preparation of moderately and severely retarded adolescents. *Journal of The Association for the Severely Handicapped, 5,* 24–37.

Davis, P., Bates, P., & Cuvo, A. J. (1983). Training a mentally retarded woman to work competitively: Effect of graphic feedback and a changing criterion design. *Education and Training of the Mentally Retarded, 18,* 158–163.

DeFazio, N., & Flexer, R. W. (1983). Organizational barriers to productivity, wages, and normalized work opportunity for mentally retarded persons. *Mental Retardation, 21,* 157–163.

Employment Committee of the Developmental Disabilities Planning Council (1981). *Employment for persons with developmental disabilities in the state of Washington.* Tacoma, WA: Department of Developmental Disabilities.

Gold, M. (1980). *Did I say that?* Champaign, IL: Research Press.

Maurer, S., Teas, S., & Bates, P. (1980). *Project AMES* (Vol. 1). Des Moines, IA: Iowa Department of Public Instruction.

Maurer, S., Bates, P., Hamre-Nietupski, S., Nietupski, J., & Teas, S. (1981). *Project AMES* (Vol. 2). Des Moines, IA: Iowa Department of Public Instruction.

Martin, J. E., Rusch, F. R., Tines, J., Brulle, A. R., & White, D. M. (in press). Work attendance in competitive employment: Comparison between nonhandicapped and mentally retarded employees. *Mental Retardation.*

McDonnell, J. J., Wilcox, B., Boles, S. M., & Bellamy, G. T. (1983). *Issues in the transition from school to adult services: A survey of parents of secondary students with severe handicaps.* Eugene, OR: Specialized Training Program, Center on Human Development.

Menchetti, B. M., Rusch, F. R., & Owens, D. (1983). Assessing the vocational needs of mentally retarded adolescents and adults. In J. L. Matson & S. E. Breening (Eds.), *Assessing the mentally retarded* (pp. 247–284). New York: Grune & Stratton.

Mithaug, D. E., & Haring, N. G. (1977). Community vocational and workshop placement. In N. G. Haring & L. J. Brown (Eds.), *Teaching the severely handicapped* (Vol. II, pp. 257–283). New York: Grune & Stratton.

Pancsofar, E., & Bates, P. (1984). Multiple baseline designs for evaluating instructional effectiveness. *Rehabilitation Counseling Bulletin, 28,* 67–77.

Pancsofar, E., Bates, P., & Bronkema, J. (1981). A survey of competitive job availability for mentally retarded workers. *Illinois Council for Exceptional Children Quarterly, 30*(3), 27–31.

Pancsofar, E., Bates, P., Krissberg, H., & Bronkema, J. (1982). Increasing the compliance of a moderately retarded worker to supervisors' instructions in a restaurant setting. *Illinois Council for Exceptional Children Quarterly, 31*(1), 19–25.

Pancsofar, E., Bates, P., & Sedlak, R. (1982). The development of task analyses for vocational training with severely handicapped students. *Illinois Council for Exceptional Children Quarterly, 31*(4), 20–23.

Rusch, F. (1983). Competitive vocational training. In M. E. Snell (Ed.), *Systematic instruction of the moderately and severely handicapped (2nd ed.)* (pp. 503–523). Columbus, OH: Charles E. Merrill.

Stanfield, J. S. (1976). Graduation: What happens to the retarded child when he grows up? In R. W. Anderson & J. G. Greer (Eds.), *Educating the severely and profoundly retarded* (pp. 403–410). Baltimore: University Park Press.

Wehman, P. (1981). *Competitive employment: New horizons for severely disabled individuals.* Baltimore: Paul H. Brookes.

Wehman, P., & Hill, M. (1982). *Vocational training and placement for the severely disabled* (Vol. 4). Richmond, VA: School of Education, Virginia Commonwealth University.

White, D. M., & Rusch, F. R. (1983). Social validation in competitive employment: Evaluating work performance. *Applied Research in Mental Retardation, 4*(4), 343–354.

Wilcox, B., & Bellamy, G. T. (1982). *Design of high school programs for severely handicapped students.* Baltimore: Paul H. Brookes.

Chapter 5

Community Services
Using the Supported Work Model within an Adult Service Agency

Thomas R. Lagomarcino

INDIVIDUALS WITH HANDICAPS face many barriers to leading self-sufficient, dignified lives. Perhaps the greatest of these barriers is their limited opportunity for gainful employment. According to national survey data (e.g., Appleby, 1978; Greenleigh Associates, 1975; U.S. Department of Labor, 1979), sheltered workshops—the primary vehicle for providing vocational rehabilitation services to these persons as adults—have been ineffective in facilitating the move from sheltered work to competitive employment. This situation becomes even more evident in a Department of Labor report (1979) revealing that 75% of the persons placed in competitive employment from sheltered workshops had received less than 1 year of workshop training. Furthermore, the largest percentage of persons placed in competitive employment from sheltered workshops remain there for 2 years or less. After 2 years, the discharge rate drops to approximately 3%. This means that persons remaining in sheltered employment have an increasingly less chance of achieving competitive employment as the duration of their "training" continues. The report also indicated that adults with mental retardation and other developmental disabilities currently constitute 91% of the persons identified as inconsequential producers by work activity centers, earning an average hourly wage of 43¢, with little opportunity for advancement in salary or job place-

ment. These wages are supplemented by public assistance, such as Supplemental Security Income (SSI). In addition to subsidized income, disabled individuals consume other public funds because many live in institutions or intermediate care facilities. Effective vocational training, leading to gainful employment in nonsheltered settings, alleviates the need of handicapped persons for public assistance by allowing them to earn at least minimum wages.

The University of Illinois in conjunction with Developmental Services Center, a local adult service agency, developed Community Services in 1978 to provide an alternative to the traditional vocational training then available to persons who were primarily mentally retarded. The ultimate goal of this program was to improve the chances of placement of these adults into competitive employment. The purpose of this chapter is to describe the community-based model utilized by Developmental Services Center and to report upon the outcomes of the model in terms of competitive employment for persons with mental retardation.

MODEL RATIONALE:
A SUPPORTED WORK PROGRAM

Historically, persons with mental retardation have been excluded from the mainstream of the labor force for several reasons. Two reasons in

particular deserve mention: (1) low expectations of parents, teachers, and employers regarding the abilities of these persons; and
(2) failure to employ a cohesive training technology to train the necessary job skills that
could lead to competitive employment. These
conditions continue in spite of recent research
demonstrating that even persons with severe
handicaps can learn complex assembly tasks
(e.g., Bellamy, 1976; Gold, 1976; Hunter &
Bellamy, 1976), community mobility skills
(e.g., Carney, Menchetti, & Orelove, 1977;
Sowers, Rusch, & Hudson, 1979; Vogelsberg
& Rusch, 1979), and vocationally relevant
social skills (e.g., Rusch, Weithers, Menchetti, & Schutz, 1980; Schutz, Rusch, &
Lamson, 1979). Parents, teachers, rehabilitation counselors, and employers who
believe handicapped persons cannot perform
with the same degree of competence as nonhandicapped individuals perpetrate a myth that
is reinforced when an untrained person fails on
the job. Such failure is not due to an inherent
lack of ability but to ineffective training programs provided by public schools and adult
local rehabilitation agencies (Rusch, Chadsey-
Rusch, Menchetti, & Schutz, 1980).

Traditionally, it has been difficult for adults
with handicaps to generalize the skills trained
in sheltered work environments to non-
sheltered, competitive employment settings.
Given this dilemma, Developmental Services
Center adopted a community-oriented behavioral approach to vocational training developed by Rusch and his colleagues at the
University of Washington (see Chapter 7)
(Rusch & Mithaug, 1980; Rusch & Schutz,
1979). This approach involves surveying potential job placements in the community to
determine the social and vocational skills employees will be expected to display on their job.
These skills are subsequently trained at community based training stations where the social
and vocational behaviors, work demands, and
the equipment are similar to those identified in
potential job placements. Finally, extensive
follow-up services are provided to teach target
employees how to remain employed.

CHARACTERISTICS OF
PARTICIPANTS ENROLLED IN TRAINING

Potential program participants must be eligible
to receive services from the Illinois Department of Rehabilitation Services and the Job
Training Partnership Act, the two primary
sources of funding for both vocational training
programs (see Figure 1). Eligibility requirements include being at least 18 years of
age, severely disabled, unemployed, and in
need of intensive skill training before entering
the job market (Table 1). Referrals have come
from a variety of sources including the sheltered workshop, rehabilitation counselors, the
local mental health agency, area special education programs, and parents. The clients' interest in participating, travel requirements, and
possible physical limitations are also given
consideration before placement in either training program is recommended.

A total of 134 persons have participated in
the program since 1978 (see Table 2). Forty-
three percent of the persons served have been
diagnosed as multiply handicapped (i.e.,
having a secondary handicapping condition).
Of the 134 persons who have participated in
training, 108 completed training and were
placed on jobs in the community. The remaining 26 individuals did not complete training for
a variety of reasons including poor attendance,
severe behavior problems, lack of interest in
obtaining employment, and health problems.

CHARACTERISTICS OF
SUPPORTED WORK MODEL

This section provides an overview of the general characteristics of the model developed by
Community Services. The four major model
components include: 1) surveying potential
employers to determine important vocational
and social survival skills that need to be
trained, 2) training individuals to perform such
skills, 3) placing trained clients into competitive employment, and 4) providing long-
term, follow-up training. Table 3 presents the
continuum of activities associated with the

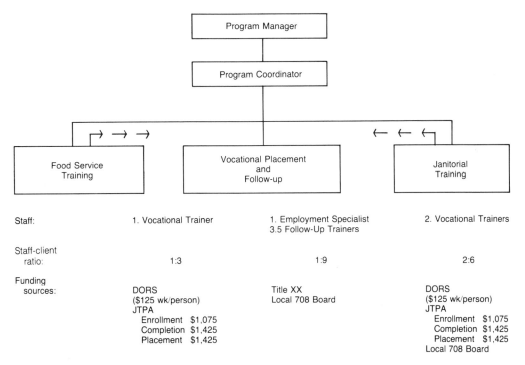

Figure 1.   Developmental Services Center Community Services.

model (Rusch, 1983). A more detailed description of each component follows.

Survey

The first component of the model, *survey*, refers to the activities related to identifying possible community job placements and the social and vocational survival skills associated

Table 1.   Client characteristics[a]

Characteristic	N	%
Age		
18–56 years of age (median age = 27)		
Sex		
Male	94	70
Female	40	30
Primary diagnosis		
Mental retardation	99	74
Mild	61	
Moderate	35	
Severe	3	
Mental illness	21	15
Learning disabilities	9	6
Visual impairment	2	2
Cerebral palsy	1	1
Other	2	2

[a]Of the 134 individuals served, 58 (43%) had a secondary handicapping condition.

with each of those jobs. It is essential to base vocational training objectives on what trainees will be expected to do upon completion of training. A community survey of this type involves contacting employers to identify possible job openings. Such contacts are fundamental to all programmatic efforts, since the range of jobs identified as viable for placement will influence the type of skills to be addressed in training. This job-requisite information is collected via verbal reports from knowledgeable persons and direct observation of worker behavior (Rusch & Mithaug, 1980).

Table 2.   Job placement statistics

Length of time on job	N	%
Janitorial/Housekeeping	Placed: 82	
3 Months	75	91
6 Months	54	66
1 Year or more	40	49
Still employed	36	44
Food Service	Placed: 26	
3 Months	20	77
6 Months	18	69
1 Year or more	16	62
Still employed	12	46

Table 3.   Continuum of major activities of community-based model

Survey	Train	Place	Maintain
1. Identify potential job placements	1. Identify skill areas in need of training	1. Identify target placement setting	1. Identify skill areas in need of training
2. Describe potential job placements to parents	2. Prioritize objectives	2. Conduct job analysis	2. Prioritize objectives
3. Conduct a job analysis	3. Provide training	3. Provide feedback to training	3. Provide training
4. Develop a community-based vocational curriculum	4. Evaluate progress	4. Place client	4. Withdraw training strategies and staff systematically

The verbal report usually involves a structured interview with an employer, a job supervisor, or an employee who is asked to describe the entry requirements for a targeted job. However, in these structured interviews, employers, supervisors, and employees often do not provide an accurate list of the skills needed for employment or do not consistently rank the importance of the behaviors. Therefore, program staff must also observe nonhandicapped employees performing the targeted jobs to validate the list of survival skills derived from the descriptive information provided in the interview with the employer or shift supervisor. In addition, by observing employed workers and noting their skill competencies, staff can identify the important characteristics of successful workers for a given employment setting.

The curriculum and assessment content areas of this model are built around the social and vocational survival skills identified through an assessment of job requisites in the local community. For example, a survey of the Champaign-Urbana area indicated a high turnover of food services and janitorial personnel. Observations of employees in janitorial positions revealed that these jobs typically involve sweeping and mopping floors, vacuuming carpets, dusting, cleaning restrooms, and other general utility work. Similarly, observations of food service workers showed that these employees performed duties such as operating industrial-size dish machines, bussing tables, and cleaning grills. The approach also necessitates identification of social skills related to

targeted jobs (e.g., grooming, greetings, and acknowledging requests made by supervisor) as well as skills required for certain tasks away from, but indirectly related to, a targeted job placement, such as riding a bus to and from work.

Train

After the survival skills have been socially validated via the comprehensive job survey, the next step consists of *training* the specified social and vocational behaviors. Unlike other vocational training programs in which individuals are placed and then provided with on-the-job training, Community Services developed time-limited preemployment training programs in which individuals are placed into community-based training stations and taught the skills needed for competitive employment for a period of time not exceeding 6 months. A primary advantage to this strategy is that persons are trained in major social and vocational skills prior to placement. That is, training is conducted in a setting solely defined for that purpose, and employers are subsequently provided a prospective employee experienced in performing many of the skills that will be required in the targeted environment.

Based on the initial survey of potential job placements in the Champaign-Urbana area, Community Services established two preemployment training programs, referred to as the Janitorial Employment Training Program and the Food Service Vocational Training Program. Both programs were established within existing businesses and took over all the re-

sponsibilities subsumed under targeted job categories (i.e., janitor, kitchen laborer) within
specific community-based settings.

The Janitorial Employment Training Program provides intensive janitorial skills training, so that at the end of the training period
participants are capable of performing the wide
range of entry-level janitorial skills necessary
for employment. Targeted vocational skills
include hand dusting, cleaning restrooms,
emptying trash, sweeping and mopping floors,
and vacuuming carpets. Trainees are also
taught how to operate and maintain equipment
such as vacuum cleaners, floor buffers, carpet
shampooers, and industrial sweepers. Training
sites, which have been operational at a number
of locations since the program started in 1978,
have included a department store, a snack bar
on the University of Illinois campus, and a
residential school for the performing arts.

The Food Service Vocational Training Program, also established in 1978, provides up to
24 weeks of individualized training in 35 social
and vocational skill areas that comprise the
position of kitchen laborer. Vocational skills
training ranges in complexity from sweeping
and mopping floors to operating industrial
dishwashing machines, cleaning grills, pots
and pans, and bussing food to the serving lines.
A variety of training sites have been utilized
since the program began, including a restaurant, the kitchen of a local hospital, and a
university dormitory kitchen.

The advantages of providing preemployment training in an ongoing industry
have far outweighed the disadvantages, including providing traditionally segregated persons an opportunity to experience the contingencies of an integrated work environment
(e.g., nonhandicapped co-workers). In addition, job-site demands often unavailable in
sheltered settings, such as time constraints,
provide significant work experiences that promote ultimate job survival. From the outset,
trainees must be on time and must competently
complete their assigned tasks. Furthermore,
while learning a specific position (e.g., janitor,
kitchen laborer), participants are surrounded
by other employees who serve as models for

acceptable behaviors and provide opportunities
for exposure to the social competencies of each
behavior in a working environment—a situation that cannot be simulated in a sheltered
environment.

Once a trainee approaches criterion on all
required social and vocational skills, she or he
is considered placement ready and is referred to
the Vocational Placement and Follow-Up
Program.

Place

The third component, *placement*, refers to the
transition process during which the trainee is
moved from the preemployment training setting to the targeted competitive employment.
At this point, individuals are referred to an
Employment Specialist, who is responsible for
the preplacement programs (i.e., Job Club) as
well as job placement. The rationale for providing placement services is that assisting
workers with handicaps in matching their skills
and needs with available jobs, and maximizing
their participation in the job search process
increase their likelihood of obtaining and maintaining competitive positions.

The first placement step consists of completing a Job Placement Plan. The purpose of
this plan is to outline the individual's vocational interests, summarize the vocational and
social skills that have been acquired in training,
identify the times the individual is available to
work, describe the current residential setting,
as well as gather information related to transportation, sources of income, and any physical
limitations the individual may have. This information is collected through interviews with
the trainee, parents, and vocational trainers.
The Job Placement Plan makes it easier for the
Employment Specialist to match available jobs
to the skills and interests of prospective employees. A copy of the Plan and monthly up-
dates are forwarded to the funding source (i.e.,
to the Department of Rehabilitation Services).

Individuals receiving placement services are
expected to participate as much as possible in
their own job search. Table 4 illustrates the
different amounts of assistance that may be
provided by the Employment Specialist. A

Table 4.   Examples of varying degrees of trainee participation in job search

	Trainee independently	Employment specialist
	Informs Employment Specialist that he or she has obtained employment	Arranges for follow-up services
	Obtains and completes application Contacts employer to schedule interview Goes through interview Reports outcome to Employment Specialist	Reviews application with trainee Provides practice before interview
Trainee participation — Least to Most	Obtains application or notification of job opening Schedules interview	Assists in completing application Provides practice before interview Accompanies trainee to interview to provide information about training program and support as needed
		Contacts employer or obtains notice of opening Guarantees position can be filled by qualified individual within 48 hours Participates in special selection process to select candidate Helps candidate prepare and accompanies candidate to interview

great deal of this assistance consists of training in skills that will help the individual participate in more stages of the search. For example, some trainees may be capable of learning job-inquiry skills such as identifying prospective employers by using the want ads or phone book, and how to contact employers by phone. However, the primary emphasis of this placement assistance has been on appropriate dress for interviews, answering questions by employers, and the kinds of questions to ask employers about potential jobs. A number of employers in the community have volunteered their time to provide prospective employees with an opportunity to practice their interviewing skills. When placement staff have made contacts, or have accompanied prospective employees to interviews, steps have been taken to ensure that lack of independence in job-seeking skills would not lower employer perceptions of the worker's independence on job-related tasks.

Realistically determining which job is most suitable for a particular person should be based upon the individual to be placed, the tasks to be performed on the job, and the willingness of the employer and co-workers to allow and accomodate retraining on the job. Before trainees are considered for a given position, the Employment Specialist visits the site and obtains information relative to wages, pay scale

and promotion criteria, benefits, and qualifications desired in applicants, with an emphasis on vocational and social skills specifically required for the position. Whenever possible, arrangements are made with the employer to observe a worker perform the duties related to the targeted position. These steps have proven extremely helpful in matching the strengths of potential employees to positions available in the community.

Maintain (Follow-up Services)

Follow-up services are provided to assist an individual, once placed, in maintaining employment in the community with its associated wages, benefits, and status beyond those that can be found in sheltered employment. Follow-up services may be needed for retraining or training of new skills, to advocate for the individual, to assist the new employee in dealing with problems that result from interactions with unfamiliar supervisors and co-workers, and to ensure that the expectations initially outlined for the position are maintained. By providing services as needed and fading them as they become less necessary, it is hoped that others in the community setting will perceive the individual as a worker qualified for the position and with all the same rights as non-handicapped individuals in the community.

Follow-up training on the new job is less

intensive and shorter in duration than training at the community-based training sites. Usually, if an individual is taught the basic skills needed for most janitorial jobs, he or she should be able to perform these tasks correctly in the placement setting with less assistance. However, the presence of different people, equipment, chemicals, and procedures in the new environment and their effect on the new employee must be taken into account. The adjustment period varies among individuals.

Before assuming the position as advocate for a person placed on a job, program staff must become familiar with the particular job. The method employed for this purpose varies somewhat from job to job, depending on how much time there is before the individual is to begin work and the employer's preference. The best way for the follow-up trainer to become familiarized with a job is to work in the position for several days, thereby receiving training from the employer or a supervisor.

The follow-up trainer may also become familiar with a given job by observing an employee who regularly works a targeted position. It is recommended that this approach be combined with consultation with the employer to ensure that the way the employee performs the job corresponds to the way the employer wants it done. If neither of these options is workable, the trainer should meet with the employer or shift supervisor to discuss the work schedule and other aspects of the job. When the new employee begins the job, he or she usually starts out working one or two shifts with an experienced employee in addition to receiving assistance from the trainer.

During the job orientation phase, the trainer analyzes each task for component steps, learns the daily schedule, identifies tasks that are performed periodically, and determines the average length of time it takes other employees to perform specific tasks. Finally, a Job Analysis Survey is completed based on the information that has been collected (Rusch & Mithaug, 1980). The purpose of the survey is to provide a complete task-by-task analysis of the job including projected time frames in which specific tasks are to be completed. Social and vocational skills that are specific to the new job site are also identified.

In addition, the follow-up trainer identifies co-workers who could serve as advocates for the new employee and observes social interaction patterns within the work site. It is crucial for the trainer to establish good working relationships with employer and staff to facilitate communication with supervisors and co-workers, making them more willing to bring up problems related to the new employee. Public relations is a significant part of a follow-up trainer's job.

Following the job orientation phase (usually lasting from 1 day to several weeks), indefinite follow-up is provided through: 1) periodic, direct observations of an individual; 2) communication with the employer by telephone and structured reports; and 3) evaluation of the results of work performance evaluation forms completed by the employer. The Work Performance Evaluation Form was developed to provide employers and job supervisors with a means of evaluating employee progress and communicating the evaluation results to placement trainers on a regular basis (see Figure 2). The form also measures employer satisfaction with the follow-up trainer and indicates whether the employer believes enough or too much contact is being maintained with the employee. After the supervisor or employer has completed the Work Performance Evaluation Form, it is shared with the employee. Whenever possible, the employer will explain the evaluation to the employee, suggesting needed improvements and telling the employee where his or her strengths lie. It is the primary responsibility of the follow-up trainer to make sure that the employee understands the comments being made by the employer and to develop individualized program plans addressing the problem areas identified by the employer.

As the employee makes progress, the follow-up trainer begins to spend less time at the work site, fading his or her presence during the times when the employee can perform tasks independently. This systematic withdrawl of trainer assistance continues until the employee

Date: _____

DSC Vocational Placement and Follow-Along Program

Name of employee _____ Name of co. _____

Supervisory person _____ Weeks on job _____

Job title and description of work performed: _____

_____

Please rate the employee on the following requirements for continuing employment:

	Good	Average	Below average	Poor	Not applicable
1. Attendance and punctuality					
2. Completes job with speed and accuracy					
3. Works independently or without much supervision					
4. Cooperates with supervisor					
5. Knows and follows safety rules					
6. Able to adjust to varied work assignments					
7. Shows an interest in the job					
8. Shows initiative					
9. Able to remember instructions, locations, etc.					
10. Able to follow directions					
11. Accepts instructions and criticism					
12. Gets along with fellow workers					
13. Exercises good judgment and is able to solve problems; asks questions when necessary					
14. Accepts responsibility					
15. Exhibits good personal grooming and hygiene habits					
16. Dresses appropriately for job					
17. Uses and cares for equipment properly					
18. Keeps work area clean					
19. Is courteous to customers					
20. Is cost conscious; aware of cost of materials needed for operation of business; does not waste materials					
21. Meets overall standards expected by you as an employer					

Trainer Evaluation Form

Please rate our follow-up services:

Trainer's name _____

	Good	Average	Below average	Poor	Not applicable
1. Trainer maintains acceptable amount of contact with employer or supervisor					
2. Trainer responds to problems, questions and concerns that employer addresses about trainee and attempts to find solutions promptly					
3. Trainer's personal appearance is acceptable for your job site					
4. Trainer conducts himself or herself in a professional manner that would present a good model of conduct for the employee he or she works with					

If any ratings are below average, please explain in detail the problem as you see it.

_____

_____

_____

Respondent's signature: _____

Figure 2.   Work Performance Evaluation Form.

73

demonstrates the ability to perform all tasks independently. During this period, the placement trainer works closely with the employer and co-workers in shifting supervisory responsibility and implementation of training strategies to them. This process further enhances long-term maintenance of the employee at the particular work site in the absence of follow-up service.

SUMMARY OF CLIENTS PLACED ON JOBS

Of the 134 persons enrolled in training, 108 were placed on jobs in the community. Table 2 provides a summary of placement based on the length of time on the job.

Individuals completing the Janitorial Vocational Training Program have been placed into a variety of settings including motels, small businesses, nursing homes, and restaurants. At these sites, the employees perform a variety of janitoral tasks dictated by the need of the individual placement. For example, some of them are required to use heavy industrial cleaning equipment such as buffers and carpet shampooers in their work, whereas others perform mostly light cleaning such as cleaning restrooms, dusting, and vacuuming carpets.

Graduates of the Food Service Vocational Training Program have been placed primarily on jobs in the dormitory kitchens at the university or in local restaurants. Most of these individuals have been employed as kitchen laborers or dishwashers, although some have been successfully placed in food preparation positions. Graduates work from 5 to 40 hours per week, most of them averaging between 20 and 25 hours per week and earning anywhere from minimum wage to $7.00 per hour.

FUNDING COMMUNITY SERVICES PROGRAM

Community Services is funded primarily by federal and state monies distributed at the local level. For example, the Department of Rehabilitation Services (DORS) and the Job Training Partnership Act (JTPA) are involved in the funding of the community-based training programs, janitorial and food service (refer to Figure 1).

Fee-for-service arrangements have been established with DORS whereby Community Services receives $125 a week for each week an individual participates in the training program. These arrangements were worked out with the vocational rehabilitation counselors at the local DORS office.

JTPA also helps support the Community Services Program. As with the DORS, individuals receiving support must be JTPA eligible. JTPA provides money through performance-based contracts established between Community Services and the local JTPA office. Specifically, Community Services is reimbursed for enrolling handicapped individuals in the training programs, having these individuals complete training, and placing them into competitive employment. The follow-up component of the program is primarily supported by the Department of Public Aid through Title XX funds and by the local mental health board.

SUMMARY AND FUTURE DIRECTIONS

Vocational competence is recognized as a critical variable in determining society's acceptance of individuals. Consequently, it represents an important consideration in the development of normalizing service alternatives (Schutz & Rusch, 1982). This chapter provides an overview of a supported work training program established jointly by a local adult service agency and the University of Illinois to place severely disabled individuals into competitive employment.

Although these innovative services exist in the Champaign-Urbana area, a group of young adults with moderate and severe handicaps are not making the transition from school to work. Moderately mentally handicapped students have received community-based vocational training while still in school, with some of them being placed into competitive employment before graduation. However, the transition has been ineffective with no direct linkage to ensure continued follow-up services after the graduates leave school. The students who are severely handicapped have also received some community-based vocational training while still in school. Due to physical limitations or eligibility requirements of the funding agencies, however, these students have not been eligible for Community Services upon leaving school.

The Illinois Competitive Employment Project, which is funded by the Office of Special Education and Rehabilitative Services (OSERS), is a 3-year project whose purpose is to examine the transition problems of these students and to develop a process to enhance their transition through cooperative programming between the local adult service agency (i.e., Developmental Services Center) and the two local education agencies. The project has enabled students to access the training programs operated by Community Services before graduation as well as to receive follow-up services after graduating from school. The adult service providers and school personnel are actively involved in developing transition plans for handicapped students aging-out of schools.

Further development of nonsheltered employment options is needed for the more severely handicapped individuals currently in adult day care or work activity programs. State agencies must continue to support innovative community-based programs as well as begin to serve those individuals previously denied access to such services. Only through these efforts will handicapped individuals become truly integrated into the community in which they live.

REFERENCES

Appleby, J. A. (1978). *Training programs and placement services*. Salt Lake City, UT: Olympics Publishing.

Bellamy, G. T. (Ed.). (1976). *Habilitation of severely and profoundly retarded adults. Monograph No. 1*. Eugene: University of Oregon, Specialized Training Program, College of Education, Center on Human Development.

Carney, I. H., Menchetti, B. M., & Orelove, F. P. (1977). Community transportation: Teaching moderately handicapped adults to ride the Champaign-Urbana Mass Transit System. In B. Wilcos, F. Kohl, & T. Vogelsberg (Eds.), *The severely and profoundly handicapped child*. Proceeding from the 1977 Statewide Institute for Education of the Severely and Profoundly Handicapped. Illinois Office of Education, Springfield, IL.

Gold, M. W. (1976). Task analysis of a complex assembly task by the retarded blind. *Exceptional Children, 43*, 78–84.

Greenleigh Associates (1975). *The role of the sheltered workshop in the rehabilitation of the severely handicapped*. Report to the Department of Health, Education, and Welfare, Rehabilitative Services Administration. New York: Greenleigh Associates.

Hunter, J. D., & Bellamy, G. T. (1976). Cable harness construction for severely retarded adults: A demonstration of training techniques. *AAESPH Review, 1*, 2–13.

Rusch, F. R. (1983). Competitive vocational training. In M.E. Snell (Ed.), *Systematic instruction of the moderately and severely handicapped* (2nd ed.) (pp. 503–523). Columbus, OH: Charles E. Merrill.

Rusch, F. R., Chadsey-Rusch, J., Menchetti, B. M., & Schutz, R.P. (1980). *Survey-train-place: Vocational preparation for the severely handicapped student*. University of Illinois at Urbana-Champaign. Unpublished manuscript.

Rusch, F. R., & Mithaug, D. E. (1980). *Vocational training for mentally retarded adults: A behavior analytic approach*. Champaign, IL: Research Press.

Rusch, F. R., & Schutz, R. P. (1979). Non-sheltered competitive employment of the mentally retarded adult: Research to reality. *Journal of Contemporary Business, 8*, 85–98.

Rusch, F. R., Weithers, J. A., Menchetti, B. M., & Schutz, R.P. (1980). Social validation of a program to reduce topic retention in a non-sheltered setting. *Education and Training of the Mentally Retarded, 15*, 208–215.

Schutz, R. P., & Rusch, F. R. (1982). Competitive employment: Toward employment integration for mentally retarded persons. In R. L. Lynch, W. E. Kiernan, & J. A. Stark (Eds.), *Prevocational and vocational education for special needs youth: A blueprint for the 1980s*. (pp. 133–159). Baltimore: Paul H. Brookes.

Schutz, R. P., Rusch, F. R., & Lamson, D. S. (1979). Evaluation of an employer's procedure to eliminate unacceptable behavior on the job. *Community Services Forum, 1*, 4–5.

Sowers, J., Rusch, F. R., & Hudson, C. (1979). Training a severely retarded young adult to ride the city bus to and from work. *AAESPH Review, 4*, 15–22.

U.S. Department of Labor. (1979). *Sheltered workshop study: A nationwide report on sheltered workshops and their employment of handicapped individuals*. Washington, DC: U.S. Department of Labor.

Vogelsberg, R. T., & Rusch, F. R. (1979). Training three severely handicapped adults to walk, look and cross uncontrolled intersections. *AAESPH Review, 1*, 264–273.

Chapter 6

University of Washington Employment Training Program

James W. Moss, John P. Dineen,
and Laurie H. Ford

THE EMPLOYMENT TRAINING Program (ETP) of the University of Washington consists of training, research, and development activities designed to enable adults with mental retardation to obtain and keep employment in the private sector (Moss, 1980). The program trains these persons for work in various food service operations and helps them keep their jobs once they are employed. In addition, program staff assist in the development of similar programs in other settings and conduct applied research to identify more effective ways to enable adults with mental retardation to obtain and keep employment. Finally, the program provides employment support services to clients placed into jobs by other facilities.

The University of Washington Employment Training Program, which started in 1975 with the first graduates employed in 1976, currently has 70 active clients (employed, temporarily unemployed, or in training). The staff includes six rehabilitation trainers, three assistant trainers, an associate director, a placement coordinator, an office manager, work-study students, and the project director.

MODEL

The ETP is a competitive employment program that utilizes a supported work model. Trainees spend a variable amount of time in a training environment before placement into competitive employment. Contrary to traditional programs in which on-the-job training is provided by the employer, the program described here offers on-the-job training provided by the ETP staff until the new worker performs to the employer's satisfaction. Retraining and support are also provided by the training program, as necessary, as long as the trainee is employed.

PROGRAM GOALS

The initial goals of the Employment Training Program were 4-fold: 1) to determine if, given training, adults with mental retardation could be employed in competitive settings; 2) to demonstrate to state agency personnel and others that workers with mental retardation could be employed in competitive jobs; 3) to convince representatives of state funding systems that employment was a reasonable alternative for many adults with mental retardation; and 4) to encourage the development of additional competitive employment programs in appropriate settings. Current goals focus on improvement of instructional techniques, development of new job opportunities, expansion of training opportunities to include persons who are severely disabled, and examination and improvement of competitive employment programs offered in secondary public schools and in sheltered workshops.

ENROLLMENT CRITERIA
AND TRAINEE CHARACTERISTICS

Prospective trainees must be able to lift and carry 20 pounds, be physically mobile, have adequate vision and hearing, and be eligible for services from the Washington State Division of Developmental Disabilities. All trainees are evaluated at the end of the first month to assess progress and to estimate the time they need to complete the program. Trainees may be dropped during the training period if eventual employment seems unlikely. Except for unusual situations, training is limited to 12 months. Referrals are accepted from any source, with most coming from the Division of Developmental Disabilities, the Department of Vocational Rehabilitation, and the public school system.

When enrolling in the program most trainees are in their 20s and have finished school. IQs of current enrollees average 56.4 with a range of 30-65. Prior trainee experience varies; of the 148 trainees who have enrolled to date, 48% (71) were previously placed in sheltered workshops (average 4 years); 28% (40) had only public school prevocational experience; 9% (14) had some prior competitive employment experience; 4% (6) came from developmental centers; and 13% (20) had no previous vocational experience. Most trainees live with their parents or independently; fewer live in group or foster homes.

Program activities are supported by fees for services from the Department of Vocational Rehabilitation and the Division of Developmental Disabilities, a federal Projects With Industry grant, and restaurant revenues. Hence, neither trainees nor employers are charged for training. Trainees are not paid during the training portion of their program; however, once employed, they are paid by their employer at the prevailing rate (at least minimum wage).

PROGRAM OPERATIONS

In-House Training

Although a small number of trainees have been placed in other industries, the ETP focuses on training for food service jobs, primarily because the high turnover rate in this industry assures an adequate number of jobs for program graduates. Equally important, the high turnover rate makes mentally retarded workers more attractive because of their relative stability (Brickey & Campbell, 1981). In addition, the continuity of necessary skills across food service jobs makes pretraining feasible.

Training is provided in three general areas: dishwashing, bussing, and cleaning. Training takes place in two settings on the University of Washington campus, which can accommodate 17 trainees at one time. One training site is a cafeteria operated by the training program, which permits maximum control over training conditions. This cafeteria serves about 400 meals a day and is representative of small restaurants. The second training site is the cafeteria of a large student center operated by the University Food Services Division. This facility serves approximately 2,500 customers per day and is typical of larger, faster restaurants. The ultimate employing restaurant may be considered a third training site. Although considerable generalization takes place from campus training sites to employing restaurants, trainees must learn to use the specific equipment of the employing restaurant and to follow the work schedule unique to the employment situation.

Training is behaviorally and competency based, with performance at criterion levels required for promotion. A trainer-trainee ratio of 1:4 allows individualized programming as necessary. Standard programs include transportation training (cf. Sowers, Rusch, & Hudson, 1979), time management (cf. Sowers, Rusch, Connis, & Cummings, 1980), grooming, responding to verbal instructions, and task sequencing (Connis, 1979) as well as task acquisition (Rusch, 1979). The training day averages 6 hours and may involve up to 14 separate tasks. Data on speed, quality, and independence are collected daily and used to make training decisions. Speed drills and other practice sessions are used in addition to restaurant production to provide more opportunities to improve skills. Only those vocational skills that are directly applicable to the positions trainees are eventually placed into are taught.

A variety of behavioral programming techniques are used, including modeling, self-monitoring and recording, peer practice and reinforcement, use of small amounts of money or tokens (such as stickers, checkmarks, or plusses), response-cost programs, and reinforcement by parents and advocates for work performance. When needed, trainees are referred for other services such as mental health services, independent living training, and medical care before being competitively employed.

Trainees are considered job ready when they meet target competitive standards for speed, quality, and attendance and receive two or fewer prompts from a trainer each day. Depending on the individual's needs and jobs available, he or she then: 1) goes directly into employment, 2) stays in training while waiting for an appropriate placement, or 3) remains at home while an appropriate job is being located.

Job Development and Matching

Job development is conducted by the placement staff on an ongoing basis using personal visits and follow-up calls to generate leads. Rather than stressing social service aspects, job developers emphasize employer advantages including pretrained and reliable employees, further on-the-job training, unlimited follow-up, program record of success, and financial benefits.

Factors considered in job screening and matching include job location, hours, pay, benefits, tasks involved, speed and flexibility required, atmosphere in the work environment (relaxed, frantic, etc.), and any special worker needs. Trainees are matched with jobs through consultation between themselves, training staff, and parents and advocates (see Chapter 13 for a thorough overview of placement procedures used by the ETP and other similar competitive employment programs).

Most trainees are placed in dishwashing jobs in medium-sized commercial restaurants where they wash dishes and pots, restock supplies, empty garbage, sweep and mop, and clean dishwashing machines and sinks. Some trainees also do bussing or food preparation. A smaller percentage work in hospitals or cafeterias. Currently, the average program graduate works 26 hours per week (range 6-40), earning $4.05 per hour (range $3.95-$5.90).

Placement

During the initial placement period, the following six services are typically provided. First, a new bus route must usually be learned. Second, it is often necessary to restructure the job since task descriptions and schedules obtained from employers prior to placement sometimes turn out to be incorrect or too general to be useful. To accurately analyze task routines and schedules without teaching the job to the trainee (now the worker) at the same time, placement trainers usually perform a given job themselves for a day before bringing in the worker. Third, once the job is structured, the trainer begins to teach the worker the required tasks and sequences. This phase may last from 2 days to 6 weeks depending on the complexity of the job and the worker's skills. Instruction is data based with the trainer using information collected on task completion, speed, quality, and independence to make training and fading decisions. Fourth, the trainer often does part of the work at first so the worker has a chance to learn new routines with fewer demands. Fifth, the trainer acts as a model for both the worker (modeling worker behavior) and the employer and co-workers (e.g., modeling of instruction techniques). Many employers have never supervised an adult with handicaps and therefore are concerned about being effective; trainers reassure them by providing directed in-service sessions. In addition, the trainer often acts as the worker's advocate in negotiating changes in the job, pointing out to the employer the progress being made, completing employment paperwork, and so forth. Sixth, the trainer provides feedback to parents and advocates, helping them adjust to the new employment situation and continue to provide support for the worker as the trainer fades out.

As the worker gains confidence and competence, the trainer withdraws from the employment situation leaving the worker alone during tasks which, according to evaluation data, he or she has successfully mastered. Throughout the initial placement period, the trainer collects and discusses written evaluations with the employer. The average worker functions independently after 6 weeks.

Follow-Up

Program staff continues to provide support and retraining after the placement period. Written supervisor evaluations will occasionally disclose a problem; at other times the employer or worker will call program staff to ask for help because of problems related to declining speed, difficulties related to changes in task assignments, problems outside of work influencing attendance, or changes in management resulting in different expectations. Open-ended follow-up has been crucial to maintaining workers in jobs; between 50% and 60% of employed program graduates require some retraining or support each year (Ford, Dineen, & Hall, 1985).

Whenever a program graduate quits, is laid off, or fired, one of three steps is taken:

1. If the termination seems to be due to something other than trainee performance (as when a restaurant closes), the trainee is placed into another job as soon as an appropriate position becomes available.
2. If vocational or social skills deficits seem to have contributed to the job loss, the trainee may be asked to return to the campus for additional training to remedy the problem and increase the chance of success in the next placement.
3. If the problems are judged to be beyond the scope of the program, the trainee is referred to another program.

ANALYSIS OF PROGRAM EFFECTIVENESS

In this section, a number of variables found to affect the likelihood of successful employment through the Employment Training Program are discussed.

Variables Contributing to Success

A total of 66% of the individuals who entered the ETP have been placed into competitive jobs. Of those, 65% were still employed at 6 months, 53% at 1 year, and 46% of all individuals placed since 1975 are still competitively employed in 1984. The primary factors contributing to job acquisition and maintenance include careful preemployment training, thorough on-the-job training, and a well-structured follow-up program.

Preemployment Training As mentioned, initial training takes place in two university cafeterias that closely resemble other commercial food service operations. Each cafeteria has a number of training slots, which can be molded to specific training needs to an extent not possible in regular competitive jobs. Most educators agree that systematically approximating target employment requirements is an effective training approach for many individuals. In practice, training criteria are graduated over time and thus trainees who may have little or no work experience are eased into increasingly demanding task schedules at ETP training sites while developing competencies.

The teacher-student ratio of 1:4 in the preemployment training site offers excellent teaching economies. For most trainees, preemployment training represents 80% of the total training service (not including long-term follow-up). Since the model typically utilizes a 1:1 training ratio during the remaining 20% of the training, the total cost of training can be held down by providing the majority of its services before actual employment.

An added advantage of having a preemployment training site is in offering practicum opportunities to graduate and undergraduate students who wish to learn the teaching technology. A final teaching advantage, at least in several replications of the ETP, is the mixing of culinary arts students with the mentally retarded students. When training programs are situated in community colleges, this natural blending of students with similar vocational goals has the long-term benefit of providing restaurant chefs and managers of tomorrow with exposure to potential co-workers with handicaps.

Preemployment training has advantages for the trainee as well. For example, an individual with severe behavior problems can often be better accommodated at a training site where there is a tolerance for wide variations in behavior than in an actual competitive situation. Also, the trainee has the opportunity to demonstrate competencies that make job matching more exacting than otherwise possible. Thus, individuals whose initial competencies are relatively low can make major gains before a job match is made.

The training process itself contributes significantly to eventual success. Specifically, using a variety of teaching procedures has been found particularly beneficial. For example, to teach speed, the ETP employs a combination of skill training; peer practice; verbal, graphic, and written feedback; and self-monitoring. To begin, the trainee is integrated into a peer-practice group consisting of three to five trainees of varying capabilities. These individuals time each other over a number of trials while performing a standard amount of work (for example, loading a tub of 30 cups and dishes into a dishwashing machine). This exercise provides both good role modeling and a reasonable amount of peer pressure to perform well. The trainee's best practice and actual work rates are measured daily by the trainer who shares this information with the trainee verbally and in written or graphic form. Since a number of tasks requiring speed lend themselves to discreet measurement, trainees are often taught to monitor their own work rate as part of the training. Thus, the training focus is on establishing effective techniques, providing repeated practice in both "fun" and actual work situations, offering clear feedback on performance, and turning over as much of the responsibility for skill maintenance to the worker as possible.

On-the-Job Training   Once on the job, the worker's chances for success are increased by several program components. Since restaurants represent different working environments, the matching process is crucial to success. The ability to train similar or identical tasks before and after employment using identical training techniques and measurement systems, plus a thorough knowledge of the trainee's strengths and weaknesses (gained through performance measurement on the job) is one of the greatest strengths of the ETP model.

The placement trainer develops a task analysis of the job during the first week of job training. Besides the obvious advantage of being able to structure training, the task analysis constitutes an agreement between the worker (represented by the trainer) and the employer regarding the exact job duties, quality standards, and sequencing of tasks. Thus, when the employer calls the ETP months or years later to request follow-up training, the task analysis serves as a benchmark for determining whether worker performance or employer standards have changed—an important consideration for the placement trainer in deciding where to focus follow-up services. Clear expectations enhance the quality of the feedback given to the worker by the employer. To the extent that a worker with mental retardation is unable to profit from the often subtle feedback available in the working environment, he or she becomes dependent on explicit supervisor intervention. The task analysis represents the basis from which the supervisor's expectations (standards) are monitored, as well as the worker's performance.

Follow-Up Services   Teaching the worker to perform a job to the employer's expectations is usually not enough to keep that individual employed for an extended period. Relatively small communication problems with a new supervisor, for example, can jeopardize the worker's job long after the work has become routine. The cost of providing open-ended follow-up services to ETP clients has ranged from $230 to $500 per worker per year after the first year of employment (Ford et al., 1985). As noted earlier, such services are required annually by half the workers. These follow-up services allow placement trainers to pinpoint problems quickly and to provide intervention specific to problems identified. Several factors make this possible, including good communication and trust between the employer and ETP trainer, task analysis information defining job expectations, a considerable amount of program staff experience in working with the restaurant industry, and the inherent effectiveness of using an applied behavior analysis approach to teaching necessary skills (Rusch & Mithaug, 1980).

Variables Contributing to Failure

Factors contributing to job losses experienced by 54% of the ETP graduates fall into four major categories. First, the worker may have not been able to learn or maintain the vocational skills needed for a given job. Second, he or she may have failed to exhibit the social behaviors supervisors and co-workers expect from fellow employees (cf. Greenspan & Shoultz, 1981). Third, the restaurant may have laid off workers or closed entirely. And finally, the worker may have chosen to quit the job.

Since the program's inception, the ETP placement trainers have been ascertaining the reasons why workers placed into competitive jobs have lost their jobs. Unlike much of the literature that suggests that social skill deficits are more likely than vocational skill deficits to be the major cause of job loss, ETP placement trainers have cited the latter most frequently (Greenspan & Shoultz, 1981; Schalock & Harper, 1978; Wehman et al., 1982). In fact, vocational problems have been cited 67% of the time as the sole or partial reason for losing a job, with work rate cited most frequently. Quality of work, attendance, and staying on-task also appear often as vocational deficits. One possible explanation for the high frequency of vocational failure is that the task analysis and subsequent task lists developed by the ETP placement trainers set up very specific vocational skill expectations for the worker, thereby making any deviation relatively easy to detect. Without the measurement system, it would be easier to attribute a job loss to more obvious social behaviors that may be accompanied by poor, but less noticeable, work performance. In addition, many entry-level jobs in the restaurant industry require superior work rates for brief periods, like during a lunch "rush," that may limit the abilities of a worker

who might otherwise competently perform. The time period for losing a job for work-rate reasons ranges from the 1st to the 182nd week, suggesting that workers may initially be unable to work fast enough, or may meet initial standards and then fail to maintain those standards, or that standards may have changed over time.

Social behaviors represent the second most frequent problem area for workers, occurring as the sole or partial reason for 28% of all job losses. The largest category centers around workers' deficits in following instructions from the supervisor. Other social problems include poor interactions with co-workers, emotional outbursts, and theft. Several factors affect these interaction difficulties. First, social behaviors are complex compared with the repetitive vocational tasks required of entry-level food service workers. Many interactions are very brief, quickly paced, and unanticipated (e.g., it may be difficult to teach a worker to accept criticism when the way in which criticism is given varies greatly). Second, generalization from a preemployment training setting to the actual job seems to be more problematic for social than for vocational skills. Trainers find themselves providing intensive training on the job for social behaviors that are not very predictable over the course of the work day. The range for losing a job due to social interactions has been found to range from a few days to 231 weeks.

Restaurant cutbacks or closures represent the third major category of job losses. The largest percentage took place in restaurant failures, followed closely by staff cutbacks that condensed or eliminated jobs. Jobs were also lost when the restaurants changed assigned tasks so significantly that the worker was unable to learn the new tasks in spite of considerable placement trainer assistance. Finally, in a few cases restaurants terminated a worker whom the ETP felt was competent and should have remained employed. Altogether, these job losses represent 28% of the total, and were usually the sole reason for terminations.

Voluntary terminations have occurred with 20% of the ETP workers, most typically because the worker was either tired of the job or because he or she did not like the working hours. Less often the worker quit for health reasons, to move to a better job, or to marry.

COSTS VERSUS BENEFITS: COMPARISON BETWEEN ETP AND OTHER PLACEMENT MODELS AND TRADITIONAL SERVICES MODELS

Because handicapped populations differ with regard to the intensity of services needed, cost comparisons between placement models may be inappropriate. Persons are usually referred to the University of Washington ETP because they are considered too disabled to benefit from other employment-oriented training programs in the Greater Seattle community. Vocational alternatives for the population served by the ETP are generally limited to traditional work activity center services.

Competitive employment programs appear relatively expensive when compared to traditional adult day care services, particularly because costs for programs like the ETP are "front-loaded," with most of the expenses occurring during the first 2 years. The current average cost of preemployment training is about $7,200; placement costs average $1,460 for the first year but drop to an average of about $300 annually per person in subsequent years of employment.

Program graduates have earned over $1,300,000 since 1976. Comparable sheltered workshop wages for the 4,242 months during which clients have been enrolled in the program would have totaled only $214,900 (based on the Washington state average activity center wage for July 1984 and assuming that all 162 clients would have been active continuously in sheltered employment). Also, competitive wages are subject to income taxes and social security deductions, which decrease the amount of unearned benefits claimed, resulting in a net gain to the economy. In addition, competitive employment provides participants such nonfinancial benefits as access to more normal work environments, exposure to non-

handicapped co-workers, improved community access, and opportunities for the community of persons who are not handicapped to interact with individuals with handicaps who are capable and productive.

PROGRAM REPLICATION

The University of Washington's competitive employment program has been replicated twice in the Seattle area; a third replication in Portland, Oregon began in January 1985. The first replication, initiated in September 1978, was operated by a local sheltered workshop. Training was conducted in a hospital kitchen and placements were subsequently made into competitive food service jobs. Of the 56 clients involved, 32 have been placed into competitive employment since its inception, demonstrating that the train-place-maintain model can be used effectively in the context of traditional adult day programming alternatives. The second replication was in a community college's culinary arts program. Trainees were registered as community college students and received training in dishwashing, potwashing, bussing, and clean-up alongside nonhandicapped persons learning to be cooks and restaurant managers. This community college program has enrolled 49 persons and has made 25 placements since June 1980.

The third replication is also based in a community college culinary arts program; however, some trainees will be placed directly into employment while others will be trained before placement. In addition, it is anticipated that a sizable number of placements will be made in nonfood service areas. With its broad range of services, the Oregon replication is designed to effectively serve a wider selection of individuals with handicaps than existing programs, which focus primarily upon serving persons with mild and moderate mental retardation.

CONCLUSIONS

Since 1976, the Employment Training Program has shown that adults with mental retardation can be competitively employed. Significantly, Washington state funding regulations have been changed, based upon the University of Washington program, to encourage high quality vocational services for this population. Thirty similar competitive employment programs have begun offering similar services since the ETP's inception. It appears that a number of conclusions are warranted, based upon the ETP's efforts:

1. Much of the research over the past half-century on moderately and severely retarded adults was done with institutional populations. Although the results of those studies may have been valid for the groups studied, there is reason to question the generalization to populations of young people who had never experienced institutional living. Much of today's knowledge about mental retardation, as reported in professional texts, may require re-examination.

2. Mental retardation can certainly be characterized by deficits in learning. Mental retardation is not necessarily characterized by deficits in performance once a task is learned. Although performance deficits clearly exist with some retarded individuals, this is not uniform across all retarded individuals.

3. Rate of performance is the outstanding cause for job losses. Unusually slow performance is one of those behaviors that make a person appear "retarded." The reason for such slow performance is not known but much of it could be caused by prior training at home and school. It is not unusual for schools to emphasize accuracy over speed and to promote undue concern over making errors. It is possible that this slow rate of performance is learned rather

than a physical consequence of the condition.

4. Social development appears to occur most rapidly after the individual leaves the training program and enters the work force. Continued exposure to socially appropriate behavior in the work place appears to provide the best opportunity for learning such skills.

5. Many of the emotional problems that interfere with employment are amenable to mental health counseling. This is an avenue that is often overlooked in securing job success.

6. Social problems are a strong second in the reasons for job losses. It is possible that some of these problems result from inadequate training prior to entry into the employment program. There is reason to question the expectations of secondary school personnel who allow youngsters to leave school with obviously inappropriate social behavior.

7. It is possible that mental retardation, *per se,* should not be considered a handicapping condition. Individuals are considered handicapped because they are unable to perform specific functions. It is this inability to perform certain functions that handicaps an individual. If people can perform most or all the needed functions to live independently in society, they may not be handicapped in spite of their disabilities. The fact that mentally retarded individuals learn slowly should not be considered a handicap as long as they learn what they need.

8. Finally, the failure of mentally retarded individuals to learn, function, and participate meaningfully in society may well be a failure of the educational system, not the retarded individual.

REFERENCES

Brickey, M., & Campbell, K. (1981). Fast food employment for moderately and mildly mentally retarded adults. *Mental Retardation, 19*(3), 113–116.

Connis, R. T. (1979). The effects of sequential pictorial cues, self-recording, and praise on the job task sequencing of retarded adults. *Journal of Applied Behavioral Analysis, 12*(3), 355–362.

Ford, L., Dineen, J., & Hall, J. (1985). Is there life after placement? *Education and Training of the Mentally Retarded, 19,* 291–296.

Greenspan, S., & Shoultz, B. (1981). Why mentally retarded adults lose their jobs: Social competence as a factor in work adjustment. *Applied Research in Mental Retardation, 2,* 23–38.

Hill, M., & Wehman, P. (1982). Cost benefit analysis of placing moderately and severely handicapped individuals into competitive employment. In P. Wehman and M. Hill (Eds.), *Vocational training and placement of severely disabled persons* (Vol. III, pp. 24–46). Richmond: Virginia Commonwealth University.

Moss, J. W. (1980). *Post secondary vocational education for mentally retarded adults.* Reston, VA: ERIC Clearinghouse on Handicapped and Gifted Children.

Rusch, F. R. (1979). A functional analysis of the relationship between attending to task and production in an applied restaurant setting. *Journal of Special Education, 13,* 399–411.

Rusch, F. R., & Mithaug, D. E. (1980). *Vocational training for mentally retarded adults: A behavior analytic approach.* Champaign, IL: Research Press.

Schalock, R. L., & Harper, R. S. (1978). Placement from community-based MR programs: How well do clients do? *American Journal of Mental Deficiency, 83,* 240–247.

Sowers, J. A., Rusch, F. R., Connis, R. T., & Cummings, L. E. (1980). Teaching mentally retarded adults to time-manage in a vocational setting. *Journal of Applied Behavior Analysis, 13,* 119–128.

Sowers, J., Rusch, F., & Hudson, C. (1979). Training a severely retarded young adult to ride the city bus to and from work. *AAESPH Review, 4,* 15–22.

Wehman, P., Hill, M., Goodall, P., Cleveland, P., Barrett, N., Brooke, V., Pentecost, J., & Bruff, B. (1982). Job placement and follow up of moderately and severely handicapped individuals: An update after three years. In P. Wehman & M. Hill (Eds.), *Vocational training and placement of severely disabled persons* (Vol. III, pp. 1–23). Richmond: Virginia Commonwealth University.

SECTION II

COMPETITIVE
EMPLOYMENT METHODS

Introduction

Robert H. Horner

COMPETITIVE EMPLOYMENT FOR more significantly disabled workers has moved from a philosophy to a reality, due in part to the development and implementation of a functional technology. Section II of this volume describes the basic procedures within that technology. These 11 chapters demonstrate how service values can drive technological development. The training, job development, and service coordination procedures described in Section II are the direct result of work by people who believe that individuals with significant disabilities not only should have access to meaningful work options, but that these workers can provide valuable labor to business and industry. The "methods" described in Section II are important because they focus on a socially valued outcome: paid work, and the life-style that paid work allows.

As the reader examines the chapters in Section II, consideration should be given to the way these chapters include and expand the traditional technology of instruction. New recognition is given to the complex demands associated with training skills that will be maintained and generalized across the full range of situations a person experiences in competitive job sites. Also of note is the extent to which the methods described in Section II represent packages with multiple procedures. The demands of competitive employment outstrip simple behavioral or instructional procedures, and command the integration of multiple methodologies in the form of packages or "systems" for employment. Given the importance of competitive employment, more research is

needed on the individual contribution of each procedure within these packages.

Section II is divided into 11 chapters that address five major themes: Assessment, Job Development, Instruction and Intervention, Research Methodology, and Systems Analysis.

ASSESSMENT

The methods of achieving competitive employment begin with attention to assessing work behavior. In Chapter 7, Pancsofar argues for an assessment process that includes the work context as well as the work behaviors that are to be employed. Building from the concept of ecological assessment, Pancsofar points to the need for including both quantitative and qualitative analysis in the process of assessment. Critical to this approach is the development of information that will have predictive validity across a range of employment settings. Pancsofar provides 10 "principles" for assessing work behavior that meet these criteria.

JOB DEVELOPMENT

For competitive employment to be a reality, there must be job sites. Two chapters deal with issues related to developing job sites. The first is written by Stainback, Stainback, Nietupski, and Hamre-Nietupski (Chapter 8), and describes procedures for building community-based training stations. This chapter carries relevance for teachers in high school special education classrooms as well as for professionals facing the task of training and employing adults with disabilities. Community-based training stations are real job sites where an individual learns employment skills before being employed in another competitive job. The chapter presents a compelling logic for why training stations are effective, and a seven-step model for developing and maintaining training stations.

A second approach to job development is provided by Martin in Chapter 13. Emphasizing the critical importance of follow-up for successful competitive employment, Martin provides a nine-step process for finding a community job and placing a person with disabilities. Important for any reader involved in competitive employment is Martin's warning to ensure that a "match" between job demands, worker ability, and available support systems indicates a high probability for success. This chapter provides readers with specific suggestions for how to proceed in the potentially intimidating task of finding appropriate competitive job options.

INSTRUCTION AND INTERVENTION

The instructional technology of competitive employment must meet uniquely difficult requirements. The most demanding of these is the need for workers to generalize and maintain work skills across settings, people, materials, and time. Wacker and Berg present an important chapter (Chapter 10) in which the dangers of "narrow skill development" are described and an array of techniques for achieving generalization and maintenance are defined. Wacker and Berg separate their list of techniques into one group that involves manipulation of antecedent events and another group that involves manipulation of consequences. In her companion chapter, Cheryl Hanley-Maxwell (Chapter 14) discusses generalization methodology from a curriculum development perspective. This chapter will be of particular interest to teachers and curriculum developers preparing materials for school programs.

The last three chapters in Section II address the critical issues related to maintaining em-ployment after placement has occurred. Competitive employment only meets our expectations and values if the worker retains his or her job over a considerable period of time. Rusch has pioneered the technology of post-placement support, and the three chapters written respectively by White, Shafer, and Rusch evidence a clear understanding of the complexity and importance of follow-up services. White (Chapter 15) emphasizes the need to use subjective evaluations that include multiple comparisons of the work life of a disabled worker with the work life of his or her non-handicapped co-workers. The discrepancies that can be identified provide critical information in building a follow-up support system. Shafer (Chapter 16) extends this notion by suggesting that co-workers be enlisted to assist the handicapped worker. Co-workers can make a significant difference in the longevity of a worker's tenure through their roles as advocates, observers, and trainers. Shafer describes specific strategies for training co-workers and motivating their ongoing support of a disabled employee. Rusch (Chapter 17) discusses the larger issue of follow-up support, emphasizing the need for both descriptive and comparative validation of information gathered about a worker.

RESEARCH METHODOLOGY

Competitive employment is still in its infancy. Considerable research and evaluation will be needed before comprehensive models are widely available. Agran provides two chapters (Chapters 11 and 12) that describe observation methods and research design methods that will be of critical value for those who continue the systematic research it this area.

SYSTEMS ANALYSIS

The technology of competitive employment is more than a technology of behavior change, it is a technology of systems change. This is apparent in Robert Schalock's chapter (Chapter 9) on service delivery coordination. Schalock draws from a theoretically sophisticated analysis of social service systems, and his substantial experience with Nebraska's vocational services, to describe the complex interconnectedness of variables that affect competitive employment. This chapter defines variables that affect a person's transitions from school to work, from school to another service delivery program, and from a workshop to a community work place. For those of us who share Schalock's frustration with a service delivery system that is "duplicative, fragmented and inefficient," this chapter offers a beacon that will prove useful in building competitive employment options.

In summary, the methodology of competitive employment is complex, encouraging, but insufficiently tested. The assessment, job development, intervention, research, and systems analysis technology that is described in Section II is the most promising set of procedures we have ever assembled. The value of these procedures will become clear as we assess their effect on the wages, integration, and independence of workers with disabilities over the next 5 years.

Chapter 7

Assessing Work Behavior

Ernest L. Pancsofar

VOCATIONAL ASSESSMENT CAN be broadly defined as the "process of obtaining information about a worker's skills and performance in order to make appropriate training decisions" (Bellamy, Horner, & Inman, 1979, p. 89). Browning and Irvin (1981) distinguished between traditional and contemporary assessment approaches. *Traditional assessment* refers to measures of prior learning "assuming that already learned aptitudes, interests, and traits can forecast subsequent learning, performance and adjustment" (Browning & Irvin, 1981, p. 375); *contemporary assessment*, in contrast, measures "applied performance within the context in which the performance is expected" (Browning & Irvin, 1981, p. 379). Several authors have provided detailed descriptions of both traditional and contemporary evaluation instruments (Bates & Pancsofar, 1985; Botterbusch, 1982; Brolin, 1982; Browning & Irvin, 1981; Field & Orgar, 1983; Menchetti, Rusch, & Owens, 1983). Whether traditional or contemporary, assessment is a value-laden process guided by the varying philosophical orientations of the professionals who are responsible for its implementation. In this chapter, 10 principles are presented that extend the current definition of contemporary assessment. Also, procedures and assessment options for handicapped persons are recommended.

PRINCIPLES OF ASSESSMENT

1. **The assessment process must be ecological**. Decisions on assessment processes must take into consideration the relationship between the specific behavior under assessment and a variety of other factors. More specifically, according to the ecological orientation, events do not happen in isolation from the context within which they are being observed. Rather, a continual interplay takes place among elements within major components of the individual's life. Figure 1 represents one example of the elements and the interactions between such elements that influence the interpretation of assessments for predictive purposes. The major components of this model include: the individual, significant others, physical environments, and culture. The *individual component* consists of such factors as descriptive medical data, psychological reports, personal likes and dislikes, role expectations, and aptitudes. *Significant others* include primary care providers, teachers, aids, schoolmates, friends, siblings, and community service personnel. Sample areas of concern within the *physical environment* encompass the school setting and materials, community work and leisure sites, and home environment and neighborhood. Finally, *cultural components* cover the operationalized philosophical orientations of representatives of the school/vocational program, the community news media's portrayal of persons with handicaps, general attitudes of nonhandicapped persons toward persons with handicaps, outcomes of judicial and legislative decisions, and the professional orientation of educators.

Instruments for assessing the variables within the four major components depicted in

Figure 1 are available; however, beyond an initial assessment, the effects of information about each element on the others must be determined. For example, documentation of family members' support of a student's realistic vocational goals will result in a significantly different approach toward community employment than when working with a trainee whose family members are unreceptive to such a vocational option.

In summary, assessment data must be evaluated in light of the relationships that exist among the four elements of an ecological model. A battery of assessment instruments is needed to obtain information about as many of the components within each element as possible. Only then will the student benefit from proactive planning of vocational opportunities and successful placement in community employment.

2. **Assessment must be conducted in settings where the student's responses can be evaluated in relation to naturally occurring environmental cues.** When assessing work

behavior, two formats may be followed. In the first, a student is requested to complete a series of steps in a task; as soon as he or she makes an error, the task is terminated whereupon the assessor records a (−) for the student's failure to complete the task. That is, when the task is not completed the student is not given credit for correct responses to preliminary steps. The second structural format allows the student to respond to the natural cue (discriminative stimulus) for each step in a task and subsequently be evaluated on each separate response. That is, for each response the assessor must identify the task-relevant cue that should set the occasion for a contingent response. After completing the response, the student has access to the task-relevant cue(s) for the next response. If the student makes an error, the assessor does not stop the task, but rearranges the environment, as needed, to introduce the task-relevant cue for the next response (Bellamy et al., 1979). By adhering to the second format for assessing specific work tasks, the assessor obtains a more accurate description of the student's functioning level and hence be-

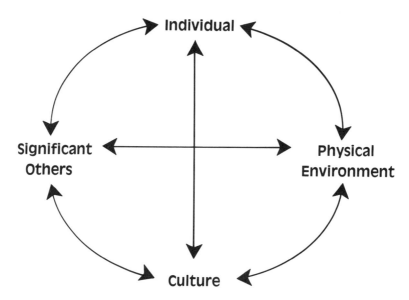

Ecological Analysis

Figure 1. Ecological analysis of significant elements within each of the components that impinges on the student. (From Pancsofar, E., & Blackwell, R. [1985]. *Community entry for the severely handicapped: A user's guide* [p. 14]. Albany: State University of New York Press. Copyright 1985 by the State University of New York Press.)

comes able to evaluate more accurately the success of subsequent training efforts.

Table 1 depicts a structural format consisting of a 10-step sequence for obtaining coffee from a vending machine. Each step (response) has a corresponding task-relevant cue (S_D). The assessment procedure begins with a brief explanation of the task followed by one demonstration by the assessor. The assesor then requests the student to obtain a cup of coffee after having determined an interval of time during which the client is expected to respond to the task-relevant cues (e.g., 3–5 seconds). If the client responds by correctly performing the response associated with the first environmental cue, the assessor records a (+) on a data form without providing any external feedback to the student. Following a correct response, the task-relevant cue for the subsequent response should be evident.

If the student fails to initiate any behavior for the first response within the allotted time, the assessor records a (−) for that response and places the correct change in the client's hand. That is, the assessor presents the next task-relevant cue as if the client had succeeded on the previous response. Again, no verbal corrective feedback is presented during this assessment phase. If the student initiates an incorrect response to the task-relevant cue, the assessor interrupts as quickly as possible and presents the cue for the following response. Again, a (−) is recorded. This sequence continues for the remaining steps in the task analysis.

3. **Assessment exemplars must have predictive validity for determining the student's ability to perform equally well on most/all instances of a given activity in anticipated work environments.** During assessment, limited samples of behavior are observed and relevant data are recorded. Based on these samples, predictions are made about a student's ability to perform equally well beyond the geographic and behavioral boundaries of the assessment environment. Accordingly, an assessor must select examples of a behavior that allow for a broad interpretation of a student's current functioning. A *general case strategy* is highly recommended for selecting examples of work behaviors to ensure adequate predictive validity in reference to a student's ability to perform equally well across diverse community settings (Horner, Sprague, & Wilcox, 1982).

In a general case approach, a limited number of examples of a work behavior sample the range of instances of the given work behavior in the student's community. By assessing a student on selected examples, the assessor gains confidence that the student will perform equally well on any example of a given work behavior. The key to selecting initial assessment examples is that they sample the range of prospective approaches to performing a given behavior within designated parameters.

Table 1. Structural format for writing task sequence of responses for baseline assessment

Task-relevant cue (S_D)	Response unit
1. Sold-out light off	1. Choose correct amount of coins
2. Change in hand	2. Place change into slot marked "coins"
3. Change makes registering "clink" sound	3. Make desired selection and depress button
4. Machine makes vibrating (humming) sound	4. Watch for cup to descend into holding compartment
5. Cup descends	5. Watch coffee fill cup
6. Cup filled	6. Listen for machine to stop brewing process
7. Machine off	7. Slide compartment door open with non-dominant hand and hold door in open position
8. Door open	8. Grasp filled cup with dominant hand and remove cup
9. Cup removed	9. Release door to closed position
10. Door closed	10. Check machine for change if correct amount was not initially placed in machine

For example, if four examples are identified as samples of the range of variation existing within the community, the student is observed responding to the task-relevant cues for the responses included for each sample. After being assessed on these probes, the student is taught to perform the behavior using examples other than the assessment probes. After acquiring a number of preselected exemplars that also sample the range of stimulus and response variation, the student is reassessed on the pretraining exemplars to verify generalization. Horner and McDonald (1982) illustrated the general case approach through an example involving 20 nontrained probe capacitors that samples the range of crimping and cutting commercially prepared biaxle capacitors. The capacitors varied in head size, distance between leads, and head shape (see Figure 2).

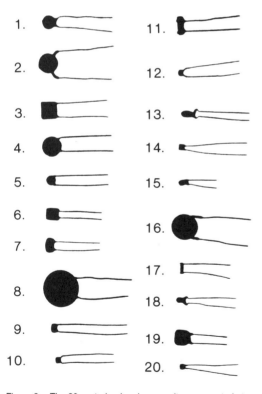

Figure 2.   The 20 nontrained probe capacitors presented at each probe session. (From Horner, R. H., & McDonald, R. S. [1982]. Comparisons of single instance and general case instruction in teaching a generalized vocational skill. *Journal of The Association for the Severely Handicapped, 7*(3), 7–20. Copyright 1982 by The Association for the Severely Handicapped. Adapted by permission.)

4. **Assessment must include both quantitative and qualitative components.** Quantitative data include measures of frequency, duration, percentage, and so forth, that can be objectively documented. Qualitative data, in contrast, refer to less objective—although no less valuable—information including comments from co-workers, weekly observation summaries by on-site managers, and parental feedback obtained through interviews and/or brief questionnaires. Although qualitative data may be biased and demonstrate limited reliability with quantitative data, their role in the success of a training program cannot be underestimated. For example, using qualitative measures, initial concerns by significant others regarding a worker's personal interactions can be resolved before they evolve into larger, more difficult-to-solve problems.

Furthermore, work supervisors may record voluminous data to document a trainee's progress only to be disappointed when the on-site manager fails to collaborate the worker's success. To achieve a more proactive assessment approach, therefore, supervisors must receive feedback about trainee progress from on-site personnel at regular intervals. Since business managers may be unfamiliar with applied behavior analysis terminology, such reports may require a specially designed format. Proficient or not, the on-site manager's subjective appraisal of trainee progress determines the probability of the continued employment of the trainee.

5. **Politics play an increasingly important role in implementing and interpreting assessment results.** Evaluators must not be naive about the role of politics in the decision-making process. *Politics* refer to those forces surrounding a decision that are not based directly on assessment results (Murphy & Ursprung, 1983). For example, if only one placement option is available in a given community, the predictive nature of a vocational assessment battery administered to determine the proper placement for an adolescent becomes irrelevant. Additionally, as a result of relationships that often develop between contracting agencies and evaluators, specific tests

may be requested to verify, for example, the referring agent's hypothesis that clerical work is the best placement for a certain student, thereby introducing a set of biasing variables in the assessment process.

Evaluation specialists work under conflicting goals (Pomerantz & Marholin, 1977). For examples, parents may have worked hard to establish a sheltered workshop in the community and, consequently, are proud of its accomplishments and services. As a result, evaluators may be reluctant to recommend placement of productive workshop employees in community work sites for fear of jeopardizing the productivity in the workshop and offending community supporters. Change can occur, but the vocational specialist needs strategies for working within the existing framework to effect changes that enhance quality work experiences for students without alienating community leaders. A docile attitude is not advocated. Rather, short- and long-range plans for change must be implemented based on cooperation and trust among all helping professionals. At the outset, the assessor needs to realize that although the current decision-making process may be out of his or her control, it need not always remain so.

6. **Baseline, formative, and summative assessment phases demand equal importance and attention.** Three distinct assessment phases are essential for documenting the success of an intervention program: baseline, formative, and summative evaluations. *Baseline measures* are designed to gather information on how a student responds to natural cues for both the task to be trained and selected probes that sample the range of opportunities to perform different instances of the task in the community. *Formative assessment,* in turn, focuses on information related to maintaining, changing, or terminating current instructional strategies. *Summative assessment* documents any functional relationships between the training strategy (independent variables) and the targeted behavior change (dependent variables). Pancsofar and Bates (1984) recommended greater reliance on variations of the multiple-baseline design as a summative as-

sessment strategy in community work sites. Thus, the work supervisor must decide on the form of the eventual summative assessment before implementing baseline and formative assessment procedures. Finally, the summative phase should contain a reassessment of generalization probes that were assessed during the baseline phase.

7. **Assessment instruments must reflect placement opportunities in present and subsequent work settings.** Elements within assessment batteries should reflect the competencies that have been identitied as necessary for successful functioning within community employment settings. Brolin (1982) recommended that job banks be established for the vocational opportunities within each community. Job bank entries would contain information about demands specific to the occupation under investigation. (Strategies for collecting this information have been recommended by Belmore and Brown (1978) and Rusch and Mithaug (1980), and in Chapter 12 of this text.)

The inclusion in a job bank of critical skills stipulated for a given job enables work supervisors to analyze similar competencies across work experiences. For example, within the math area, a range of skills might be required for time management across 10 work sites. A listing of specific behavioral objectives for time management acquires a functional nature by documenting the need within actual work settings in this area.

To secure relevant information about the demands of specific job sites, a job analysis specialist may set up structured interviews with prospective employers and request information about social, reading, math, and strength/stamina requirements for success within a designated job. The data form presented in Figure 3 has been helpful in initial contacts with employers. The sample interview with a supervisor of cleaning persons at a motel reflects the supervisor's subjective appraisal of the vital skills related to the position under consideration. As a result of conducting interviews with 15 additional motel supervisors in the local community, the job analysis specialist

Job Skill Inventory

Location: DAYS INN

Activity: CLEANING PERSON

Requisite skills: A COURTEOUS TO CUSTOMER

B GETS ALONG WITH MGR. AND FELLOW WORKERS

C FRIENDLY TO CUSTOMER

D ON TIME TO WORK

E WILLING TO WORK HARD

F HAS GOOD ATTITUDE

G

H

Reading: A READS APPLICATION

B READS LABELS FOR WORK PRODUCTS

C READS CHARTS AND IS ABLE TO CHECK IN PROPER COLUMN

D

E

F

G

H

Math: A COUNTS LINENS NEEDED FOR ROUND

B

C

D

E

F

G

H

Strength/ A WALKS A LOT—UP STAIRS

Stamina: B CARRIES BUNDLES OF LINENS

C PUSHES CARTS WITH SUPPLIES

D BENDS ALL DAY

E MOVES ROOM FURNITURE

F ABLE TO WITHSTAND VARYING WEATHER CONDITIONS

H

Figure 3. Modified job skill inventory of selected requisite skills for a cleaning person.

arrived at a cluster of common skills. Based upon such data, a more objective, quantified analysis may be documented of the areas selected by a given supervisor as representing requisite work skills.

8. **Developmentally organized assessment instruments are inappropriate for predicting vocational success.** Work supervisors are advised to avoid developmentally sequenced inventories of work behaviors in developing vocational objectives. Since these instruments are intended to evaluate a level of difficulty factor in performing increasingly more complex work behaviors, specific inventory items may not directly relate to behaviors evident in the immediate community. To demonstrate effective instructional progress, trainers tend to target behaviors the student missed on the inventory. Thus, acquisition of prerequisite vocational skills in a hierarchical order is not related to a functional derivation of a student's work experience objectives. Administratively, individuals with similar disabilities can be compared on their ability to perform skills in a developmental hierarchy. However, such information does not reflect the competencies necessary in a functional context.

Table 2 contains 20 items from the vocational domain of a developmentally sequenced assessment. The assessor rates each behavior using one of four options: *always, more than half the time, less than half the time,* and *never.* The difficulty level of general work behaviors is sequenced from *easy* to *hard.* Predicting a student's eventual functioning in a community work setting based on the results of this behavior sampling is inappropriate. As illustrated by comparing the elements of this assessment with the behaviors listed in Figure 3, limited similarity exists between work requisite skills and the more global ratings found in Table 2.

9. **Workers are more apt to lose their jobs due to work-related deficits than inability to perform work tasks.** Factors related to performing a specific work task including behaviors such as tardiness, interactions with co-workers, responses to change in task demands, and general personality characteristics are significant predictors of a trainee's chances of maintaining competitive employment. As a result, sensitive assessment instruments are needed to document work-related behaviors that could impede the employee's acceptable performance. Table 3 contains a list of work-related behaviors based on a review of the related literature (Rusch, 1983).

10. **Assessment measures must become increasingly specific as the student prepares for gainful employment.** Hawkins (1979)

Table 2. Elements within a sample developmentally sequenced vocational assessment

1. Assumes a body position at a task or at play such that both hands are available for use.
2. Participates in a single activity for 10 minutes (if protected from interruption).
3. Attends to a single activity in a room with people.
4. Assembles two-part objects that fit together in a simple but secure way.
5. Attends to an assigned task or activity for ½ hour (may need to be encouraged).
6. Attempts to do an assigned task without resistance.
7. Puts away own tools and materials at the end of a task (may need a reminder up to one-half of the time).
8. Tosses hand-sized objects into an open box or wastebasket at a distance of 3 feet.
9. Stops a task when it is done.
10. Attends to work in a group without distracting others.
11. Changes activity without showing discomfort when assigned from one task to a different task.
12. Goes to an assigned area without reminder in a routine daily program.
13. Undertakes and completes a task in order to receive money.
14. Indicates if own performance meets the standards set for an activity (these standards may be very low).
15. Uses a hammer to pound, pliers to grasp, and a screwdriver to turn (need not be skillful).
16. Increases speed of work when told to do so.
17. Arises and leaves residence so as to reach work or activity on time.
18. Assembles objects with five parts that must be put together in a particular order.
19. Uses public transportation on one local route such as from residence to work and back.
20. Operates power hand tools such as a drill or food mixer without a supervisor present.

From Bock, W., & Weatherman, R. (1978). *Minnesota developmental programming system.* Minneapolis, MN: Bock Associates.

Table 3. Worker characteristics that have been the subject of employer evaluations

Acceptance of criticism	Instructional assistance, level of
Acknowledgment	Maintenance of positive attitude about work
Arrival behaviors	Moping
Requests for assistance	Noncompliance
Attending	Pages turned independently, percent of recipe
Not attending	Response to prompts and praises
Attending-to-task behavior	Production—speed of task completion
Bus riding (from home to work)	Staff feedback
Complaining	Stereotypic behavior
Completion of assigned tasks	Sweeping responses with a broom
Completion of job on time	Time management
Compliance	Topic repetition
Cooperation with employees and employers	Verbal abuse
Disagreements	Work behavior, compliant
Drooling	Working alone
Following a schedule	Working fast during rush times
In motion (looking busy)	Working safely
Not in motion	

Adapted from Rusch, F. R. (1983). Competitive vocational training. In M. E. Snell (Ed.), *Systematic instruction of the moderately and severely handicapped* (2nd ed.) (pp. 503–523). Columbus, OH: Charles E. Merrill. Copyright 1983 by Bell & Howell Company. Reprinted by permission.

used the image of a funnel to represent the quantity and quality of assessment information required by the trainer as a student becomes involved in a work experience program. Figure 4 illustrates the elements of a funnel approach as applied to community employment. Initially, the trainer reviews general information including previous student records, anecdotal reports, general physical health, general characteristics, and parental input. Data from these sources, in turn, set the parameters for the environmental surveys of stage two. Here current and future environments are assessed to validate the importance of priority behaviors

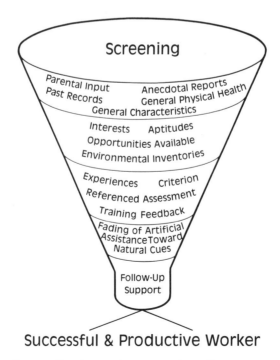

Figure 4.   Funnel approach to increasingly specific assessment.

leading toward successful functioning in community work settings. Following the environmental analyses, the student is assessed on selected high priority responses to natural cues. That is, to establish an accurate baseline response rate, criterion-referenced assessments are conducted under circumstances that are as close as possible to those in the natural environment. During the following formative assessment phase, the fading of artificial cues is documented as the student responds to task-relevant cues. The final stages of the funnel approach include continued, on-the-job follow-up using instruments developed specifically for co-workers, natural supervisors, and probes for generalization to similar work settings.

SUMMARY

Following this presentation of guidelines for adhering to a contemporary approach to assessment of work behavior, examples of assessment instruments in specific content areas are reviewed in subsequent chapters. A student's entry into competitive employment should not be based on traits that have limited validity for predicting progress throughout a training program. Rather than limiting work options, contemporary assessment focuses on delineating requisite behaviors that are sub-

sequently targeted for training. The principles of contemporary assessment include:

Collect and interpret data within an ecological framework.

Identifiy environmental cues to be associated with specific responses.

Follow a general case approach to selecting assessment examples that sample the range of placement opportunities in the community.

Include both quantitative (objective) and qualitative (subjective) measures.

Be aware of the externalities (politics) associated with the assessment process.

Give equal emphasis to baseline, formative, and summative phases of assessment.

Complete Job Skill Inventories of requisite behaviors associated with community work opportunities.

De-emphasize reliance on developmentally sequenced assessments.

Focus assessment on work-related skills that influence longevity of work experience.

Increase the specificity of assessment as a worker advances through work experiences.

Adherence to these guidelines makes community employment a viable work option for students with diverse handicapping conditions.

REFERENCES

Bates, P., & Pancsofar, E. (1985). Assessment of vocational skills. In A. F. Rotatori & R. Fox (Eds.), *Assessment for regular and special education teachers: A case study approach* (pp. 335–359). Austin, TX: PRO-ED.

Bellamy, G. T., Horner, R. H., & Inman, D. P. (1979). *Vocational habilation of severely retarded adults: A direct service technology.* Baltimore: University Park Press.

Belmore, K., & Brown, L. (1978). A job skill inventory strategy designed for severely handicapped potential workers. In N. G. Haring & D. D. Bricker (Eds.), *Teaching the severely handicapped* (Vol. 3, pp. 223–262). Columbus, OH: Special Press.

Bock, W., & Weatherman, R. (1978). *Minnesota developmental programming system.* Minneapolis, MN: Bock Associates.

Botterbusch, K. F. (1982). *A comparison of commercial vocational evaluation systems* (2nd ed.). Menomonie, WI: Materials Development Center.

Brolin, D. E. (1982). *Vocational preparation of persons with handicaps* (2nd ed.). Columbus, OH: Charles E. Merrill.

Browning, P., & Irvin, L. K. (1981). Vocational evaluation, training, and placement of mentally retarded persons. *Rehabilitation Counseling Bulletin, 25,* 374–409.

Field, T. F., & Orgar, W. (1983). *Measuring worker traits.* Athens, GA: VDARE Service Bureau.

Halpern, A. S., & Fuhrer, M. J. (Eds.). (1984). *Functional assessment in rehabilitation.* Baltimore: Paul H. Brookes.

Haring, N. G., Liberty, K. A., & White, O. R. (1980). Rules for data-based strategy decisions in instructional programs: Current research and instructional implications. In W. Sailor, B. Wilcox, & L. Brown (Eds.), *Methods of instruction for severely handicapped students* (pp. 159–194). Baltimore: Paul H. Brookes.

Hawkins, R. P. (1979). The functions of assessment: Implications for selection and development of devices for assessing repertoires in clinical, educational, and other settings. *Journal of Applied Behavior Analysis, 12,* 501–516.

Horner, R. H., & McDonald, R. S. (1982). Comparisons of single instance and general case instruction in teaching a generalized vocational skill. *Journal of The Association for the Severely Handicapped, 7*(3), 7–20.

Horner, R. H., Sprague, J., & Wilcox, B. (1982). General case programming for community activities. In B. Wilcox & G. T. Bellamy, *Design of high school programs for severely handicapped students* (pp. 61–98). Baltimore: Paul H. Brookes.

Menchetti, B. M., Rusch, F. R., & Owens, D. (1983). Assessing the vocational needs of mentally retarded adolescents and adults. In J. L. Matson & S. E. Bruening (Eds.), *Assessing the mentally retarded* (pp. 247–284). New York: Grune & Stratton.

Murphy, S. T., & Ursprung, A. (1983). The politics of vocational evaluation: A qualitative study. *Rehabilitation Literature, 44* (1–2), 2–12.

Pancsofar, E., & Bates, P. (1984). Multiple-baseline designs for evaluating instructional effectiveness. *Rehabilitation Counseling Bulletin, 28,* 67–77.

Pomerantz, D., & Marholin, D. (1977). Vocational habilitation: A time for change. In E. Sontag, J. Smith, & N. Certo (Eds.), *Educational programming for the severely and profoundly handicapped* (pp. 129–141). Reston, VA: Council for Exceptional Children.

Rusch, F. R. (1983). Competitive vocational training. In M. E. Snell (Ed.), *Systematic instruction of the moderately and severely handicapped* (2nd ed.) (pp. 503–523). Columbus, OH: Charles E. Merrill.

Rusch, F. R., & Mithaug, D. E. (1980). *Vocational training for mentally retarded adults: A behavior analytic approach.* Champaign, IL: Research Press.

Vash, C. L. (1981). *The psychology of disability.* New York: Springer.

Chapter 8

Establishing Effective Community-Based Training Stations

William Stainback, Susan Stainback,
John Nietupski, and Sue Hamre-Nietupski

TRADITIONALLY, MANY PERSONS with handicaps, particularly those with severe handicaps, have not been trained for employment. At the present time, when training does occur, it often takes place in institutional settings or sheltered workshops in community settings. When the ultimate goal is for the person being trained to work in an institutional or sheltered workshop setting, such training sites are appropriate. In other words, it is realistic to train a person in an institution or sheltered workshop if the employment goal is for him or her to work in that type of setting. However, the goals for persons with handicaps, even severe handicaps, are changing. Such goals now include living in community settings and holding competitive jobs to the greatest extent possible (Brown, Nietupski, & Hamre-Nietupski, 1976; Schutz & Rusch, 1982). Thus, alternatives to traditional training settings must be explored, including the development of training settings that prepare persons with all types of handicaps for competitive employment in "actual" community settings.

Establishing community-based training stations in actual employment settings is one way of providing realistic and functional training for competitive employment. A community-based training station is a vocational training site within an ordinary community work setting (e.g., in dishwashing rooms in restaurants, in

industrial plants). Community-based training stations have been successfully established and maintained by special education teachers and vocational education personnel (Alper, 1981; Nietupski, Hamre-Nietupski, Welch, & Anderson, 1983; Rusch & Mithaug 1980; Wehman, 1981).

Several researchers (Brown et al., 1983; Rusch, 1983; Wehman, 1983) have recommended that persons with handicaps begin receiving training in community-based training stations at the earliest possible age, preferably during the early high school years. Early preparation for employment can ease the transition between school and work and increase the chances of vocational success.

The purposes of this chapter are: 1) to provide a rationale for increased use of community-based training stations as vocational training sites, and 2) to outline and discuss the procedures involved in developing and maintaining such training settings.

RATIONALE FOR COMMUNITY-BASED TRAINING STATIONS

Community-based training stations are considered good vocational training sites for a number of reasons, some of which are reviewed here.

103

1. Ensures Training of Vocational Survival Skills

Although efficient use of instructional time is important for everybody, it is particularly critical for persons with handicaps because of the difficulties many of them encounter in mastering new skills (Rusch & Schutz, 1981). Thus, training time must not be wasted on nonfunctional or irrelevant tasks (e.g., sorting, assembling, and resorting and reassembling manufacturing parts obtained from a local industry). Community-based training stations used as vocational training sites ensure the functionality of the tasks being trained. Business people, and others in the community who need a job done, usually do not have the tolerance or time for their employees to work on made-up or superficial tasks. Tasks such as washing dishes at a restaurant, clearing and cleaning tables at a fast food chain establishment, making beds in a motel, serving as a maid, and/or cutting someone's grass serve a purpose—they are *functional, useful,* and *real.*

2. Provides Opportunity to Learn Social Interaction Skills

Working with co-workers, supervisors, and, if necessary, the general public in a business establishment within the community requires social skills that are not generally the same as those needed in sheltered workshops or in-school work sites. In segregated and/or artificial training sites, most co-workers also experience handicaps, some of them severe. Thus, the social interaction pace is generally slower than in the community at large. In addition, supervisors and/or trainers in artificial work settings are often less concerned about and more tolerant of the worker's social behaviors since social interaction skills tend not to be as critical to co-worker and customer satisfaction in a segregated as in a competitive employment situation. Thus, the social skills needed to interact in competitive employment situations with nonhandicapped co-workers, supervisors, and/or the general public are often inadvertently not taught in artificial settings and thus not acquired by students. If competitive employment is to be a realistic goal for individuals

with handicaps, training that prepares them for social situations in the real world is critical (Rusch, 1983). Community-based training stations can facilitate the development of such social skills.

3. Provides Opportunities to Learn Ancillary Survival Skills Needed for Competitive Employment

Working in community-based training stations requires that persons with handicaps learn to perform a variety of ancillary survival skills needed in competitive employment (Sowers, Rusch, Connis, & Cummings, 1980). That is, in community-based training stations, persons with handicaps are generally required to engage in activities that are often not required of them in more segregated, simulated vocational training settings. For example, they must often learn to manage their time, to get to and from the job, plan for lunch and/or break times, groom appropriately, punch a time clock, and display an attitude appropriate to the work place. Although important to job success (Rusch, 1983), these types of survival skills often are not required (and thus frequently not taught) as an integral part of vocational training within a sheltered setting or other environments foreign to competitive employment. Skills such as riding a bus, crossing a street, or determining the time to meet a carpool, for example, usually only become critical, and thus a priority for instruction, when they are needed.

4. Provides Opportunities for Co-Workers to Serve as Role Models

As in learning any task, being around individuals who are engaged in the same task or exhibiting a behavior a student is being directly instructed to master provides worthwhile training input. Thus, in a community-based training station, an individual with a handicap constantly is exposed to persons actually engaging in work tasks within a competitive employment setting. Furthermore, the student also has an opportunity to model necessary skills such as being polite, going to and riding on a bus, being on time, and/or using a time clock correctly. In more artificial training sites, on the other hand, most co-workers are fellow students who generally have not yet mastered such skills themselves and, thus, cannot serve as appropriate role models.

5. Provides Opportunities for Nonhandicapped Co-Workers to Gain a Better Understanding of Persons Who Experience Handicaps

In the future, many nonhandicapped persons will likely be required to live and work in integrated community settings together with persons experiencing different handicaps, including severe handicaps. In this respect, community-based training stations have the indirect benefit of directly exposing non-handicapped persons to individuals who experience handicaps. Under supervised conditions, nonhandicapped co-workers can learn to interact positively with and understand persons with handicaps as fellow workers and as individuals with various personalities, feelings, and skills who can contribute in some productive way to their community. Most importantly, such exposure and interaction can correct many false assumptions, such as individuals with handicaps: 1) are dangerous and should be feared, 2) are incompetent and cannot contribute to society, and/or 3) do not "understand" and thus can be ridiculed, treated cruelly, taken advantage of, or ignored without any "real harm" to them.

6. Provides Training Personnel with Information about Community Work

Another benefit of community-based training stations is that special educators and/or vocational specialists are continually exposed to and can observe community work situations. These situations provide a rich source of information regarding the type of classroom and/or field instruction that persons with handicaps need to perform in competitive employment situations. In other words, community-based training stations help ensure that direct service personnel receive the real-world input necessary for them to provide realistic vocationally related instruction to persons with handicaps.

7. Provides Opportunities to Learn Interdependence

The goal of vocational training programs for persons with handicaps is often defined as to prepare them to function independently in competitive employment. More realistically, however, the goal probably should be to prepare them for *interdependence*. As noted by Voeltz, McQuarter, and Kishi (1985):

Society is comprised of interdependent networks of persons with whom we live and work, and few of us could maintain that we are independent in the sense of living and working and recreating in isolation from other persons. What must now occur is preparation so that the individual with handicaps becomes a normalized member of such mutually rewarding interdependencies. (p. 84)

In most competitive employment situations, interdependence networks develop. Work stations within these settings can provide persons with handicaps opportunities to learn how to fit within such networks. The situation is often complex; it is frequently dynamic and fluid as opposed to static or never changing. Thus, it is difficult, if not impossible, to duplicate the nuances and complexities of actual interdependence networks in competitive employment situations within simulated environments.

8. Reduces Complexity of Necessary Generalizations

Generalization has long been a major concern in vocational education of persons with handicaps (Bellamy, Horner, & Inman, 1979; Cuvo, Leaf, & Borakove, 1978; Horner, Sprague, & Wilcox, 1982; Wehman, 1981; Wehman & McLaughlin, 1980). Many of these individuals have difficulty generalizing skills across settings or performing a task that differs from a task they have learned to perform in the past (Rusch, 1983; Rusch & Schutz, 1981).

When teaching students to perform vocational tasks in community-based training stations, the task, as well as the specific antecedent and consequent conditions for performing it, are likely to be similar to those encountered in competitive employment. That is, working at a job in a community-based training station is similar to competitive employment—the only difference being the more systematic instruction and close supervision given to the person learning to do a given job. Thus, unlike sheltered work settings, the natural cues for exhibiting a task and the natural consequences inherent in competitive employment settings are part of the environment and can be incorporated into the vocational training sequence. As a result, the generalizations required when moving from a community-based training station into actual competitive employment are minimal. In short, generalization is less complex since setting conditions in community-based training are more similar to actual community work than setting conditions in simulated or sheltered environments.

9. Provides Opportunity for More Normalized Vocational Preparation

Training within community settings is not a new concept (Rusch, 1983). It has long been standard practice in vocational education for many nonhandicapped students to receive at least part of their training in community job sites (e.g., traditional cooperative work programs). Thus, providing training to persons with handicaps within community job sites may be viewed as just another normalized kind of activity, that is, one in which many non-handicapped persons traditionally have had an opportunity to participate.

10. Provides Opportunity to Raise Community Members' Expectations

When a person with a handicap learns to function successfully in a community-based training station, community members become aware of the "handicapped" person's ability to contribute to society. As this occurs repeatedly and on a large scale, recognition that persons with handicaps can provide needed services can be expected to increase while the common stereotype of these individuals as being totally dependent upon the community can be expected to decrease. Community members including co-workers, employers, supervisors, parents, and even trainers and fellow trainees will potentially develop respect for what individuals with handicaps can accomplish in the work world. In community-based training stations where individuals with handicaps are called upon to deal directly with or be exposed to the general public, the impact on expectations can be even greater. In turn, the elevated expectations on the part of all community members can lead not only to greater respect for persons with handicaps but to increased interaction opportunities that might be unattainable without these positive expectations.

11. Enhances Likelihood of Competitive Employment

The probability that persons with handicaps will be able to secure competitive employment is considerably enhanced after they have successfully completed a vocational training sequence in a community-based, rather than a simulated training environment. By mastering the goals involved in working in a community-based training station, students in essence demonstrate their ability to function in competitive employment. Consequently, potential employers can be more confident that the survival skills critical to job success, such as dependability, as well as the social interaction requirements involved in competitive employment have most likely been acquired. In addition, the potential employee with a handicap or handicaps will have had actual experience working successfully in a competitive employment setting. Experience is often a prerequisite for job opportunities; such "on-the-job" training may be acceptable to some employers to fulfill this requirement.

Finally, as a consequence of community-based training stations, many potential employers, co-workers, and community members will become more familiar with the work skills of persons with handicaps who have successfully contributed to the work force. As a result of this exposure, many nonhandicapped employees may feel more confident of the potential of individuals with handicaps and their own ability to communicate and interact with them. Advantages such as these can do much to increasing further the acceptance of persons with handicaps into a community employment structure.

Summary

Compared to sheltered, segregated, and/or work-simulated settings, community-based training stations offer many advantages. See Table 1 for a summary of the advantages. As much as possible, special educators and vocational personnel should capitalize on these advantages by trying to establish community work stations as primary settings for vocational training of persons with all types of handicapping conditions, including severe handicaps. In the next section, procedures for developing and maintaining training stations within the community are outlined and discussed.

DEVELOPING AND MAINTAINING COMMUNITY-BASED TRAINING STATIONS

School districts attempting to provide community-based vocational training should treat the establishment of community training stations as a systematic process, one that requires careful planning (Cuvo et al., 1978; Rusch & Mithaug, 1980). The procedural outline presented in Table 2 exemplifies an effective approach to developing community-based training stations (Maurer, Teas, & Bates, 1981; Nietupski et al., 1983; Wehman, 1981; Wehman & McLaughlin, 1980). Each aspect of the model is detailed below.

Table 1. Advantages of community-based training stations

1. Training of vocational survival skills is ensured
2. Opportunities to learn social interaction skills are provided
3. Opportunities to learn ancillary survival skills supportive of competitive employment are provided
4. Co-workers can serve as role models
5. Co-workers begin to understand persons who experience handicaps
6. Direct service personnel become familiar with employment
7. Interdependent networks develop
8. Generalization is enhanced
9. More normalized learning experience
10. Positively influences community members' expectations
11. Enhances the likelihood of competitive employment

Table 2. Procedural model for developing and maintaining community training stations

1. Develop program goals and rationale
2. Compile a potential training station listing
3. Contact employers and establish training stations
4. Determine training station skills demands
5. Place and train students
6. Transfer supervision to nonschool staff
7. Maintain and expand training stations

1. Develop Program Goals and Rationales

The first, extremely critical, step in establishing community-based training stations involves the development of program goals and rationales. School district personnel must have a clear conception of the outcomes desired for their students and the reason(s) why those outcomes are desirable in order to convince employers to participate in the vocational program and/or to avoid misconceptions or problems once training stations have been established. If the purpose of the program is not clear, 1) employer involvement will be difficult to obtain; or 2) once stations are established, difficulties may be encountered due to differing program expectations.

Although individual districts may have unique program goals, several common goals can be identified. For example, school districts may emphasize that their primary intent is to provide students with the opportunity to acquire skills necessary to become productive workers upon graduation from the program. A second goal may be that the district wishes to provide a variety of training experiences in order to help students identify the type(s) of option(s) best suited for them. Closer cooperation between the school program and the business community may be a third program goal. Finally, a fourth general objective might be to provide the community with an opportunity to witness students with handicaps, including those with severe handicaps, interacting with nonhandicapped persons in an appropriate, capable, and productive capacity in the community.

For each of the general goals, a rationale should be provided. For example, the rationale offered for the first goal, preparing students for postschool vocational productivity, might be that to achieve competent adult performance, training must be provided while students are still in school. The rationale offered for providing a variety of training experiences might be that this represents the most effective means of determining the type of vocation best suited for students—that a lack of vocational experience makes it difficult for many students to identify their vocational preferences. The rationale offered for closer school and business community ties might stem from a desire on the part of the school district to modify its program to ensure that it provides students with valid skills for capable performance in the world of work. The rationale offered for the fourth goal might be that, due to past isolation, many persons with handicaps have had limited contact with the community and, thus, may erroneously be viewed by nonhandicapped persons as incapable of community involvement.

The above program goals and rationales are intended to serve as examples. The development of an informational brochure containing goals and rationales is recommended. Such a brochure may be distributed to employers during preliminary contact and, thus, can become an invaluable tool in recruiting employer involvement.

2. Compile Potential Training Station Listing

Once program goals and rationales have been articulated, school districts should develop a compendium of potential vocational training stations within the district. In order to accomplish this task, personnel must be familiar with their community, particularly with existing employment options (e.g., industrial, service) and key contact persons (e.g., personnel directors, owners, supervisors) within local business establishments.

In addition to personal familiarity with the business community, other sources might be drawn upon to identify potential training sites. These include obtaining business contacts from other school district personnel (e.g., teachers, administrators, school secretaries, custodians), identifying employers suggested by

Experience-Based Career Education (EBCE) instructors serving handicapped pupils, obtaining Chamber of Commerce/Jaycee directories and Job Service Employer listings, and/or consulting the telephone directory and classified advertisement section of the local newspaper. School districts need not develop a definitive listing prior to contacting potential employers. However, a reasonably sized pool of representative businesses might be targeted initially. This preliminary list should be continually updated as training stations are established.

3. Contact Employers and Establish Training Sites

Once a potential training site listing has been developed, employer contacts should be initiated. We suggest that school personnel initially contact businesses in which they have an acquaintance or contact person. It might be advisable to discuss the desire to establish a training station with the contact person and solicit his or her reaction prior to approaching the business owner, manager, or personnel director. If their contact person reacts favorably, he or she may be asked to raise the possibility of program participation with the employer. Such inside leverage has been described as a useful strategy in securing owner willingness to discuss program participation (Nietupski et al., 1983). Furthermore, the contact person may be able to relate employer concerns prior to school personnel contact with that individual.

Once preliminary communication has been established with or without a contact person, the employer should be contacted by telephone to describe the training program in general terms and to arrange for a meeting. Personnel making phone contact should identify themselves and their affiliation, briefly explain their desire to establish a training station in the business, and suggest a meeting in the near future to discuss program participation. If the employer indicates an interest in program participation and/or a willingness to meet, a meeting should be scheduled. In addition, the informational brochure, discussed previously, might be sent prior to the meeting.

If the employer appears reluctant to meet regarding program participation, he or she might be directed to other business persons whose firms have been successfully involved in the vocational program. It might also be suggested that he or she discuss the program further with the contact person. A follow-up phone call might be made after the employer has had an opportunity to make inquiries about the program.

A face-to-face meeting with the potential employer provides school district personnel with an opportunity to make an indepth presentation of their program and thereby "sell" it to the employer. Program representatives should reiterate program goals and rationales, perhaps augmented with slides showing students involved in work experiences. School personnel should also emphasize that they, not the employer, are initially responsible for the necessary training and supervision, with transfer of supervision to the employer only after the student demonstrates satisfactory work performance. Such assurances are important, especially if the employer expresses concern over his or her staff's ability to deal effectively with handicapped workers. Finally, if possible, presentors might provide the employer with "testimonials" from other business persons as to the benefits of program participation. If such testimonials are not available, letters from school district personnel such as the supervisor of the food service workers, the secretary, or custodians who have been involved in supervising in-school training, might lend support to the program. The presentation might culminate with a question and answer period, followed by a request for employer representation in the program.

School personnel must be prepared to handle both positive and negative employer responses to their requests for participation. Although school personnel might choose not to pursue employers who refuse to consider involvement, initial employer refusal often takes the form of hesitancy or a reluctance to become involved "at this time." In such instances,

several strategies might be employed, including: 1) encouraging employers to contact businesses that have been successfully involved in the program, 2) inviting them to observe students with handicaps engaged in vocational training, 3) suggesting a "trial" period of specified length in order to determine if program participation could be worked out, or 4) allowing the employer additional time to consider the offer. The key in dealing with a reluctant potential employer is *congenial persistence*. That is, school personnel must be able to "stick with" a reluctant employer, and yet do so in a nonconfrontative, nonthreatening manner, seeking creative solutions to the apparent obstacles to program participation.

An employer's decision to participate in the program should be followed by the completion of a training agreement form specifying the respective responsibilities of the school and the employer, and signed by both parties. The value of this form is that it reiterates the expectations for both parties and can be filed for future reference. A sample training agreement form (Maurer et al., 1981) is presented in Figure 1.

4. Determine Training Station Skill Demands

Once a training station has been secured, school personnel should identify the work and ancillary skills required for successful performance. Two sources of information might be utilized for this purpose. To gain a general notion of the skill requirements for various occupations, the U.S. Department of Labor's (1977) *Dictionary of Occupational Titles* (DOT) may be consulted.

The DOT outlines job requirements; however, it does not describe requirements unique to individual business establishments, nor can it specify the social and interpersonal behavior demands of a particular work setting. For this reason, information obtained from the DOT must be augmented with that gathered through direct observation and inventory of the business establishment.

A process of determining the vocational requirements at particular business establishments has been proposed by Alper (1981),

This agreement is made and entered into (date) by and between (training site) and (school), (city, state).

It is the mutual desire of the parties of this agreement to provide on-the-job training of (student) to enable (student) to gain practical knowledge and experience in the occupation of (job title/description) from (beginning date) to (ending date).

(Training site) agrees as follows:

1. To provide an experienced employee who will act as (student's) advocate.
2. To provide the equipment, tools, materials, and/or special clothing necessary.
3. To provide a written evaluation of (student's) performance as requested by (vocational training) school.
4. To abide by school holidays, excusing (student) from training on the following days: (dates).
5. To notify insurer for purposes of coverage under the Worker's Compensation Act and to provide prompt first aid and medical attention as needed in case of an injury on the work site.
6. To alter (student's) work schedule or assignment, with the school staff's cooperation, as needed.

(Vocational training) school agrees as follows:

1. To provide a trainer to supervise, counsel, and instruct.
2. To maintain and be responsible for all records relative to (student's) performance.
3. To provide all benefits to (student).
4. To provide and/or arrange for transportation to and from (training site).
5. To maintain close and open communication with all (training site's) personnel.
6. To alter (student's) work schedule or assignments with (training site's) cooperation, as needed.

It is recognized that this training agreement can be terminated immediately based upon the request of (student), (his/her) parents, training site personnel, or school staff.

By: _____   By: _____
Title: _____   Title: _____
Date: _____   Date: _____

Figure 1.   A sample training agreement. From Nietupski, J., Hamre-Nietupski, S., Welch, J., & Anderson, R. J. (1983). Establishing and maintaining vocational training sites for moderately and severely handicapped students: Strategies for community/vocational trainers. *Education and Training of the Mentally Retarded, 18*(3), 169–175.

Belmore and Brown (1978), Rusch and Mithaug (1980), and Wehman (1981), as well as Agran (Chapter 12). In essence, this process involves a careful inventory of the work environment to determine specific work skill demands, working conditions unique to the business establishment (e.g., noise level, co-worker proximity, physical layout), and ancillary skills considered important for success (e.g., communication skills, breakroom skills, transportation skills, use of restroom and other self-care skills such as dress requirements).

5.   Place and Train Students

Upon completion of a thorough inventory of the training site, one or more students should be selected as initial trainees. Since an employer's experience with the *first* student can greatly affect his or her participation in the program, it is important that the first student(s)

selected for training closely match the job requirements of the particular site. Subsequent students need not be as skilled as the initial student(s), however, thus avoiding the common practice of providing community-based instruction only to more capable students.

Once students have been selected, instruction should be provided on the job for the specific tasks and ancillary skills identified through the inventory process. Training procedures found to be effective with students with handicaps include task analysis, chaining techniques (forward, backward, and total cycle chaining), shaping, cue redundancy, prompting hierarchies (verbal, gestural, modeling, and physical guidance), and contingency management techniques. Such procedures need to be applied in order to facilitate vocational skill *acquisition, fluency, maintenance,* and *generalization.* An indepth discussion of training procedures is beyond the scope of this chapter. However, the reader is referred to Chapter 12 of this text as well as to the writings of Bellamy, Horner, and Inman (1979), Rusch and Mithaug (1980), Wehman (1981), and Wehman and McLaughlin (1980) for further information.

As training is conducted, school personnel should maintain frequent contact and communication with supervisors and employers regarding student performance. In this regard, data indicating task acquisition and/or increased production rates should be shared with both the supervisor and the employer as evidence of program success. In addition to feedback regarding student progress, input might be sought in the form of: 1) supervisor or employer evaluation of student performance and 2) ways to improve the program. For example, a supervisor might be asked to suggest a more efficient means of performing a task, or co-workers may be requested to propose how a task arrangement might be redesigned to make it easier for a student to perform. The advantage of seeking input from employers is that they may develop greater "ownership" in the program, thus facilitating continued program involvement. Furthermore, employer involvement during the training phase should make supervisors more comfortable working with students with handicaps, thus reducing potential problems related to the transfer of supervision, which is discussed in the following section.

In addition to maintaining close employer contact during training, school personnel must keep the classroom teacher (if he or she is not the vocational instructor) informed of student progress. Such communication can be extremely important when students need instruction on skills such as grooming, which might be provided more intensively in the classroom.

6. Transfer Supervision to Nonschool Staff

As students become more capable workers, it is necessary to reduce the amount of supervision and shift control to business establishment personnel. This transition can be difficult; thus, it should be carried out systematically. Wehman

(1981) outlined a number of useful strategies for transferring supervision to nonschool personnel. First, teachers might gradually thin the reinforcement schedule provided to students in an effort to reduce student dependence on teachers as sources of reinforcement. If possible, teachers might also teach students to self-reinforce, thus further reducing dependency upon the trainer.

Wehman (1981) suggested that teachers, through modeling, provide the work supervisor with the skills necessary to effectively manage the student. In addition, school personnel may need to gradually reduce the frequency of contact between the teacher and supervisor during the transfer process, especially if the supervisor is relying too heavily upon the teacher in dealing with the student.

Finally, Wehman (1981) recommended the recruitment of a co-worker advocate who might be provided with the necessary information and skills to assist a student when problems arise and to provide social contact in the business establishment. The use of such an advocate has the 2-fold advantage of: 1) assisting in the transfer of supervision, and 2) providing a student with a potential friend in the work setting. In our zeal to train vocational competency, we often forget the social aspects of a student's lifespace. Since one of the goals behind the establishment of community-based vocational training stations is to develop positive interactions between handicapped and nonhandicapped persons, attention to the social aspects of work seems especially warranted.

7. Maintain and Expand Training Stations

School personnel should attach the same degree of importance to station maintenance and systematic expansion of training station options as they do to initial site establishment. Too often, community vocational training stations are lost due to a lack of a positive working relationship between the school district and the business establishment. Furthermore, a program may limit its options for students and/or become "stale" if it does not expand beyond the initial training stations. Therefore, strategies must be implemented both to maintain appropriate stations and to develop new ones.

With respect to station maintenance, several strategies can be employed. One group of strategies is designed to foster business establishment "ownership" in the vocational program by continuing to provide employers with feedback regarding the success of the program and seeking their input. Ownership also can be enhanced by having business establishment personnel assist in the recruitment of new training sites. Finally, by sharing the success of *their* program with business peers, employers are more likely to maintain a vested interest in the program's continued operation and success.

A second set of strategies involves reinforcing employers and helpful employees for their efforts. In discussing community integration, Wehman and Hill (1984) stressed the importance of rewarding the community for its participation and interest. These rewards can take many forms, such as:

1. School districts have held appreciation banquets for employers, with students, parents, staff, and upper-level school district administrators in attendance to illustrate the importance placed upon the program.
2. School personnel have patronized the business establishments that have provided training sites.
3. Feature articles in local newspapers have highlighted business establishments involved in the program, thus giving both the employer and the district invaluable publicity.

4. Letters and thank-you notes have been written to employees and owners on behalf of students.

These and other forms of acknowledgment can serve to strengthen the bonds between school and business, thus enabling continued program participation and growth.

In addition to training maintenance, new stations should gradually be added. The strategies for establishing initial training stations apply to the development of new stations. However, favorable employer response and any positive publicity that may have ensued should make the establishment of new training stations easier.

Summary

This section presents several points to be considered when establishing and maintaining community-based vocational training stations. The guidelines form a procedural model that has been successfully employed in many communities throughout the country.

SUMMARY

More attention needs to be paid to preparing persons with handicaps for competitive employment. Establishing community-based training stations is one way of providing realistic and functional training for competitive employment. In this chapter, the authors provide a rationale for the more frequent use of community-based training stations and suggest a set of guidelines for how to develop and maintain such stations.

REFERENCES

Alper, S. (1981). Utilizing community jobs in development vocational curriculum for severely handicapped youth. *Education and Training of the Mentally Retarded, 16*, 317–221.

Bellamy G., Horner, R., & Inman, D. (1979). *Vocational habilitation of severely retarded adults: A direct service technology.* Baltimore: University Park Press.

Belmore, K., & Brown, L. (1978). A job skill inventory designed for severely handicapped potential workers. In N. G. Haring & D. D. Bricker (Eds.), *Teaching the severely handicapped* (Vol. 3, pp. 223–262). Columbus, OH: Special Press.

Brown, L., Ford, A., Nisbet, J., Sweet, M., Shiraga, B.,

York, J., & Loomis, R. (1983). The critical need for nonschool instruction in educational programs for severely handicapped students. *Journal of The Association for the Severely Handicapped, 8*, 71–77.

Brown, L., Nietupski, J., & Hamre-Nietupski, S. (1976). *Hey! Don't forget about me: Education's investment in the severely, profoundly and multiply handicapped* (pp. 2–15). Reston, VA: Council for Exceptional Children.

Cuvo, A., Leaf, R., & Borakove, L. (1978). Teaching janitorial skills to mentally retarded: Acquisition, generalization, and maintenance. *Journal of Applied Behavior Analysis, 11*, 345–355.

Horner, R. H., Sprague, J., & Wilcox, B. (1982). General

case programming for community activities. In B. Wilcox & G. T. Bellamy, *Design of high school programs for severely handicapped students* (pp. 61–98). Baltimore: Paul H. Brookes.

Maurer, S., Teas, S., & Bates, P. (1981). *Project AMES* (Vol. 1). Des Moines, IA: Iowa Department of Public Instruction.

Nietupski, J., Hamre-Nietupski, S., Welch, J., & Anderson, R. (1983). Establishing and maintaining vocational training sites for moderately and severely handicapped students: Strategies for community/vocational trainers. *Education and Training of the Mentally Retarded, 18,* 169–175.

Rusch, F. (1983). Competitive vocational training. In M. E. Snell (Ed.), *Systematic instruction of the moderately and severely handicapped* (2nd ed.) (pp. 503–523). Columbus, OH: Charles E. Merrill.

Rusch, F. R., & Mithaug, D. E. (1980). *Vocational training for mentally retarded adults: A behavior analytic approach.* Champaign, IL: Research Press.

Rusch, F. R., & Schutz, R. P. (1981). Vocational and social work behavior research: An evaluative review. In J. L. Matson & J. R. McCartney (Eds.), *Handbook of behavior modification with the mentally retarded* (pp. 247–280). New York: Plenum.

Schutz, R. P., & Rusch, F. R. (1982). Competitive employment: Toward employment integration for mentally retarded persons. In R. L. Lunch, W. E. Kiernan, &

J. A. Stark (Eds.), *Prevocation and vocational education for special needs youth: A blueprint for the 1980s* (pp. 133–159). Baltimore: Paul H. Brookes.

Sowers, J., Rusch, F., Connis, R., & Cummings, L. (1980). Teaching mentally retarded adults to time manage in a vocational setting. *Journal of Applied Behavior Analysis, 13,* 119–128.

U.S. Department of Labor (1977). *Dictionary of occupational titles* (4th ed.). Washington, DC: U.S. Department of Labor.

Voeltz, L., McQuarter, R., & Kishi, S. (1985). Assessing and teaching social interaction skills. In W. Stainback & S. Stainback (Eds.), *Integration of students with severe handicaps in regular schools: A handbook for teachers* (pp. 66–86). Reston, VA: Council for Exceptional Children.

Wehman, P. (1981). *Competitive employment: New horizons for severely disabled individuals.* Baltimore: Paul H. Brookes.

Wehman, P. (1983). Toward the employability of severely handicapped children and youth. *Teaching Exceptional Children, 15,* 220–225.

Wehman, P., & Hill, J. (1984). Integrating severely handicapped students in community activities. *Teaching Exceptional Children, 16,* 142–145.

Wehman, P., & McLaughlin, P. (1980). *Vocational curriculum for developmentally disabled persons.* Baltimore: University Park Press.

Chapter 9

Service Delivery Coordination

Robert L. Schalock

DESPITE ATTEMPTS TO provide competitive employment opportunities to persons with handicaps, most handicapped individuals are still far from functioning within the "mainstream" of competitive employment. These individuals' failure to attain competitive employment stems from several reasons, including: 1) lowered expectations for employment potential, 2) assumptions that sheltered workshops provide viable training and placement services, 3) disincentives to gainful employment, and 4) failure to utilize a community-referenced, problem-solving orientation to instruction during the school years and thereafter. These reasons, and many more, are explored in the following discussion. In this chapter, the author introduces problems that relate to the current state of our service delivery system—a system that can best be described as duplicative, fragmented, and inefficient (Schalock, 1985).

The fragmented nature of current services to persons with handicaps is the result of:

1. Needed services that go beyond the boundaries of traditional generic community services such as health care and education
2. Continued controversy regarding categorical versus functional definitions
3. Overlapping legislation and lack of a clear national policy
4. Multiple funding sources without financial coordination
5. Multiple planning bodies accompanied by inadequate control and responsibility
6. Lack of reliable data on program benefits and effectiveness

7. Lack of adequate resources including facilities, technology, experience, and trained staff
8. Public attitude that the handicapped person (or his or her family) is responsible for independently obtaining effective services
9. Competition among service providers for resources

Despite lack of consistency and uniformity, competitive employment opportunities can be made increasingly available to persons with handicaps, primarily through *interagency* coordination and *intersector* (public and private) cooperation. This coordination and cooperation is improved through the individualized transition plan (ITP) process, which can be used to improve both service delivery coordination and program evaluation.

Transitions are an essential part of everybody's life, requiring adaptations at various times to new roles, locations, and relationships. As currently conceived (Bellamy, 1983), transitions: 1) apply to everyone with a disability; 2) should be outcome oriented such that a successful transition into employment, for example, results in normalized wage levels, working conditions, life style, and benefits; 3) represent a longer time span than 1 year and should be viewed as "bridging services" over a number of years (Office of Special Education, 1984); 4) are based on interagency services offered, their appropriateness and quality; and 5) differ among people. Some individuals may require no special services (and, therefore, no systematic transitional plans), whereas others may require either time-limited or ongoing services, with corresponding ITPs.

The ITP concept facilitates a person's transition or adaptation to other environments. According to the ITP process, significant others in the handicapped individual's *current* and *future* lifespaces secure meaningful information about environments for which the individual needs to be prepared, and subsequently provide services to enhance the probability of a smooth adjustment to such settings. ITPs are developed for critical life stages according to specifications discussed in Brown et al. (1981), Schalock (1983), and Stainback, Stainback, Nietupski, and Hamre-Nietupski (Chapter 8). The ITP should:

1. Be developed on the basis of a continuously updated person-environment analysis
2. Be comprehensive, specifying the preparatory experiences needed to function independently and productively in the new environment
3. Be individualized, containing precisely stated transition objectives, training activities, and materials and evaluation strategies functionally related to a unique "lifespace"
4. Involve parents and/or guardians
5. Require participation of both sending and receiving personnel who jointly design and assist in implementing a series of experiences designed to maximize appropriate functioning
6. Include the expertise of professionals who visit and obtain information about the wide range of environments for which the individual is being prepared
7. Require direct instruction in a variety of subsequent environments because of some individuals' difficulties in stimulus and response generalization
8. Integrate activities that prepare the person with handicaps for subsequent living-working-recreation environments
9. Focus on behavioral skill development, prosthetic procurement and/or usage, and environment modifications required to live and function successfully in the least re-

strictive and most productive environments

Over the past 3 years, the ITP approach has been used by the author to help: 1) students transition from school to competitive employment, 2) students transition from school to another service delivery program, and 3) adult developmental disabled persons transition from workshop to work place. Each use is described briefly in ensuing sections.

TRANSITIONING FROM SCHOOL TO WORK

When assisting students in transitioning from school to work, the resource teacher temporarily leaves the classroom to enter the community as a job trainer and advocate. The critical student level and systems level activities required in this process are outlined in Table 1 and described more fully in Stainback et al. (see Chapter 8). To ensure that the ITP interfaces properly with the individualized education program (IEP), which is required by both state and federal agencies, the IEP should focus on short-term (yearly) objectives, while the ITP targets long-range (4–5 years) transitional plans (see Table 2 for a sample).

As illustrated in Table 2, the ITP process normally begins when the student is 16 years old, and involves parents' acceptance of the long-range goal of employment. Procedures are based on the student and systems level activities outlined in Table 1. Finally, the ITP frequently involves interagency coordination already from its early phases, since the eventual follow-along assistance typically involves an agency other than the school system, such as vocational rehabilitation services or community-based mental retardation programs.

TRANSITIONING FROM SCHOOL TO ANOTHER SERVICE DELIVERY PROGRAM

Transitioning a student from school to work is not always possible due to such factors as parental opposition and local employment con-

Table 1. Critical activities involved in transitioning students from school to work

Systems level activities

1. Survey community employers concerning desired skills and behaviors for entry-level employees.
2. Develop a *Student Competency Checklist* that incorporates the desired employee skills and behaviors.
3. Develop *Vocational Curriculum Teaching Modules* based on skill and behavior priorities identified by local employers.
4. Implement a *Resource-Teacher Training Plan* that develops teacher competencies in job analysis, job development, and on-the-job support activities.
5. Develop a *Program Handbook* of vocational services and activities that provide specific procedures to:
    a. Facilitate a cooperative working relationship between community employers, schools, and teachers.
    b. Encourage program ownership at the school district level through solicitation of school administrator and teacher participation, and input in program-related decision-making processes and activities.
    c. Maintain a data base related to student and school characteristics, vocational education/training services, and specific outcome measures.

Student level activities

1. Start the ITP process at 16 years of age in cooperation with the parents.
2. Evaluate the student's interests, aptitudes, and temperament in reference to the entry-level skills outlined by the employer and obtained from a job analysis.
3. Provide job exploration and short-term on-the-job training before final commitment. Assist the student considerably at first, but fade assistance as soon as possible.

---

ditions. Hence, an alternative transitioning process is often needed. The model presented here was developed jointly by the local Educational Service Unit and Mid-Nebraska Mental Retardation Services (a community-based mental retardation program). Service delivery coordination between these two agencies has been significantly enhanced by four critical elements: 1) a common language, 2) informed interagency agreements, 3) person-environment congruence analysis, and 4) systematic transitional planning.

Common Language

An essential catalyst in the ITP process is the development and use of a common language. One aspect of such a common language involves the use of the same behavioral domains and criterion-referenced assessment instruments to evaluate the student's behavioral skill profile and the environment's behavioral skill requirements (see Figures 1 and 2). The procedures for completing behavioral skills and environmental profiles can be found in Schalock and Koehler (1984) and Schalock and Jensen (in press).

The second aspect of a common language relates to staff service functions that relate to measurable staff activities. Activities can be converted to *units of service,* which is time associated with staff functions as follows: one unit of service consists of 15 minutes of one-to-one activity, 30 minutes of two to three clients/students to one instructor, or 1 hour of four or more students/clients to one instructor. Specific staff functions include:

1. *Training:* running a direct training program.
2. *Assistance:* activities whose purpose is to facilitate skill maintenance and/or generalization. The intent of assistance units is not to run habilitative training programs, but to provide the assistance necessary to ensure skill generalization and clients' success in their current placement.
3. *Case management:* contact with the client or 15 minutes expended by case management on behalf of the client.
4. *Support:* activities performed *for* the client. The intent of support units is to carry out for the client the task he or she cannot do, or has not been able to learn, but which is still required by the client's current environment.
5. *Supervision:* time spent monitoring clients, accompanying a client to his or her personal appointments, or recreational

Table 2. Individual transition plan[a]

Year	Goal(s)[b]	General procedure	Projected needed resources	Responsible persons	Completion date
1983	Arrange orientation meeting with parent regarding ITP goal for job placement in 5 years	ITP team contacts parents	Community job training site and supervision	Vocational consultant Resource teacher	
1984	Locate job training site for Chris (1–2 days per week during last part of school year)	Advise superintendent of need Contact community employers	Job site transportation	Home school superintendent Vocational consultant	
1985	Have Chris in half-day job training	Orient employer Place and do work adjustment Conduct-on-the-job-assistance	Job site transportation	Facilitator-enabler Employer	
1986	Coordinate job placement/training and transportation with community-based mental retardation program	Develop interagency agreement	Job site transportation	Vocational consultant CBMR job supervisor and case manager	
1987	Have Chris participate in high school graduation program	Place name on office list Inform home district superintendent		Parent Resource teacher School principal	
1987	Have Chris maintain full-time employment with occasional follow-along assistance	Provide assistance units by CBMR staff	10 assistance units per month	CBMR job facilitator/assistant	

[a]Attached to the student's regular individualized education plan.
[b]Begin at age 16.

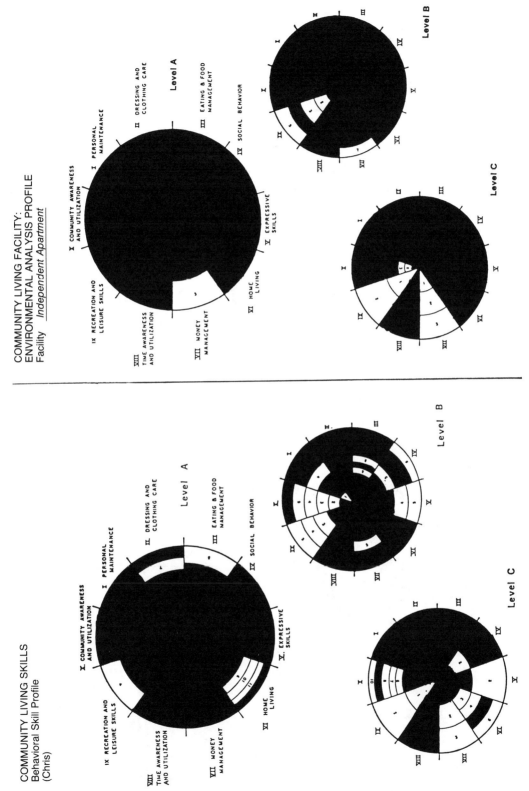

COMMUNITY LIVING SKILLS
Behavioral Skill Profile
(Chris)

COMMUNITY LIVING FACILITY:
ENVIRONMENTAL ANALYSIS PROFILE
Facility *Independent Apartment*

Figure 1. Client skills versus environmental requirement profiles (community living).

119

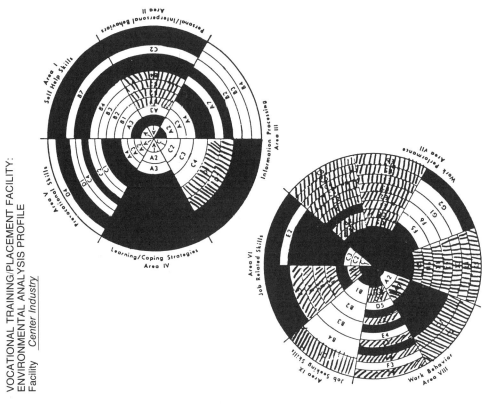

VOCATIONAL TRAINING/PLACEMENT FACILITY:
ENVIRONMENTAL ANALYSIS PROFILE
Facility   *Center Industry*

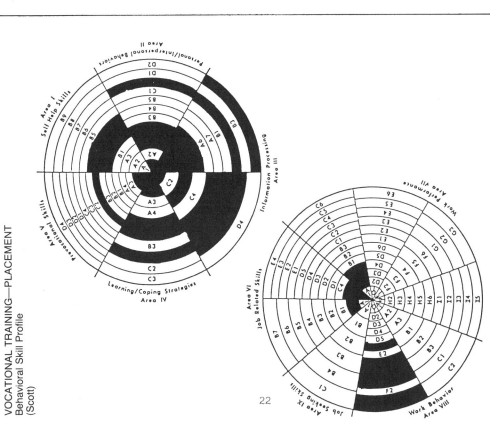

VOCATIONAL TRAINING—PLACEMENT
Behavioral Skill Profile
(Scott)

Figure 2.   Client skills versus environmental requirement profiles (vocational).

and community activities. The intent of these units is to supervise and monitor—not to provide skill training, assistance, or support.

Interagency Agreements

Agreements can vary from a broad statement of commitment to work together, to a detailed description of each party's roles and responsibilities relative to the agreement. The following components should be considered:

1. Delineation of goals and measurable objectives
2. Delineation of specific programs and services involved in the ITP so as to facilitate clear communication
3. Each party's specific actions, roles, and responsibilities relative to the agreement, including sharing of staff and resources
4. Designation of specific staff within each agency to implement and monitor the ITP process
5. Evaluation procedures and guidelines for the utilization of evaluation data

Person-Environment Congruence Analysis

Student or client characteristics are critical for both community placement and job success. A number of behavioral skill assessment instruments can be used to determine a person's *behavioral skill profile*. For example, the left-hand section of Figures 1 and 2 summarizes how a behavioral skill profile is developed (Schalock & Koehler, 1984). The skills assessed reflect the behavioral skills generally required for increased independence and vocational productivity. Darkened areas represent those skills the person can do "independently"; the slashed, those performed "with assistance"; and the blank areas, those skills the person "cannot do."

Evaluating the behavioral requirements of different environments constitutes the second component of a person-environment analysis. This analysis requires that the environment be evaluated to determine whether the behavioral skills on which the person was previously assessed are required for successful performance in that environment. If they are, do they need to be performed independently or is assistance provided? This concept of environmental analysis is shown in the right-hand section of Figures 1 and 2 that summarizes the behavioral skills required to function in: 1) an independent apartment, and 2) a center industry. The darkened area represents skills required to be done "independently"; the slashed, activities "done with assistance"; and the blank area, "skill not required." Specific techniques for completing a person-environment analysis can be found in Schalock and Koehler (1984); procedures for quantifying the goodness-of-fit between person and environment are outlined in Schalock and Jensen (in press).

The person-environment analysis is conducted when the student is 16, and repeated as often as necessary. Once completed, it can be used for the following purposes.

Establishing Long-Term Placement Goals

Many parents worry about the nature of subsequent environments available to their handicapped adolescents, and the requirements of these environments. Consequently, parents frequently become overprotective and resist vocational placement of their child. Also, the IEP-ITP process is frequently met with apprehension by parents who have always anticipated that their child will "go into the group home and the sheltered workshop." The data represented in Figure 1 were used to dispel Chris's parents' apprehensions and erroneous anticipations. Based on her behavioral skill profile, it is apparent that Chris can live independently, but that she will need some assistance and additional training to do so. Furthermore, she would obviously not fit into a group home for which the environmental analysis profile indicated the presence of few required skills.

Remediating Important Mismatched Skills

Matches and mismatches of specific skills can be categorized as "important" or "not important," with importance being defined by the vocational or living situation requirements. An "important match," therefore, is a skill rated as being required for successful adaptation to the environment, and performed independently by the client. An "important mismatch," on the other hand, denotes a skill or behavior required for successful adaptation, which the person does not demonstrate. "Mismatched" skills should constitute the priority training areas during the ensuing IEP-ITP years (see Figure 3).

Systematic Transitional Planning

The procedures for transitioning a student from school to another service delivery program are mechanically similar to those described for the transition from school to work. As illustrated in Figure 2, a rather large discrepancy was found between Scott's behavioral skill profile and the skills required by the job training environment. Due to a significant number of risk factors, the IEP-ITP team's decision was to place Scott in the Mid-Nebraska center industry job training program. Table 3 outlines the yearly goals and long-range transitional plans involved in the process.

TRANSITIONING FROM WORKSHOP TO WORK PLACE

As mentioned, the availability of competitive employment opportunities is enhanced by interagency cooperation, as reflected in the previously described ITP example, and intersector (public and private industry and business) cooperation. One approach to this type of service delivery coordination was described in the initial ITP example (see "Transitioning from School to Work"). A second approach involves work training stations (WTS) that provide an opportunity to train for a particular job in the setting where that job is usually performed. In addition to being specific and client referenced, the utilization of industrial, service, and business settings offers several benefits for job training and placement including:

1. Special partnerships with business and industry demonstrating the range of work the developmentally disabled can perform in jobs outside those typically assigned to this population

2. Work training opportunities in a variety of occupational areas
3. Reduction of job training time and costs by training in the natural environment
4. Integrated work provided in the least restrictive environment
5. Increased placements and success rates increased from those experienced in traditional sheltered workshop programs

Among the steps involved in the development and operation of a work training station, the following four appear to be the most critical.

Procuring Work Training Stations

To date, we have employed a traditional marketing approach to obtaining placements involving *product* (the labor force), *price* (making a competitive bid for services performed), *promotion* (advertising and selling), and *placement-distribution* (establishing and operating the WTS). The guidelines for procuring a WTS are outlined in Table 4. Some of the incentives that can be used include the opportunity to capitalize, tax incentives, handling overflow production, provision of a "super trainer" that can be shared, establishing a data system for the company, and helping to move the company into a Type Z organization (Ouchi, 1981; President's Committee, 1983).

Negotiating the WTS Contract

Before finalizing a contract, the following parameters must be determined (Hagner & Como, 1982): 1) the work to be performed, 2) the means for measuring the work to be performed, 3) agency resources to be committed to the WTS, and 4) the rate to be charged for the work (a fair rate includes the wages, FICA, FUTA, Workers' Compensation, and employee benefits [i.e., health insurance, retirement plans] which would normally be part of an employment agreement with the company). Once these parameters are determined, a contract can be negotiated. Critical responsibilities for both the agency and company are summarized in Table 5.

Assessed Environmental Requirements	Assessed Student Skills: Independent	Assistance/Supervision	Does Not Do
Independence Required	Important match[a]	Important	Mismatch[b]
Required, but Assistance Provided	Unimportant mismatch	Match	Important mismatch[b]
Not Required	Potentially important mismatch	Unimportant mismatch	Unimportant match

Figure 3. Assessing the match between assessed student skills and environmental requirements. (*a:* focus for maintenance and generalization training; *b:* focus for behavioral skill training.)

Operating WTS

Successful WTS operation requires "serving the account" through established customer service principles. Some of the more important of these principles include:

1. Standing behind the products being produced (labor force and product per se)
2. WTS supervisors acting "as if" they were company employees, even though they officially are employees of the agency involved
3. WTS trainers/supervisors acting as "customer service representatives" handling day-to-day problems and liaison
4. WTS trainer/supervisors being on duty whenever trainees are at the company. Agency staff are responsible for handling social behavior and job-related behaviors.

Using ITP as Catalyst

Successful transitioning of clients into a work training station requires careful and creative planning regarding the client's goals and objectives. At the agency level, the ITP is frequently based on a forecast of client movement into programs that would fulfill those goals and objectives (Schalock, 1983). Coordination of services at this level requires not only intersector cooperation, but also coordinated marketing and programmatic services. As illustrated in Table 6, the ITP process interfaces with the three phases of Work Training Station development, operation, and continuance. The ITP format used is the same as that presented in Figure 3 and Table 3.

The "data requirements" mentioned in Table 6 relate to the need to evaluate the effectiveness, efficiency, and cost outcome of the WTS concept. That need, and its relationship to service delivery coordination, is discussed more fully in Schalock and Hill (1986).

CONCLUSION

As stated at the beginning of this chapter, competitive employment opportunities should be provided to all individuals, regardless of handicap. For this to occur, major changes will need to take place not only in our perception of handicapped persons, but also in the way in which we transition these persons from one environment to another. The ITP process represents an effective approach to facilitating

Table 3. Individual transition plan (yearly goals and long-range transitional plan)

Year	Goal(s)[a]	Measurable objectives	Techniques/ procedures	Projected needed resources	Responsible persons	Evaluation criterion	Completion date
1984	Develop interagency agreement Develop the following skills: 1. Self-feeding 2. Community awareness and utilization 3. Self-grooming	Signed agreement ITP Feeds self independently Walks to workshop from residence Bathes independently	Prescriptive programming and staff assistance	10 hours of staff time 50 training units 25 staff assistance units	Case managers Classroom teacher	Signed agreement ITP Feeds self independently Walks to workshop Bathes independently	
1985	Complete a person-environmental analysis	Analysis completed and mismatched skills identified	Ecobehavioral analysis	10 hours of staff time	Diagnostic programmers	Analysis completed and mismatched skills identified	
1986	Desensitize Scott to center industry (job training site)	Attends workshop for 2 hours per day	Desensitization programming (DRO, DRA, DRI)	8 units of training and 2 units of assistance per day	Diagnostic programmers	Attends workshop for 2 hours per day	
1987	Desensitize Scott to residence	Remains in residence overnight once a month	Desensitization programming (DRO, DRA, DRI)	1 unit of residential and 5 assistance units per month	Case managers and community living alternatives coordinator	Remains in residence overnight once per month	
1988	Have Scott successfully enrolled in Mid-Nebraska training program	Attends workshop daily and resides in the residence	Certification	Daily units of service: 8 Training 10 Assistance 1 Maintenance 1 Transportation 2 Residential 1 Case management	Case managers and diagnostic programmers	Attends workshop daily & resides in the residence	

[a]Most likely to be yearly goals beginning at age 16.

Table 4.   Guidelines for work training station procurement

1.   Identify those jobs available in the community which are of sufficient quantity to ensure placement opportunities after training in the WTS.

2.   Target those businesses (industries) to whom you will be marketing the WTS. A great deal of research will go into this phase of the *marketing plan.* The local Chamber of Commerce may be a good place to start gathering data. They will provide a list of area businesses as well as future commercial and industrial trends and development for your area. Key contacts and relationships with potential customers can be developed through memberships in local Chamber of Commerce, service organizations, and business associations.

3.   Develop a marketing approach or strategy. This is the key to successful establishment of a WTS. The individual responsible for marketing must project a professional business attitude and approach to the targeted markets. A good marketing approach or strategy includes:
     a.   An informed assessment of the targeted company, including its financial position, its standing in the community, and its attitudes toward workers. Look for characteristics of a "Theory Z" business attitude (Ouchi, 1981). You are not to request financial statements, but to tactfully get a feel for the company.
     b.   The initial sales call. At this point, identify the company's employment needs and problems, assess the physical condition of the potential WTS, and determine any fears or apprehensions company officials have about disabled workers. This stage provides an opportunity to begin discussing what the agency can offer the company. Avoid "selling the disabled" or calling attention to how badly work is needed. Immediately after the initial call, write a thank you note reiterating one way in which the agency may be helpful to the company.
     c.   Assess the potential work and the environment. Is it an appropriate setting for a WTS? Can instructors and trainees master the skills necessary to successfully complete the work? What commitment can the agency make in terms of staff and resources? Will the WTS be integrated such that it will provide for interaction with other employees?
     d.   Follow-up on the initial sale contact as often as necessary. Do not feel that you must establish a WTS within a certain time. It can take up to a year of "stroking" and talking up the "Theory Z" notion before reaching the WTS contract negotiating stage.

Table 5.   Work training station contract provisions

Agency responsibilities

1.   Work to be provided stated in terms of outcomes with the appropriate quality and quantity requirements.

2.   Supervision/training to be provided by the agency. Since the agency is operating as an independent contractor, issues such as salary, benefits, payroll taxes, and Workmen's Compensation are the agency's responsibility.

3.   Trainee selection. The agency will be responsible for screening and selecting the workers to be placed at the WTS. Some companies may like veto power over workers they feel are not appropriate. Although such a clause may be added, it should not be encouraged. Instead, point out that any worker who is not making progress at the WTS will be terminated by the trainer.

4.   Transportation of workers.

5.   Guarantee statement. The agency assumes responsibility for completion of the work tasks spelled out in the agreement.

Company responsibilities

1.   Equipment, material, and supplies. Details should be specified in the contract.

2.   Work schedules and lines of communication. The company should notify the agency WTS trainer of changes in work schedules and any problems encountered by the WTS.

3.   Terms of reimbursement. The company will pay the agency a given amount for work completed as stated in the agreement (usually per number of pieces, or per day or per week—not per hour or per person). The payment schedule should also be stated to clarify how and when payment will be received.

Terms of agreement

The agreement should specify that it will be in effect for at least 90 days to allow time for the WTS to prove itself. Thereafter, it will continue indefinitely unless terminated by either party with a 30-day written notice, or by mutual consent of both parties.

Note: Examples of actual contracts are available from the author or in Stainback, Stainback, Nietupski, and Hamre-Nietupski (see Chapter 8).

Table 6. Interfacing the individual program plan (ITP) and data requirements with the phases of work training station development and operation

Component	Phase I (Development)	Phase II (Operation)	Phase III (Continuance)
Marketing	1. Procuring WTS 2. Negotiating WTS contract	1. Customer service 2. Ongoing evaluation of training site	1. Job placement 2. Ongoing customer service, evaluation and renegotiating contract(s)
Programmatic	1. Initial job analysis 2. Short-term pretraining 3. Part-time transitioning into WTS	1. Job analysis 2. Person-environment congruence analysis 3. Specialized on-the-job training 4. Providing assistance units of service	1. Place into regular employment 2. Fade assistance and supervision 3. Provide ongoing assistance and generalization training
ITP	1. Formulate ITP based on a client's interests, skills, and goals 2. Develop ITP (as outlined in chapter)	1. Monitor ITP and evaluate client's progress toward regular employment 2. Modify ITP according to necessary training, assistance, and supervision units of service	1. Continue monitoring and modifying the ITP 2. Terminate client from active programmatic service when assistance is no longer necessary

Data requirement	1. Types of jobs/occupational areas
	2. Types of segregated/integrated working environments including:
	  Accessibility
	  Integrated work/eating areas
	  Learning of marketable skills
	  Work routines and schedules
	  Negative connotations or stereotypes
		1. Employment records of workers including:
		  Number in program
		  Number in fulltime, part-time and temporary employment
		  Total work hours/month
		  Wages and fringe benefits
		  Skill acquisition indices
		  Skill maintenance indices
		  Units of assistance/supervision required by employee/job classification
			1. Employment records (as per Phase II)
			2. Support units required for long-term placement

these transitions, while at the same time improving service delivery coordination. The success of the ITP results from the requirements it places on service delivery systems including: 1) creative thinking and planning regarding a person's movement-placement goals and objectives, 2) agreements between various public and private components of a service network, 3) person-environment congruence analysis designed to reduce or eliminate the mismatch between people and their environments, 4) specialized skill acquisition and generalization training in the natural environment, 5) providing services in a business-like fashion, and 6) ongoing program monitoring and evaluation. Fulfillment of these requirements will not only increase service delivery coordination, but also improve the quality, quantity, and validity of the competitive employment opportunities for handicapped citizens.

REFERENCES

Bellamy, T. (1983, June). *Bridges from school to working life*. Paper presented at the 103rd Annual AAMD meeting, Dallas, TX.

Brown, L., Pumpian, I., Baumgart, D., VanDeventer, P., Ford, A., Nisbet, J., Schroeder, J., & Gruenewald, L. (1981). Longitudinal transition plans in programs for severely handicapped students. *Exceptional Children, 47,* 624–631.

Hagner, D., & Como, P. (1982). *Resource manual for work stations in industry*. Menomonie, WI: Stout Vocational Rehabilitation Institute.

Office of Special Education. (1984). *OSERS programming for the transition of youth with disabilities: Bridges from school to working life*. Draft.

Ouchi, W. (1981). *Theory Z: How American business can meet the Japanese challenge*. Reading, MA: Addison-Wesley.

President's Committee on Mental Retardation. (1983). *Report to the President: The mentally retarded worker an economic discovery*. Washington, DC: U.S. Department of Health and Human Services, Office of Human Services.

Schalock, R. L. (1983). *Services for the adult developmentally disabled: Development, implementation and evaluation*. Baltimore: University Park Press.

Schalock, R. L. (1985). Comprehensive community services: A plea for interagency collaboration. In R. H. Bruininks & K. C. Lakin (Eds.), *Living and learning in the least restrictive environment* (pp. 37–63). Baltimore: Paul H. Brookes.

Schalock, R. L., & Hill, M. L. (1986). Evaluating employment services. In W. E. Kiernan & J. A. Stark (Eds.), *Pathways to employment for adults with developmental disabilities* (pp. 285–302). Baltimore: Paul H. Brookes.

Schalock, R. L., & Jensen, M. (in press). Assessing the goodness-of-fit between persons and their environments. *Journal of The Association for Persons with Severe Handicaps*.

Schalock, R. L., & Koehler, B. (1984). *Ecobehavioral analysis and augmentative habilitation techniques*. Hastings, NB: Mid-Nebraska Mental Retardation Services.

Chapter 10

Generalizing and Maintaining Work Behavior

David P. Wacker and Wendy K. Berg

GIFFORD, RUSCH, MARTIN, AND WHITE (1984) proposed that competitive employment training programs be considered along two dimensions: 1) *adaptability* (student performs correctly across work environments and tasks), and 2) *autonomy* (student works without need for extra intervention). Within this conceptual framework, the relative success of a program is determined not only by the student's acquisition of specific skills, but also by the student's performance in novel (untrained) settings and novel tasks. The purpose of this chapter is to describe training procedures that facilitate generalization (i.e., adaptability) and maintenance (i.e., autonomy) of work behaviors in community settings.

To date, the most common approach to vocational training has been to rely extensively on task analytic procedures (Mithaug, 1979). If training consists entirely of task analytic procedures, however, the student may only learn specific responses on specific tasks. This is not a concern if: 1) the job task a student is to perform following graduation is known, 2) the student never changes jobs, or 3) the job task never changes. However, since jobs and work tasks frequently change (Wehman & Kregel, 1985), it is important to teach generalized work skills.

TRAINING TECHNIQUES FOR PRODUCING GENERALIZATION AND MAINTENANCE

Definition and Types

According to Stokes and Baer (1977), generalization takes place when desired behavior occurs in: "non-training conditions (i.e., across subjects, settings, people, behaviors and/or time)" and when "no extra training manipulations are needed; or may be claimed when some extra manipulations are necessary, but the cost or extent is clearly less than that of direct intervention" (p. 350). The definition consists of two critical components: 1) different types of generalization, and 2) amount of subsequent training.

In the most complete conceptual analysis of generalization to date, Drabman, Hammer, and Rosenbaum (1979) identified 16 separate types of generalization. These types of generalization, which include those identified by Stokes and Baer (1977) and various combinations (e.g., across settings and time), may each require different training procedures (or combinations of procedures). Most commonly, several types of generalization are required in order that training conducted in school programs will directly facilitate placement. Assume, for example, that a student is taught to sweep floors in the school during the student's senior year based on a survey of potential community jobs in the student's community. The rationale may be that if several janitorial positions are available in the student's community—each of which requires the worker to sweep floors—teaching the student to sweep floors will facilitate placement. Even if training in the school setting is augmented by community-based instruction, the student may still need to generalize his or her skills across settings (school and/or training site to actual job setting), across people (educational staff to work supervisors and co-workers), across materials (different types of brooms and containers), and over time (senior year to beginning of work).

Procedures that promote acquisition of skills are not necessarily the same as those that promote generalization (Gifford et al., 1984). Consequently, acquiring a specific skill in a specific context does not imply: 1) that the student can perform variations of that skill, 2) that the student can perform the same skill in different settings or in the presence of different people, or 3) that the student will continue to perform the same skills in the same context over time. Instead, the opposite should be assumed unless specific procedures have been utilized to increase the probability of generalization (Stokes & Baer, 1977).

The second component of the definition proposed by Stokes and Baer (1977) relates to the amount of training students will need following the initial training. Too often, we have assumed that students do not generalize because they do not perform errorlessly (or at criterion) on new tasks, in new settings, or after some interval of time following training. Most workers, handicapped or nonhandicapped, require at least minimal training to learn specific job tasks. Generalization has occurred when *either*: 1) a student independently completes a job task in novel (untrained) situations, or 2) the amount of training a student needs to perform subsequent job tasks is substantially reduced. For example, in a recent study by Berg, Wacker, Berrie, and Swatta (1984), three students functioning within the severe-to-profound range of mental retardation were taught to complete various work and daily living tasks using picture prompts. On the average, students required 101 sessions to perform the training task at criterion. Following training, all students performed errorlessly when completing the same task in different settings, and required an average of 18 sessions to learn novel tasks when provided with pictures to guide their performance. In this case, generalization was documented by substantially reduced training time across tasks.

In the following subsections, training techniques that produce generalization of vocational skills are described. These strategies, which have been described in greater detail elsewhere (Drabman et al. 1979; Gifford et al., 1984; Stokes & Baer, 1977), are divided into two categories: antecedent and consequence procedures. The final section contains an overview of considerations for enhancing generalization across supervisors, work settings, work tasks, and time (traditionally referred to as maintenance or autonomy) (Gifford et al., 1984).

Antecedent Procedures

An antecedent stimulus may be any feature of the environment the student is in, including the placement of objects, the presence of a given individual, or the type of cue, prompt, or instruction provided to a student. Such antecedent stimuli can come to control subsequent behavior (become discriminative stimuli) through consistent pairing with reinforcement. For example, if a student is reinforced for cleaning tables in the lunchroom only when the cleaning materials are placed on the teacher's desk, and the teachers says "Go to work," both the placement of the materials and the verbal instruction of the teacher may control responding.

At least four training procedures based on the antecedents of behavior may be useful in producing generalization of vocational behavior. In each of these procedures, the demonstration of a functional relationship between the presence of an antecedent stimuli and the occurrence of a desired response is a critical component.

Common Discriminative Stimuli When a systematic attempt is made to match the discriminative stimuli (S^Ds) used during training with S^Ds routinely available in a work setting, a "common stimuli" procedure (Stokes & Baer, 1977) is being utilized. In work environments, multiple antecedents are present, any of which may come to guide behavior. The purpose of training, therefore, is to teach the student to respond appropriately to naturally occurring S^Ds.

In the example given previously, the students cleaned tables only when the cleaning materials were on the teacher's desk, and when told by the teacher to start working. Neither of these antecedents will be available in most work settings. In a restaurant, for example, the student must clean tables whenever a table is dirty and, of even more importance, when the patrons have left (or are leaving) the restaurant. If the student only cleans a table when specifically told to do so by a work supervisor, or attempts to clean tables before the patron is finished, he or she will probably not be retained. However, if during training the student learns to independently clean tables at appropriate times, the common features between the training situation and the actual work setting may produce generalization across these two situations. In other words, the S^Ds guiding behavior are similar (common) within the two situations and should promote generalization.

The use of common S^Ds is an especially important component of simulated training programs. If training cannot be conducted in an actual work setting, it is imperative that the critical features of those environments be incorporated into training. Too often, analysis of common features includes only the materials used while ignoring the antecedents and consequences that guide and motivate behavior.

In addition, training students to respond to common S^Ds also provides the trainer with a specific context for a student's independence (autonomy) in performing a given work task. *Independence* can be defined as functioning without need for extra intervention; that is, independence occurs when the student performs job tasks under the naturally occurring antecedent and consequent conditions available in a work setting. For example, if a community work supervisor routinely provides gestures (points) to show workers where they are to work, independent functioning consists of functioning under gestural cues. Rather than attempting to make students "independent" without reference to known conditions (identified antecedents and consequences), school personnel should determine such conditions prior to training. To accomplish this goal, observations of job tasks in community settings or surveys (Sowers, Rusch, Connis, & Cummings, 1980) completed by community work supervisors may be used.

Sufficient Exemplars   One pragmatic difficulty with a common discriminative stimuli approach is that the antecedents used in work environments frequently vary. For example, work supervisors often use slightly different instructions at different times to direct workers, different restaurants may utilize different cleaning materials, and the location and presence of various other antecedents vary within and across settings.

Given this situation, vocational trainers have three choices: 1) train the student on a specific task(s) and "hope" that generalization occurs (Stokes & Baer, 1977), 2) attempt to train under all possible conditions, or 3) train a sufficient number of examples of the possible antecedent conditions (and/or corresponding responses) required by a potential job. This latter approach to training has been termed "training sufficient exemplars" (Stokes & Baer, 1977).

In the context of vocational training, *sufficient exemplars* refers to providing the student with a number of examples of the antecedents, desired target responses, settings, or supervisors during the training program. For example, rather than training a student to clean tables only in the school cafeteria, with only one set of cleaning materials, one set of directions, and in the presence of only the teacher, a sufficient exemplars approach includes using more than one example of tables, materials, directions, settings, and supervisors. Conducting training with multiple examples increases the probability that the student will generalize his or her cleaning skills to untrained examples.

Wacker and Berg (1984) taught four junior high students functioning within the moderate range of mental retardation to perform various cleaning tasks (e.g., dusting tables, cleaning windows, cleaning sinks, etc.). The students were initially taught to perform two of these tasks with different materials. After the students reached criteria on both training tasks, generalization occurred across different settings and cleaning tasks (students now performed the untrained tasks at criteria), resulting in no further training being required.

The number of examples needed by a given student to achieve generalization cannot always be predicted prior to training. However, frequently as few as two examples are required (Stokes & Baer, 1977). When conducting baseline, attempt to assess the student in several different settings, using different materials, and with different supervisors. Following baseline, conduct training on one or more of these examples, and determine whether or not generalization has occurred across untrained conditions (by intermittently probing the student's performance in the untrained conditions). Continue training until the student generalizes his or her performance across all remaining (untrained) conditions.

General Case Instruction An extension of the sufficient exemplars approach is to use what Horner and McDonald (1982) and Sprague and Horner (1984) referred to as *general case instruction*. General case instruction is conducted by first defining an instructional universe, selecting examples from that universe, and then training those examples sequentially. The instructional universe is defined by determining those stimulus features of a task (stimulus class) that either cause the same response (response class) or different responses. Ensuring that students receive instruction on examples of all relevant members of the stimulus class increases the probability that they will generalize their responding to untrained members.

A *stimulus class* is defined by the stimulus characteristics that members of the class have in common. For example, all spray bottles share certain features such as the presence of a nozzle. A *response class* is based on two criteria. First, members of the same response class have the same outcome (e.g., a clean surface). Second, members share similar motoric characteristics (e.g., spraying or wiping). Consequently, general case instruction is successful when all members of a given stimulus class (spray bottles) produce specific responses (spraying a surface). For example, Horner and McDonald (1982) trained four high

school students to crimp and cut electronic capacitors varying in size, shape, color, and lead separation space. Rather than simply attempting to train students on examples of capacitors, the authors selected examples representing each of these dimensions. The results indicated that training specific examples (defined by the stimulus characteristic of the task) increased the probability of generalization across all remaining capacitors.

In general case programming, the examples to be trained are defined by variations in the task. Spray bottles, for example, might vary by size, color, and type of spray nozzle. Rather than training students to use spray bottles that share each of these characteristics, it is important to train students utilizing different types of spray bottles.

Antecedent Cue Regulation *Antecedent cue regulation* refers to responses a student makes to limit the potential range of S^Ds controlling behavior (Gifford et al., 1984). As discussed previously, multiple antecedent stimuli are available in work settings, any of which may come to control responding. Teaching students to regulate which of the antecedent stimuli control their behavior (i.e., which stimuli function as S^Ds) increases the probability that the students will continue to perform correctly following training (maintenance).

Antecedent cue regulation is one of a series of procedures that promote self-control. Goetz and Etzel (1978) defined self-control as responses made by an individual that, in turn, modify the individual's own behavior. Self-control procedures may be especially viable in community settings, because they may facilitate generalization when other, externally imposed procedures are not available (Gifford et al., 1984).

Antecedent cue regulation procedures fall into two general classes: self-generated mediators and externally generated mediators (Gifford et al., 1984). The use of self-instructions is the most common example of *self-generated mediators*. Self-instructions with students who are mildly and moderately mentally retarded have been used to improve social behavior

(Matson & Adkins, 1980), academic performance (Albion & Salzberg, 1982), and speed of completing vocational tasks (Crouch, Rusch, & Karlan, 1984).

In each of the above cases, the self-instructions produced by the student constituted a stimulus that controlled a previously acquired response (Gifford et al., 1984; Karlan & Rusch, 1982). Typically, students are first trained to complete a task to criterion. They are then taught to self-instruct correct performance, and finally to complete the task (say-then-do). Training students to consistently produce a verbal instruction prior to completing a task may increase maintenance of responding (Karlan & Rusch, 1982).

Another self-generated mediator consists of teaching students to produce a verbal label (instead of an instruction) that serves to guide their performance by making certain aspects of the task more salient, rather than explicitly stating what the students should do (Wacker & Berg, 1983a; Wacker & Greenebaum, 1984). Wacker and Greenebaum (1984) taught seven adolescents with moderate and severe mental retardation to complete a sorting task by training them to verbalize (label) the relevant dimension of the objects they were sorting. As a result of using the self-generated labeling procedure, all students acquired the original target response and generalized their sorting skills across untrained tasks.

Externally generated mediators are antecedent stimuli originally provided by training staff, but which the student is taught to independently control to modify his or her own behavior. The most common example of an externally generated mediator is picture cues. Picture cues have been used to facilitate the performance of moderately or severely mentally retarded persons on complex daily living and vocational tasks (Johnson & Cuvo, 1981; Martin, Rusch, James, Decker, & Trtol, 1982; Sowers et al., 1980). During training, the client learns to imitate the performance depicted in a picture, turn to the next picture and imitate that performance (look-then-do), and so forth, until all steps in a task are completed (Martin et al., 1982; Wacker & Berg, 1983b).

Berg and Wacker (1983) taught a severely mentally retarded adolescent to follow picture cues (bound into a book) to independently locate and empty wastebaskets as part of a janitoral job training site (see Figure 1). Prior to the introduction of the picture cues (baseline), the student selected wastebaskets in a random fashion, frequently "forgetting" to empty several wastebaskets. Picture cues were introduced into the job site with a three-step training procedure: 1) the student turned the pages in a sequential order, 2) the student turned the pictures in the picture book and located the wastebasket shown, and 3) the student turned the pictures, located the wastebaskets, and emptied the wastebaskets into a custodian's trash cart. Following training (Post 1) the student independently used the picture prompts to guide his performance, completing the task with at least 90% accuracy. Following the completion of posttraining (Baseline 2), the pictures were removed to determine if the student was relying upon the picture prompts to complete the target task. As shown during Baseline 2, the student's accuracy of performance decreased substantially when the picture cues were not available to guide his performance. Finally, the picture cues were returned to the student during Post 2, and his performance returned to acceptable levels of accuracy. In addition, during both post conditions the student reliably turned most pages of the picture book, further suggesting that the student actively used the pictures to guide his performance.

Connis (1979) and Sowers et al. (1980) also used picture prompts to train mentally retarded clients to become more independent in vocational settings. Connis's (1979) clients, who were moderately mentally retarded, learned to use picture sequences to change work tasks independently. Similarly, Sowers et al. (1980) used picture prompts to train adults to go to and from work break and lunch independently.

Picture prompts have also been utilized to train more complex tasks. Wacker and Berg (1983b) used picture prompts to train five adolescents, who were moderately or severely retarded, to complete complex assembly tasks.

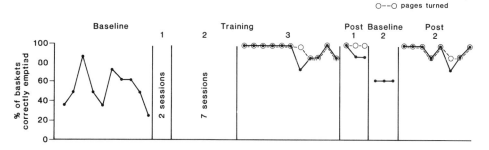

Figure 1. Percentage of steps completed correctly in locating and emptying wastebaskets.

In addition, the adolescents generalized their use of the picture prompts to independently complete untrained vocational tasks. Berg et al. (1984) achieved similar results with dusting and cleaning tasks, and also reported that students continued to effectively use the pictures to guide their behavior over a 3-month period. Finally, Berg and Wacker (1983) reported similar effects when pretaped instructions and tactual prompts were used with adolescents who were blind, or deaf and blind, respectively.

Like self-instructions or labels, permanent prompts (picture cues, pretaped instructions, and tactual prompts) may promote generalization by providing stable discriminative stimuli that the student can use to guide his or her performance across tasks or settings. As workers learn to use these antecedent stimuli to guide their own performance (develop self-control), they become increasingly more independent in vocational settings and more likely to generalize their skills across settings, tasks, and time.

Summary In this section we described procedures that arrange antecedent events to promote a student's ability to be more independent and to adapt to new situations. Although the use of these procedures has not been widely reported in the competitive employment literature, they hold considerable promise based upon the results of several research efforts described in the work behavior literature.

Consequence Procedures

The consequences of behavior can serve to both motivate continued responding and cor-

rect inappropriate responding. The emphasis in this chapter is on the application of consequences to motivate (reinforce) continued responding. At least three consequence procedures should be included in vocational training.

Natural Maintaining Contingencies As with antecedents, only naturally occurring consequences (Stokes & Baer, 1977) should be used during training if at all possible. Students who are trained to work for reinforcers that are routinely available in work settings (e.g., money, items available during work breaks, contact with co-workers) are much more likely to maintain their skills over long periods of time in those settings.

Three training approaches should be considered that utilize naturally available contingencies. First, students should be trained to engage in behavior that normally receives reinforcement (Stokes & Baer, 1977). Rusch, Schutz, and Agran (1982), for example, reported that community work supervisors frequently specify entry-level requirements for their workers. Therefore, by first surveying the expectations of work supervisors, and then training students to perform relevant skills (defined by the work supervisors), we increase the probability of students receiving reinforcement.

Second, naturally occurring consequences may not initially serve to reinforce behavior. If this is the case, training should be continued until naturally occurring consequences serve as reinforcers for desired behavior. This is accomplished by pairing the natural consequences of behavior with previously established reinforcers. Once behavior is under control using these types of reinforcers, the extraneous reinforcers are systematically withdrawn until the student is working only for the naturally occurring reinforcers. For example, if a student initially cleans tables only when he or she is continuously praised by the teacher, teacher praise might be paired with money and/or items at work break. Before training is terminated, the student should be working at criterion only for money and/or for break times after teacher praise has been gradually withdrawn.

Finally, students may be trained to appropriately solicit reinforcement from the natural work environment (Seymour & Stokes, 1976). Most workers, at least occasionally, solicit praise from supervisors in appropriate ways and hence increase the amount of reinforcement received. Students with severe handicaps rarely have the necessary skills to engage in this type of behavior, and must be specifically trained to do so. Perhaps even more important, they must learn to identify appropriate occasions for seeking reinforcement. As an example, students might be taught to make an acceptable greeting response or gesture whenever their supervisor is nearby, and they have completed a job task. In this way, students may increase their probability of receiving praise or social reinforcement from supervisors.

Intermittent Reinforcement Schedules A related issue concerns the delivery of reinforcement. Training usually begins with continuous reinforcement, which is not a common feature of many work environments. In addition, reinforcement in training settings is usually response based (contingent on correct performance), while in community work settings it tends to be time based (weekly checks, regularly scheduled break times).

An obvious approach to facilitating maintenance is to gradually increase the reinforcement schedule (change from continuous to intermittent reinforcement). Control of behavior may be shifted from continuous to intermittent schedules for two main reasons. First, intermittent schedules, if based on the schedules used in probable work environments, provide the student with similar conditions across training and work settings. As discussed previously, the probability of producing generalization is increased when the conditions used during training match the conditions routinely available in natural settings (Kazdin, 1978).

Second, intermittent reinforcement schedules are more resistant to extinction than are continuous schedules (Rusch, Connis, & Sowers, 1978). As students begin to work more independently in job settings, they will probably not receive the same amount of praise and attention as during training. By increasing the amount of time worked (or the number of correct responses made) before receiving reinforcement, we may decrease the probability of extinction (i.e., decrease the likelihood of the students decreasing their rate or accuracy of performance).

Consequence Regulation For some students, contingencies may be shifted from external administration to self-administration (Kazdin, 1978); that is, students are trained to evaluate their own behavior and to independently deliver reinforcers to themselves. For example, Helland, Paluck, and Klein (1976) compared self-reinforcement to supervisor-delivered reinforcement on production rates in a workshop setting. The clients (mildly and moderately mentally retarded) were to reinforce themselves (compliment themselves and select a reinforcer) upon completing prespecified amounts of work. While both reinforcement conditions led to higher performance levels, the clients in the self-reinforcement group worked independently of staff.

Reinforcer regulation procedures offer many of the potential advantages identified for antecedent cue regulation procedures. Thus, both types of procedures develop self-control in students, which increases their autonomy in work settings. In addition, self-administration of reinforcers may potentially facilitate maintenance in two ways. First, the student receives potentially greater amounts of reinforcement, which can be important when naturally occurring reinforcement schedules are insufficient to maintain responding.

Second, as students learn to control their

own behavior through self-delivered consequences, changes in the natural environment
may not be as disruptive to their performance.
For example, if work supervisors change, resulting in substantially reduced social reinforcement for a student, he or she may continue to perform at acceptable levels because he
or she already controls many of the consequences that maintain behavior.

Summary We have introduced three procedures that focus upon consequence procedures, including use of: 1) natural contingencies, 2) intermittent reinforcement
schedules, and 3) consequence regulation.
Each procedure has been reported in the work
behavior literature.

DEVELOPING
GENERALIZATION PACKAGES

To date, few attempts have been made to systematically evaluate the effects of combining
various procedures to produce generalization
(Gifford et al., 1984). Table 1 presents a preliminary analysis of the types of generalization
that may be facilitated by individual training
procedures. The types of generalization facilitated by the training procedures were selected
based on previous findings in the literature, and
on a conceptual analysis of the purposes of the
procedures. Therefore, the outcomes of the
procedures, especially when used in combination, are not known and may be variable.
By considering the types of generalization
needed and the purposes of the training pro-

cedures, more systematic efforts may be attempted to produce the desired outcomes.

In our view, none of the procedures is singularly sufficient to produce all the potentially
needed types of generalization, thus requiring
some combination, or package of procedures.
For example, antecedent cue regulation procedures potentially facilitate all types of generalization, but only within certain contexts.
For students to use picture prompts across
tasks, they must have generalized skills in
following novel (untrained) pictures, which
may necessitate that they be trained to use
pictures with a sufficient exemplars or general
case procedure. In addition, although picture
prompts may facilitate maintenance by providing the student with consistent S^Ds over
time, the student may still need to be trained
with one of the consequence procedures to
facilitate continued use of the pictures.

Consideration must also be given to combining procedures that produce the same type
of generalization. For example, the combined
use of common stimuli and sufficient exemplars may lead to more successful generalization
across settings than either procedure alone,
because this combination provides the student
with increased opportunities to respond to relevant antecedent stimuli. In some settings, a
common stimuli approach may be most efficient in producing generalization, whereas in
other settings multiple examples are needed
because of variations (types of materials available) in those stimuli.

Rules for selecting and combining pro-

Table 1.   Types of generalization facilitated by training procedures

Generalization procedures	Types of generalization			
	Across supervisors	Across work settings	Across work tasks[a]	Over time
Antecedent procedures				
1. Common stimuli		+		
2. Sufficient exemplars	+	+	+	
3. General case		+	+	
4. Antecedent cue regulation	+	+	+	+
Consequent procedures				
1. Natural contingencies	+	+		+
2. Intermittent schedules				+
3. Consequence regulation	+			+

[a]Includes variations in work materials and responses.

cedures are needed to continue the development of an effective generalization technology. In the following section, an initial attempt to establish some decision rules is provided.

SELECTION OF TRAINING TECHNIQUES

The decision of what procedure(s) to use with which student is dependent on several interrelated factors, including the specific responses to be produced, the probable settings in which those responses will ultimately occur, and the interaction between the skills the student currently possesses and those required by a particular technique. In the following subsections, each of these factors is discussed.

Selecting Target Behavior

Although traditional vocational programs have provided training in a variety of complex skills (usually involving multistep assemblies or multichoice discriminations), these skills are frequently not directly relevant to community employment. As a result, they do not generalize to community work settings because of a lack of common stimuli or natural contingencies to prompt and maintain those skills.

The first step in transitional programs, therefore, is to train skills that have some probability of being encouraged in work settings (see Table 2). Potential jobs may initially be determined based on occupations that traditionally have high turnover rates and are available in a student's community. For example, food service, janitorial, and maid service jobs have been successfully trained (Rusch et al., 1982).

The second step is to determine the naturally occurring or tolerated antecedents and consequences for performance. Readers are referred to Chapter 15 for a description of procedures to follow to ascertain naturally occurring or tolerated antecedents and consequences. By specifying the conditions as well as the responses required in a work setting, the trainer can begin to determine the training techniques that most closely match a potential work setting.

Third, work supervisors' entry-level requirements must be determined. Although workers may display a variety of skills and various competency levels, it is important to establish which of these skills are critical to work supervisors (Rusch et al., 1982). Use of a checklist, such as the *Vocational Assessment and Curriculum Guide* (Rusch et al., 1982), may be sufficient for this purpose.

Selecting Training Procedures

Once the specific behaviors and the necessary conditions for those behaviors have been determined, training procedures can be selected systematically. In this process, four variables should be considered. First, assessment (baseline) should be conducted to determine which skills a student currently possesses. Since students sometimes display more skills in actual work settings than in simulated or training environments, baseline should be conducted at the proposed work site as well as in the training setting. In addition, by having several opportunities to demonstrate skills under the natural conditions present in a work setting, students

Table 2. Factors and steps to consider in selecting training techniques

Factor	Steps
1. Select relevant target behavior	1A. Behavior is required/encouraged by work supervisors 1B. Jobs that require the behavior are available in the community. 1C. Behavior is trained under naturally occurring or acceptable antecedents and consequences 1D. Entry-level requirements have been determined
2. Select effective and efficient training procedures	2A. Baseline performance in both training and actual work settings 2B. Train variations in work tasks, materials, procedures, and settings 2C. Determine the range of generalization expected across conditions 2D. Determine the types of training procedures that are acceptable to work supervisors

may independently acquire many of the necessary work or work-relevant (e.g., social) skills.

Second, variations in work tasks, materials, and procedures within and between settings may necessitate the use of multiple procedures during training. For example, after training students to use picture prompts to assemble two different types of vocational items, Wacker and Berg (1983b) assessed generalization on untrained items (and untrained pictures) representing each of the tasks initially trained. By utilizing both picture prompts (antecedent cue regulation) and examples of different types of tasks (general case instruction), two different generalization procedures were combined. This approach was adopted because the job tasks required that the students independently perform relatively complex assembly tasks (18–43 separate steps) that were not sequenced, and that they perform two variations of the task. Antecedent cue regulation was selected to facilitate their maintenance of responding ("remembering" to do each step), whereas general case instruction was selected to facilitate their generalization across different tasks.

Third, the training time needed to teach students must be evaluated with respect to the use of a particular strategy. For example, an analysis of a potential job task may reveal that as many as 20 different varieties of materials are possible across settings. The issue here concerns the criteria established for successful generalization. Should training time be extended to increase generalization across a wide range of potential settings for a particular type of job, or should training be conducted on various jobs, each with a narrower range of generalized responses across potential settings?

With respect to picture prompts, Wacker and Berg (1983b) recommended that training be considered effective only when: "(a) extensive training is not required to teach students to use pictures to guide their performance, (b) once students learn to use picture prompts, the amount of training on other tasks is reduced when pictures are available, (c) picture prompts promote generalization or maintenance of performance or both, and (d) supervision of students is reduced when picture prompts are available" (pp. 431–432).

The guidelines proposed by Wacker and Berg suggest that students be trained to use picture prompts depending on the relative difficulty they have in acquiring the necessary skills; that is, not all students will benefit from such learning. Spellman, DeBriere, Jarboe, Campbell, and Harris (1978), for example, reported that several of their students never acquired the skills necessary to use picture prompts. Similar criteria are needed for other generalization procedures to guide our decision as to when training should be terminated. This is especially important since the initial acquisition of specific skills may not be sufficient to determine the success of training.

Finally, the training procedures that will most likely be tolerated in the work environment should be considered. For example, Menchetti, Rusch, and Owens (1983) found that food service employers would allow only certain select training and management strategies for use in competitive employment (see Table 3). Such information may be critical to job placement, particularly when "ignoring an error," commonly considered an appropriate extinction procedure, would not be allowed.

Summary

In this section we discussed the need to combine generalization procedures for maximum efficiency as well as specific examples of such generalization packages. The decision to choose a certain procedure should be determined by the specific responses to be produced, the probable settings in which the responses will occur, and the interaction between the skills the student possesses and those required by a particular technique.

CONCLUSIONS

Training procedures that produce both acquisition and generalization of vocational skills are increasingly recognized as a necessary part of transitional programs. In most circumstances it is no longer sufficient simply to demonstrate that a student can learn a specified

Table 3. Training and management strategies for use in competitive employment

Employers would allow:
1. Keeping monthly records
2. Keeping weekly records
3. Telling the employee what he or she did wrong
4. Verbally or physically instructing the employee while he or she corrects an error
5. Asking the employee why he or she is acting socially inappropriately
6. Allowing a performance rate of faster than 50% when the employee is receiving training
7. Working for money
8. Praise from a supervisor
9. Immediate reinforcement
10. A combination of food, points, access to preferred activities, physical contact, or praise and money
11. Verbal instruction, demonstrations, and physical assistance when learning a new job
12. Repeating an instruction.
13. Teaching one task at a time
14. Teaching the easiest jobs first
15. Color coding job-related equipment

Employers would never allow:
1. Ignoring an error
2. Yelling at an employee
3. Yelling at the employee when he or she acts socially inappropriately
4. Ignoring socially inappropriate behavior
5. Points for work that can later be traded for material objects
6. Teaching all tasks at one time

Adapted from Menchetti, B. M., Rusch, F. R., & Lamson, D. S. (1981). *Journal of The Association for the Severely Handicapped, 6*, 6–16.

vocational skill. Rather, the student must be both autonomous in performing the skill and adaptable to environmental changes in work settings following training (Gifford et al., in press). Programs that emphasize generalization of skills directly facilitate both of these training goals. Although a variety of procedures have been reported to successfully produce generalization, decision rules for their selection—either singularly or in combination—have not been developed. A related issue concerns what criteria should be used to evaluate a program in terms of the generalization produced.

REFERENCES

Albion, F., & Salzberg, C. (1982). The effects of self-instructions on the rate of correct addition problems with mentally retarded persons. *Education and Training of Children, 5,* 121–131.

Berg, W., & Wacker, D. (1983). *Effects of permanent prompts on the vocational performance of severely handicapped individuals.* Paper presented at the Association for Behavior Analysis, Milwaukee, WI.

Berg, W., Wacker, D., Berrie, P., & Swatta, P. (1984). *Assessing generalization with picture prompts.* Paper presented at the Association for Behavior Analysis, Nashville, TN.

Connis, R. (1979). The effects of sequential pictorial cues, self-recording, and praise on the job task sequencing of retarded adults. *Journal of Applied Behavior Analysis, 12,* 355–361.

Crouch, K. P., Rusch, F. R., & Karlan, G. R. (1984). Competitive employment: Utilizing the correspondence training paradigm to enhance productivity. *Education and Training of the Mentally Retarded, 19*(4), 268–275.

Drabman, R., Hammer, D., & Rosenbaum, M. (1979). Assessing generalization in behavior modification with children: The generalization map. *Behavioral assessment, 1,* 203–219.

Gifford, J., Rusch, F., Martin, J., & White, D. (1984). Autonomy and adaptability: A proposed technology for maintaining work behavior. In N. Ellis & N. Bray (Eds.), *International review of research on mental retardation* (Vol. 12, pp. 285–314). New York: Academic Press.

Goetz, E., & Etzel, B. (1978). A brief review of self-control procedures: Problems and solutions. *Behavior Therapy, 1,* 58.

Helland, C., Paluck, R., & Klein, M. (1976). A comparison of self and external reinforcement with the trainable mentally retarded. *Mental Retardation, 14,* 22–23.

Horner, R., & McDonald, R. (1982). Comparison of single instance and general case instruction in teaching a generalized vocational skill. *Journal of The Association for the Severely Handicapped, 7,* 7–20.

Johnson, B., & Cuvo, A. (1981). Teaching mentally retarded adults to cook. *Behavior Modification, 5,* 187–202.

Karlan, G., & Rusch, F. (1982). Correspondence between saying and doing: Some thoughts on defining correspondence and future directions for application. *Journal of Applied Behavior Analysis, 15*, 151–162.

Kazdin, A. (1978). Behavior modification in retardation. In J. Neisworth & R. Smith (Eds.), *Retardation: Issues, assessment, and intervention* (pp. 299–339). New York: McGraw-Hill.

Martin, J., Rusch, F., James, V., Decker, P., & Trtol, K. (1982). The use of picture cues to establish self-control in the preparation of complex meals by mentally retarded adults. *Applied Research in Mental Retardation, 3*, 105–119.

Matson, J., & Adkins, J. (1980). A self-instructional social skills training program for mentally retarded persons. *Mental Retardation, 18*, 245–248.

Menchetti, B. M., Rusch, F. R., & Lamson, D. S. (1981). Employer's perception of acceptable procedures for use in competitive employment settings. *Journal of The Association for the Severely Handicapped, 6*, 6–16.

Menchetti, B. M., Rusch, F. R., & Owens, D. (1983). Assessing the vocational needs of mentally retarded adolescents and adults. In J. L. Matson & S. E. Breening (Eds.), *Assessing the mentally retarded* (pp. 247–284). New York: Grune & Stratton.

Mithaug, D. (1979). The relationship between programmed instruction and task analysis in the prevocational training of severely and profoundly handicapped persons. *American Association for the Education of the Severely/Profoundly Handicapped Review, 4*, 162–178.

Rusch, F. R., Connis, R. T., & Sowers, J. (1978). The modification and maintenance of time spent attending to task using social reinforcement, token reinforcement and response cost in an applied restaurant setting. *Journal of Special Education Technology, 2*, 18–26.

Rusch, F. R., Martin, J. E., & White, D. M. (1985). Competitive employment: Teaching mentally retarded employees to maintain their work behavior. *The Mentally Retarded, 20*(3), 182–189.

Rusch, F., Schutz, R., & Agran, M. (1982). Validating entry-level survival skills for service occupations: Implications for curriculum development. *Journal of The Association for the Severely Handicapped, 7*, 32–41.

Seymour, F., & Stokes, T. (1976). Self-recording in training girls to increase work and evoke staff praise in an institution for offenders. *Journal of Applied Behavior Analysis, 9*, 41–54.

Sowers, J., Rusch, F., Connis, R., & Cummings, L. (1980). Teaching mentally retarded adults to time-manage in a vocational setting. *Journal of Applied Behavior Analysis, 13*, 119–128.

Spellman, C., DeBriere, T., Jarboe, D., Campbell, S., & Harris, S. (1978). Pictorial instruction: Training daily living skills. In M. E. Snell (Ed.), *Systematic instruction of the moderately and severely handicapped* (pp. 391–411). Columbus, OH: Charles E. Merrill.

Sprague, J., & Horner, R. (1984). The effects of single instance, multiple instance, and general case training on generalized vending machine use by moderately and severely handicapped students. *Journal of Applied Behavior Analysis, 17*, 273–278.

Stokes, T., & Baer, D. (1977). An implicit technology of generalization. *Journal of Applied Behavior Analysis, 10*, 349–367.

Wacker, D., & Berg, W. (1983a). *Use of a verbal labeling procedure with severely handicapped adolescents on two vocational tasks.* Paper presented at the Association for Behavior Analysis, Milwaukee, WI.

Wacker, D., & Berg, W. (1983b). Effects of picture prompts on the acquisition of complex vocational tasks by mentally retarded adolescents. *Journal of Applied Behavior Analysis, 16*, 417–433.

Wacker, D., & Berg, W. (1984). *Evaluation of response outcome and response topography on generalization of skills.* Unpublished manuscript, Division of Developmental Disabilities, The University of Iowa, Iowa City, IA.

Wacker, D., & Greenebaum, F. (1984). Efficacy of a verbal training sequence on the sorting performance of moderately and severely retarded adolescents. *American Journal of Mental Deficiency, 88*, 653–660.

Wehman, P., & Kregel, J. (1985). A supported work approach to competitive employment of individuals with moderate and severe handicaps. *Journal of The Association for Persons with Severe Handicaps, 10*, 3–11.

Chapter 11

Observational Reporting of Work Behavior

Martin Agran

AS PART OF preparing students for competitive employment, effective data collection systems are necessary to extract maximum information about the quality and level of the students' social and vocational survival skills. The ecological complexities of work environments, including some employers' ambivalence and resistance to using certain procedures, underscore the need to utilize data collection systems that are adaptable to competitive work environments while providing representative estimates of students' demonstration of survival skills (Menchetti, Rusch, & Lamson, 1981). Ultimately, the true measure of a student's competence will be determined by the precision and efficiency of the data collection system employed.

Observational recording represents the most suitable procedure for assessing students' competence in competitive employment and evaluating the effectiveness of interventions designed to facilitate acquisition of criterion goals. The purpose of this chapter is to examine several observation and recording systems, the types of information they yield, and their suitability for competitive work environments. The following observational recording systems are examined: 1) event recording, 2) interval recording, 3) time sampling, 4) latency recording, and 5) duration recording. In spite of their potential accuracy, observational systems are subject to error and biases that, in turn, may lead to distorted and unrepresentative data. Potentially confounding variables such as chance agreement are discussed along with suggestions on how to reduce the threat of these variables.

Observational methodology provides a direct and efficient means of obtaining objective data on work performance (Hartmann & Wood, 1982). Traditionally, such ratings have been used for evaluation purposes whereby respondents (i.e., employers, supervisors) provide judgments on an employee's competence. However, though such judgments may yield valuable information about consumer acceptability of training efforts (Rusch & Mithaug, 1980), evaluative data derived from ratings are suspect in at least two ways. First, as Cairns and Green (1979) noted, rating systems are based on the assumption that the rater has "a theoretical concept of the quality or attribute to be rated" (p. 211). That is, the rater must be cognizant of the specific behaviors or responses that reflect the quality or attribute being measured. Hence, any misunderstanding or misinterpretation of the items to be rated may result in biased ratings. Second, since raters must be knowledgeable about an employee's work behavior in order to give an informed statement, biased ratings may result (White & Rusch, 1983).

Observers, on the other hand, do not need any special knowledge of employees; furthermore, they can be trained to record all specified code categories. In addition, observation systems are flexible, relatively easy to use, and widely applicable (Hartmann & Wood, 1982).

Generally, observation methods are either event or time based (Rusch & Mithaug, 1980). The selection of one method over another is determined by behavior type and frequency of the behavior(s) to be observed. Since reported data are restricted to the unit of measurement recorded, unsuitable recording procedures or irrelevant data will yield either unrepresentative or unreliable information.

Work behavior can be measured and assessed along several dimensions, including *frequency* and *rate of occurrence, checklist recording, duration,* and *latency.* Observations of the *frequency* of occurrence of discrete behaviors are typically event based (e.g., the number of times an employee complies with the supervisor's commands). Frequency may also be reported as a *percentage correct* measure, that is, the percentage of appropriate responses an employee emits. Finally, frequency measures may be reported as rate measures. *Rate* refers to the frequency of occurrence of a given behavior within specified time periods; as such, it is particularly useful for reporting productivity-related behavior (i.e., number of products completed by the employee in a given period of time). *Checklist recording* is also a frequency count involving the recording of whether or not a target behavior(s) occurred. *Duration* measures the length of time an employee takes to demonstrate a discrete behavior (e.g., completing an assigned task). Finally, *latency* relates to the amount of time an employee requires to initiate a desired response (i.e., compliance).

Selection of a recording system is determined by the dimension that is deemed most appropriate for the intent of the educational or rehabilitational program. In the following sections several observation and recording procedures and their suitability for obtaining information about each of the previously listed dimensions are examined.

SPECIFYING AND
MEASURING BEHAVIORAL OBJECTIVES

Prior to selecting an observation and recording system, it is essential to specify and define the observational targets (work behaviors). This task requires clear and unambiguous response definitions that focus on the observable characteristics of a response, not the assumed purpose of the response. Bernstein and Ziarnik (1984) suggested that observers need to attend to the topography of a behavior (how it looks), rather than its function. The former will be clearly observable and measurable, whereas the latter involves some degree of inference and, consequently, may produce biased data. Category definitions may either be molar or molecular (Hartmann & Wood, 1982). *Molar categories* refer to global measures of behavior (e.g., assists co-workers). By requiring that the observer make inferences (i.e., judgments about whether or not an observed response category did or did not occur), these definitions are susceptible to observer bias. *Molecular categories,* on the other hand, are more narrowly defined and describe specific responses. Although molecular behaviors require more precise discriminations, they are easily recorded by trained observers and reduce the chance of bias. The process of writing behavioral objectives will not be reiterated here as it has been adequately described in several available texts (cf. Alberto & Troutman, 1982). Nevertheless, it should be emphasized that response definitions must be objective (specify observable characteristics), clear (understandable, requiring little or no inference), and complete (clearly define the beginning and end of a response) (Kazdin, 1982).

SELECTING OBSERVATION
AND RECORDING SYSTEMS

As mentioned, selection of an appropriate observation and recording system depends upon the number of behaviors to be observed; the anticipated frequency of the observed behavior(s); and whether a frequency count, percentage of occurrence, or time measure is needed. The first decision to be made when selecting an observation and recording system is whether the target behavior(s) is numerical or temporal (Alberto & Troutman, 1982). If numerical, the behavior(s) to be assessed will be measured in number of units or percentage completed; the former is used when opportunities to demonstrate the target behavior(s) remain constant, while the latter measurement unit is applied when such opportunities are not held constant. If temporal, the target behavior(s) are measured in time units.

Second, it must be determined whether the target behavior is discrete or continuous. *Discrete behaviors* have clear boundaries (a beginning and an end), thus they can be identified and subsequently recorded as either occurring or not occurring. *Continuous behaviors*, in contrast, do not have a clear beginning or an end. Such behaviors may be complex (i.e., consist of several response units) or may consist of one or few behaviors that occur at high frequency and, subsequently, preclude a determination of when one behavior stops and another starts.

Third, the frequency level (high, medium, or low occurrence rates) must be determined regardless of the nature of the behavior (i.e., discrete or continuous). Fourth, if the chosen measurement unit is temporal, a decision must be made on whether a latency or duration measure should be recorded.

TYPES OF OBSERVATION AND RECORDING SYSTEMS

Five observation and recording systems can be used to assess work behavior in competitive work environments. These include *event recording, interval recording, time sampling, latency recording,* and *duration recording.* Figure 1 provides an overview of the selection process.

The following examples illustrate the process of selecting the most appropriate observation and recording system based on the four decision-making steps outlined above (Alberto & Troutman, 1982).

Example 1 The number of instructions a student follows in a given work period needs to be estimated. First, since a frequency count is desired, the appropriate unit of measurement is numerical. Second, since "instruction following" has a clear beginning (request to perform a task) and end (completion of the requested task), it is a discrete behavior. Third, prior to intervention, pilot observations (informal data collection) would reveal that instructions are typically delivered at a medium or low

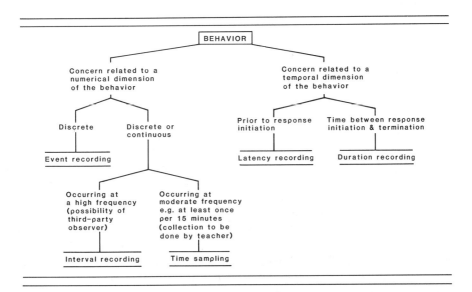

Figure 1. Selecting observation and recording systems. (From Alberto, P. A., & Troutman, A. C. [1982]. *Applied behavior analysis for teachers*, p. 113. Columbus, OH: Charles E. Merrill. Copyright 1982 by Charles E. Merrill Publishing Co.; reprinted by permission.)

rate throughout the day. Based upon this information, it would be appropriate to select an event-recording procedure to record the frequency of occurrence of the target behavior.

Example 2 A trainer wants to record a student's attention-to-task behavior. Although the student has a good work record, co-workers have recently indicated that his work is too slow. Furthermore, the trainer wishes to observe the student at varying times during the day to determine if he or she responds differentially at various times of day. First, a time measurement is clearly needed. Second, attending behavior is by nature continuous and occurs at a high frequency. Third, since several observational sessions will be conducted, a time sampling recording procedure is most appropriate.

Specific information on how to utilize these procedures is provided in the following sections.

Event Recording

This frequently used recording procedure provides unbiased estimates of target behaviors and has been recommended as yielding the most accurate count of discrete events (Repp, Roberts, Slack, Repp, & Berkler, 1976). Event recording, which is used when time is not critical, involves tallying the number of times a target behavior did or did not occur in a given observation period. A counting device, such as a wrist golf counter, is often used. However, Menchetti et al. (1981) pointed out that since employers may be resistant to the use of wrist counters in competitive work environments, service providers should assess consumer acceptability of observation and recording procedures prior to their implementation.

Rusch, Weithers, Menchetti, and Schutz (1980) investigated the effectiveness of a program involving co-workers as change agents to decrease the number of topic repetitions made by a mentally retarded employee during breaks. Training consisted of preinstruction and instructional feedback. Co-workers were instructed to provide feedback to the target employee when he repeated topics; in addition, trainers also delivered feedback. Two dependent measures and one independent measure were collected. The dependent measures were the number of topic repeats and the total number of topics. The independent measure consisted of staff feedback representing the number of times a trainer or co-worker expressed that he repeated a topic. These variables were recorded during 30-minute lunch and dinner meals.

Data indicated that the program effectively reduced the number of topics; however, co-workers were unable to modify the employee's behavior without trainer assistance. Despite direct observational measures indicating decreased frequency of topic repetitions, co-workers reported that the subject's number of repetitions remained the same. Several reasons were suggested for this discrepancy. First, the trainers and co-workers may not have been measuring the exact same behavior. Second, the co-workers may have been influenced by the number of topic repetitions made throughout the day rather than those heard during meal times. Third, the co-workers may have feared retaliation by supervisors, who were very interested in the program's results, and thus waited for the last day to give their honest opinions; due to summer lay-offs, supervisor feedback could not be obtained. Nevertheless, the effectiveness of the intervention was verified by the decreased number of topic repeats, without a decrease in the total number of topics contributed to conversation during lunch and dinner periods.

Chadsey-Rusch, Karlan, Riva, and Rusch (1984) also investigated the modification of conversational behavior. Utilizing a social skills training package, these researchers investigated a program designed to increase the question-asking behavior of three mentally retarded kitchen laborers. Additionally, two collateral behaviors—topic initiations (i.e., introducing a new topic) and topic continuations (i.e., continuing or maintaining an established topic)—were measured. Training involved use of a structured conversational format consisting of a rationale, modeling, and feedback. The intervention was delivered in both un-prompted (baseline) and prompted (i.e., a prompt delivered every 2 minutes) conditions. Frequency was coded from 10-minute tape recordings of conversational samples. The re-sults indicated that prompted training increased the frequency of conversational questions for each subject and that question-asking differ-entially influenced topic continuations and topic initiations.

Event-recording procedures have also been used in investigations of the effectiveness of programs designed to increase the compliance of employees in competitive jobs. For exam-ple, Karlan and Rusch (1982) examined the relationship between acknowledgment and compliance in the work performance of two moderately mentally retarded adults receiving postplacement training as kitchen laborers. *Ac-knowledgment* was defined as emitting an ap-propriate verbal response within 3 seconds after a command, whereas *compliance* was identified as the initiation of actions in re-sponse to a request or command. The treatment first consisted of verbal prompts, followed by a contingent token points system. Data were collected on the number of acknowledgments and compliant responses and the number of instructions delivered by the staff; these mea-sures were reported in percentages. The results indicated that while the verbal prompts af-fected compliance positively, they were in-effective at increasing instances of ac-knowledgment. Token points, in turn, were found to increase instances of acknowledgment for two subjects and compliance for one sub-ject. The data suggested a relationship between acknowledgment and compliance, and that in-creases in the former (i.e., acknowledgment) may result in increases in the latter (i.e., com-pliance) (see Figure 2).

Pancsofar, Bates, Krissberg, and Bronkema (1982) also investigated compliance. Their training program, which was designed to in-crease the compliance of a moderately men-tally retarded individual working in a restau-rant, consisted of verbal praise for following

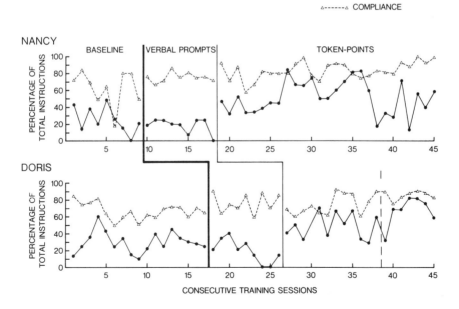

Figure 2. Percentage of total instructions receiving acknowledgment and the percentage of total instruc-tions for which compliance resulted. (From Karlan, G.R., & Rusch, F.R. [1982]. Analyzing the relationship between acknowledgment and compliance in a nonsheltered work setting. *Education and Training of the Mentally Retarded, 17,* 205. Copyright 1982 by Education and Training of the Mentally Retarded; reprinted by permission.)

instructions, ignoring noncompliant behavior, and a tangible reward (certificate awarded at end of day). Data were collected during two work periods. The first period, which was 45 minutes to 1 hour long, involved washing pots and pans. The second work period—1–2 hours in length—involved washing dishes and unloading bus carts. Data were taken on the number of instructions emitted by the supervisor and the number of compliances. Since opportunities to demonstrate the target behavior varied, data were reported in percentages of compliance to instructions. Increased compliance was reported. In addition, generalization across behaviors (washing pots and pans to unloading bus carts and washing dishes) was also noted.

Checklist Recording

This type of recording has also been suggested as an event-based measure (Rusch & Mithaug, 1980). *Checklist recording* involves noting whether or not a particular behavior(s) occurred, prior to or during a given observation period, using yes or no responses. Checklist procedures permit the observer to record the occurrence of a behavior(s) that occurs at a low rate (e.g., once a day), but at a relatively constant time (e.g., when the employee arrives at work). For example, a checklist may be used to record whether a student is appropriately groomed and dressed for work (Rusch & Mithaug, 1980); that is, the observer records on a recording sheet whether the student's hair was combed, clothes were pressed, or hands were clean.

Lignugaris/Kraft, Rule, Salzberg, and Stowitschek (in press) utilized a checklist-recording procedure to obtain information about the pattern and content of social interactions during work and break times in two businesses that refurbished household goods (i.e., thrift shops). To supplement the information obtained via naturalistic observation on the interactions of handicapped and nonhandicapped employees, observers responded to a 35-item checklist that included such questions as whether the interactions observed were work or nonwork related, whether they involved cooperation or criticism, and how many co-workers, if any, were interacting with the target subject at the same time. The data indicated that handicapped and nonhandicapped workers demonstrated similar interaction patterns. For both, most interactions during work periods were work related, primarily consisting of giving assistance and working cooperatively; criticism of co-workers was rarely observed. This field observation checklist supported the findings of the observational data.

Rusch and Mithaug (1980) suggested that responding rates should be calculated when events and time vary. *Rate* is a combined event- and time-based recording procedure determined by dividing an employee's number of completed products or responses by the length of the work period or observation session. Thus, if an employee's productivity is to be estimated, a rate measure would be appropriate. For example, Wehman (1981) wished to increase to a criterion of .42 pots per minute the number of pots a mentally retarded food service worker needed to scrub. Baseline data indicated that the employee scrubbed pots at a rate of .29. A program involving prompts, assistance, and reinforcement eventually increased her productivity rate to criterion.

In summary, event recording is an accurate and relatively simple method of measuring increases or decreases in target behaviors. Event recording provides representative estimates of the effects of interventions upon behavior change and is suitable to use with discrete behaviors that occur at low or medium rates.

Interval Recording

This recording system provides estimates of the occurrence of behavior in time units rather than frequency counts. Instead of providing a tally of discrete behavioral events, interval recording involves recording whether or not the target behavior occurs within a short period of time. Observation sessions are divided into intervals of equal length (e.g., 10 or 15 seconds) during which the target behavior is observed. If the behavior occurs during the interval, occurrence is noted. Even if the response occurs more than once during an interval, it is only scored as occurring once. Although interval recording is not as accurate as event recording, the advantage of this recording system is that it allows an observer to collect a representative estimate of a target behavior in a relatively short period of time. Interval recording has been recommended as the second most accurate method of recording observational data (Repp et al., 1976).

As with event recording, interval recording has wide applicability and provides a time-based measure that requires relatively short blocks of observational time. Using interval recording, Schutz, Rusch, and Lamson (1979) investigated the effectiveness of two procedures designed to decelerate the verbally abusive behavior of three mentally retarded kitchen laborers. Treatment consisted of: 1) a warning plus suspension, and 2) a warning only. Observers recorded the occurrence of verbal abuse in 22 15-minute intervals across a work day. The treatment program resulted in a decrease in the percentage of intervals with verbal abuse incidents for all subjects. Thus, the study suggests the feasibility of using an externally delivered, employer-validated contingency (i.e., suspension) in a placement setting.

In another study, Connis and Rusch (1980) examined the effectiveness of a training program designed to reduce the drooling, noncompliance, and complaining of three mentally retarded food service employees. Target behaviors were observed and recorded during a 1-hour and ½-hour period, respectively. That is, drools and complaints were observed for 60 1-minute intervals, whereas noncompliance was observed for 30 1-minute intervals. Although an interval-recording procedure was used, data were reported in terms of daily frequencies, not percentages of occurrence. The training resulted in a deceleration for all inappropriate responses to near zero levels during training and a 4-week follow-up condition.

Time Sampling

As in interval recording, time-sampling observations are conducted in brief intervals (Kazdin, 1982). However, unlike interval recording, such observations are made several times a day rather than during a single observation period. Time sampling is particularly suitable for multiple or high-frequency behaviors. The percentage of time the target behavior occurs is usually reported. Powell, Martindale, Kulp, Martindale, and Bauman (1977) suggested three methods for time sampling: *whole interval, momentary interval,* and *partial interval.* Selection of the appropriate method is determined by the nature of the behavior and the intent of the investigation.

In *whole interval time sampling,* behavior is recorded as having occurred only if it is observed as occurring for the duration of a whole interval. Subsequently, whole interval recording tends to underestimate the occurrence of behavior and may yield a conservative estimate of a deceleration program. For example, Rusch (1979) investigated the relationship between attending to task and productivity in a nonsheltered vocational setting utilizing whole interval time sampling. Six mentally retarded employees involved in an on-the-job food service training program were randomly assigned to two experimental groups. One group was reinforced for speed of task completion (production), the other for attending to task (attending). *Attending* was defined as task-related physical activity during an entire 30-second interval; *speed of task* (production) was measured as the time it took an employee to clean 15 tables. Results indicated that failure to adequately produce was associated with failure to attend; however, increases in attending behavior were not necessarily occasioned by increased production. Thus, Rusch suggested that, depending on the nature of the target behavior, either dimension may be treated (i.e., attending or producing).

In another study, Rusch et al. (1984) analyzed the extent to which trainer presence may produce reactive effects (i.e., employees work more when trainers observe them). Estimates of continuous time spent working were reported in percentages of whole intervals of working to provide a conservative estimate of time spent working. As expected, results of the study suggested that employees worked more when trainers observed them.

Partial interval time sampling involves recording a behavior(s) as occurring if any part of the response occurs in any part of the interval. Consequently, it has been suggested that partial interval recording provides an overestimation of the occurrence of a behavior (Powell et al., 1977). Thus, this recording system is suitable for behavior that occurs in a continuous stream of events (e.g., social interactions) and does not have an easily discernible beginning and end. Partial interval time sampling is particularly appropriate for multiple behaviors or a single behavior that occurs at a high frequency (e.g., sorting items during assembly). For example, Lignugaris/Kraft et al. (1984) investigated the interaction patterns of handicapped and nonhandicapped persons during work and break periods. Observation codes included verbal and physical initiations to and from the target subjects. Data were recorded on the rate and direction of initiations, the participants involved in the interactions, the extent of active participation, and the general content of interactions. A partial interval time-sampling recording procedure was chosen to obtain maximum information about interactions.

Last, *momentary interval time sampling* requires recording a behavior as occurring if it is observed at the end of a given interval and has been recommended as a more accurate estimate of occurrence than whole interval or partial interval methods. Rusch, Morgan, Martin, Riva, and Agran (1985) examined the effects of self-instructional training on the work performance of two mentally retarded food service employees. Momentary interval time sampling was used to assess the target behavior—time spent working. Additionally, comparative data were collected; an observer looked at the target employee of a co-worker and recorded whether the employee was working at the end of each 10-second interval during a 20-minute session.

Through self-instructional training, subjects were successfully trained to emit specific task-related verbalizations prior to their work performance as a means of effectively increasing time spent working. In another study, Wehman, Hill, and Koehler (1979) selected a momentary interval procedure to assess an employee's percentage of work time on task. The employee's behavior was observed at the end of a 10-second interval until 5 minutes elapsed. Additionally, the frequencies of trainer-delivered verbal, gestural, or physical prompts (event-based procedures) were recorded. Assistance was provided and later faded to increase the percentage (see Figure 3).

In summary, time-sampling and the various interval-recording procedures provide representative time-based estimates of work behavior. They have been found particularly suitable for multiple behaviors or behaviors that occur at a high frequency.

Duration Recording

This type of recording procedure has also been employed in several investigations in the work behavior literature. Duration recording involves the length of time needed to demonstrate a target behavior; it is suitable for discrete behaviors that have distinguishable beginnings and ends. For example, Sowers, Rusch, Connis, and Cummings (1980) trained three moderately mentally retarded employees in time management skills by using time cards—an antecedent cue regulation procedure. The subjects, who were food service employees, were trained to go and return from lunch and breaks on time. Training involved preinstruction, instructional feedback, and the use of a time card with clock faces pictured on one side. Specifically, the subjects were trained to match the times on the card with times on a real clock. To assess treatment effectiveness, the duration of break and lunch periods was measured and the number of minutes the subjects were either early or late was recorded. The differences between time assigned and actual times were subsequently measured. The intervention was found effec-

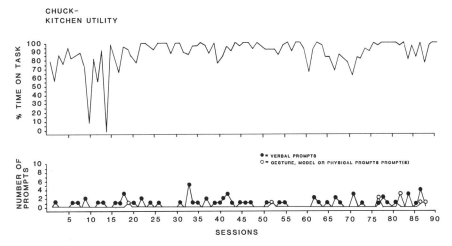

Figure 3. Percent of time on task and degree of prompts required. (From Wehman, P., Hill, J. W., & Koehler, F. [1979]. Placement of developmentally disabled individuals into competitive employment: Three case studies. *Education and Training of the Mentally Retarded, 14,* 271. Copyright 1979 by Education and Training of the Mentally Retarded; reprinted by permission.)

tive for teaching the employees time management skills.

Latency Recording

The use of *latency recording,* which involves measuring the length of time a person takes to demonstrate a work behavior, has been reported in only a few instances in the work behavior literature. In one such study, Crouch, Rusch, and Karlan (1984) examined the effects of correspondence training upon the time three mentally retarded kitchen laborers spent performing work tasks. Training was initiated in response to work supervisors' reports that these individuals did not start or complete assigned tasks at specified times. Hence, target behaviors included workers' start time, task duration, and supervisor ratings. A stopwatch was used to measure start and completion times; in addition, assigned and actual times were compared. Training consisted of: 1) having the employees receive prompts on how to use a wristwatch to complete tasks on time, 2) reinforcing employees for saying when they would start and complete the target task, and 3) reinforcing employees only for positive correspondence between their time statement and task performance, followed by verbal training again. The results indicated that the initial verbal training phase was sufficient to establish

and/or maintain verbal control of the task completion behavior.

Summary

Specifically identified target behaviors may be accurately recorded by use of observational systems including: 1) event recording, 2) interval recording, 3) time sampling, 4) duration recording, and 5) latency recording. Each recording procedure yields information that is either related to a numerical (i.e., event or interval recording, or time sampling) or a temporal dimension of the behavior (i.e., latency or duration recording). The choice of observation system is determined by the nature and frequency of the behavior(s) to be observed.

INTEROBSERVER AGREEMENT

In spite of the availability of various observation and recording systems, observation of behavior is a difficult process (Yarrow & Waxler, 1979). Since observing is a human process and human beings are poor scientific instruments, behavioral observations are frequently inconsistent, uncalibrated or imprecise, and unreliable. Hence, some measure of predictability or reliability is needed. A complete discussion of observer agreement is not presented here since this topic has been thoroughly examined in the observational literature (cf. Johnson & Bolstad, 1973; Kazdin, 1982). Nevertheless, several points relevant to preparing students with handicaps for competitive employment are highlighted.

The intent of collecting agreement data is to ensure that observers are seeing the same behavior(s) at the same time that it occurs, thereby preventing measurement error and the failure to discover important phenomena or functional relations. Agreement does not guarantee accuracy, however. Thus, the former may be achieved but not the latter. To be effective, therefore, agreement measures must be checked for each behavior and within each phase, preferably several times.

Several agreement methods have been reported in the work behavior literature. For example, in their investigation of topic repeats, Rusch et al. (1980) calculated observer agreement by using a *frequency ratio,* (i.e., dividing the smaller frequency total by the larger frequency total). Although this procedure has been criticized for reporting agreement on total number of behaviors rather than particular instances (Kazdin, 1982), it is suitable for frequency counts—the unit of measurement for the above study.

Due to its ease of computation and interpretation, *percentage agreement* represents the most popular method of estimating agreement (Hollenbeck, 1978). Rather than totals, agreement is determined on a response-by-response or point-by-point basis. That is, the number of observer agreements on specific intervals or trials is divided by the total number of agreements and disagreements and multiplied by 100 (Kazdin, 1982). Several of the studies previously cited have utilized a point-by-point agreement method (Connis & Rusch, 1980; Rusch, 1979; Rusch et al., 1984; Sowers et al., 1980).

Although convenient and popular, percentage agreement does not report chance agreement levels and thus may produce biased data (Hartmann, 1977; Hollenbeck, 1978; Johnson & Bolstad, 1973). This problem may be exacerbated when a behavior occurs at a high frequency, since it may be recorded as occurring solely on the basis of chance. *Kappa,* which is

calculated by subtracting expected agreements from observed agreements, has begun to receive some attention in applied research as a method to estimate agreement that corrects for chance (Cohen, 1960). For example, Schutz, Jostes, Rusch, and Lamson (1980) calculated kappas to assess interobserver agreement of observations of sweeping and mopping tasks. The kappas yielded a high agreement score (0.94), corrected for chance.

Despite its growing popularity in applied research, the use of kappa to measure interobserver agreement of work performance is new to the work behavior literature. Hollenbeck (1978) indicated that kappa represents an agreement statistic of choice to handle chance agreement. Thus, kappa corrects for chance based on the frequency of occurrence and nonoccurrence intervals. Kappa ranges from -1.00 to $+1.00$. If observers agree solely on the basis of chance (i.e., observational judgments are random), kappa equals 0.00. If agreement surpasses chance, kappa will exceed 0 and approach a maximum of $+1.00$ (Kazdin, 1982). Data in the Schutz et al. (1980) investigation reported acceptable agreement measures corrected for chance.

Kazdin (1982) noted that low agreement scores (i.e., lower than the conventional 80% criterion) are not necessarily unacceptable if potential biases have been accounted for and identified, and if the conditions under which they were obtained minimize sources of bias and artifact. Kazdin indicated that estimates of agreement should include information on how the estimate was obtained and under what conditions. By providing an estimate of agreement that corrects for chance, kappa addresses potential biases resulting from chance. Further use of kappa is encouraged in the employment education literature.

Summary

Effective preparation of students with handicaps for competitive employment requires reliable measurement procedures to ensure that relationships between interventions and behavioral outcomes can be understood and accepted with some degree of confidence. In this brief overview several methods of estimating agreement are suggested and the advantages and limitations associated with each are identified.

SUMMARY

This chapter focuses on several observation and recording systems found useful in the process of preparing students with handicaps for competitive employment. Specifically, the following observational recording systems are examined: 1) event recording, 2) interval recording, 3) time sampling, 4) latency recording, and 5) duration recording. In addition, four decision-making steps are outlined as a means of arriving at the most appropriate recording system.

REFERENCES

Alberto, P. A., & Troutman, A. C. (1982). *Applied behavior analysis for teachers*. Columbus, OH: Charles E. Merrill.

Bernstein, G. S., & Ziarnik, J. P. (1984). *The behavior management observation system*. Manuscript submitted for publication.

Cairns, R. B., & Green, J. A. (1979). How to assess personality and social patterns: Observations or ratings? In R.B. Cairns (Ed.), *The analysis of social interactions: Methods, issues, and illustrations* (pp. 209–226). Hillsdale, NJ: Lawrence Erlbaum Associates.

Chadsey-Rusch, J. C. Karlan, G. R., Riva, M. T., & Rusch, F. R. (1984). Teaching mentally retarded adults conversational skills in employment settings. *Mental Retardation, 22,* 218–225.

Cohen, J. (1960). A coefficient of agreement for nominal scales. *Educational and Psychological Measurement, 20,* 37–46.

Connis, R. T., & Rusch, F. R. (1980). Programming maintenance through sequential-withdrawal of social contingencies. *Behavior Research of Severe Developmental Disabilities, 1,* 249–260.

Crouch, K. P., Rusch, F. R., & Karlan, G. R. (1984). Utilizing the correspondence training paradigm to enhance productivity in an employment setting. *Education and Training of the Mentally Retarded, 19,* 268–275.

Hartmann, D. P. (1977). Consideration in the choice of interobserver reliability estimates. *Journal of Applied Behavior Analysis, 10,* 103–116.

Hartmann, D. P., & Wood, D. D. (1982). Observational methods. In A. S. Bellack, M. Hersen, & A. E. Kazdin (Eds.), *International handbook of behavior modification and therapy* (pp. 109–138). New York: Plenum.

Hollenbeck, A. R. (1978). Problems of reliability in observational research. In G. P. Sackett (Ed.), *Observing behavior* (Vol. 2, pp. 79–98). Baltimore: University Park Press.

Johnson, S. M., & Bolstad, O. D. (1973). Methodological issues in naturalistic observations: Some problems and solutions for field research. In L. A. Hamerlynck, L. C. Handy, & E. J. Mash (Eds.), *Behavior change: Methodology, concepts, and practice* (pp. 7–67). Champaign, IL: Research Press.

Karlan, G. R., & Rusch, F. R. (1982). Analyzing the relationship between acknowledgement and compliance in a non-sheltered work setting. *Education and Training for the Mentally Retarded, 17,* 202–208.

Kazdin, A. E. (1982). *Single-case research designs*. New York: Oxford University Press.

Lignugaris/Kraft, B., Rule, S., Salzberg, C. L., & Stowitschek, J. J. (in press). A descriptive analysis of social interpersonal skills among handicapped and non-

handicapped adults in an employment setting. *Journal of Employment Counseling*.

Menchetti, B. M., Rusch, F. R., & Lamson, D. S. (1981). Social validation of behavioral training techniques: Assessing the normalizing qualities of competitive employment training procedures. *Journal of The Association for the Severely Handicapped, 6,* 6–16.

Pancsofar, E., Bates, P., Krissberg, H., & Bronkema, J. (1982). Increasing the compliance of a moderately retarded worker to supervisor's instructions in a restaurant setting. *Illinois Council for Exceptional Children Quarterly, 31,* 19–25.

Powell, J., Martindale, B., Kulp, S., Martindale, A., & Bauman, R. (1977). Taking a closer look: Time sampling and measurement error. *Journal of Applied Behavior Analysis, 10,* 325–332.

Repp, A. C., Roberts, D. M., Slack, D. J., Repp, C. F., & Berkler, M. S. (1976). A comparison of frequency, internal, and time-sampling methods of data collection. *Journal of Applied Behavior Analysis, 9,* 501–508.

Rusch, F. R. (1979). A functional analysis of the relationship between attending to task production in an applied restaurant setting. *Journal of Special Education, 13,* 399–411.

Rusch, F. R., Menchetti, B. M., Crouch, K. P., Riva, M., Morgan, T., & Agran, M. (1984). Competitive employment: Assessing employee reactivity to naturalistic observation. *Applied Research in Mental Retardation, 5,* 339–351.

Rusch, F. R., & Mithaug, D. E. (1980). *Vocational training for mentally retarded adults: A behavior analytic approach*. Champaign, IL: Research Press.

Rusch, F. R., Morgan, T., Martin, J. E., Riva, M., & Agran, M. (1985). Competitive employment: Teaching mentally retarded employees self-instructional strategies. *Applied Research in Mental Retardation, 6,* 389–407.

Rucsh, F. R., Weithers, J. A., Menchetti, B. M., & Schutz, R. P. (1980). Social validation of a program to reduce topic repetition in a non-sheltered setting. *Education and Training of the Mentally Retarded, 15,* 208–215.

Schutz, R. P., Jostes, K., Rusch, F. R., & Lamson, D. (1980). The contingent use of pre-instruction and social validation in the acquisition, generalization, and maintenance of sweeping and mopping responses. *Education and Training of the Mentally Retarded, 15,* 306–311.

Schutz, R. P., Rusch, F. R., & Lamson, D. S. (1979). Evaluation of an employer's procedure to eliminate unacceptable behavior on the job. *Community Service Forum, 1,* 4–5.

Sowers, J. A., Rusch, F. R., Connis, R. T., & Cummings,

L. E. (1980). Teaching mentally retarded adults to time-manage in a vocational setting. *Journal of Applied Behavior Analysis, 13,* 119–128.

Wehman, P. (1981). *Competitive employment: New horizons for severely disabled individuals.* Baltimore: Paul H. Brookes.

Wehman, P. H., Hill, J. W., & Koehler, F. (1979). Placement of developmentally disabled individuals into competitive employment: Three case studies. *Education and Training of the Mentally Retarded, 14,* 269–276.

White, D. M., & Rusch, F. R. (1983). Social validation in competitve employment: Evaluating work performance. *Applied Research in Mental Retardation, 4,* 343–354.

Yarrow, M. R., & Waxler, C. Z. (1979). Observing interaction: A confrontation with methodology. In R. B. Cairns (Ed.), *The analysis of social interactions: Methods, issues, and illustrations* (pp. 37–65). Hillsdale, NJ: Lawrence Erlbaum Associates.

Chapter 12

Analysis of Work Behavior

Martin Agran

THIS CHAPTER EXAMINES analytic procedures (i.e., experimental designs) to assess functional relationships between interventions and observed behaviors. Given this information, the effectiveness of interventions can be ascertained and decision making facilitated. The following analytic procedures are examined: 1) reversal or ABAB design, 2) multiple-baseline designs, 3) changing-criterion design, and 4) simultaneous-treatment designs. Specifically, the suitability of these designs to assess treatment and outcome relationships in competitve work environments is examined. Additionally, a withdrawal strategy to assess generalization is discussed.

INTRODUCTION TO ANALYSIS

To assess the effectiveness of an intervention, it is essential that analytic procedures are used that can rule out confounding variables and can demonstrate, instead, a functional relationship between the intervention and the desired behavior change. The purpose of this chapter is to examine procedures that can be used to apply experimental control so that relationships between dependent variables (behaviors that will be measured) and independent variables (interventions) can be ascertained. These procedures include experimental designs that include repeated measures across experimental conditions. Suggestions on selecting procedures appropriate for investigations in competitive work environments are provided.

ANALYTIC PROCEDURES INCORPORATING REPEATED MEASURES EXPERIMENTAL DESIGNS

Analytic procedures incorporating repeated measures report repeated observations of performance across different experimental conditions (Kazdin, 1982). Thereby, changes in dependent variables or target behaviors can be related to the manipulations of the independent variable or intervention across different experimental conditions. The function of the analytic procedure or design is to demonstrate that a functional relationship exists between the observed behavior change and the intervention so that confounding variables (e.g., practice effect, history) not under the control of the teacher can be ruled out as not contributing to the change. This information is obtained via continuous assessment of the student's performance of the target behavior in a baseline phase, then monitored as the intervention is applied. In baseline, data are collected to illustrate the student's present level of performance and the performance pattern if the intervention were not to be provided. As the intervention is applied, its effects on the target behavior are monitored. Collected data indicate the direction and extent of influence the intervention has on work performance.

The following designs are examined: 1) a reversal or ABAB design, 2) the multiple-baseline design, 3) the changing-criterion design, and 4) the simultaneous-treatment design. The advantages and limitations of each design are examined.

Reversal or ABAB Design

A reversal or ABAB design allows for repeated observations of a student's performance across experimental conditions. The reversal design allows the teacher to analyze the difference in a student's work performance in two baseline conditions, before and after an intervention is applied. Intervention effects are clear if performance increases or decreases from baseline when the intervention is applied, reverts back to baseline level when the intervention is withdrawn, then changes again as the intervention is reinstated (Kazdin, 1982).

A reversal design represents a powerful analytic procedure for analyzing functional relationships. For example, Kazdin and Polster (1973) investigated the effectiveness of a token economy system in increasing and maintaining the social interactions of two mildly mentally retarded sheltered workshop employees. An ABAB design was employed to assess the effects of the token economy on increasing the frequency of peer social interactions made during breaks from work. The intervention consisted of tokens and praise. Whenever the two workers' self-reports concerning social interactions (i.e., verbal interactions with another co-worker) were verified by a supervisor, they were given a token; conversely, they were fined when their self-reports were not verified. The intervention was subsequently withdrawn in the second baseline, then reinstated. Significant differences between conditions were demonstrated.

Although an ABAB design provides strong evidence of functional relationships, there are several problems associated with it that have made it unsuitable for investigations to prepare students for competitive employment. Among the problems associated with reversal designs include concerns regarding the withdrawal of interventions, irreversibility of the response, and staff resistance (Hersen & Barlow, 1976). The design requires that the behaviors modified have to make rapid reversals. If the response fails to return to baseline levels, it is difficult to draw conclusions about the effectiveness of the intervention. Indeed, it is often

unlikely that, after bringing the performance of a target work behavior to criterion, it will return to a baseline level. Furthermore, a withdrawal of treatment may result in a student's regression to an undesirable or maladaptive performance level. Application of the design dictates that, despite identified needs, a student must stay in baseline at least two times. This may prolong the student's performance of inappropriate behavior(s) in his or her work setting and may debilitate his or her teacher's efforts to facilitate the acceptance of supervisors and co-workers. It is thus likely such a design will receive staff resistance.

Despite its limitations, a reversal design represents a methodologically powerful experimental tool (Kazdin, 1982). Subsequently, several recommendations have been made to alleviate the difficulties associated with the design. First, it has been suggested that a reversal design include a short second baseline. A brief reversal (e.g., 1 or 2 days) permits a teacher to assess the effects of an intervention using a return-to-baseline phase, without keeping a student in an extended baseline condition. As Kazdin notes, this may partially alleviate concerns about temporarily suspending an intervention. Needless to say, a brief reversal is suitable only when the target behavior can make a rapid reversal. Additionally, a teacher may be reluctant to withdraw an intervention, even though the return to baseline is quite brief. Second, combining an ABAB design with another analytic procedure has been suggested. For example, Chadsey-Rusch, Karlan, Riva, and Rusch (1984) combined a multiple-baseline design with a reversal component to contrast the effects of prompted and unprompted training on conversation behavior and prompted training and baseline measures for one subject; this reversal was not replicated for the other subjects. If a functional relationship between an intervention and a target behavior is not clear, a combined design may be helpful in demonstrating such a relationship. Inclusion of a reversal phase resulting in a reversion of the behavior to a baseline level may provide evidence that a functional relationship exists, despite data that suggest otherwise. Needless to say, a decision to include a reversal phase with another analytic procedure is predicated on the belief that the advantages for the student derived from demonstrating that a functional relationship exists outweigh the disadvantages associated with withdrawing the intervention. Despite such recommendations, the necessity of withdrawing treatment and the unlikelihood that the target behavior will revert back to baseline levels, as well as potential staff resistance, have precluded the use of the design in the preparation of persons with handicaps for competitive employment.

Multiple-Baseline Designs

A multiple-baseline design permits analysis of the effects of the intervention on more than one behavior, person, or situation. Unlike the reversal or ABAB design, a return to baseline is not needed; consequently, a multiple-baseline design does not have associated problems with staff resistance regarding the withdrawal of the intervention. Instead, experimental control is demonstrated when behavior changes are evidenced immediately after an intervention is applied to different behaviors at different points in time. Multiple-baseline designs represent the most frequently used analytic procedure in the work behavior literature.

In multiple-baseline designs, the intervention is introduced in two or more baselines (i.e., behaviors, persons, or settings) at different points in time. If baseline levels change when the intervention is applied, these effects are attributed to the intervention. The baselines that have not yet been treated serve as control conditions. If effects can be demonstrated each time the intervention is applied, without contemporaneous changes in other baselines, such confounding factors as history and maturation can be ruled out. For example, Cuvo, Leaf, and Borakove (1978) trained six moderately mentally retarded students in entry-level janitorial skills; in all, 181 component responses were trained. A multiple-baseline design across subjects and responses was employed. The training was introduced sequentially across subjects and tasks. The results indicated that all students

acquired, after an average of approximately 2.67 hours of training, all of the 181 component responses. The design demonstrated that skill performance did not improve until the intervention was initiated for each student and subtask. Likewise, Connis (1979) used a multiple-baseline design across subjects ($N = 4$) to increase the task-change behaviors of four moderately mentally retarded food service employees. The subjects were trained to refer to a picture schedule, look at the appropriate photo in sequence, mark an X on a square of paper beneath the photo, and begin the task represented on the photo within a 40-second time limit. The combined use of the picture schedule and self-recording procedure resulted in the acquisition of independent task-change behaviors for all subjects. These changes occurred directly after the introduction of the intervention.

Although multiple-baseline designs are frequently used, several problems have been associated with their use. The sequential introduction of the intervention across subjects or responses necessitates that one or more baselines are extended, thus resulting in an extended no-treatment condition (Noonan & Bickel, 1981). Cuvo (1979) has suggested that, although the longer the baseline the stronger the effect of the demonstration, a minimum of only two baseline points is required, assuming the data are stable. Baseline conditions can thus be shortened. Another potential problem cited is that extended baselines alone, independent of the effects of the intervention, may provide students with increased opportunities to perform the response and may result in behavior change. Likewise, extended baselines may be punishing to students and debilitate their performance of desired behaviors. To counter this factor, probe assessments of baseline data can be collected; that is, data can be collected once every 2–3 days, rather than on a daily basis. Furthermore, the intervention may differentially affect baselines. These inconsistent effects will detract from the overall power of the intervention. The incorporation of another design, along with the multiple-baseline, has been suggested as a way to reduce such ambiguity and clarify conclusions about the intervention. For example, Chadsey-Rusch et al. (1984) included a reversal component for one subject to contrast training conditions. Also, Schutz, Rusch, and Lamson (1979) combined a multiple-baseline design across subjects with a simultaneous-treatment component to investigate the effectiveness of two procedures to decelerate the verbally abusive behavior of three moderately mentally retarded kitchen laborers. The intervention consisted of a warning plus suspension, and a warning only. The treatment procedure resulted in a deceleration of aggressive behavior for all subjects. The multiple-baseline design demonstrated that verbally abusive behavior decreased when the intervention was applied. The simultaneous-treatment component compared the effect of the warning plus suspension, and a warning only.

Last, experimental control is demonstrated in a multiple-baseline design when behavior change is observed only when an intervention is introduced. If changes in other baselines occur, clear conclusions about functional relationships cannot be drawn. Consequently, the interdependence of baselines may represent a potential problem in a multiple-baseline design. However, if covariation exists, this may not necessarily suggest that intervention effects are not clear. As Kazdin (1982) notes, dramatic treatment effects for other baselines may present clear evidence of the strength of the intervention, regardless of covarying data. For example, Agran, Salzberg, and Stowitschek (1985) utilized a multiple-baseline design across persons and behaviors to examine the effects of a self-instructional training package in facilitating the acquisition and generalization of two topographically similar social behaviors, i.e., self-initiated contacts with a work supervisor when an employee runs out of work materials, and self-initiated contacts when an employee needs assistance (e.g., has wrong-sized part). Three mentally retarded and two behaviorally handicapped employees of a sheltered workshop participated in the investigation. The training resulted in rapid and dramatic gains in the first target behavior for all

participants. A within-subject replication was conducted to assess the effects of the training package on producing changes in a second target behavior for three participants. For two of the three participants, increases in the first target behavior did not produce changes in the second behavior; thus, experimental control was demonstrated. For the third participant, though, increases in the first target behavior resulted in corresponding increases in the second behavior. If this generalized effect were replicated across the other participants, conclusions about the effectiveness of the intervention would be difficult to draw. However, since this effect was observed only for one participant, and the data revealed dramatic and rapid behavior changes for all participants, the effectiveness of the intervention was clearly demonstrated.

Changing-Criterion Design

The changing-criterion design has been useful in examinations in the work behavior literature. This design involves the use of several subphases (i.e., at least two replications). Each subphase requires that the student achieve successive approximations of the target behavior. Experimental control is demonstrated when the student meets or surpasses the criterion set for each subphase. The design is particularly appropriate for a shaping procedure. There is no need to withhold (as in the multiple-baseline design) or to withdraw (as in the reversal design) the intervention.

A changing-criterion design is appropriate for behaviors that can show stepwise increases. Subsequently, it is useful for investigations examining acceleration problems, e.g., increasing work productivity. For example, Davis, Bates, and Cuvo (1983) investigated the effects of a changing-criterion design on increasing the work rate of a kitchen laborer. The employee was responsible for tray stripping, waste disposal, stacking dishes, and soaking silverware. Three criterion changes were included in the design. The results indicated that the employee increased her work rate from below standard to within an acceptable range. Likewise, Wehman (1981) reported that changing-criterion designs were used to increase the productivity of several employees associated with Project Employability. In one example, the compliance of one employee was increased from a baseline rate of 360 minutes a day to 475 minutes. For two other employees, increases in wrapping silverware and scrubbing pots were achieved via the application of the design.

When using a changing-criterion design, it is essential that baseline and intervention phases be sufficiently long to demonstrate changes. Also, changes need to be large enough so that a relationship can be seen, but not so large that the student is unable to achieve it. If the correspondence between the criterion and the observed performance is not clear, the effects of the intervention are difficult to evaluate. In all, the changing-criterion design represents a methodologically sound and useful procedure.

Simultaneous-Treatment Design

Although the simultaneous-treatment design has rarely been used in work behavior investigations, it represents a potentially effective procedure to compare the effectiveness of two or more different interventions. In a simultaneous-treatment design, the same behavior is exposed to different interventions under different stimulus conditions (e.g., two times per day) in the same phase; the conditions are presented an equal number of times. Then, the effects of the different interventions are compared. If one intervention is more effective than the other, a last phase consisting of only one intervention is introduced. This intervention is administered across all stimulus conditions. An advantage of this design is that, unlike reversal or multiple-baseline designs, a withdrawal or suspension of treatment is not required. Additionally, the design requires less time than reversal or multiple-baseline designs. Unlike these designs, baseline trends do not present a problem in a simultaneous-treatment design as long as differential effects result from the interventions.

Simultaneous-treatment designs can be employed as a single analytic procedure or as a combined design to enhance the clarity of a demonstrated functional relationship. For example, Schutz et al. (1979) included a simultaneous-treatment component in a multiple-baseline design to assess the effects of a warning only to a warning plus suspension procedure in reducing the verbal abuse of a food service employee. The simultaneous-treatment design demonstrated that the warning alone procedure was not effective in reducing verbal abuse incidents, whereas the warning plus suspension was.

As with the other designs, the simultaneous-treatment design has several problems associated with it. First, the behavior examined must be susceptible to rapid changes. That is, if a given target behavior is not amenable to rapid change, utilization of this design may not be appropriate. Second, there may be potential problems with carryover effects or multiple-treatment interference. If there is a possibility that one intervention may be influenced by another, the effects of one or the other intervention cannot be clearly assessed. As Kazdin (1982) suggests, efforts need to be made to ensure that interventions will be discriminable to students so they know when each is in effect. Third, it is essential that interventions are balanced across stimulus conditions. Failure to do so beclouds conclusions about functional relationships because intervention effects may be confused with stimulus conditions. Despite these limitations, the design represents a potentially powerful procedure to demonstrate the effectiveness of one intervention over another, and further use in competitive work environments is encouraged.

ANALYTIC PROCEDURES TO ASSESS GENERALIZATION

Despite the effectiveness of systematic training programs in training persons with mental retardation to acquire critical skills needed for employment success, many mentally retarded employees have been unable to generalize these newly acquired skills across tasks, settings, persons, and time (Martin & Agran, in press). Procedures are needed to ensure that acquired skills extend and maintain beyond termination of training (Rusch & Schutz, 1981).

Rusch and Schutz (1981) reported that the vocational habilitation research has primarily looked at task-related skill acquisition and indicated that, despite the generally acknowledged importance of maintenance and generalization, these issues have received little attention in the work of behavior literature. As Baer, Wolf, and Risley (1968) suggested, response maintenance and generalization must be included in the teaching process. Clearly, research needs to more stringently address the long-term behavior through maintenance and generalization of work behavior. This section describes withdrawal design methodology.

Withdrawal Designs

Rusch and Kazdin (1981) suggested three designs for withdrawing training components to facilitate and assess generalization: 1) sequential withdrawal, 2) partial withdrawal, and 3) partial-sequential withdrawal. In a sequential withdrawal design, one training component, then another, are withdrawn in consecutive experimental phases. If, at any time, the performance level decreases to below acceptable levels, a component (or all components) can be replaced; when the behavior is built back to its previous level, a different order of withdrawal can be instigated. This strategy was employed by Connis and Rusch (1980) to assess the maintenance of reduced levels of three inappropriate behaviors. In a multiple-baseline design across subjects and behaviors, the effects of training on reducing the drooling, noncompliance, and complaining of three mentally retarded food service employees were investigated. Training consisted of praise, instructions, and reprimands. The training resulted in a deceleration of all inappropriate responses to near zero levels during training and a 4-week follow-up condition. To assess maintenance, treatment components were sequentially withdrawn. This procedure provided a preview of which components were critical to response durability.

In a partial withdrawal design, either a single component, several, or all components of an intervention are withdrawn from one of the baselines of a multiple-baseline design. This withdrawal strategy is a means of determining what can happen if similar withdrawals are replicated across the remaining baselines. The results of an initial partial withdrawal provides information in determining if the withdrawal of other components should be advanced across the same baseline, or replicated across the other baselines. Once again, if the withdrawal results in a loss of behavior, the components can be replaced; following reinstatement, a different withdrawal order may be tried across the same or another baseline. For example, Vogelsberg and Rusch (1979) trained three students with severe handicaps to cross intersections. The intervention consisted of instructions, corrective feedback, and selective repeated practice of approaching, looking, stepping, and walking skills. After the students achieved criteria, a partial withdrawal was conducted. Feedback was withdrawn for one student as an intervention component. This resulted in a decrease in looking for cars in each of four directions. This provided a preview of what might happen if this withdrawal was replicated across the other students. Behavioral rehearsal and modeling facilitated the reacquisition of the skill for the student.

Last, in a partial-sequential withdrawal, the two previously described strategies are combined. First, all or part of an intervention is withdrawn from one baseline of a multiple-baseline design. Then, if the behavior maintains, the withdrawal may be advanced to include other components, or replicated across other baselines. However, if the behavior does not maintain, the withdrawn components may be reintroduced simultaneously with the withdrawal of the same or different components across one or more of the other baselines.

As Martin and Agran (in press) noted, the successful implementation of withdrawal methodology is dependent upon the teacher's responsiveness to the presence or absence of changes in the dependent measure. In effect, this methodology advocates the systematic withdrawal of components to decrease the probability of students discriminating the absence of training components, in other words, to facilitate maintenance. In total, these designs may facilitate the generalization of desired behavior change without prolonged loss of desired behavior (Kazdin, 1982).

Data Analysis

Analytic procedures incorporating repeated measures (i.e., single-subject research) examine changes in dependent variables or target behaviors over time. Consequently, such analytic procedures control for variance by experimental design rather than by relying on statistical procedures (Kratochwill, 1978). Although statistical analysis may be used, visual inspection of graphic displays is often the most effective means of determining the effects of an intervention (Parsonson & Baer, 1978). Such visual examination of graphed data provides the basis for judgment about reliability or consistency of intervention effects (Kazdin, 1982).

To enhance accurate and efficient data display, the following criteria are recommended: 1) provision of a concise title describing the nature and purpose of the intervention, 2) explicit captions establishing the identity and meaning of the variables (dependent and independent), and 3) appropriate scale units on the ordinate and abscissa scales (Jones, Vaught, & Weinrott, 1977). With this information, clear and concise summaries of data can be displayed.

To determine the magnitude of change resulting from an intervention, visual examinations of graphic displays to identify changes in *level* and/or *trend* are conducted. *Changes in*

level refer to a shift or discontinuity of performance from the end of one phase (or experimental condition) to the beginning of a next phase (or experimental condition) (Kazdin, 1982). Level changes may represent changes in which the target response either increases (i.e., step-up) or decreases (i.e., step-down) after the introduction of an intervention (Rusch & Mithaug, 1980). Figures 1 and 2 show such changes. Note the increase in number of responses in Figure 1 and the decrease in Figure 2.

Changes in trend refer to changes in data (i.e, either increases or decreases) systematically over time. Figure 3 displays an increase trend. Inspection of these data suggests a change in performance from a baseline phase (Condition A) to an intervention phase (Condition B). Figure 4 displays a decrease trend. Note that introduction of the intervention produced a decrease in performance.

Inspection of changes in level or trend provides a useful analytic procedure to assess intervention effects. By comparing changes in performance levels across experimental conditions, intervention effects can be assessed. Changes in level and/or steps after an intervention is introduced or modified (e.g., a component is added to or withdrawn from a training package) yield clear information about the strength of an intervention. For example, performance levels that appear to be unchanged across conditions either in level or trend clearly suggest that the intervention is not producing desired behavior changes, as in Figure 5. However, definite changes in performance in desired direction (i.e., increase or decrease), as in Figures 6 and 7, strongly demonstrate inter-

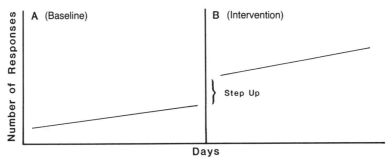

Figure 1.   Step-up level change. (From Rusch, F R., & Mithaug, D. E. [1980]. *Vocational training for mentally retarded adults*, p. 61. Champaign, IL: Research Press; reprinted by permission.)

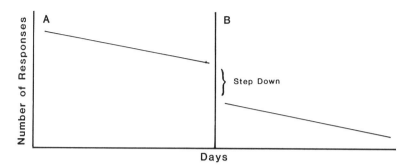

Figure 2.   Step-down level change. (From Rusch, F R., & Mithaug, D. E. [1980]. *Vocational training for mentally retarded adults,* p.61. Champaign, IL: Research Press; reprinted by permission.)

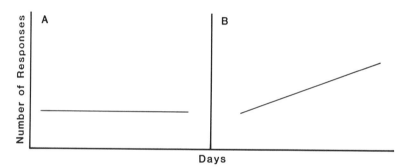

Figure 3.   Change in trend (increase). (From Rusch, F R., & Mithaug, D. E. [1980]. *Vocational training for mentally retarded adults,* p.59. Champaign, IL: Research Press; reprinted by permission.)

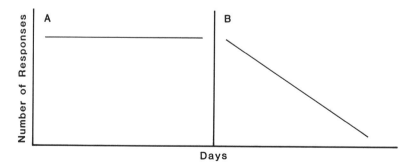

Figure 4.   Change in trend (decrease). (From Rusch, F R., & Mithaug, D. E. [1980]. *Vocational training for mentally retarded adults,* p.59. Champaign, IL: Research Press; reprinted by permission.)

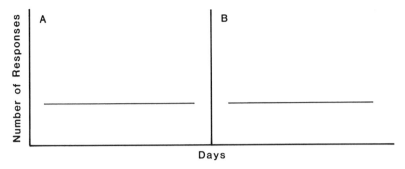

Figure 5. No trend change.

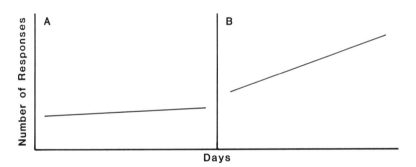

Figure 6. Changes in level and trends (increase). (From Rusch, F R., & Mithaug, D. E. [1980]. *Vocational training for mentally retarded adults,* p.63. Champaign, IL: Research Press; reprinted by permission.)

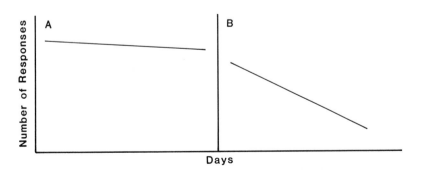

Figure 7. Changes in level and trends (decrease). (From Rusch, F R., & Mithaug, D. E. [1980]. *Vocational training for mentally retarded adults,* p.63. Champaign, IL: Research Press; reprinted by permission.)

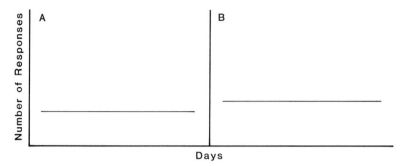

Figure 8.   Slight change in level.

vention effects. Figure 6 illustrates a step-up change in level and a change (i.e., increase) in trend, and Figure 7 illustrates a step-down change in level and a change (i.e., decrease) in trend.

Generally, a clear demonstration of intervention effects is apparent under the following conditions: 1) dramatic level changes, 2) steep slopes of trend changes, and 3) a combination of both. Such patterns present convincing information about the efficacy of the intervention in producing desired behavior changes. Less convincing demonstrations of intervention effects include slight changes in level or trend, or changes in one variable (either level or trend) without changes in the other. Note Figure 8 illustrates a slight change in level (without a change in trend), and Figure 9 illustrates changes in level and trend, but both changes are slight.

In summarizing, analysis of changes in level and/or trend present clear demonstrations of intervention effects and suggest the efficiency

of visual analyses to determine the strength and consistency of intervention effects.

SIMPLIFIED TIME SERIES ANALYSES FOR EVALUATING INTERVENTION EFFECTS

Analytic procedures incorporating repeated measures assess changes in target behaviors over time. Consequently, biases resulting from serial dependency may occur. Evaluations of intervention effects (particularly changes in level) may be obfuscated by trends or systematic departures from random variation (Tryon, 1982). That is, data may be correlated over time. These data may suggest a trend and thus delimit the strength of an intervention.

To extract serial dependency from data to evaluate treatment effects, time series analysis procedures are used. The procedure most often recommended is one that involves a complex mathematical model (e.g., autoregressive integrated moving average) (Glass, Willson, &

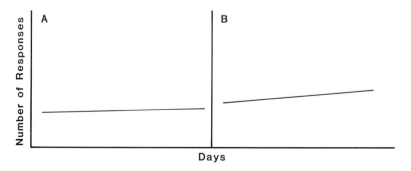

Figure 9.   Slight change in level and trend.

Gottman, 1975), using a computer program. Such a procedure requires many data points (i.e., at least 50–100 data points per experimental phase), with less confidence on the model if fewer data points are used (Hartmann, et al., 1980).

Tryon (1982) has recommended a simple method of time series analyses to evaluate intervention effects that can be used with small data sets (as few as 8 points per phase). This method provides a useful analytic procedure to assess intervention effects on work behavior. The method produces a C statistic, which evaluates variability in successive data points relative to changes in trend across experimental conditions. As Tryon indicated, the C statistic evaluates how large squared deviations from the mean are relative to the sum of the squared consecutive differences.

The C statistic represents a simple method that can be used with small data sets and can be easily calculated by hand. The C statistic involves creating a comparison series, then testing for a trend. Two methods can be used. The first and more powerful involves fitting a regression line to the data in a prior phase, then subtracting the trend line values from the data points in a previous phase to data in a subsequent phase. The C statistic is then applied to test for any trends. The second method involves subtracting corresponding baseline points from intervention points, then testing for any trends using the C statistic as in the first method. Likewise, data within a phase can be analyzed.

Simplified time series analyses were conducted in the Agran et al. (1985) investigation to determine if there were statistically significant trends in the baseline data prior to the introduction of the intervention. These analyses were conducted to assist the visual analysis of the data. Table 1 displays baseline performance data for one participant. Baseline points were first subtracted consecutively from each other (i.e., first baseline point from the second baseline point, etc.). The differences were then squared and totaled. Next, differences between baseline points and the mean were calculated. These differences were squared, totaled, then

Table 1. Calculation of the C statistic

$\times$ (% of appropriate initiations)	D^2
0	400
20	0
20	400
40	400
20	400
0	400
20	400
0	

$D^2 = 2400$

$2SS(X) = 2800$

$$C = 1 - \frac{2400}{2800} = 0.142$$

$$Sc = \frac{N-2}{(N-1)(N+1)} = \frac{6}{(7)(9)} = 0.308$$

$$Z = \frac{0.142}{0.308} = 0.461, \text{ n.s.}$$

multiplied by 2. The C statistic and its standard error was then calculated, based on the number of data points. Last, the Z statistic was calculated. The value of $Z = 0.461$ indicated the absence of a trend in baseline for this participant.

As Tryon (1982) noted, the C statistic represents a simple yet elegant method to evaluate intervention effects in serially dependent time series data. As such, this statistic serves as an easily calculated method that allows work behavior researchers more confidence in the interventions they implement when trend differences are not readily apparent and/or data are serially dependent. Further use of this statistic supplies service providers with a simple procedure that allows them to credit changes in work behavior to the effects of the interventions implemented, not to existing trends in serially dependent time series data.

SUMMARY

This chapter examines several analytic procedures to examine functional relationships between interventions and desired behavior change. These procedures incorporate repeated measures and include: 1) an ABAB or reversal design, 2) multiple-baseline design, 3) changing-criterion design, and 4) a simultaneous-treatment design. The advantages and limitations of each in regard to investigations in competitive work environments are discussed. Also, a discussion of withdrawal methodology to facilitate the generalization of work behavior over time is presented. Last, several methods to analyze the magnitude of behavior change and to evaluate intervention effects are suggested.

REFERENCES

Agran, M., Salzberg, C. L., & Stowitschek, J. J. (1985). *An analysis of the effects of a self-control training program on the acquisition and generalization of social behaviors in a work setting.* Manuscript submitted for publication.

Baer, D. M., Wolf, M. M., & Risley, T. R. (1968). Some current dimensions of applied behavior analysis. *Journal of Applied Behavior Analysis, 1,* 91–97.

Chadsey-Rusch, J. C., Karlan, G. R., Riva, M. T., & Rusch, F. R. (1984). Teaching mentally retarded adults conversational skills in employment settings. *Mental Retardation, 22,* 218–225.

Connis, R. T. (1979). The effects of sequential pictorial cues, self-recording, and praise on the job task sequencing of retarded adults. *Journal of Applied Behavior Analysis, 12,* 355–361.

Connis, R. T., & Rusch, F. R. (1980). Programming maintenance through sequential-withdrawal of social contingencies. *Behavior Research of Severe Developmental Disabilities, 1,* 249–260.

Cuvo, A. J. (1979). Multiple-baseline design in instructional research: Pitfalls of measurement and procedural advantages. *American Journal of Mental Deficiency, 84,* 219–228.

Cuvo, A. J., Leaf, R. B., & Borakove, L. S. (1978). Teaching janitorial skills to the mentally retarded: Acquisition, generalization, and maintenance. *Journal of Applied Behavior Analysis, 11,* 345–355.

Davis, P., Bates, P., & Cuvo, A. J. (1983). Training a mentally retarded woman to work competitively: Effect of graphic feedback and a changing criterion design. *Education and Training of the Mentally Retarded, 18,* 158–163.

Glass, G. V., Willson, V. I., & Gottman, J. M. (1975). *Design and analysis of time series experiments.* Boulder: Colorado Associated University Press.

Hartmann, D. P., Gottman, J. M., Jones, R. R., Gardner, W., Kazdin, A. E., & Vaught, R. (1980). Interrupted time-series analysis and its application to behavioral data. *Journal of Applied Behavior Analysis, 13,* 543–559.

Hersen, M., & Barlow, D. H. (1976). *Single case experimental designs.* New York: Pergamon Press.

Jones, R. R., Vaught, R. S., & Weinrott, M. (1977). Time-series analysis in operant research. *Journal of Applied Behavior Analysis, 10,* 151–166.

Kazdin, A. E. (1982). *Single-case research designs.* New York: Oxford University Press.

Kazdin, A. E., & Polster, R. (1973). Intermittent token reinforcement and response maintenance in extinction. *Behavior Therapy, 4,* 386–391.

Kratochwill, T. R. (Ed.) (1978). *Single-subject research: Strategies for evaluating change.* New York: Academic Press.

Martin, J. E., & Agran, M. (in press). Factors that impede competitive employment of mentally retarded workers. In J. L. Matson & R. P. Barrett (Eds.), *Advances in developmental disorders.* Greenwich, CT: JAI Press.

Noonan, M. J., & Bickel, W. K. (1981). The ethics of experimental design. *Mental Retardation, 19,* 271–274.

Parsonson, B. S., & Baer, D. M. (1978). The analysis and presentation of graphic data. In T. R. Kratochwill (Ed.), *Single-subject research: Strategies for evaluating change.* New York: Academic Press.

Rusch, F. R., & Kazdin, A. E. (1981). Toward a methodology of withdrawal designs for the assessment of response maintenance. *Journal of Applied Behavior Analysis, 14,* 131–140.

Rusch, F. R., & Mithaug, D. E. (1980). *Vocational training for mentally retarded adults: A behavior analytic approach.* Champaign, IL: Research Press.

Rusch, F. R., & Schutz, R. P. (1981). Vocational and social work behavior research: An evaluative review. In J. L. Matson & J. R. McCartney (Eds.), *Handbook of behavior modification with the mentally retarded.* New York: Plenum.

Schutz, R. P., Rusch, F. R., & Lamson, D. S. (1979). Evaluation of an employer's procedure to eliminate unacceptable behavior on the job. *Community Service Forum, 1,* 4–5.

Tryon, W. W. (1982). A simplified time-series analysis for evaluating treatment interventions. *Journal of Applied Behavior Analysis, 15,* 423–429.

Vogelsberg, T., & Rusch, F. R. (1979). Training severely handicapped students to cross partially controlled intersections. *AAESPH Review, 4,* 264–273.

Wehman, P. (1981). *Competitive employment: New horizons for severely disabled individuals.* Baltimore: Paul H. Brookes.

Chapter 13

Identifying Potential Jobs

James E. Martin

JOB PLACEMENT HAS traditionally been considered the end point of the vocational rehabilitation process (Gannaway & Wattenbarger, 1979; Schutz & Rusch, 1982; Wasil, 1974; Wehman, 1981). As Vandergoot, Jacobsen, and Worrall (1979) indicate:

> Placement is an event and not a process . . . it is the crucial event in the rehabilitation process; it indicates that a client has accepted a job offer that yields appropriate career enhancement opportunities . . . all other rehabilitation activities can be related to it. In this sense, there is a rehabilitation process leading to placement, but not a distinct placement process. (p. 7)

Sheltered workshop-based evaluation, experience, and counseling are services deemed important to facilitate placement (Katz, 1968). In contrast, placement activities are given little emphasis by rehabilitation counselors. Usdane (1976) reports that rehabilitation counselors spend about 7% of their time in actual placement activities; few are trained to work with persons who are mentally retarded, especially those who are moderately and severely disabled (Hill, 1982). The operating practices of many rehabilitation centers reflect this view. Walls, Tseng, and Zarin (1976) indicated that often client cases are closed 30 days after placement into competitive employment, during which time little follow-up is provided. If mentally retarded individuals are placed, they are usually in the mild range.

In the not too distant past, vocational rehabilitation focused primarily upon serving those persons who were physically or mildly mentally handicapped (Whitehead, 1979). In many instances these clients were "work ready" when they were referred to a local rehabilitation facility, as many of them left for competitive employment positions after a few months of entering the workshop (Rusch & Mithaug, 1980). Traditionally, one-to-one or small group counseling sessions combined with "sheltered workshop experiences" were sufficient to achieve competitive employment. However, during the 1960s and 1970s, as moderately and severely mentally retarded individuals were deinstitutionalized and joined those who stayed in their communities, they became involved with community rehabilitation workshops (cf. Bruininks, Meyers, Sigford, & Lakin, 1981; Novak & Heal, 1980). With a changed clientele, the traditional rehabilitation placement model failed (Pomerantz & Marholin, 1977). These new clients did not acquire needed skills through counseling or by just being in a sheltered environment, but rather they required intensive training, coordinated placement efforts, and long-term follow-up to move from a sheltered rehabilitation setting to competitive employment (Rusch & Mithaug, 1980). A different vocational training model was needed—one that could be utilized by the existing adult

Special thanks are extended to James V. Husch, Program Coordinator for the Comprehensive Transition Training Project at the University of Colorado at Colorado Springs, for his suggestions and careful review of this chapter. The preparation of this chapter was in part supported by a Transition Research Grant from the U.S. Department of Education, Office of Special Education and Rehabilitative Services.

service network, and by developing public school programs.

The "survey-train-place-maintain" approach was introduced as a curriculum model for preparing individuals who are moderately and severely mentally retarded for employment (Rusch, 1983). According to this model, placement was no longer considered to be the endpoint of vocational preparation, as retraining and continued follow-up was conceived as needed for an indefinite time after placement (Rusch, 1983). This chapter examines the placement process and related issues. Specifically, nine components of the placement process are presented.

PLACEMENT PROCESS

Job placement is the process of matching an individual's abilities and interests to the requirements of a specific full- or part-time competitive community job. In order to avoid the criticism of not including steps to follow to maintain the placement once a worker is employed (Schutz & Rusch, 1982), job placement here refers only to obtaining a job; follow-up after placement is a separate process (see Chapters 15 and 16 for an expanded discussion of follow-up procedures). The remainder of this section reviews the nine steps involved in job placement.

Step 1: Identifying Community Placement Options

It is axiomatic that not all moderately and severely mentally retarded individuals of working age will be placed into competitive employment positions. Many school and community programs have not yet established competitive employment training programs (Wehman & McLaughlin, 1980), and not all individuals have the "work ready" skills to enable them to be successfully placed (Minton, 1977; Schalock, Harper, & Genung, 1981). The public schools and postsecondary rehabilitation centers have available, however, several program options besides competitive employment. Tables 1 and 2 briefly describe the most common programs utilized across various sections of the country. Although student or client

involvement in these programs is not considered a placement, the services provided enable many to receive some preparation for competitive employment. Each of these options has its advantages and disadvantages, but it is beyond the scope of this chapter to explore them.

Local Job Market   Each community possesses its own entry-level opportunities, and placements are usually made within the local job market (Rusch & Mithaug, 1980). For instance, a resort area will have more motel and restaurant positions available than a small rural community. As a means to assist placement staff in understanding local employment conditions, a placement advisory board, made up of community leaders, employers, and representatives from other vocational training programs, should be established. The committee could serve as a forum for public relations and, as Rusch (1983) indicates, "This committee might help a placement coordinator find job vacancies; gain entrance into various job sites; communicate with co-workers . . . and conduct local surveys" (p. 514).

Step 2: Undertaking a Community Placement Survey

Once workers have met the performance criteria from the training site, they are ready to advance into competitive employment. To ensure that such placements can be made, job development activities must have taken place beforehand. A placement coordinator could attempt to contact potential employers in person, but this approach would be very time consuming and inefficient. Instead, a mail survey with phone follow-up should be undertaken, whereby a large number of potential employers could be inexpensively contacted.

Mail Survey   Perhaps the quickest means of establishing a pool of potential employers is through a mail survey. Personalized letters should be sent to the potential employers in a community area. Lists of possible employers can be obtained through the phone book, Job Service, Chamber of Commerce, and advisory board members, to name a few. For instance, in the Comprehensive Transitional Training Project operated through the University of Colorado at Colorado Springs and the local

Table 1. School-based training options for moderately and severely mentally retarded students

Prevocational Class Activity Social, self-help, and work-related behaviors needed for entrance into vocational training programs are taught.

Sheltered Workshop A program where students work on either simulated or paid assembly contracts. Some schools send students to community workshops, while others have a workshop within the school building.

In-School Mainstreaming Integration into existing junior or senior high industrial arts or vocational education classes. Major modifications in class routine would need to be made.

Job Cluster Training Students are taught within the school to perform related skills found within a job cluster, such as those skills needed for light manufacturing or janitorial work.

Work Experience Students spend short periods of time for part of their school day at different realistic jobs either at school or community sites.

Specific Job Training Students go to a community-based job training station (like a motel), where the social and vocational skills associated with the job are learned while the students work at the job.

Adapted from Bellamy, Rose, Wilson, and Clarke (1982). Their chapter provides a detailed discussion of the pros and cons associated with each of these placements.

public school special education program, various employers were targeted. First, a call was made to check if the firm was still in operation, and to obtain the name of the person responsible for hiring entry-level staff. Second, an original-looking typed letter (done on a word processing machine) addressed to the contact person from each firm was sent prior to the time students finished their training program (see Form 1 in the Appendix). A self-addressed, stamped reply card was also included in the mailing (see Form 2 in the Appendix). The card was designed so that employers could quickly check off their response. Rusch and Mithaug (1980) indicate that a response card that is designed to be quickly and easily filled out will increase the response rate.

A brochure that further explains the program should be enclosed with each letter. Instead of relying upon the employers' goodwill toward those with handicapping conditions, the brochure would highlight the beneficial aspects of hiring a "trained" worker, and how this would be a financial asset to the employer. Relying upon employers' feelings of mercy toward persons with handicaps will result in few placements. In order to make an impact, the beneficial aspect of hiring a trained worker must be stressed instead. A brochure utilized by "On the Job Incorporated" includes these points (see Form 3 in the Appendix). Notice how the information is presented to the employer as if a service is being sold. "OJ Incorporated" is not asking for handouts, but instead operates as a broker system much as any other service that an employer purchases. The brochure used by the

Table 2. Postsecondary (adult) training options for moderately and severely mentally retarded clients

Developmental (Day Care) Centers A prework activity program that provides training in self-care and prevocational skills.

Work Activity Programs A preworkshop center at which a worker's level of productivity is less than 25% of normal productivity rates. Focus is upon prevocational skills and leisure activities.

Sheltered Workshops Usually multi-component programs where one component is extended employment. In extended employment, workers produce more than 25% of the normal productivity rate but have not yet mastered the vocational and social skills needed for community employment.

Sheltered Industry A business where products are produced for profit, usually by high functioning handicapped individuals working alongside a few nonhandicapped co-workers and supervisors.

Enclaves A small group of handicapped individuals working together in an industrial setting under the supervision of production staff.

Specific Job Training Workers are involved at a community-based job training station (like a restaurant kitchen) where they learn the needed social and vocational skills while working on the job.

Competitive Community Employment A placement where the individual "is working for at least minimum wage, or better, with non-handicapped co-workers at a job that provides room for advancement in settings that produce valued goods or services" (Rusch, 1983, p. 504).

Based in part upon the options discussed by Rusch and Mithaug (1980).

Comprehensive Transition Training Project at the University of Colorado at Colorado Springs offers another example (see Form 4 in the Appendix).

In order to keep on top of the flow of information as the mail survey is returned, a record system must be used. This ledger needs to include the names and addresses to whom letters were sent, their responses, the date their responses were received, the action that will be taken by the placement coordinator, and the outcome. The ledger should be kept readily available to record the information from the employers who may choose to call rather than send back the response card. If they do call, simply ask the questions contained on the response card and record this information in the ledger. These data will provide valuable information for many months, as they will indicate the pool of employers who will in all likelihood be more receptive to the establishment of additional training sites and/or placements.

Telephone Follow-Up During the process of conducting a mail survey, many people intend to reply but misplace the response form before they have had a chance to mail it. A follow-up telephone call to those who did not respond 2 weeks or so after the letters were sent is an appropriate way to complete the survey. As before, the calls should be documented. During the first part of the phone interview, the placement coordinator should briefly explain the program. Then, if the employer is still interested, the questions that were included on the response form should be asked. The opportunity to ask more questions about the business could arise. In this case, determine the number of entry-level positions, their job descriptions, and typical length of employment. If the previous employee was terminated, try to determine the reason as this could be useful when trying to match candidates to a job.

Step 3: Evaluating Employment Opportunities

The entry-level jobs that potential employers identify must be examined in terms of the demands the position places upon the workers (Gannaway & Wattenbarger, 1979). As Mith-aug, Hagmeier, and Haring (1977) indicated, the most probable placement opportunities have to be analyzed to determine the work skills and habits needed for employment. Rusch and Mithaug (1980) outlined four main components that must be included in a job analysis: 1) work environment, 2) tasks to be completed, 3) conditions of employment, and 4) work requirements. Form 5 in the Appendix presents a completed job survey analysis from the Illinois Competitive Employment Project at the University of Illinois.

Rusch and Mithaug (1980) discuss in detail the various aspects involved in undertaking a job analysis. To summarize their points, the analysis should be completed by: 1) interviewing the person who will be the direct supervisor, 2) having a conversation with the person who is currently doing the tasks, 3) observing the interactions and work environment while touring the job site, and 4) actually doing the job. Since it seems that job placements succeed better when the job tasks are outlined and agreed to before the placement occurs, the supervisor should (in writing) verify the task analysis and/or job duties. This can be done by having the supervisor sign off on the completed job analysis sheet (which can be attached to the placement contract). This way, if additional tasks are added or duties changed after employment, training time can be more easily negotiated. Finally, the form should be saved for future reference. As placement staff change, the original analysis can be useful long after it is completed.

One of the biggest errors that can be made in placement is to accept immediately any offer for competitive employment (Wehman & McLaughlin, 1980). This opportunity may seem inviting, especially if community job slots are difficult to obtain, but several factors may exist that could make the job a poor placement—and this is where the job analysis becomes so important. If the employer has had constant short-term turnover in the position, this may suggest that the environment is less than desirable. The work load may be unreasonable, the supervisor unfair, or the co-workers may be too demanding. Taking the time to do a careful analysis of the job will determine if the work environment is positive, the tasks that are required as a part of the job, and if the job is one that has adequate benefits to compensate for the possible loss of other medical or living support.

Each vocational placement program will need to design its own analysis form so as to include information relevant to local needs. Most programs should at a minimum, however, include most of the informational categories outlined in the example from Form 5 in the Appendix. Each of the five parts of the analysis are used to obtain different types of information, and for the most part the items within each part are self-explanatory; a few do need a more in-depth examination.

Classification of Position (Section I) The *Dictionary of Occupational Titles,* published by the U.S. Department of Labor in 1977, gives each job available in America today a specific title. The position being analyzed must use the title found in the *Dictionary,* as it is the official standard by which jobs are classified and, among other uses, various assessment instruments and interest inventories are keyed to the titles (see Chapter 7 for more information about assessment devices).

Stability of Job (Section I) As Rusch and Mithaug (1980) indicate, this item refers to the 2-year employee turnover rate for the position being analyzed. This figure can best be noted in an average monthly (or yearly if the rate is very low) term. For instance, in the job survey analysis example the average turnover rate is once every 4 months. This figure needs to be considered along with the data on previous firings and abandonments.

Reasons for Previous Firings and Abandonments (Section I) Reasons for leaving can often be related to supervisory style or other unique demands associated with a position. Thus, specific reasons as to why the previous workers left must be obtained. For example, as in Form 5, most workers left because of their dislike of weekend employment, not because of supervisory style. The worker identified for this site should be made well aware of his or her work schedule, and not

mind working on Saturday, Sunday, and holidays.

Importance of Speed (Section II) The need to complete a job quickly varies across firms. For instance, in the example, each hotel room had to be cleaned in less than 30 minutes. Or, on an assembly line operation, a worker would have to keep up with the pace. As Rusch and Mithaug (1980) suggest, these two examples require different methods of feedback and different trainee skills.

General Social Environment (Section II) Since getting along with co-workers is a survival need, be sure to note the types of interaction, especially during break times, that occur.

Physical Conditions (Section II) When a trainee moves from a sheltered school or rehabilitation setting for the first time, a harsh physical environment may make the transition more difficult. For instance, going to work in a meat cutting room where the temperature is kept in the low 40s may cause undue problems. Also note any possible physical barriers that could impede someone who may have a physical handicap. The example provided in Form 5 indicates that the physical environment would be pleasant for all but a worker confined to a wheelchair.

Job Task Analysis (Section III) The task analysis needs to be detailed enough so the major steps of the job are identified. Some jobs are keyed to time, others to the changing demands of the situation. The example in Form 5 indicates that the first few steps at the start of the shift need to be done in a certain order and within a broad time frame. The remainder of the shift is divided into cleaning rooms in less than 30 minutes. It is possible to develop an analysis for the entire day and also separate analyses for various tasks that must be done during the day. A good job task analysis provides the foundation for accountable programming.

Pay Scale (Section IV) Unless pay is decided upon at the start of the project, confusion will certainly develop later on. Note the starting salary, who is providing it, and provisions for future pay increases. Depending upon the age of the student, if he or she is placed through a school training program, or other factors, make sure the arrangements are in accordance with state and federal labor laws (see Martin and Husch, 1986, for more information about labor laws in relation to various vocational training and placement options).

Union (Section IV) If a union is present, contact the local union representative to explain the program. Many national unions have established policy statements that commit them to advancing the employment opportunities of workers who have handicapping conditions (see Weisgerber, Dahl, & Appleby, 1981).

Travel (Section IV) Note the existence of car pools, availability of mass transportation, or other options. The lack of an adequate transportation plan can prevent a placement from occurring.

Criteria for Promotion (Section IV) Many firms have an evaluation form that supervisors complete; if so, try to obtain this form and use it to evaluate the worker. If a formal procedure for promotion does not exist, attempt to determine what the supervisor considers as crucial.

Functional Academic Skills (Section V) Determine the exact type of academic skill required and if a worker would be allowed to use aids to complete the tasks. For instance, in the example in Form 5 in the Appendix, the maid must check off on a written work sheet the items completed in each room. Rather than using a written form, the use of a picture-coded check sheet could accomplish the same goal.

Step 4: Matching Candidates and Jobs

Once possible jobs have been analyzed and a decision has been made as to the suitability of each, the next process is to match the positions to those candidates who have met training criterion. As Goodall, Wehman, and Cleveland (1983) indicate, successful job placement relies upon the process of carefully matching a client's abilities to the requirements of a specific job. Ideally, if the trainees had been involved in a food service laborer training program, then the placement possibilities should be in this area. The only exception would be a case in which the trainee determined that he or she no longer wanted to work in food service. At all times, consideration

must be given to the preferences of the trainees. No surer way exists to set up failure than to place a person in a job that he or she does not want to do. But placement coordinators need to be careful not to mistake a dislike for the fear often associated with undertaking the first job or returning to competitive employment after a long absence.

The actual matching of available positions to candidates is both an objective and subjective process. First, the information obtained from the job analysis must be reviewed in relation to the abilities and preferences of the trainees. Among others, the shift that will be worked and the location of the firm will be crucial objective variables. Maybe one worker likes early morning jobs, while another performs best in the afternoon or evening. Likewise, one trainee may be able to ride a bus any place about town so location is less of an issue. In another case, bus service may not be available to the location and, unless alternative modes of transportation (like a car pool) are found, placement in that job would not be feasible. From a subjective stance, the information from the job analysis suggests that the co-worker associated with the position under consideration is one who would be understanding of a person who might be socially awkward—for example, the co-worker once worked in a place that hired mentally retarded workers and he supported them as much as possible.

Step 5: Redesigning Jobs

Job redesigning, or job engineering, is "the process by which jobs are constructed or modified to meet the specific needs of people . . ." (Gannaway & Wattenbarger, 1979, p. 52). It is also where the nature of the work environment is altered to minimize the work barriers (Vandergoot et al., 1979). Once a particular worker has been matched with a potential job, if needed, that job can be redesigned in two ways. First, the job descriptions can be modified. For instance, Brown et al. (1984), describe a worker named John whose hospital job description is modified from that of any other workers. He folds towels, unpacks supplies, and attaches printed labels to supplies. Most of the tasks that regular employees do, John doesn't perform. He does not, among other tasks, set dials on the washing and drying machines, operate sterilizers, or fill orders for supplies. In this particular case, John does not get paid for his work. On the other hand, Wehman's Virginia project (see Chapter 2) will negotiate during the placement process to modify a job description so that it may be reduced in tasks or complexity, or so that the shift could be extended in order for the work to be completed. Unlike Brown et al.'s example, these workers are paid. Regardless as to what is decided, make sure the details of the placement correspond to state and federal labor laws.

Second, additional cues or prosthetic devices can be added to assist in the scheduling of tasks to be completed throughout the day, or in the completion of a task. Menchetti, Rusch, and Lamson (1981) surveyed the participants attending a professional food service conference to determine what training techniques they would allow to be used in their kitchens. They found that almost all kitchen supervisors would permit the development and display of picture-coded job schedules. These sequenced photos would enable the mentally retarded workers to look at each picture, do what was seen, and then look at the next, and so on until all tasks were completed (see Gifford, Rusch, Martin, and White [1984] for more information about use of picture cues). Also, the majority would allow color coding of work equipment, for instance, placing red dots on the dishwasher controls to denote those that must be turned on at the start of a shift.

Step 6: Developing Employer Expectations

During discussions with an employer prior to the placement, the coordinator must finalize the information about: 1) the placement, and 2) the services that will be provided during the follow-up phase. This information will be the data that the employer uses to formulate his or her expectations about the placement and follow-up process. Once the placement has been established, one method to finalize the situation is to draw up a placement contract. It will outline the responsibilities of all parties

involved, and detail the follow-up procedures (see Form 6 in the Appendix for an example contract). This document is one that should be flexible enough to include information unique to a particular placement site. For instance, in one setting an employer may request that co-workers be provided information about training procedures. Or, it may outline how a job was restructured. In any case, the document should always include a description of the duties that the person will be expected to perform, and how he or she will be evaluated.

An agreement should, whenever possible, be included in the contract to preserve the job position for the placement program. This can be established by reaching an understanding with the employer that in the event the person placed fails, another worker will be placed in that position (Rusch, 1983). Each community job placement should be regarded as a "slot"; that is, as a placement that can always be filled by a candidate from the training program. At times, the person placed in the position will be asked to leave (terminate his or her placement) because of production, attendance, or social reasons. When this happens, the placement coordinator will always want to be able to have the option of placing someone else into the position.

Step 7: Discussion with Parents or Guardians

Before a placement is finalized, parents and/or guardians need to be informed (see Chapter 21 for more information about family contacts). This must be done for several reasons. First, parents need to know the details of the placement: what the work environment is like, the tasks that need to be completed, co-worker acceptance, and pay. Second, if applicable, the impact upon public financial support payments needs to be discussed. As a worker's income increases, for instance, the amount of Supplemental Security Income can decrease to the point where the person is no longer eligible. Kochany and Keller (1981) found that one of the major reasons many people left competitive employment was the negative impact their earnings had upon SSI, and their subsequent loss of publicly provided medical coverage. Third, as Rusch and Mithaug (1980) suggest, the advantages of the placement must be pointed out; these include, among others, working with nonhandicapped peers and the opportunity to become a productive citizen.

Step 8: Interviewing for the Job

The job application and interview process has been identified as a crucial component of placement efforts for individuals who have mild handicapping conditions; that is, the initial interview often determines whether or not the person becomes employed (Hill, Wehman, & Pentecost, 1980; Kelly & Christoff, 1984). Hollandsworth, Glazeski, and Dressel (1978) indicated the importance of the interview in their finding that competent workers who have poor interview abilities often have difficulty in obtaining work. Job interview training packages have been developed to increase the probability of a favorable interview. Martin (1986), for instance, used a training package comprised of preinstruction, role playing, and videotape feedback to improve 15 job interview skills of four mildly mentally retarded individuals.

A placement program for individuals who are moderately to severely mentally retarded, however, must utilize the interview process differently than what would be done with less disabled job candidates. In most instances, the completion of an application form is too complex an academic operation. Likewise, the ability to respond appropriately in an in-depth interview is limited. The placement coordinator, through matching the requirements of a specific job to the talents found in a pool of trainees who have been involved in a training program, plays the major role in negotiating the placement with an employer. For all practical purposes, the person is placed upon the decision of the placement coordinator or placement team. What is needed, Rusch and Mithaug (1980) refer to as a preinterview. During this visit to the job site, the prospective worker meets his or her co-workers, begins the process of learning his or her way around the setting, and has the opportunity to see what the respon-

sibilities are. Prior to this time, the worker should have received training or met the criterion for appropriate social behavior.

Step 9: Establishing Work Performance Evaluation Form

During the trial work period, the placed worker will be evaluated to determine if he or she meets at least the minimum criteria for acceptable performance. Firms undertake this process in various ways. Some may have a formal evaluation system comprised of checklists completed at different times. Others will be informal, that is, based upon the impression of the supervisor. In order to increase the likelihood of success and as a means to pinpoint problem areas, a work performance evaluation form must be developed and completed frequently during the trial work period.

According to Rusch and Mithaug (1980), the work performance evaluation form will consist of social, vocational, and special skill areas. Most of the needed skill information can be obtained from the job survey analysis and from the employer evaluation form, if one is available. Perhaps as important, it will be helpful to obtain from the person in charge of hiring what he or she considers the most important worker traits. These areas, if not already included on the task analysis, must be incorporated into the work performance evaluation form. The top three or four traits should be highlighted and extra attention given to the worker's performance in these areas. For instance, as noted in the job analysis from Form 5 in the Appendix, one of the most important qualifications was to be socially "tact" with hotel guests. Next was the ability to clean a room well within the 30-minute limit. This will provide the follow-up staff with information that will help maintain the placement.

In a unique and interesting study, White and Rusch (1983) found that when co-workers, supervisors, managers, and the mentally retarded workers themselves rated performance, a marked difference was obtained among the various groups. Co-workers rated the mentally retarded workers' performance better than the shift supervisors or managers; with the managers' ratings being the lowest of all. The mentally retarded workers' ratings of themselves were the best of all. These results point out the need to have constant communication flow between the workers and those whose responsibility it is to hire and fire. This should be done in the following manner. A work performance evaluation form must be completed each week based upon input from the supervisor and co-workers. This information would then be shared with the manager and the worker, and areas of disagreement or concern would receive immediate attention. Often a manager only receives information about a given worker from the shift supervisors. A supervisor's perception of a worker's ability could be shaded by one or two negative events, that is, unless a communication flow exists to provide information about improved performance.

Form 7 in the Appendix depicts the work performance evaluation form utilized by the Food Service Training Project at the University of Illinois. This form was made specific to that food service operation, with the items being those deemed most important by the supervisors and managers. Note that this form is divided into four main categories: 1) work quality, 2) level of responsibility, 3) relationship to supervisors and co-workers, and

4) ability to manage time. When this form was completed by the mentally retarded workers, the questions were read to them and difficult words were explained. The 1 to 4 scale was highlighted by the use of sad, neutral, and happy faces. Although the work performance evaluation forms should differ from firm to firm, this example provides a model in how to create the basic form.

SUMMARY

This chapter provides an overview of the placement process from both the traditional vocational rehabilitation model and from the survey-train-place-maintain perspective. In relation to the latter, nine aspects of the placement process are discussed. What is unique about the placement process as compared to the other stages of the survey-train-place-maintain model is that so little hard, data-based research has been undertaken to guide the development of best practices. Until this situation is resolved, placement will remain an "art," a practice that relies upon the instincts and experiences learned from a few very good people who make placements occur. The development of a placement curriculum is discussed in the next chapter.

REFERENCES

Bellamy, G. T., Rose, H., Wilson, D. J., & Clarke, J. Y. (1982). Strategies for vocational preparation. In B. Wilcox & G. T. Bellamy, *Design of high school programs for severely handicapped students* (pp. 139–152). Baltimore: Paul H. Brookes.

Brown, L., Shiraga, B., York, J., Kessler, K., Strohm, B., Sweet, M., Zanella, K., VanDeventer, P., & Loomis, R. (1984). Integrated work opportunities for adults with severe handicaps: The extended training option. *The Journal of the Association for Persons with Severe Handicaps, 9,* 262–269.

Bruininks, R. H., Meyers, C. E., Sigford, B. B., & Lakin, K. C. (Eds.). (1981). *Deinstitutionalization and community adjustment of mentally retarded people.* Washington, DC: American Association on Mental Deficiency.

Gannaway, T. W., & Wattenbarger, W. (1979). The relationship of vocational evaluation and vocational placement functions in vocational rehabilitation. In D. Vandergoot & J. D. Worrall (Eds.), *Placement in*

rehabilitation (pp. 43–58). Baltimore: University Park Press.

Gifford, J. L., Rusch, F. R., Martin, J. E., & White, D. M. (1984). Autonomy and adaptability: A proposed technology for maintaining work behavior. In N. Ellis & N. Bray (Eds.), *International review of research in mental retardation* (Vol. 12, pp. 285–318). New York: Academic Press.

Goodall, P. A., Wehman, P., & Cleveland, P. (1983). Job placement for mentally retarded individuals. *Education and Training of the Mentally Retarded, 18,* 271–278.

Hill, J. W. (1982). Vocational training. In L. Sternberg & G. L. Adams (Eds.), *Educating severely and profoundly handicapped students* (pp. 269–312). Rockville, MD: Aspen Systems.

Hill, J. W., Wehman, P., & Pentecost, J. (1980). Developing job interview skills in mentally retarded adults. *Education and Training of the Mentally Retarded, 15,* 179–186.

Hollandsworth, J. G., Jr., Glazeski, R. C., & Dressel, M. E. (1978). Use of social skill training in the treatment of extreme anxiety and deficient verbal skills in the job-interview setting. *Journal of Applied Behavior Analysis, 11,* 503–510.

Katz, E. (1968). *The retarded adult in the community.* Springfield, IL: Charles C Thomas.

Kelly, J. A., & Christoff, K. A. (1984). Job interview training for the mentally retarded: Issues and application. *Applied Research in Mental Retardation, 4,* 355–367.

Kochany, L., & Keller, J. (1981). An analysis and evaluation of the failures of severely disabled individuals in competitive employment. In P. Wehman, *Competitive employment: New horizons for severely disabled individuals* (pp. 181–198). Baltimore: Paul H. Brookes.

Martin, J. E. (1986). *Development of job interview skills through video-tape feedback.* Manuscript submitted for publication.

Martin, J. E., & Husch, J. (1986). *U.S. Department of Labor rules in relation to school-based vocational training programs.* Manuscript submitted for publication.

Menchetti, B. M., Rusch, F. R., & Lamson, D. S. (1981). Social validation of behavioral training techniques: Assessing the normalizing qualities of competitive employment training programs. *Journal of The Association for the Severely Handicapped, 6,* 6–16.

Minton, E. B. (1977, December). Job placement: Strategies and techniques. *Rehabilitation Counseling Bulletin,* pp. 141–149.

Mithaug, D. E., Hagmeier, L., & Haring, N. (1977). The relationship between training activities and job placement in vocational education of the severely and profoundly handicapped. *AAESPH Review, 2,* 89–109.

Novak, A. R., & Heal, L. W. (1980). *Community integration of developmentally disabled individuals.* Baltimore: Paul H. Brookes.

Pomerantz, D. J., & Marholin, D. (1977). Vocational habilitation: A time for change. In E. Sontag, J. Smith, & N. Certo (Eds.), *Educational programming for the severely and profoundly handicapped* (pp. 129–141). Reston, VA: Council for Exceptional Children, Division on Mental Retardation.

Rusch, F. R. (1983). Competitive vocational training. In M. E. Snell (Ed.), *Systematic instruction of the moderately and severely handicapped,* (2nd ed.) (pp. 503–523). Columbus, OH: Charles E. Merrill.

Rusch, F. R., & Mithaug, D. E. (1980). *Vocational training for mentally retarded adults: A behavior analytic approach.* Champaign, IL: Research Press.

Schalock, R. L., Harper, R. S., & Genung, T. (1981). Community integration of mentally retarded adults: Community placement and program success. *American Journal of Mental Deficiency, 85,* 478–488.

Schutz, R. P., & Rusch, F. R. (1982). Competitive employment: Toward employment integration for mentally retarded persons. In K. L. Lynch, W. E. Kiernan, & J. A. Stark (Eds.), *Prevocational and vocational education for special needs youth* (pp. 133–159). Baltimore: Paul H. Brookes.

Usdane, W. (1976). The placement process in the rehabilitation of the severely handicapped. *Rehabilitation Literature, 37,* 162–165.

U.S. Department of Labor (1977). *Dictionary of occupational titles* (4th ed.). Washington, DC: U.S. Department of Labor.

Vandergoot, D., Jacobsen, R., & Worrall, J. D. (1979). New directions for placement practice in vocational rehabilitation. In D. Vandergoot & J. D. Worrall (Eds.), *Placement in rehabilitation* (pp. 2–41). Baltimore: University Park Press.

Walls, R. T., Tseng, M. S., & Zarin, H. N. (1976). Time and money for vocational rehabilitation of clients with mild, moderate, and severe mental retardation. *American Journal of Mental Deficiency, 80,* 595–601.

Wasil, R. A. (1974). Job placement: Keystone of career development. *American Vocational Journal, 49,* 32.

Weisgerber, R. A., Dahl, P. R., & Appleby, J. A. (1981). *Training the handicapped for productive employment.* Rockville, MD: Aspen Systems.

Wehman, P. (1981). *Competitive employment: New horizons for severely disabled individuals.* Baltimore: Paul H. Brookes.

Wehman, P., & McLaughlin, P. J. (1980). *Vocational curriculum for developmentally disabled persons.* Baltimore: University Park Press.

White, D. M., & Rusch, F. R. (1983). Social validation in competitive employment: Evaluating work performance. *Applied Research in Mental Retardation, 4,* 343–354.

Whitehead, C. (1979). Sheltered workshops in the decade ahead: Work and wages, or welfare. In G. T. Bellamy, G. O'Connor, & O. C. Karan (Eds.), *Vocational rehabilitation of severely handicapped persons: Contemporary service strategies* (pp. 71–84). Baltimore: University Park Press.

Appendix

The following forms will assist in job development. These examples need to be modified to fit local conditions.

**Sample Mail Survey Letter Used
to Obtain a Pool of Placement Opportunities**

Current Date

Mrs. Betty Smith
Director of Human Resources Development
Penrose Community Hospital
3205 N. Academy Blvd.
Colorado Springs, Co. 80907

Dear Mrs. Smith:

Are the applicants for your entry level positions well
qualified? Do you have a high rate of turnover in these
positions? If you are not satisfied with the answers to
these and other similar questions, then please read on.

The University of Colorado at Colorado Springs in
conjunction with the Special Education Program of School
District #11 has started a project to facilitate the
transition of mentally handicapped students from home and
school into the world of work.

A primary goal of this project is to systematically train
these students at community job sites to independently
perform all of the specific tasks and to meet the social
demands associated with entry level postions. These
training sites will be under the supervision of the project.

However, we can provide you with these well trained
individuals only with your help. Please take a few minutes
to fill out and return the pre-stamped reply card. This
information will enable us to begin the process of training
needed skills to fulfill the demands of potential entry
level positions.

Thank you for your time and interest.

Sincerely,

James V. Husch
Placement Coordinator

Enclosures

Form 2
Mail Survey Response Card

BUSINESS REPLY MAIL
FIRST CLASS PERMIT NO. 1387 COLORADO SPRINGS, CO

NO POSTAGE
NECESSARY
IF MAILED
IN THE
UNITED STATES

Postage will be paid by addressee.

School of Education
Department of Special Education
Attn: Jim Husch
University of Colorado at Colorado Springs
Austin Bluffs Parkway
Colorado Springs, CO 80907

REPLY CARD

Please check those that apply:
_____ I would like more information.
_____ I would like to be considered for a training site.
_____ I am willing to meet with you to discuss my
entry level positions.
_____ I am willing to speak to your students with
regard to careers.

Name: _____ Phone: _____

Address: _____

City/State/Zip: _____

Form 3
"On the Job Incorporated" Informational Brochure

Attention employers: Why take chances when you hire?

You wouldn't risk buying a new car
without a test drive...

Demonstrated Performance is the Key

On the Job, Inc.

Takes the risk out of hiring

And here's how...

- -

Like buying, hiring is a major investment

When you buy a car...

When you hire through On the Job...

You shop around...

On the Job, Inc. (OJ) saves you shopping time.
OJ recruits, screens, and trains entry level workers.

You consider the cost...

OJ's customers are eligible for substantial savings
under the Targeted Job Tax Credit program. (We'll
even do the paperwork!) OJ's workers are disabled
and disadvantaged persons who truly want to work.

OJ will save you money—by lowering your cost
of recruiting, screening and training employees.

Turnover goes down—productivity goes up.

You examine the track record...

OJ is bringing to California employers a service
which has already proven highly effective in other
states.

We'll be happy to put you in touch with satisfied
clients such as The Bank of Boston, Aetna
Insurance Co., and Sheraton Corporation.

You choose the model you want...

Tell us the requirements of your jobs—OJ will
ensure that the applicants you see are the ones
you're looking for.

You order custom options...

Your OJ worker will be trained—on the job,
in your company with the help of OJ staff—
to suit your specific needs.

You check the warranty...

OJ guarantees high quality, reliable, dedicated
workers and good performance—at no risk to you.

(During the training and "test-drive" period,
your workers are on our payroll. You pay us,
we pay them.)

You test drive...

OJ gives you a way to test a person's performance
on the job—before you hire.

[Above portion of employer brochure reprinted with permission from On the Job, Inc., Berkeley, CA.]

Form 4

Brochure used by the Comprehensive Transition Training Project

The Comprehensive Transition Training Project

The U.S. Office of Education, Department of Special Education and Rehabilitation Services is sponsoring, through the University of Colorado and School District #11 a demonstration and research project to increase the independence of mentally handicapped youth. A primary goal of the project is to facilitate the transition of mentally handicapped students from home and school into the working community by improving their abilities to independently perform a wide range of tasks.

Major Project Objectives in Relationship to Employers:

* To establish a vocational training program that will facilitate the transition of students between school, supported work, and competitive employment settings.

* To survey community employers to determine potential jobs and job training stations.

* To conduct analyses of potential jobs from which identified, specific criteria can be developed for students to move from school to work.

* To develop curricula for training skills and behaviors necessary for advanced training and competitive employment.

* To involve well prepared students in appropriate community training sties.

* To place well trained students from the training sites into appropriate community jobs.

Needed Employer Involvement:

* To assist in the process of job analysis so the performance and behavioral requirements for various entry level positions can be identified.

* To speak to special students with regard to careers.

* To provide possible contract work and/or materials needed to set up simulated work stations in the schools.

* To provide community job training stations, so students can be taught specific job requirements at the work site.

* To assist in the process of matching well prepared students with appropriate jobs.

What Employers Can Expect from Project:

* Development of well prepared students for specific entry level jobs.

* Development of independent workers.

* Matching of appropriate students with appropriate jobs.

* Assistance, if eligible, in obtaining targeted jobs tax credit.

* Once placed, continued follow-up by project staff.

Form 5

Completed Job Survey Analysis from the
Illinois Competitive Employment Project

I. Firm and Position Overview

Name of firm: Jumer's Castle Lodge

Address: 209 S. Broadway, Urbana, IL 61801

Phone: 384-8800 X119

Type of industry: Hotel/Motel industry

Name and title of person interviewed: Betty Jones—Executive Housekeeper

Title of position: Housekeeper/Maid

Total number of people employed: 167

Hotel employees in position: 12 maids

Stability of job: Turnover averages once every four months

Reasons for previous firings/abandonments: Firings have rarely occurred. Schedule default is the main reason. People leave their job to go to school, for more pay, problems at home, deciding not to work weekends.

"Not a desirable job" says the supervisor, "the only thing is we work out of a basement and there is *always* work to be done."

II. Work Environment

Type of firm: Hotel/lodge running at 60% occupancy per month. Football weekends, special weekends, e.g., Mom's Day, Dad's, etc., and shows in area increase occupancy.

Importance of speed: Worker must be able to completely clean a room/bathroom "to standard"* in ½ hour.

Number of co-workers trainee will work directly with: Direct contact will be with the Executive Housekeeper/2 assistants, but trainee will be acquainted with 11 housekeepers/maids.

Supervision available: Executive housekeeper prorates minimal supervision. Runs checks from time to time as well as front desk checks to see if rooms are ready from time to time.

Probable cooperation of other employees: Co-workers have their own work to complete in designated 8 hours but would be willing to help in necessity. *Not* doing trainee's work, however.

General social environment: "Family environment within department"—Hotel friendly warm, pleasant.

Physical appearance: Maids wear white shoes, hose, Jumer's uniform; blue dress, white apron, white hat. Must wear hat and be well groomed; clean hair, no odor, must make good impression on public being served.

Form 5 adapted with permission from Rusch, F.R., & Mithaug, D. (1980). *Vocational training for mentally retarded adults: A behavioranalytic approach,* Figures 7.6, 7.9, 7.10, and 7.11. Champaign, IL: Research Press.

*"to standard"—Jumer's guests pay higher rates for quality rooms done with a special flair (extras) and Lodge expects the utmost in cleanliness and neatness in rooms. Measured by guest approval (no comments) or complaints, as well as Executive Housekeeper.

III. Job Task Analysis

	Approximate Times		*Task Performed*
1.	8:00 a.m. (9:00 Sat./Sun.)	1.	Punch in
2.	8:05 a.m.	2.	Load cart with all maid supplies (see bottom)
3.	8:10 a.m.	3.	Check vacuum to see if in working condition
4.	8:13 a.m.	4.	Sign out master key for room entry/sign time
5.	8:15 a.m.	5.	Pick up linen sheet (see below)
6.	8:15 a.m.	6.	Begin room check to see what rooms are vacant/ready to be cleaned
7.	8:30 a.m.	7.	Begin cleaning 1st room on linen sheet that is vacant
8.	8:30–9:00 (see list attached)	8.	Jumer's checklist of things to be done in each room in ½ hour
9.	9:00 a.m.	9.	Move to next room
10.	9:30 a.m.	10.	Move to next room
11.	10:00 a.m.	11.	Break 10 minutes in employee lounge
12.	10:10 a.m.	12.	Move to next room
13.		13.	And so on until lunch
14.	11:00 a.m.	14.	Lunch
15.		15.	Move to next room
16.		16.	And so on until 10-minute break at 2:00
17.	2:00 p.m.	17.	Move to next
18.		18.	And so on until 4:30 p.m.
19.		19.	Make sure all 15 rooms on sheet are vacant and ready to sell Clock out.

Comments: These times are approximate; Mrs. Steele emphasized importance of cleaning rooms quickly on days lodge is booked.

Night maid works from 3:00–9:00 p.m. and has fewer rooms to clean. Takes care of Lodge restrooms and central areas.

Maid Supplies—Camay, Safeguard, body towels, hand towels, washcloths, tissues, glasses, toilet paper, matches, sheets, chocolates (gift boxes), cleaning supplies, etc.

Linen Sheet—A listing of 15 rooms* to be cleaned by shift's end. Used to account for what maid was in what room, when it is ready for occupancy, and to keep track of rooms done.

*15—Could be reduced for efficient but slower handicapped employee; 8–10 rooms might be a possible goal for such an employee.

JUMER'S CASTLE LODGE ROOM CHECKLIST

(can be pictured cued)

Guest rooms

1. Check bed pads, linens, blankets and spreads. Reject if torn or stained.
2. Make bed neatly and correctly. Corners hospital style with sheet (top) and blanket loose under quilt.
3. Empty wastebasket and wipe clean.
4. Wash ashtrays in bathroom with water. Place one on table, one on desk, and one in bathroom. Replace matches to standard. See example.
5. If a check out, check drawers for lost and found items. If items found turn in to Executive Housekeeper.
6. Check and replace in desk drawer: stationery, menu, and phone book.
7. Check and replace the Bible in the bedside drawer.
8. Clean and replace tray, ice bucket, and four room glasses. Place on table or in the bathroom.
9. Check operation of radio, TV, lamps, and drapery rods. May work with music or TV on.
10. Sweep down cobwebs on walls, large chandelier, and behind drapes.
11. Clean off mirror and TV screen with glass cleaner and paper towel.
12. Brush down all lamp shades, bed hangings, and drapes.
13. Wipe out all drawers.
14. Wipe telephone and phone index.
15. Wipe fingermarks from all doors.
16. Replace coat hangers and place one laundry bag on top of the coat rack.
17. Dust all furniture and fixtures.
18. If a check out, place doilies, candy, and welcome card on the desk.

Bathrooms

1. Put liquid cleaner on brush and swab entire bowl.
2. Check faucets, toilet bowl, shower, and lights for operation.
3. Remove all used soap if a check out.
4. Empty waste basket. Wipe clean.
5. Scour and sanitize shower wall, tub, soap dish, wash basin, counter top, toilet seat, and outside of toilet bowl.
6. Keep vent over tub free of dust.
7. Dust mirror frame and light globes.
8. Clean mirror and chrome Kleenex cover with glass cleaner.
9. Dry all surfaces. Chrome should be free of water spots.
10. Check shower curtains and hooks. Replace if needed.
11. Check and replace soap (one bar of Camay and one bar of Safeguard), toilet tissue, Kleenex, one shoe shiner, two sani bags, and one ashtray with matches.
12. Replace bathmat on towel holder over toilet.
13. Replace towels and washcloths to standard.
14. Scrub bathroom floor.
15. Turn off lights.
16. Spray with deodorant.

Must all be completed within ½ hour.
Each can be broken down into steps; maids may use this checklist.

Insurance and other benefits: One week paid vacation after 1 year. Free group insurance after 90 days.

Employee gets one meal in shift—lunch day shift, dinner night shift. It is the employee meal and it is free— entree, salad, soup, and milk or coffee.

Physical conditions: Work out of basement, no sunlight; noisy hot in laundry. Requires use of elevator and some stairs. Rooms too small for a worker in a wheelchair—no room for making beds, cleaning bathrooms except in handicapped rooms.

IV. Conditions of Employment

Work hours per day: 8½ hours   Per week: 35–40 hours (5-day work weeks)

Shift: 8:00 a.m.–4:30 p.m. day maids   3:00 until about 9:00 or 10:00 when work is done.

Pay scale: All maids begin at $3.35. After 90 days raise to $3.45: pay rate increases after this point are not common because of management.

Bonuses/overtime pay: Overtime—time and a half if one works a holiday and day before or day after, and 20 or more hours in week.

Union operating
  Name: none

  Address:

Union representative
  Name: n/a

  Phone number:

Travel requirements: Worker can get to lodge by red, green, orange, grey, Orchard Downs, and yellow bus or must have own dependable source of transportation.

Training: Executive housekeeper said experience is important but not necessary. Will train for 2 to 3 days working along with another maid. Trainers could work in room within Lodge on slow days (under 60% occupancy).

Criteria for promotion: To move up, a person must be "aggressive," hard working, must take initiative to get work done, "do work without being told," be dependable, and work weekends willingly.

V. Worker Requirements

Education requirements: Preferably high school graduate; not necessary—will accept those with only 2 years high school. Age requirement: 20 years. Looking for maturity, social tact with guests.

Previous Experience: Not necessary but helpful. Training period is short (2–3 days).

Licenses/certificates: None required.

Special Social/Functional Academic/Vocational Skills: It would be necessary for the employee to be pleasant and tactful with guests. Some form of acceptable communication; writing or word cards or speaking mandatory.

Vocational skills: Some knowledge of washing machine/dryers, vacuums for operation would be helpful. Skills needed, vacuum operation, elevator operation, dusting, scrubbing. Attention to detail—bedmaking.

Tests: None for day maid unless suspect of theft—the lie detector test may be required. Night maid is subject to lie detector test for security purposes. Night maid works "more alone." "Temptations are more easily given in to at night."

Form 6
Sample Placement Contract

Placement Contract

This contract represents an agreement and outlines the areas of responsibility between the Comprehensive Transitional Training Project of the University of Colorado at Colorado Springs, School District #11, the student and employer named below.

Student

I, _____ agree to do the following during the time that I am placed at _____.

1. Arrive to and leave from work per schedule
2. Do the tasks included in my schedule
3. Work hard and do a good job
4. Listen to the boss and do what I am told
5.
6.

Employer

I, _____ agree to employ _____ in a part-time job as long as his work quality and behavior are acceptable and I have work for him to do.

1. Follow-up staff from the program will work with _____ during his time on duty until he masters the assigned tasks, and then the staff will be available to retrain as needed.

2. If the present placement does not work out, the placement program will have the first chance at providing another worker for that position.

3. I will meet with the follow-up staff on at least a weekly basis for a brief meeting to review the worker's progress.

4. The worker will be evaluated per our usual evaluation form. In addition, any other data collected by the follow-up staff will be considered during his evaluation period.

Follow-up Staff

The follow-up staff of the Comprehensive Transitional Training Project will:

1. Provide training to enable the worker to complete assigned work tasks as needed
2. Meet with supervisor to discuss performance
3. Provide additional assistance to the worker or co-workers as requested by the site supervisor

_____ Date

Worker _____
Employer _____
Placement Coordinator _____

Form 7
Work Performance Evaluation Form
Utilized by the University of Illinois Food Service Training Program

1 Poor	2 Needs Improvement	3 Average	4 Good	5 Exceptional
Shows no effort to meet requirements. Would not pass probation	Makes effort to meet requirements but needs additional training to pass probation	Meets most requirements normally associated with job description and requires average amount of supervision	Meets all requirements and works independently with few exceptions	Model employee, exceeds requirements in most areas, takes pride in job

1. Overall job skills/work quality 1 2 3 4 5
   A. Obtains/returns materials for task 1 2 3 4 5
   B. Uses correct approach technique to complete tasks 1 2 3 4 5
   C. Takes care of equipment and materials 1 2 3 4 5
   D. Attends to task 1 2 3 4 5
   E. Works fast during rush times 1 2 3 4 5
   F. Meets sanitation requirements 1 2 3 4 5
   G. Takes pride in job 1 2 3 4 5

2. Overall level of responsibility 1 2 3 4 5
   A. Works alone 1 2 3 4 5
   B. Works safely 1 2 3 4 5
   C. Completes all assigned tasks 1 2 3 4 5
   D. Follows procedures and policies 1 2 3 4 5

3. Overall relationship to supervisors and co-workers 1 2 3 4 5
   A. Cooperates 1 2 3 4 5
   B. Is considerate of others 1 2 3 4 5
   C. Maintains a positive attitude about work 1 2 3 4 5
   D. Accepts criticism 1 2 3 4 5
   E. Asks for assistance when necessary 1 2 3 4 5
   F. Communicates with supervisors and co-workers 1 2 3 4 5

4. Overall ability to manage time 1 2 3 4 5
   A. Attendance 1 2 3 4 5
   B. Completes job on time 1 2 3 4 5
   C. Follows a schedule 1 2 3 4 5
   D. Manages time appropriately 1 2 3 4 5
   E. Follows directions to do a task at a given time 1 2 3 4 5

ADDITIONAL STRENGTHS

ADDITIONAL WEAKNESSES

From White, D. M., & Rusch, F. R. (1983). Social validation in competitive employment: Evaluating work performance. Applied Research in Mental Retardation, 4, 343–354. Copyright 1983 by Pergamon Press. Adapted by permission.

Chapter 14

Curriculum Development

Cheryl Hanley-Maxwell

CHILDREN ENTER SCHOOL with a variety of abilities and disabilities. Through the schooling process, educators attempt to develop existing abilities and remediate or compensate for disabilities with the end goal of producing independently functioning adults. Typically, adults are expected to contribute to society, be self-supporting, and be capable of self-maintenance. As educators, we mold such individuals by what we teach, how we teach, and where we teach. An important element in this process is the curriculum, which is the focus of the following discussion.

CURRICULUM

The word *curriculum* engenders images of manuals and handbooks—the "cookbooks" that specify what students need to know, in what order, and when. "A curriculum represents the goals and expected outcomes of the schooling process. It specifies the knowledge and competencies that school leavers are expected to have achieved" (Wilcox & Bellamy, 1982a, p. 23). The curriculum translates these expectations into specific goals, objectives, and activities. It provides a sense of direction in education by providing the framework that ties together the various steps in the educational process and directing these steps toward the end goals. A well developed curriculum is critical to the comprehensive education of all students, including those with handicaps.

Programs designed to foster and enhance adult functioning of persons with mental re-

tardation typically focus on three major domains: employment, leisure-recreation, and residential (Rusch, Chadsey-Rusch, White, & Gifford, 1985; Rusch, Schutz, & Agran, 1982). Brown et al. (1979) have suggested that four domains be considered in educating persons with severe handicaps, including: employment, leisure/recreation, community, and domestic. Although this chapter centers on curriculum development as it relates to employment training, it goes beyond this domain as adequate functioning in competitive employment environments requires adjustment in several domains. For example, an individual must know not only how to perform the functions specific to the job, but he or she must be able to: independently travel to and from work (community); appropriately fill break or lunch time (leisure); and wear clean, appropriate work clothing (domestic). The proposed curriculum strategies (see Figures 1 and 2) for achieving these goals consist of the following steps: 1) examining present environments for possible functioning needs, 2) surveying the community for potential job placements, 3) assessing skill requirements in relevant environments, and 4) selecting specific skill clusters and the division of these skill clusters based on curricular focus (maintenance or generalization). Determining what skills are necessary for functioning in competitive employment settings is based on the "survival skills" perspective (Rusch, 1979). In this chapter, the way in which these skills are incorporated into the curriculum are discussed in two contexts:

Survey community for possible current environments

ID present environment

Assess job/environment requirements (social/vocational survival skills)

"Expert" information   Direct observation

Inventory: general information, specific work skill clusters,
supportive skills

Delineate and inventory subenvironments

Divide skill clusters into specific job skills

Task analyze

Systematically instruct

Develop transition plans

Withdraw

Maintain

Figure 1.   Steps in curriculum development when targeted job placement is known.

1) when the targeted job placement is known, and 2) when the targeted job placement is unknown.

CURRICULAR CONSIDERATIONS

When developing curricula for students with handicaps, educators often find an absence of manuals or handbooks that meet the needs of all their students. While this lack of instructional support may appear to be a hindrance, it is a reflection of the individual needs of such students.

A variety of curricular models are available for educating young students with handicaps. Wilcox and Bellamy (1982a) describe four models of curriculum. These models are: eliminative, developmental, early academics, and demands of adult life. Eliminative curricular models are designed to eliminate inappropriate behaviors. Once the maladaptive behaviors

have been purged from the individual's repertoire, adaptive responses can be developed. The major danger with this type of curriculum is that the student is being deprived of any form of environmental control. Additionally, this model delays the learning of functional skills. Unfortuantely, this type of model is frequently seen in the experimental literature dealing with individuals with severe handicaps.

Developmental models of curricular content are based on the development of the normal infant. Skills are taught in the same sequence as that which is demonstrated by nonhandicapped children. Haring and Bricker (1976) discussed the need for this type of curricular model. They felt it gave an appropriate curricular framework. The developmental model is intended to help in the identification of those skills that are being performed at a near-normal levels, as well as those skills that are in need of intervention. This type of identification would as-

Survey community for potential jobs

ID possible placements

Assess job/environment requirements (social/vocational survival skills)

"Expert" information   Direct observation

Inventory: general information, specific work skill clusters, supportive skills

Delineate and inventory subenvironments

ID probable placements

ID common survival skills

Select target skills

Define instructional examples

Define range of examples

Select examples

Sequence examples

Systematically instruct

Probe

Withdraw

Maintain

Figure 2. Steps in curriculum development when targeted job placement is unknown.

sist in the development of long-range goals and short-term objectives, as well as provide for the sequencing of skills. Finally, it tells the teacher where to start. Unfortunately, many severely handicapped children do not follow normal sequences of development. Additionally, severely handicapped students develop more slowly than nonhandicapped peers. Developmental models assume that unlimited instructional time is available for the student. Given the learning characteristics of individuals with severe handicaps and time limits of school, this is not true (Wilcox & Bellamy, 1982a). Another concept that does not necessarily apply to the severely handicapped student is readiness. The developmental model implies that some skills are necessary before other skills may be acquired. Severely handicapped students may never acquire some of these "prerequisite skills" and will never be ready to progress to more relevant activities. Developmental models provide no functional alternative if the student fails to acquire the "basic" skills (Brown et al., 1979). Finally, developmental curricular models do not have content that is necessarily related to ultimate adult functioning or daily life. Objectives are derived from assessment and screening devices that may not relate to daily functioning. And the domains around which the developmental model is centered (gross motor, fine motor, perceptual, cognitive, social, and self-help) are not integrated and necessarily helpful in adult functioning (Wilcox & Bellamy, 1982a).

Curricular models based on early academic content utilize the basic skills approach. Normal behavior is thought to be a cumulative product based on a set of core skills (time telling, change making, basic reading). Haring, Liberty, and White (1980) indicate that these behaviors can be taught, and that many of them are necessary for the eventual functioning of the individual. However, this approach fails to integrate these behaviors into functional units that can be utilized in community settings. Skills are splintered and never drawn together. This model focuses on the form of behavior rather than the function (Wilcox & Bellamy, 1982a).

Models based on the demands of adult life (Brown et al., 1979; Belmore & Brown, 1976; Rusch et al., 1985) integrate these basic skills into functional units. These curricular models base their content on competencies needed to function both inside and outside the school. They propose a top-down model in which the environment is inventoried to identify survival skills. Table 1 depicts an environmental inventory matrix. Various present and future settings (home, school, place of employment, community) are examined across skill domains (employment, residential/domestic, leisure/recreation). Survival skills are identified within each domain in relation to each setting. Such a framework enables the educator to take a comprehensive view of potential functioning opportunities. Through the identification of survival skills, this model takes into account the limited time available to the student with severe handicaps, and the image that such students often present (Wilcox & Bellamy, 1982a).

Secondary students require a curriculum and educational opportunities that transcend the usual high-school-to-vocational-rehabilitation sequence. The traditional sequence often represents two separate programs operating with separate goals and opportunities that do not necessarily match one another. Students with handicaps, however, need a program that embodies similar goals and opportunities while also providing for an orderly transition from high school programs to vocational opportunities and long-term employment.

A curriculum development strategy should not produce a fixed curriculum sequence that can be applied to all students in all settings; rather, it should be unique to each student and each community. In an effort to provide some direction to the developement of appropriate curricula for severely handicapped students, Brown et al. (1979) listed three assumptions on which curriculum should be founded: 1) students with handicaps should be prepared for maximally independent, productive participation in many "least restrictive" community

Table 1. Environmental inventory matrix

| Setting | Domain | | |
	Employment	Residential/domestic	Leisure/recreation
Home			
School			
Place of employment			
Community			

settings; 2) the ability to generalize skills learned in one setting to novel settings cannot be assumed; and 3) students with handicaps do *not* represent a homogeneous population with fixed characteristics and abilities. Curricula that take into account the above assumptions will provide tailor-made programs designed to meet students' specific skill needs in present and future environments, including students with mild handicaps. For all students with handicaps this top-down model of curriculum development is particularly well suited because the goals and objectives are based on the skill demands present in adult environments (Brown et al., 1979).

One curriculum development strategy consists of identifying potential job sites and their prerequisite survival skills, the topic of the next section.

SURVIVAL SKILLS

Survival skills for individuals with handicaps are generally thought of as those behaviors that facilitate functioning in community settings (Martin, Rusch, & Heal, 1982). Such skills are of particular importance to individuals preparing for competitive employment (Rusch, 1979). In relation to employment, survival skills are "those skills that when acquired increase the likelihood of work placement and/or employment maintenance" (Rusch et al., 1982). Survival skills can be divided into two categories: social survival skills and vocational survival skills. *Social survival skills* fall in the Brown et al.'s (1979) interaction-with-nonhandicapped-peers domain, that is, skills that require or are required in interactions with others (e.g., co-workers, supervisors). *Vocational survival skills,* in turn, refer to the non-social interaction skills required by the job (e.g., completing work on time, performing quality work) (Rusch et al., 1982).

Identifying Potential Job Sites

Determining what social and vocational survival skills are necessary for success in community jobs requires that potential job placements be identified. Bates and Pancsofar (1981) described six methods of determining

available community jobs: 1) listing previously successful employment sites, 2) keeping track of the frequency with which specific types of jobs appear in the classified ads, 3) obtaining a list of employment openings from the local Job Service, 4) developing a list of potential job sites in conjunction with local business and service clubs, 5) utilizing personal contracts with employers, and 6) reviewing other successful training programs in the community and other similar communities. (See Chapter 15 for a more thorough discussion of methods to use to identify potential job sites.)

Once a listing of potential job placements has been generated, the specific skills required for success in each of the potential job sites must be identified (Bates & Pancsofar, 1981). This task can be accomplished by means of verbal reports from individuals who know the job and direct observations of employees who are presently performing a similar or the same job.

Verbal reports from individuals who know the job (e.g., co-worker, supervisor, rehabilitation expert) will yield a list of skills that are essential to that particular job. Such reports may consist of responses to an interview or a questionnaire. Verbal reports should be supplemented by direct observation to validate the list of survival skills provided by the knowledgeable person, and to obtain an accurate ranking of the importance of each of these skills (Rusch, Rusch, Menchetti, & Schutz, 1980). Direct observation requires on-site observation of workers who are performing a similar or the actual targeted job. Through direct observation, survival skills are listed and ranked in order of importance (Rusch et al., 1980).

The identification of survival skills and the utilization of such skills as the basis for curricular content enhance the probability that learners with severe handicaps will receive instruction in content areas that are relevant to their future functioning needs. As with any curriculum development strategy, curriculum assets must be matched to learner needs.

Mithaug, Hagmeier, and Haring (1977) developed a framework for identifying requisites for placement in community jobs consisting of

10 steps, including surveying potential community job placements, selecting probable placements, assessing job requirements, and assessing learner competencies in relation to these requirements. Rusch et al. (1980) and Rusch (1983) expanded Mithaug et al.'s (1977) proposed framework to include training and maintenance. According to the ensuing model, survey-train-place-maintain, the first step in a training program for learners with severe handicaps is to *survey the community,* including identification and validation of social and vocational survival skills.

Job Inventory Strategy

Belmore and Brown (1976) proposed a strategy for conducting community surveys. This method, the Job Inventory Strategy, is designed to identify specific skill needs and provide precise information about the appropriateness of the match between a particular job and the needs and skills of a student with handicaps. The inventory covers three major areas: (1) general information, (2) specific work skills required, and (3) supportive skills and other required information.

General information relates to the reasons why a given job is being considered for students with severe handicaps. Thus, a rationale should be established regarding the job's appropriateness for the student, what it can contribute to the student's growth, and how it matches the student's unique capabilities. Besides a task analysis of the job and a description of the products produced, such factors as basic performance criteria, work hours, work days, overtime, breaks, etc. should also be specified. The physical plant and work area (including a diagram), as well as the social environment (specifying the nature and extent of all possible social interactions with co-workers, supervisors, etc.), should also be described in addition to any special rules the employer may have that are applicable to all employees.

The second general area of the Job Inventory Strategy, *specific work skills required,* is used most often to determine whether or not a student has the skills necessary for a particular job. Specifically, student work skills should be examined in relation to job requirements in the following areas: 1) physical/sensory motor skills (e.g., ability to lift heavy objects or complete tasks requiring good eye-hand coordination); 2) functional academic skills (e.g., minimal reading or math level required); 3) interpersonal skills (e.g., ability to follow multi-step directions or ask for help); 4) machine and tool usage (e.g., operating a dishwasher or floor polisher); and 5) hygiene (e.g., general cleanliness of clothing, body, and hair).

The third general area specified by Belmore and Brown (1976), *supportive skills and other required information,* deals with skills that are not directly related to the job, but are required for success at the job site. This component should include information about transportation and mobility (e.g., access to public transportation, student's ability to use public transportation independently); skills related to work preparation (e.g., making and packing a lunch, selecting clean and appropriate clothing, securing a hairnet); basic money management skills (e.g., banking payroll checks, writing personal checks, budgeting, purchasing items, paying for public transportation, filing income tax return); time-telling skills (e.g., knowing when to arrive at or depart from work, break time, job schedule); health code requirements (e.g., hair length, use of a hairnet or smock, TB test); and informed consent and other legal requirements (e.g., filling out W-4 forms, signing work contract).

Particular sections of the survey process can be supplemented by more information obtained through further systematic observation of the specific work environment. Once a job site has been targeted as a potential place of employment, subenvironments that are particular to the specific job should be delineated and inventoried (e.g., the work site, the lunchroom/breakroom, the bathroom, etc. [Brown et al., 1979]). Each of these subenvironments is composed of unique skill clusters or activities. These, in turn, become the basic curriculum units for students with severe handicaps (Wilcox & Bellamy, 1982a).

CURRICULAR FOCUS

Since time and resource limitations make it impossible to teach students with handicaps all the skills they need for every potential future environment, educators must select the content and method of instruction that are most appropriate for each student's curricular sequence. Frequently such a decision is based on whether the student's future placement is known or not. If the placement is known, skill maintenance becomes the relevant curriculum focus. However when the targeted job placement is unknown, generalization is the relevant focus.

Maintenance: Developing a Curriculum Based upon a Target Placement

When the targeted job is known, skill clusters or activities can be divided into specific skills that are directly related to the performance demands of a particular job. For example, if the targeted job placement for a student will be a janitorial position in a small restaurant or bar, job-specific skills might include: cleaning and sanitizing two restrooms, cleaning the bar and an adjoining eating area, maintaining the floor in the entry, and disposing of trash. Specific vocational survival skills include: cleaning and sanitizing toilets and urinals, replacing toilet paper, washing bathroom walls, cleaning and polishing mirrors, cleaning sinks, replenishing paper towels, sweeping and mopping floors, emptying trash, vacuuming, washing tables and chairs, and cleaning windows, video-games, and pinball machines. There are a variety of social survival skills also required. These skills include: greeting co-workers, supervisor, and employer; requesting more supplies; accomodating customers; responding to requests or greetings from customers; and obtaining lunch during the work day. Each specific skill is task analyzed, and programs are designed to accommodate specific student abilities and disabilities.

For example, the activity of table washing could then be divided into the following steps:

1. Obtain supplies
   a. Rag
   b. Small bucket
   c. Measuring cup
   d. Bleach
2. Fill bucket ¾ full with warm water
3. Measure ¼ cup bleach
4. Pour bleach into water
5. Rinse measuring cup
6. Put away bleach and measuring cup
7. Take supplies to first table in eating area
8. Wet rag
9. Squeeze out excess water
10. Using large circular motion, wipe entire table top
11. Check for food stuck to table top
12. If food found, scrub area until particle is loosened or dissolved
13. Repeat steps 8–12
14. If table top clean, proceed to next table
15. Repeat steps 8–14 until all tables are clean
16. Throw rag in laundry bag
17. Empty bucket
18. Put bucket away

Modification could be made in measuring, task sequencing, etc., to adjust to the student's needs. Acquisition is facilitated through systematic assessment and teaching procedures (e.g., levels of assistance, prompting, fading, reinforcement and correction procedures, etc.). Maintenance is ensured through the use of systematic withdrawal procedures.

Rusch and Kazdin (1981) describe three withdrawal designs: 1) sequential withdrawal, 2) partial withdrawal, and 3) combined withdrawal. Sequential withdrawal consists of gradually withdrawing different components of an intervention. Components are withdrawn in consecutive phases. The partial withdrawal design is similar to the sequential withdrawal design in that components of an intervention are gradually withdrawn. However, it differs in that the intervention is gradually withdrawn across different persons, behaviors, settings, or baselines. Combined partial-sequential withdrawal designs provide a blend of the other two designs. Components of an intervention are gradually withdrawn for a given baseline or an individual subject, and the procedure for withdrawing the intervention is attempted one baseline, person, behavior, etc. at a time.

Each of these designs utilizes five basic steps. The steps in withdrawal include: 1) identification of program components, 2) withdrawal of antecedents, 3) assessment of maintenance, 4) withdrawal of consequences, and 5) assessment of maintenance.

If it is determined that "washing tables" is a skill that is critical in a particular job site, the student must acquire the skill and continue to perform in the absence of the trainer. The acquisition and maintenance programs for this particular activity might include several steps. The acquisition could employ a least-intrusive to most-intrusive prompting system that allows student behavior to control the amount of assistance from the trainer. As the student acquires the skill, trainer assistance is faded. A similar system would be used in the delivery of reinforcement. During the initial stages of acquisition, the student is often reinforced for every correct response. As the student acquires skills in the chain, larger and larger chunks of behavior are required to obtain reinforcement. When the entire chain is acquired and performed independent of program cues or prompts, the maintenance phase begins. Trainer presence is faded as the student demonstrates the ability to independently perform the activity.

Students should be placed on the job using well designed transition plans based on students' generalization and maintenance needs. Generalization needs can be kept to a minimum if students are trained for a particular job with same or similar materials (e.g., cleaning supplies) and in the same or similar settings in which they will be expected to perform upon employment (e.g., cafeteria, restaurant, small electronics firm). Maintenance should be specifically programmed for by the specification of the withdrawal procedures to be used (Rusch & Kazdin, 1981).

Generalization: Developing Curriculum Based upon Unknown Future Placement

When the targeted job placement is unknown, educators must plan the most efficient program using the information gathered from job inventories to develop their curriculum. Specifically, skills that are relevant to a student's survival in more than one vocational setting must be identified and included in addition to skills essential for survival in any community setting. Also, skills that are unique to probable placements must be identified as potential areas of skill development.

A skill that can be performed in one setting only is of little use to an individual if that setting is not the target placement setting, hence the importance of generalization. For students who are handicapped, curriculum activities that increase the probability that skills learned in one setting will be successfully performed in settings different from those used during training must be the focus (Horner, Sprague, & Wilcox, 1982). Teaching the "general case" is attained when correct performance across a full range of trained and nontrained examples is achieved.

One curriculum strategy that shows promise for teaching the "general case" is *general case programming,* which focuses attention upon the selection and sequencing of "examples" within and among teaching sessions (Horner et al., 1982). The basic steps in teaching general case include: 1) defining relevant and potential placement settings in which students may be required to work, 2) identifying the range of task and performance requirements in the potential work settings, 3) selecting examples of tasks to be used during instruction, 4) sequencing and teaching the task, and 5) assessing generalization to untrained examples (Horner et al., 1982). Each of these steps are summarized in Table 2 and described below.

Defining Relevant and Potential Placement Settings The number of relevant and potential placement settings is determined through the job analysis survey (Rusch & Mithaug, 1980). These settings include jobs that share major characteristics, such as food service jobs or janitorial positions. The teacher must systematically survey the community to identify the potential jobs. These surveys include careful observation of potential settings, interviews with experts (e.g., a supervisor at an employ-

Table 2. Steps of general case programming

Define the instructional universe
  (amount of behavior and all relevant stimulus
    situations)
  Observation of target settings
  Interview with experts
  Use of one's own knowledge
Identify the range of relevant stimulus and
    response variation
  Identify generic response chain
  Determine generic discriminative stimuli
  Document variation across generic stimuli
  Document variation across generic responses
  Identify exceptions or potential errors
Select examples for use on teaching and
    probe testing
  Determine minimum number of training examples
  Choose examples
Sequence selected teaching examples
  Teach multiple examples with multiple
    components
  Use cumulative programming procedures
  Teach skills concurrently
  Teach general case before exceptions
Teach the examples
Test using nontrained probe examples

ment site), or by relying on one's own knowledge of the requirements of the setting (Horner et al., 1982).

If, through observation, it is determined that "washing tables" is an activity performed in many of the target settings, then this skill should be learned by students who may be placed in one of these settings. Careful observation often reveals that there is a great deal of variation in how tables should be washed. For example, tables vary in size (small, long), shape (square, rectangular, oval, round), and surface texture (smooth, rough, "fabric") and, therefore, require different skills. Also, locations could include kitchens, dining rooms, cafeterias, bars, and restaurants; cleaning materials may differ in the type of cleaner used (premixed, ready to mix) and the activity required to apply it (spray and wipe; wet, squeeze, and wipe); and equipment could vary from rag to sponge to towel, and buckets and measuring cups (if needed) vary in size, composition (glass, plastic, metal), weight, color, and measuring line markings. Each of these variations must be identified, and representative examples must be chosen to ensure maximum generalization of the skills.

Identifying Range of Tasks and Performance Requirements The second step, *identifying the range of tasks and performance requirements in potential work settings,* is similar to a task analysis in that the chain of generic performance requirements is described. These performance requirements usually encompass identifying and listing what events, actions, or objects will function as cues or information sources for correct performance.

Selecting Task Examples Task selection must be based upon the following criteria: 1) they must contain equal amounts of information, and 2) they must teach the student what not to do as well as what to do. Washing a table may include: an example using a premixed spray bottle with a rag to wash table tops in a semi-crowded cafeteria; an example requiring the student to measure and mix bleach and water in a bucket, and use a sponge to clean table tops in a deserted bar; and an example using a disinfectant cleaner and water in a small bucket, and a white towel to clean tables in a small crowded restaurant.

Much of the literature indicates that training multiple examples, especially if they are carefully chosen, increases generalization. "Best examples" should be selected from "actual" examples (Hupp & Mervis, 1981). For students with handicaps, simulated examples have not been shown to reliably result in generalization (Wilcox & Bellamy, 1982b).

Sequencing and Teaching Task Examples Multiple examples should be taught within individual teaching sessions. If a task requires a large number of steps, a subset of those steps may be selected for individual instructional sessions. The "general case" should be taught before any exceptions since the student's ability to identify the relevant characteristics common to all examples is reduced if exceptions are taught simultaneously with other examples. In the table-washing example, the teacher should teach the entire task, varying the materials and equipment as much as possible.

Many factors have been shown to facilitate generalization. According to Guess (1980), generalization tends to be more successful if the presentation of examples incorporates:

1) multiple trainers, 2) "sufficient" examples, 3) varied settings, 4) appropriate (real life) content, 5) "sufficient" duration, and 6) an adequate reinforcement schedule. Furthermore, Engelmann and Carnine (1982) identified five structural conditions that will potentially influence an individual's ability to generalize what is being learned. The first included identifying the quality of sameness throughout all examples (e.g., given several examples of tables varying in size and shape, the learner should identify the quality of "tableness" as being the same). Second, during teaching the teacher should provide a signal (e.g., a verbal cue) that accompanies each example demonstrating the quality to be generalized. Third, the physical variation of the examples that contain the common quality is shown by presenting a range of examples (e.g., large round tables, small square tables, and long rectangular tables). Fourth, the teacher must present negative examples (e.g., red box), so that the learner will be able to determine the limits of permissible variation (a signal for nonexamples should also be presented). And fifth, testing must include both positive and negative examples not previously presented in training.

The training site must be considered a critical part of training for generalization. Currently, many programs for students with handicaps are provided in environments that differ drastically from "normal" situations. For example, nonhandicapped peers are rarely present, social demands are contrived or absent, emphasis is on skill acquisition rather than regular performance, and students assume little responsibility for their own behavior. Yet, we expect these students to acquire behaviors to be used in "normal" settings. Presuming generalization between such different settings is little more than the "train and hope" approach (Bellamy, Rose, Wilson, & Clarke, 1982). In contrast, generalization is enhanced if examples

are taught in the natural context. ". . . if generalization is the professed goal of a treatment program, the best treatment situation is one that shares as many common elements as possible with other non-treatment situations" (Rose, 1979, p. 199).

Assessing Using Nontrained Examples *Probes* are used to obtain information about error patterns and to help modify teaching examples to eliminate such errors. *Probes* are conducted after the student has learned some or all the teaching examples.

SUMMARY AND CONCLUSIONS

The curricular focus (maintenance versus generalization) is important to the development of a curriculum. When the targeted job placement is known, the curricular focus becomes one of maintenance. For such situations there is more time for specific skill development and the maintenance of skills. Typically, a highly specialized skill development package is characterized by this type of curriculum. When the targeted job placement is unknown, generalization becomes the curricular focus. Frequently, the *type* of targeted job placement is known, whereas the exact site is not (e.g., janitorial, food service, electronics). Educators must select tasks that are relevant to as many job sites as possible. For generalization purposes, particular tasks tend to be less defined than corresponding skills found in curricula focusing on maintenance. Teaching the "general case" is recommended as a method for selecting, sequencing, and evaluating acquisition of survival skills.

Many factors must be considered in deciding on instructional arrangement, including: 1) what skills will be taught and where, 2) influence of staff and student time constraints on selected examples, and 3) availability of examples. Typically, there is not enough time to teach all the skills needed to adequately function in postschool years' environments.

REFERENCES

Bates, P., & Pancsofar, E. (1981). Longitudinal vocational training for severely handicapped students in the public schools. In R. York, W. K. Schofield, D. J.

Donder, D. L. Ryndak, and B. Reguly (Eds.), *Organizing and implementing services for students with severe and multiple handicaps: Proceedings from the 1981*

Illinois Statewide Institute for Educators of the Severely and Profoundly Handicapped (pp. 105–122). Springfield, IL: Department of Specialized Educational Services, Illinois State Board of Education.

Bellamy, G. T., Rose, H., Wilson, D. J., & Clarke, J. Y. (1982). Strategies for vocational preparation. In B. Wilcox and G. T. Bellamy, *Design of high school programs for severely handicapped students* (pp. 144–150). Baltimore: Paul H. Brookes.

Belmore, K., & Brown, L. (1976). A job skill inventory strategy for use in public school vocational training programs for severely handicapped potential workers. In L. Brown, N. Certo, K. Belmore, & T. Crowner (Eds.), *Madison's alternative for zero exclusion: Papers and programs related to public school services for secondary age severely handicapped students (Volume VI: Part 1)* (pp. 143–218). Madison, WI: Madison Metropolitan School District.

Brown, L., Branston, M. B., Hamre-Nietupski, S., Pumpian, I., Certo, N., & Gruenewald, L. (1979). A strategy for developing chronological age-appropriate and functional curricular content for severely handicapped adolescents and young adults. *Journal of Special Education, 13,* 81–90.

Englemann, S., & Carnine, D. (1982). *Theory of instruction: Principles and applications.* New York: Irving Publishers.

Guess, D. (1980). Methods in communication instruction for severely handicapped persons. In W. Sailor, B. Wilcox, & L. Brown (Eds.), *Methods of instruction for severely handicapped learners* (pp. 213–221). Baltimore: Paul H. Brookes.

Haring, N. G., & Bricker, D. (1976). Overview of comprehensive services for the severely/profoundly handicapped. In N. J. Haring & L. J. Brown (Eds.), *Teaching the severely handicapped,* (Vol. 1). New York: Grune & Stratton.

Haring, N. G., Liberty, K. A., & White, O. R. (1980). Rules for data-based strategy decisions in instructional programs: Current research and instructional implications. In W. Sailor, B. Wilcox, & L. Brown (Eds.), *Methods of instruction for severely handicapped students* (pp. 159–192). Baltimore: Paul H. Brookes.

Horner, R. H., Sprague, J., & Wilcox, B. (1982). General case programming for community activities. In B. Wilcox & G. T. Bellamy, *Design of high school programs for severely handicapped students* (pp. 61–89). Baltimore: Paul H. Brookes.

Hupp, S. C., & Mervis, C. B. (1981). Development of generalized concepts by severely handicapped students.

Journal of The Association for the Severely Handicapped, 6, 14–21.

Martin, J. E., Rusch, F. R., & Heal, L. W. (1982). Teaching community survival skills to mentally retarded adults: A review and analysis. *Journal of Special Education, 3,* 105–119.

Mithaug, D. E., Hagmeier, L. D., & Haring, N. G. (1977). The relationship between training activities and job placement in vocational education of the severely and profoundly handicapped. *AAESPH Review, 2,* 89–109.

Rose, H. (1979). Effectiveness and generalization of overcorrection procedures with the stereotyped behavior of a severely retarded adult. *AAESPH Review, 2,* 196–201.

Rusch, F. R. (1979). Toward the validation of social/vocational survival skills. *Mental Retardation, 17,* 143–145.

Rusch, F. R. (1983). Competitive vocational training. In M. E. Snell (ed.), *Systematic instruction of the moderately and severely handicapped* (2nd ed.) (pp. 503–523). Columbus, OH: Charles E. Merrill.

Rusch, F. R., Chadsey-Rusch, J., White, D. M., & Gifford, J. L. (1985). Programs for severely mentally retarded adults: Perspectives and methodologies. In D. Bricker & J. Filler (Eds.), *The severely mentally retarded: From research to practice* (pp. 119–140). Reston, VA: Council for Exceptional Children.

Rusch, F. R., & Kazdin, A. E. (1981). Toward a methodology of withdrawal designs for the assessment of response maintenance. *Journal of Applied Behavior Analysis, 14,* 131–140.

Rusch, F. R., & Mithaug, D. E. (1980). *Vocational training for mentally retarded adults: A behavior analytic approach.* Champaign, IL: Research Press.

Rusch, F. R., Rusch, J. C., Menchetti, B. M, & Schutz, R. P. (1980). *Survey-train-place: Developing a school-aged vocational curriculum for the severely handicapped student.* Unpublished manuscript.

Rusch, F. R., Schutz, R. P., & Agran, M. (1982). Validating entry-level survival skills for service occupations: Implication for curriculum development. *Journal of the Association for the Severely Handicapped, 7,* 32–41.

Wilcox, B., & Bellamy, G. T. (1982a). *Design of high school programs for severely handicapped students* (pp. 23–40). Baltimore: Paul H. Brookes.

Wilcox, B., & Bellamy, G. T. (1982b). *Design of high school programs for severely handicapped students* (pp. 99–120). Baltimore: Paul H. Brookes.

Chapter 15

Social Validation

David M. White

THE PURPOSE OF the present chapter is to introduce and provide an overview of the concepts and methods of social validation as applied to the evaluation of work behavior research. As a methodology utilized to evaluate the acceptability of applied interventions (Kazdin, 1977; Kazdin & Matson, 1981; Wolf, 1978), social validation has been used in a variety of contexts, including training appropriate eating behavior in mentally retarded individuals (Nutter & Reid, 1978) and, in delinquent youth, training interpersonal skills (Minkin et al., 1976) and appropriate interactions with police (Werner et al., 1975).

In the area of competitive employment, social validation has involved assessment of the social acceptability of interventions with respect to: 1) the intervention focus, 2) procedures used to change behavior, and 3) intervention effectiveness. Social validation of *intervention focus* involves assessing whether work behavior selected for training is important for enhancing employability. Many procedures may be potentially effective in altering behavior; some, however, such as timeout from reinforcement, may be viewed as unacceptable in the community where the employment intervention is to be implemented. Thus, the social acceptability of intervention procedures is an important basis for selection among *potentially* effective techniques. The *effectiveness* of planned interventions is validated, in turn, by examining behavior change in the light of the performance of peers or in comparison to that of nonhandicapped peers in the work environment.

Two procedures, social comparison and subjective evaluation, have been used to evaluate the social validity of goals (focus), procedures, and results. *Social comparison* involves comparing a student's behavior before and after habilitation with similar behavior of nonhandicapped peers. Social validation is demonstrated when, after treatment, a trainee's job performance is as valued as that of nonhandicapped peers (i.e., co-workers). Using the method of *subjective evaluation*, a target behavior is evaluated by experts or significant others with whom the student has contact (e.g., employers, supervisors, co-workers) to determine that change resulting from the intervention is perceived as important.

The three social validity components (goals, procedures, and results) and the two methods for establishing social validity (social comparison and subjective evaluation) suggest six areas of importance to employability efforts (see Table 1).

To be effective, subjective evaluation requires that a Work Performance Evaluation Form (WPEF) be developed. The WPEF is a questionnaire displaying many of the social and vocational skills that are of concern to employers, supervisors, and co-workers. The sample WPEF presented in Table 2 was used in a study on the concordance of ratings provided by employers, supervisors, and co-workers (White & Rusch, 1983). The substantial disagreement observed among the three rating groups concerning student employees' performance suggested the need to obtain opinions from all three (White & Rusch, 1983). The

Table 1. Illustration of six forms of social validation

Procedure	Goal	Procedures	Results
Social comparison	Identification of a range of skills exhibited by nonhandicapped co-workers who perform comparable tasks during similar work periods. Co-workers are compared along both social and vocational dimensions. The objective is to specify upper and lower limits for acceptable work behavior in the employment setting, and adjust or manage the student's behavior to fall within tolerable limits. Behavior that falls outside the treatment focus serves as an intervention target.	Identification of procedures typically used by employers in training non-handicapped co-workers. Co-workers compared are those who perform similar tasks during similar work periods. The primary objective is to specify the procedures that are acceptable to the job setting. This component of social validation is implemented to identify a set of management techniques for use in training.	Evaluation of whether changes resulting from an intervention are clinically important. The procedure involves comparison of the student's work after instruction with that of nonhandicapped co-workers considered to be functioning adequately in the job environment. A significant change is defined as one in which the student's performance falls within the acceptable range.
Subjective evaluation	Solicitation of opinions of others in the setting who are capable of making meaningful decisions about the student based on their expertise in the occupational area or their relationship to the student. Opinions might be solicited to identify aspects of vocational and/or social behaviors required for survival in the job setting. Initial screening is used to develop prescriptions for training.	Assessment of the social acceptability of behavioral management techniques to be used in training. Management techniques include both those planned for use and those presently used in an ongoing program. Opinions of administrators, supervisors, and co-workers may be solicited. Social acceptability is typically evaluated with regard to ethics, cost, and practicality. Although a wide range of techniques are initially effective in changing behaviors (e.g., verbal praise or timeout from reinforcement), only a subset is likely to be viewed as acceptable or appropriate to a given employment setting.	Solicitation of the opinions of administrators, supervisors, and co-workers to evaluate the effects produced by the employment training program. Significant others are asked whether changes resulting from instruction are important. The objective is to assess whether training has led to qualitative changes in how the client is viewed by others.

200

Table 2. Work Performance Evaluation Form (WPEF)

	1 Poor	2 Needs Improvement	3 Average	4 Good	5 Exceptional
	Shows no effort to meet requirements. Would not pass probation	Makes effort to meet requirements but needs additional training to pass probation	Meets most requirements normally associated with job description and requires average amount of supervision	Meets all requirements and works independently with few exceptions	Model employee, exceeds requirements in most areas, takes pride in job

		1	2	3	4	5
1.	Overall job skills/work quality	1	2	3	4	5
A.	Obtains/returns materials for task	1	2	3	4	5
B.	Uses correct approach technique to complete tasks	1	2	3	4	5
C.	Takes care of equipment and materials	1	2	3	4	5
D.	Attends to task	1	2	3	4	5
E.	Works fast during rush times	1	2	3	4	5
F.	Meets sanitation requirements	1	2	3	4	5
G.	Takes pride in job	1	2	3	4	5
2.	Overall level of responsibility	1	2	3	4	5
A.	Works alone	1	2	3	4	5
B.	Works safely	1	2	3	4	5
C.	Completes all assigned tasks	1	2	3	4	5
D.	Follows procedures and policies	1	2	3	4	5
3.	Overall relationship to supervisors and co-workers	1	2	3	4	5
A.	Cooperates	1	2	3	4	5
B.	Is considerate of others	1	2	3	4	5
C.	Maintains a positive attitude about work	1	2	3	4	5
D.	Accepts criticism	1	2	3	4	5
E.	Asks for assistance when necessary	1	2	3	4	5
F.	Communicates with supervisors and co-workers	1	2	3	4	5
4.	Overall ability to manage time	1	2	3	4	5
A.	Attendance	1	2	3	4	5
B.	Completes job on time	1	2	3	4	5
C.	Follows a schedule	1	2	3	4	5
D.	Manages time appropriately	1	2	3	4	5
E.	Follows directions to do a task at a given time	1	2	3	4	5

ADDITIONAL STRENGTHS   ADDITIONAL WEAKNESSES

From White, D. M., & Rusch, F. R. (1983). Social validation in competitive employment: Evaluating work performance. *Applied Research in Mental Retardation, 4*, 343–354. Copyright 1983 by Pergamon Press. Adapted by permission.

resulting WPEF was developed to obtain subjective evaluations of work performance in the
following areas: 1) job skills and work quality,
2) level of responsibility, 3) relationship to
supervisors and co-workers, and 4) ability to
manage time. Work Performance Evaluation
Forms can be developed for any occupational
area and any set of work behaviors. (For WPEF
development, scoring, and interpretation information, see Rusch and Mithaug [1980,
pp. 175–180; 199–203].)

SOCIAL VALIDATION IN
COMPETITIVE EMPLOYMENT

This section focuses on empirical research on
the social validation of competitive employment training programs in an effort to convey
the principles of social validation. The overview is organized according to the six types of
social validation introduced in Table 1.

Intervention Focus

Social Comparison The social comparison method may be used to identify the
goals of interventions designed to teach skills
needed for survival in competitive employment. Crouch, Rusch, and Karlan (1985) used
social comparison in a university food service
setting. Three students enrolled in a competitive employment program were responsible
for completing various tasks in a cafeteria,
such as setting up a lunch line and sweeping a
dinner serving line. Social comparison data on
the range of time (speed) with which nonhandicapped workers performed similar tasks
suggested that all three students completed
their tasks too slowly. Consequently, the intervention goal of the program became to increase
the speed with which the target students completed their tasks.

The intervention, *correspondence training*
(cf. Karlan & Rusch, 1982), consisted of reinforcing students for saying when they would
start and complete an assigned task. In a subsequent experimental phase, subjects were reinforced for positive correspondence between
the stated times and task performance, that is,
for doing what they said they would do.

The verbal training procedure increased the

time spent working on assigned tasks for two of
the three students. Although the third student's
productivity also increased noticeably, the student was unable to attain the criterion performance level established by his supervisor.
Objective data demonstrated, however, that
nonhandicapped co-workers were also unable
to meet the criterion time established by the
supervisor. In fact, the third student's average
task time was found to exceed that of his
co-workers. The authors interpreted these data
as indicating that the supervisor's criterion of
adequate performance was too strict. They
argued, further, that a more reasonable criterion would have sensitized those around the
student to the noticeable shift in speed with
which this individual completed tasks. As a
result of the social comparison data, the supervisor agreed that the previous standard was too
stringent and, subsequently, imposed a more
reasonable standard.

Subjective Evaluation Subjective evaluations are likewise used to identify the focus of
employment instruction. Opinions are solicited
from persons capable of making meaningful
decisions about a student's behavior based
upon their exposure to the student (e.g., a
parent or an advocate) or their professional
expertise. Rusch, Schutz, and Agran (1982)
used subjective evaluation to identify the skills
required of individuals for entry into competitive employment. They sent questionnaires
to 120 potential employers representing food
service, janitorial, and maid service occupations throughout the state of Illinois. Questionnaire items were based on previous research on entry-level skills required for
acceptance into prevocational training programs (Mithaug & Hagmeier, 1978). Based
upon potential employers' responses, 28 specific skills necessary for survival in competitive
employment were identified (see Table 3).

The results of this survey provided important
information about the skills that are required of
individuals with handicaps. All respondents
unanimously agreed, for example, that new
employees must be able to: 1) recite their full
name when requested, 2) demonstrate the basic
addition skills, 3) keep their hair neat and
combed, 4) follow instructions, and 5) com-

Table 3. Skills employers deem important for entry into food service or janitorial and maid service occupations

Social skills

1. Follow one instruction provided at a time (100%).
2. Recite verbally upon request:
   a. Full name (100%)
   b. Home address (98%)
   c. Home telephone number (98%)
   d. Previous employer (91%)
3. Maintain proper grooming by:
   a. Dressing appropriately for work (98%)
   b. Cleaning self before coming to work (96%)
4. Maintain personal hygiene by:
   a. Keeping hair combed (100%)
   b. Shaving regularly (98%)
   c. Keeping teeth clean (96%)
   d. Using deodorant (96%)
   e. Keeping nails clean (93%)
5. Communicate such basic needs as:
   a. Sickness (98%)
   b. Toileting necessities (94%)
   c. Pain (92%)
6. Speak clearly enough to be understood by anyone on the second transmission (97%).
7. Respond appropriately and immediately after receiving 1 out of every 2 instructions (96%).
8. Remember to respond to an instruction that requires compliance after a specific time interval with 1 reminder (95%).
9. Respond appropriately to safety signals when given verbally (94%).
10. Initiate contact with supervisor when cannot do job (94%).
11. Initiate contact with co-worker when needing help on task (94%).
12. Work without displaying or engaging in major disruptive behaviors (e.g., arguments) more frequently than 1–2 times per month (94%).
13. Initiate and/or respond verbally in 3–5-word sentences (92%).
14. Work without initiating unnecessary contact with strangers more frequently than 3–5 times per day (92%).
15. Reach places of work by own transportation arrangements (e.g., walking, taxi, personal car) (92%).
16. Follow instructions with words such as *in* and *on* (90%).

Vocational skills

1. Complete repetitive tasks previously learned to proficiency within 25% of average rate (100%).
2. Demonstrate basic addition skills (100%).
3. Move safely about work place (98%).
4. Understand work routine by not displaying disruptive behaviors when routine task or schedule changes occur (98%).
5. Demonstrate understanding of rules (set down by supervisor) by not deviating from them more frequently than 3–5 times per month (98%).
6. Work at job continuously, remaining on task for 30- to 60-minute intervals (95%).
7. Demonstrate basic arithmetic skills to subtract (93%).
8. Want to work for money (92%).
9. Write 3–5-word sentences (91%).
10. Learn new job tasks explained by watching co-workers/supervisors perform tasks (90%).
11. Continue working without disruptions when co-workers are observing (90%).
12. Correct work on task after second correction from supervisor (90%).

From Rusch, F. R., Schutz, R. P., & Agran, M. (1982). Validating entry-level survival skills for service occupations: Implications for curriculum development. *Journal of The Association for the Severely Handicapped, 7,* 37–38. Copyright 1982 by The Association for the Severely Handicapped. Adapted by permission.

plete previously learned tasks to proficiency within 25% of the average rate. Furthermore, skills required for competitive employment were found to differ from those considered necessary in sheltered workshops. Polled supervisors unanimously agreed, however, with such sheltered workshop requirements as being able to communicate basic needs, including those involved in thirst and hunger, and being capable of communicating basic needs receptively and expressively by means of verbal expression, signs, or gestures (Mithaug & Hagmeier, 1978).

The demands placed upon students in sheltered workshops appear less stringent than those in competitive employment settings. Employer's standards also seem higher. Consequently, to enhance their effectiveness, community-based employment training efforts, including public school programs for secondary-age students, should be focused upon the unique set of skills required in the community. Rusch et al. (1982) were careful to note that the focus of any employment program must ultimately be decided upon at the local level. Their study surveyed a representative sample of potential employers in Illinois, and identified skills that served as a general guideline to the requirements and expectations of many employers. However, in implementing any subjective evaluation of treatment focus, the selection of a focus must be based upon subjective evaluations appropriate to the unique work environment in which community placement is an objective.

Summary Both social comparison and subjective evaluation are utilized in establishing the goals and focus of competitive employment programs. Social comparison is used to observe and record the behavior of nonhandicapped workers considered by employers or supervisors to perform adaptively in the competitive employment setting. The primary objective of this method is to specify the upper and lower limits of acceptable on-the-job behavior and, subsequently, manage or adjust trainees' performance to fall within these limits. Using the method of subjective evaluation, opinions are solicited from individuals in the employment setting who, as a result of their relationship with the student or expertise in the occupational area, are in a position to make meaningful recommendations about the treatment focus, that is, the skills demanded for employment survival. These opinions are used to develop prescriptions for subsequent employment training.

Treatment Procedures

Increasing attention has recently been given to public reaction to the procedures used in employment interventions. Consumers appear concerned that such procedures represent ac-

ceptable means for changing behavior. Verifying that planned intervention procedures are acceptable to consumers is important for several reasons. First, it may be of little use to develop effective treatment procedures if they are highly objectionable to those with whom they will be used (e.g., employers). Second, research evidence shows that application of aversive behavioral techniques results in higher participant dropout rates, not because such techniques are ineffective, but because they are not acceptable. Third, since instructional programs are more likely to be adopted if the procedures involved are viewed as desirable, preferred, or acceptable, program success may depend upon the acceptability of the techniques. In the following section, selected studies are used to illustrate the validation of intervention procedures through social comparison and subjective evaluation.

Social Comparison Applied to treatment procedures, social comparison consists of identifying behavior management techniques normally used within employment settings to train nonhandicapped co-workers who perform tasks similar to those of target trainees during similar work periods (Rusch, Morgan, Martin, Riva, & Agran, 1985). The primary objective of the social comparison method is to identify a set of management techniques that are *presently utilized* by employers, and that are acceptable to employers within the job setting. These techniques may then be utilized by teaching staff in training students.

Menchetti, Rusch, and Lamson (1981) used the social comparison method to identify procedures deemed acceptable to employers in training students as workers in food service occupations. They distributed a questionnaire to college and university food service employers in nine states. The questionnaire provided respondents with a description of either a mentally retarded or a nonhandicapped worker, and asked them to indicate their acceptance or nonacceptance of various behavior management procedures. Potential employers were found clearly to prefer certain procedures, while rejecting others. For example, employers reported that the use of a token economy system would *never* be an acceptable treatment procedure in their work settings, although they approved of frequent use of reinforcement with a new employee. Furthermore, some procedures viewed as acceptable for training mentally retarded workers were found to be unacceptable for training nonhandicapped workers. Thus, the use of a golf counter as a data collection device was reported to be *un*acceptable in the training of nonhandicapped workers, but acceptable in training mentally retarded workers. Table 4 lists procedures found to be acceptable (Menchetti et al., 1981).

Menchetti and his colleagues (1981) also found that a number of behavior management strategies commonly viewed as effective and acceptable in prevocational training settings (e.g., sheltered workshops) were considered unacceptable in community-based food services training settings. Community employers reported, for example, that ignoring socially inappropriate behavior, such as yelling at others, would be an unacceptable treatment strategy in their work settings—yet, extinction is known to be a powerful and useful intervention strategy in prevocational settings. Menchetti et al. (1981) reported that, while demonstrably effective, many behavioral procedures currently used in applied behavior analysis are unacceptable in most community-based employment settings. To increase the probability of placing and maintaining students in competitive employment, teachers should: 1) refrain from implementing socially unacceptable training procedures; 2) develop new, more socially acceptable interventions; and 3) when particularly effective procedures are found to be socially unacceptable, educate consumers about their effectiveness before implementing them. A fourth option might be added: teachers should become aware of effective behavior change strategies that may already be intact and in operation in the employment setting, that is, effective techniques that employers normally use in training nonhandicapped workers. Such flexibility on the part of teachers maximizes normalizing opportunities to students through the use of procedures often encountered in everyday life.

Furthermore, bringing behavior under the control of natural contingencies has long been advocated in applied behavior analysis as useful for achieving maintenance and generalization (Ayllon & Azrin, 1968; Baer & Wolf, 1970; Stokes & Baer, 1977). Thus, the behavior of significant others in the employment context can play a critical role in the maintenance and potential transfer of students' skills. One of the most obvious procedures for ensuring that behavior will maintain and transfer to new situations is to bring the behavior under the control of consequences that exist naturally in the target environment.

Subjective Evaluation The subjective evaluation method is also useful for assessing employment intervention procedures. Similar to social comparison, the subjective evaluation method relies upon opinions solicited from persons who are exposed to the trainer and have expertise in the occupational area under consideration. Subjective evaluations are most often used to determine the acceptability of planned instructional procedures. Yet, as noted, social validation may be helpful in sensitizing interventionists to the potential effectiveness of procedures *already accepted* and currently used by employers. It is helpful, therefore, to consider subjective evaluation as a starting point and to request information about employee training procedures already in use. The effectiveness of such procedures can then be objectively assessed.

Schutz, Rusch, and Lamson (1979) used the subjective evaluation method to identify procedures normally used by employers in dealing with inappropriate aggressive behavior in their employees. Three students receiving instruction as kitchen laborers in a community-based, food service employment training station were found to frequently exhibit aggressive behavior on the job. Specifically, they often made aggressive physical gestures such as fist shaking, and aggressive verbal behavior such as talking back. Subjective evaluation data suggested that, if observed in nonhandicapped workers, such aggressive behavior would normally be punished by a warning and a 1-day suspension. The results of imposing this consequence on

Table 4. Percentage of employers endorsing treatment procedures as acceptable in training of handicapped and nonhandicapped workers

Survey items	Always allow		Sometimes allow		Never allow	
	Handicapped	Nonhandicapped	Handicapped	Nonhandicapped	Handicapped	Nonhandicapped
When a new employee is acting socially inappropriate (i.e., shouting at people in the room) allow the training supervisor to:						
1. Ask the employee why she or he is acting this way	29	71	14	29	0	0
2. Bring the behavior to the attention of someone with more authority	21	64	64	21	7	21
3. Verbally reprimand the employee	0	36	57	38	21	21
4. Yell at the employee	0	0	7	0	93	100
5. Tell the person to go home	7	0	50	57	43	43
6. Ignore the behavior	0	7	7	7	93	56
Allow a performance rate of:						
7. Faster than normal rate		50	14	14	29	29
8. 100%	50	50	50	29	0	14
9. 75%	43	57	64	36	0	7
10. 50%	14	7	21	71	43	14
11. 25%	29	7	14	36	50	50
Allow new employees to work for:						
12. Money	29	64	7	36	7	0
13. Praise from a training supervisor	56	59	29	29	0	14
14. Physical contact, such as a pat on the back	71	36	57	57	0	7
15. Access to a preferred activity, such as working at a favorite job station	43	7	50	79	21	14

Item						
16. Points that later can be traded for material objects	29	7	29	36	64	57
17. Food (i.e., Cokes and lunch)	7	0	43	50	36	50
18. A combination of any of the above with money	21	57	14	29	14	14
Reward the new employee:						
19. Only on designated pay days	71	36	29	7	36	57
20. Periodically, such as after 2 or 3 days	29	14	63	36	14	43
21. After each work day	14	29	36	43	14	29
22. Immediately, i.e., after successful completion of each task	36	36	7	36	7	29
Allow training of new jobs when a training supervisor:						
23. Verbally describes	71	29	21	7	7	0
24. Demonstrates	86	21	14	0	0	0
25. Physically assists	57	7	43	7	7	0
Allow the training supervisor to acquire training assistance from other permanent employees in the form of:						
26. It is unacceptable for any employees to assist in the training	21	36	43	36	36	
27. Repeating an instruction	50	36	50	0	0	
28. Showing the new employee what to do	79	28	21	0	0	
29. Physically assisting the new employee	79	43	21	0	0	

57

the three students were evaluated by direct, objective measurement. The application of a warning and suspension was found to be successful in reducing aggression. Thus, subjective evaluation proved valuable for identifying a procedure to which students clearly responded, although it was not commonly used in employment training. The implication is that individuals in training may respond to consequences that occur naturally in community-based employment.

Summary The social validation of treatment procedures is a critical component of any competitive employment program. Clearly, it constitutes a serious waste of teaching staff's time and effort, as well as employers' money, to develop effective training procedures if, ultimately, they will be found objectionable and if employers will not allow them to be implemented. As mentioned, many behavior management techniques (e.g., extinction, physical punishment) lead to high participant dropout rates, not because they are ineffective, but because they are unacceptable. Social comparison and subjective evaluation are useful methods for assessing the social acceptability of treatment procedures. Social comparison focuses on the procedures employers use in training nonhandicapped workers. Whenever possible, the teaching staff should implement behavior management strategies that are already intact and in operation in competitive employment situations in order to maximize the normalizing properties of the trainee's experiences.

In addition, subjective evaluation should be used to solicit the opinions of employers, supervisors, and co-workers regarding the ethics, cost, and practicality of planned treatment procedures.

Intervention Effects

Social Comparison The social comparison method has also proven useful for the social validation of treatment effects. Rusch, Martin, and White, (1985) used social comparison to evaluate the efficacy of self-instruction in improving two students' performance of tasks associated with their jobs in a food service setting. The students were responsible for serving meals during lunch and dinner hours. However, they commonly failed to complete all their responsibilities, for example, wiping counters and checking and restocking supplies. Evaluation of the intervention through direct observation indicated that self-instruction was effective with both students spending more time working and meeting or exceeding non-probationary, nonhandicapped co-worker production standards. This study showed the utility of directly observing the performance of nonhandicapped co-workers, establishing a standard by which to compare trainee performance and measure intervention effectiveness.

Subjective Evaluation In the subjective evaluation of treatment outcome, global assessments are used to ascertain whether treatment is effective in developing behaviors valued by significant others in the employment setting. Rusch, Weithers, Menchetti, and Schutz (1980) used the subjective evaluation method in assessing the efficacy of a training program designed to modify the conversational speech of a student who was employed in a university food service setting. Initially, the investigators consulted supervisors and co-workers in the setting to identify troublesome behavior that might require postplacement training. Supervisors and co-workers agreed that the student repeated topics excessively during conversations. Consequently, they received preinstruction in how to use instruction, feedback, and mild social censure as consequences when the student repeated a topic. Direct measures obtained during the intervention showed that the treatment was effective by markedly reducing topic repetitions. However, co-workers reported that they believed the topical repeats had *not* been reduced. Rusch et al. (1980) offered several potential reasons for this discrepancy, including: 1) topical repetition as rated by trained observers (direct measure) differed from the behavior rated by the co-workers, that is, *topic repetition* for co-workers may have comprised a broader definition than for observers; 2) co-workers may have let the student's topic repetitions throughout the day influence their ratings during meals; and 3) the co-workers may have worried that their ratings would not be kept anonymous, possibly leading to retaliation by supervisors and/or others interested in employing mentally retarded workers. Regardless of the reason for the discrepancy, treatment effects were insufficient to influence co-workers' ratings, hence they failed to effect a *clinically important* change. Co-worker opinions are an important evaluative criterion since the trainee will continue to encounter such evaluations after treatment is terminated.

Summary Evaluation of treatment effectiveness constitutes an essential component of competitive employment programs. That is, it is important to establish that a given program has effected the changes and the degree of impact it initially intends. The social comparison method is particularly valuable in gauging treatment effectiveness. Evaluation of treatment effectiveness using social comparison involves anchoring the assessment of a student's performance by comparing it, before and after treatment, with the performance of nonhandicapped peers who perform comparable tasks during similar work periods and are considered by employers to perform adaptively. A socially validated change is established if the trainee's performance falls within the normal range. The subjective evaluation method performs a complementary function by assessing whether a given intervention has led to *qualitative* changes, as reflected in how the student is viewed by others in the setting with whom the student frequently interacts. A socially validated change, therefore, is one that has resulted, according to the view of others, in enhancing the student's everyday functioning and ameliorating problems for which the student initially received the training.

Implications of Social Validation: Community Integration

Social validation has significant implications for integration of students into the community. As pointed out in the previous section, the perceived value of competitive employment programs may be established by asking significant others to evaluate the outcomes of the programs. Social criteria, based upon the expectations and opinions of community members, ensure that applied interventions are both

important to the student and valued by society. *Social validation ensures that intervention priorities regarding focus, procedures, and results are not arbitrarily or stipulatively described, but are preferred and consensually agreed upon by community members.*

Traditionally, vocational training has been insulated from the community in which students obtain jobs, focusing on teaching various production-oriented skills put to use primarily in sheltered, segregated work environments. For example, adults with various levels of mental retardation have been taught how to pull a plunger (Evans & Spradlin, 1966), fold boxes (Loos & Tizard, 1955), drop marbles (Tramontana, 1972), stuff envelopes (Brown & Pearce, 1970), and thread labels (Teasdale & Joynt, 1967). Although not without merit, these demonstrations have contributed little to our understanding of how to prepare students for community adjustment. Indeed, early research suggested methods useful in teaching complex vocational tasks requiring multiple discriminations of form, color, color-form compounds, and size, as well as judgment and use of tools (Bellamy, Peterson, & Close, 1975; Crosson, 1969; Friedenburg & Martin, 1977; Gold, 1972, 1976; Hunter & Bellamy, 1976; Irvin, 1976; Martin & Flexer, 1975). Research has also shown that stimulus control, shaping, and chaining techniques were effective in vocational training (Bellamy, 1976).

The primary limitation of the traditional approach, however, was its insulation from the needs and concerns of the community into which students were ultimately placed. It was not at all clear that the skills students learned in workshops prepared them for successful participation in the community. Many researchers have argued that employment instruction be directed toward the development of behaviors that have immediate social value — survival skills (Rusch, 1979a). *Survival skills* refer to relevant, functional skills that increase a person's chances of enjoying services that are typically available to all members of a community (Kenowitz, Gallagher, & Edgar, 1977). With respect to employment training, both social and vocational survival skills appear necessary for effective employment integration

(Rusch & Schutz, 1981). Specifically, *social survival skills* include interactive behavior such as exchanging greetings, following directions, or complying with requests, whereas *vocational survival skills* refer to behaviors directly related to performing job-related tasks (e.g., sweeping).

Social validation has been used to identify skills that are important for community integration. Increasingly, social validation is employed in community integration efforts in such diverse areas as teaching persons with retardation to play board games (Wehman, Renzaglia, Berry, Schutz, & Karan, 1978), purchase color-coordinated clothing (Nutter & Reid, 1978), cross partially controlled intersections (Vogelsberg & Rusch, 1979), and ride a bus to and from work (Sowers, Rusch, & Hudson, 1979) and around the community (Marholin, O'Toole, Touchette, Berger, & Doyle, 1979). In an employment context, social validation has been utilized to identify skills that supervisors consider necessary for entrance into sheltered workshops (Johnson & Mithaug, 1978; Mithaug & Hagmeier, 1978; Mithaug & Hanawalt, 1978). More recently, social validation studies have centered upon variables required for survival in competitive employment, such as rate of task completion (Crouch et al., 1985), continuous work (Rusch, 1979b; Rusch et al., 1985), and social interactions (Chadsey-Rusch, Karlan, Riva, & Rusch, 1984; Rusch et al., 1980). As mentioned, the use of social validation in competitive employment has the corroboration of potential consumers, including administrators, employers, supervisors, co-workers, and the trainees themselves, in assessing the community relevance of the training focus (Rusch et al., 1980), treatment procedures (Schutz et al., 1979), and results (White & Rusch, 1983) of competitive employment programs.

ISSUES AND LIMITATIONS

Social validation represents an important advance in the assessment of effects of competitive employment training. However, several potential limitations are implicit in its use.

Issues and limitations pertain both to social comparison and subjective evaluation.

Social Comparison

For social comparison, the use of normative data in determining acceptability of the goals, procedures, and results of applied interventions is of concern. The use of normative performance levels implies satisfaction with these levels; utilizing normative data as the basis for deciding treatment goals and judging treatment against what is normally done is to tacitly endorse the status quo. The use of normative levels as evaluative criteria is not always appropriate. One objection rejects the need for rank-ordering people on a single criterion, and instead posits maximization of each person's potential for living according to a standard of life selected by the individual, not by those in power (cf. Rappaport, 1977). Indeed, an argument could be made for *changing* normative levels. For example, attendance rates of nonhandicapped workers may be used as a criterion for evaluation job performance of mentally retarded employees. However, research shows that mentally retarded workers trained in competitive employment often have attendance records that equal and even exceed those of nonhandicapped workers (Martin, Rusch, Tines, Brulle, & White, in press). If competitive employment programs brought attendance records within the normative range, there would be little cause for celebration. Thus, normative data should be used, *not as an absolute criterion,* but as a general standard or working guideline.

Subjective Evaluation

Subjective evaluations of work performance also pose potential problems by being more susceptible to rater bias than overt behavioral measures. Such ratings occasionally reflect changes in cases where actual behaviors have not changed (Kent, O'Leary, Diament, & Dietz, 1974). That is, global ratings may change even when more objective measures indicate that no change has been made. Kazdin (1973) and Schnelle (1974) showed that when people are led to believe that performance will improve with training, they tend to rate behavior as having improved. Thus, even if subjective evaluations of a student employee's work behavior suggest that treatment has led to improvements in global ratings, it is possible that the student did not change. This problem can be circumvented by having subjective evaluators observe *videotapes* of students' performance without knowing whether certain behaviors occurred before or after treatment (e.g., Rusch, 1983).

Another concern related to using subjective evaluation to assess treatment effects involves the meaning that can be attributed to improvements in rated behaviors. Specifically, following competitive employment training, global, subjective evaluations may indicate a qualitative change in behavior. However, the question remains, "has a *clinically significant* change been achieved?" (cf. Risley, 1970). A perceived change in behavior is not necessarily an important change. "Noticeable difference," as reflected in global ratings, does not neces-

sarily reflect adequate work performance. Thus, post intervention performance rated as improved or superior compared to pretraining does not guarantee that posttraining performance should not be modified further, or that the treatment has produced a level of change necessary for improvement in the student's everyday functioning in the employment environment.

CONCLUSION

Social comparison and subjective evaluation appear to be critical methodological additions to overt behavioral data in evaluating work behavior. The primary issue in integrating students into community-based employment is how well they perform assigned tasks relative to others and how they are perceived by others. Simple measures of students' overt behavior cannot adequately address these crucial issues, hence the importance of social validation.

REFERENCES

Ayllon, T., & Azrin, N. H. (1968). *The token economy: A motivational system for therapy and rehabilitation.* New York: Appleton-Century-Crofts.

Baer, D. M., & Wolf, M. M. (1970). The entry into natural communities of reinforcement. In R. Ulrich, T. Stachnick, & J. Mabry (Eds.), *Control of human behavior* (Vol 2, pp. 319–324). Glenview, IL: Scott, Foresman, and Co.

Bellamy, G. T. (1976). Habilitation of the severely and profoundly retarded: A review of research on work productivity. In G. T. Bellamy (Ed.), *Habilitation of severely and profoundly retarded adults* (pp. 53–64). Rehabilitation Research and Training Center in Mental Retardation, University of Oregon.

Bellamy, G. T., Peterson, L., & Close, D. (1975). Habilitation of the severely and profoundly retarded: Illustration of competence. *Education and Training of the Mentally Retarded, 10,* 174–186.

Brown, L., & Pearce, E. (1970). Increasing the production rate of trainable retarded students in a public school simulated workshop. *Education and Training of the Mentally Retarded, 5,* 15–22.

Chadsey-Rusch, J. C., Karlan, G. R., Riva, M. T., & Rusch, F. R. (1984). Competitive employment: Teaching conversational skills to adults who are mentally retarded. *Mental Retardation, 22,* 218–225.

Crosson, J. E. (1969) A technique for programming sheltered workshop environments for training severely retarded workers. *American Journal of Mental Deficiency, 73,* 814–818.

Crouch, K. P., Rusch, F. R., & Karlan, G. P. (1985). Utilizing the correspondence training paradigm to enhance productivity in an employment setting. *Education and Training of the Mentally Retarded, 19,* 268–275.

Evans, G., & Spradlin, J. (1966). Incentives and instructions as controlling variables in productivity. *American Journal of Mental Deficiency, 71,* 129–132.

Friedenburg, W. P., & Martin, A. S. (1977). Prevocational training of the severely retarded using task analysis. *Mental Retardation, 15,* 16–20.

Gold, M. (1972). Stimulus factors in skill training of the retarded on a complex assembly task: Acquisition, transfer, and retention. *American Journal of Mental Deficiency, 76,* 517–526.

Gold, M. (1976). Task analysis of a complex assembly task by the retarded blind. *Exceptional Children, 43,* 78–84.

Hunter, J. D., & Bellamy, G. T. (1976). Cable harness construction for severely retarded adults: A demonstration of training techniques. *AAESPH Review, 1,* 2–13.

Irvin, L. K. (1976). General utility of easy to hard discrimination training procedures with the severely retarded. *Education and Training of the Mentally Retarded, 11,* 247–250.

Johnson, J. L., & Mithaug, D. E. (1978). A replication of sheltered workshop entry requirements. *AAESPH Review, 3,* 116–122.

Karlan, G. R., & Rusch, F. R. (1982). Analyzing the relationship between acknowledgement and compliance in a non-sheltered work setting. *Education and Training of Mentally Retarded, 17,* 202–208.

Kazdin, A. E. (1973). Role of instructions and re-inforcement in behavior change in token reinforcement programs. *Journal of Educational Psychology, 64,* 63–71.

Kazdin, A. E. (1977). Assessing the clinical or applied importance of behavior change through social validation. *Behavior Modification, 1,* 427–451.

Kazdin, A. E., & Matson, J. L. (1981). Social validation in mental retardation. *Applied Research in Mental Retardation, 2,* 39–53.

Kenowitz, L. A., Gallagher, J., & Edgar, E. (1977). Generic services for the severely handicapped and their families: What's available? In E. Sontag, J. Smith, & N. Certo (Eds.), *Educational programming for the severely and profoundly handicapped* (pp. 31–39). Reston, VA: Council for Exceptional Children.

Kent, R. M., O'Leary, K. D., Diament, C., & Dietz, A. (1974). Expectation biases in observational evaluation of therapeutic change. *Journal of Consulting and Clinical Psychology, 42,* 774–780.

Loos, F., & Tizard, J. (1955). The employment of adult imbeciles in a hospital workshop. *American Journal of Mental Deficiency, 59,* 394–403.

Marholin, D., O'Toole, K. M., Touchette, P., Berger, P., & Doyle, D. (1979). "I'll have a Big Mac, large fries, large coke, and apple pie," . . . or teaching adaptive community skills. *Behavior Therapy, 10,* 236–248.

Martin, A. S., & Flexer, R. W. (1975). *Three studies on training work skills and work adjustment with the severely retarded.* Texas Tech, University, Research & Training Center in Mental Retardation.

Martin, M. E., Rusch, F. R., Tines, J. J., Brulle, A. R., & White, D. M. (in press). Work attendance in competitive employment: Comparison between non-handicapped and mentally retarded employees. *Mental Retardation.*

Menchetti, B. M., Rusch, F. R., & Lamson, D. S. (1981). Employers' perceptions of acceptable training procedures for use in competitive employment settings. *Journal of The Association for the Severely Handicapped, 6,* 6–16.

Minkin, N., Braukmann, C. J., Minkin, B. L., Timbers, G. D., Timbers, B. J., Fixsen, D. L., Phillips, E. L., & Wolf, M. M. (1976). The social validation and training of conversational skills. *Journal of Applied Analysis, 9,* 127–139.

Mithaug, D. E., & Hagmeier, L. D. (1978). The development of procedures to assess prevocational competencies of severely handicapped young adults. *AAESPH Review, 3,* 94–115.

Mithaug, D. E., Hagmeier, L. D., & Haring, N. G. (1977). The relationship between training activities and job placement in vocational education of the severely and profoundly handicapped. *AAESPH Review, 2,* 89–109.

Mithaug, D. E., & Hanawalt, D. A. (1978). The validation of procedures to assess prevocational task preferences in retarded adults. *Journal of Applies Behavior Analysis, 11,* 153–162.

Nutter, D., & Reid, D. H. (1978). Teaching retarded women in clothing selection skill using community norms. *Journal of Applied Behavior Analysis, 11,* 475–487.

Rappaport, J. (1977). *Community psychology: Values, research, and action.* New York: Holt, Rinehart & Winston.

Risley, T. R. (1970). Behavior modification: An experimental-therapeutic endeavor. In L. A. Hamerlynck, P. O. Davidson, & L. E. Acker (Eds.), *Behavior modification and ideal mental health services* (pp. 103–127). Calgary, Alberta, Canada: University of Calgary Press.

Rusch, F. R. (1979a). Toward the validation of social/vocational survival skills. *Mental Retardation, 17,* 143–145.

Rusch, F. R. (1979b). A functional analysis of the relationship between attending to task and production in an applied restaurant setting. *Journal of Special Education, 13,* 399–411.

Rusch, F. R. (1983). Evaluating the degree of concordance between observers' versus employers' evaluation of work behavior. *Applied Research in Mental Retardation, 4,* 95–102.

Rusch, F. R., Martin, J. E., & White, D. M. (1985). Competitive employment: Teaching mentally retarded employees to maintain their work behavior. *Education and Training of the Mentally Retarded, 20*(3), 182–189.

Rusch, F. R., Morgan, T. K., Martin, J. E., Riva, M., & Agran, M. (1985). Competitive employment: Teaching mentally retarded adults self-instructional strategies. *Applied Research in Mental Retardation, 6,* 389–407.

Rusch, F. R., & Mithaug, D. E. (1980). *Vocational training for mentally retarded adults: A behavior analytic approach.* Champaign, IL: Research Press.

Rusch, F. R., & Schutz, R. P. (1981). Vocational and social work behavior research: An evaluative review. In J. L. Matson & J. R. McCartney (Eds.), *Handbook of behavior modification with the mentally retarded* (pp. 247–280). New York: Plenum.

Rusch, F. R., Schutz, R. P., & Agran, M. (1982). Validating entry-level survival skills for service occupations: Implications for curriculum development. *Journal of The Association for the Severely Handicapped, 7,* 32–41.

Rusch, F. R., Weithers, J. A., Menchetti, B. M., & Schutz, R. P. (1980). Social validation of a program to reduce topic repetition in a non-sheltered setting. *Education and Training of the Mentally Retarded, 15,* 208–215.

Schnelle, J. F. (1974). A brief report on invalidity of parent evaluations of behavior change. *Journal of Applied Behavior Analysis, 7,* 341–343.

Schutz, R. P., Jostes, K. F., Rusch, F. R., & Lamson, D. S. (1980). The use of contingent preinstruction and social validation in the acquisition, generalization, and maintenance of sweeping and mopping responses. *Education and Training of the Mentally Retarded, 15,* 306–311.

Schutz, R. P., Rusch, F. R., & Lamson, D. S. (1979). Evaluation of an employer's procedure to eliminate unacceptable behavior on the job. *Community Services Forum, 1,* 4–5.

Sowers, J., Rusch, F. R., & Hudson, C. (1979). Training a severely retarded young adult to ride the city bus to and from work. *AAESPH Review, 4,* 15–22.

Stokes, T. F., & Baer, D. M. (1977). An implicit technology of generalization. *Journal of Applied Behavior Analysis, 10,* 349–367.

Teasdale, R., & Joynt, D. (1967). Some effects of incentives on the behavior of adolescent retardates. *American Journal of Mental Deficiency, 71,* 925–930.

Tramontana, J. (1972). Social versus edible rewards as a function of intellectual level and socio-economic class. *American Journal of Mental Deficiency, 77,* 33–38.

Vogelsberg, R. T., & Rusch, F. R. (1979). Training severely handicapped students to cross partially controlled intersections. *AAESPH Review, 4,* 264–273.

Wehman, P., Renzaglia, A., Berry, G., Schutz, R., & Karan, O. (1978). Developing a leisure skill repertoire in severely and profoundly handicapped persons. *American Association for the Education of the Severely and Profoundly Handicapped, 3,* 162–171.

Werner, J. S., Minkin, N., Minkin, B. L., Fixsen, D. L.,

Phillips, E. L., & Wolf, M. M. (1975). "Intervention package": An analysis to prepare juvenile delinquents for encounters with police officers. *Criminal Justice and Behavior, 2,* 55–83.

White, D. M., & Rusch, F. R. (1983). Social validation in competitive employment: Evaluating work performance. *Applied Research in Mental Retardation, 4,* 343–354.

Wolf, M. M. (1978). Social validity: The case for subjective measurement or how applied behavior analysis is finding its heart. *Journal of Applied Behavior Analysis, 11,* 203–214.

Chapter 16

Utilizing Co-workers as Change Agents

Michael S. Shafer

ALMOST EVERY CHAPTER in this book emphasizes the importance of providing comprehensive services to ensure long-term retention. The critical nature of providing such services may best be understood by recognizing that while most persons who are mentally retarded may acquire a particular skill, they may not be able to perform it in different settings or long after training. These issues, traditionally referred to as generalization and maintenance (Stokes & Baer, 1977a), are critical to all phases of competitive employment training as evidenced by the wide variety of settings, persons, and tasks that are commonly encountered in nonsheltered, competitive employment environments. For example, the interactions occurring among co-workers may be topographically similar to those occurring between workers and employers or customers; however, subtle cues such as facial expression or voice intonation may dictate how similar the required response needs to be. Failure to attend to and, in turn, respond to these cues could result in inappropriate and potentially job-threatening responses.

Traditional strategies of programming generalization and maintenance for the mentally retarded worker have relied on systematically fading the job trainer from the work site (Wehman, 1981), fading reinforcement or feedback schedules (Rusch, Connis, & Sowers, 1978;

Rusch & Mithaug, 1980), partially withdrawing treatment packages (Rusch & Kazdin, 1981), or providing general case programming (Horner & McDonald, 1982). Although these strategies have proven effective within the confines of relatively brief experimental periods, their failure to deal with issues that arise long after job placement (such as new or different job duties) leads one to agree with Rusch's (1983) conclusion that, in many respects, we are still plagued by a "place and pray" approach to job placement in competitive settings.

To eradicate this "place and pray" job placement approach, long-term follow-up services must be provided. For example, students served through the supported work model introduced by Rusch (1983) and Wehman (1981) are assessed on a regular basis to ensure that performance of all job-relevant skills are being maintained at acceptable levels. Typical assessment procedures include periodic site visits and direct observation by job trainers, phone interviews with the student's employers, and written employer evaluations collected at regular intervals. Based upon these evaluations, potential job-threatening behaviors are brought to the attention of the placing agency and dealt with in an expedient manner, thereby facilitating continued employment.

During the follow-up process, the job trainer may be called upon to deal with a variety of

Preparation of this chapter was supported by Grant GO28301124 from the National Institute of Handicapped Research, U. S. Department of Education. The opinions expressed in this chapter are those of the author and no official endorsement by the Department should be inferred.

issues, ranging from designing and implementing behavioral analytic programs to performing family-related activities. Examples of the latter include helping alter a student's public bus route because of a change in the work schedule, assisting the student in opening a bank account, or identifying appropriate work accessories for the student (e.g., apparel, lunchbox, jewelry). This topic is discussed in greater detail in Chapter 21.

Additionally, follow-up activities may require the job trainer to re-enter the job site to increase, decrease, or maintain job-related behaviors. Activities such as these typically require the analytic skills and clinical precision of a highly trained individual. Recently, however, a number of individuals involved in competitive employment of mentally retarded individuals have suggested that, in many instances, some of the follow-up functions routinely assigned to the job trainer can be assumed by nonhandicapped co-workers on the job site (Rusch, 1983; Rusch & Mithaug, 1980; Rusch & Schutz, 1981; Wehman, 1981; Wilcox & Bellamy, 1982).

Utilization of co-workers to facilitate follow-up efforts has often been suggested as a more desirable programming option than traditional trainer- or teacher-mediated efforts (Rusch, Martin, & White, 1985). The utilization of peers has long been recognized as a natural and practical technique for programming generalization and maintenance among children (Stokes & Baer, 1977b). The primary advantage of peer-mediated programs is the continuing presence of the peer. Second, involving co-workers to assist in evaluating student performance may provide a more valid assessment of responding than that obtained from the typical obtrusive observations of a job trainer (White & Rusch, 1983). Third, co-worker–assisted programming efforts appear to represent a less restrictive and more normalizing approach to providing comprehensive follow-up strategies. Finally, involvement of co-workers in follow-up activities could potentially reduce the program costs incurred during this phase of job placement (Hill & Wehman, 1983).

In summary, solicitation of co-worker assistance to facilitate comprehensive follow-up services for competitively employed, mentally retarded individuals appears to offer an appropriate approach for agencies placing students who are handicapped. In the preceding chapter on social validation, two areas were identified in which co-workers have proven helpful by: 1) serving as normative references by which to compare student performance with target employees, and 2) providing subjective evaluations of student performance. The present chapter expands this list of potential co-worker assistance functions by adding the roles of advocate, observer, and intervention agent. Collectively, these separate functions represent a continuum of co-worker–assisted follow-up efforts that require progressively more involvement and sophistication on the part of the co-worker (see Table 1).

CO-WORKERS AS ADVOCATES

The potential success of competitive job placements is often determined by the job trainer's ability to enlist the support and understanding of co-workers at the job site. If employees with mental retardation are perceived as lazy, favored, incompetent, undependable, or any of several other sterotypes, their potential for long-term placement success is greatly diminished, regardless of job proficiency (Albin, Stark, & Keith, 1979; Rusch & Mithaug, 1980; Wehman, 1981). Therefore, it is imperative that at least one co-worker be identified at a job site who will serve as an on-site advocate for the student.

Advocate Roles

Co-worker advocacy may take many forms. For example, while serving in a protective role, the co-worker advocate may:

1. Ensure that the student's rights are not compromised by unsupporting co-workers.
2. Help prevent the student from getting stuck performing all the less prestigious jobs that are typically shared by all of co-workers (e.g., scrubbing trash cans).

Table 1. Continuum of co-worker–assisted follow-up strategies

Co-worker function	Skill development	Motivational concerns	Level of involvement	Degree of sophistication
Serve as normative reference	None	None	Passive	Low
Provide subjective evaluation	None	None	↑	↑
Serve as co-worker advocate	Minimal	Minimal		
Serve as co-worker observer	Specific training required	May be needed		
Serve as co-worker trainer	Specific training required	Required	Active	High

3. Minimize the frequency of practical jokes directed at the student.
4. Handle any confrontations that may occur between the student and other co-workers.

In addition to serving in a protective role, co-worker advocates may function to provide a communicative interface between the student, the student's parents or residential counselor, and the employer. Quite often, an employer may be willing to hire a student with mental retardation, but is unable (or unwilling) to provide the communication necessary to maintain that student at a competitive standard. In such situations, the aid of a co-worker who works alongside or near the student may be beneficial, particularly for the nonverbal student. The co-worker might speak up for the client with the supervisor, communicate schedule changes with the client and his or her parents, or assist the client in obtaining specific information such as the location of a specific item.

Advocate Characteristics

To date, no information is available on what characteristics are indicative of a good co-worker advocate. Given the nature of the task, three characteristics appear to be crucial. First, the co-worker advocate should be a veteran employee in good standing with the employer. This individual should have a thorough understanding of his or her own position and the student's, as well as the overall operations of the job site. Second, since the co-worker advocate may be required to mediate problem situations between the student and other co-workers, he or she should enjoy relatively good social status within the work environment. Third, a co-worker advocate must be understanding, particularly of individuals with disabilities. In this regard, co-workers who are themselves handicapped or have a handicapped relative are often the best prospects. Quite often, the best co-workers advocates bring themselves to the job trainer's attention by volunteering assistance or through past personal experience with persons who are handicapped.

Summary

The role of a co-worker advocate can be relatively passive and unskilled, whereby the co-worker advocate is simply asked to "keep an eye on the student" and report to the job trainer in the event of any potential job-threatening problem. Follow-up services based on this approach using appropriate co-workers (see Table 2) have been shown to result in higher numbers of students remaining employed. Hence, co-worker advocacy is a critical facet of a comprehensive follow-up program.

CO-WORKERS AS OBSERVERS

The effectiveness of using co-workers to socially validate intervention methods and outcomes has been repeatedly demonstrated by applied researchers in competitive employment settings (Rusch, Weithers, Menchetti, & Schutz, 1980; Schutz, Jostes, Rusch, & Lam-

Table 2.   Identification of co-worker who will serve as advocate

Advocate roles
Ensure that job tasks are assigned fairly
Discourage practical jokes
Serve as mediator if confrontations occur
Facilitate communication
Advocate characteristics
Nonprobationary employee in good standing with employee
Socially accepted by co-workers
Understanding and willing to assist

son, 1980; Schutz, Rusch, & Lamson, 1979). One facet of social validation, as delineated in the previous chapter, consists of collecting subjective ratings from co-workers and supervisors in an attempt to evaluate the acceptability of intervention goals, outcomes, or procedures (Kazdin, 1977; White & Rusch, 1983; Wolf, 1978). The information generated in this manner provides the applied researcher with a social referent by which the necessity for, the projected method of, as well as the resultant outcome of certain interventions may be gauged.

Utilizing co-workers to subjectively validate intervention programs may represent greater involvement of these individuals than that associated with co-worker advocacy. Evidence suggests that co-workers may be utilized to *objectively* evaluate student performance as well. Previous investigations have demonstrated the success of utilizing participant observers such as parents, classroom peers, and teachers to accurately observe and record the behavior of others (Hall et al., 1971; Kubany & Slogett, 1973). To date, however, only two investigations have utilized co-worker observational strategies in vocational settings. Kazdin and Polster (1973) and Rusch and Menchetti (1981) surveyed co-workers to verify the occurrence of target behaviors in sheltered and competitive settings, respectively. Kazdin and Polster questioned handicapped co-workers to verify the occurrence of target social responses that had been verbally reported by the subjects. The information obtained from the co-workers was subsequently used in conjunction with more precise observational data to evaluate treatment effectiveness.

In contrast, Rusch and Menchetti (1981) assessed treatment effectiveness solely on the basis of co-workers' reports. Supervisors, cooks, and fellow kitchen laborers were questioned on a daily basis to assess the occurrence and quality of compliant responding by a worker with mental retardation. In this investigation, the effect of warnings of suspension from work and actual suspension due to noncompliance was assessed via a multiple-baseline design across subjects (i.e., cooks, then supervisors). When only warnings were issued by the supervisors, compliance to requests from the cooks remained unchanged. However, when the supervisors subsequently carried out the suspensions, spillover effects were obtained as compliance to supervisor and cook requests improved dramatically, although the latter had never provided warnings or suspension. Figure 1 displays the results of the warnings and actual suspension due to noncompliance.

As reported by Rusch and Menchetti (1981), the use of co-workers to observe and report the occurrence of target behaviors is one example of co-worker–assisted follow-up efforts surely to be applied with greater frequency in the future. Utilizing co-workers as observers has been widely supported in recent investigations assessing the reactive effects of obtrusive job trainer observations (Fischer, Wehman, & Young, 1980; Rusch et al., 1984). *Reactivity* is said to occur when individuals under observation alter their responding patterns due to their awareness of being observed (Haynes, 1978). Rusch et al. (1984) systematically assessed reactivity among five employees with mental retardation by comparing rates of on-task behavior during periods of obtrusive and unobtrusive observation. Obtrusive observations were designed to approximate typical follow-up observation processes; as such, they were carried out by special educators who are not typically present in the work environment. Unobtrusive observations, on the other hand, were intended to simulate the conditions of co-worker observations; hence, they were characterized by data collectors posing as co-workers.

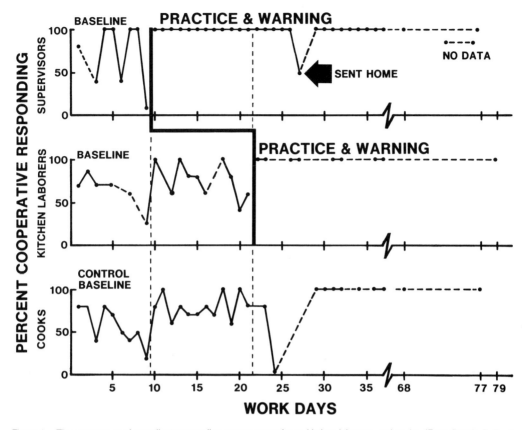

Figure 1. The percentage of compliant responding across supervisors, kitchen laborers, and cooks. (From Rusch, F. R., & Menchetti, B. M. [1981]. Increasing compliant work behaviors in a non-sheltered work setting. *Mental Retardation, 19,* 107–112.)

Rates of on-task behavior were consistently observed to be higher during obtrusive observations, suggesting that the students were not only aware that they were being observed but, as a result of this knowledge, they altered their typical work behavior patterns. In interpreting these results, Rusch et al. suggested that utilizing co-workers to collect data may minimize student reactivity due to the co-workers' natural presence on the job.

While the use of co-workers to observe and record student work performance may minimize the potential for reactivity, a number of other issues may adversely affect the validity of co-worker observational data. In particular, observer bias (Kent, Diament, Dietz, & O'Leary, 1974) and observer drift (Johnson & Bolstad, 1973), which have plagued traditional observational systems, appear to be accentuated when utilizing a reiatively untrained pool

of data collectors such as co-workers. (Readers are referred to Chapter 11 for a discussion of special considerations to be included in the observation process.)

Observer bias has been defined as an inaccuracy in observationally generated data that reflects a bias or expectancy on the part of the observer (Kent et al., 1974). Such bias may be the result of: 1) the observer knowing if the student is currently receiving some form of training, 2) a desire to please the job trainer, or 3) an attempt to "cover up" for the student. In addition, observer bias may result from a co-worker working against the student and attempting to portray performance as being worse than it actually is.

Observer drift, on the other hand, is said to occur when the observations made by an individual change over time due to the development of idiosyncratic definitions of the target behavior (Johnson & Bolstad, 1973). For example, a co-worker assigned to evaluate a student's sweeping performance may inadvertently become more stringent about defining acceptable performance. As a result, improvement would not be noted, although significant gains may have been made according to the original definition of acceptable sweeping performance.

Due to the potential adverse effects of observer drift and observer bias, the training provided to co-worker observers is critical to the collection of accurate information. As with any observational system, great care should be taken to ensure that the co-worker observer is attending to the same behavior and dimensional properties as the job trainer. Verbally describing the behavior, pointing it out when it occurs, modeling the behavior, or providing appropriate (acceptable) and inappropriate (unacceptable) examples of the target behavior are all methods the job trainer may use to ensure that the co-worker is attending to relevant aspects of the target behavior. In addition, interobserver reliability, either among co-worker observers or between co-worker observers and the job trainer, should be assessed periodically to minimize the potential for observer drift.

When devising a data collection system for use by co-worker observers, the process of observing and recording student performance should be designed so that it intrudes minimally upon the co-worker's regular job duties. As a result, specific observational systems such as frequency counts and event or time sampling should be kept as simple as possible while still yeilding a robust evaluation. The number of behaviors to be observed by the co-worker observer, for example, should be kept to a minimum, in part, to minimize disruption of job responsibilities, but also to strengthen accuracy. A number of investigations have indicated that the validity (accuracy) of observations is negatively related to the number of behaviors observed. Consequently, co-worker observers should be expected to attend to no more than one or two different responses. Finally, the transfer of

information from co-worker observer to job trainer should be carefully engineered to guard against inadvertently biasing the co-worker's response definitions (O'Leary, Kent, & Kanowitz, 1975). Specific feedback that indicates the job trainer's pleasure (or displeasure) with the information conveyed by the data should be avoided. Instead, general praise to the co-worker for collecting the data should be delivered.

Summary

Evaluation of student performance in competitive employment settings by nonhandicapped co-workers is suggested as one means of alleviating the reactive effects often attributed to job trainer observations. Utilization of co-workers in this role should be considered a supplement to other information-gathering systems typically employed during follow-up. Two potential threats to the validity of co-worker observations are identified: observer bias and observer drift. Although these threats should not limit co-worker observation-based systems, they do dicate the supplemental nature of co-worker observational information.

CO-WORKERS AS TRAINERS

The involvement of co-workers in the follow-up process, as advocates or observers, will enhance the student's prospect for long-term competitive employment. This progressively complex co-worker–assisted follow-up is primarily dependent upon the job trainer's ability to enlist willing individuals. In certain circumstances where willing co-workers may be identified, evidence suggests that these individuals may also be utilized to mediate follow-up programs designed to facilitate generalization and maintenance of student work performance.

Previous demonstrations of peer-mediated interventions have been primarily restricted to applications with children for the purpose of facilitating social behavior (Shafer, Egel, & Neef, 1984; Strain, Kerr, & Ragland, 1979) and improving academic performance (Trovato & Bucher, 1980) or speech articulation (Johnston & Johnston, 1972). For example, a great deal of research has been carried out in which children have been taught to model, prompt, or reinforce desirable behavior with their behaviorally deficient peers (Egel, Richman, & Koegel, 1981; Parson & Heward, 1979; Trovato & Bucher, 1980). Similarly, parents (Adubato, Adams, & Budd, 1981; Isaacs, Embry, & Baer, 1982) and siblings (Schreibman, O'Neil, & Koegel, 1983) of behaviorally deficient children have been trained to employ a variety of operant techniques. Collectively, these investigations have demonstrated that individuals of varying intellectual capacities can be trained to effectively engage in complex behavioral skills and, as a result, effect generalized changes in the repertoires of their peers, children, or siblings.

Comparable demonstrations using co-workers in competitive employment settings have been reported in only a handful of studies (DeMars, 1975; Rusch et al., 1980; Stanford & Wehman, 1980). DeMars (1975), for example, described a program that used nonhandicapped co-workers to teach janitorial skills to three moderately retarded students. Although exemplary in its innovative approach to job training, DeMar's program was not described sufficiently to allow for adequate replication. Without additional information about: 1) the process for selecting co-workers to serve as trainers, 2) specific types of correction procedures used by the co-workers, and 3) specific training effects upon the interactions between the co-workers and the students, similar programs cannot be implemented.

In the only systematic evaluation of a co-worker–mediated intervention reported to date, Rusch et al. (1980) attempted to reduce the frequency of topic repetitions in a moderately mentally retarded student working in a university cafeteria. In this study, the three co-workers with whom the student ate his meals were instructed to inform the student each time he repeated a statement that had previously been made by himself or the co-workers. In addition to this instruction, the experimenters discussed with the co-workers what constituted a topical repeat, and role played some common topical repeats. Resulting observational data, which were collected by the experimenters, indicated that the co-workers were only minimally effective in reducing the student's repeats. Subsequently, the co-workers were cued by the experimenters to provide feedback when they failed to do so independently. This additional component resulted in a dramatic and sustained decrease in repeats by the student, suggesting that the co-workers may not have been adequately trained to attend to all topical repeats, or they they were not motivated to respond consistently to the repeats.

Based upon the reports of DeMars (1975), Rusch et al. (1980), and others, a number of important implications may be drawn regarding the application of co-worker–mediated programs, including co-worker training strategies, motivating co-worker trainers, and determining apropriate applications for co-worker–assisted programs.

Co-worker Training Strategies

Previous demonstrations of peer-mediated interventions with children have utilized a variety of training strategies such as modeling, role playing, direct prompting, and shaping to prepare peer trainers (cf. Strain, 1981). In contrast, the few co-worker–mediated programs reported have typically relied upon discussion as the sole training mechanism. The limited results obtained by Rusch et al. (1980), who utilized a combination of discussion and role playing, point to the need for a more structured training program that emphasizes behavioral rehearsal, as reported in the peer-mediated literature.

Co-worker training sessions should be scheduled during the co-worker's own time, unless employer approval can be obtained to conduct training during work. Rusch (1983) suggested training co-workers during short, 10-minute inservice sessions before or after work. Break or lunch time may also be appropriate training times. To maximize the potential for generalized behavior change, sessions should occur on the job site, where the co-worker will be interacting with the student (Stokes & Baer, 1977a).

Based upon the results of procedures utlized

in previous peer-mediated programs, co-worker training sessions should consist of three segments: 1) discussion, 2) modeling with verbal description, and 3) behavioral rehearsal. During the first part of each session, the job trainer should identify the behavioral characteristics in need of change and specify the behavioral technique(s) to be utilized by the co-worker. Technical terms such as "reinforcement" or "extinction" should be avoided in favor of lay terms to avoid intimidating the co-worker. In addition, the trainer should stress the importance of the co-worker trainer's participation in the program and the positive impact this participation will have upon the target student.

During the second part of each training session, the job trainer should model and verbally describe the behavior being taught. For example, if reinforcement strategies are being trained, the job trainer could model examples of physical contact (e.g., handshakes) or praise while verbally describing *when* reinforcement is given (after a desirable response), *why* reinforcement is given (to increase a response), and *how* reinforcement is given (frequently and positively). The co-worker trainer should be questioned periodically to ensure that he or she understands the content material.

The final component of co-worker training sessions should consist of behavioral rehearsal. During this phase, the co-worker may be asked to practice the behavior being taught. In order to more closely approximate natural conditions, the job trainer could role play the part of the student, or the co-worker trainer could practice with the student directly, while receiving feedback from the trainer. In addition to providing prompts, the job trainer might also provide intermittent praise or additional instruction to the co-worker, based upon performance.

The number of training sessions to be conducted should be related to the performance of the co-worker trainer during training sessions as well as during natural interactions with the student. Consequently, periodic and unobtrusive observations of the student's performance and the interactions of the co-worker trainer should be conducted. Based upon these observations, decisions regarding additional or revised training sessions should be warranted.

Developing Motivational Systems

In addition to the procedures used to train co-worker trainers, the development of appropriate motivational systems is critical to the long-term success of co-worker–assisted follow-up programs. Although reinforcement strategies have been largely ignored in previous peer-mediated studies, edible reinforcement (Ragland, Kerr, & Strain, 1978) and experimenter praise (Shafer et al., 1984) have been effectively employed with children. When motivating nonhandicapped adult co-workers, reinforcers should be identified that are not only reinforcing to the co-worker, but also socially appropriate (see Table 3). Examples may include the personal satisfaction the co-worker trainer derives from helping another individual, personal recognition by the employer, an official letter of commendation, or small monetary rewards provided by the placement agency. As with co-worker advocacy, individuals may spontaneously avail themselves of the job trainer, thus minimizing any motivational concerns. If, however, a co-worker trainer does not respond immediately and enthusiastically to the requests of the job trainer, and if no other appropriate co-workers are available, a specific motivational plan should be developed.

The behavioral skills to be used by co-worker trainers will, to some extent, dictate the need for structured reinforcement strategies. For example, behaviors already present in a co-worker's repertoire, which may function to facilitate the performance of a student, are

Table 3. Potential reinforcers for co-workers

Free coffee or soft drink
Increased vacation days
Increased responsibility
Job completion by job trainer
Job redesign
Letter of commendation
Money
Pay increase
Personal recognition from employer
Personal recognition from job trainer
Time off

more likely to be maintained in the absence of trainer-delivered reinforcement (Strain, 1981). For this reason, co-worker–mediated programs may be more appropriate for follow-up interventions as opposed to initial skill training (DeMars, 1975). The clinical skills required to teach complex vocational behaviors to individuals with mental retardation (e.g., time-delay prompting, general case programming, intermittent reinforcement schedules) are typically not used by paraprofessionals. Hence, they are also beyond the scope of co-worker trainer efforts. In contrast, follow-up programming centering on maintaining desired student behavior, for example, requires less technical and precise skills such as verbal reinforcement and verbal prompting (cf. Karlan & Rusch, 1982). These skills are already used by most nonhandicapped individuals in normal interactions and, as a result, are much easier to develop and maintain in order to facilitate work performance of the student.

Summary

Based upon previous demonstrations of peer-mediated interventions with children, utilizing nonhandicapped co-workers to facilitate follow-up efforts represents an effective adjunct to job trainer intervention. Co-worker training is conceptualized as a three-tier process consisting of discussion, modeling with verbal discussion, and behavioral rehearsal. It is recommended that use of co-worker trainers be restricted to maintenance programming efforts and that co-worker training pay special attention to the motivational needs of the co-workers.

CONCLUSION

All too often, people with handicaps who are placed into competitive employment lose their jobs because the placing agency provides little or no follow-up. Recent demonstration efforts have emphasized the critical nature of providing long-term, follow-up services to facilitate job retention. This chapter focuses upon utilizing co-workers as one means of enhancing follow-up. Based upon related research, the use of co-workers in the roles of advocates, observers, and trainers is suggested. In conjunction with co-worker–assisted social validation techniques, these functions represent a continuum of co-worker–assisted follow-up efforts requiring increasing levels of co-worker cooperation and sophistication. Collectively, these efforts appear to be promising components of comprehensive follow-up services.

REFERENCES

Adubato, S. A., Adams, M. K., & Budd, K. S. (1981). Teaching a parent to train a spouse in child management techniques. *Journal of Applied Behavior Analysis, 14,* 193–205.

Albin, T. J., Stark, J. A., & Keith, K. D. (1979). Vocational training and placement: Behavior analysis in the natural environment. In G. T. Bellamy, G. O'Connor, & O. C. Karan (Eds.), *Vocational rehabilitation of severely handicapped persons* (pp. 161–180). Baltimore: University Park Press.

DeMars, P. K. (1975). Training adult retardates for private enterprise. *The American Journal of Occupational Therapy, 29,* 39–42.

Egel, A. L., Richman, G., & Koegel, R. L. (1981). Normal peer models and autistic children's learning. *Journal of Applied Behavior Analysis, 14,* 3–12.

Fischer, J. J., Wehman, P., & Young, R. (1980). Reactivity and its effect on performance of severely handicapped food service workers. In P. Wehman & M. Hill (Eds.), *Vocational training and placement of severely disabled persons* (Vol. 2, pp. 151–164). Richmond, VA: Virginia Commonwealth University.

Hall, R. V. Fox, R., Willard, D., Goldsmith, L., Emerson, M., Owen, M., Davis, F., & Porcia, E. (1971). The teacher as observer and experimenter in the modification of disputing and talking out behavior. *Journal of Applied Behavior Analysis, 4,* 141–149.

Haynes, S. M. (1978). *Principles of behavioral assessment.* New York: Plenum.

Hill, M., & Wehman, P. (1983). Cost benefit analysis of placing moderately and severely handicapped individuals into competitive employment. *Journal of The Association for the Severely Handicapped, 8,* 30–38.

Horner, R. H., & McDonald, R. S. (1982). Comparison of single instance and general case instruction in teaching a generalized vocational skill. *Journal of The Association for the Severely Handicapped, 8,* 7–20.

Isaacs, C. D., Embry, L. H., & Baer, D. M. (1982). Training family therapists: An experimental evaluation. *Journal of Applied Behavior Analysis, 15,* 505–520.

Johnson, S. M., & Bolstad, O. D. (1973). Methodological issues in naturalistic observations: Some problems and solutions for field research. In L. A. Hamerlynck, L. C. Handy, & E. J. Mash (Eds.), *Behavior change:*

Methodology, concepts, and practice (p. 26). Champaign, IL: Research Press.

Johnston, J. M., & Johnston, G. T. (1972). Modification of consonant speech sound articulation in young children. *Journal of Applied Behavior Analysis, 5,* 233–246.

Karlan, G. R., & Rusch, F. R. (1982). Correspondence between saying and doing: Some thoughts on defining correspondence and future directions for application. *Journal of Applied Behavior Analysis, 15,* 156–162.

Kazdin, A. E. (1977). Assessing the clinical or applied importance of behavior change through social validation. *Behavior Modificaton, 2,* 39–54.

Kazdin, A. E., & Polster, R. (1973). Intermittent token reinforcement and response maintenance in extinction. *Behavior Therapy, 4,* 386–391.

Kent, R. M., Diament, C., Dietz, A., & O'Leary, K. D. (1974). Expectation biases in observation of therapeutic change. *Journal of Consulting and Clinical Psychology, 42,* 774–780.

Kubany, E., & Slogett, B. (1973). Coding procedures for teachers. *Journal of Applied Behavior Analysis, 6,* 339–344.

O'Leary, K. D., Kent, R. M., & Kanowitz, J. (1975). Shaping data collection congruent with experimental hypothesis. *Journal of Applied Behavior Analysis, 8,* 43–51.

Parson, L. R., & Heward, W. L. (1979). Training peers to tutor: Evaluation of a tutor training package for primary learning disabled students. *Journal of Applied Behavior Analysis, 12,* 309–310.

Ragland, E. U., Kerr, M. M., & Strain, P. S. (1978). Effects of peer social initiations on the behavior of withdrawn autistic children. *Behavior Modification, 2,* 565–578.

Rusch, F. R. (1983). Competitive vocational training. In M. Snell (Ed.), *Systematic instruction of the moderately and severely handicapped* (2nd ed.) (pp. 503–523). Columbus OH: Charles E. Merrill.

Rusch, F. R., Connis, R. T., & Sowers, J. (1978). The modification and maintenance of time spent attending to task using social reinforcement, token reinforcement, and response cost in an applied restaurant setting. *Journal of Special Education Technology, 2,* 18–26.

Rusch, F. R., & Kazdin, A. E. (1981). Toward a methodology of withdrawal designs for the assessment of response maintenance. *Journal of Applied Behavior Analysis, 14,* 131–140.

Rusch, F. R., Martin, J. E., & White, D. M. (1985). Competitive employment: Teaching mentally retarded employees to maintain their work behavior. *Education and Training of the Mentally Retarded, 20*(3), 182–189.

Rusch, F. R., & Menchetti, B. M. (1981). Increasing compliant work behaviors in a non-sheltered setting. *Mental Retardation, 19,* 107–112.

Rusch, F. R., Menchetti, B. M., Crouch, K., Riva, M., Morgan, T. K., & Agran, M. M. (1984). Competitive employment: Assessing employee reactivity to naturalistic observation. *Applied Research in Mental Retardation, 5*(3), 339–351.

Rusch, F. R., & Mithaug, D. E. (1980). *Vocational training for mentally retarded adults: A behavior analytic approach.* Champaign, IL: Research Press.

Rusch, F. R., & Schutz, R. P. (1981). Vocational and social work behavior research: An evaluative review. In J. L. Matson & J. R. McCartney (Eds.), *Handbook of behavior modification with the mentally retarded* (pp. 247–280). New York: Plenum.

Rusch, F. R., Weithers, J. A., Menchetti, B. M., & Schutz, R. P. (1980). Social validation of a program to reduce the topic repetition in a non-sheltered setting. *Education and Treatment of the Mentally Retarded, 15,* 208–215.

Schreibman, L., O'Neill, R. E., & Koegel, R. L. (1983). Behavioral training for siblings of autistic children. *Journal of Applied Behavior Analysis, 16,* 129–138.

Schutz, R. P., Jostes, K. F., Rusch, F. R., & Lamson, D. S. (1980). Acquisition, transfer, and social validation of two vocational skills in a competitive employment setting. *Education and Treatment of the Mentally Retarded, 4,* 306–311.

Schutz, R. P., Rusch, F. R., & Lamson, D. S. (1979). Evaluation of an employer's procedure to eliminate unacceptable behavior on the job. *Community Service Forum, 1,* 5–6.

Shafer, M. S., Egel, A. L., & Neef, N. A. (1984). Training mildly handicapped peers to facilitate changes in the social interaction skills of autistic children. *Journal of Applied Behavior Analysis, 17*(4), 461–476.

Stanford, K., & Wehman, P. (1980). Improving the social interactions between moderately retarded and non-retarded coworkers: A pilot study. In P. Wehman & M. Hill (Eds.), *Vocational training and placement of severely disabled persons* (Vol. 3) Richmond, VA: Virginia Commonwealth University.

Stokes, T., & Baer, D. (1977a). An implicit technology of generalization. *Journal of Applied Behavior Analysis, 10,* 349–367.

Stokes, T., & Baer, D. M. (1977b). Preschool peers as mutual generalization-facilitating agents. *Behavior Therapy, 7,* 549–556.

Strain, P. S. (1981). *The utlization of classroom peers as behavior change agents.* New York: Plenum.

Strain, P. S., Kerr, M. M., & Ragland, E. U. (1979). Effects of peer-mediated social interaction and prompting/reinforcement on the social behavior of autistic children. *Journal of Autism and Developmental Disabilities, 9,* 41–54.

Trovato, J., & Bucher, B. (1980). Peer tutoring with or without home based reinforcement for reading remidiation. *Journal of Applied Behavior Analysis, 13,* 129–141.

Wehman, P. (1981). *Competitive employment: New horizons for severely disabled individuals.* Baltimore: Paul H. Brookes.

White, D. M., & Rusch, F. R. (1983). Social validation in competitive employment: Evaluating work performance. *Applied Research in Mental Retardation, 4,* 343–354.

Wilcox, B., & Bellamy, G. T. (1982). Program administration and support. *Design of high school programs for severely handicapped students* (pp. 211–220). Baltimore: Paul H. Brookes.

Wolf, M. M. (1978). Social validity: The case for subjective measurement or how applied behavior analysis is finding its heart. *Journal of Applied Behavior Analysis, 11,* 203–214.

Chapter 17

Developing a Long-Term Follow-Up Program

Frank R. Rusch

EACH OF THE preceding chapters in this section focuses upon the many essential characteristics of a supported work approach to competitive employment. The present chapter introduces methods to use to maintain employment after placement. Remaining employed depends upon many factors, most of which are related to consumer satisfaction and the efforts made to ensure that the placement is satisfactory to everybody involved. Social validation has surfaced as a means of evaluating whether behavior changes are important to the consumer for whom the changes are intended (i.e., the employer). The concept of social validation and its application to competitive employment is overviewed by White in Chapter 15. Indeed, within the present context, the employer, supervisor, co-worker(s), *and* the target employee form a complex, intricate social arrangement based upon expectations and perceived behaviors.

This chapter presents a rationale for follow-up programs and describes procedures for developing follow-up services by identifying needed follow-up resources. Topics include specifying and evaluating perceived and actual deficits, establishing priorities for deficits in need of remediation, and implementing the follow-up program, with final emphasis on decreasing follow-up services.

REASONS FOR ESTABLISHING FOLLOW-UP PROGRAM

Follow-up services after a person has been placed are important for several reasons, including: 1) early identification of problems, 2) establishing a follow-up schedule, 3) providing on-the-job intervention, 4) seeking validation by significant others, 5) planning interventions by others, 6) withdrawing follow-up, and 7) evaluating adjustment.

Early Identification of Problems

One fundamental reason for establishing follow-up services is to identify problems in need of remediation to prevent the target employee from losing his or her job. Often employers' and supervisors' expectations are such that they perceive competencies of persons who are handicapped (prior to and immediately after placement) as being below those of other co-workers. Consequently, the performance of newly placed employees tends to be checked closely. Such close scrutiny, in turn, has led to job performance demands that are often greater than those placed on co-workers who are not handicapped. In instances when the target employee cannot meet the increased job performance demands, the employer's and/or supervisor's lowered expectations are confirmed. If this situation continues, the employee may ultimately come to the erroneous perception that his or her abilities are inadequate for a given job.

Establishing Follow-Up Schedule

In an effort to identify postplacement problems, the Work Performance Evaluation Form was developed (see Chapter 15; also White & Rusch, 1983). The Work Performance Evaluation Form (WPEF) is initially distributed to co-workers, supervisors, and employers, who are asked to rate the new employee weekly for the first month. Follow-up staff, in turn, monitor and evaluate any differences between the rater groups and the target employee in terms of perceived performance problems in light of acceptable performance. After the first month, follow-up staff request that the company employee, who has evaluative responsibilities over all personnel, rate the target employee monthly using the WPEF. Ultimately, the evaluator is asked to complete semi-annual evaluations (usually after 6 months of continuous employment).

Providing On-the-Job Intervention

Persons with handicaps will require some on-the-job training after placement. This training is critical for ensuring continued employment. The procedures delineated in the preceding chapters in this section are recommended for identifying problems and providing on-the-job training. Almost 10 years ago, Mithaug and Haring (1977) proposed a similar approach to evaluating performance on the job, consisting of the following eight steps: 1) analyzing the skills required to complete a job, 2) pinpointing behaviors expected by the supervisor, 3) specifying the motivational system on the job, 4) encouraging conformity to rules, 5) discouraging deviant behavior, 6) assessing skill level relevant to the job, 7) specifying behavioral objectives for each identified deficiency, and 8) developing and implementing a training program.

Seeking Validation by Significant Others

Because existing job performance standards do not always match those encountered on the job, it is important to obtain supervisor feedback to validate whether follow-up efforts are positively influencing performance. Programs developed to facilitate training of survival skills, therefore, are often based upon input from supervisors. Procedures for obtaining such feedback are discussed in detail in Chapter 15.

Planning Intervention by Others

Since it is impossible to intervene every time a target employee requires training or retraining on a task, it must be specified early in the placement stage that employing staff (e.g., co-workers) will need to occasionally teach new skills or eliminate unwanted behavior (see Chapter 16). Training on the job necessitates the development of the most often used training strategies. In a restaurant, for example, training on the job may require that the new employee is trained to be responsive to a demonstration and one instance of simple corrective feedback from a co-worker while performing a task *before* the person is placed or allowed to work alone without follow-up program-personnel assistance.

To date, little attention has been paid to job placement follow-up provided by co-workers. Based on our findings, we recommend that co-workers be trained to work with target employees via short inservice workshops that focus upon training and managing behavior. For example, 10-minute sessions could be scheduled during breaks or before or after work to demonstrate effective training procedures and to allow co-workers to practice. Behavior descriptions and the goal of the Work Performance Evaluation Form also could be addressed. In essence, the follow-up staff are responsible for monitoring placement. Consequently, time should be devoted to a series of well planned and coordinated inservice activities for all employees at the job site.

Withdrawing Follow-Up

The supported work model assumes that follow-up is provided for all persons placed on a job. The difficulty of determining when to withdraw follow-up checks without losing acquired, maintained, and generalized survival skills is an important reason for establishing follow-up support. No supported work program is successful if loss of behavior results in job loss. Methods of follow-up withdrawal and withdrawal evaluation have been discussed in the applied literature (Connis & Rusch, 1981;

Rusch, Chadsey-Rusch, & Lagomarcino, in press; Rusch & Kazdin, 1981).

Several factors should be considered when estimating how soon to withdraw staff from a placement setting. Foremost among these is the newly placed employee's ability to perform the job without trainer feedback and in the trainer's absence. Rusch and Kazdin (1981) suggested using partial withdrawals when estimating levels of dependence. *Partial withdrawal* refers to the procedure of removing one component of the training package or the complete training package from any combination of situations (e.g., from the morning session but not the afternoon session), behaviors (e.g., from greetings at the start of the day but not during lunch), or persons (e.g., from one target employee but not from another target employee who may be working on the same job). Vogelsberg and Rusch (1979) incorporated a partial withdrawal approach in assessing whether elimination of feedback from one of three severely handicapped adolescents who had learned to cross streets would lead to loss of acquired skills. Upon removal of feedback, the authors found that one class of behaviors (looking for traffic) was not maintained. Therefore, assuming that similar withdrawals from the other two adolescents would result in similar behavior losses, they introduced a second training strategy—modeling—in place of feedback.

Rusch and Kazdin (1981) also recommended the use of sequential withdrawals to maintain responses. *Sequential withdrawal* refers to removing, initially, one component of a multiple-component training package, then a second, and so on, until all components have been withdrawn. Rusch, Connis, and Sowers (1978) used this strategy with a mildly mentally retarded woman, who was instructed to attend to the task of cleaning tables. Attending was taught via prompts, praise, and a token economy that incorporated points that could be earned throughout the day and exchanged for items the woman selected from a department store. Initially, the token economy required the employee to exchange her points twice a day.

Rusch and his colleagues withdrew the token economy one component at a time, and then the prompts and praise, until the training package consisted of the target employee receiving wages every 2 weeks.

When withdrawing on-the-job intervention, follow-up trainers must evaluate whether the absence of intervention and/or the person(s) who introduce interventions result in loss of behavior. If so, the withdrawal approach must be: 1) repeated more slowly so that the new employee eventually does not discriminate between the absence or presence of the intervention or trainer, 2) supplemented with a second strategy (e.g., self-monitoring) or, possibly, 3) only partially withdrawn (i.e., part of the procedures remain). In the last instance, the strategy might include training other employees on the job to maintain performance (Rusch & Menchetti, 1981).

Evaluating Adjustment

Several sources may be consulted to determine if follow-up efforts are effective, such as the target employee's parents, guardians, employers, supervisors, co-workers, and many others. It is, for example, essential to work with parents once their son or daughter has been placed. Employees who have never managed their own earnings will require assistance in learning how to bank, save, and spend. Parents are likely sources of informing follow-up staff of whether money is important to their son or daughter. To this end, it may be necessary to promote shopping trips, trips to movies, and dinners out with the new employee relying upon his or her own money for parents to believe that their son or daughter has meaningfully adjusted to being employed. (The reader is referred to Chapter 21 for a discussion of the roles of parents.)

DEVELOPING A FOLLOW-UP PROGRAM

Although some new employees may do extremely well after placement, suggesting the need for little, if any, follow-up, as stated above, most persons are more likely to require some form of follow-up services. Such services may range from occasional visits across several weeks to extensive sessions over a period of a year or longer. Regardless of their frequency and duration, these contacts will most likely represent follow-up program efforts to provide additional training. The remainder of this chapter deals almost exclusively with discrepancies between expectations that result in the need for follow-up support.

When providing follow-up, it should be remembered that: *Every time a follow-up contact is made, for whatever reason, the new employee's strengths should always be discussed by the follow-up personnel and members of the employing agency.* We cannot overemphasize the importance of stressing an employee's strengths. Too often we get so involved with a particular problem, such as how fast someone performs during the morning schedule or how poorly he or she cleans a floor, that the person's overall competencies are overlooked.

The follow-up staff's primary goal is to coordinate their own objective assessments with evaluations of the employing staff in an effort to evaluate actual performance on the job. Provided with the employing staff's typically subjective evaluations, follow-up staff must determine the extent of correspondence between the two sets of evaluations. Two types of validation guided our social validation program—subjective evaluation and social comparison.

Subjective Evaluation

Subjective evaluation refers to efforts to evaluate training based upon judgments about qualitative aspects of work behavior. For example, work behavior that has been changed by a trainer may be evaluated by significant others who are in a position to judge the effects of training (e.g., supervisors). Typically, employers evaluate their staff at least annually, with new staff being evaluated during the first 3–6 months of employment. Sometimes, existing work performance evaluations are used as the sole subjective evaluation measure. However, existing evaluations are often not sufficiently expansive or behaviorally oriented to

provide the information needed to develop individual training plans. Therefore, follow-up staff should utilize a behaviorally based work performance measure during the first year in addition to any evaluation form that may be used by the employing agency.

The behaviorally based work performance evaluation form must be completed by an employee who has responsibility for staff evaluations and, possibly, hiring and firing. It should not solely be filled out by co-workers in positions similar to that of the new employee or by the new employee. Recent research has revealed gross discrepancies between evaluations conducted by experienced supervisory staff and those completed by handicapped employees or employees who are considered peers (White & Rusch, 1983). Employees who are handicapped and co-workers who are not handicapped evaluate performance significantly higher than supervisors.

Social Comparison

Social comparison refers to efforts to compare the target employee's work performance with that of his or her peers (e.g., nonhandicapped co-workers) for the purpose of determining whether target behavior (e.g., how fast the target employee works) is distinguishable from peer behavior. Social comparisons entail direct observation of an employee's work performance to compare his or her performance with that of a target employee (cf. Rusch, Weithers, Menchetti, & Schutz, 1980). Rather than training the target employee to work just like his or her peers, the goal is to adjust or manage target behavior so that the new employee works within tolerable limits. Employees behave variably; some days they work faster than on other days. This variability may be due, in part, to setting conditions (e.g., heat, tension), subject characteristics (e.g., how one feels), or a combination of the two. Social comparison defines the boundaries of acceptable work performance.

Correct use of social comparison entails selecting an employee who peforms tasks that are comparable to those of the target employee during similar work periods. It is crucial to collect direct, repeated measures of work performed under similar conditions for both employees. For example, it would be appropriate to collect data on a target employee within 30 minutes of a break if the comparison employee is observed during the same period. If both are working in the same location, the evaluator may either observe one employee for a brief period (e.g., 10 seconds) and then the other (also for 10 seconds), alternating until the work sample is completed. If the two employees work in separate locations in the same building, the observer may watch one employee for a period of time and then the other for exactly the same length of time (e.g., for 10 minutes). If a comparable employee is not working at the same time as the target employee, the peer should be observed performing the same tasks during the same periods on days when the target employee is off work. For example, if the target employee works 5 days a week with a part-time employee working on his or her days off (or the reverse), both employees may be observed under the same conditions but at alternating times. (The reader is referred to Chapter 11 for more discussion of observation methodology.)

Social comparison is useful when combined with subjective evaluations. As mentioned, subjective evaluations will be made in placement sites. Particularly when poor, such evaluations must be considered when determining whether the target employee is adjusting to his or her job. Social comparison is particularly useful when supervisors provide subjective evaluations that are below their perceived standard. Instances where subjective evaluations show high performance but social comparison measures indicate low performance are not as important as when the reverse occurs. Simply stated, if the employer believes an employee is doing well and follow-up staff disagree, based upon objective data, it may not be essential to correct or lower the employer's evaluations.

Intervention is crucial only in those instances when the employer believes there is a problem. For example, if an employer, who is also the supervisor, rates an employee poorly on "completes all assigned tasks," the follow-up staff should objectively evaluate "completes all assigned tasks" and, when (or where) a problem is found, remediate the difference. Perhaps the employee does not complete a particular task daily or performs it differently than traditionally. In either case, feedback to the employer and acceptable training of the employee should result in a higher evaluation on "completed all assigned tasks" the next time the evaluator rates the target employee.

Summary

Subjective evaluations and social comparisons are critical vehicles for determining how well a target employee is performing. More importantly, these evaluations directly relate to how well target employees are adjusting to the demands of a new job. Although the new employee may fail to meet some of the performance criteria, follow-up staff may be able to increase the likelihood of the employer, supervisor, and/or co-worker not paying undue attention to perceived problems. Agreements and disagreements must be documented and shared with the employing staff during scheduled and structured verbal reports (see Table 1).

During these meetings, follow-up staff should identify areas that require training and set priorities (see Table 2). First, the agreed-upon competencies should be discussed to ensure that they are not overlooked in light of deficits or problems. Second, agreed-upon deficits identified *initially* by subjective evaluation and confirmed by direct observation should receive attention. Third, subjectively specified deficits that are not objectively identified as deficits should be addressed. Finally,

Table 1. Listing agreements and disagreements

	Agreements	Disagreements
Deficits	1.	1.
	2.	2.
	3.	3.
	4.	4.
	5.	5.
Competencies	1.	1.
	2.	2.
	3.	3.
	4.	4.
	5.	5.

Table 2.   Setting priorities

1. Agreed-upon competencies
2. Agreed-upon deficits
3. Subjectively specified deficts that were not objectively validated
4. Objectively specified deficits that were not subjectively validated

all cases require that the *conditions* under which the perceived or actual deficits were evident be specified. This is done by identifying the time of day, type of work, and social conditions (e.g., who is present) during which any of the areas requiring possible retraining of the new employee occurred. See Table 3 for a representative form used for this purpose.

SPECIFYING PLACEMENT TRAINING OUTCOMES

The results of subjective and objective evaluations require that follow-up staff set priorities for deficits in need of remediation and specify placement training objectives based upon these deficits. Three steps should be followed for each identified deficit: 1) getting input from the employer, supervisor, and/or co-workers regarding the work behavior in question and determining what level of performance (e.g., quality and quantity) will be acceptable after a

specified period of training; 2) determining the level of improvement that is possible in the time available for (re)training; and 3) negotiating with the employee, supervisor, and/or co-worker about a performance level that can be reasonably expected in the time available. For example, somebody may have been placed conditionally because the employer, supervisor, and/or co-worker were interested in employing a person from the training program but had some reservations about working with persons with handicaps. Three weeks after the placement, several minor discrepancies emerged, and efforts to remedy them led to additional discrepancies between what was expected and what was obtained. In this case, it may become necessary to set a date for terminating employment. Specifically, the target employee will be fired if she or he does not meet the employing staff's expectations within the specified time period.

DELIVERING FOLLOW-UP SERVICES

The number of deficits and their relative importance determine schedules for providing follow-up services. Before a placement is made, employers, supervisors, and/or co-workers must agree that the training program's

Table 3.   Possible retraining areas

	Areas	Time of day	Type of work	Social condition
Agreed-upon deficits (subjective/objective agreement)				
1.				
2.				
3.				
4.				
5.				
Subjectively specified deficits (objectively identified as competencies)				
1.				
2.				
3.				
4.				
5.				
Objectively specified deficits (subjectively identified as competencies)				
1.				
2.				
3.				
4.				
5.				

goal is for the target employee to do well enough that follow-up staff's services *are not necessary or required* in the future, except on a consulting, periodic basis. Furthermore, it is important to agree upon the follow-up schedule before the placement. Rusch and Mithaug (1980) suggested two follow-up schedules: 1) the adjusted follow-up schedule, and 2) the fixed follow-up schedule.

Adjusted Follow-Up

An *adjusted schedule* is determined solely by the success of the program being monitored and the target employee's success in meeting the expectations of the employer, supervisor, and/or co-worker. Initially, the adjusted schedule make take the form of 8 hours of direct, daily contact with the target employee. Eventually, the follow-up schedule may be reduced to weekly checkups. However, the move from direct, daily contact to occasional weekly checkups is not arbitrary. Table 4 contains a sample adjusted follow-up schedule.

As illustrated, the follow-up trainer was either on-site or off-site. When on-site, the trainer was either in clear view of the target employee (observable) or not observable. In our example, the target employee required 8 hours of direct service for the first 3 days. However, this intense schedule was reduced to 7 hours per day after the 3rd day, 6 hours the 6th through the 9th day, and so on, until 7 weeks later a trainer was required on the job only 2 hours a day. One of these hours was spent directly observing the target employee while the other was devoted to talking with the employer, supervisor, and co-worker about ratings and overall progress. Eventually, follow-up services took the form of a 1-hour visit to the site to discuss the evaluation form *only* (subjective evaluation). While the sample schedule depicted in Table 4 proved successful with one target employee, it needs to be adjusted in other instances depending on the target employee's performance and the employing staff's perception of performance.

Fixed Schedules

The *fixed schedule* is negotiated with the employing agency to establish preset visitations by follow-up personnel. While such an arrangement is less desirable than the adjusted schedule, it may be the only schedule the employing agency will tolerate due, possibly, to perceived untimely interruptions. When utilizing the fixed schedule, follow-up staff should negotiate for as much time as possible, to be reduced as slowly as possible over the course of several weeks or months. Negotiating a stringent follow-up schedule is advisable with an employer wishing to know, in advance, when and how much time will be required. The time may be decreased after the schedule is set up. However, the opposite, that is, increasing the number and duration of visits, may be more difficult. Table 5 displays a sample fixed schedule.

Table 4.   Sample adjusted follow-up schedule

Date	Observable to employee	Not observable to employee	Off-site
January 21–23	8	0	0
January 24–25	7	1	0
January 28–31	6	2	0
February 1	5	3	0
February 4–8	4	3	1
February 11–15	3	2	3
February 18–22	2	2	4
February 25–March 1	1	2	5
March 4–8	1	1	6
March 11–September 1 (per week)	1	1	6
September forward (per week)	0	1	7

Table 5. Sample fixed follow-up schedule

Weeks	Observable to employee	Not observable to employee	Off-site
1	8	0	0
2	6	2	0
3	5	2	1
4	4	3	1
5	4	2	2
6	3	3	2
7	3	2	3
8	2	3	3
9–12	2	2	4
13–16	2	1	5
17–20	1	2	5
21–24	1	1	6

SUMMARY

This chapter focuses upon many of the issues that may surface after a person with handicaps has been placed in competitive employment, and the follow-up procedures that should be adhered to regardless of whether or not serious problems occur. Follow-up should not be taken lightly, nor should it center solely on problems and deficits. Follow-up services are a necessary function of a supported work program attempting to create employment opportunities for persons with handicaps. Training staff's response to the employing agency *after* placement is central to the target employee's long-term adjustment. Following many of the suggestions offered in this text and adopting new approaches to surveying, training, and placing trainees will increase the likelihood that persons with handicaps will begin to share in the many experiences we tend to take for granted.

REFERENCES

Connis, R. T., & Rusch, F. R. (1981). Programming maintenance through sequential withdrawal of social contingencies. *Behavior Research of Severe Developmental Disabilities, 1,* 249–260.

Mithaug, D. E., & Haring, N. G. (1977). Community vocational and workshop placement. In N. G. Haring & L. J. Brown (Eds.), *Teaching the severely handicapped* (Vol. II, pp. 257–283). New York: Grune & Stratton.

Rusch, F. R., Chadsey-Rusch, J., & Lagomarcino, T. R. (in press). Preparing students for employment. In M. Snell (Ed.), *Systematic instruction for persons with severe handicaps.* Columbus, OH: Charles E. Merrill Publishing Co.

Rusch, F. R., Connis, R. T., & Sowers, J. (1978). The modification and maintenance of time spent attending to task using social reinforcement, token reinforcement and response cost in an applied restaurant setting. *Journal of Special Education Technology, 2,* 18–26.

Rusch, F. R., & Kazdin, A. E. (1981). Toward a methodology of withdrawal designs for the assessment of response maintenance. *Journal of Applied Behavior Analysis, 14,* 131–140.

Rusch, F. R., & Menchetti, B. M. (1981). Increasing compliant work behaviors in a non-sheltered setting. *Mental Retardation, 19,* 107–112.

Rusch, F. R., & Mithaug, D. E. (1980). *Vocational training for mentally retarded adults: A behavior analytic approach.* Champaign, IL: Research Press.

Rusch, F. R., Weithers, J. A., Menchetti, B. M., & Schutz, R. P. (1980). Social validation of a program to reduce topic repetition in a non-sheltered setting. *Education and Training of the Mentally Retarded, 15,* 208–215.

Vogelsberg, R. T., & Rusch, F. R. (1979). Training severely handicapped students to cross partially controlled intersections. *AAESPH Review, 4,* 264–273.

White, D. M., & Rusch, F. R. (1983). Social validation in competitive employment: Evaluating work performance. *Applied Research in Mental Retardation, 4,* 343–354.

SECTION III

COMPETITIVE EMPLOYMENT ISSUES

Introduction

John L. Gifford

THE SEVEN CHAPTERS in Section III address issues that impinge upon employment of persons with disabilities at diverse system levels. In Chapter 18, Karan and Knight underscore the importance of achieving an ecological understanding of the individual within the work groups to which he or she belongs. Bellamy, Rhodes, Bourbeau, and Mank provide a policy analysis in Chapter 19 and describe a two-tiered system, CEPs (Competitive Employment Programs) and SEPs (Supported Employment Programs), which are time-limited and long-term support programs, respectively. In Chapter 20, Chadsey-Rusch discusses the social competence of individuals with mental retardation within dyads and small group settings. Schutz discusses interventions to facilitate family interactions in Chapter 21, as well as suggesting the importance of identifying the community's perceived needs and values. Within Chapter 22, Renzaglia addresses shortcomings in personnel preparation and proposes that these deficiencies can be surmounted through the concept of an educational team manager to bridge diverse specialities serving the individual with handicaps and to coordinate educational programs. Chapter 23, by Walls, Zawlocki, and Dowler, like Chapter 19, is a policy analysis. However, its emphasis is upon economic disincentives that reduce the likelihood of individuals with mental retardation entering competitive employment. In Chapter 24, Matson and Rusch are concerned with what might be considered philosophical issues, such as self-esteem, self-worth, and independence, while at the same time they are very much interested in the operationalization and realization of these abstract goals by individuals with mental retardation within their day-to-day lives.

The rest of this Introduction provides an integration of these papers. First, Chapters 18, 20, and 21, whose common themes are support groups, communication, interaction within dyads and small groups, and person-environment fit, are discussed together. Next, Chapters 19 and 23, which discuss current policy and proposals for change in the area of competitive employment, are summarized. The theme of Chapter 22, the educational manager, is discussed with respect to the issues of interagency coordination and policy development. Finally, the topic of Chapter 24, quality of life, is considered as an underlying principle that can guide development of interventions with individuals, personnel preparation models, and policy development.

PERSON-ENVIRONMENT FIT

In Chapter 18, Karan and Knight introduce an ecological perspective within which to view competitive employment (Karan & Schalock, 1983). The individual is considered with respect to the environment; appropriate person-environment match is the goal, achievable by focusing interventions on either the person, the environment, or both. Karan and Berger focus first on the individual, identifying the characteristics of "high-risk" individuals (e.g., social-interpersonal difficulties, excessively influenced by external forces; difficulties in emotional expression and negative self-concept [Gardner & Cole, 1983]; poor social role development [Martin, Flexer, & Newberry, 1979]; and low motivation [Karan & Gardner, 1973]. Next, the authors identify components of socially accessible environments, which are often essential for successful competitive employment by individuals who are mentally handicapped. Such socially accessible environments include links to key support persons or groups, quality interpersonal transactions, informational feedback focused on satisfying basic psychological and social needs, and reciprocity of need satisfaction. By identifying the characteristics of individuals and environments crucial to successful person-environment fit, the authors have made possible the next step: identification of the critical interactions between persons and environment. People influence each other in complex and subtle ways. Karan and Knight emphasize the critical importance of communication in establishing the reciprocal relationships that are the key to developing a support network. To facilitate improved communication, the authors propose "The Awareness Wheel" model (Miller, Nunnally, & Wackman, 1975), whose components include interpretations, sensations, feelings, intentions, and actions.

Like Karan and Knight, Chadsey-Rusch in Chapter 20 begins with an ecological perspective. More specifically, the author proposes an ecobehavioral (Rogers-Warren & Warren, 1977; Willems, 1977) perspective within which to consider social competence. The chapter includes summaries of social behaviors necessary for successful employment (e.g., ability to communicate at least basic needs, compliance, nondisruption of work setting, and ability to follow directions [Rusch, Schutz, & Agran, 1982]), as well as social behaviors associated with job loss (e.g., character or moral reasons, temperament or affective reasons, and social awareness or not understanding people and work settings [Greenspan & Shoultz, 1981]).

In order to unify findings and provide understanding of social competence, Chadsey-Rusch utilizes the conceptual framework of McFall (1982). Within the framework, social competence and social skills are differentiated. Social competency relates to adequacy of performance on a particular social task. Social skills are specific behaviors needed to perform competently on a particular social task. Furthermore, social skills can be divided into three

types: 1) social decoding skills, 2) social decision skills, and 3) social performance skills. Social decoding involves understanding the social situation and what the context implies. Social decision involves choosing the appropriate response for the given context. Social performance includes judging whether the response met the demands of the social task. Interventions based upon the model depend upon identifying social tasks that are critical to the individual in question. Next, the task must be analyzed, which will involve consideration of variables that could potentially influence the task, such as its purpose, task constraints, setting, and performance criteria. Then, assessment of the individual should be conducted on the social tasks identified. The interventions discussed by Chadsey-Rusch are primarily focused on the individual, as opposed to environmental interventions. The author identifies several social skill training packages and relates them to the McFall (1982) model of social competence.

Because Chadsey-Rusch's focus is primarily on the individual and Karan and Berger's emphasis is upon environmental intervention, the two chapters complement each other effectively. Specifically, the social skill packages—which contain the following components: 1) rationale as to why a given social behavior is desirable, 2) an opportunity to observe examples of the behavior, 3) an opportunity to practice the behavior, and 4) feedback regarding performance—complement Karan and Knight's suggested steps to make an environment more socially accessible. These steps include: 1) identify key individuals to function as support people, 2) assist in improving successful interactions within the work environment between the high-risk individual and his or her supervisor and co-workers, 3) observe the individual with mental retardation across settings and time to identify both temporally proximate and distant events that may be influencing the individual's inability to function effectively on the job, 4) attempt to ensure that the responsibility for behavioral-change programs is shared by the individual and significant others, and 5) ensure that those providing support to the high-risk person have their own sources of support. Combining the two sets of strategies provides a powerful approach toward facilitating person-environment match.

Many of the same issues addressed within the areas of support networks and social competence also potentially apply to the topic of parent training and involvement. Again, the ecobehavioral approach allows a systematic analysis of the person with mental retardation and his or her significant others. In addition to behavioral interventions focusing upon the individual and the environment, social validation (White, Chapter 15) provides a powerful means to enhance person-environment match and development of support networks. In Chapter 21, Schutz identifies inventorying the needs of parents, assessing their values, and evaluating their level of satisfaction with program delivery as a means to promote the transition process into competitive employment. The parent frequently provides the most important support that an individual with mental retardation has. Parental support for the child's entrance into competitive employment is critical for success on the job. By utilizing parents to socially validate employment choices, training means, and placement procedures, the likelihood of success on the job is enhanced.

POLICY

Often, successful interventions directed toward individuals with mental retardation and their environment are thwarted by existing fiscal and administrative policies. In Chapter 19, Bellamy, Rhodes, Bourbeau, and Mank describe an alternative approach to service delivery that could more adequately satisfy constituencies served by workshops. Historically, workshop programs for persons with mental retardation have developed into dual-purpose entities: 1) to provide sheltered employment, and 2) to move individuals on to competitive jobs. These two functions often are combined in one agency within a flow-through model of services. In theory, individuals move through the continuum of ser-

vices until they become competitively employed. In practice, 75% of all consumers placed in competitive employment are transferred during their first 3 months (Moss, 1979). The annual likelihood of placement for individuals who have been in workshop programs longer than 2 years is 3%. The time-limited nature of support for individuals entering competitive employment has reduced the likelihood of more severely handicapped individuals entering into competitive employment. Bellamy et al. propose a two-tiered system, CEPs and SEPs. CEPs are time-limited programs designed to move jobless individuals with disabilities into self-supporting, open employment. SEPs, on the other hand, provide longer term, publicly supported jobs for individuals with handicaps. Through the dual framework, each individual referred to an agency has a chance to obtain work and the conflicting goals of the agency are reduced considerably.

Even if the policy alternative proposed by Bellamy et al. is successful, an additional policy hurdle is identified by Walls, Zawlocki, and Dowler in Chapter 23. Movement into competitive employment may be significantly curtailed because of social benefits paid to individuals with disabilities. Both a behavioral analysis of disincentives (Rusch & Mithaug, 1980) and a microeconomics approach predict decreased job-seeking and work behaviors when tax-free benefits are high. When guaranteed social benefit pay is balanced against pay from competitive employment, which has several uncertainties related to it, the social benefit pay is highly attractive. The continued availability of work is uncertain, the ability to be successful on the job is uncertain, and the effects of increased wages upon current benefits is particularly uncertain in the eyes of the recipient. Walls et al. suggest that a major overhaul of the social benefit system is needed to produce a consistent system that provides incentives, rather than disincentives. However, the authors indicate the magnitude of such a restructuring in the face of entrenched agencies and political inertia.

PERSONNEL PREPARATION

Due to the complexity of the task facing practitioners serving individuals with disabilities, personnel preparation will have to provide a more comprehensive and systematic curriculum. Renzaglia notes in Chapter 22 that the quality of educational programs for students with handicaps is still poor (Alper & Alper, 1980). There is a critical need for the practices developed in model demonstration programs to be incorporated into preservice and inservice preparation programs. The author notes that because of the variety of specialists serving individuals who are mentally handicapped, educators and rehabilitation personnel must become educational team managers (Haring, 1982; Mori, Rusch, & Fair, 1982). In addition, a model personnel preparation curriculum should be competency based, field based, behaviorally grounded, include community-referenced curriculum development, and provide a focus on transition issues. Furthermore, there should be a broadened awareness of medical, legal, and advocacy issues, as well as an understanding of service delivery systems that promotes interagency cooperation. Due to the varying types and degrees of handicaps experienced by vocational training program participants, educators must have a wider and more sophisticated range of skills.

QUALITY OF LIFE

In Chapter 24, Matson and Rusch address the issue of quality of life. They identify general descriptors of quality of life, such as self-esteem, self-worth, and independence. These are considered in more operationalized form as the ability to live where one chooses, equal access to services, and opportunity to attend community schools and to engage in other normalized activities. Additionally, the ability to work, experience the feeling of accomplishment, and have the respect of supervisors and co-workers is a major step toward achieving quality of life. Articulating the concept of the quality of life is a first step toward its realization. However, policy decisions must come to reflect this concept, community attitudes must be influenced by its message, and its implications must find their way into the day-to-day lives of individuals who are mentally handicapped.

REFERENCES

Alper, S., & Alper, J. (1980). Issues in community-based vocational programming: Institutionalization of staff. In C. Hansen (Ed.), *Expanding opportunities: Vocational education for the handicapped* (pp. 121–143). University of Washington: PDAS.

Gardner, W. I., & Cole, C. L. (1983). A structured learning habilitation approach: Use with the mentally retarded presenting emotional and behavioral disorders. In O. C. Karan & W. I. Gardner (Eds.), *Habilitation practices with the developmentally disabled who present behavioral and emotional disorders* (pp. 39–60). Madison, WI: Rehabilitation Research and Training Center in Mental Retardation.

Greenspan, S., & Shoultz, B. (1981). When mentally retarded adults lose their jobs: Social incompetence as a factor in work adjustment. *Applied Research in Mental Retardation, 2,* 23–38.

Haring, N. (1982). Review and analysis of professional preparation for the severely handicapped. In B. Wilcox & R. York (Eds.), *Quality education for the severely handicapped* (pp. 180–201). Falls Church, VA: Counterpoint Handcrafted Books.

Karan, O. C., & Gardner, W. I. (1973). Vocational rehabilitation practices: A behavioral approach. *Rehabilitation Literature 34,* 290–298.

Karan, O. C., & Schalock, R. L. (1983). An ecological approach to assessing vocational and community living skills. In O. C. Karan & W. I. Gardner (Eds.), *Habilitation practices with the developmentally disabled who present behavioral and emotional disorders* (pp. 121–173). Madison, WI: Rehabilitation Research and Training Center in Mental Retardation.

Martin, A., Flexer, R., & Newberry, J. (1979). The development of a work ethic in the severely retarded. In T. Bellamy, G. O'Connor, & O. Karan (Eds.), *Vocational rehabilitation of severely handicapped persons: Contemporary service strategies* (pp. 136–159). Baltimore: University Park Press.

McFall, R. M. (1982). A review and reformulation of the concept of social skills. *Behavioral Assessment, 4,* 1–33.

Miller, S., Nunnally, E., & Wackman, D. B. (1975). *Alive and aware: Improving communication in relationships.* Minneapolis, MN: Interpersonal Communication Programs, Inc.

Mori, A., Rusch, F., & Fair, G. (1982). *Vocational education for the handicapped: Perspectives on special populations/severely and moderately handicapped* (Personnel Development Series: Document 1). Champaign, IL: Office of Career Development for Special Populations, University of Illinois.

Moss, J. W. (1979). *Post secondary vocational education*

for mentally retarded adults. Final Report to the Division of Developmental Disabilities, Rehabilitation Services Administration, Department of Health, Education and Welfare, Grant No. 56P 50281/0.

Rogers-Warren, A., & Warren, S. F. (1977). The developing ecobehavioral psychology. In A. Rogers-Warren & S. F. Warren (Eds.), *Ecological perspectives in behavior analysis* (pp. 3–8). Baltimore: University Park Press.

Rusch, F. R., & Mithaug, D. E. (1980). *Vocational training for mentally retarded adults: A behavior-analytic approach.* Champaign, IL: Research Press.

Rusch, F. R., & Schutz, R. P., & Agran, M. (1982). Validating entry-level survival skills for service occupations: Implications for curriculum development. *Journal of The Association for the Severely Handicapped, 1,* 32–41.

Willems, E. P. (1977). Steps toward an ecobehavioral technology. In A. Rogers-Warren & S. F. Warren (Eds.), *Ecological perspectives in behavior analysis* (pp. 39– 61). Baltimore: University Park Press.

Chapter 18

Developing Support Networks for Individuals Who Fail to Achieve Competitive Employment

Orv C. Karan and Catherine Berger Knight

RESULTS OF THE employment models described in this text have demonstrated that persons with various handicaps are capable of becoming productive members of the national work force (Schutz & Rusch, 1982). In spite of the noteworthy strides made in this respect to date, a large number of individuals continue to be unsuccessful in nonsheltered employment. This chapter focuses on persons who are unable to retain nonsheltered, competitive employment as well as those who fail initially to be considered for such placement (Shiraga, 1983; Wehman et al., 1982).

Table 1 lists many of the factors that have been identified as contributing to failure in competitive employment. A full discussion of each of these is beyond the scope of this chapter, but the interested reader is referred to Kochany and Keller (1981) and Bernstein and Karan (1979) for more detail.

Considerable evidence suggests that the major reason why people with mental retardation fail vocationally relates to social-interpersonal difficulties (Crawford, Aiello, & Thompson, 1979; Edgerton & Bercovici, 1976; Foss & Bostwick, 1981; Foss & Peterson, 1981; Greenspan & Shoultz, 1981; Niziol & DeBlassie, 1972; Richardson, 1978; Rosen,

Clark, & Kivitz, 1977; Rusch, 1979, 1983; Sowers, Thompson, & Connis, 1979; Wehman, 1981). As White and Rusch (1983) noted, one's impressions of another's vocational skills are related to impressions of their social skills.

As a result, program developers typically include social skills training as a regular part of overall employment preparation (Rusch, Schutz, & Agran, 1982; Schutz & Rusch, 1982; Stanford & Wehman, 1982). Although important, such training usually addresses only part of the identified need since social-interpersonal competency is not unidimensional; rather, it involves complex interactions with others. In recognition of the complexity of the issues, attempts have been made to incorporate significant others in the immediate environment as change agents (Rogers-Warren & Warren, 1977; Rusch & Schutz, 1981; Rusch, Schutz, & Heal, 1983; Schoggen, 1978). However, even these efforts have tended to place the emphasis for change on the individual rather than on ways to increase successful interactions (Bottorf & De Pape, 1982). The broader viewpoint needed in addressing those who are failing vocationally constitutes the focus of this chapter.

This work was supported, in part, by Grant 008300148 to the Research and Training Center in Community Integration of the Mentally Retarded, University of Wisconsin-Madison, from the National Institute of Handicapped Research, Department of Education. The authors thank Donna Pauls for her unselfish assistance in the preparation of this manuscript.

241

Table 1. Factors associated with failure in competitive employment

Behavior	Reference
Maladaptive behavior(s) including noncompliance, off-task, bizarre and/or aggressive, stereotypic, self-destructive, etc.	Clarke, Greenwood, Abramowitz, and Bellamy, 1980 Foss and Peterson, 1981 Kochany and Keller, 1981
Extreme dependence on direct supervision	Foss and Peterson, 1981 Schalock and Harper, 1981 Wehman, 1981
Inappropriate interactions with supervisor(s) and/or co-worker(s)	Foss and Peterson, 1981 Wehman, 1981
Excessive tardiness	Brickey and Campbell, 1981 Kochany and Keller, 1981
Inadequate attendance	Kochany and Keller, 1981
Insufficient speed and/or accuracy	Brickey and Campbell, 1981 Kochany and Keller, 1981 Schalock and Harper, 1978 Sowers, Thompson, and Connis, 1979
Failure to notify employer when unable to report to work	Wehman, 1981
Unacceptable personal appearance	Foss and Peterson, 1981
Transportation difficulties	Bernstein and Karan, 1979 Brickey and Campbell, 1981 Wehman, 1981
Opposing pressure from family and significant others	Kochany and Keller, 1981 Karan and Schalock, 1983b
Lack of interagency support and/or cooperation	Karan and Schalock, 1983b Kochany and Keller, 1981
Supervisory vacillation	Kochany and Keller, 1981 Sowers, Thompson, and Connis, 1979
Medical problems	Clarke, Greenwood, Abramowitz, Bellamy, 1980
Lack of strength or stamina	Wehman, 1981
Negative side effects of medication	Karan, Bernstein, Harvey, Bates, Renzaglia, and Rosenthal, 1979
Financial difficulties of the company	Wehman, 1981

From Karan, O. C. & Schalock, R. L. (1983a). An ecological approach to assessing vocational and community living skills. In O. C. Karan & W. I. Gardner (Eds.), *Habilitation practices with the developmentally disabled who present behavioral and emotional disorders* (pp. 121–173). Madison, WI: Rehabilitation Research and Training Center in Mental Retardation.

Our major premise is that in employment settings where retention has occurred, reasonable to good matches exist between people and their environments. Furthermore, the environments have provided sufficient support to help the individual meet the demands placed on him or her. Where failure or lack of growth exists, however, available resources have not been sufficient to help the individual meet job demands (French, 1968). While several conceptual streams of thought will be combined as this premise is developed, the ecological or "person-environment" perspective (Karan & Schalock, 1983a) provides the unifying theme.

As soon as one adopts an ecological perspective with its comprehensive concern for interactions between people and their environment (Jeger & Slotnick, 1982), the inherent limitations of focusing behavior change efforts on only one of the participants of the interactional process become evident. Interactions are multidimensional, multichanneled phenomena in which the interactants' behaviors are coordinated across many temporal dimensions (Higginbotham & Yoder, 1982).

Within an ecological perspective, the unique qualities of a person and his or her environment are matched to promote a person-environment congruence that optimizes functional levels (Chadsey-Rusch, 1985; Richardson, 1981; Rusch & Mithaug, 1985; Stucky & Newbrough, 1981; Sutton, Michael, & Wanner, 1981). This approach recognizes the importance of the individual's characteristics, the characteristics of the environment, and their interactions. Each of these components is explored in the sections that follow.

First, we address the personal characteristics of persons with mental retardation who are susceptible to social-interpersonal problems, and thus at "high risk" for failure in employment settings. Second, we discuss environmental characteristics with an emphasis on those aspects that make them socially accessible. This discussion includes a review of relevant social support literature. Third, we incorporate into the usual conceptualization of social-interpersonal problems the consideration that one's behavior is not always under the influence of temporally proximate factors. A phenomenon remains inexplicable as long as the range of observation is too narrow to include the context in which the phenomenon occurs. Thus, temporally distant factors may play considerably more influential roles than the vocational literature has yet to fully recognize. Finally, we reconceptualize social-interpersonal problems by considering them communication problems because of people's reciprocal influences on each other.

After combining these streams of thought, we describe a model for improving communication in relationships. "When one person is aware of the other's presence, it is impossible for communication not to occur" (Bassett & Smythe, 1979, p. 5). Yet, if one attributes false meaning to another's behavior or interprets another's actions to mean something other than what the person intended, the chances for miscommunication are high. *We believe that improving the communicative interactions of high-risk persons and significant others within their ecological systems is the key to their successful nonsheltered employment, because communication is the essence of relationships (Rubin, 1983) and relationships are the primary ingredients of supportive environments.*

The Awareness Model (Miller, Nunnally, & Wackman, 1975) presented in the last section of this chapter can help improve communication by forcing us to reconsider our interpretations of the behavior(s) of others.

PERSONAL CHARACTERISTICS OF PERSONS WITH MENTAL RETARDATION SUSCEPTIBLE TO SOCIAL-INTERPERSONAL PROBLEMS

Certain psychological characteristics of some persons with mental retardation render them "at risk" for displaying various social-interpersonal difficulties (Gardner & Cole, 1983). Such individuals are often excessively influenced by external stimulation and tend to view others as being in charge while they have little responsibility for themselves or their own behavior. According to Gardner and Cole (1983), such individuals are also more likely to have poorly developed and predominantly negative self-concept attributes.

These personal features create difficulty as they serve as the impetus for avoiding or withdrawing from various interpersonal-social situations that potentially could contribute to the development of more positive features (Peters, Pumphrey, & Flax, 1974). Additionally, individuals evidencing these characteristics have often shown poorly differentiated social roles; that is, they do not demonstrate an awareness of what is expected in various situations (Martin, Flexer, & Newberry, 1979).

Among persons with mental retardation who are likely to have the greatest difficulty in sustaining and maintaining nonsheltered employment, emotional expression presents a particular problem (Gardner & Cole, 1983). These individuals often show little emotional differentiation and their predominant emotional tone is negative. They may strike out in a random and disorganized fashion, verbally or physically attacking whomever or whatever happens to be present. Also, relatively minor sources of irritation or frustration may produce unusually strong emotional reactions. Few events, situations, or activities in the person's environment produce positive emotional reactions, and even events that result in positive or neutral emotional reactions in most persons may instead stimulate negative emotional reactions.

Finally, a general class of difficulties relates to motivation. Thus, the range and type of events that serve as effective incentives are usually limited (Karan & Gardner, 1973). Furthermore, the value of incentives may vary considerably from time to time, and only minimal delay of gratification and postponement of satisfaction may be tolerable.

Although we firmly believe in positive interventions that actively teach alternative behaviors and skills that one can use to adapt to the expectations, stresses, or demands of one's social and physical environments, we also believe that high-risk individuals need continuing support, guidance, promoting, and redirection to avoid falling into one of the many emotional and behavioral traps that are so deeply entrenched in their behavioral repertoires. Such a supportive attitude is not easy to adopt, however. It is very difficult, for example, to act kindly toward someone who only days, hours, or even minutes ago physically or verbally aggressed against you or someone you cared about (Karan, 1983). We all have biases and value systems that will affect our interactions with others, particularly when the other person's behavior is an affront to our own interpretations of "normal" behavior.

CHARACTERISTICS OF ENVIRONMENT: IMPORTANCE OF SOCIAL SUPPORT SYSTEMS

Our assertion that high-risk individuals need continuing support from significant others relates to the broader concept of social supportiveness that has been receiving increased attention (O'Connor, 1983). Within an ecological framework, the importance of such supportiveness is noted in the assessment of environmental characteristics including staff attitudes, family/benefactor involvement, and peer support (Karan & Schalock, 1983a).

Social support has been cited in numerous studies as a major factor in the successful community adjustment of persons with mental

retardation (O'Connor, 1983). Its importance is no less critical for employment. In reviewing the literature on the social adaptation of persons who are mentally retarded, Romer and Heller (1983) concluded that: "We should consider the possibility that the social milieu is as powerful a determinant of social adjustment as individual social skills are" (p. 311).

Although social support was first described in the literature some time ago (Axelrod, 1956), it has not yet been precisely defined (O'Connor, 1983). The various definitions that have been proposed emphasize, to varying degrees, the importance of: 1) linkages to key people or groups, 2) interpersonal transactions, 3) informational feedback that increases an individual's capacity to satisfy basic psychological and social needs, and 4) reciprocity of need satisfaction (Barrera & Ainlay, 1983; Caplan, 1974, 1976; Cassel, 1974; Cobb, 1976; Heller, 1979; House, 1981; Kaplan, Cassel, & Gore, 1977; Leavy, 1983). In an attempt to consolidate the numerous definitions, O'Connor (1983) identified social support as being "made up of the emotional, informational, and material support provided by friends, relatives, neighbors, service providers, and others with whom one has an ongoing relationship, and to whom one can turn in times of need or crisis" (p. 187).

The general concept of social support is distinguished from social networks by specific sets of interpersonal linkages that are used to interpret social behavior (Mitchell, 1969; Mitchell & Trickett, 1980; Moos & Mitchell, 1982; Mueller, 1980). Research employing social network analyses has provided most of the tools and methods for identifying, albeit imprecisely, the most salient characteristics of social support (Barrera, 1981; Bott, 1971; Heller, 1979; Mitchell, 1969; Moos & Mitchell, 1982; Mueller, 1980).

Much of the research on social support involves naturalistic studies that claim that social support protects or "buffers" an individual against the adverse effects of stress. Other studies have addressed the consequences of loss of support among individuals who were previously supported (Heller, 1979). According to O'Connor's (1983) summarization, social support contributes to: 1) reduced stress; 2) better outcomes of physical health problems, and 3) enhanced mental well-being.

Among the numerous studies that have found relationships between aspects of personal social networks and psychological disorders (Leavy, 1983; Mitchell & Trickett, 1980; Mueller, 1980), perhaps the most consistent finding is that the absence of social supports is associated with increased psychological distress (Mueller, 1980). In spite of methodological problems within many of these studies, results indicate that social support plays an important role in the healthy adjustment of both clinical and nonclinical populations.

Social support has also received attention in the literature on work stress and health. Recent studies indicate that certain kinds of social support from certain kinds of people can reduce certain kinds of occupational stress, improve certain health indicators, and buffer certain relationships between stress and health (House, 1981). Although not large, this body of data is remarkably consistent (House, 1981).

The beneficial effects of social support have, thus, been noted in an abundance of naturalistic and correlational research. Individuals with social ties have been found to show less vulnerability to stress and to be more socially adjusted; that is, social support appears to be a vital ingredient for positive mental and physical health (Heller, 1979; Mitchell, Billings, & Moos, 1981).

A successful social life and interactions with others are vital parts of everyone's lives— including persons who are mentally retarded (Baker, Seltzer, & Seltzer, 1977; Bercovici, 1981; Bjaannes & Butler, 1974; Butler & Bjaanes, 1977; Edgerton, 1967; Edgerton & Bercovici, 1976; Heal, Sigelman, & Switzky, 1978; Heller, Berkson, & Romer, 1981; Weiss, 1974). Noting that peer relationships play a critical role in the successful adjustment of adults with mental retardation in community settings, Romer and Heller (1983) cited evidence that individuals with higher degrees of peer contact are more likely to: 1) remain in the community (Gollay, Freedman, Wyngaarden, & Kurtz, 1978), 2) transfer to less restrictive settings, 3) demonstrate independence in self-care skills (Heller & Berkson, 1982), 4) earn more money, and 5) transfer out of vocational workshops for positive reasons (Melstrom, 1982).

The literature also indicates that, regardless of their level of intelligence, individuals are likely to belong to a peer network (Landesman-Dwyer, Berkson, & Romer, 1979; Landesman-Dwyer, Stein, & Sackett, 1978; MacAndrew & Edgerton, 1966; Romer & Berkson, 1980, 1981). Furthermore, an individual's tendency to develop peer relationships has been found to depend in part on the sociability of the person's milieu (Romer & Heller, 1983). With the exception of Wehman's (1981) finding that nonhandicapped co-workers were generally indifferent toward the placement of workers with mental retardation in their settings, the role of the larger community of nonhandicapped adults in promoting the adjustment of adults with mental retardation has not been fully examined (Romer & Heller, 1983).

In addition to emphasizing the importance of social relationships and networks for the successful adjustment of persons with mental retardation, the findings of the social support research also have direct implications for high-risk individuals who are failing to enter or retain nonsheltered employment. In recognition of the importance of the social milieu for human functioning, it seems clear that, for high-risk individuals in particular, efforts must be directed toward building more social supports *into* and *around* their work environment.

TRANSACTIONS ACROSS TIME AND SETTINGS

Each of us is "enmeshed in a complex social system, as both a giver and receiver (an exciter and responder) in social transactions with other . . . [individuals] in a variety of roles and settings" (Kauffman, 1981, p. 27). Failure to realize the intricacies of these relationships often leads us to attribute certain properties to an individual that he or she may not possess. For example, a person may demonstrate good task orientation, high productivity, positive mood, and appropriate social behavior for days, weeks, or even months at a time. Then, for no apparent reason, he or she may start displaying erratic production, negative mood, and explosive social behaviors. Aggressive behavior towards co-workers may occur only once every 6 months, but only one or two occurrences may be enough for the person to lose his or her job.

Such complex behavior patterns are often of low frequency but high intensity. Because these behaviors often do not occur with any apparent functional regularity, attempts to develop appropriate behavior-change programs have proven difficult if not impossible, partly because of the limitations of the current technology related to such problems. If, however, the limits of an inquiry are extended to include the effects of one's behavior on others, their reactions to it, and the context in which this takes place, the focus shifts to the relationship between the parts of a wider system (Watzlawick, Beavin, & Jackson, 1967).

In an assessment of an individual's (John) verbal aggression on the job, Gardner, Karan, and Cole (1984) extended the field of their inquiry to include a range of events outside the immediate job environment. The need to do so became apparent when the authors found that even under closely monitored conditions in which they recorded events that coincided in time with John's verbal aggression, they were still unable to predict with greater-than-chance accuracy if his next verbal aggression would occur coterminously with any of these identified events. However, upon broadening the scope of inquiry to include person-environment interchanges occurring at earlier times outside the employment setting, certain temporally distant setting events were found to influence the effects more than immediate setting events. The authors found, for example, that when John either spent the weekend with his family while his brother was also visiting, or when he had difficulty getting up in the morning, or when a particular male staff member was on

duty in his group home, and/or when negative interactions with peers took place on the bus prior to arriving at the job, the probability was much greater that he would display verbal aggression coinciding with the occurrence of any of the temporally proximate setting events at his job that on most other days would not affect him.

Once temporally distant events become more identifiable, service delivery must focus on direct intervention within the wider ecological systems level, if possible, while simultaneously attempting to minimize the stress at the employment setting on those occasions when the probability of problems is high. In John's situation, for example, the male staff member at the group home could be trained to relate differently to John. And, upon arrival at the vocational setting on those occasions when John was likely to be particularly vulnerable, opportunities could be created to shift his mood from negative to positive by allowing him to discuss his views and feelings with a support person over a cup of coffee before the work day began.

Figure 1 represents the wider system we have conceptualized as interacting with, affecting, and being affected by a high-risk individual's behaviors. We have purposefully balanced the individual's social-interpersonal behaviors on a rather precarious base to convey how fragile such behaviors sometimes are and how easily they can be shifted as a function of changing ecological conditions.

Each of the revolving components of an individual's ecological system may take on significant functional roles, which at any point could shift the balance. Thus, with transportation, for example, if one had difficulty getting to and from work, one's job could be in jeopardy. This problem could simultaneously jeopardize an individual's residential placement since in many cases the individual must be employed or participating in daily vocational services as a condition for living there.

As further indicated in Figure 1, we have conceptualized employment, residence, and family, friends, and support persons as the primary influences within a given individual's

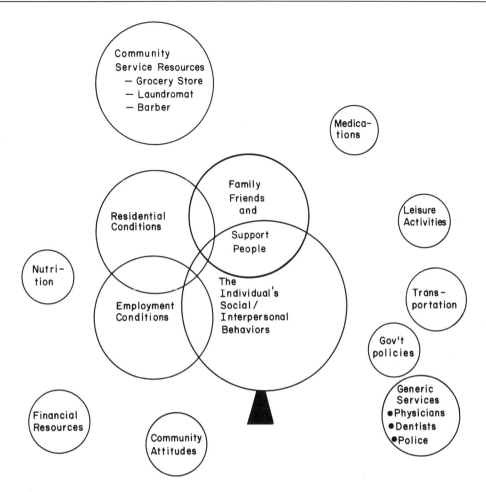

Figure 1.   An individual's ecological system.

ecological system. Each of these influences includes its own unique set of ecological variables. Figure 2, for example, depicts a community residence (a group home) as both a work place for the staff and as a home for its residents. Among other things, staff are responsible for contributing to a healthy psychosocial environment for the residents (i.e., by providing support, training, security, comfort, etc.). Yet, staff simultaneously have their own employment needs, which relate to satisfaction or dissatisfaction with their jobs due to salary, growth opportunities, working conditions, supervisory support, etc. As conceptualized in Figure 2, the greater the overlap between the two circles, the greater the degree of compatibility between staff and resident needs.

Within our proposed framework, every part of the system (see Figures 1 and 2) is related to its fellow parts, and changes in one part may cause a change in other parts, which, in turn, could affect the total system (Jeger & Slotnick, 1982). It is our contention that the social-interpersonal problems of high-risk individuals are often an indication of broader systems problems. Yet, standard practice has usually focused remediation attempts on the individual rather than on the broader system of persons, places, and things that may be directly (and indirectly) contributing to the presenting difficulties.

Attempting to create change in a person's behavior without simultaneously recognizing, respecting, and, at times, modifying the balance between the person's behavior and the persons, places, and things that interact with him or her has been a serious limitation of work conducted to date with high-risk individuals (Karan & Schalock, 1983b). A logical starting point, therefore, is to attempt to increase one's successful interactions with others and vice versa—an issue that is discussed in the following two sections.

INTERACTION WITH ENVIRONMENT: INTERPERSONAL BEHAVIOR AS COMMUNICATION

People influence each other in complex and subtle ways, as illustrated in the following case example:

> Sam is helping Joe learn a new job and has just explained how two different pieces fit together. Joe indicates that he does not understand. Sam grits his teeth, shakes his head, and brusquely explains the procedures again. Joe begins to pout. Sam demands to know why Joe is pouting. "Because you are mad," Joe cries out. "I am not mad at you," Sam explains. Joe continues to look sad and yells at another worker to stop staring at him. Sam takes away Joe's parts and tells him that he will not be able to work on any new jobs until he starts acting like an adult.

Sam and Joe are obviously influencing each other. Their interactions are not atypical—we have all experienced similarly difficult encounters. Unfortunately, interactional difficulties such as these have not received much

attention in the contemporary employment literature. This reciprocity of influence has led us to reconceptualize social-interpersonal problems as communication problems. An elaboration of our viewpoint follows.

In the special education and vocational habilitation fields, communication has traditionally been relegated to the status of monophonic messages. From the broader perspective advocated here, however, communication occurs whenever people assign meaning to each other's behavior. Thus, as soon as one person is aware of another's presence, communication occurs, and regardless of one's intention it is impossible to keep people from attributing meaning in behavior. When two people interact, both are simultaneously behaving and attributing meaning to the behavior of the other. One cannot *not* communicate; indeed, all behavior is communication (Watzlawick et al., 1967). No matter what an individual is doing, he or she is behaving, and one cannot be aware of this behavior without interpreting it (Basset & Smythe, 1979).

Thus, communication is a dynamic and multifaceted compound of many behavioral modes—verbal, tonal, postural, contextual— all of which qualify or confuse the meaning of all the others. For example, what we say can be incompatible with what we mean, which, in turn, can be incompatible with how we act.

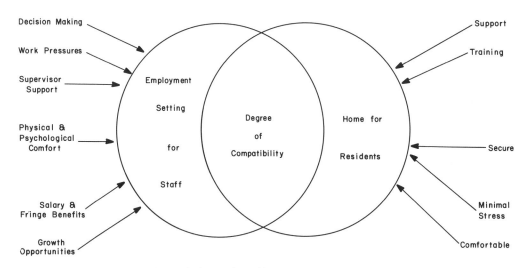

Figure 2.   The group home as both a work place and a residence.

Considering that an estimated 65% of all communication is based on nonverbal behavior (Birdwhistell, 1970), the way we act can significantly influence how others perceive us. Indeed, people often assign greater weight to the perceived feelings communicated nonverbally than to the feelings expressed verbally (Mehrabian, 1972).

For reasons that are only vaguely understood, most people possess an immense amount of knowledge about the rules and calibration of customary or acceptable behavior, e.g., society's laws (Mehrabian, 1972). Most of us use this knowledge to evaluate, influence, and predict behavior, and we are particularly sensitive to inconsistencies. Thus, if another's behavior is out of context or shows a certain kind of randomness or lack of constraint, it immediately strikes us as inappropriate. The difference between a person's behavioral patterns and those of the social norm may significantly affect his or her ability to develop relationships (Higginbotham & Yoder, 1982; Tjosvold & Tjosvold, 1983; Wills, 1973).

Higginbotham and Yoder (1982) suggested that communication competency entails: 1) the ability to produce socially acceptable and interpretable behavior through coordinating and regulating one's own behaviors, 2) the ability to employ behaviors to influence other persons in a socially acceptable manner, and 3) the ability to successfully interpret others' behavior.

Many persons with mental retardation, and in particular those who have spent years in institutions, have deficiencies in one or all of these areas. Problems of this type are particularly acute among those who are the least likely to obtain or retain nonsheltered, competitive employment. As discussed in a preceding section, such individuals may have difficulty reading cues and using feedback to organize their behavior in addition to displaying verbal and nonverbal communication that generates incongruent information (Birenbaum & Seiffer, 1976; Stucky & Newbrough, 1981).

The complexity of such individuals' interaction patterns requires solutions that are equally complex and capable of shifting, depending on the moods and conditions represented by the participant and the settings (Karan, 1982). Thus, in establishing intervention programs it is necessary to be concerned not only with the effects an individual's behavior has on somebody else's behavior, but also with *what effects the other person's reaction has*. Miscommunication cycles may result in totally deteriorated relationships.

In the next section we describe a model for improving communication in relationships. The model, referred to as "The Awareness Wheel" (see Figure 3) (Miller et al., 1975), has been found very useful in helping us to identify and clarify our own communication patterns and, as importantly, helping us to become more aware of the patterns of others.

AWARENESS MODEL FOR IMPROVING COMMUNICATION

As noted earlier, whenever people interact they are simultaneously behaving and attributing meaning to the behavior of others. "When one person is aware of the other's presence it is impossible for communication not to occur" (Bassett & Smythe, 1979, p. 5). Our value systems, developed through social-cultural learning experiences, influence how we interpret and react to another's behavior, particularly if the other person is behaving in ways we think we understand. For example, at one time or another we have probably all said something like, "he knows damn well what he is doing" or "she is doing that just to spite me," when describing another's repetitive and irritating (to us) behavior patterns. Such expressions convey intentions on the part of the other individual that may or may not exist. Yet, if we believe the intent is present, our reaction to it and/or programs for it will incorporate such a perspective. If, however, the individual's behavior is not a function of the alleged intention, our misguided reactions or programs may only intensify the person's problematic behavior, put us into no-win power struggles with him or her, and for some, even result in exclusion from the setting (i.e., loss of job). The Awareness Model (see Figure 3) is intended to raise our consciousness so that we are not so blinded

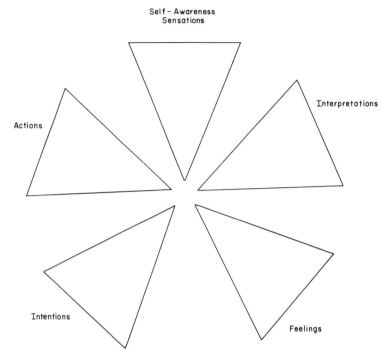

Figure 3.   A model of self-awareness.

by our own biases that we react emotionally, rather than therapeutically, when interacting with high-risk persons (Karan, 1983). The components of the model are described below.

Interpretations

Interpretations refer to all of the different kinds of meanings we attribute to things to help us understand ourselves, other people, and situations. They are constructed out of our past, present, and anticipated experiences. Our interpretations depend upon what our senses take in, how we are feeling, and what we desire. Furthermore, interpretations are influenced by past interpretations, especially our beliefs and assumptions. They are not simply based on the way things are—on some "reality out there"— but on reality as we make it (Watzlawick et al., 1967).

Sensations

It has been estimated that a person receives 10,000 sensory impressions (exteroceptive and proprioceptive) per second (Watzlawick et al., 1967). Decisions about what is essential and

what is irrelevant vary from individual to individual, and much is clearly missed. Basically, senses report raw data and act as the funnel through which information comes in. It is important to separate sense data from interpretations because of the subjectivity inherent in the latter. If, however, we remember that our interpretations are different from our observations, we are less likely to conclude that what we think is correct. Our awareness can be increased by reconsidering sensory data to see how we arrived at a particular interpretation.

Feelings

Our feelings represent our spontaneous responses to our interpretations and expectations. Feelings are the emotional reactions conditioned by our life experiences. They serve two important functions. First, they can act as a barometer and help alert us to what is going on and help us to better understand our reactions to situations. In programming, therefore, we should try to tune into our feelings and realize that just because a particular course of action feels right, it does not mean that it is (Karan,

1983). Often, appropriate treatment programs have just the opposite impact, namely, they may be effective but do not feel right to those designing or implementing them (Karan, 1983).

Second, feelings can help us clarify expectations because some feelings occur due to a difference between what is expected and what is actually experienced. Such discrepancies result in either positive or negative feelings. Although feelings cannot be controlled by simply ignoring or denying them, they can change subject to our reassessment of sense data and interpretations. Reconstructing expectations and interpretations can give rise to new and different feelings.

Intentions

Intention has a broad meaning; in this model, however, it is usually taken to mean a general attitude of moving toward or away from something. It can be used to signify anything from an immediate desire to some long-range goal. Intentions are difficult to identify because they can be mixed up with what we would like others to do. They are powerful because they can have a great impact on our actions. When something important is happening between people or when one person feels satisfied or dissatisfied, identifying our intentions can be helpful for clarifying what is happening.

Actions

Most people make the false assumption of thinking that they are aware of what they are doing. Yet, frequently some of our actions are not part of our awareness. Thus, we are often unaware of a number of important behaviors that others observe. In normal conversation, for example, we are probably unaware of many of our actions that may affect others in a variety of ways such as our vocal pitch, range, and height; articulation control; rhythm control; resonance; tempo; laughs; cries; yawns; sneezes; coughs; vocal clicks; intensity; pauses; head shakes; gestures; body movements; eye contact; distance between ourselves and the person with whom we communicate, etc. Obviously, it is difficult to be aware of all our

actions because so much happens at one time, *but our actions are sense data from which others make interpretations!*

Limited Self-Awareness

Limited self-awareness exists when one or more dimensions of the Awareness Wheel are not present. At such times we experience incomplete self-awareness, that is, the messages we send to others are probably misleading and the risk of getting into miscommunication cycles with others is high.

Awareness of Others

Using this same model, awareness of others means tuning into their Awareness Wheel. Just as it is not easy to become completely aware of ourselves, it is even more difficult to be completely aware of another person. Complete awareness may be impossible, *but we can become more aware.*

Increased awareness of others can be achieved in several ways, for example, by paying close attention to the sense data we receive from others and the interpretations we make from these data. The Awareness Wheel provides a helpful guide in this respect. Before acting, ask yourself such questions as: What do I think the other person is sensing? What do I think the other is thinking (i.e., what interpretations is he or she drawing from his or her sensations)? What do I think he or she is feeling? What do I think his or her intentions are? What does he or she want to happen? What do I think his or her actions mean? What do I think he or she is doing?

Any time we try to conclude what others are thinking or feeling we are making guesses. In our everyday dealings we are doing this all the time. For high-risk persons whose self-control is relatively fragile, the cost for communication errors may be life experiences within environments that are more restricted than necessary.

The value of presenting this model is that it may raise the consciousness of those who interact with high-risk persons, and hence help break through some of the miscommunication cycles that may be contributing to their failure in nonsheltered employment.

SUMMARY

Although many of the points expressed in this chapter have general applicability, we have focused on a select group of persons with mental retardation whose social-interpersonal behaviors have contributed to their failure to secure or retain competitive employment. For these individuals, our conventional behavior-change approaches have been too narrow and must be supplemented so as to incorporate the influences of their daily transactions across time and settings. Consequently, we advocate extending current conceptions to include greater consideration for the interdependency among the elements within one's ecological system and for the reciprocal influences people have on each other. Recognizing the theoretical nature of the concepts addressed in this chapter, we offer the following specific suggestions as preventive steps toward reducing the likelihood that a given high-risk individual will be removed from his or her job.

1. *Identify key individuals to function as support people.* To accomplish this, consider some of these questions: What are the attitudes of co-workers toward this person? What is the nature of the relationships between this person and his or her supervisor and co-workers? How does this person perceive these relationships? Are support networks already in existence in the work setting that could easily incorporate this individual? To what extent does the individual have the opportunity to participate in social situations (coffee and lunch breaks) on the job? To what extent is this person included in parties or social gatherings beyond the immediate environment of the work setting? Who are the most significant persons in the individual's immediate support network (family, friends, residential staff, "benefactor" [Edgerton, 1967])?

2. *Assist in improving successful interactions within the work environment between the high-risk individual and his or her supervisor and co-workers.* Try to acquire information on existing attitudes, behavioral styles, and potential sources of miscommunication.

3. *Observe the high-risk individual across settings and time to identify both temporally proximate and distant events that may be influencing the individual's inability to function effectively on the job.*

4. *If behavior-change programs seem to be required, attempt to ensure that the responsibility for change is shared by the individual and significant others.* Thus, when designing behavioral interventions consider such issues as: Is the behavior-change program designed for the individual's well-being or for the convenience of others? Will the program lead to successful interactions or is it only designed to change the behavior of the person with mental retardation? Beyond making specific behavioral recommendations, assist significant others who deal with the high-risk individual in identifying their sources of miscommunication and teach them how to become more sensitive to the reciprocal influences they share. This may be the most difficult task since those who interact daily with the individual may believe they understand him or her. Consequently, they may be resistant to any suggestions, either implied or direct, that they may have to change.

5. *Ensure that those providing support to the high-risk person have their own sources of support.* In relationships with high-risk individuals there may be an uneven balance between meeting one's own needs as well as the needs of the person with mental retardation. For this reason, additional support relationships for these important significant others will help ensure that needs that are not being met by the high-risk person are being met by others.

REFERENCES

Axelrod, M. (1956). Urban structure and social participation. *American Sociological Review, 21*, 14–18.

Baker, B. L., Seltzer, G. B., & Seltzer, M. M. (1977). *As close as possible: Community residences for retarded adults.* Boston, MA: Little, Brown.

Barrera, M., Jr. (1981). Social support in the adjustment of pregnant adolescents: Assessment issues. In B. H. Gottlieb (Ed.), *Social networks and social support* (pp. 69–96). Beverly Hill, CA: Sage.

Barrera, M., Jr., & Ainlay, S. L. (1983). The structure of

social support: A conceptual and empirical analysis. *Journal of Community Psychology, 11*, 133–143.

Bassett, R. W., & Smythe, M. J. (1979). *Communication and instruction.* New York: Harper & Row.

Bercovici, S. M. (1981). Qualitative methods in cultural perspectives in the study of deinstitutionalization. In R. H. Bruininks, C. E. Meyer, B. B. Sigford, & K. C. Lakin (Eds.), *Deinstitutionalization and community adjustment of mentally retarded people* (Monograph No. 4, pp. 133–144). Washington, DC: American Association on Mental Deficiency.

Bernstein, G. S., & Karan, O. C. (1979). Obstacles to vocational normalization for the developmentally disabled. *Rehabilitation Literature, 40*(3), 66–71.

Birdwhistell, R. L. (1970). *Kinesics and context.* Philadelphia, PA: University of Pennsylvania Press.

Birenbaum, A., & Seiffer, S. (1976). *Resettling retarded adults in a managed community.* New York: Praeger.

Bjaannes, A. T., & Butler, E. W. (1974). Environmental variation in community care facilities for mentally retarded persons. *American Journal of Mental Deficiency, 78*, 429–439.

Bott, E. (1971). *Family and social networks* (2nd ed.). New York: Free Press.

Bottorf, L., & De Pape, D. (1982). Initiating communication systems for severely speech-impaired persons. *Topics in Language Disorders, 2*, 55–72.

Brickey, M., & Campbell, K. (1981). Fast food employment for moderately and mildly retarded adults: The McDonald's project. *Mental Retardation, 19*, 113–116.

Butler, E. W., & Bjaannes, A. T. (1977). A typology of community care facilities and differential normalization. In P. Mittler (Ed.), *Research to practice in mental retardation: Vol. 1. Care and intervention* (pp. 337–347). Baltimore: University Park Press.

Caplan, G. (1974). Support systems. In G. Caplan (Ed.), *Support systems and community mental health* (pp. 1–40). New York: Behavioral Publications.

Caplan, G. (1976). The family as a support system. In G. Caplan & M. Killilea (Eds.), *Support systems and mutual help: Multidisciplinary explorations* (pp. 19–36). New York: Grune & Stratton.

Cassel, J. (1974). Psychosocial processes and "stress": Theoretical formulations. *International Journal of Health Services, 4*, 471–482.

Chadsey-Rusch, J. (1985). Community integration and mental retardation: An ecobehavioral approach to service provision and assessment. In R. H. Bruininks and K. C. Lakin (Eds.) *Living and learning in the least restrictive environment*, (pp. 245–260). Baltimore: Paul H. Brookes.

Clarke, J. Y., Greenwood, L. M., Abramowitz, D. B., & Bellamy, G. T. (1980). Summer jobs for vocational preparation of moderately and severely retarded adolescents. *Journal of The Association for the Severely Handicapped, 5*, 24–37.

Cobb, S. (1976). Social support as moderator of life stress. *Psychosomatic Medicine, 38*, 300–314.

Crawford, J. L., Aiello, J. R., & Thompson, D. (1979). Deinstitutionalization and community placement: Clinical and environmental factors. *Mental Retardation, 17*, 59–63.

Edgerton, R. B. (1967). *The cloak of competence: Stigmas in the lives of mentally retarded.* Berkeley, CA: University of California Press.

Edgerton, R. B., & Bercovici, S. M. (1976). The cloak of competence: Years later. *American Journal of Mental Deficiency, 80*, 485–497.

Foss, G., & Bostwick, F. (1981, December). Problems of mentally retarded adults: A study of rehabilitation service consumers and providers. *Rehabilitation Council Bulletin.*

Foss, G., & Peterson, S. L. (1981). Social-interpersonal skills relevant to job tenure for mentally retarded adults. *Mental Retardation, 19*, 108–106.

French, J. R. P., Jr. (1968). The conceptualization and measurement of mental health in terms of self-identity theory. In S. B. Sells (Ed.), *The definition and measurement of mental health* (pp. 135–159). Washington, DC: U.S. Government Printing Office.

Gardner, W. I., & Cole, C. L. (1983). A structured learning habilitation approach: Use with the mentally retarded presenting emotional and behavioral disorders. In O. C. Karan & W. I. Gardner (Eds.), *Habilitation practices with the developmentally disabled who present behavioral and emotional disorders* (pp. 39–60). Madison, WI: Rehabilitation Research and Training Center in Mental Retardation.

Gardner, W. I., Karan, O. C., & Cole, C. L. (1984). Assessment of setting events influencing the functional capacities of mentally retarded adults with behavior difficulties. In A. Halpern & M. Fuhrer (Eds.), *Functional assessment in rehabilitation* (pp. 171–186). Baltimore: Paul H. Brookes.

Gollay, E., Freedman, R., Wyngaarden, M., & Kurtz, N. R. (1978). *Coming back: The community experience of deinstitutionalized mentally retarded people.* Cambridge, MA: ABT Books.

Greenspan, S., & Shoultz, B. (1981). Why mentally retarded adults lose their jobs: Social competence as a factor in work adjustment. *Applied Research in Mental Retardation, 2*, 23–28.

Heal, L., Sigelman, C., & Switzky, H. (1978). Research on community residential alternatives for the mentally retarded. In N. Ellis (Ed.), *International review of research in mental retardation* (Vol. 9, pp. 209–249). New York: Academic Press.

Heller, K. (1979). The effects of social support: Prevention and treatment implications. In A. P. Goldstein & F. H. Kanfer (Eds.), *Maximizing treatment gains* (pp. 353–382). New York: Academic Press.

Heller, T., & Berkson, G. (1982, April). *Friendship and residential relocation.* Paper presented at the Gatlinburg Conference on Research in Mental Retardation, Gatlinburg.

Heller, T., Berkson, G., & Romer, D. (1981). Social ecology in supervisd communal facilities for mentally retarded adults: VI. Initial social adaptation. *American Journal of Mental Deficiency, 86*, 43–49.

Higginbotham, D. J., & Yoder, D. E. (1982). Communication within natural conversational interaction: Implications for severe communicatively impaired persons. *Topics in Language Disorders, 2*(2), 1–20.

House, J. S. (1981). *Work stress and social support.* Reading, MA: Addison-Wesley.

Jeger, A. M., & Slotnick, R. S. (1982). *Community mental health and behavioral-ecology.* New York: Plenum.

Kaplan, B. H., Cassel, J. C., & Gore, S. (1977). Social support and health. *Medical Care, 15*, 47.

Karan, O. C. (1982). From the classroom into the community. In K. P. Lynch, W. E. Kiernan, & J. A. Stark (Eds.), *Prevocational and vocational education for spe-*

cial needs youth: A blueprint for the 1980's (pp. 169–182). Baltimore: Paul H. Brookes.

Karan, O. C. (1983). Habilitation programming for behaviorally disordered mentally retarded adults: Just because it feels right does not mean it is. In O. C. Karan & W. I. Gardner (Eds.), Habilitation practices with the developmentally disabled who present behavioral and emotional disorders (pp. 29–38). Madison, WI: Rehabilitation Research and Training Center in Mental Retardation.

Karan, O. C., Bernstein, G. S., Harvey, J., Bates, P., Renzaglia, A., & Rosenthal, D. (1979). An extended evaluation model for severely handicapped persons. AAESPH Review, 4, 374–398.

Karan, O. C., & Gardner, W. I. (1973). Vocational rehabilitation practices: A behavioral approach. Rehabilitation Literature, 34, 290–298.

Karan, O. C., & Schalock, R. L. (1983a). An ecological approach to assessing vocational and community living skills. In O. C. Karan & W. I. Gardner (Eds.), Habilitation practices with the developmentally disabled who present behavioral and emotional disorders (pp. 121–173). Madison, WI: Rehabilitation Research and Training Center in Mental Retardation.

Karan, O. C., & Schalock, R. L. (1983b). Who has the problem? An ecological perspective on habilitation programming for behaviorally involved persons. In O. C. Karan & W. I. Gardner (Eds.), Habilitation practices with the developmentally disabled who present behavioral and emotional disorders (pp. 77–91). Madison, WI: Rehabilitation Research and Training Center in Mental Retardation.

Kauffman, J. M. (1981). Characteristics of children's behavior disorders (2nd ed.). Columbus, OH: Charles E. Merrill.

Kochany, L., & Keller, J. (1981). An analysis and evaluation of the failures of severely disabled individuals in competitive employment. In P. Wehman, Competitive employment: New horizons for severely disabled individuals (pp. 181–198). Baltimore: Paul H. Brookes Publishing Co.

Landesman-Dwyer, S., Berkson, G., & Romer, D. (1979). Affiliation and friendship of mentally retarded residents in group homes. American Journal of Mental Deficiency, 83, 571–580.

Landesman-Dwyer, S., Stein, J. G., & Sackett, G. P. (1978). A behavioral and ecological study of group homes. In G. P. Sackett (Ed.), Observing behavior: Vol. 1. Theory and applications in mental retardation (pp. 349–377). Baltimore: University Park Press.

Leavy, R. L. (1983). Social support and psychological disorder: A review. Journal of Community Psychology, 11, 3–21.

MacAndrew, C., & Edgerton, R. B. (1966). On the possibility of friendship. American Journal of Mental Deficiency, 70, 612–621.

Martin, A., Flexer, R., & Newberry, J. (1979). The development of a work ethic in the severely retarded. In T. Bellamy, G. O'Connor, & O. Karan (Eds.), Vocational rehabilitation of severely handicapped persons: Contemporary service strategies (pp. 136–159). Baltimore: University Park Press.

Mehrabian, A. (1972). Nonverbal communication. Chicago, IL: Aldine-Atherton.

Melstrom, M. A. (1982). Social ecology of supervised communal facilities for mentally disabled adults: VII.

Productivity and turnover rate in sheltered workshops. American Journal of Mental Deficiency, 87, 40–47.

Miller, S., Nunnally, E., & Wackman, D. B. (1975). Alive and aware: Improving communication in relationships. Minneapolis, MN: Interpersonal Communication Programs, Inc.

Mitchell, J. C. (Ed.). (1969). Social networks in urban situations. Manchester, England: University Press.

Mitchell, R. E., Billings, A. G., & Moos, R. H. (1982). Social support and well-being: Implications for prevention programs. Journal of Primary Prevention, 3, 77–98.

Mitchell, R. E., & Trickett, E. J. (1980). Task force report: Social networks as mediators of social support: An analysis of the effects and determinants of social networks. Community Mental Health Journal, 16, 27–44.

Moos, R. H., & Mitchell, R. E. (1982). Social network resources and adaptation: A conceptual framework. In T. A. Wills (Ed.). Basic processes in helping relationships (pp. 213–232). New York: Academic Press.

Mueller, D. P. (1980). Social networks: A promising direction for research on the relationship of the social environment to psychiatric disorder. Social Science and Medicine, 14A, 147–161.

Niziol, O. M., & DeBlassie, R. R. (1972). Work adjustment and the educable mentally retarded adolescent. Journal of Employment and Counseling, 9, 158–166.

O'Connor, G. (1983). Presidential address 1983: Social support of mentally retarded persons. Mental Retardation, 21, 1987–196.

Peters, E. N., Pumphrey, M. W., & Flax, B. (1974). Comparison of retarded and nonretarded children on the dimensions of behavior in recreation groups. American Journal of Mental Deficiency, 79, 87–94.

Richardson, S. A. (1978). Careers of mentally retarded young persons: Services, jobs, and interpersonal relations. American Journal of Mental Deficiency, 82, 349–358.

Richardson, S. A. (1981). Living environments: An ecological perspective. In H. C. Haywood & J. R. Newbrough (Eds.), Living environments for developmentally retarded persons (pp. 15–30). Baltimore: University Park Press.

Rogers-Warren, A., & Warren, S. F. (Eds.). (1977). Ecological perspectives in behavior analysis. Baltimore: University Park Press.

Romer, D., & Berkson, G. (1980). Social ecology of supervised communal facilities for mentally disabled adults: II. Predictors of affiliation. American Journal of Mental Deficiency, 85, 229–242.

Romer, D., & Berkson, G. (1981). Social ecology of supervised communal facilities for mentally disabled adults: IV. Characteristics of social behavior. American Journal of Mental Deficiency, 86, 228–238.

Romer, D., & Heller, T. (1983). Social adaptation of mentally retarded adults in community settings: A social-ecological approach. Applied Research in Mental Retardation, 4, 303–314.

Rosen, M., Clark, G. R., & Kivitz, M. S. (1977). Habilitation of the handicapped: New dimenesions in programs for the developmentally disabled. Baltimore: University Park Press.

Rubin, T. I. (1983). One to one understanding of personal relationships. New York: Viking Press.

Rusch, F. (1979). Toward the validation of social/

vocational survival skills. *Mental Retardation, 17,* 143–145.

Rusch, F. R. (1983). Competitive vocational training. In M. Snell (Ed.), *Systematic instruction for the moderately and severely handicapped* (pp. 503–523). Columbus, OH: Charles E. Merrill.

Rusch, F. R., & Mithaug, D. E. (1985). Competitive employment education: A systems-analytic approach to transitional programming for the student with severe handicaps. In K. C. Lakin & R. H. Bruininks (Eds.), *Strategies for achieving community integration of developmentally disabled citizens* (pp. 177–192). Baltimore: Paul H. Brookes.

Rusch, F. R., & Schutz, R. P. (1981). Vocational and social work behavior: An evaluative review. In J. L. Matson & J. R. McCartney (Eds.), *Handbook of behavior modification with the mentally retarded* (pp. 247–280). New York: Plenum.

Rusch, F. R., Schutz, R. P., & Agran, M. (1982). Validating entry-level survival skills for service occupations: Implications for curriculum development. *Journal of the Association for the Severely Handicapped, 7*(3), 32–41.

Rusch, F. R., Schutz, R. P., & Heal, L. W. (1983). The validity of sheltered and nonsheltered work behavior research: A review and discussion. In J. L. Matson & J. A. Mulick (Eds.), *Comprehensive handbook on mental retardation* (pp. 455–466). New York: Pergamon Press.

Schalock, R. L., & Harper, R. S. (1978). Placement from community-based mental retardation programs: How well do clients do? *American Journal of Mental Deficiency, 83,* 240–247.

Schalock, R. L., & Harper, R. S. (1981). A systems approach to community living skills training. In R. H. Bruininks, C. W. Meyers, B. B. Sigford, & K. C. Lakin (Eds.), *Deinstitutionalization and community adjustment of mentally retarded people* (Monograph No. 4, pp. 316–336). Washington, DC: American Association on Mental Deficiency.

Schoggen, P. (1978). Ecological psychology and mental retardation. In G. P. Sackett (Ed.), *Observing behavior: Vol. 1. Theory and applications in mental retardation* (pp. 33–62). Baltimore: University Park Press.

Schutz, R. P., & Rusch, F. R. (1982). Competitive employment: Toward employment integration for mentally retarded persons. In K. Lynch, W. Kiernan, & J. Stark (Eds.), *Prevocational and vocational education for special needs youth: A blueprint for the 1980's* (pp. 133–159). Baltimore: Paul H. Brookes.

Shiraga, B. (1983). *A follow-up examination of severely handicapped graduates of the Madison Metropolitan School District from 1979–1983.* Unpublished master's thesis, University of Wisconsin-Madison.

Sowers, J., Thompson, L., & Connis R. (1979). The food service vocational training program: A model for training and placement of the mentally retarded. In T. Bellamy, G. O'Connor, & O. Karan (Eds.), *Vocational rehabilitation of severely handicapped persons: Contemporary service strategies* (pp. 181–205). Baltimore: University Park Press.

Stanford, K. K., & Wehman, P. (1982). Improving the social interactions between moderately retarded and nonretarded coworkers: A pilot study. In P. Wehman & M. Hill (Eds.), *Vocational training and placement of severely disabled persons: Vol. III. Project employability,* (pp. 141–159). Richmond, VA: Virginia Commonwealth University.

Stucky, P. E., & Newbrough, J. R. (1981). Mental health of mentally retarded persons: Social-ecological considerations. In H. C. Haywoood & J. R. Newbrough (Eds.), *Living environments for developmentally retarded persons* (pp. 31–56). Baltimore: University Park Press.

Sutton, G. W., Michael, J. G., & Wanner, J. A. (1981). *The least restrictive living alternative. Toward behavioral criteria for appropriate placement of mentally retarded persons.* Paper presented at the American Association on Mental Deficiency Annual Convention, Detroit, MI.

Tjosvold, D., & Tjosvold, M. M. (1983). Social psychological analysis of residences for mentally retarded persons. *American Journal of Mental Deficiency, 88,* 28–40.

Watzlawick, P., Beavin, J. H., & Jackson, D. D. (1967). *Pragmatics of human communication.* New York: W. W. Norton and Co.

Wehman, P. (1981). *Competitive employment: New horizons for severely disabled individuals.* Baltimore: Paul H. Brookes.

Wehman, P., Hill, M., Goodall, P., Cleveland, P., Brooke, V., & Pentecost, J. H. (1982). Job placement and follow-up of moderately and severely handicapped individuals after three years. *Journal of the Association for the Severely Handicapped, 7,* 5–16.

Weiss, R. S. (1974). The provisions of social relationship. In Z. Rubin (Ed.), *Doing unto others: Joining, molding, conforming, helping, loving* (pp. 17–26). Englewood Cliffs, NJ: Prentice-Hall.

White, D. M., & Rusch, F. R. (1983). Social validation in competitive employment: Evaluating work performance. *Applied Research in Mental Retardation, 4,* 343–354.

Wills, R. H. (1973). *The institutionalized severely retarded: A study of activity and interaction.* Springfield, IL: Charles C Thomas.

Chapter 19

Mental Retardation Services in Sheltered Workshops and Day Activity Programs
Consumer Benefits and Policy Alternatives

G. Thomas Bellamy, Larry E. Rhodes,
Philip E. Bourbeau, and David M. Mank

THE PURPOSE OF the chapter is to appraise the employment and related services status of individuals with mental retardation who are served in sheltered workshops and day activity programs. Two important developments of the last decade facilitate and, at the same time, complicate the task. The first consists of an extensive set of descriptive studies about sheltered workshop performance; the second relates to the emergency of "best practices" based upon applied behavior research.

During the last few years, national studies of sheltered workshops have proliferated (General Accounting Office, 1980; Greenleigh Associates, 1975; U.S. Department of Labor, 1977, 1979; Whitehead, 1981), providing detailed descriptions of the practices and outcomes of sheltered workshop programs along with recommendations for workshop operation and government policy (e.g., Whitehead, 1979, 1981). Though drawing from the same data base, the present chapter is unique by focusing on service consumers with mental retardation and analyzing day activity programs typically not considered in earlier works. The inclusion of day activity programs is a logical outgrowth of the demonstrated vocational competence of persons with mental retardation in such settings (Bellamy, Peterson, & Close, 1975; Crosson, 1966; Gold, 1972, 1973; Loos & Tizard, 1955).

Employment services that produce wages significantly above workshop norms have been provided in both sheltered programs (Bellamy, Horner, Sheehan, & Boles, 1981) and competitive employment (Bates & Pancsofar, 1983; Cook, Dahl, & Gale, 1977; Moss, 1979; Rusch & Mithaug, 1980; Sowers, Thompson, & Connis, 1979; Washington Division of Developmental Disabilities, 1984; Wehman, 1981). The volume and variety of existing evidence make it unlikely that such work successes represent exceptional cases; rather, the compelling conclusion is that all or most individuals now served in sheltered workshops and day programs are capable of performing well-paid work. Consequently, distinctions between day activity and sheltered work programs cannot be defined on the basis of service consumers' potential or readiness for work. An even more important implication of the evidence of the vocational competence of persons with mental retardation in such settings is its affirmation that difficulties experienced by people with mental retardation in obtaining and maintaining work cannot be attributed simply to the presence of mental retardation or other factors associated with the individual service consumer. Instead, such difficulties must be traced largely to characteristics of the service delivery system and the larger employment context. A similar inerpretation has been suggested by Dart, Dart, and Nosek (1980), who argued that individuals with disabilities often are limited far more by social attitudes and unnecessary services than by their own physical disabilities.

The present analysis focuses on how the structure of workshops and day activity programs may be modified to support employment, not how the condition of mental retardation hinders employment. This review is one among a number of commentaries on service improvement strategies. Data on workshop operation and individual work potential have led to a variety of suggestions for how to adapt services to the needs of changing consumer groups and rising employment expectations. Unfortunately, these suggestions show little consensus, primarily because of the diverse nature of the constituents affected. Workshops and day activity programs serve a wide range of consumers. Programs affect local businesses, labor groups, public service, and a growing group of service professionals in addition to the families and advocates of disabled individuals. Furthermore, implications may be drawn for public policy as well as education, rehabilitation, disability insurance, income security, medical assistance, civil rights, housing, labor business regulation, and taxation. All government levels are involved in funding or regulating such services and can be substantially affected by cost-transfer effects in program changes. As national data on workshop operations have become available, the positions of various groups have become increasingly well defined.

Within the context of the negotiation, compromise, and consensus building that now is occurring among many of these groups, the present chapter addresses three specific issues. First, it outlines the development of current services and summarizes available data on the experiences and benefits of consumers with

mental retardation within those services. Second, the chapter defines the major interests of mentally retarded service consumers that should serve as criteria for evaluating proposed changes. Third, the chapter presents a framework for a system design that, if implemented through consistent governemnt policy, could satisfy the major interests of most constituencies affected by workshops.

FOUNDATIONS OF CURRENT SERVICES

The current system of employment services for consumers with mental retardation is rooted in programs initiated between 1850 and 1950 by a variety of residential institutions, charities, and parent organizations. Generally, these programs were based on the assumption that difficulty in obtaining or maintaining competitive work stemmed from inadequate abilities of individuals with handicaps. Implicitly, if not explicitly, assuming that competitive employment was impossible, programs sought to provide a sheltered setting in which some work would be possible. Thus, most programs operated as not-for-profit organizations with volunteer boards of directors, using donations and other charitable funds to supplement the revenue generated by commercial operations.

Over time, the federal government began to assist service providers. For example, the 1983 amendments to the Vocational Rehabilitation Act permitted workshops to pay subminimum wages to workers with handicaps, thereby allowing workshops to compete with other businesses for contracts. By the mid-1940s, additional revisions to the Act allowed for the provision of services to adults with mental retardation. Significant changes in workshop operation resulted from further amendments to the Vocational Rehabilitation Act in 1954, expanding the funding of state rehabilitation programs and making grants available to private organizations to develop new techniques for serving persons with disabilities (U.S. Department of Labor, 1977). The resulting incentives turned the traditional workshop attention from employment to preparation of handicapped individuals for independent competitive jobs (DuBrow, 1957, 1959). Workshop services designed to foster work readiness stressed evaluation, adjustment, and counseling. Consequently, sheltered work assumed the role of a therapeutic modality used to build tolerance to competitive employment (Ruegg, 1981).

The subtle and cumulative result of the history of employment services for consumers with mental retardation was the development of dual objectives for workshop programs—they were expected to: 1) provide sheltered employment, and 2) move individuals into competitive jobs. Neff (1970) separated these objectives by distinguishing between rehabilitation workshops, intended to function as a transitional service for competitive placement, and sheltered workshops, designed to provide remunerative employment to those who presumably could not compete with non-handicapped members of the work force. Despite Neff's attempts to differentiate these goals, both functions were typically undertaken by a single agency. In time, federal program support encouraged the development of staffing patterns and program objectives that added greater emphasis to the competitive placement function, eventually leading to the 1966 amendments to the Fair Labor Standard Act, which authorized the establishment of work activity centers within sheltered workshops for the purpose of serving those individuals who were not considered ready to benefit from placement preparation.

The sheltered workshop's emphasis on preparation for competitive employment, in conjunction with the vocational rehabilitation agency's mandate to serve those handicapped individuals for whom employment was feasible, most likely contributed to excluding from workshops many individuals with severe handicaps. As a result, concerned parents, family members, and other advocates led pioneering efforts to create day activity centers based on donations and volunteer efforts paralleling earlier chapters in the development of sheltered workshops (Bergman, 1976; Cortazzo, 1972). Like those earlier efforts, private day programs eventually attracted government

support. With federal funding under the Developmental Disabilities and Social Service programs, day activity centers expanded rapidly in most states, becoming an integral part of community service delivery for individuals with mental retardation.

The advent of day activity programs complicated the task of community providers even more. Added to the historical conflict in the workshop between employment and preparation for competitive employment was the need to provide day programs to previously unserved individuals in order to prevent them from becoming institutionalized. As a group, service providers became entangled in a network of guidelines, regulations, and funding contingencies that stipulated that they: 1) provide services for most, if not all, individuals requiring community programming; 2) function as employers of those served; and 3) move as many of their clients as possible into competitive jobs in the community. In order to meet any one of these goals, a single service agency virtually would have to ignore the other two.

To accomodate these conflicting service needs most states developed a flow-through model or continuum model of services. Within this model, which still persists in some form, individuals not considered ready or able to benefit from job preparation are referred to day activity programs or work activity centers, which are expected to develop readiness to benefit form workshop programs. As such readiness comes about, consumers are expected to move through the continuum of vocational services until they reach the goal of independent employment in the competitive sector. This flow-through model has displaced the initial employment function of sheltered workshops to such an extent that Greenleigh Associates (1975) reported that only 5% of sheltered workshops in the country provided strictly renumerative employment for handicapped workers. Instead, a variety of educational and therapeutic programs are provided to individuals at lower levels of the service continuum, whereas sheltered work is used as means of job preparation for individuals at higher levels.

Today, more than 30 federal programs affect sheltered workshops and day activity programs. Principal funding is provided under the Vocational Rehabilitation, Job Training Partnership, Developmental Disabilities, Social Services, and Medicaid programs. These programs, in turn, provide general regulatory direction for state and/or local governments that commonly contract services from private local providers. Some programs, like the Handicapped Assistance Loans of the Small Business Administration and the Federal Contracts Set-Aside Program established by the Javits-Wagner-O'Day Act, focus on commercial operations support in workshops.

One of the most important federal programs affecting workshops is purely regulatory. Thus, under the authority of the Fair Labor Standards Act amendments of 1967, the U.S. Department of Labor regulates all workshops and day programs that pay subminimum wages to individuals with handicaps. This regulation occurs within the context of three types of workshops that correspond roughly to the steps in the flow-through model described earlier: regular program workshops, work activity centers, and training and evaluation programs.[1]

In most states, adult day programs, work activity centers, and regular progam workshops form the service continuum through which handicapped individuals are expected to progress. Consumers entering the vocational service system undergo an evaluation, the outcome of which determines program placement.

Generally, individuals considered to lack vocational potential or readiness are directed into day activity programs. As individual development occurs, consumers are theoretically referred to work activity centers for training in more work-like settings. Then, as vocational readiness becomes evident, the consumer moves into a training program and performs real work in a regular workshop until his or her performance is judged to indicate readiness for competitive placement. At that time, an independent job in the community is located and the individual is placed in the private sector.

SERVICE AND OUTCOMES

This section summarizes available data on the status of consumers with mental retardation within the continuum of vocational services. Of central importance are a definition of who receives which type of service, the status of these consumers with respect to competitive job placements, wages, and progress through the continuum.

Service Received

Consumers of the vocational services system display diverse needs. Obtaining accurate information on the number of these individuals who are mentally retarded is complicated by differences in methodology across available studies and the definitions of retardation typically used by vocational rehabilitation agencies to establish eligibility and classify service re-

---

[1]Definitions of workshop types used by the U.S. Department of Labor are as follows. *Sheltered workshop* or *workshop* means a charitable organization or institution conducted not for profit, but for the purpose of carrying out a recognized rehabilitation program for handicapped workers, and/or providing such individuals with remunerative employment or other occupational rehabilitating activity of an educational or therapeutic nature.

Work activities center means a workshop, or a physically separated department of a workshop, having an identifiable program, separate supervision and records, planned and designed exclusively to provide therapeutic activities for handicapped workers whose physical or mental impairment is so severe as to make their productive capacity inconsequential. Therapeutic activities include custodial activities (such as activities that focus on teaching basic living skills), and any purposeful activity so long as work or production is not the main purpose. No individual worker whose productivity substantially exceeds 50% of average minimum wage shall be employed at less than the statutory minimum wage under a work activities center certificate.

Training program means a program of not more than 12 months' duration. Longer periods may be approved in unusual circumstances, designed to: 1) develop the behavior patterns that will help a client adjust to a work environment, or 2) teach the skills and knowledge related to a specific occupational objective of a job family, meeting state agency or equivalent standards.

Evaluation program refers to a program of not more than 6 months' duration. Longer periods may be approved in unusual circumstances, using the medium of work to determine a client's potential, and meeting state agency or equivalent standards.

cipients. According to the American Association on Mental Deficiency (Grossman, 1973), mental retardation refers to everybody whose measured intelligence quotient is below 70. An older category of borderline retardation (IQ 70–85) has been dropped, since individuals within this range typically showed no organic impairment and often functioned more adequately in society when free of the possibly stigmatizing label of mental retardation. Despite this shift in the definition of mental retardation, Vocational Rehabilitation guidelines still identify all persons whose measured IQ falls below 85 as mentally retarded (Laski, 1979). The inclusion of borderline individuals within Vocational Rehabilitation guidelines alters any interpretation of sheltered workshop data. The borderline category includes many more individuals than any other level within the mental retardation range, and, generally, these individuals require less intervention and training than people with more severe mental retardation. For these reasons, outcome data typically reported on the sheltered workshop system probably reflect an optimistic picture of current services and benefits for persons with mental retardation.

The number of persons with mental retardation placed in workshops has grown tremendously in recent years. According to Department of labor figures, 13,772 or 34% of all workshops participants in 1963 were mentally retarded. In 1973, participants with mental retardation totaled 38,671, accounting for 46.5% of the total workshop population. By 1976, over 88,000 persons with mental retardation were receiving services in sheltered workshops. This number represents 61% of the toal number of workshop participants for the year. Thus, from 1968 to 1976, the number of persons with mental retardation served in shel-

tered workshops increased 545%. As illustrated in Table 1, most of these individuals were served in work activity centers.

However, workshop data do not account for the large number of individuals who are mentally retarded and are served in day activity programs, or not served at all. Cortazzo (1972) reported that in 1964, 64 day activity programs were in operation nationwide; by 1971, the number had risen to 422. A 1979 survey by Bellamy, Sheehan, Horner, and Boles (1980) revealed 1,989 such centers serving approximately 105,500 clients. Integration of these workshop data is made difficult by the fact that programs funded as day activity progams within a state are eligible for certification from the U.S. Department of Labor as work activity centers. The extent of this overlap is unknown. However, since states with approximately 40% of all day activity centers disallow work through state guidelines, it can be safely assumed that at least 40,000 individuals now served in adult activity centers are not included in the Department of Labor data base. The best available estimate of the status of individuals with mental retardation in the services continuum uses this conservative estimate from the 1979 day activity program survey (Bellamy et al., 1980) and the 1976 data collected on workshops by the U.S. Department of Labor. Figure 1 shows the resulting distribution by program type.

Competitive Job Placement

The rate of placement from sheltered workshops to competitive employment has been reported at about 12% of the total workshop population annually (U.S. Department of Labor, 1977, 1979). For consumers with mental retardation, reported placement rates did not vary greatly from this figure. Thus, individuals with mental retardation were placed into com-

Table 1. Distribution of mentally retarded clients across types of workshop programs

Type of program	1968	1973	1976
Regular program workshops	832	2,251	13,732
Work activity centers	9,997	30,429	63,917
Training and evaluation programs	1,872	3,923	10,882

From U.S. Department of Labor. (1977). *Sheltered workshop study*, Table 10; U.S. Department of Labor. (1979). *Study of handicapped clients in sheltered workshops*, Table 2.

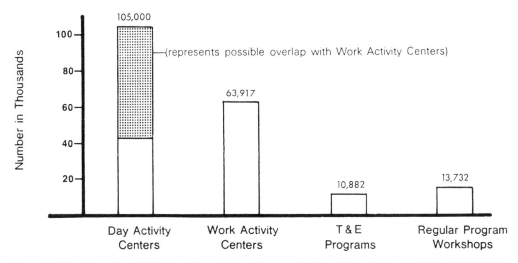

Figure 1.   Estimated number of individuals with mental retardation served in day activity centers, work activity centers, training and evaluation programs, and regular program workshops. (From Bellamy, Sheehan, Horner, and Boles, 1980; U.S. Department of Labor, 1979.)

petitive employment by program type as follows: training and evaluation programs (6%); regular program workshops (11.3%); and work activity centers (7.4%).

Moss (1979) extracted data from the U.S. Department of Labor (1977) report that provide a rather complete picture. His analysis showed that 75% of all consumers placed into competitive employment are transferred during their first 3 months. The annual likelihood of placement for individuals who have been in workshop programs longer than 2 years is 3%. Thus, consumers who remain in workshop programs beyond a minimum length of time have less opportunity of acquiring a job in the competitive sector. This finding is particularly disturbing since 23% of consumers with mental retardation in regular program workshops (RPWs) and work activity centers (WACs) have been in their respective programs for more than 5 years.

Progress through the Continuum

National data on movement between vocational service programs are difficult to isolate for persons with mental retardation. Nevertheless, given the extent to which WACs are populated with consumers with mental retardation, the figures for all WAC clients serve as a conservative estimate. Thus, the U.S.

Department of Labor (1979) reported for 1976 that less than 3% of the individuals served to work activity centers moved on to regular program workshops. These data are corroborated by a report from the California Department of Finance (1979) indicating that in 1978 only 3.3% of WAC clients moved into regular program workshops. According to the same report, 2.7% of day activity program participants moved on to more vocationally oriented programs during the year. Figures from the New Jersey Bureau of Adult Training Services (1981) indicated that during 1980, only 31 of 385 (3.5%) of day activity clients moved to work programs.

The overwhelming majority of individuals who are mentally retarded are served in the two bottom levels of the vocational service continuum—day activity programs and work activity programs—where the probability of progression toward competitive employment is nearly nonexistent. If each consumer had an equal probability of movement along this continuum and was placed in a day activity program, he or she would require an average of between 47 and 58 years to move through program levels before realizing community employment; for clients in work activity centers it would take, on the average, 10–19 years to obtain a job. Figure 2 presents client

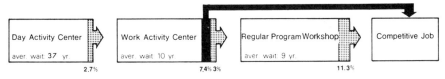

percent of clients moving to higher level program during a year

Figure 2. Client movement through the continuum of vocational service. (From California Department of Finance, 1979; U.S. Department of Labor, 1979.)

movement through the continuum of vocational services.

Wages

Table 2 presents the mean hourly, monthly, and yearly wages of all workshop consumers when in production. These data suggest that consumers in workshop programs are not working a full day, since the hourly wage data indicate greater productivity then do the monthly and yearly earnings. Table 2 also shows that sheltered workshop wages are low. Wages for participants with mental retardation are uniformly lower than those of other consumer groups.

Table 3 presents mean hourly wages earned by consumers with mental retardation and the corresponding percentage of minimum wage for 1968, 1973, and 1976 across RPWs, WACs, and training and evaluation programs.

The differences in wages paid to consumers may be attributable, at least in part, to the fact that individuals with mental retardation have less access to work than do clients in general shops. Figure 3 shows a comparison between hours worked per week in workshops serving other consumers and those serving adults with mental retardation. Relative to other disability groups in workshops, consumers with mental retardation have not enjoyed equal opportunities to earn wages.

Data on job placement, wages, and program movement provide a bleak outlook for adults with mental retardation placed in sheltered workshops and day activity program. In response to requests to function as small businesses, service providers have attempted to: 1) pay reasonable wages to employees, 2) hire nearly everyone who wants a job, and 3) place the best workers with competing firms. The

many conflicts created by these expectations have not been erased by public funding. Based on widespread demonstrations of employment success, even with individuals labeled moderately, severely, and profoundly mentally retarded, placement in day activity and work activity programs cannot be justified in terms of individual limitations. Instead, placement must be addressed as an issue of equity in service provision and work allocation within the service system.

CURRENT PROPOSALS FOR REFORM

Not surprisingly, data on wages, job placement, and program movement by consumers of vocational services have contributed to the growing concerns of consumers, professionals, and the general public. Many proposed reforms appear to address the problems of low wages and job placement probabilities. Among these, three frequently expressed proposals advocate a major shift away from sheltered workshops. The first calls for nonvocational progamming; the second involves individuals with mental retardation working in integrated settings as volunteers if pay is not considered feasible; the third suggests replacement of sheltered work with competitive employment programs.

Insignificant progress in developing acceptable employment alternatives has contributed to reform suggestions in the United States and abroad focusing on nonvocational objectives (Australia Department of Social Security, undated; Whelan & Speake, 1977). Tizard and Anderson (1979) argued that for people with severe mental retardation, alternatives to work must be urgently sought because a dwindling supply of work threatens to exclude them from

Table 2. Mean hourly, monthly, and yearly earnings of workshop clients across program types

Program type	Hourly earnings			Monthly earnings			Yearly earnings		
	All consumers	Mentally retarded consumers	All other consumers	All consumers	Mentally retarded consumers	All other consumers	All consumers	Mentally retarded consumers	All other consumers
All shops	$ .80	$ .57	$1.23	$ 74	$ 47	$118	$ 666	$ 417	$1,083
Regular program workshops	1.54	1.21	1.73	179	131	206	1,677	1,175	1,970
Work activity centers	.42	.39	.56	31	29	36	288	268	350
Training and evaluation programs	.78	.61	.91	62	52	75	333	327	343

From U.S. Department of Labor. (1979). *Study of handicapped clients in sheltered workshops*, Tables 30, 34, and 38.

Table 3. Mean hourly wage and percentage of minimum wage earned by clients with mental retardation in three program types

Program type	1968 ($1.15)[a]		1973 ($1.60)[a]		1976 ($2.30)[a]	
	Mean wage of MR	% minimum wage	Mean wage of MR	% minimum wage	Mean wage of MR	% minimum wage
Total	$ .40	35%	$ .43	27%	$ .57	27%
Regular program workshop	.93	81%	1.11	69%	1.21	53%
Work activity center	.33	29%	.35	22%	.39	17%
Training and evaluation programs	.44	38%	.52	33%	.61	27%

From U.S. Department of Labor. (1977). *Sheltered workshop study*, Table 11; U.S. Department of Labor. (1979). *Study of handicapped clients in sheltered workshops*, Table 30.
[a]Minimum wage.

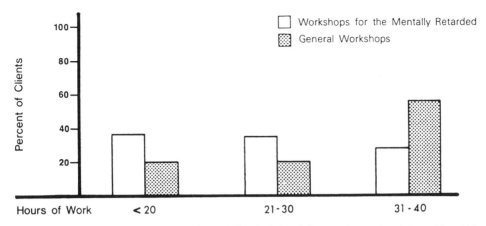

Figure 3. Weekly hours of work for clients in mentally retarded workshops and general workshops. (From U.S. Department of Labor, 1979.)

the work force. A similar viewpoint was expressed by Brown et al. (1985), who maintained that creation of volunteer jobs in integrated settings is an acceptable form of employment of people labeled severely mentally retarded, and that any form of segregated programming is unacceptable. According to this position, unpaid work is considered appropriate because: 1) limited skills and behavioral deficiencies frequently make pay inpractical, 2) working without pay provides opportunity for partial repayment to taxpayers for public services received, and 3) unpaid work is an effective method of preparing adults with severe mental retardation for further paid employment. (Pursuant to this line of logic, the quality of life resulting from unpaid work is greater than that in segregated settings.)

The third major proposal for reform calls for replacing sheltered workshops with competitive employment training programs. It is an attractive alternative because both public and individual benefits are enhanced when a recipient of public services successfully is placed in competitive employment. A growing body of literature supports the position that many people with severe disabilities are capable of competitive employment, and that such employment leads to both greater integration and higher wages than sheltered or day activity programs (Moss, 1979; Rusch & Mithaug, 1980; Schneider, Martin, & Rusch, 1981;

Sowers, Thompson, & Connis, 1979; Wehman, 1981).

Two obstacles prevent complete replacement of current service models with competitive employment programs, however. The first relates to the limitations placed by local economics and businesses on the number of individuals employed. A second barrier stems from the degree of support some individuals require relative to what is available in the competitive work environment. For example, limitations currently placed upon follow-up support and employer incentive create a disadvantage both to employers and the large groups of now unemployed individuals who are severely disabled and require ongoing support to sustain a high productivity level or to meet the changing demands of the work place.

As a result, the most common recommendations for reform of day services involve improving, rather than replacing, the existing sheltered workshop system (Lilly, 1979; Redkey, 1979; Whelan & Speake, 1977; Whitehead, 1981). Some recommend excluding individuals with severe disabilities in order to focus more effectively on placement objectives and to maintain high benefit-to-cost returns on investment in rehabilitation programs (Levitan & Taggart, 1977, 1982). Others have advocated direct wage subsidies to rectify inadequate wages (Rubin, 1982). Many propose tightening national standards to increase performance in current services, such as creating uniform data reporting, increasing the focus upon individual service plan requirements, and setting standards for determining a person's readiness for competitive employment (e.g., Whitehead, 1981).

Taken in isolation, no reform suggestions seem capable of solving the complex problems underlying incompatible program objectives and the conflicting interests of various groups. Instead, a number of changes must be integrated into a comprehensive government policy that addresses the full spectrum of issues affecting national employment policies for people with mental retardation. Rather than attempting costly piecemeal reforms, change efforts should address the underlying policies that sustain the ineffective flow-through model of vocational services. At issue is government policy and system design, not simply details of service provision.

REFORM INTERESTS OF CONSUMERS WITH MENTAL RETARDATION

Employment for persons with severe disabilities has just begun to receive political attention, despite the research activity and demonstration of successful employment of the last two decades. The problem facing the professional and advocacy community is how to establish policies and accompanying service systems to ensure equitable services and opportunities for consumers having mental retardation. Initially, a statement of the basic interests of service consumers would provide a set of criteria upon which reform proposals could be evaluated and policy activities be initiated. Many authors have described the interests of adults with mental retardation (e.g., Bellamy et al., 1980; Bernstein & Karan, 1979; Brown et al., 1985; Gold, 1972; Wehman, 1981; Wolfensberger, 1967). Four critical interests repeatedly emerge; vocational services should be: 1) inclusive, 2) accountable for work-related consumer benefits, 3) combined with programs that expand work opportunities, and 4) secure. Each concern is discussed briefly below.

Inclusive Programs

The employment potential of individuals with severe disabilities is no longer in doubt as complex work skills and significant productivity have been documented across diverse work environments. Consequently, an acceptable system must give equal work opportunities to individuals with severe disabilities. Current barriers to equal work opportunity for severely disabled individuals include: unnecessarily restrictive entrance requirements to vocationally oriented programs (Mithaug, Hagmeier, & Haring, 1977); regulations in some states that prevent work in entry-level day services (Bellamy et al., 1980); and program practices that typically give those with mild handicaps first access to available work.

Many are willing to sacrifice employment opportunities for individuals with severe disabilities in order to serve consumers with mild handicaps who require the least intervention. Cost-benefit analyses, such as those commonly applied to vocational rehabilitation programs (Berkowitz, Englander, Rubin, & Worrall, 1975; Rubin, 1982), demonstrate high returns for investments in services to individuals with mild handicaps. However, these traditional analyses do not take into account the rapidly rising costs of *not* providing vocational opportunities and services to those with severe handicaps (General Accounting Office, 1981; Moss, 1979).

Serving the vocational and employment interests of citizens with mental retardation requires a design that includes all individuals now served in work activities and day activity programs. Thus, services are needed that emphasize work and productivity for all individuals while providing an alternative to nonproductive services at the bottom of the service continuum.

Accountability for Work-Related Consumer Benefits

Successful vocational services should result in employment, *employment* being defined as activity that generates wages and related job benefits. The interests of mentally retarded service consumers will be best served when the quality of all vocational options are indexed by the same standards as those used by others, including such general questions as: What income level will the job provide?; How attractive is the work life itself?; and What security benefit does the job provide? Instead, current program goals typically address a variety of skills and behaviors that appear important for future participation in work settings. Much of this emphasis on *preparation* for work derives from a rehabilitation model that focuses on independent employment. According to this model, preparation and dependency on service continue until an individual is able to succeed in the competitive work force without further support. Consequently, individuals who do not attain complete independence or normal productivity are relegated to indefinite preparation, with little or no opportunity to participate in the economic mainstream.

Expansion of Work Opportunities

The employment interests of persons with mental retardation would be poorly served if government policy addressed only the provision of services to individual consumers. Unemployment and underemployment of persons who have retardation cannot be attributed entirely to the presence of disabling conditions and the quality of services provided. Of at least equal importance is the availability of work opportunities. Thus, no policy or program reform will be effective without significant changes in public incentives for employers to expand work opportunities for all citizens with disabilities. At least two kinds of incentives are needed: 1) those that reimburse employers for excess costs related to *initial* employment of individuals who are later able to contribute normally to productivity, and 2) those that expand the availablilty of supported employment to individuals now denied access to sheltered workshops and job training programs.

Security

Reliable out-of-home day services are critical to the community residence and adjustment of many individuals. Interruptions of services are both disruptive to families and costly to community service providers. Thus, the prospect of periodic lack of services may force families to consider institutionalization or other unnecessarily expensive and restrictive alternatives. From a family perspective, it is not sufficient for vocational programs to serve only those who can be competitively employed. Except in unusual circumstances the local service need will be greater than the market for a program's labor force. To respond to the interests of consumers having retardation, reform of vocational services must include sound alternatives within every sector of the labor market and provide stability without excluding individuals with severe handicaps from available work opportunities.

FRAMEWORK FOR REFORM

One way to achieve systemwide change that addresses the full range of concerns discussed here involves replacing the flow-through model of traditional vocational services with a two-part system—one focusing on supported employment, and the other emphasizing temporary preparation and support leading to unsupported competitive employment. The intended goal of such an approach is employment-related outcomes at all service levels, elimination of unnecessary prerequisites for vocational programs, and encouragement of greater private sector efforts.

Program Elements

Competitive employment training programs (CEPs) are transitional programs designed to move jobless individuals with disabilities into self-supporting, open employment. CEPs should be held specifically accountable for the number of individuals placed in open employment and the cost of required services, without regard for wages earned during training. CEPs may be operated by private provider agencies, by industries or other employers, in joint efforts like many Projects With Industries (Jewish Vocational Service, 1978), in special job placement services, in community colleges and vocational-technical schools, or in a variety of other arrangements.

Supported employment programs (SEPs), in turn, provide longer term publicly supported jobs for individuals with handicaps. Supported employment is intended for persons normally served in day activity and work activity centers. Supported employment programs, unlike CEPs, are designed to provide publicly funded support throughout a period of employment; they are intended for persons who can only work when such support is available. Public support could be provided in many environments with varying degrees of integration with nonhandicapped co-workers. Support may involve funding of nonprofit organizations, long-term wage subsidies for private employers, priority access to public contracts, low-interest loans, and so forth. SEPs would be held specifically accountable for wages provided to participants with the available level of public support.

Through the CEPs and SEPs, the proposed policy framework replaces existing day activity programs, work activity centers, and sheltered workshops. Instead of basing program levels on indefensible attributions about individual potential, the recommended approach assumes that all service recipients are capable of working. As a result, work objectives are met either by providing extended, supported work, or by training for open employment. Quality of work in both programs is measured on the basis of wages, lifestyle impact, work-life quality, and security.

Rationale

Both competitive and supported employment programs are necessary. The separation of supported employment and job preparation services is based upon the fundamental incompatibility between outcomes often expected of vocational programs. This incompatibility is evidenced by the flow-through model's failure to provide equitable opportunities or quality services to individuals with severe disabilities. Supported employment programs would be best measured by immediate and ongoing contributions made to consumer income, integration, security, and satisfaction. Transitional services, on the other hand, are better measured by the speed and effectiveness with which these services change an individual's

status from unemployed to employed. The service structures needed to effectively achieve these separate objectives require major differences in: 1) organization and staffing patterns, 2) learning and teaching strategies involved, and 3) type of commercial interface that must take place between programs and their respective communities.

To be efficient, supported employment and competitive employment preparation require different organizational and staffing patterns. A combination of the two results in duplication of functions and higher administrative and overhead costs. For example, the U.S. Department of Labor (1977) reported that nearly 64% of salaries in workshops serving people with mental retardation are spent on administrative, technical, and professional functions. No true estimate of costs for direct services can be made based on the available data. A recent study of adult programs in one state reported a public cost of $82 in adult day services for each staff hour spent in direct service with program participants (McDonnell, 1981).

The need to separate SEPs and CEPs is also supported by differences in the way in which learning theory can best be applied to each. Thus, CEPs are transition programs preparing clients for jobs in environments different from those where training occurs. Consequently, these programs involve: 1) predicting how specific skills will serve individuals within the community's job market, 2) targeting skills most likely to be transferable across jobs, and 3) training for a variety of experiences across a defined range of jobs. Ultimately, procedures for effective transition must emphasize systematic programming for generalization (e.g., Colvin & Horner, 1983) and careful selection of jobs (Sowers, Thompson, & Connis, 1979). Extended supported employment, on the other hand, does not have to prepare individuals for job performance in radically different environments. Instead, a narrow range of work in a supported environment accommodating individual differences is most likely to maximize productivity and increase worker wages.

Both SEPs and CEPs meet their objectives only when they are active partners in a community's labor pool. However, the strategy by which each type of service becomes a viable part of this labor force varies markedly. Whereas the supported employment program must be competitive as a subcontractor or prime manufacturer, or operate within the structure of a host company, the placement program, by marketing a personnel service to businesses, must interact primarily with those who have responsibility for personnel functions in local employment.

System Characteristics

These considerations suggest that replacing the flow-through model or service continuum with two distinct types of services—one providing extended employment in publicly supported work settings, the other preparing clients for self-sustaining employment—could solve many of the problems that now hinder or restrict employment and related services for individuals with mental retardation. To operate, coordinate, and regulate these two programs, a vocational service system must resolve additional operating issues, incuding those discussed below.

1. *Program Placement* In spite of a tendency to serve those with severe handicaps in SEPs while directing more capable individuals to CEPs, such placement is not inherent in the proposed model. Depending on job availability, presence of supportive family members, transportation, and individual consequences of loss of public support, individuals with severe handicaps could be served in CEPs, while many consumers with only mild disabilities might choose SEPs. Such a program decision should reflect the values of family members, information on available work opportunities, and local support for either option. An Individual Habilitation Plan process appears to be a reasonable vehicle for such decision making and a means of ensuring that no consumer is constrained below his or her potential employment level. It seems unwise to limit SEPs to individuals who have failed in CEPs; nor should CEPs be limited to those who have succeeded in SEPs. In many communities, a limited and variable number of jobs places

natural restrictions on the size of successful CEPs. Conversely, under some circumstances government services create powerful incentives to avoid the risks associated with competitive employment, especially when job security is low. Appropriate services should be determined and reviewed on an individual basis without the constraints imposed in a fixed sequence of service.

2. *Work Allocation* To the extent that all individuals needing community service are placed in either CEPs or SEPs, the volume of available work may not match participants' ability to perform. In SEPs, for example, one option would be to always give preference to clients with the most severe handicaps. Not only would this ensure that individuals with the fewest options receive some work benefits, it could also create incentive for more capable individuals to perform in CEPs instead.

3. *Cost Analysis* Traditional benefit-cost analyses used by vocational rehabilitation agencies appear appropriate for CEPs. SEPs, on the other hand, might be more appropriately evaluated with an alternative investment analysis comparing costs and benefits to alternative, nonvocational programs.

4. *Accountability for Outcomes* Holding CEPs accountable for a number of individuals who enter open employment while making SEPs responsible for the average monthly wage received by participants could provide several program advantages. Unnecessary process regulations could be eliminated, consumer power enhanced, and alternative program models encouraged.

SUMMARY

As evidenced by nearly a decade of data, no functional continuum of training and employment services is available to consumers with mental retardation, despite dramatic increases in funding and the heroic efforts of service providers and advocates. It is clear, however, that substantive change requires that a reconceptualization must be made at the broadest policy levels.

Both the opportunity and the necessity to redesign services stem from the growing fiscal crisis faced by states and providers and a need for increased consumer services. The proposal for reform set forth here advocates the differentiation of short-term transition services leading to employment in the competitive sector from long-term structured employment opportunities for individuals requiring ongoing support. Work and productivity are emphasized at all service levels, with a focus on current, work-related benefits for consumers.

REFERENCES

Australia Department of Social Security (undated). *The ATC handbook.* Development and Special Projects Section, Rehabilitation and Subsidies Division, Department of Social Security, P.O. Box 1, Woden, Australia.

Bates, P., & Pancsofar, E. (1983). Project EARN (Employment and Rehabilitation = Normalization): A competitive employment training program for severely disabled youth in the public schools. *British Journal of Mental Subnormality, 29*(57), 97–107.

Bellamy, G. T., Horner, R. H., Sheehan, M. R., & Boles, S. M. (1981). Structured employment and workshop reform: Equal rights for severely handicapped individuals. In J. Lapadakis, J. Ansley, & J. Lowitt (Eds.), *Work, services and change: Proceedings from the National Institute on Rehabilitation Facilities* (pp. 59–76). Washington, DC: National Association of Rehabilitation Facilities.

Bellamy, T., Peterson, L., & Close, D. (1975). Habilitation of the severely and profoundly retarded: Illustration of competence. *Education and Training of the Mentally Retarded, 10,* 174–186.

Bellamy, G. T., Sheehan, M. R., Horner, R. H., & Boles, S. M. (1980). Community programs for severely handicapped adults: An analysis of vocational opportunities. *Journal of The Association for the Severely Handicapped, 5*(4), 307–324.

Bergman, A. (1976). *A guide to establishing an activity center for mentally retarded persons.* Washington: U.S. Government Printing Office.

Berkowitz, M., Englander, V., Rubin, U., & Worrall, J. D. (1975). *An evaluation of policy-related rehabilitation research.* New York: Praeger.

Bernstein, G. S., & Karan, O. C. (1979). Obstacles to vocational normalization for the developmentally disabled. *Rehabilitation Literature, 40*(3), 66–71.

Brown, L., Shiraga, B., York, J., Kessler, K., Strohm, B., Sweet, M., Zanella, K., VanDeventer, P., & Loomis, R. (1985). Integrated work opportunities for adults with severe handicaps: The extended training option. *Journal of The Association for Persons with Severe Handicaps, 9*(4), 262–269.

California Department of Finance. (1979). *A review of sheltered workshops and related programs (Phase II): To assembly concurrent resolution* (No. 206, Vol. II, Final report). State of California, Sacramento.

Colvin, G. T., & Horner, R. H. (1983). Experimental analysis of generalization: An evaluation of a general case program for teaching motor skills to severely handicapped learners. In D. Hogg & P. Mittler (Eds.), *Advances in mental handicap research: Vol. 2. Aspects of competence in mentally handicapped people* (pp. 309–345). Chichester, England: John Wiley & Sons.

Cook, P., Dahl, P., & Gale, M. (1977). *Vocational training and placement of the severely handicapped: Vocational opportunities.* Palo Alto: The American Institute for Research in the Behavioral Sciences.

Cortazzo, A. (1972). *Activity centers for retarded adults.* Washington, DC: President's Committee on Mental Retardation.

Crosson, J. (1966). The experimental analysis of vocational behavior in severely retarded males (Doctoral dissertation, University of Oregon, 1966). *Dissertation Abstracts International, 27,* 3304.

Dart, J., Dart, Y., & Nosek, P. (1980). A philosophical foundation for the independent living movement. *Rehabilitation Gazette, 23,* 16–18.

Dubrow, M. (1957). *Report of the institute held for the creative use of sheltered workshops in rehabilitation.* New York: Altro Health and Rehabilitation Services, Inc.

Dubrow, M. (1959). Sheltered workshops for the mentally retarded as an educational and vocational experience. In *New Trends in rehabilitation.* Washington, DC: Department of Health, Education and Welfare, Office of Vocational Rehabilitation.

General Accounting Office. (1980). *Better reevaluations of handicapped persons in sheltered workshops could increase their opportunities for competitive employment.* Washington, DC: General Accounting Office.

General Accounting Office. (1981). *Stronger federal efforts needed for providing employment opportunities and enforcing labor standards in sheltered workshops.* Controller General's report to the Honorable Barry M. Goldwater, Jr., HRD-81-99.

Gold, M. W. (1972). Stimulus factors in skill training of the retarded on a complex assembly task: Acquisition, transfer and retention. *American Journal of Mental Deficiency, 76,* 517–526.

Gold, M. W. (1973). Research on the vocational habilitation of the retarded: The present, the future. In N. R. Ellis (Ed.), *International review of research in mental retardation* (Vol. 6, pp. 97–147). New York: Academic Press.

Greenleigh Associates (1975). *The role of the sheltered workshop in the rehabilitation of the severely handicapped.* Report to the Department of Health, Education and Welfare, Rehabilitation Services Administration, New York.

Grossman, H. (Ed.). (1973). *Manual on terminology and classification in mental retardation.* Washington, DC: American Association on Mental Deficiency.

Jewish Vocational Service. (1978). *Rule #9: Program models for Projects With Industry.* Chicago: Research Utlization Laboratory, Jewish Vocational Service.

Laski, F. J. (1979). Legal strategies to secure entitlement to services for severely handicapped persons. In T. Bellamy, G. O'Connor, & O. Karan (Eds.), *Voca-*

tional rehabilitation of severely handicapped persons: Contemporary service strategies (pp. 1–32). Baltimore: University Park Press.

Levitan, S., & Taggart, R. (1977). *Jobs for the disabled*. Baltimore: Johns Hopkins University Press.

Levitan, S., & Taggart, R. (1982). Rehabilitation, employment and the disabled. In J. Rubin (Ed.), *Alternatives in rehabilitating the handicapped* (pp. 89–149). New York Human Science Press.

Lilly, K. L. (1979). Redefining the purpose of sheltered workshops. *Amicus, 4,* 277–280.

Loos, F., & Tizard, J. (1955). The employment of adult imbeciles in a hospital workshop. *American Journal of Mental Deficiency, 59,* 395–403.

McDonnell, A. (1981). *Work environments of severely handicapped adults*. Eugene, OR: University of Oregon, Division of Special Education and Rehabilitation.

Mithaug, D. E., Hagmeier, L. D., Haring, N. G. (1977). The relationship between training activities and job placement in vocational education of the severely and profoundly handicapped. *AAESPH Review, 2,* 89–109.

Moss, J. W. (1979). *Post secondary vocational education for mentally retarded adults*. Final Report to the Division of Developmental Disabilities, Rehabilitation Services Administration, Department of Health, Education and Welfare, Grant No. 56P 50281/0.

Neff, W. (1970). Vocational assessment: Theory and models. *Journal of Rehabilitation,* 36(1), 27–29.

New Jersey Bureau of Adult Training Services (1981, June). *Movement of adult activities clients to vocational programs*. Paper presented at New Jersey Bureau of Adult Training Services Regional Supervisor's Meeting, Trenton.

Redkey, M. (1979). A different kind of workshop. *Amicus, 4,* 270–272.

Rubin, J. (Ed.). (1982). *Alternatives in rehabilitating the handicapped*. New York: Human Sciences Press.

Ruegg, P. (1981). The meaning and use of work as a modality in habilitation and rehabilitation of disabled persons in facilities providing vocational programs. In J. Lapadakis, J. Ansley, & J. Lovitt (Eds.), *Work, services and change: Proceedings from the National Institute on Rehabilitation Facilities* (pp. 5–22). Washington, DC: National Association of Rehabilitation Facilities.

Rusch, F., & Mithaug, D. (1980). *Vocational training for

mentally retarded adults: A behavior analytic approach*. Champaign, IL: Research Press.

Schneider, K. E., Martin, J. E., & Rusch, F. R. (1981, November). An initial investigation into the costs and benefits between a sheltered and non-sheltered vocational program for mentally retarded adults: Are we sacrificing quality? *Counterpoint, 2,* 1 and 24.

Sowers, J., Thompson, L., & Connis, R. (1979). The food service vocational training program. In T. Bellamy, G. O'Connor, & O. Karan (Eds.). *Vocational rehabilitation of severely handicapped persons: Contemporary service strategies* (pp. 15–23). Baltimore: University Park Press.

Tizard, J., & Anderson, E. (1979, June). *The education of the handicapped people*. Paris, France: Organization of Economic Cooperation and Development, Center for Educational Research and Innovation.

U.S. Department of Labor. (1977). *Sheltered workshop study: A nationwide report on sheltered workshops and their employment of handicapped individuals* (Vol. 1). Washington, DC: U.S. Department of Labor.

U.S. Department of Labor (1979, March). *Study of handicapped clients in sheltered workshops* (Vol. II). Washington, DC: U.S. Department of Labor.

Washington Division of Developmental Disabilities. (1984). *Employment support data*. Olympia, WA.

Wehman, P. (1981). *Competitive employment: New horizons for severely disabled individuals*. Baltimore: Paul H. Brookes.

Whelan, E., & Speake, B. (1977). *Adult training centres in England and Wales*. Manchester, England: Revell & George Limited.

Whitehead, C. W. (1979). Sheltered workshops in the decade ahead: Work and wages, or welfare. In T. Bellamy, G. O'Connor, & O. Karan (Eds.), *Vocational rehabilitation of severely handicapped persons: Contemporary service strategies* (pp. 71–84). Baltimore: University Park Press.

Whitehead, C. (1981). *Final report: Training and employment services for handicapped individuals in sheltered workshops*. Washington, DC: Office of Social Services Policy, Office of the Assistant Secretary for Planning and Evaluation, U.S. Department of Health and Human Services.

Wolfensberger, W. (1967). Vocational preparation and occupation. In A. Baumeister (Ed.), *Mental retardation* (pp. 232–273). Chicago: Aldine Atherton.

Chapter 20

Identifying and Teaching Valued Social Behaviors

Janis Chadsey-Rusch

TO SECURE AND maintain employment, individuals with mental retardation must exhibit behaviors that are valued and considered appropriate in employment settings. Two major behavioral categories for ensuring employment success include production skills performed at some acceptable criterion and effective social skills. Without adequate skills in these areas, individuals with mental retardation are likely to encounter difficulties finding and/or maintaining a job. Although both production and social skills are necessary for job survival (Rusch, 1979), there is ample evidence to suggest that the major reason for job loss for persons with mental retardation may be their lack of appropriate social skills rather than poor job performance (Gold, 1975; Greenspan & Shoultz, 1981; Kochany & Keller, 1981; Schalock & Harper, 1978). Both Brown et al. (1981) and Will (1984) implied that the standards used to measure adults' success in job situations should also serve as the criteria for the skills to be acquired by individuals with mental retardation in employment training situations. Consequently, valued social skills displayed by successfully employed adults must be identified and taught to individuals with mental retardation to help them secure and maintain competitive employment.

Although research results suggest that effective social skills are related to job success, little agreement has been reached on how to define, measure, assess, and teach social skills. Probably the primary reason for this lack of consensus stems from the difficulty of operationally defining social skills. For example, the socially skilled individual has been described as someone who easily interacts with others, is a good conversationalist, can communicate and elicit information, and leaves others with a positive feeling after the interaction (Kelly, 1982). In addition, the socially skilled individual knows how to change his or her behavior as a situation changes, and is perceptive and flexible enough to respond appropriately to existing social rules and cultural norms. These types of descriptions, although intuitively accurate, are too broad to lend themselves easily to curricular and instructional components. For example, what does it mean to "easily interact with others," and how does one teach this skill—especially to individuals with cognitive impairments? In the vocational realm, job trainers are more likely to successfully teach job production behaviors that can be easily operationalized (e.g., running a dishwashing machine), than social behaviors that are difficult to break down into instructional components.

The primary focus of this chapter is on a discussion of valued social skills that have been identified in employment settings and a description of a framework that can be used to operationalize social skills, thus making them more effectively assessed and taught. In addition, a number of unresolved philosophical and research issues related to social skills in employment contexts are presented. The chapter is based on the premise that valued social skills should be identified and taught from an ecobehavioral perspective. A brief overview of this perspective follows.

ECOBEHAVIORAL PERSPECTIVE

An ecobehavioral perspective has been suggested as an over-arching framework from which to consider intervention programs for individuals requiring behavioral change (Rogers-Warren & Warren, 1977; Willems, 1977) and, specifically, persons with mental retardation (Chadsey-Rusch, 1985; Rusch, Chadsey, White, & Gifford, 1985). Essentially, an ecobehavioral perspective integrates principles and methods from ecological and behavioral psychology. *Ecological psychology* studies the interrelationships and interdependencies between individuals, their behavior, and their physical and social environments (Barker, 1968; Schoggen, 1978). *Behavioral psychology,* and in particular the applied behavior analytic approach (Baer, Wolf, & Risley, 1968), emphasizes that behaviors are learned through experiences with the environment, and that socially important behaviors can be changed in their usual contexts via behavior principles. As a result of combining these two approaches, individual behavior is viewed as a dynamic part of the interaction between the person and his or her environment, that is, people influence environments and environments influence people. Interdependencies between a person and the environment can be studied either at a molecular level (e.g., studying the social relationships between co-workers during a break from work) or from a molar level (e.g., the federal influence of SSI benefits on employment patterns). Regardless, all behavior is viewed from a systems perspecitve and any change in the person-environment relationship will influence other parts of the system. This systems approach to the study to behavior, which has become the zeitgeist in the field of mental retardation (Chadsey-Rusch & Rusch, in press), has far-reaching implications for assessment and intervention programs.

The goal of the ecobehavioral approach is to maximize the *fit* (Rappaport, 1977) or congruence (Thurman, 1977) between the person and the environment. According to Thurman, congruence occurs when an individual's behavior is in harmony with the social norms of his or her environment. When individuals with mental retardation enter into different environments, they may display behaviors that vary considerably from established social norms, or they may lack the skills necessary to function adequately. If incongruences occur, three options exist: 1) the behavior of the person with mental retardation must be changed, 2) the context in which the deviant or incompetent behavior occurs must be altered, or 3) both the person and the environment need to be transformed. Ecological congruence does not necessarily imply *normal,* instead it should be viewed as "maximal adaptation to the environment" (Thurman, 1977, p. 332). Each environment or context defines a continuum of behavioral responses that not only promote adaptation, but are also accepted and/or tolerated by others in those environments.

Summary

Drawing its perspective from both ecological and behavioral psychology, the ecobehavioral approach views the interaction between persons and environments as interdependent. Thus, any change in the person or the environment will affect other parts of the relationship. The goal of the ecobehavioral approach is to enhance the congruence between the person and his or her environment by changing the person, the environment, or both. The ecobehavioral perspective has considerable merit for studying social skills in employment settings by offering a methodology for identifying the continuum of social skills that promote adaptation to employment environments and by providing a methodology to teach those behaviors.

RESEARCH IDENTIFYING
VALUED SOCIAL BEHAVIORS
IN EMPLOYMENT SETTINGS

The ecology of employment settings needs to be studied in order to define the continuum of social behaviors that will maximize person-environment congruence. Although prior research has delineated a variety of social behaviors that are valued in sheltered workshop settings (Cheney & Foss, 1984; Foss & Peterson, 1981; LaGreca, Stone, & Bell, 1982; Mithaug & Hagmeier, 1978), little research of this type has been conducted in the competitive employment sector. One of the few studies to date that have identified valued social behaviors associated with competitive employment was conducted by Rusch, Schutz, and Agran (1982). In this investigation, questionnaires were sent to 120 potential employers from food service and janitorial/maid service occupations in Illinois to solicit information about their expectations for entry into employment. Survey questions were taken from Mithaug and Hagmeier's (1978) original list of items used to validate the social and vocational behaviors needed for sheltered workshop entry.

Survey results indicated that respondents (66% of the sample) considered 70 behaviors to be necessary for entry into competitive employment. Of these 70 behaviors, 16 social behaviors were agreed upon by 90% of the employers as being important. Two social behaviors (verbally reciting full name on request and following one instruction provided at a time) were mentioned by every employer as being critical for competitive employment.

In spite of its limitations (e.g., job survival skills may be a local issue, small sample range and size), the Rusch et al. (1982) study represents a first attempt to validate a group of social behaviors that are valued by employers. In addition, it is probable that the absence of these behaviors is likely to increase ecological incongruence.

In another study, Salzberg, Agran, and Lignugaris/Kraft (1985) surveyed employers from five different jobs to obtain their opinions regarding social behaviors important for entry-level work and behaviors that may differ in importance across jobs. The results from this study indicated that social behaviors related to worker productivity (e.g., asking supervisors for assistance, following directions, respond-ing to criticism, getting information before a job, offering to help co-workers) were rated higher in importance than general personal social behaviors (e.g., listening without interrupting, acknowledging, and expressing appreciation to co-workers). Interestingly, the mean rating for nonsocial production-related behaviors (e.g., getting to work on time) was significantly higher than the mean rating for task-related social behaviors and personal social behaviors. Furthermore, little relationship was noted between the frequency of occurrence of a behavior and its rated importance.

While Salzberg et al. (1985) confirmed the assumption that social factors are critical for success in all the jobs studied, differences between jobs emerged. For example, social behaviors were considered more important for kitchen helpers and food service workers than for janitors, dishwashers, and maids. Such differences were attributed to the fact that some jobs (i.e., kitchen helpers and food service workers) were carried out in more of a social context, where workers frequently interact with co-workers and customers.

Although the Rusch et al. (1982) and the Salzberg et al. (1985) studies are among only a few investigations that have begun to identify valued social behaviors in competitive employment settings, there are a number of other studies that have specified the social behaviors *not* valued in employment settings. These social behaviors (discussed below) have been associated with job loss and therefore with ecological incongruences.

Social Behaviors Associated with Job Loss

In 1981, Greenspan and Shoultz conducted a study to determine the primary reason for job termination from competitive employment of 30 mildly and moderately mentally retarded individuals in Nebraska. Data were collected from employment records and from interviews with caseworkers, job placement staff, and former employers. The reasons for job loss were categorized as either social or nonsocial (e.g., production, health, economy). Greenspan and Shoultz found that 17 of the 30 subjects lost their jobs for nonsocial reasons.

In a more fine-grained analysis, these authors further sorted the social reasons for job loss into three categories: 1) character or moral reasons (e.g., stealing, assaulting others, sporadic work attendance), 2) temperament or affective reasons (e.g., yelling, banging head, hallucinations), and 3) social awareness reasons, or not understanding people and work settings (e.g., walking into a meeting and talking about a TV program, being inquisitive about other people's business). The data from this sorting procedure revealed that three persons lost their jobs for reasons related to character and five for temperament reasons, whereas nine lost their jobs because of social awareness problems.

The results from this study led Greenspan and Shoultz (1981) to conclude that social incompetence was at least as important for job termination as were nonsocial factors. In addition, social awareness incompetence accounted for more job losses than either character or temperament. The ability to understand what other people think and feel, to social problem solve, and to interpret social rules, situations, and norms were suggested by Greenspan and Shoultz as behaviors that needed to be targeted for remediation in efforts to enhance job placement and maintenance.

Kochany and Keller (1981) examined the job loss reasons for clients served by Project Employability (Wehman, 1981), a job placement and supported work program for individuals with severe disabilities. Among the numerous reasons given for job termination, many could be classified as social. For example, the majority of handicapped individuals lost their jobs for displaying maladaptive behaviors (e.g., complaining, screaming, destroying property, interacting inappropriately with supervisors and co-workers, displaying stereotypical and self-abusive behavior, being noncompliant). In addition, several individuals were fired for being excessively tardy or for poor attendance. A third category used to classify reasons for job termination, critical nonvocational reasons, included the social behaviors of poor communication and conversation ability.

Subsequent to Kochany and Keller's study (1981), Wehman, Hill, Goodall, Cleveland, and Pentecost (1982) evaluated the results of Project Employability after 3 years of ongoing services. The social reasons for job loss reported in their investigation included: 1) noncompliance, 2) failure to notify an employer when unable to report for work, and 3) bizarre and/or aggressive behavior.

Several social reasons were also found to account for job loss in an investigation conducted by Brickey, Browning, and Campbell (1982). In this follow-up study, the authors examined the employment history of 53 mildly and moderately mentally retarded adults who had been placed in Projects With Industry or competitive employment. Behaviors that could be considered social, and which contributed to job terminations, included relations with peers and supervisors, inappropriate behaviors, absenteeism and tardiness, and poor motivation and attitude. In an extension of this study, Brickey, Campbell, and Browning (1985) identified other reasons given by employers for job termination. The social behaviors leading to job loss included hypochondria, gross insubordination and abusive behavior, and refusal to accept instructions.

In a recent study, Ford, Dineen, and Hall (1984) investigated the long-term job maintenance problems among the graduates from the Employment Training Program at the University of Washington. According to the job-loss records examined, social life skills accounted for 42% of all job losses. In particular, poor social interactions with employers and/or co-workers (12%), emotional outbursts (6%), and inappropriate language (3%) contributed to job terminations.

Summary

Although past research efforts have yielded little information regarding valued social behaviors in competitive employment settings, it has provided information regarding some social behaviors that are not valued. Essentially, the results from the Rusch et al. (1982) study suggest that employers want their workers:

1) to be able to communicate at least their basic needs (especially by verbal means), 2) to be compliant, 3) not to disrupt the work setting, and 4) to follow directions. Similarly, Salzberg et al. (1985) found that following directions, asking for assistance, and responding to criticism were important behaviors. Consistent with these findings, lack of several of the same behaviors was cited as a reason for job loss, that is, individuals lost their jobs for being noncompliant and for evidencing maladaptive or inappropriate behaviors. Thus, employers not only value compliance and appropriate behavior, they are likely to fire their employees for not displaying these behaviors.

Several other points are important when considering the research findings discussed above. First, all of the investigations used different systems for categorizing social behaviors. In addition, many of the categories were so broadly defined (e.g., peer relations) that they would not be useful for assessment or intervention purposes. These broad categorization systems underscore the general difficulty in the field of reaching a consensus on the definition of social skills. Unless there is some uniformity in the way social skills are defined and categorized, it will be difficult to make comparisons and generalizations between future research efforts (Martin, Rusch, Lagomarcino, & Chadsey-Rusch, in press).

Prior research efforts have also made no attempt to describe the continuum of social responses that would be acceptable in employment settings. For example, how many times can an employee talk to another co-worker while performing a job task before he or she is verbally reprimanded by a supervisor? (Supervisors may tolerate a certain amount of conversation between co-workers before reprimanding them.) Future research endeavors must begin to specify the continuum of responses that will be accepted (or tolerated) in employment settings before ecological incongruence results.

In the next section of this chapter, a framework is presented as a means to operationalize the concept of social skills. This framework is suggested as a beginning point to be able to more effectively assess and teach social skills in employment settings.

OPERATIONAL FRAMEWORK FOR CONCEPTUALIZING SOCIAL SKILLS

Most people agree that the primary goal of social skills training for persons with mental retardation is that they be viewed by employers and co-workers as socially competent. Borrowing from the work of McFall (1982), a distinction can be made between the terms *social competence* and *social skill*. According to McFall, "competence is a general evaluative term that refers to the quality or adequacy of a person's overall performance in a particular task" (p. 12). Thus, in order to be viewed as socially competent, a person does not have to exhibit exceptional social performance, only adequate social performance. Social skills, on the other hand, refer to more specific behaviors needed to perform a task competently. Before the issue of social skills can be addressed further, however, it is necessary to discuss the framework in which social competence is judged (McFall, 1982).

Framework for Social Competence

In discussing social competence, McFall (1982) stressed several factors that can influence the evaluation of social competence. First, since it is a general evaluative term, social competence reflects someone's judgment of performance according to a particular criterion—competence does not reside in performance. Thus, when someone judges performance, his or her judgment is subject to error and bias. For example, unless explicit criteria are stipulated, one person may judge a given performance to be competent, while somebody else may judge the same performance as being incompetent. Second, judgments of competence are made in relation to a specific task; if the conditions of the task change, the evaluation of the performance may change accordingly. Third, the personal characteristics of the individual (e.g., age, sex, experience) may influence judgment. And lastly, a judgment of a person as being socially competent implies a certain degree of performance consistency within a task, that is, a consistent performance is maintained over time.

Identifying Social Tasks According to McFall (1982), the most important component of the social competence framework is the task involved. The task serves as the unit with which to organize or chunk events. The best way to identify tasks is by answering the question, "What are you doing?" Thus, "washing dishes," "sweeping the floor," and "carrying out the garbage," are all examples of production-related tasks that exist in employment settings. Tasks must be easily observable and amenable to being broken down into subtasks by hierarchically analyzing their components. Conducting task analyses is not a new idea for personnel involved in providing services to individuals with mental retardation. What is new, and what has not been done extensively in the past, is to identify the social tasks that exist in employment settings, and to consider the variables that may affect the task analysis. As stated, only limited research has focused on the valued social tasks that exist in competitive employment settings (e.g., Rusch et al., 1982; Salzberg et al., 1985). Table 1 presents a partial list of valued social tasks generated from these studies. Table 2 illustrates a possible task analysis of the social task, "having a conversation."

Variables that Affect Task Analysis Conducting an analysis of a social task involves more than breaking the task down into individual components. Other features may influence the task, such as the purpose of the task, task constraints, setting, the rules governing task performance, criteria associated with

Table 1.   Social tasks that may exist in employment settings

Asking for assistance
Responding to criticism
Following directions
Having a conversation
Offering to help co-workers
Providing information about the job
Using social amenities
Extending greetings
Giving positive comments

Table 2.   Analysis of social task, "having a conversation with co-workers"

Initiating a topic
↓
Listening to co-workers
↓
Asking a question
↓
Listening to co-workers
↓
Answering a question
↓
Exiting the conversation

successful and unsuccessful performance, and the relationship between the task and other aspects of the individual's life (McFall, 1982). Consider the example of the social task, "extending greetings." The need to extend greetings occurs frequently in most employment situations. Although the purpose of extending greetings may vary, probably the primary purpose of greeting others is to acknowledge their presence or to recognize that they exist. Constraints that may be placed upon greeting others might include how well two people know each other or how long it has been since they last saw each other. For example, when we enter a work place in the morning, we are likely to greet our co-workers with "Hi. How are you?" Yet, if we were to come across one of the same co-workers a short time later (e.g., 2 minutes) and were to extend the same greeting, our performance would probably not be judged as very competent. In this situation, a brief smile would probably be the greeting of choice. Thus, task analysis must take into consideration constraints that may be placed upon a task.

The setting is another factor to consider when analyzing social tasks. Behavior judged as being competent in one setting, may be viewed as incompetent elsewhere, even though it may be performed in the same manner. For example, while it is appropriate to say, "Hi. How are you?" to others in the work place, it is inappropriate to extend the same greeting to everyone encountered in a shopping mall. Similarly, it may be appropriate to shout and yell at a football game, but it is not appropriate to engage in the same behavior in most churches. According to McFall (1982), setting accounts for a major portion of the variance found in evaluations of social performance.

All social tasks are governed by sets of social

rules. Although most individuals understand and follow social rules, it is often difficult to articulate them. Social rules imply the ability to evaluate the rightness and wrongness of social behavior—applied to the previous example, the right and wrong way to extend greetings. McFall (1982) considered the study of social behavior, in part, to be an attempt to identify and build formal models based upon social rules.

For social behavior to be judged as competent, it is important to know the criteria that separates an adequate task performance from an inadequate performance. In many instances, there may be more than one way to successfully accomplish a specific task. That is, as mentioned, a continuum of responses may be judged as being acceptable before ecological incongruence occurs. In the previous case of extending greetings, verbal greetings (e.g., saying hello) will probably be judged as being the most competent behavior. However, nonverbal behavior (e.g., smiling) can also be considered a competent way of performing the task. Thus, while there may be more than one way to accomplish a social task, it is important to know the criteria that distinguish competent from incompetent performance.

Lastly, the social task should always be considered from a systems perspective; that is, it is important to determine how the performance of a given task relates to other aspects of the individual's life. For example, if an individual greets co-workers appropriately at work, does that also mean that he or she will greet others in a different setting in equally appropriate ways? Similarly, should the type of greetings extended to others change with time? Considering how a task fits into other aspects of the individual's life constitutes an important part of studying social behaviors from an ecobehavioral perspective.

In summary, there are a number of variables that must be considered when analyzing a social task. These variables include the purpose of the task, task constraints, the setting in which the task occurs, the social rules governing task performance, criteria associated with successful and unsuccessful performance, and the relationship between the task and other aspects of the individual's life.

Assessing Social Competence Assessing social competence involves a series of steps. First, all social tasks that are critical and relevant (McFall, 1982) to the individual need to be identified. Critical and relevant tasks are those tasks that have been associated with successful job placement and maintenance, or are those tasks that are likely to lead to job loss when they are not performed in a competent manner. Critical social tasks can be identified by directly observing the employment settings and the behaviors of others (e.g., co-workers), or by soliciting the opinions of others via surveys or interviews (e.g., Rusch et al., 1982).

Once identified, critical and relevant social tasks must be task analyzed into components with consideration given to: purpose of the task, constraints, setting, rules, criteria, and congruence with the person's life system. As McFall (1982) suggested, tasks can be analyzed independent of the individual, whereupon the individual can be studied in relationship to task components. This procedure precludes the necessity of analyzing social tasks for every person. It is highly likely that many, but not all, social tasks identified in one employment setting may also be relevant in other employment settings. One major training goal is that instruction on one set of tasks generalizes to other employment settings in which the same set of social tasks exists.

When social tasks have been identified and analyzed, the individual is assessed in relation to the tasks within the natural environment. If a natural environment assessment is difficult, significant others in the employment setting (e.g., co-workers, supervisors) may be asked to judge the individual's usual performance on a task, or performance may be assessed via role play vignettes in analogue settings. Finally, performance samples must be evaluated against specific criteria for competent performance.

Summary One of the primary goals of social skills training is that the individual receiving training be judged as socially competent by significant others (e.g., co-workers and supervisors). Being viewed as socially competent does not mean that an individual displays exceptional social performance—only *adequate* social performance. Since social competence is a general evaluative term, judgment of such behavior is open to error and bias. In order to make judgments regarding social competence, performance is always judged against certain criteria on a particular task. The unit of measurement used to chunk or organize events is the social task. Social tasks can be identified by answering the question, "What are you doing?"

Although few social tasks have been identified and validated in the competitive employment training literature, social validation procedures (Wolf, 1978) may represent one valid method of identifying critical and relevant tasks (Chapter 16). Once relevant social tasks have been identified, they can be analyzed into components with considerations given to purpose of the task, constraints, setting, rules, and congruence with the person's life system. Finally, the individual's competence on the targeted tasks can be assessed according to explicit criteria associated with competent performance.

Conceptualizing Social Skills

As indicated, McFall (1982) distinguished between social competence and social skills. Whereas social competence is defined as the adequacy of performance on a social task, social skills are defined as more specific behaviors—specific abilities needed to perform competently on a particular social task. Table 3 presents an adaptation of McFall's (1982) model of social skills. As illustrated, when presented with a social task, an individual must engage in three types of social skills: 1) social decoding skills, 2) social decision skills, and 3) social performance skills.

Social Decoding Skills When presented with a social task, an individual must first perceive and interpret the task requirements. That is, he or she must be able to: 1) understand people and the environemnt, 2) interpret the nonverbal behavior of others, and 3) discriminate and interpret important cues (e.g., social rules) in social contexts. Social decoding skills include many of the behaviors referred to in

Table 3. Social skills model

Social cue decoding skills
Shows an understanding of people and environments
Perceives and interprets the nonverbal and verbal behavior of others
Discriminates and interprets cues (and rules) in social contexts

Social decision skills
Searches for possible responses that would meet requirements of social task
Selects appropriate response from own repertoire

Social performance skills
Delivers effective social response
Self-monitors (evaluates) own behavior
Benefits from feedback to facilitate future response selection and delivery

Adapted from McFall (1982).

Greenspan's (1981) conceptualization of social awareness, for example, being able to assume the role of others, being able to read social situations accurately, and being able to understand and evaluate social events. As Greenspan and Shoultz (1981) discovered, the majority of adults with mental retardation were fired from their jobs for lack of appropriate social awareness behaviors—that is, they were judged, in part, as being socially incompetent due to an inability to correctly decode social situations (e.g., walking into a meeting and talking about a TV program). However, even if an individual interprets a social task correctly, he or she may not necessarily be judged as socially competent. Rather, a judgment of social incompetence may be incurred if the individual had difficulties with social decision or performance skills.

Social Decision Skills After having interpreted the demands of a given social task, individuals must be able to use social decision skills to search for responses that would meet the requirements of the social task, and, from such a list of responses, decide upon the most appropriate response(s). To succeed in these efforts, the individual must have the ability to decide upon effective ways of accomplishing a social task and to evaluate the effectiveness of each possible solution or response. For example, if criticized on the job, employees could react in several ways: they could get mad and say they quit; they could start crying; they could fail to respond; they could say they understand and that they will try to do a better job in the future; or they could blame someone else for their poor performance. Recognizing these response alternatives and deciding which response would be the most appropriate for meeting the demands of a particular social task exemplifies successful use of social decision skills.

Social Performance Skills   After deciding upon the appropriate response, the individual must use social performance skills to effectively deliver the chosen response and judge whether or not it appropriately met the demands of the social task. For example, during a conversation, asking a question is a good way of showing interest in what another person has to say. However, some questions are more appropriate than others. For example, in most instances, it would be inappropriate to ask a person who was just introduced how much money he or she made. Thus, future response selection (in this case, directing questions to a newly met person) will be modified based upon the feedback encountered in a previous, but similar, situation. As McFall (1982) pointed out, this self-monitoring strategy actually initiates the need to use social decoding skills again.

Assessing Social Skills   Before social skills can be assessed, the social task must be thoroughly analyzed in order to identify a socially competent performance. Subsequently, the individual's performance on the social task must be established. If performance is judged to be incompetent, it becomes necessary to determine whether the incompetent performance is due to difficulties related to social decoding skills, social decision skills, social performance skills, or some combination thereof. McFall (1982) suggested several assessment procedures. For example, in order to assess social performance skills, the individual could be presented with a social task in which the decoding and decision steps had already been carried out so that he or she only had to complete the performance step. Similarly, in assessing social decision skills, the individual could be presented with a task in which he or she was asked to generate a list of solutions to the problem.

No currently available measurement device exists that will aid in assessment of social skills. Consequently, direct service providers must construct criterion-referenced instruments as needed. The previous discussion on assessment of social competence is germane to the assessment of social skills. Assessment devices need to be constructed based upon the critical social tasks identified in employment settings. Although social performance skills can most likely be assessed in the natural environment, the assessment of social decoding and decision skills may require the use of role play.

Summary   Social skills are those specific behaviors that are necessary to perform competently on a particular social task. Social decoding, decision, and performance skills are suggested as three important specific behaviors that, when performed, lead to favorable social judgments. This conceptualization of social skills represents only a beginning. Extensive research is needed to arrive at definitional refinements as well as appropriate ways to assess and teach each skill.

INTERVENTION STRATEGIES

Social incompetence (or ecological incongruence) can be viewed as a mismatch between a person's abilities and the demands of the task (McFall, 1982). The focus of this chapter has primarily been on increasing an individual's ability to perform competently on a social task. In some cases, however, it may be more appropriate to change the task demands than the person's abilities. For example, if an employer requires that employees be able to verbally indicate when they have run out of materials, he or she may be persuaded to accept the same communication nonverbally (e.g., by pointing to a picture in a communication book that indicates that more materials are needed). In this case, the demands of the social task (requesting more materials verbally) are altered rather than the person's abilities.

In the area of social skills training, intervention research has focused primarily on strategies designed to alter a person's social abilities rather than altering the demands of the environment. A line of research has investigated strategies to decrease inappropriate social behaviors (e.g., Dwinell & Connis, 1979; Rusch, Weithers, Menchetti, & Schutz, 1980; Schutz, Rusch, & Lamson, 1979). The focus of the following section, however, is on a body of research that has studied intervention strategies designed to increase the social competence abilities in persons with mental retardation required for jobs in competitive employment settings.

Most investigations of strategies for increasing social competence in persons with mental retardation have used social skills training packages, typically consisting of some combination of the following components: 1) a rationale as to why a given social behavior is desirable, 2) an opportunity to observe examples of the behavior (i.e, modeling), 3) an opportunity to practice the behavior, usually in role play situations, and 4) feedback regarding performance. Although most studies have employed these packages in analogue settings, several researchers have trained and taken measures of the social behavior in the natural environment.

Kelly, Wildman, and Berler (1980) used a social skills training package to improve the job interview skills repertoire of four adolescents with mild retardation. Rather than applying the social skills training package to individual trainees, the package was applied to the group across behaviors in a multiple-baseline design. Immediately after a 45-minute training session, individual members of the group participated in a mock interview. Social validation techniques were used to construct the mock interviews (i.e., role plays) and to judge the training effects. Results of the study demonstrated that a group social skills package was effective for increasing the frequency of job interview behaviors. In addition, these behaviors generalized to an *in vivo* job interview at a fast food restaurant and were judged by a panel of employers as being improved after training.

In a similar investigation, Hall, Sheldon-Wildgen, and Sherman (1980) used a social skills training package (plus a token economy) to teach six adults with mild and moderate retardation office and interview skills, and skills needed to fill out a job application form. All training sessions were conducted in a group home. Once criteria on the skills were met, performance was found to generalize to a different office, application form, and interviewer.

Rusch and Menchetti (1981) used portions of a social skills training package to teach compliance to directions to a male with moderate mental retardation employed as a kitchen laborer. After receiving instructions on how to follow directions, the employee was allowed time to practice those behaviors prior to his work shift. He was also told that if he did not comply during the day, his shift supervisor would send him home. Data were collected by asking a supervisor, kitchen laborer, and a cook questions about the employee's compliance throughout the day. Results indicated that instructions, practice, and a warning were sufficient to increase compliance across coworkers and supervisors. Generalized treatment effects were also noted from supervisors and professional kitchen laborers to a third nontreated group, cooks.

In a recent investigation, Chadsey-Rusch, Karlan, Riva, and Rusch (1984) used a social skills training package plus prompts to increase the frequency of question asking during conversation. Participants in the study were three adults with moderate mental retardation who were receiving training as kitchen laborers in a competitive employment site. All training and performance took place in an analogue setting; no generalization measures were taken in the natural environment.

Three social tasks (handling criticism, taking a joke or sarcastic remark, and soliciting assistance) were taught to an employee with moderate mental retardation by using modeling, role plays, and feedback (Shafer, Brooke, & Wehman, 1985). In this investigation, systematic procedures based on the work by Goldfried and D'Zurilla (1969) and Bates (1980) were used to construct the role plays. The procedures consisted of: 1) conducting a situation analysis to determine the critical and relevant social tasks and problematic situations associated with those tasks, 2) identifying appropriate responses to the situations, and 3) rating the effectiveness of the responses. Performance measures were probes taken on a series of six role plays developed for each social task prior to training. All training sessions were conducted in an analogue setting. Results from the study showed increased mean effectiveness scores on the role plays along with generalization to untrained role play scenes. In addition, generalization to the natural environment was also probed by having the employee's supervisor set up situations that called for use of the social behaviors being trained. Partial generalization to the natural environment was found.

Elements of a social skills training package were used in a study by Karlan and Rusch (1982) to investigate the realtionship between acknowledgment and compliance. In this study, a combination of rationale, modeling, verbal prompts, and tokens were used in training two kitchen employees with moderate mental retardation. All training and performance occurred in the natural environment. Results showed that verbal prompts to acknowledge receipt of an instruction increased compliance, but negatively affected acknowledgment. Use of token points resulted in increases in the acknowledgment of instruction for both employees, greatly increased compliance with one employee, but only slightly for the other.

Two studies reviewed used no social skills training packages. Instead, one study used a combination of techniques to teach a break time sequence of social behaviors to four high school students with autism. Breen, Haring, Pitts-Conway, and Gaylord-Ross (1984) used nonhandicapped high school students as training co-workers during a simulated break time; in addition, generalization effects to an *in vivo* break time with natural co-workers were also measured. During the simulated break time, the task-analyzed sequence of social behaviors was taught using instructional assistance along with massed practice for steps that were difficult to learn. Once the sequence was learned, generalization to a natural co-worker was

measured. If generalization did not occur, a second peer was used as a training co-worker until generalization effects were demonstrated. All four youths learned the social skill sequences and achieved generalization to natural co-workers. Interestingly, the natural co-workers were not coached to respond in any specific manner to the youths' social initiations. The majority of responses emitted by the natural co-workers to the youths with autism were positive, but passive.

Finally, Stanford and Wehman (1982) used verbal prompts and reinforcement to successfully increase the social interactions of two employees with moderate mental retardation with their nonhandicapped co-workers during lunch. Stanford and Wehman also coached the nonhandicapped workers to be receptive to the initiations from the employees with mental retardation. All training and performance occurred in the natural environment.

Relationship between Intervention Strategies and Social Competence

A comparison of the preceding intervention strategies to the social competence framework proposed by McFall (1982) leads to the following conclusions. First, all studies pinpointed social tasks except for Chadsey-Rusch et al. (1984), who trained a social task component (i.e., question asking), and Stanford and Wehman (1982), whose descriptions of the targeted behavior (i.e., social interactions) were extremely broad. Second, little information was given about the hierarchical analysis of the task except for the studies by Hall et al. (1980), Kelly et al. (1980), Breen et al. (1984), and Rusch and Menchetti (1981). However, even in these studies, the social task was only analyzed to one level. It probably is unnecessary (and too time consuming) to analyze social tasks into nth components. McFall (1982) stated that task units such as "blinking an eye" or "lifting a finger" are too microscopic the majority of the time to be considered very important. Further research is needed to identify the level of task analysis necessary to be useful for training.

Third, few of the studies reviewed here described other variables that could affect competent performance on a social task, such as the purpose of the task, task constraints, setting, the rules governing task performance, criteria associated with successful and unsuccessful performance, and the relationship between the task and other aspects of the individual's life. No available empirical evidence suggests that a careful analysis of social tasks along these dimensions would contribute to training effects and generalization. Yet, ecological analyses such as these have been recommended in the past as important assessment components for other tasks (e.g., Falvey, Brown, Lyon, Baumgart, & Schroeder, 1981; Ford & Mirenda, 1984).

Fourth, except for Kelly et al. (1980) and Chadsey-Rusch et al. (1984), no measures were given regarding the judgment of social performance by significant others. Although objective measures are criticial for validating effects, subjective measures are also important for socially validating effects. For example, consider the Rusch et al. (1982) study designed to reduce topic repetition. Even though Rusch et al. (1982) found a reliable decrease in the frequency of topic repetitions after training, subjective measures from co-workers revealed that they believed that topic repetitions had not declined as a result of training. Many variables (e.g., psychometric) may have affected this relationship, hence the need for further research in this area. However, the ultimate judgment of social competence in employment settings is that given by supervisors, co-workers, and consumers.

Relationship between Intervention Strategies and Social Skills

The intervention studies reviewed focused primarily upon teaching social performance skills; few studies focused upon teaching social decoding or decision skills. However, those studies that included a rationale and modeling component (e.g., Chadsey-Rusch et al., 1984) and socially validated their role play assessments in order to determine a continuum of competent responses (Shafer et al., 1985) may inadvertently have been training social decoding and decision behaviors.

In spite of the focus on social performance skills, no study addressed the role of self-monitoring on acquisition and generalization of behaviors. As discussed previously, self-monitoring constitutes an important part of social performace skills by allowing the individual to judge the effectiveness of his or her response to determine the future response selection. Teaching of self-monitoring and other self-control strategies has been recommended in order to promote generalization and independent behavior (Gifford, Rusch, Martin, & White, 1984; Chapter 10, this text). Further research is needed in this area to validate the importance of self-monitoring behaviors in relation to social competence. Research is also needed to determine reliable procedures for assessing and teaching these behaviors.

Summary

The intervention strategies described in this section have proven successful for teaching a variety of social tasks to individuals with mental retardation in competitive employment settings. In particular, social skills training packages have been found to be effective with employees with mild and moderate mental retardation. These packages may also prove successful with individuals having more severe mental retardation, especially when combined with other training techniques, such as those used by Breen et al. (1984).

In addition to noted training effects, nearly all studies probed for generalization effects in the natural environment. Although not as pronounced as direct training effects, generalization was often seen to occur. These results are encouraging, because some social tasks (e.g., handling criticism) will be difficult to train in the natural setting, and therefore require training in simulated settings using role plays as exemplars. If training is not conducted in the natural environment, generalization measures must be taken, and found, in the natural environment.

A number of investigations used supervisors, co-workers, or peers in training and data collection. It is highly probable that these indidviduals will play an important role in the development of social competence of employees with mental retardation in the future.

SUMMARY AND FUTURE RESEARCH ISSUES

Past research has clearly demonstrated a relationship between effective social skills and job acquisition and maintenance. Many employees with mental retardation have lost their jobs due to social incompetence, and in the few studies available, employers have consistently rated social behaviors as being important on the job. Even though social behaviors are important in job situations, little agreement exists on how to define, measure, assess, and teach social skills. In this chapter, an operational framework for conceptualizing social skills based on the work of McFall (1982) is presented. McFall distinguished between social competence and social skills, stating that social competence is a general evaluative term that refers to the adequacy of performance on a particular social task, whereas social skills are specific behaviors needed to perform competently on a task. A framework for social competence is presented, including a description of the social task and the variables that may influence it. Social decoding, decision, and performance skills are described as behaviors that may contribute to social competence. Finally, studies in which social behaviors were taught to employees with mental retardation in employment settings are reviewed.

A variety of research issues in this area need to be addressed. Foremost among these is the need to validate the framework of social competence and social skills suggested by McFall (1982). Currently, little is known about the importance or the usefulness of the components described. For example, the important social tasks that exist in employment settings must be identified and adequately described. Social tasks need to be described in relation to specific jobs, generalities across jobs, and variables (e.g, setting, criteria) that may affect them.

More research is also needed in the area of intervention strategies. For example, if training must be conducted in analogue settings under simulated conditions, what can be done to ensure generalization to the natural environment? If general case programming (e.g., Horner & McDonald, 1982) is applied to the construction of role plays, is generalization more likely to occur? If positive social behaviors are taught, will the frequency of negative social behaviors decrease? What kinds of intervention techniques can be used to change the demands of the social task, rather than the abilities of the individual? How can co-workers and supervisors be more effectively used in training situations? If these individuals are used, how will their training involvement affect their future interactions and attitudes toward workers with mental retardation?

Finally, how will social skills training affect people with mental retardation themselves? If they are not at risk for losing their jobs because of inappropriate social behaviors, should they receive social skills training anyway? Should we change the social skills of someone who just seems to be naturally shy? Will this make him or her happier? Will social skills training enable individuals with mental retardation to have more friends and support on the job? How can we be assured that social skills training will result in mutually reinforcing interactions between handicapped and nonhandicapped persons? These and other questions suggest the magnitude of the research that remains to be conducted in the area of social skills training for persons with mental retardation employed in competitive work settings.

REFERENCES

Baer, D. M., Wolf, M. M., & Risley, T. R. (1968). Some current dimensions of applied behavior analysis. *Journal of Applied Behavior Analysis, 1,* 91–97.

Barker, R. G. (1968). *Ecological psychology.* Stanford, CA: Stanford University Press.

Bates, P. (1980). The effectiveness of interpersonal skills training on the social skill acquisition of moderately and mildly retarded adults. *Journal of Applied Behavior Analysis, 13,* 237–248.

Breen, C., Haring, T., Pitts-Conway, V., & Gaylord-

Ross, R. (1984). The training and generalization of social interaction during breaktime at two job sites in the natural environment. In R. Gaylord-Ross, T. Haring, C. Breen, M. Lee, V. Pitts-Conway, & D. Roger (Eds.), *The social development of handicapped students*. San Francisco. San Francisco State University.

Brickey, M., Browning, L., & Campbell, K. (1982). Vocational histories of sheltered workshop employees placed in Projects With Industry and competitive jobs. *Mental Retardation, 20,* 52–57.

Brickey, M. P., Campbell, K. M., & Browning, L. J. (1985). A five-year follow-up of sheltered workshop employees placed in competitive jobs. *Mental Retardation, 23,* 67–83.

Brown, L., Pumpian, I., Baumgart, D., VanDeventer, P., Ford, A., Nisbet, J., Schneider, J., & Gruenwald, L. (1981). Longitudinal transition plans in programs for severely handicapped students. *Exceptional Children, 47,* 624–630.

Chadsey-Rusch, J. C. (1985). Community integration and mental retardation: The ecobehavioral approach to service provision and assessment. In R. H. Bruininks & K. C. Lakin (Eds.), *Living and learning in the least restrictive environment* (pp. 245–260). Baltimore: Paul H. Brookes.

Chadsey-Rusch, J., Karlan, G. R., Riva, M., & Rusch, F. R. (1984). Competitive employment: Teaching conversation skills to adults who are mentally retarded. *Mental Retardation, 22,* 218–225.

Chadsey-Rusch, J., & Rusch, F. R. (in press). Habilitation programs for mentally retarded persons with severe behavior problems. In R. P. Barrett (Ed.), *Treatment of severe behavior disorders: Contemporary approaches with the mentally retarded*. New York: Plenum.

Cheney, D., & Foss, G. (1984). An examination of the social behavior of mentally retarded workers. *Education and Training of the Mentally Retarded, 19,* 216–221.

Dwinell, M. A., & Connis, R. T. (1979). Reducing inappropriate verbalizations of a retarded adult. *American Journal of Mental Deficiency, 84,* 87–92.

Falvey, M., Brown, L., Lyon, S., Baumgart, D., & Schroeder, J. (1981). Strategies for using cues and correction procedures. In W. Sailor, B. Wilcox, & L. Brown (Eds.), *Methods of instruction for severely handicapped students* (pp. 109–133). Baltimore: Paul H. Brookes.

Ford, A., & Mirenda, P. (1984). Community instruction: A natural cues and corrections decision model. *Journal of the Association for Persons with Severe Handicaps, 9,* 79–88.

Ford, L., Dineen, J., & Hall, J. (1984). Is there life after placement? *Education and Training of the Mentally Retarded, 19,* 291–296.

Foss, G., & Peterson, S. L. (1981). Social-interpersonal skills relevant to job tenure for mentally retarded adults. *Mental Retardation, 19*(3), 103–106.

Gifford, J. L., Rusch, F. R., Martin, J. E., & White, D. M. (1984). Autonomy and adaptability in work behavior of retarded clients. In N. Ellis & N. Bray (Eds.), *International review of research on mental retardation* (Vol. 12, pp. 285–318). New York: Academic Press.

Gold, M. W. (1975). Vocational training. In J. Wortis (Ed.), *Mental retardation and developmental disabilities: An Annual Review* (Vol. 7, pp. 254–264). New York: Brunner/Mazel.

Goldfried, M. R., & D'Zurilla, J. J. (1969). A behavior-analytic model for assessing competence. In C. D. Spielberger (Ed.), *Current topics in clinical and community psychology* (Vol. 1, pp. 151–196). New York: Academic Press.

Greenspan, S. (1981). Defining childhood social competence: A proposed working model. In B. Keogh (Ed.), *Advances in special education* (Vol. 3, pp. 1–39). Greenwich, CT: JAI Press.

Greenspan, S., & Shoultz, B. (1981). Why mentally retarded adults lose their jobs: Social incompetence as a factor in work adjustment. *Applied Research in Mental Retardation, 2,* 23–38.

Hall, C., Sheldon-Wildgen, J., & Sherman, J. A. (1980). Teaching job interview skills to retarded clients. *Journal of Applied Behavior Analysis, 13,* 433–442.

Horner, R. H., & McDonald, R. S. (1982). Comparison of single instance and general case instruction in teaching a generalized vocation skill. *Journal of The Association for the Severely Handicapped, 7*(3), 7–20.

Karlan, G. R., & Rusch, F. R. (1982). Analyzing the relationship between acknowledgement and compliance in a non-sheltered work setting. *Education and Training of the Mentally Retarded, 17,* 202–208.

Kelly, J. A. (1982). *Social-skills training: A practical guide for interventions*. New York: Springer.

Kelly, J. A., Wildman, B. G., & Berler, E. S. (1980). Small group behavioral training to improve the job interview skills repertoire of mildly retarded adolescents. *Journal of Applied Behavior Analysis, 13,* 461–471.

Kochany, L., & Keller, J. (1981). An analysis and evaluation of the failures of severely disabled individuals in competitive employment. In P. Wehman, *Competitive employment: New horizons for severely disabled individuals* (pp. 181–198). Baltimore: Paul H. Brookes.

LaGreca, A. M., Stone, W. L., & Bell, C. R. (1982). Assessing the problematic interpersonal skills of mentally retarded individuals in a vocational setting. *Applied Research in Mental Retardation, 3,* 37–53.

Martin, J. E., Rusch, F. R., Lagomarcino, T., & Chadsey-Rusch, J. (in press). Comparison between workers who are nonhandicapped and mentally retarded: Why they lose their jobs. *Applied Research in Mental Retardation*.

McFall, R. M. (1982). A review and reformulation of the concept of social skills. *Behavioral Assessment, 4,* 1–33.

Mithaug, D. E., & Hagmeier, L. D. (1978). The development of procedures to assess pre-vocational competencies of severely handicapped young adults. *AAESPH Review, 3,* 94–115.

Rappaport, J. (1977). *Community psychology: Values, research and action*. New York: Holt, Rinehard, & Winston.

Rogers-Warren, A., & Warren, S. F. (1977). The developing ecobehavioral psychology. In A. Rogers-Warren & S. F. Warren (Eds.), *Ecological perspectives in behavior analysis* (pp. 3–8). Baltimore: University Park Press.

Rusch, F. R. (1979). Toward the validation of social/vocational survival skills. *Mental Retardation, 17,* 143–145.

Rusch, F. R., Chadsey, J., White, D., & Gifford, J. L. (1985). Programs for severely mentally retarded adults: Perspectives and methodologies. In D. Bricker &

J. Filler (Eds.), *Severe mental retardation: From theory to practice* (pp. 119–140). Lancaster, PA: Division on Mental Retardation of the Council for Exceptional Children.

Rusch, F., & Menchetti, B. M. (1981). Increasing compliant work behaviors in a non-sheltered work setting. *Mental Retardation, 19*(3), 107–111.

Rusch, F. R., Schutz, R. P., & Agran, M. (1982). Validating entry-level survival skills for service occupations: Implications for curriculum development. *Journal of The Association for the Severely Handicapped, 1*, 32–41.

Rusch, F. R., Weithers, J. A., Menchetti, B., & Schutz, R. P. (1980). Social validation of a program to reduce topic repetition in a non-sheltered setting. *Education and Training in Mental Retardation, 15*(3), 187–194.

Salzberg, C. L., Agran, M., & Lignugaris/Kraft, B. (1985). *Behaviors that contribute to entry-level employment: A profile of five jobs.* Manuscript submitted for publication.

Schalock, R. L., & Harper, R. S. (1978). Placement from community-based mental retardation programs: How well do clients do? *American Journal of Mental Deficiency, 83*, 240–247.

Schoggen, P. (1978). Ecological psychology and mental retardation. In G. P. Sackett (Ed.), *Observing behavior: Vol. 1. Theory and applications in mental retardation* (pp. 33–62). Baltimore: University Park Press.

Schutz, R. P., Rusch, F. R., & Lamson, D. S. (1979). Evaluation of an employer's procedure to eliminate unacceptable behavior on the job. *Community Services Forum, 1*, 4–5.

Shafer, M. S., Brooke, V., & Wehman, P. (1985). Developing appropriate social-interpersonal skills in a mentally retarded worker. In P. Wehman & J. W. Hill (Eds.), *Competitive employment for persons with mental retardation: From research to practice* (Vol. 1, pp. 358–375). Richmond, VA: Virginia Commonwealth University, Rehabilitation Research and Training Center.

Stanford, K., & Wehman, P. (1982). Improving the social interactions between moderately retarded and non-retarded coworkers: A pilot study. In P. Wehman & M. Hill (Eds.), *Vocational training and job placement of severely disabled persons* (pp. 141–158). Richmond, VA: Virginia Commonwealth University.

Thurman, S. K. (1977). Congruence of behavioral ecologies: A model for special education. *Journal of Special Education, 11*, 329–333.

Wehman, P. (1981). *Competitive employment: New horizons for severely disabled individuals.* Baltimroe: Paul H. Brookes.

Wehman, P., Hill, M., Goodall, P., Cleveland, V. B., & Pentecost, J. (1982). Job placements and follow-up of moderately and severely handicapped individuals after three years. *Journal of The Association for the Severely Handicapped, 7*, 5–15.

Will, M. (1984, March/April). Bridges from school to working life. *Programs for the Handicapped, 2*, 8–9.

Willems, E. P. (1977). Steps toward an ecobehavioral technology. In A. Rogers-Warren & S. F. Warren (Eds.), *Ecological perspectives in behavior analysis* (pp. 39–61). Baltimore: University Park Press.

Wolf, M. M. (1978). Social validity: The case for subjective measurement or how applied behavior analysis is finding its heart. *Journal of Applied Behavior Analysis, 11*, 203–214.

Chapter 21

Establishing a Parent-Professional Partnership to Facilitate Competitive Employment

Richard P. Schutz

MANY PARENTS OF children with severe disabilities are expressing resistance to recent programmatic changes reflecting a greater emphasis on the preparation of their son or daughter for entry into competitive job placements (Hill, Seyfarth, Orelove, Wehman, & Banks, 1985). While the specific reasons for their reluctance to support this new initiative are just beginning to be systematically studied, it is understandable given the conflicting advice parents have received from professionals over the past two decades. For example, 20 years ago, many of these same parents were being counseled to institutionalize their child. In recent years, parents have been advised to seek integrated public school services and community-based adult services. However, as recently as 1 year ago, the majority of educational and rehabilitation professionals were emphasizing the limitations of individuals with severe disabilities and were not preparing them for meaningful work within integrated employment settings. Even today, professionals, taken in total, continue to present confusing messages concerning appropriate service de-livery and design, reflecting the conflict between traditional and contemporary expectations for individuals with severe disabilities.

Another contributing factor to the current lack of parental support may be their unfamiliarity with the vocational program planning and delivery process. Typically, parents have not been involved with this process nor have professionals supplied adequate information regarding competitive employment preparation programs to parents. This situation is not particularly surprising, considering the previous lack of attention competitive job training for individuals with severe disabilities has received.

Although some professionals may consider parental input to be irrelevant to vocational program development, data are available that suggest employment programs will not be successful without parental support (e.g., Kochany & Keller, 1981). This chapter begins with a review of the effect parental involvement has upon vocational preparation programs. From this basis, issues and concerns regarding the parent-professional partnership

The development of this chapter was supported in part by the following: U.S. Department of Education Contract No. 300-85-0160; U.S. Department of Education Grant No. G-0084-01325; Illinois Department of Rehabilitation Services; Illinois Department of Mental Health and Developmental Disabilities; and the Illinois Governor's Planning Council on Developmental Disabilities. The opinions expressed herein do not necessarily reflect the position or policy of these agencies.

and general recommendations for improving the partnership are discussed. Finally, specific strategies for allying parents with program staff are presented.

EFFECT OF PARENTAL INVOLVEMENT

The primary obligation of any social service professional is the selection of a social unit to change as a means of solving a presenting problem (Haley, 1976). When the issue is vocational preparation, professionals may choose to intervene at a number of levels including the individual, the family system, a component of the family system such as parents, a larger social system like a school or community, or some combination of these units. Traditionally, professionals have chosen to concentrate on the individual with vocational training needs as the primary unit, either by intentional selection or through routine practice (cf. Rusch & Schutz, 1981; Rusch, Schutz, & Heal, 1983).

Contrary to this relatively narrow approach to vocational preparation, the importance of the broader concept of social support has been cited in numerous studies as a major factor in successful community adaptation (Edgerton, 1967; O'Connor, 1983; Sigelman, Novak, Heal, & Switzky, 1980). Specifically, a number of authors have pointed out the powerful influence the family exerts on the career attitudes and options of the member with a handicap (Darling, 1979; Kernan & Koegel, 1980; Kochany & Keller, 1981; Schneider, 1968). In a recent follow-up study, Hasazi, Gordon, and Roe (1985) indicated that over 80% of former special education students who were working obtained employment through a "self-family-friend" network.

Kernan and Koegel (1980) examined the effect of the family and delivery system support on the competitive employment status of 48 individuals labeled as mildly mentally retarded. Essentially, their analysis revealed the following:

1. Where there was an active and involved family or service delivery support system

impelling an individual toward competitive employment, the individual was likely to be competitively employed, or making his or her way up the employment ranks.
2. Where there was some encouragement from either the family or service delivery system but little active involvement, individuals were less likely to be successful in attaining employment, or took longer to do so.
3. Where family support was not intact and support potentially forthcoming from the delivery system failed to emerge, individuals were likely to remain in a sheltered workshop or not seek any kind of employment (Kernan & Koegel, 1980).

Kernan and Koegel (1980) found that those individuals who were not exposed to a family support system that stressed the value of competitive employment were far less active and successful in finding employment, regardless of the support received from a service provider.

The provision of aid and encouragement in the job-seeking process represents only one factor associated with the family's effect on an individual's involvement in competitive employment. Regardless of the degree and type of an individual's disability, the family operates as a mediating unit between the individual and society (Okun & Rappaport, 1980). As the primary unit of socialization, the family is the means through which social expectations are communicated to the individual. Consequently, the family can affect, either positively or negatively, such job-related areas as the individual's basic orientation toward work, job aspirations, and beliefs concerning what the world (i.e. government-sponsored programs in particular) owes a person (Kernan & Koegel, 1980).

Family members (i.e., specifically parental attitudes) may also strongly influence the outcomes of specific interventions (Edge, Strenecky, & McLaughlin, 1979; Ferrara, 1979; Goldstein, 1979; Walthal & Love, 1974) across a variety of programmatic areas ranging from recreational (Katz & Yekatiel, 1974) to work-oriented settings (Kernan & Koegel, 1980; Koegel, 1978; Nitzberg, 1974). The family can also convey messages to society regarding how to change policy or programs to accomodate the needs of individual family members (Dybwad, 1983). This has been demonstrated in such areas as parental activism in the movement toward free and appropriate public school services for all handicapped children.

Summary

From the above discussion, it should be obvious that parental input into the vocational preparation process is an influencial force for many individuals with special needs. Parents may, through positive feelings and support, encourage their child to participate fully in all aspects of a vocational preparation program. Conversely, parents who are not supportive of a program or who are overprotective may hinder their child's participation in vocational training opportunities.

ISSUES AND CONCERNS

Given the powerful influence parents may exert on the career preparation of their child, the parent-professional partnership may be viewed as one of the most critical elements in a vocational education or training program. Despite the importance of this partnership, communication between parents and professionals is often limited. Furthermore, when communication does exist, the parent-professional partnership may be less than productive. This section discusses such issues and concerns related to the parent-professional partnership as the status of parental involvement with programs, parental fears and doubts, psychological barriers to a partnership, and the lack of adequate preparation of parents and professionals to work cooperatively.

Status of Parental Involvement

Consumerism, in general, has been growing in recent years. As part of this larger social movement, parents of children with handicaps have become more involved in school-age programs, at least in the development of individual education plans. This increased involvement has been aided by legislation such as the Education for All Handicapped Children Act of 1975 (Public Law 94-142), and by a number of publications that instruct parents in organizing and advocacy techniques (e.g., Anderson, Chitwood, & Hayden, 1982; Biklen, 1974; Markel & Greenbaum, 1979). There has also been an increase in the awareness of professionals serving all age levels of persons with handicaps for the need of parental involvement in programmatic efforts; a perspective long held in preschool programs (Zigler & Valentine, 1979).

Despite the movement toward increased parental involvement, the data on the degree of parental involvement are not encouraging. For example, Stile, Cole, and Garner (1979) suggest there is evidence that attrition is often high in parental involvement programs. The data indicate a higher percentage of preschool parents are involved in programs than parents of elementary-age children, and the least parental involvement is at the secondary level. Attrition appears to be occurring at each level, becoming more pronounced as the child becomes older.

In addition to the attrition factor, data from several studies suggest parental attendance at program planning meetings cannot be equated with participation in decision making. A rather encouraging level of parental attendance at individualized education program (IEP) meetings has been reported, ranging from 66% to 83% (Goldstein, Strickland, Turnball, & Curry, 1980; Marver & David, 1978). However, an analysis of observational data collected during IEP conferences indicated the topic most addressed by parents was family life (e.g., sibling interactions) as opposed to topics such as educational goals, instructional objectives, and placement alternatives (Goldstein et al., 1980). Despite the assumption of a passive role in decision making, parents generally report an extremely high level of satisfaction with their input into the decision-making process (Lynch & Stein, 1982; Goldstein et al., 1980).

The issue of parental involvement is further clouded by our lack of knowledge regarding how participating parents differ from those who do not participate. However, most parental involvement programs do tend to be oriented toward the comparatively well-educated, middle to upper income family. For example, Hargis and Blechman (1979) surveyed the parent training literature and reported that lower socioeconomic status families have been underrepresented in the literature. In one study concerning parent participation (Baker, Clark, & Yasuda, 1981), a parent training program was offered to 74 families with a child diagnosed as moderately to severely mentally retarded; 24% joined the program. A comparison of participants with nonjoiners revealed that participants were already more involved in school activities and were better educated. According to Budoff (1979), minority and low income parents are usually less well educated, may have language problems, and probably conceive of the problems of their child differently than service providers. Consequently, it is unlikely that these parents would interact with or press service providers for the most appropriate programs, unless provided with considerable outside support (Budoff, 1979).

As indicated by the data on attrition, there is another group of parents who tend to be less involved with programmatic efforts. Many parents of adolescents and young adults with developmental disabilities, particularly those who never institutionalized their child, express that they are somewhat discouraged and disappointed. Their discouragement and disappointment comes, in part, from their observation of the emphasis that has been placed on preschool and elementary education. They realize these programs were not available for their child and, perhaps more importantly, now see children similar to their own functioning at a higher level and having greater potential because of the benefits of such programs. Many of these same parents spent years advocating for programs and conducting their own preschool and school programs in church basements or in private homes, with little professional as-

sistance. Now these parents are older and many state they are tired of the stress and time-consuming activities associated with interacting with professionals in order to obtain appropriate services for their child.

Parental Fears and Doubts

When parents do become involved with vocational programs, their lack of realism concerning their child's vocational potential becomes a frequent and vexing problem for vocational instructors and habilitation service personnel. Parents may either expect greater achievement from their child than professionals do or frequently parents are not willing to have their child take risks associated with community job placements. In the former case, parents may not support a vocational training program offering potential placements in entry-level jobs such as janitorial positions. In the latter case, parents may not believe their child can acquire and maintain competitive employment or fear their child would be exposed to abuse or embarrassment in a work situation.

The difficulty of being able to arrive at realistic expectations is often associated with parental concerns about the availability of services for their child after they leave school. Vocational training programs leading to competitive employment or supported employment placements (e.g., see Chapters 2 through 6) are relatively new and still unavailable in many communities. When such services are available in a local community, they frequently have waiting lists. In addition, many vocational training programs address a limited number of job types. In many communities, adequate space in sheltered workshops is also not available. These situations can create anxieties among parents that confuse their postschool expectations. Families and persons with developmental disabilities who do attempt to plan for vocational actualization beyond adolescence are often left with uncertainly and a limited range of career options. Add to this the narrow range of stereotypically available low status jobs for individuals with handicaps (Brolin & Gysbers,

1979), and the issue of career development becomes an esoteric abstraction for many families with children with severe disabilities, instead of a reality.

Another concern of many parents is the financial security of their offspring. Many young adults with severe disabilities are dependent upon public assistance, which may cause parents anxiety because of the tenuous nature of federal or state social assistance programs. Given the maze of regulations governing Supplemental Social Security Income (SSI) payments, many parents express concern about their child being disqualified. This concern, coupled with the possibility that a job placement may not work out over time, leads some parents to provide lukewarm, if any, support to competitive vocational training efforts.

As youth with severe disabilities leave the public school system, parents are confronted with a variety of issues in addition to those directly associated with vocational programs. Parents may face such questions as: 1) where will my child live; 2) who will supervise his or her leisure time; and 3) how will long-term financial support (e.g., wills and trusts) be arranged? Issues such as these may compound potential problems concerning parental support for vocational training.

In addition to anxiety aggravated by pressing issues conerning the future, parents of youth with severe disabilities often encounter impediments and postponements due to problems in the local service delivery system. Perhaps most disconcerting for these parents is the experience of losing the systematic provision of educational and related services sponsored through the public school. For many families, the loss of the school as the focus and monitor of their child's services is tantamount to falling into a void. The service void experienced by many parents is directly related to the fragmented and duplicative nature of the adult service system (Schalock, 1983). In addition to uncoordinated interagency efforts, Phelps and Thornton (1979) cited the failure of agencies to involve employers in their programmatic efforts as a major hindrance to the vocational training process.

Psychological Barriers to Effective Partnership

Relations between parents and professionals have been marred by conflict (Foster, Berger, & McLean, 1981). Often the root of such conflict appears to be related to psychological barriers. As discussed here, psychological barriers refer to the attitudes and perceptions of parents and professionals concerning a shared decision-making process. In regard to educational program development, psychological barriers have been reported for both groups.

Research conducted on the stress experienced by regular and special education teachers indicated that teachers rank interaction with parents as a major source of job stress (Bensky et al., 1980). A potential reason for this stress is the limited training teachers generally receive to prepare them to interact effectively with parents (Schuck, 1979). It is interesting to note that while teachers report feeling intimidated and stressed when working with parents, likewise, parents report similar feelings of intimidation and stress when working with teachers. Clearly, the psychological component of the parent-professional partnership can be a barrier to an effective working relationship.

A perceived "trainer-trainee" relationship between professionals and parents may also lead to conflict. Many professionals assume that parents know little or nothing about the educational needs of their child. For example, in a survey of over 1,500 planning team professionals, only two activities of a possible 24 were chosen as appropriate for parent involvement (Yoshida, Fenton, Kaufman, & Maxwell, 1978). A further indication of professional perspectives was provided by Morgan and Rhode (1980) in a survey of approximatey 300 special education teachers conducted in 1978 and again in 1980. The authors reported that teachers' attitudes ranged from ambivalent to negative regarding the value of parent participation in the educational planning process.

Some attempts to establish interactions between parents and professionals are doomed to failure from the start. For example, Turnbull

(1983) reported that a parent involvement program used the slogan, "Parents are Educable." Undoubtedly, it was not the intent of professionals to label parents as possessing IQs roughly between 55 and 70; however, it is understandable how parents could view this as an insult. In part, such a slogan points out the lack of understanding and empathy some professionals possess for parents. However, it also points to what many parents refer to as the superiority (professional)-inferiority (parent) status that they believe characterizes their interactions with professionals.

The attitudes and behaviors of parents have also contributed to negative interactions. For example, professionals have been excluded from community interest groups because it is felt that it is impossible for them to understand parental needs and feelings. Sometimes, parents form tight cliques with the primary goal of ostracizing and criticizing professionals (Turnbull, 1983). There have also been instances where, having fought for and eventually received appropriate services, parents continue intensive advocacy efforts focused on minor issues that lead to major confrontations (Turnbull, 1983).

Conflict in parent-professional relations may also arise from parental expectations regarding their role in educational programs. The results of several studies indicate that parents prefer to engage in informal information exchange as opposed to assuming an active educational decision-making role (Lusthaus, Lusthaus, & Gibbs, 1981; Nadler & Shore, 1980). If parents choose not to actively participate, professionals may view it as lack of commitment to the child. When professionals place demands on parents and expect them to become intensely involved in a child's program, parents may feel guilty or resentful. Parents may experience the feelings of guilt if they do not spend a great deal of time working with the child, or they may feel resentment because the "helping" professional is viewed as not helping enough.

Lack of Preparation to Participate

Expectations for effective parental-professional participation in programmatic decision making and vocational training efforts are meaningless if the two groups are not prepared to work cooperatively. To date, the preparation of professionals to work with parents as partners has not been a priority of preservice (Schuck, 1979) or inservice educational programs. While numerous efforts have focused on preparing teachers to provide training to parents in such areas as behavior management, there has been little emphasis on communicating with and engaging in joint decision making with parents.

There is an interesting distinction between an emphasis on professionals providing training to parents and professionals working collaboratively with parents. In the first case, professionals are placed in a superior role, and in the latter case, professionals and parents function in an equal role. The perceived status between these two roles has important implications for future professional preparation efforts. In general, there is an apparent need to move beyond the preparation of professionals to provide training and, instead, to focus efforts on improving communication skills and group decision-making strategies.

Deficits in parents' skills to effectively engage in cooperative efforts appear to be even more acute than those of professionals. For example, many parents either do not know or do not understand the educational entitlements contained in public laws (Budoff, 1979) and the service options available in a local community. This deficit in a knowledge base is compounded further because parents must often discover sources of information for themselves. Consequently, obtaining necessary information to participate in a partnership with professionals can be a time-consuming and frustrating experience for parents.

Active parental involvement with vocational training programs may also be hampered by a parent's lack of strategies for negotiating with professionals. Parents are often unfamiliar with the established procedures used in a public school or rehabilitation system, educational and rehabilitation terminology, and the application of legal and policy guidelines to the level of service provided. For parents who possess such knowledge, active participation may still be problematic due to the time and energy required.

Summary

The degree to which parents actively participate in their son or daughter's vocational preparation program will ultimately vary according to each individual parent's needs, desires, skills, or personal situation. However, the wise program administration will provide parents with opportunities to explore a diversity of roles and permission to participate to the degree they wish. Training and support services may also be offered so parents who wish to expand the scope of their participation can obtain the skills and confidence to do so.

Unfortunately, the reality is that parents of children with severe disabilities often encounter a pervasive skepticism about their potential contributions to programmatic efforts. Parents' interactions with a fragmented service delivery system may also further exacerbate their sense of being unwelcome. This may in turn lead to self-doubt and parents underrating their own abilities.

Of course, parents are not the only victims. Professionals who have not had opportunities to work *with* parents, as opposed to for or against them, also suffer. The balance of power between professionals and parents is beginning to change. Professionals who cling to their "turf" are missing out on an opportunity to join with parents who are learning to act on their own behalves.

Is rapprochement possible between parents and professionals? Certainly, neither group will ever totally share the other's experiences. However, as long as we are capable of empathy, change in the direction of greater mutual understanding and support appears to be possible.

FOUNDATIONS FOR PARTNERSHIP

Based upon the influence parents may exert on the vocational preparation of their child, the degree to which parents are currently participating in programmatic efforts, and the current barriers to parent participation, two recommendations for improving the parent-professional partnership are presented in this section. First, program administrators should consider the development, or revision, of a parent involvement policy that provides options for participation. Second, educational opportunities should be expanded for both professionals and parents.

Alternatives in Parental Involvement Policy

The transition from school to work and other facets of adult life often requires adjustments for the parents of a person with severe disabilities that may be as difficult as those required of the individual. As Mittler, Cheseldine, and McConachie (1980) have suggested, many families of handicapped adolescents have developed patterns of interaction and organization that promote stability and diminish disruptions to normal family activities. This homeostatic tendency of families may be severely stressed when parents are faced with the loss of the secure and regular schedule provided by school and confronted by decisions with lifelong implications in such areas as employment. These transitional issues, coupled with the influence parents exert on the vocational preparation of the child, suggest participation of and support for parents would be a critical component of vocational preparation programs.

The assertion that parents may assume an important role in vocational preparation programs does not infer that every parent should be expected to participate with equal intensity or at the same level. Expecting all parents to be equal participants establishes goals that many parents may fail to meet, frustrating parents and professionals alike. Consequently, secondary and adult vocational preparation programs should consider the development of a parental involvement policy that provides for options that can be adjusted to parents' needs, interests, abilities, preferences for involvement, and time availability. As Turnbull and Turnbull (1982) suggest, parents should have the opportunity not to be involved, to be involved at a passive level, or to be involved as a full and equal partner with professionals.

Six types of parental involvement to consider in the development or revision of a program's parental participation policy are presented in Table 1. The types of potential participation and the corresponding nature of the involvement should not be interpreted as strictly hierarchical or mutually exclusive in nature. For example, a parent may choose to have only minimal involvement with program staff, while actively participating in the counseling of other parents. The important point for professionals to consider is the development of a sufficient range of options for the parental involvement to adequately reflect parents' priorities and concerns.

While the development of a parental involvement policy that affords parents the opportunity to select the level and intensity of their participation is important, the manner in which a specific program's policy is developed may be equally important. Parental input should be utilized as much as possible in the development of the policy and the corresponding involvement alternatives. This manner of policy development should facilitate the establishment of a parent-professional partnership in which specific objectives can later be pursued in a cooperative fashion.

Development of Expanded Educational Opportunities

Both parents and professionals need to increase their knowledge and skills in such areas as collaboration and programmatic decision making if effective partnerships are to develop. Educational opportunities for both groups should focus on constructive communication techniques (e.g., listening, nonverbal communication, and assertiveness) and group decision-making skills (e.g., establishing agendas, planning, and reaching closure). Another priority topic for both groups is an awareness of the variety of social services available in any given community and how access to services is obtained.

The area of parent-professional collaboration should receive increased attention within professional preservice and inservice curricula. Instruction should focus on strategies for altering communication and involvement options to the preferences and skill levels of parents. Furthermore, most trainees in the human services professions are not parents, and demographic trends toward deferred childbearing increase the likelihood that young pro-

Table 1.   Types of parental involvement

Type	Nature of involvement
1. Passive receptivity	Parents consent to allow their child to participate in a vocational education or training program. Additional involvement would be limited to adherence to minimal program requirements for parental participation, such as attending mandatory Individual Education/Program Planning conferences.
2. Minimal involvement	Parental involvement is characterized by periodic discussions with professionals concerning the adolescent's program alternatives and/or progress. Communication may take such forms as parent group meetings, periodic telephone calls, and written monthly report exchanges.
3. Training program participant	Training programs for parents may take many forms (e.g., didactic and experiential). Similarly, topics addressed in programs might vary from constructive communication strategies and group decision-making skills to home-based intervention strategies.
4. Active planning team member	This type of involvement is characterized by parents and professionals working closely to select program goals, teaching selected skills, and evaluating program effectiveness.
5. Counselor of other parents	Parental participation is characterized by providing program information, emotional support, and encouragement to new families. Involvement may take such forms as individual contact with new families and coordinating a parent support group.
6. Advocate and policymaker	As an advocate, parents may become involved with identifying community needs, building alliances with other groups, identifying and responding to those who resist change, and taking action on issues through such forms as letter-writing campaigns. As policymakers, parents might assist in the formulation of agency and program policy and interpret policy to the community at large.

fessionals will have limited personal experience with parenting issues (Shonkoff, 1983). Consequently, there appears to be a critical need for a major teaching commitment in this area. Generally, service providers should be taught to focus their attention beyond the individual with vocational training needs, and to consider the needs of their families.

In addition to the topics cited as important for both groups, parent education programs might also focus on such topics as advocacy skills, training in relations with community service agencies, and techniques for enhancing the independence of their child. The specific content of a parent education program must be based upon the needs of individual families and provided at a level that is within the parents' capacity to respond. Professionals must not assume that they know what parents need in the way of information or training. Parental education is most effective if professionals and parents work cooperatively to determine needs, define and set priorities for goals, and plan activities to reach stated goals.

Summary

Parents and professionals have an opportunity to refine the process of parental involvement with vocational programmatic efforts. The future presents numerous opportunities for meaningful partnerships based on mutual support that could yield increased benefits for parents, professionals, and individuals with special vocational training needs.

ALLYING PARENTS WITH PROGRAM STAFF

The implementation of a parent involvement policy that provides options for participation and the expansion of educational opportunities for professionals and parents should enhance a partnership between the two groups. Beyond these foundations, however, programs may initiate additional strategies to ally parents with program staff. This section discusses several strategies related to parental information and awareness, collaborative planning efforts, and parents' potential support service needs.

Information and Awareness

The selection of vocational preparation goals for persons with developmental disabilities is a value-laden process of choosing among future vocational possibilities and identifying appropriate services for targeted employment placements. Consequently, a parent-professional partnership in such areas as collaborative planning and decision making occurs most effectively when there is mutual understanding of what is possible within the local labor market and immediate service delivery system.

Knowledge of the potential employment options in a local community allows parents to actively participate in the development of a systematic plan for their son's or daughter's job opportunities. To make informed choices, parents should be provided with information regarding such topics as: 1) the types of job opportunities that exist locally, 2) characteristics of these jobs (e.g., seasonal, part-time, job security, benefits, and required skills), 3) job training and other services that could affect employment success, and 4) the success of individuals with developmental disabilities in entering the local job market. In addition, professionals should provide parents with information concerning the effect of employment on support programs such as Supplementary Security Income.

The provision of information regarding vocational preparation programs will also assist parents in identifying options logically related to employment plans and possibilities. Generally, professionals should attempt to address parents' concerns centered on their unfamiliarity with the program in relation to their son's or daughter's safety, success, and future. Specific types of program-related information that might be communicated to parents include: 1) the goals and description of the program, 2) the relationship of tasks and jobs utilized in training to future employment options, 3) the manner in which individual vocational goals are selected, 4) staffing and supervision provided during training and after placement, and 5) the past success of the vocational program. The manner in which this information is provided to parents might include a parent handbook, individual and/or group parent meetings, and job training site visits.

Collaborative Planning

The primary vehicle available to parents for influencing the vocational preparation of their son or daughter is the individualized education program at the secondary level or the individualized program plan (IPP) at the postsecondary level. However, as discussed previously, parents tend to assume a passive role in the decision-making process. Furthermore, when professionals attempt to obtain information concerning the vocational development of the family member with a handicap, they may become easily sidetracked by other issues confronting the family or thoroughly confused by the family's communication pattern and organization. One strategy that may be utilized to alleviate these potential planning problems is a structured parent interview.

The parent interview is a strategy that can be used for maximizing parental input into the IEP or IPP, developing a parent-professional communication system, and identifying parent information and support needs. Structured parent interviews can be conducted to address such items as:

1. Parents' perceptions of general educational or training needs
2. Parents' perceptions of specific vocational preparation needs
3. The types and extent of participation in home and community activities
4. Delineation of high priority goals and objectives directly related to general and specific vocational training needs
5. Parents' perceptions of their child's future

6. Parental preferences for a system for maintaining ongoing contact with the professional
7. Parents' information and support needs related to advocating and caring for their child

Illustrative examples of questions related to individual vocational program planning are presented in Table 2. An example of another potential component—parental preferences for ongoing contact with professionals—of a structured interview is presented in Figure 1. The specific content of a structured parent interview will, in part, be dependent upon the location of the vocational preparation program (i.e., secondary school programs or adult service agency). Regardless of the program's location, the development of a structured parent interview should reflect the combined efforts of professionals and parents.

When flexibly applied, the structured parent interview process assists the professional to enter the family system while maintaining an outsider's sense of direction and purpose. As typically used, structured interviews are conducted with the parents of new or potential program participants and then updated on an annual basis. Generally, it is advantageous to schedule a meeting in advance, so both parents may participate in the interview and to conduct the interview at the parents' home. Care should also be taken to utilize the structured interview as a guide for the meeting, with interviewers rephrasing questions to use words they feel comfortable with and the parents will understand.

The structured parent interview strategy should not be viewed as a replacement for

Table 2. Parent interview: Sample vocationally related questions

1. What types of work settings would you like to see your son/daughter participating in?
2. Do you have any concerns regarding your son's/daughter's future vocational needs?
3. What are your preferences for your son's/daughter's occupation? Are there any activities from past vocational programs or work training experiences that you feel should be included in your son's/daughter's current program?
4. Are there any occupations that you object to your son/daughter participating in?
5. Are there any jobs in which your son/daughter is particularly interested, either at home (e.g., chores) or in the community?
6. Are there any jobs that are particularly aversive or unpleasant to him/her?

	Use		How often			
	Yes	No	Daily	Weekly	Monthly	Other (please specify)
a. Log book						
b. Informal phone contact						
c. Phone call night						
d. Newsletters						
e. Home visits						
f. School or program visits						
g. Parent inventory						
h. Other						

Figure 1. Structured parent interview: Assessment of parent/professional contact preferences.

parental participation in IEP or IPP meetings. However, when employed prior to such meetings, the structured parent interview can yield information valuable in the development of specific vocational training goals and objectives. Consequently, the structured parent interview should be seen as complementary to program planning meetings and a strategy to facilitate increased parental involvement in the planning and decision-making stages of programmatic efforts.

Support Services

Vocational preparation programs should consider the inclusion of support services for fam-

ilies. Frequently, professionals become so involved with the provision of services to the individual with vocational training needs that they fail to see potential needs of the family. Communicating an interest in the entire family is often crucial to the ongoing parent-professional partnership. However, care and encouragement are not always sufficient; parents also expect professionals to be well informed about other community services. Consequently, vocational program staff should be prepared to respond to information requests ranging from the availability of respite services to additional information on SSI.

It is not uncommon for some parents to

devote a great deal of time and resources to their child's program. For example, some parents attempt to reinforce work skills by assigning their son or daughter chores at home. Parents may also assist in locating a job placement for their child, serve on a vocational program's advisory board, or coordinate a program-related parent group. Participation in such activities may detract from other family involvements. Professionals should not only be cognizant of this potentiality, but endeavor to assist parents in achieving a balance between overall family needs and the needs of the child with a severe disability.

Generally, it is important for professionals to be aware of the local resources available to a family and to assess the extent to which a family can utilize them. Professionals and parents must also evaluate which parental needs cannot be met by existing resources. This procedure may extend the search for services, lead to the modification of current services, or stimulate the creation of new ones.

As suggested previously, the use of a structured parent interview strategy can facilitate the identification of parental support and information needs. A program may then address identified informational needs through such procedures as the development and distribution of a local service directory and individual or group meetings with parents. The development of a program-related parent group may also serve to provide parents with information and support.

Summary

Strategies for allying parents with professionals, such as those discussed in this section, are not particularly new. However, rarely are these types of strategies systematically utilized in vocational preparation programs. Nevertheless, the quality of parent-professional partnerships ultimately have impact on the success of individuals being prepared to enter competitive employment positions. Professionals should not expect parents to effectively participate in vocational programmatic efforts without the benefit of a firm knowledge base. In addition to addressing the informational needs of parents, professionals should endeavor to solicit the input of parents during the planning and implementation of vocational training programs. Finally, professionals must remember that the needs of parents, and families, may transcend those concerning the child with a severe disability, and attempt to assist in addressing these needs.

CONCLUSION

The parent-professional partnership is a crucial variable affecting the preparation of individuals with developmental disabilities for entry into competitive employment positions within a local community. Undoubtedly, it is important for both parents and vocational service providers to become more knowledgeable about each other's involvement in this relationship. Professionals will have to learn of the needs of the parents with sons or daughters with developmental disabilities. Parents, on the other hand, will have to become familiar with professionals' approaches to vocational service delivery and the advances in training and placement technology that can fruitfully be brought to bear on their child's needs. Moreover, both parents and professionals should approach the partnership with a sense of flexibility and a willingness to attempt alternative methods to reach a collaborative working relationship. A parent-professional partnership reflecting mutual understanding and support should enhance the benefits for both groups as well as for individuals with special vocational training needs.

REFERENCES

Anderson, W., Chitwood, S., & Hayden, D. (1982). *Negotiating the special education maze.* Englewood Cliffs, NJ: Prentice-Hall.

Baker, B., Clark, D., & Yasuda, P. (1981). Predictors of success in parent training. In P. Mittler (Ed.), *Frontiers of knowledge in mental retardation.* Baltimore: University Park Press.

Bensky, J., Shaw, S., Gouse, A., Bates, H., Dixon, B., &

Beane, W. (1980). Public Law 94-142 and stress: A problem for educators. *Exceptional Children, 47*(1), 24–29.

Biklen, D. (1974). *Let our children go: An organizing manual for advocates and parents.* Syracuse, NY: Human Policy Press.

Brolin, D., & Gysbers, N. (1979). Career education for persons with handicaps. *Personnel and Guidance Journal, 58*(4), 258–262.

Budoff, M. (1979). Implementing due process safeguards: From the user's point of view. In Department of Health, Education, and Welfare, Office of Education, *Due process: Developing criteria for the evaluation of due process procedural safeguard provisions.* Philadelphia: Research for Better Schools, Inc.

Darling, R. B. (1979). *Families against society: A study of reaction to children with birth defects.* Beverly Hills, CA: Sage Publications.

Dybwad, G. (1983). The achievements of parental organizations. In J. Mulick and S. M. Pueschel (Eds.), *Parent-professional partnerships in developmental disability services* (pp. 197–206). Cambridge, MA: Academic Guild Publishers.

Edge, D., Strenecky, B., & McLaughlin, J. (1979). Parent involvement: A consumer perspective in the home and community. *Education and Training of the Mentally Retarded, 14,* 143–144.

Edgerton, R. (1967). *The cloak of competence: Stigma in the lives of the mentally retarded.* Berkeley: University of California Press.

Ferrara, D. (1979). Attitudes of parents of mentally retarded children toward normalization activities. *American Journal of Mental Deficiency, 84,* 145–151.

Foster, M., Berger, M., & McLean, M. (1981). Rethinking a good idea: A reassessment of parental involvement. *Topics in Early Childhood Special Education, 1,* 55–65.

Goldstein, E. (1979). The influence of parental attitudes on psychiatric treatment outcomes. *Social Casework, 60,* 350–359.

Goldstein, S., Strickland, B., Turnbull, A., & Curry, L. (1980). An observational analysis of the IEP conference. *Exceptional Children, 46*(4), 278–286.

Haley, J. (1976). *Problem solving therapy.* San Francisco: Jossey-Bass.

Hargis, K., & Blechman, E. (1979). Social class and training of parents as behavior change agents. *Child Behavior Therapy, 82,* 194–203.

Hasazi, S., Gordon, L., & Roe, C. (1985). Factors associated with the employment status of handicapped youth exiting high school from 1979 to 1983. *Exceptional Children, 51*(6), 455–469.

Hill, J., Seyfarth, J., Orelove, F., Wehman, P., & Banks, P. (1985). Parent/guardian attitudes toward the working conditions of their mentally retarded children. In P. Wehman & J. Hill (Eds.), *Competitive employment for persons with mental retardation: From research to practice* (pp. 285–314). Richmond: Rehabilitation Research and Training Center, Virginia Commonwealth University.

Katz, S., & Yekatiel, E. (1974). Leisure time problems of mentally retarded graduates of training programs. *Mental Retardation, 12*(3), 54–57.

Kernan, K., & Koegel, R. (1980). *Employment experiences of community-based mildly retarded adults.* Working paper No. 14, Socio-Behavioral Group, Men-

tal Retardation Research Center, School of Medicine, University of California, Los Angeles.

Kochany, L., & Keller, J. (1981). An analysis and evaluation of the failures of severely disabled individuals in competitive employment. In P. Wehman, *Competitive employment: New horizons for severely disabled individuals* (pp. 181–198). Baltimore: Paul H. Brookes.

Koegel, R. (1978). *The creation of incompetence: Socialization and mildy retarded persons.* Working paper No. 6, Socio-Behavioral Group, Mental Retardation Research Center, School of Medicine, University of California, Los Angeles.

Lusthaus, C., Lusthaus, E., & Gibbs, H. (1981). Parents' role in the decision process. *Exceptional Children, 48*(3), 256–257.

Lynch, E., & Stein, R. (1982). Perspectives on parent participation in special education. *Exceptional Education Quarterly, 3*(2), 56–63.

Markel, G., & Greenbaum, J. (1979). *Parents are to be seen and heard: Assertiveness and educational planning for handicapped children.* San Luis Obispo, CA: Impact Publishers.

Marver, J., & David, J. (1978). *The implementation of individualized education program requirements of P.L. 94-142.* Menlo Park, CA: SRI International.

Mittler, P., Cheseldine, S., & McConachie, H. (1980). *Roles and needs of parents of handicapped adolescents.* Paris: Organization for Economic Cooperation and Development, Center for Educational Research and Information.

Morgan, D., & Rhode, V. (1980). Attitudes of Utah's special education teachers toward IEPs. In *Individualized education programs: A handbook for the school principal.* Logan: Utah State University, Department of Special Education.

Nadler, B., & Shore, K. (1980). Individualized education programs: A look at realities. *Education Unlimited, 2*(3), 30–34.

Nitzberg, J. (1974). The resistive parent behind the resistive trainee at a workshop training center. *Special Children, 6,* 5–29.

O'Connor, G. (1983). Social support of mentally retarded persons, *Mental Retardation, 21,* 187–196.

Okun, B., & Rappaport, L. (1980). *Working with families: An introduction to family therapy.* North Scituate, MA: Duxbury Press.

Phelps, L. A., & Thornton, L. J. (1979). *Vocational education and handicapped learners: Perceptions and inservice needs of state leadership personnel.* Urbana: University of Illinois, College of Education.

Rusch, F., & Schutz, R. (1981). Vocational and social work behavior: An evaluative review. In J. Matson & J. McCartney (Eds.), *Handbook of behavior modification with the mentally retarded* (pp. 247–280). New York: Plenum.

Rusch, F., Schutz, R., & Heal, L. (1983). Vocational training and placement. In J. Matson & J. Mulick (Eds.), *Handbook of mental retardation* (pp. 455–466). New York: Pergamon Press.

Schalock, R. L. (1983). *Services for developmentally disabled adults: Development, implementation, and evaluation.* Baltimore: University Park Press.

Schneider, D. L. (1968). *Perceptions of family atmosphere and the vocational interests of physically handicapped adolescents: An application of Anne Roe's theory.* (Doctoral dissertation, New York University.) Dissertation

Abstracts International, 1967, 29, 2574-AA. University Microfilms No. 69-3195.

Schuck, J. (1979). The parent-professional partnership: Myth or reality? *Education Unlimited, 1*(4), 26–28.

Shonkoff, J. (1983). A perspective on pediatric training. In J. Mulick & S. Pueschel (Eds.), *Parent professional partnerships in developmental disability services* (pp. 75–88). Cambridge, MA: Academic Guild Publishers.

Sigelman, C., Novak, A., Heal, L., & Switzky, H. (1980). Factors that affect the success of community placement. In A. Novak & L. Heal (Eds.), *Integration of developmentally disabled individuals into the community* (pp. 57–74). Baltimore: Paul H. Brookes.

Stile, S., Cole, J., & Garner, A. (1979). Maximizing parental involvement in programs for exceptional children: Strategies for education and related service personnel. *Journal of the Division of Early Childhood, 1,* 68–82.

Turnbull, A. (1983). Parent-professional interactions. In M. Snell (Ed.), *Systematic instruction of the moderately and severely handicapped* (2nd ed., pp. 18–44). Columbus, OH: Charles E. Merrill.

Turnbull, H., & Turnbull, A. (1982). Parent involvement: A critique. *Mental Retardation, 20*(3), 115–122.

Walthal, J., & Love, H. (1974). *Habilitation of the mentally retarded individual.* Springfield, IL: Charles C Thomas.

Yoshida, R., Fenton, K., Kaufman, M., & Maxwell, J. (1978). Parental involvement in the special education pupil planning process: The school's perspective. *Exceptional Children, 44*(7), 531–534.

Zigler, E., & Valentine, J. (Eds.). (1979). *Project Head Start: A legacy of the war on poverty.* New York: Free Press.

Chapter 22

Preparing Personnel to Support and Guide Emerging Contemporary Service Alternatives

Adelle Renzaglia

ALTHOUGH SECONDARY EDUCATION programs for students with handicaps have emerged as a national priority (Bellamy & Wilcox, 1980; Wehman, Renzaglia, & Bates, 1985; Will, 1984), existing programs have not, for the most part, adequately prepared these students for meaningful work in community settings. In fact, most adolescents and adults with severe handicaps are continuing to be denied employment in segregated, sheltered work settings, much less being given the opportunity for competitive employment in integrated community businesses and industries (Revell, Wehman, & Arnold, 1985).

Even though vocational training programs are less than adequate, the vocational competence of students with handicaps has been established. During the 1970s, researchers provided numerous demonstrations of the ability of persons with severe handicaps to acquire industrial, benchwork jobs and to produce at acceptable rates (e.g., Bellamy, 1976; Bellamy, Peterson, & Close, 1976; Gold, 1972; Karan, Wehman, Renzaglia, & Schutz, 1976). In the late 1970s and the 1980s, these demonstrations of competence grew to include successful training and placement of persons with moderate and severe handicaps in competitive, nonskilled jobs such as janitorial and food

service positions (e.g., Rusch & Mithaug, 1980; Wehman, 1981).

As the number of demonstrations of vocational competence has increased through model demonstration projects, increases in the number of successful locally funded vocational training programs would be expected. However, this is not the case. Although there are more training programs preparing students with handicaps for meaningful nonsheltered employment, the majority of vocational programs continue to train and place persons with handicaps in sheltered, segregated settings where remuneration is minimal, if at all (OSERS, 1984). Even more disturbing, the U.S. Commission on Civil Rights (1983) reported that between 50% and 80% of the adults reporting disabilities are unemployed. These facts would suggest that the strategies found effective in the demonstration programs for successfully training and placing persons with handicaps in meaningful, nonsheltered settings are not being adequately disseminated to those professionals (e.g., special educators and rehabilitation personnel) providing direct service to the majority of persons with handicaps (Mori, Rusch, & Fair, 1982). Professionals currently serving persons with handicaps continue to have low expectations and, consequently, fail to provide the opportunities for meaningful, nonsheltered employment (Alper & Alper, 1980).

IMPETUS BEHIND DEVELOPMENT OF PERSONNEL TRAINING PROGRAMS

Training programs for personnel serving all students with handicaps, including those with severe handicaps, began to multiply with the passage of Public Law 94-142, the Education for All Handicapped Children Act of 1975. This piece of legislation mandated the right of all school-age children and adolescents to an appropriate education. In addition to this law, the Rehabilitation Act of 1973 (Public Law 93-112) mandated the rights of all adolescents and adults, regardless of the degree of handicap, to be served in vocational rehabilitation programs. As a result of the passage of these laws, the need for trained personnel has grown immensely. However, university training programs have not yet met these demands.

In response to the increasing demands for trained personnel, many institutions of higher education have developed personnel training programs (Haring, 1982). However, in many cases these programs were hastily developed by persons who also had little expertise in educating students with handicaps (especially severe handicaps). Consequently, the level of expertise of many professionals remains unacceptable, and the quality of educational programs for students with handicaps is still poor (Alper & Alper, 1980). Similarly, as students with severe handicaps are referred to vocational rehabilitation personnel working in adult service programs, these direct service personnel need assistance in acquiring the strategies necessary for appropriately serving this newly identified group of clients (OSERS, 1984).

FOCUS ON TRANSITION

The ultimate goal of special education for persons with handicaps is employment. Frequently, students in public school programs acquire adequate job skills and the necessary related social skills but are unemployed or are served in nonproductive day programs after graduating from school (Moon, 1984; Will, 1984). As a result, the Federal Office of Special Education and Rehabilitative Services (OSERS) has identified transition from public school to work as a priority for persons with handicaps. OSERS has stated that current practices in transitioning students with handicaps from school to work are unacceptable (OSERS, 1984). This is due, at least in part, to the lack of adequately trained personnel providing public school education and adult services.

Although adult training programs are not mandated, educators have identified these services as essential (Bellamy, Sowers, & Bourbeau, 1983; Rusch & Mithaug, 1985; Wehman, Kregel, & Barcus, 1985). In addition, program initiatives and funding through Public Law 98-199, Education for Handicapped Children amendments, are available for the development of formal transitional services. Unfortunately, there are few personnel preparation programs (preservice or inservice) that train personnel specifically to develop transitional services. Furthermore, the need for trained personnel to provide adult services is even greater since long-term employment for many persons with handicaps is dependent on continued training and follow-up throughout an individual's adult working years (Rusch & Mithaug, 1985).

In summary, the need for trained personnel to provide appropriate employment education programs for persons with handicaps is great and continues to grow. In fact, McAlees (1984) stated that the development of training programs and facilities designed to equip persons with handicaps with marketable vocational skills is rapidly expanding, and by the year 1990, preservice and inservice personnel training programs must prepare at least 14,595 new vocational/job skills development personnel alone to meet the needs of persons with handicaps who will need some form of vocational training to become employed.

PERSONNEL TRAINING MODELS

Education for persons with handicaps crosses disciplines as well as social service personnel.

Public school special education teachers and adult service rehabilitation personnel are all involved in developing vocational training, placement, and follow-up services for persons with handicaps. Therefore, personnel preparation programs must be designed to provide all of these personnel with the competencies necessary for providing students, regardless of the severity of their handicaps, with marketable job skills.

Preservice Training

As stated by McAlees (1984), there is a growing need for newly trained professionals in the area of vocational training for persons with handicaps. Special education teachers as well as rehabilitation personnel must acquire the skills to orchestrate service plans for individual students. Effective services involve input from a variety of disciplines, including educators, language clinicians, occupational and physical therapists, psychologists, adult service providers, funding agencies, and parents. Consequently, educators and rehabilitation personnel must become educational team managers (Haring, 1982; Mori et al., 1982). Ultimately, it is the responsibility of the teacher or the rehabilitation counselor to coordinate all of the necessary services and to make sure the students' needs are met.

Preservice training programs have traditionally emphasized elementary-age students with mild to moderate handicaps (Grosenick & Huntze, 1980; Kokaska & Brolin, 1985). Therefore, a new emphasis must be placed on serving adolescents and adults and, specifically, those with severe handicaps. The objective of preservice training programs should be to provide the theoretical base in combination with the practical skills necessary for competent vocational training (Haring, 1982). Sontag, Burke, and York (1973) suggested that the greater the degree of handicap of the persons being served, the more precise and specific the competencies must be of a teacher attempting to provide effective educational programming. Additionally, Wehman (1979) asserts that the needs of students with severe handicaps in the areas of curriculum, instruction, and follow-up services are significantly

different than the needs of students with lesser handicaps. Therefore, direct service personnel who were specifically trained to develop and implement educational programs for persons with severe handicaps are necessary.

Inservice Training

Since effective personnel preparation programs designed to train vocational trainers for students with handicaps have been and continue to be in small number, there are many teachers and adult service providers who were never trained specifically for work with persons who have moderate, severe, profound, or multiple handicaps. However, they are now charged with providing training programs for these individuals, and, consequently, do not have the necessary skills (Bates, Hamre-Nietupski, Nietupski, Maurer, & Teas, 1984; Haring, 1982; Snell, Thompson, & Taylor, 1979). Therefore, inservice training programs designed to provide the same conceptual base and practical skills as provided in preservice training programs must be developed. In addition, changing attitudes of personnel currently providing day programming resulting in increased expectations for persons with handicaps may be necessary (Alper & Alper, 1980).

Unlike preservice training, inservice training is constrained by time, which would necessitate an instructional format that differs from most preservice training programs. Personnel trainers must work very closely with the school or service agency administrators and staff to establish a format compatible with the persons being served. In addition, in many instances personnel development activities may require that the instructors (e.g., university professors) travel to the inservice participants rather than requiring the participants to convene on the instructor's territory.

GUIDELINES FOR DEVELOPING PERSONNEL TRAINING PROGRAMS

Competency-Based Training

Current practices in teacher education for students with handicaps include the provision of competency-based training programs (Haring,

1982; Mori et al., 1982). Several authors have detailed competencies that must be included in comprehensive teacher training programs (e.g., Burke & Cohen, 1977; Haring, 1982; Perske & Smith, 1977; Weissman-Frisch, Crowell, & Inman, 1980; Wilcox, 1977). However, the process for selecting teacher competencies has not always been based on empirical evidence, including the long-range effects on student behavior (Mori et al., 1982; Thurman & Hare, 1979).

Fredericks et al. (1978) conducted one of the few studies designed to identify the needed competencies for teaching students with severe handicaps. Their results suggested that two variables accounted for the differences between special educators whose students made significant gains and those whose students made small gains: 1) the number of minutes spent in instruction, and 2) the percentage of instructional programs that were task analyzed. In a follow-up study, Fredericks, Anderson, and Baldwin (1979) found an additional variable that influenced student gains—the teacher's skills in providing instructional feedback. Although these studies do not provide a large body of data, the findings do support the need for systematic organizational skills of teachers for students with severe handicaps (Mori et al., 1982).

With the growing emphasis on transitional programs and the recent demonstrations of vocational competence of persons with handicaps, personnel training programs must identify the competencies required for successful training and placement of individuals with varying degrees of handicaps in meaningful work (Mori et al., 1982). A number of competencies have been identified as necessary for teachers who specialize in secondary-level vocational training, including:

1. Identifying realistic, community-specific vocational skills
2. Developing systematic, task-analyzed instructional programs
3. Working cooperatively with special educators, rehabilitation personnel, and parents in an interdisciplinary fashion
4. Training students to adapt to the social

environment of work settings including interactions with supervisors and fellow workers
5. Training students in supportive skills such as transportation, appropriate use of leisure time, telling time, and money management
6. Procuring competitive employment or supported employment placements
7. Providing maintenance and follow-up services to ensure long-term employment (Feinberg & Wood, 1978; Fredericks et al., 1978, 1979; Horner & Bellamy, 1978; Kokaska & Brolin, 1985; McCormick, Cooper, & Goldman, 1979; Mori et al., 1982; Perske & Smith, 1977; Pomerantz & Marholin, 1977; Rusch & Mithaug, 1980; Wehman, 1981; Will, 1984).

The issues related to each of these identified competencies are discussed in more detail in the following section.

After graduation from public school settings, most students with handicaps are referred to vocational rehabilitation services. Consequently, rehabilitation personnel are required to take on the responsibilities for providing appropriate vocational services to their newly referred clients. Most rehabilitation counselors, however, are not trained to provide services to students with moderate, severe, or multiple handicaps (Mori et al., 1982; Van Etten, Arkell, & Van Etten, 1980). Therefore, training programs for these professionals must also identify the competencies required for successful provision of services (Mori et al., 1982). Since many of the clients referred will not have been previously placed in meaningful, productive jobs, rehabilitation counselors may need many of the same competencies as special educators. Current personnel preparation programs for rehabilitation personnel do have course sequences in which the information and practical skills needed could certainly be infused (Mori et al., 1982). Additionally, the content of inservice training programs may not differ greatly from those provided for special educators involved in vocational training.

Identifying Realistic, Community-Specific Vocational Skills   The foundation of a successful vocational training program is a sound curriculum based upon the skills that are needed to function in the community (Wehman, Kregel, & Barcus, 1985). Therefore, personnel preparation programs must provide trainees with the skills necessary to develop relevant, community-referenced curricula. Methods of surveying a specific community for potential jobs and identifying the skill clusters necessary for success on those jobs (e.g., Belmore & Brown, 1978) must be target skills for participants in inservice or preservice training programs. In addition, a graduate of a personnel training program must also have the skills necessary to evaluate student skills in relation to job possibilities and the desirability of potential jobs in order to make decisions about appropriate training and placement for individual students. (See also Chapter 13.)

Developing Systematic, Task-Analyzed Instructional Programs   As stated previously, Fredericks et al. (1978, 1979) identified the minutes spent in instruction, the percentage of task-analyzed programs, and the ability of a teacher to provide instructional feedback as three competencies that discriminated between teachers who achieved large gains and those who achieved small gains with their students. These skills are basic to a systematic instructional approach in an applied behavior analytic framework. As a technology for teachers, applied behavior analysis has provided teachers with student success that other approaches have not. Therefore, a behavioral technology must be the base for professional preparation for direct service positions (Perske & Smith, 1977; Wehman et al., 1985). Teachers must be able to analyze skills, develop assessment procedures, develop and write systematic instructional intervention procedures, consistently implement the programs as written, and continuously evaluate program success (Haring, 1982).

Working Cooperatively with Special Educators, Rehabilitation Personnel, and Parents   Since there are a number of agencies and professionals involved in providing services to any individual with handicaps, cooperation and coordination among professionals is essential (Kokaska & Brolin, 1985; Moon, 1984;

Mori et al., 1982). If successful transition from school to work is to be realized, teachers and adult service providers must interact on a regular basis prior to a student's graduation from public school programming. Therefore, professionals must demonstrate the skills to work cooperatively with a variety of agencies and disciplines. As stated previously, primary service providers must act as team managers for persons with whom a variety of professionals are involved (Haring, 1982; Mori et al., 1982). An understanding of the disciplines with which the service provider interacts must also be demonstrated. Therefore, special educators and rehabilitation personnel should be given comparable information regarding the other agency's services and constraints. Information about funding sources should also be acquired.

In addition to an understanding of the two major service providers, the services available through and the potential for cooperation with other disciplines must also be recognized. For example, rehabilitation engineers and industrial engineers have a great deal of information and many skills that could assist primary service providers in developing effective vocational training programs for persons with a variety of handicaps.

Basic to the successful delivery of services to individuals with handicaps is the *interaction between home and school* or rehabilitation personnel (Haring, 1982; Mori et al., 1982; Wehman et al., 1985). If vocational success is to be realized for any individual with handicaps, support from his or her home environment is crucial. Thus, newly trained educators must demonstrate the ability to interact successfully with significant persons in an individual's home environment. These educators must have skills to systematically examine the needs and desires of a home environment, develop a process for home (e.g., parent) involvement in a training program, and provide assistance to significant persons in the home in strengthening the skills of, and providing support to, the family member who is handicapped.

Since competitive employment requires involvement in numerous disciplines, the primary service provider will likely be required to provide information to other disciplines less familiar with the problems of the persons being served and the components of good programs. Consequently, educators must be prepared to provide *inservice* to other professionals and to family members regarding vocational training strategies and supportive information (Haring, 1982; Mori et al., 1982).

Training Students to Adapt to Social Environments A major factor in job success of persons with handicaps has been their ability to engage in socially appropriate interactions with employers and co-workers (Greenspan & Shoultz, 1981; Hanley-Maxwell, Rusch, Chadsey-Rusch, & Renzaglia, in press). Therefore, educators must be equally as prepared to develop instructional interventions designed to increase appropriate social skills as they are to develop work skill acquisition programs. Educators must be able to assess work environments to identify the crucial social skills necessary for successful employment and assess student/trainee skills to identify training objectives. Both behavioral excesses and deficits must be identified and remediated to ensure employment success.

Training Students in Supportive Skills Vocational success in most cases requires that an individual demonstrate skills in a range of areas supportive to the actual employment site. An individual's ability to use transportation to get to and from work, use leisure time (e.g., work breaks) appropriately, budget and use money in a variety of community settings, tell time or follow a schedule, etc., may influence vocational success (Mori et al., 1982; Wehman et al., 1985). Therefore, personnel preparation programs must equip program participants with the knowledge and practical skills necessary for assessing the demands on an individual job in these supportive skill areas, assessing an individual's skill level, and developing and implementing effective training programs to facilitate the necessary skill performance in the required areas.

Procuring Competitive or Supported Employment Placements A key factor in vocational success for persons with handicaps is a match between the worker and the specific work site and demands of the position. Vocational trainers must be competent in identifying good job matches for individual students and, in order to do so, must be aware of all possible employment options. Knowledge of the types of competitive employment options, their wages, and benefits would be necessary for a trainer to make successful placements.

Information regarding supported employment is also necessary, including: 1) methods of providing ongoing support in a competitive job, 2) strategies for developing work crews, 3) procedures necessary for establishing work stations in industry (enclaves), 4) situations in which job sharing is an option, and 5) the process necessary to establish an integrated industrial workshop in which workers are paid at acceptable rates. (The reader is referred to Chapter 19 for a discussion of supported employment.) Additionally, vocational trainers must demonstrate a working knowledge of the regulations outlined by the U.S. Department of Labor in training and placement of persons with handicaps and a knowledge of labor unions and their interactions with potential job options.

With a knowledge base regarding regulations and potential options, vocational service providers will be able to make appropriate job-student/trainee matches. Therefore, personnel preparation programs should provide participants with this information or with strategies for obtaining the information.

Providing Maintenance and Follow-Up Services The transition from vocational training to successful employment requires careful planning on the part of the trainer. For many persons with handicaps, ongoing support may be necessary for an indefinite period of time (Wehman, 1981; Wehman et al., 1985). Therefore, trainers must have the skills to identify the support needed and provide the necessary services. Maintenance of job and related skills is also a concern for many workers with handicaps. Strategies designed to promote skill maintenance must be readily identifiable and used by vocational trainers. These may include the gradual withdrawal of the training conditions (Rusch & Kazdin, 1981) and the development of self-management skills in the employee to facilitate independence and skill maintenance. (The reader is referred to Chapter 17 for a more thorough discussion of job maintenance.)

Knowledge- and Field-Based Personnel Preparation

Haring (1982) suggested that effective personnel preparation programs must include both a strong theoretical base and an emphasis on practical skills. Many of the above-stated competencies require a knowledge base upon which practical skills are built. While a knowledge base can be demonstrated through coursework or inservice workshops, practical skills must be demonstrated and verified in competitive employment programs where trainees work directly with students with handicaps, other professionals, and student family members (Mori et al., 1982; Umbreit, Karlan, York, & Haring, 1980).

Knowledge Base A strong theoretical or knowledge base is important to effective competitive employment. With a strong base in theory, an individual providing direct service has a framework within which to make decisions regarding programming. In order to develop a strong theoretical or knowledge base, a trainee must become familiar with current literature and research related to the issues of importance (Haring, 1982; Mori et al., 1982). An understanding of the variables related to conducting strong or methodologically sound research should also be acquired by the participants in a personnel training program. This would allow the participants to continue reading research as it is produced and to critically evaluate and integrate relevant findings into their programs.

A *preservice* training program should include coursework from which the knowledge or theoretical base is obtained. The following courses or content areas have been discussed by numerous personnel trainers and should be included in a training program to ensure a strong theoretical base:

1. Applied behavior analysis
2. Systematic instruction
3. Educational assessment and data-based programming
4. Curriculum development for persons with handicaps
5. Emergency medical procedures
6. Physical aspects of persons with multiple handicaps
7. Interagency coordination: Working with professionals and parents
8. Vocational education and transition for persons with handicaps
9. Legal issues and advocacy

Knowledge in these areas can be evaluated through course examinations and projects or papers. However, as stated previously, knowledge does not stand on its own. Ultimately, this knowledge base must have an impact on practical or direct service skills of trainers. Therefore, practical skills must be evaluated continuously and in conjunction with evaluation of a trainees knowledge.

Field Base In *preservice* training programs, the placement of trainees in ongoing practicum sites enables the evaluation of practical skills or the application of knowledge in direct service programming (Mori et al., 1982). The provision of practicum placements concurrent with coursework allows an evaluation of course competencies in practical applications.

Given the potential demands placed on vocational trainers once employed, preservice training would best prepare competent educators by requiring multiple practicum experiences rather than a single classroom placement (Van Etten et al., 1980). Participants involved in preservice programs should have the opportunity to interact with persons with a variety of handicapping conditions and in a variety of instructional settings. Providing trainees with practicum experiences in both public school vocational programs and adult services would sensitize them to the opportunities and constraints of these programs as well as potential strategies for systems change resulting in quality service delivery.

Practical skills, in many cases, are most appropriately evaluated in clusters. For example, systematic instructional skills, including student assessment, curriculum development, task analysis, and provision of instructional feedback and evaluation of student progress, might best be evaluated in the context of a total instructional program as opposed to in isolation from each other. These clusters, however, must be applied and evaluated repeatedly under changing conditions (multiple settings and with a variety of students) in order to guarantee that a trainee has acquired them.

Inservice Models   As stated previously, inservice training programs for personnel already involved in competitive employment for persons with handicaps should also include both theoretical and practical skill components. However, the format for developing knowledge and practical skills of inservice participants would necessarily differ from a preservice model (Haring, 1982). Inservice models can range from group workshops, designed to provide participants with theory and practical skills with application in their current employment sites, to individual consultation (e.g., the Active Response Inservice Training Model [Snell et al., 1979]) that is provided in the participant's actual employment site. An additional alternative is the combination of group workshops and individual consultation. Regardless of the model selected, inservice trainers should build in a procedure for evaluating the effects of the inservice training on the participant's job performance. Weissman-Frisch et al. (1980) delineated four general guidelines for the provision of effective inservice training: 1) using a variety of methods for evaluation; 2) including a small number of participants in group sessions; 3) incorporating lecture, discussion, modeling, direct applications of intervention strategies, simulation, feedback, and reinforcement; and 4) using a competency-based model.

Prior to designing an inservice training program, instructors must assess the needs of inservice participants. This needs assessment should be used to structure the inservice training and determine the inservice content. As a result of a needs assessment, instructors may choose to develop a technical assistance plan with each participant. This plan would delineate the inservice activities to be conducted and would be designed to meet the needs of individuals or groups of individuals.

For example, if a group of participants had been assessed and the results indicated that their needs were for information or skills related to curriculum development, procuring employment placements, and providing maintenance and follow-up services, a schedule for inservice workshops related to these topics could be developed (see Table 1). The sessions would be approximately 2½–3 hours in length and could be run sequentially for 2 full days or could be spread across time if a 2-day workshop was not feasible.

In conjunction with the workshops described in Table 1, inservice trainers might conduct on-site consultation with participants to provide assistance with individual concerns that may be unique to an employment site.

PROGRAM EVALUATION

Given the new emphasis on training personnel to deliver vocational services to students with handicaps, personnel training programs are still in the developmental stage. Therefore, personnel preparation procedures should be carefully and continuously evaluated (Mori et al., 1982). In addition, program evaluation should be multifaceted, designed to address all components of a personnel training program (Weissman-Frisch et al., 1980). Evaluation of the theory or knowledge base of trainees and trainee performance in providing services to persons with handicaps should be included. Additional evaluation activities should be conducted to assess trainee satisfaction with the program and employer satisfaction once trainees secure employment after leaving the training program. Table 2 presents the environments in which evaluation activities should be conducted and the data to be collected.

The theory- or knowledge-based competencies included in a training program will be targeted in coursework. Therefore, these competencies should be evaluated in courses or didactic inservice sessions. *Written exams* and

Table 1. Sample inservice workshop sequence

Session 1: Identifying vocational and social survival skills
  Advantages of including employers and co-workers as sources of information about nonsheltered
    employment settings
  Types of information that should be collected
    Verbal reports
    Observations
  Identifying vocational survival skills
    Performance suggested by study
    Validation by employers/co-workers
  Identifying social survival skills
    Performance suggested by study
    Validation by employers/co-workers
  Identifying acceptable training procedures
    Purposes of assessment
    Procedures suggested by study
    Validation by employers/co-workers

Session 2: Placement
  Identifying possible job placements
  Selecting probable job placements
  Surveying job placements
  Types of placements
  Conducting a placement survey
    Mail survey
    Telephone survey
  Conducting a job analysis
    Type of firm
    Importance of speed
    Number of co-workers with whom trainee will work directly
    Supervision available
    Probable cooperation of other employees
    General social environment
    Physical appearance
    Physical conditions
  Task analysis
    Job behaviors
  Conditions of employment
    Work hours
    Shift
    Pay scale
    Bonuses/overtime pay
    Union membership
    Travel requirements
    Training
    Promotional criteria
    Insurance, health, and other benefits
  Worker requirements
    Education
    Experience
    Licenses/certificates
    Special social/vocational skills
    Tests
    Reason(s) for previous firings or abandonments
    Contact person
  Analysis of employer, supervisor, and co-worker concerns and expectations
    Ideal employee characteristics
  Developing a Work Performance Evaluation Form
    Collecting the forms
    Data analysis
    Providing feedback
    Behavioral observations at the employment site

(continued)

Table 1. *(continued)*

Placement process
    Contacting the employee
    Reviewing the job analysis survey
    Contacting parents/guardians
    Interviewing for the job
    Contacting the placement committee

Session 3: Total service planning (TSP)
    Introduction to the TSP
    Advantages to establishing goal
    Components of a TSP (which meet care standards)
    The TSP staffing
        The participants at TSP staffings should include:
            The case manager will chair the staffing. The participants will bring into the staffing identified trainee needs
            based upon the skills needed for successful performance.
            The group will set priorities for future placement and need for interaction with other programs or agencies.
    Individual program plans (IPP)

Session 4: Follow-Up
    Reasons for establishing a follow-up program
        Early identification of problems
        Providing on-the-job intervention
        Seeking validation by significant others
        Planning intervention by others
        Fading follow-up checks
        Evaluating adjustment
    Developing a follow-up program
    Selecting training resources
    Developing training resources
        Structured verbal report
    Specifying placement training outcomes
        Three steps to follow for identified deficits
        Setting priorities for deficits
    Delivering follow-up services
        Adjusted follow-up
        Fixed follow-up
    Implementing follow-up services
    Administering the Work Performance Evaluation Form
    Providing feedback on employee progress
    Maintaining a placement log

Adapted from inservice program developed by Frank Rusch.

projects (e.g., literature reviews or critical reviews of research, position papers) provide a measure of a trainee's knowledge upon which the skills for acquiring competencies in many practical skills are based. A *pretest-posttest* format may be selected for assessing the knowledge or theory base of trainees participating in inservice training.

Evaluation activities designed to assess program effectiveness in providing trainees with the necessary practical skills should be conducted while the trainees are using the designated skills. This occurs in practicum sites, during preservice training, or in "hands-on" activities provided during inservice training. *Direct observation of trainee performance* should be conducted repeatedly to assess trainee competence in delivering appropriate services to persons with handicaps. Behavioral observations should be systematic with performance criteria clearly defined prior to observations. This can be accomplished by developing a performance checklist that a practicum supervisor is directed to use consistently across observations. Repeated observations will provide the observer with data regarding a trainee's progress toward meeting competencies and a trainee's continued needs for training. Since inservice participants are employed while participating in training activities, behavioral observations may be conducted in employment sites.

Table 2. Evaluation activities conducted across training and employment environments

	Environment		
Evaluation activities	Class or workshop	Practicum	Employment
Written exams	X		
Written projects	X		
Pretests and posttests	X	X	
Behavioral observation		X[a]	X[a](Ins.)[b]
Student/client performance data		X[a]	X[a](Ins.)[b]
Trainee satisfaction	X[a]	X[a]	X[a]
Employer satisfaction			X[a]

[a]Repeated measures should be collected.

[b](Ins.), Activities conducted in inservice training programs only.

The ultimate goal of personnel training is to increase the quality of vocational services provided to persons with handicaps. Therefore, program evaluation should include an analysis of the effect of personnel training on student/client performance (Thurman & Hare, 1979). *Student/client performance data* should be evaluated to determine if program trainees have, in fact, acquired the competencies necessary for successful vocational training. Performance data should also be collected repeatedly to monitor cumulative effects of service delivery as well as effects across time as the program trainees acquire more skills.

A final component of program evaluation is an assessment of *consumer satisfaction*. Consumers, in this context, include both the program trainees and those persons employing program graduates. *Trainee satisfaction* data can be collected across a variety of settings and activities. Course or inservice workshop evaluations should indicate trainees' satisfaction with the content and format of instruction. Practicum evaluations completed by trainees should yield satisfaction with practicum sites, requirements, supervision, and the evaluation procedures used to assess trainee performance. Additional trainee satisfaction measures should be collected once a trainee is employed and has had the opportunity to use the skills acquired in the personnel preparation program. At this point, a trainee may be able to give realistic critical feedback based on the application of his or her skills in an actual employment situation. Assessing program graduates across years may also provide insightful infor-

mation regarding the long-range effects of the training program.

Another component of evaluating consumer satisfaction involves assessing employers of program graduates to determine their views of program graduate competence. *Employer satisfaction* can be assessed by evaluating employers' perceptions of the competencies of the employees in performing their jobs. Additional questions might address employers' view of employees' strengths and weaknesses, and include asking employers if they would be willing to hire program graduates in the future. As with trainee satisfaction, assessment of employer satisfaction across years would provide pertinent information regarding the durability and adaptability of trainee skills across time.

Although this multifaceted approach to evaluation may be costly and time consuming (Weissman-Frisch et al., 1980), the information obtained will provide personnel trainers with valuable feedback. Additionally, the data that will be collected on the competencies required by effective vocational trainers and the personnel training strategies that prove effective should guide professionals in designing personnel preparation programs resulting in highly trained program graduates, who ultimately will increase the quality and success of vocational training programs for persons with handicaps.

SUMMARY

Research in the area of competitive employment for persons with handicaps has demonstrated that these individuals are capable of being productive members of integrated communities (Rusch & Mithaug, 1980; Wehman et al., 1985). Consequently, a recent emphasis has been placed on improving the quality of vocational training programs (e.g., OSERS, 1984; Will, 1984). However, there is a paucity of trained professionals who have the knowledge base and practical skills necessary for developing competitive employment programs. Additionally, the need for new professionals who are trained to provide competitive employment options is continuing to grow due to the growing numbers of persons with handicaps entering training programs (McAlees, 1984). Therefore, personnel preparation programs must address these needs by developing, implementing, and evaluating training activities that produce competent professionals.

Although little research has been conducted to evaluate the necessary components of effective personnel preparation, a number of educators have suggested that training programs should be competency based as well as field based. Theoretical foundations should be rooted in a behavioral technology, and curriculum development strategies should be community referenced. Given the lack of a data base supporting these components, a continuous multifaceted evaluation plan should be designed and implemented.

Both preservice needs and inservice needs must be addressed by personnel training programs. The need for inservice is emphasized because of the vast number of service providers in public school and adult service programs who lack training, especially in the newly identified strategies for promoting competitive employment resulting in students/clients obtaining meaningful, nonsheltered employment. Because of the varying types and degrees of handicaps experienced by vocational training program participants, educators must have a wide range of skills. Interagency cooperation is imperative if a smooth transition from school to work is to be realized, and vocational training and support services should continue to be available to persons with handicaps throughout their working years. Special educators, vocational rehabilitation personnel, and other adult service providers must receive training if the needs of those referred for services are to be met.

REFERENCES

Alper, S., & Alper, J. (1980). Issues in community-based vocational programming: Institutionalization of staff. In C. Hansen (Ed.), *Expanding opportunities: Vocational education for the handicapped* (pp. 121–143). University of Washington, PDAS.

Bates, P., Hamre-Nietupski, S., Nietupski, J., Maurer, S., & Teas, S. (1984). *Statewide implementation of a community/vocational education model for moderately/ severely handicapped students*. Unpublished manuscript.

Bellamy, G. T. (Ed.). (1976). *Habilitation of severely and profoundly retarded adults* (Vol. 1). Eugene, OR: University of Oregon Center on Human Development.

Bellamy, G. T., Horner, R. H., & Inman, D. P. (1979). *Vocational habilitation of severely retarded adults: A direct service technology*. Baltimore: University Park Press.

Bellamy, G. T., Peterson, L., & Close, D. (1976). Habilitation of the severely and profoundly retarded: Illustrations of competence. *Education and Training of the Mentally Retarded, 10,* 174–186.

Bellamy, G. T., Sowers, J., & Bourbeau, P. (1983). Work and work-related skills. In M. Snell (Ed.), *Systematic instruction of the moderately and severely handicapped*

(2nd ed.) (pp. 290–502). Columbus, OH: Charles E. Merrill.

Bellamy, G. T., & Wilcox, B. (1980). *Secondary education for severely handicapped students: Guidelines for quality services*. Eugene, OR: Center on Human Development.

Belmore, K., & Brown, L. (1978). A job skill inventory strategy designed for severely handicapped potential workers. In N. G. Haring & D. D. Bricker (Eds.), *Teaching the severely handicapped* (Vol. 3, pp. 223–262). Columbus, OH: Special Press.

Burke, P., & Cohen, M. (1977). The quest for competence in serving the severely/profoundly handicapped: A critical analysis of personnel preparation programs. In E. Sontag, T. Smith, & N. Certo (Eds.), *Educational programming for the severely and profoundly handicapped* (pp. 445–464). Reston, VA: Council for Exceptional Children.

Feinberg, F., & Wood, F. (1978). Goals for teachers of seriously emotionally disturbed children. *Preparing teachers to develop and maintain therapeutic educational environments: The proceedings of a workshop*. Minneapolis: University of Minnesota.

Fredericks, H. D., Anderson, R., & Baldwin, V. (1979).

Identifying competency indicators of teachers of the severely handicapped. *AAESPH Review, 4,* 81–95.

Fredericks, H. D., Anderson, R., Baldwin, V., Grove, D., Moore, M., Moore, W., & Beard, J. (1978). *The identification of competencies of teachers of the severely handicapped.* Project report (Grant # 0EG-0-74-2775).

Gold, M. (1972). Stimulus factors in skill training of retarded adolescents on a complex assembly task: Acquisition transfer and retention. *American Journal of Mental Deficiency, 76,* 517–526.

Greenspan, S., & Shoultz, B. (1981). Why mentally retarded adults lose their jobs: Social competence as a factor in work adjustment. *Applied Research in Mental Retardation, 2,* 23–38.

Grosenick, J., & Huntze, S. (1980). *National needs analysis in behavior disorders: Severe behavior disorders.* Columbia, MO: University of Missouri.

Hanley-Maxwell, C., Rusch, F. R., Chadsey-Rusch, J., & Renzaglia, A. (in press). Factors contributing to job terminations. *Journal of the Association for Persons with Severe Handicaps.*

Haring, N. (1982). Review and analysis of professional preparation for the severely handicapped. In B. Wilcox & R. York (Eds.), *Quality education for the severely handicapped* (pp. 180–201). Falls Church, VA: Counterpoint Handcrafted Books.

Horner, R., & Bellamy, G. T. (1978). A conceptual analysis of vocational training. In M. E. Snell (Ed.), *Systematic instruction of the moderately and severely handicapped* (pp. 441–455). Columbus, OH: Charles E. Merrill.

Karan, O., Wehman, P., Renzaglia, A., & Schutz, R. (Eds.). (1976). *Habilitation practices with the severely developmentally disabled.* Madison, WI: R & T Center.

Kokaska, C., & Brolin, D. (1985). *Career education for handicapped individuals,* (2nd ed.). Columbus, OH: Charles E. Merrill.

McAlees, D. (1984). The need for trained personnel in rehabilitation facilities by 1990. *The RTC Connection, 5,* 1–5.

McCormick, L., Cooper, M., & Goldman, R. (1979). Training teachers to maximize instructional time provided to severely and profoundly handicapped children. *AAESPH Review, 4,* 301–310.

Moon, S. (1984). *Project Transition into Employment.* Grant proposal funded by the Office of Special Education and Rehabilitative Services, Special Education Programs, U.S. Department of Education, Grant No. G008430058.

Mori, A., Rusch, F., & Fair, G. (1982). *Vocational education for the handicapped: Perspectives on special populations/severely and moderately handicapped* (Personnel Development Series: Document 1). Champaign, IL: Office of Career Development for Special Populations, University of Illinois.

OSERS (1984). *Supported employment for adults with severe disabilities: An OSERS program initiative.* Washington, DC: U.S. Office of Special Education and Rehabilitative Services.

Perske, R., & Smith, J. (1977). *Beyond the ordinary: The preparation of professionals to educate severely and profoundly handicapped persons.* Seattle, WA: The American Association for the Education of the Severely/Profoundly Handicapped.

Pomerantz, D. J., & Marholin, D. (1977). Vocational habilitation: A time for change. In E. Sontag, J. Smith, & N. Certo (Eds.), *Educational programming for the severely and profoundly handicapped* (pp. 129–141). Reston, VA: Council for Exceptional Children.

Revell, G., Wehman, P., & Arnold, S. (1985). Supported work model of competitive employment for mentally retarded persons: Implications for rehabilitative services. In P. Wehman & J. Hill (Eds.), *Competitive employment for persons with mental retardation: From research to practice* (pp. 46–64). Richmond, VA: Virginia Commonwealth University, RRTC.

Rusch, F., & Kazdin, A. (1981). Toward a methodology of withdrawal designs for the assessment of response maintenance. *Journal of Applied Behavior Analysis, 14,* 131–140.

Rusch, F., & Mithaug, D. (1980). *Vocational training for mentally retarded adults: A behavior analytic approach.* Champaign, IL: Research Press.

Rusch, F., & Mithaug, D. (1985). Competitive employment education: A systems-analytic approach to transitional programming for the student with severe handicaps. In K. C. Lakin & R. H. Bruininks (Eds.), *Strategies for achieving community integration of developmentally disabled citizens* (pp. 177–192). Baltimore: Paul H. Brookes Publishing Co.

Snell, M., Thompson, M., & Taylor, K. (1979). Providing inservice to educators of the severely handicapped: The active response inservice training model. *Education and Training of the Mentally Retarded, 14,* 25–33.

Sontag, E., Burke, P., & York, R. (1973). Considerations for serving the severely handicapped in the public schools. *Education and Training of the Mentally Retarded, 8,* 20–26.

Thurman, S., & Hare, B. (1979). Teacher training in special education: Some perspectives circa 1980. *Education and Training of the Mentally Retarded, 14,* 292–295.

Umbreit, J., Karlan, G., York, R., & Haring, N. (1980). Preparing teachers of the severely handicapped: Responsibilities and competencies of the teacher trainer. *Teacher Education and Special Education, 3,* 57–72.

U.S. Commission on Civil Rights (1983). *Accommodating the spectrum of disabilities.* Washington, DC: U.S. Commission on Civil Rights.

Van Etten, G., Arkell, C., & Van Etten, C. (1980). *The severely and profoundly handicapped: Programs, methods and materials.* St. Louis: C. V. Mosby Co.

Wehman, P. (1979). *Curriculum design for the severely and profoundly handicapped.* New York: Human Sciences Press.

Wehman, P., (1981). *Competitive employment: New horizons for severely disabled individuals.* Baltimore: Paul H. Brookes.

Wehman, P., Kregel, J., & Barcus, M. (1985). School to work: A vocational transitional model for handicapped youth. In P. Wehman & J. Hill (Eds.), *Competitive employment for persons with mental retardation: From research to practice* (pp. 169–196). Richmond, VA: Virginia Commonwealth University, RRTC.

Wehman, P., Renzaglia, A., & Bates, P. (1985). *Functional living skills for moderately and severely handicapped individuals.* Austin, TX: Pro-Ed.

Weissman-Frisch, N., Crowell, F., & Inman, D. (1980).

Inservicing vocational trainees: A multiple perspective evaluation approach. *Journal of The Association for the Severely Handicapped, 5,* 158–172.

Wilcox, B. (1977). A competency-based approach to preparing teachers of the severely/profoundly handicapped: Perspective I. In E. Sontag, J. Smith, & N. Certo (Eds.), *Educational programming for the severely and pro-foundly handicapped* (pp. 418–428). Reston, VA: Council for Exceptional Children.

Will, M. (1984). *OSERS programming for the transition of youth with disabilities: Bridges from school to working life.* Washington, DC: U.S. Office of Special Education and Rehabilitative Services.

Chapter 23

Economic Benefits as Disincentives to Competitive Employment

Richard T. Walls,
Richard J. Zawlocki, and Denetta L. Dowler

WORK INCENTIVES ENCOURAGE or motivate a person to engage in productive employment. Work disincentives, on the other hand, discourage, check, or restrain a person from seeking or engaging in productive employment. All persons of working age encounter both work incentives and disincentives. For example, many want leisure time that can be obtained by not working but also want money that can be gained by working. Work disincentives tend to be more numerous and chronic for persons with handicaps than for persons who are not handicapped.

The purpose of this chapter is to present theory and research related to work disincentives for persons with handicaps. Two predominant theoretical views—microeconomics and the psychology of behavior analysis—are introduced. Furthermore, the chapter contains an overview of specific disability benefits that may detract from employment-oriented efforts.

THEORETICAL VIEWS

Microeconomics and Disincentives

Microeconomics theory is based around the choices people make to maximize utility. *Max-*
imizing utility means striving to attain the highest level of satisfaction from a set of circumstances. For example, a child in a candy store with a dime in her pocket chooses 2 Mary Janes (2¢), 1 Tootsie Pop Drop (3¢), and 1 jaw breaker (5¢). She would rather have this combination than 15 Mary Janes or any other combination that her money will buy. That is, this combination has highest utility for her, given her budget constraint. Utility is represented in microeconomics by a preference curve depicting the points at which a person is equally satisfied with the combination of circumstances presented. At all these points along the preference or utility curve, the given choices are equally acceptable. The utility function for the child is such that she would just as soon have: 1) an ice cream bar (25¢), 2) 3 jaw breakers (15¢), or 3) 2 jaw breakers and a Tootsie Pop Drop (13¢) as 4) what she chose. All four choices have an equally satisfying value to the girl. She maximized utility since the choice she made was the only one of these four she could afford. In economic terms, her decision was based on the point at which her utility function (preference curve) touched her price or income line.

Preparation of this manuscript was supported, in part, by the National Institute of Handicapped Research through the West Virginia Rehabilitation Research and Training Center (West Virginia University and West Virginia Division of Vocational Rehabilitation). We express appreciation to Debra Evansky for manuscript preparation.

The girl in our example would rather have had a Milky Way, a Snickers, or a 5th Avenue, but she could not afford them. These three potential choices are on a different utility curve that is higher in satisfaction. She had equal preference for the three candy bars, but no point on this higher utility function touched her price line.

Although the stakes are much higher, disincentives and work choices may be represented using the same concepts as the candy store examples. A preference curve for workers who are handicapped would show whether they prefer specified benefit levels rather than earnings. From an economics perspective, when given a choice between $600 in tax-free benefits and $600 in take-home wages for working full time, the person would likely remain on benefits if possible. However, if the same person could choose between the $600 in benefits and a sure job paying $2,000, he or she would probably try to work. Utility functions representing the choices an individual would likely make can only be determined empirically, but limited research has been conducted in this area. Economists generate such curves mathematically, but several assumptions are involved in doing so.

Figure 1 represents three possible preference curves (utility functions), the highest for a job yielding $2,000 take-home pay per month (after taxes and withholding). For a person getting $1,400 in cash and in-kind benefits, a sure job (100% chance of getting and retaining the job) at a $2,000 take-home pay would be attractive. The attractiveness, however, would decrease as the perceived chance of getting and holding the job decreased. When the chances of getting a job, even a high-paying job (such as this $2,000 one) are slim, very little in sure tax-free benefits would be sacrificed in a rehabilitation attempt. A similar interpretation accompanies the middle preference curve, depicting a $1,000 take-home pay situation. The lowest preference curve represents a job at about the minimum wage ($400 take-home). Only individuals receiving very low benefits would be better off economically by sacrificing benefits to take the minimum wage job. A

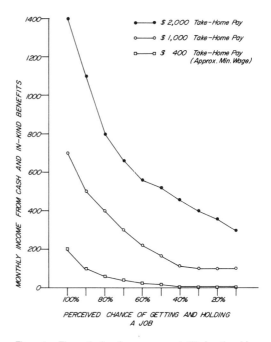

Figure 1. Theoretical preference curves (utility functions) for three salary levels. Each curve represents the points at which 1) certain benefits and 2) perceived chance of getting and holding a job at that salary are equally acceptable.

person receiving $300 or more in benefits per month would not be in a better economic position by working at this income level. In 1981, only 36% of the clients who were rehabilitated by the Vocational Rehabilitation Agency in the United States entered jobs paying the minimum wage or more (Walls, Moriarty, McLaughlin, & Dowler, 1984). Coupled with the preference curves shown in Figure 1, this fact paints a dismal picture of people who would prefer to work but cannot afford to.

Behavior Analysis of Disincentives

The employment disincentives effects stemming from disability benefits can also be explained from a behavior analytic perspective (Rusch & Mithaug, 1980). According to the behavior analytic model, behavior is under the control of its consequences. That is, reinforcement increases the frequency of behavior; punishment decreases it. These two basic principles are involved in most people's actions and may explain why some people do not seek, obtain, and maintain competitive employment. Reinforcement and punishment may be subdivided into positive reinforcement, negative reinforcement, positive punishment, and negative punishment.

Positive reinforcement occurs when a behavior is increased because of the presentation of some stimulus following the behavior. The amount of effort an individual might exert to get and keep benefits is likely to be partly dependent upon the positively reinforcing consequences of such activity. For example, if basic necessities like cash, food, housing, and medical care result from qualifying for benefits, individuals should continue to try to maintain qualification for benefits. Thus, they will learn to behave in ways that guarantee receipt of these benefits. They will wait in line, apply for benefits, attempt to demonstrate and maintain eligibility, and live on benefits if such behaviors have been positively reinforced.

Negative reinforcement occurs when a behavior is increased because of the removal of some stimulus following the behavior. A response that removes an aversive or noxious stimulus will be strengthened. For example, when an injured worker no longer has access to a salary and basic necessities, receipt of benefits constitutes relief from this noxious situation. Applying for, gaining, and maintaining benefits provides escape from the disabled person's otherwise grim prospects. Avoidance of hunger, exposure, and untreated illness through active pursuit of benefits would increase, since such behaviors have been negatively reinforced.

Positive punishment occurs when a behavior is decreased because of the presentation of some stimulus following the behavior. A response that brings on an aversive or noxious stimulus will be weakened. For example, the response of employers and workers to the vocational attempts of persons with handicaps is often one of subtle or overt rejection. Therefore, difficulties associated with seeking or resuming productive employment can be much more punishing than the social service system that is attuned to the needs of handicapped persons. When the employment environment constitutes a threat and approaches to it are met with less positive consequences than un-

employment, work behaviors are positively punished.

Negative punishment occurs when a behavior is decreased because of the removal of some stimulus following the behavior. A response that removes a positive stimulus will be weakened. For example, if working does not adequately compensate for the loss of necessities provided by benefits, a reluctance to work should follow. If money, food, shelter, and medical care are removed or reduced when a person engages in competitive employment, there is little incentive to continue. Expensive medical care is particularly hard to replace for many workers who are handicapped. Loss of extra leisure time by working 40 hours a week is also a consideration. Behaviors that lead to losses in physical and psychological well-being are negatively punished.

Thus, until individuals are encouraged to be employed rather than discouraged from it, there is little reason to expect them to seek employment. Individuals who are handicapped are reacting in the most adaptive fashion to their environment according to the behavioral principles of reinforcement and punishment.

Summary

Microeconomics and behavior analysis represent two theoretical positions from which cash and in-kind benefits may be viewed as disincentives to competitive employment. Microeconomics theory is based on the choices people make to maximize utility. Behavior analytic theory considers the consequences of behaviors associated with employment and unemployment. Both theoretical approaches lead to predictions of decreased job seeking and work behaviors when tax-free benefits are high.

DISABILITY BENEFITS

Workers' Compensation, Social Security Disability Insurance (SSDI), Supplemental Security Income (SSI), and a variety of cash and in-kind benefits may directly influence efforts of persons with handicaps to become competitively employed. Each of these sources of benefits is discussed.

Workers' Compensation

The Workers' Compensation program exists to provide dollars and/or services to compensate workers for illness or injury due to employment. This is not a single unified program but a collection of public, private, or employer-managed no-fault insurance arrangements. The workers' compensation premiums paid by employers are determined by factors such as size and type of the business, past accident record, and the insurance agreement. Premiums are paid to private insurance carriers or state-managed insurance funds. Private companies can run their own workers' compensation program by maintaining a sufficiently large security fund. Although state programs are mandated by federal law, regulations concerning determination of benefits vary from state to state. Provisions typically include a range of payments scheduled according to severity and duration of disability. Five types of claims may be filed. These are medical coverage only, temporary total disability, permanent partial disability, permanent total disability, and death.

Usually, all medical expenses are covered and cash benefits are provided for the period during which an individual is unable to work. Cash benefits are not intended to be full replacement of wages but are often based on a ⅔ wage replacement figure. This wage replacement rule assures a minimum dollar amount for low wage earners and uses the ⅔ guideline up to prescribed amounts. Since these benefits are not taxed and must fall between minimum and maximum prescribed amounts, wage replacement under workers' compensation may be less than ⅔ or more than 100% of the predisability salary.

The generic economic disincentive in workers' compensation is a remuneration or compensation level that closely matches or exceeds the worker's predisability earnings (or potential postdisability earnings). In recent years, workers' compensation premiums paid in by employers and benefits paid out to injured workers have been increasing dramatically. Thus, "it appears that the 'more adequate'

benefits may have affected workers' safety behavior, their propensity to file a workers' compensation claim, and time recuperating after an accident and thus have tended to increase the costs of the workers' compensation system" (Worrall, 1983, p. 62). Given the differing provisions of the workers' compensation program, eight potential sources of economic disincentives may be identified.

1. *State Laws and Regulations Specifying Relatively High Wage Replacement Rates* Burton (1983) suggested that a replacement rate greater than 75–85% of a worker's wage losses creates a serious disincentive. Florida experienced disincentive effects when the replacement rate was set at 95%. Typically, however, the wage replacement rate is set at 66.6% of wages lost.

2. *Nontaxable Nature of Cash Benefits* Because benefits are not taxed, some individuals may be better off receiving workers' compensation than their salary (Worrall, 1983). For example, under the Federal Employee's Compensation Act (FECA), high salary workers may receive more income than their former take-home pay (Staten & Umbeck, 1983). The tax-free nature of these benefits yields inequitable disincentives to return to work for different income levels.

3. *Programs Indexed to State Average Weekly Wages and Sensitive to Inflation* Workers who receive benefits that automatically increase as a result of inflation will be more reluctant to actively engage in rehabilitation and job search than if their benefits remained stable over time. Totally incapacitated workers, however, require adjustments in benefits since they do not have the opportunity to return to the world of work.

4. *Benefits Based on Amount of Lost Wage* In "scheduled" benefit programs, cash awards of specific amounts and durations have been predetermined for particular illnesses or injuries without regard to any wage losses by the worker. In contrast, "wage-loss" programs attempt to provide more equitable remuneration for workers who make different salaries. Based on a study of labor force participation, Johnson (1983) proposed that a shift from

scheduled to wage-loss benefit programs would reduce the likelihood of employees returning to work. Evidence also suggests that awards based on a schedule may be fairer to the worker because they are less subject to the unpredictability of litigation (Conley & Noble, 1979). In addition, workers with handicaps but not lost wages would suffer from a wage-loss program (Burton, 1983).

5. *Variability in Determining a Disability and Its Associated Benefits* Worrall and Appel (1982) found that less serious disabilities are often associated with more flexibility and movement in claim categories. Disabled workers may be tempted to try to self-label and justify a more serious claim. This process will probably require staying off the job until the claim is settled. If permanent partial disability of a substantial nature has been certified with accompanying wage replacement, significant economic disincentives may occur. Burton (1983) noted that permanent partial disability claims make up more than 60% of all money paid for benefits, even though they account for less than 25% of all cases filed. Furthermore, a high proportion of former workers with some level of permanent disability have not been re-employed (Conley & Noble, 1979). Temporary total disability is the most frequent type of claim and has been found to be related to wage replacement rates (Butler & Worrall, 1983). For example, higher benefits are received and more temporary total disability claims are made in the west and northeast regions of the United States than in the north-central and south regions where replacement rates are lower.

6. *Legal Advice* To maximize potential settlements, attorneys may advise their clients not to return to work (Johnson, 1983) and not to accept vocational rehabilitation services (Conley & Noble, 1979). Permanent partial disability claims make up the majority of controversial litigated cases (Burton, 1983). While the attorneys may only be seeking to preserve their client's rights in such cases, attorneys also benefit from high settlements, since they typically receive 20–25% of the award (Conley & Noble, 1979; Staten & Umbeck, 1983).

7. *Retroactive Payment for Waiting Period* States require a waiting period of 2–7 days after injury before cash payments may be made to the worker. Payment for this waiting period can only be recovered if a worker is unable to work for a minimum prescribed period (usually 14 days). Some workers, therefore, are tempted to stay out a few extra days in order to qualify for retroactive benefits (Conley & Noble, 1979).

8. *Union Rules and Regulations* In some unions, when a disabled worker returns to work and takes another position with the same employer, he or she loses all seniority acquired before the injury (Eaton, 1979). Furthermore, the typical union-versus-management adversary role encourages the injured worker to maximize potential benefits. The finding that proportionally more claims are filed in unionized occupations than in non-union jobs led Butler and Worrall (1983) to conclude that either: 1) riskier occupations are associated with unions, or 2) unions promote the claim-filing process.

SSDI and SSI

Social Security Disability Insurance (SSDI) and Supplemental Security Income (SSI) are programs of the Social Security Administration designed to provide a minimum standard of living to persons with handicaps. SSDI (Title II of the Social Security Act) determines benefit awards based on former wage levels for workers who have paid into the Social Security system. SSI (Title XVI), on the other hand, provides cash benefits to individuals based on their level of need, provided they do not have sufficient previous work experience to entitle them to SSDI benefits.

Several disincentives to participate in vocational rehabilitation and full employment were addressed in the 1980 Amendments to the Social Security Act. As a result, SSI began to allow benefits (e.g., Medicaid, cash supplements, attendant care) to continue even though a person's earnings exceeded the substantial gainful activity level. Such benefits were retained for any workers earning less than $714 per month (federal break-even point). Prior to this change, benefits were terminated at the end of the 9-month trial work period if the worker's salary exceeded the substantial gainful activity level ($300) after that period was over. During the 9 nonconsecutive months of the trial work period, there was (and continues to be) no ceiling on earnings. A month was (and continues to be) counted as one of the nine if a specified minimum dollar amount was earned. During a 3-year experimental period legislated in 1980, beneficiaries could continue to receive cash benefits after the trial work period, if their earnings remained lower than the federal "break-even" amount. This amount is based on a reduction of $1 in benefits for each $2 earned.

A second change resulting from the 1980 Amendments to the Social Security Act was allowance of deductions for impairment-related work expenses. Prior to this, the cost of disability-related adaptations (e.g., medical devices, adapted transportation) was not subtracted from earnings when figuring SSI benefits.

A third change is automatic re-entitlement to benefits within a specific time after SSI payments have stopped. That is, SSI recipients who go back to work (terminating their benefits) and then find themselves unable to work can be reinstated without a waiting period. Formerly, there was a substantial delay between the time recipients stopped working and resumption of benefits (Hommertzheim, 1983; Noble, 1984). Although the effects of these changes have not been completely analyzed, the intent was to make employment more attractive and to reduce the benefit rolls.

The Social Security Disability Insurance program also underwent changes in 1980. Medicare benefits were extended for 3 years after cash benefits ceased, and the waiting period for former SSDI beneficiaries who again became eligible for benefits was eliminated. As in the revised SSI program, if medical recovery does not occur, the disability status of SSDI beneficiaries can be maintained for up to 15 months after the 9-month trial work period. This provision guarantees a certain amount of income security, since benefits can

be immediately reinstated if a person is no longer able to work.

The disincentives to employment and termination of benefits that may result from the SSI/SSDI programs have been the focus of several studies. For example, Shea, Rogers, Langlois, and Mancini (1980) reported the results of a survey undertaken to determine client perceptions of disincentives to employment. Shea et al. found that concern about earning enough wages to meet living expenses was listed most often as a primary disincentive. Client fear concerning ability to keep a job was ranked as second in importance. Loss of medical benefits was rated as a larger source of disincentive for SSI clients than for SSDI clients. Furthermore, nonworkers stated that the biggest obstacle to employment was fear of not finding a permanent job. Also, clients saw the money-related rules concerning the trial work period as inadequate

Regardless of severity of disability, vocational rehabilitation clients who are receiving SSI/SSDI benefits are placed in competitive employment less often than nonbeneficiaries (Better et al., 1979). Using national data from fiscal year 1975, Better et al. (1979) also demonstrated that beneficiaries are less likely to achieve an earnings level that allows self-sufficiency. Based on analyses of these data, the authors concluded that receipt of SSI/SSDI benefits acts as a disincentive to competitive employment.

In another investigation, Wesolowski and Zawlocki (1980) noted a relationship between the amount of cash SSI or SSDI benefits received and clients' ability to secure and maintain competitive employment. Of 43 clients participating in a Job Club placement program, 15 getting an average of $219 per month dropped out of the program, 5 receiving a mean of $178 per month terminated employment within 2½ months, while the remaining 23 clients receiving an average of $84 per month obtained and kept jobs. That is, clients who received the lowest dollar amounts in benefits successfully secured and maintained competitive employment. Presumably, persons receiving highest SSI and SSDI benefits are also the most severely handicapped. It is, however, plausible that a disincentives effect also is operating.

Lando, Coate, and Kraus (1979) discussed the increased number at SSDI applications in terms of the rate of which SSDI benefits replace predisability spendable earnings. The ratio of average monthly award to average spendable earnings rose from about 26% in 1968 to more than 40% in 1978 (see Figure 2). At the same time, the number of clients leaving the rolls during this period was found to decrease.

Hommertzheim (1983) developed an "economic disincentives model" for examining the effects of changes in the values of five kinds of assistance programs: 1) SSI, 2) food stamps, 3) Medicaid, 4) Section 8 Housing, and 5) Title XIX aide and attendant care. According

to Hommertzheim, current legislation has reduced disincentives. For those who must pay for attendant care, however, disincentives do exist since there is little or no incentive to seek employment when the cost of attendant care absorbs a substantial proportion of an individual's salary. Furthermore, high attendant care costs relative to certain income levels act as a disincentive despite the allowance for some attendant care costs to be classified as excluded income when determining SSI eligibility. Even considering the 1980 changes in Social Security legislation, several sources of work disincentives exist.

1. *High Tax-Free Benefits* Despite laudable intentions, the provision of substantial services to those in need has proven in some cases to serve as a work disincentive (Carley, 1975). For example, most SSI beneficiaries would achieve employment in the secondary

Figure 2. Ratio of disabled worker average monthly award to average spendable earnings, quarterly 1964–78. (From Lando, M. E., Coate, M. B., & Kraus, R. [1979]. Disability benefit applications and the economy. *Social Security Bulletin, 42*[10], 3–10. Reprinted with permission.)

labor market where they would gain little or perhaps even lose financially by sacrificing tax-free benefits to hold a minimum-wage job (Noble, 1984). Similarly, most SSDI beneficiaries must earn considerably more than the substantial gainful activity level in order for employment to be economically advantageous (Subcommittee on Social Security, 1976). The ratio of the value of benefits from SSDI to benefits from net earnings rose from about 30% in 1969 to about 40% in 1978, along with a rise in applications for SSDI benefits (Lando et al., 1979). In summary, the current relatively high level of tax-free benefits encourages some potential rehabilitants to remain on the SSI and SSDI rolls (Berkowitz, Horning, McConnell, Rubin, & Worrall, 1982).

2. *Short Duration and Low Monthly Earnings Criterion During Trial Work Period* Even though the months required for the trial work period need not be consecutive, a worker may exhaust these months before demonstrating consistent work performance. Carley (1975) noted the disincentive effects of such "sputtering" attempts at employment. In addition, Berkowitz et al. (1982) stated that "Valuable months of trial work are used up in earning a level of income that would be unlikely to lead to the termination of benefits. In addition, many beneficiaries, after their trial work period at low wages has expired, lack the assurance that they can sustain participation in the labor force; consequently, they do not risk losing their benefits by seeking out more hours of work or work at a higher wage" (p. 76). Although the trial work period was designed to buffer the transition from dependence on SSI and SSDI to independent employment, the low earnings criterion defining a trial work month undermines work confidence as the end of the period approaches.

3. *Criterion for Determining Dependency Status for Students (ages 18–21)* Benefit eligibility is based on combined parent and student incomes since 18- to 21-year-old students are considered dependents. A student (seen as a dependent) from a low-middle SES family would probably not be eligible for benefits to assist paying the costs of education.

Consequently, such a person would be discouraged, if not prevented, from training for a high level job in the primary labor market (Texas Rehabilitation Commission, 1978).

4. *Loss of Other Family Benefits* The family may lose benefits if the member of the family who is handicapped goes back to work. For example, if the wife of a disabled worker goes to work, benefits continue to be paid to the family's children and the disabled person. If, however, the husband became employed at the same wage as the wife and the wife did not work, all cash benefits to the family would be lost. In the former case, the family gets the same total benefits as before plus the wife's salary, whereas the family would lose the income from benefits if the disabled worker became employed (Texas Rehabilitation Commission, 1978).

5. *Sense of Dependency and Negative Outlook Fostered by Pursuit of Eligibility* Grimaldi (1980) noted the stringent requirements for qualifying. During the application process, all of the applicant's efforts, and possibly his or her social support network, focus on demonstrating an inability to work (Noble, 1984). Once accepted, however, the client is expected to minimize the disability that he or she sought to demonstrate (Berkowitz et al., 1982). Such a process may be debilitating by itself because the person is certified disabled by the agency and labeled unable to work by all concerned.

6. *Complex and Confusing SSI and SSDI Rules* The extensive requirements for eligibility, trial work period, substantial gainful activity, medical benefits, waiting periods, suspension of benefits, termination, and the like are virtually unintelligible to most applicants. Clients are frightened that any action they take may make their situation worse. Wise (1974) described his own difficulties in dealing with the system. In spite of extensive participation in rehabilitation, he did not return to work because of uncertainty about the consequences of his actions. Recently, legislative attempts have been made to eliminate disincentives; however, until both applicants and street-level social service workers clearly understand the

law and its provisions, disincentives will remain (Noble, 1984). If remedial legislation, designed to reduce disincentives, compounds the existing confusion, it may only serve to further increase disincentives. Ambiguity and misunderstanding are major sources of work disincentives that scare, frustrate, and anger potential rehabilitants.

Multiple Benefits

A person with an employment handicap may be eligible for a variety of cash and in-kind benefits. Paglin (1979) noted the importance of including in-kind benefits (e.g., rent supplements and food stamps) in figuring income level. Many cash-poor families are above the poverty level if the values of in-kind benefits received are taken into account. About 60% of benefits income is derived from such in-kind sources. Walls, Masson, and Werner (1977) listed a number of cash and in-kind federal benefit programs in which persons who are handicapped and/or their families might participate. These sources of benefits are listed in Table 1. According to Walls et al. (1977), eligibility restrictions range from no-income rules to limits on wages, other income, and some public benefits. The list includes cash, food, health, housing, education, job, and social benefits. Even though certain benefits may not be received while others are in effect, many benefits programs are not mutually exclusive (Muller, 1981). Thus, a person or family may have multiple sources of benefit income.

The central question is how multiple sources affect disincentives for rehabilitation and work (Berkowitz, 1980). Muller (1980) studied disabled workers who received benefits from SSDI and at least one other source (including veterans' payments, private pensions, government pensions, aid to the blind, workers' compensation, and others). He found that replacement rates for clients receiving multiple benefits were about 50% higher, overall, than for those who received only SSDI. For example, as illustrated in Figure 3, about 22% of clients getting only SSDI reached a .50 replacement rate (half of their former income) as

compared with only about 10% of multiple-benefit recipients. At the high replacement rate end of the scale (1.60 = 160% of former income), however, the figures are reversed. That is, while only about 8% of those with one benefit received the high replacement rate, about 30% of multiple beneficiaries did.

Persons who receive multiple benefits are less likely to be rehabilitated and employed. Walls (1982) studied 200 vocational rehabilitation clients of which 134 had some cash or in-kind benefits. Of these persons, 87 received benefits from two or more sources, the most frequent combination being welfare and food stamps. The various combinations of benefits, the numbers of clients receiving them, and the percentages of clients rehabilitated for each combination of two benefit sources are reported in Table 2. Combinations of three or more sources were so numerous that they are not reported. Percent rehabilitated is not synonomous with competitive employment; usually it is higher than the percentage of competitively employed clients. Figure 4 depicts the percentage of clients rehabilitated and the percent competitively employed at closure by the number of sources of benefits. As illustrated, the percentage of clients rehabilitated and employed decreases dramatically as the number of benefit sources increases from 1 to 2, to 3, to 4, to 5, and to 6. Although more than 25% of those who received no benefits were rehabilitated and employed competitively, none of those receiving benefits from three or more sources got a job.

Just as the payments and numbers of beneficiaries continue to climb (Berkowitz, 1981), the amounts and numbers of persons receiving multiple benefits have no doubt increased. The motivation to actively seek rehabilitation services and subsequent employment may be blunted by the following sources of disincentives created by the conjunction of different benefits.

1. *Aggregated Effect of Multiple Cash and In-Kind Benefits* The aggregate effect of multiple cash and in-kind benefits may produce a substantial support system for disabled individuals. When in-kind benefits such as

Table 1. Federal programs for income security by eligibility rules on current income

No-Income Rules	
Medicare—for aged and disabled persons	*Health benefits*
Veterans' compensation for service-connected disability	Medicaid
	Medical care for veterans with nonservice-connected disability
Veterans' compensation for service-connected death	Comprehensive health services
Veterans' housing loans	Children's programs—dental comprehensive health, infant care projects, and crippled children's services
Veterans' medical care for service-connected disability	
Veterans' educational assistance for veterans, dependents, and survivors	*Housing*
	Low-rent public housing
Veterans' vocational rehabilitation allowance for 30% disability	Rent supplements
	Homeownership loans, urban and rural, private and rental
Retirement—federal civil service and military	
Social security for persons aged 72 and over	Rural housing—technical assistance, site loans, repair loans
Federal employees' compensation for job-related injuries	Indian housing—improvement and technical assistance
Meals for certain persons aged 60 and over	
	Appalachian housing program
Limit on Wages (for beneficiaries under age 72)	*Education*
Social Security—Old Age, Survivors, and Disability Insurance (SSDI)	Basic educational grants
	College work-study
Limit on Wages and Some Public Benefits	Student loans—various kinds of special fields
Railroad retirement, disability, and survivor benefits	Head Start and Follow-Through for primary-school children
Unemployment insurance—federal, state, railroad, and trade adjustment	Upward Bound and Talent Search for high school students
Black lung benefits for miners, dependents, and survivors	Work-study vocational education
	Jobs and training
Limit on Wages, Some Public Benefits, and Unearned Private Income	Comprehensive Employment and Training Act (CETA)
Cash aid	Work incentive projects
Aid to Families with Dependent Children (AFDC)	Vocational Rehabilitation Services
	ACTION-sponsored programs—Foster Grandparents and Senior Companions
Supplemental Security Income (SSI)	Career opportunities program
Veterans' pensions for nonservice-connected disability or death	*Social services*
General assistance to specific groups—Cubans, Indians, disaster populations, and emergency assistance	Services to needy families on welfare—counseling, day care, homemaker service, health care
Food benefits	Services to needy aged, blind, or disabled
Food stamps	Legal services for the poor
School programs—breakfast, lunch, and milk	
Special supplemental feeding for women, infants, and children	

From Walls, R. T., Masson, C., & Werner, T. J. (1977). Negative incentives to vocational rehabilitation. *Rehabilitation Literature*, *38*, 143–150. Reprinted with permission from the National Easter Seal Society.

food stamps, housing assistance, and medical cards are "cashed-in" at the market value, the total support level may discourage acceptance of any job not providing adequate compensation for the loss of this high dollar value of combined benefits.

2. ***Reduction Rate for Multiple-Benefit Combinations*** Reduction rate acts as a disincentive for clients receiving a single type of benefit, but multiple-benefit combinations compound the problem. The interrelationships of some programs are such that eligibility for one program increases the likelihood of meeting requirements for others. Similarly, loss of one will likely lead to loss of others. This means that if two persons received equal dollar amounts of benefits, one of them might lose more by going to work than the other because his or her benefits come from multiple sources rather than one source.

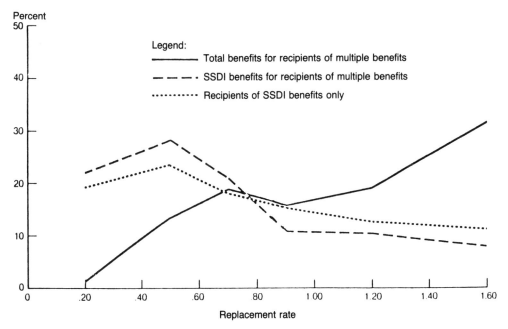

Figure 3. Distribution of replacement rates by multiple-benefit status (lifetime earnings formulation). (From Muller, L. S. [1980]. Receipt of multiple benefits by disabled-worker beneficiaries. *Social Security Bulletin, 43*(11), 3–19, 43. Reprinted with permission.)

3. *Confusing Interaction between Disincentives*

Receipt of more than one type of benefit can intensify and confound many of the disincentives noted previously in this chapter. Such disincentives include interactions with taxes and inflation, high replacement rates, variability in determining benefits, advice from lawyers, retroactive payments, trial work periods, other family benefits, sense of dependence, as well as complex and confusing rules.

Summary

A number of disincentives related to benefits operate to discourage people from working. This situation is particularly acute for individuals who are severely handicapped, since they require substantial support over a longer period time. Although there "is not a great army of malingerers out there, somehow taking advantage of these social benefit programs" (Berkowitz, 1981, p. 53), people usually choose not to work when economic conditions favor not working. When people are rewarded for demonstrating an inability to work and, conversely, are punished for working, they

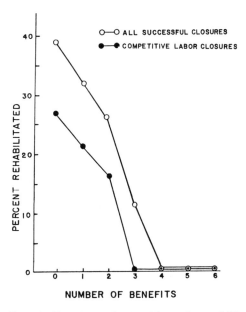

Figure 4. Percentages of successful case closures (all Vocational Rehabilitation status 26 closures and competitive labor closures, a subset of Vocational Rehabilitation status 26) for the number of sources of benefits (numbers of clients with 0 through 6 sources of benefits, respectively, were 66, 47, 50, 28, 4, 4, 1). (From Walls, R. T. [1982]. Disincentives in vocational rehabilitation: Cash and in-kind benefits from other programs. *Rehabilitation Counseling Bulletin, 26*, 37–46. Copyright AACD. Reprinted with permission. No further reproduction authorized without permission of AACD).

Table 2. Combinations of benefits and rehabilitation outcome

Combination	Number of clients	Percent rehabilitated
Welfare and food stamps	25	8
Food stamps and other medical	20	0
Welfare and other medical	16	0
SSI and food stamps	8	38
SSDI and food stamps	6	0
Welfare and Medicaid	6	0
SSI and Medicaid	5	60

usually will not work. When the rules are so complex and confusing that they appear capricious, people become fearful about giving up sure cash and in-kind benefits to risk uncertain employment.

CONCLUSION

A major overhaul rather than a patchwork solution is needed, but it is not likely to happen. Agencies are entrenched, livelihoods would be destoyed, and proposals for this type of massive social reform would be political suicide. It appears that such an overhaul would have to include dismantling of the social service agencies as we know them. Restructuring would require technological, legislative, economic, and social organizations to provide responsible service to those in need balanced with the recognition that most people are capable of some level of productive employment. Building this new incentive-producing machinery would be a costly and painful process.

REFERENCES

Berkowitz, M. (1980). *Work disincentives*. Falls Church, VA: Institute for Information Studies.

Berkowitz, M. (1981). Disincentives and the rehabilitation of disabled persons. *Annual Review of Rehabilitation, 2*, 40–57.

Berkowitz, M., Horning, M., McConnell, S., Rubin, J., & Worrall, J. D. (1982). An economic evaluation of the beneficiary rehabilitation program. In J. Rubin (Ed.), *Alternatives in rehabilitating the handicapped: A policy analysis* (pp. 1–87). New York: Human Sciences Press.

Better, S. R., Fine, P. R., Simison, D., Doss, G. H., Walls, R. T., & McLaughlin, D. E. (1979). Disability benefits as disincentives to rehabilitation. *Health and Society, 57*, 412–427.

Burton, J. F., Jr. (1983). Compensation for permanent partial disabilities. In J. D. Worrall (Ed.), *Safety and the work force: Incentives and disincentives in workers' compensation* (pp. 18–60). Ithaca, NY: ILR Press, Cornell University.

Butler, R. J., & Worrall, J. D. (1983). Workers' compensation benefit and injury claims rates in the seventies. *The Review of Economics and Statistics, 65*, 580–589.

Carley, E. J. (1975). *Ways to improve the trust fund and SSI programs: Final Report*. Rhode Island: Vocational Rehabilitation Agency, SSA-RSA Ad Hoc Committee.

Conley, R. W., & Noble, J. H., Jr. (1979). *Workers' compensation reform: Challenge for the 80's* (Research Report of the Interdepartmental Workers' Compensation Task Force, Vol. 1, No. 0-522-032/6835). Washington, DC: U.S. Government Printing Office.

Eaton, M. W. (1979). Obstacles to the vocational rehabilitation of individuals receiving workers' compensation. *Journal of Rehabilitation, 45*, 59–63.

Grimaldi, P. L. (1980). *Supplemental Security Income: The new federal program for the aged, blind, and disabled*. Washington, DC: American Enterprise Institute for Public Policy Research.

Hommertzheim, D. (1983). *Economic disincentive analysis of H.R. 3236 and proposed public assistance programs* (Tech. Rep.). Wichita, KS: Rehabilitation Engineering Center, Cerebral Palsy Research Foundation of Kansas.

Johnson, W. G. (1983). Work disincentives of benefit payments. In J. D. Worrall (Ed.), *Safety and the work force: Incentives and disincentives in workers' compensation* (pp. 138–153). Ithaca, NY: ILR Press, Cornell University.

Lando, M. E., Coate, M. B., & Kraus, R. (1979). Disability benefit applications and the economy. *Social Security Bulletin, 42*(10), 3–10.

Muller, L. S. (1980). Receipt of multiple benefits by disabled-worker beneficiaries. *Social Security Bulletin, 43*(11), 3–19, 43.

Muller, L. S. (1981). *Receipt of multiple benefits by disabled-worker beneficiaries* (SSA Publication No. 13-11870). Washington, DC: U.S. Government Printing Office.

Noble, J. H. (1984). *Rehabilitating the SSI recipient: Overcoming disincentives to employment of severely disabled persons*. Unpublished manuscript prepared for the U.S. Senate Special Committee on Aging.

Paglin, M. (1979). Poverty in the United States: A reevaluation. *Policy Review, 2*, 7–24.

Rusch, F. R., & Mithaug, D. E. (1980). *Vocational* *training for mentally retarded adults: A behavior analytic approach.* Champaign, IL: Research Press.

Shea, S., Rogers, J. M., Langlois, S., & Mancini, J. (1980). *The client perspective on performance in the special SSDI and SSI vocational rehabilitation programs.* Berkeley, CA: Berkeley Planning Associates.

Staten, M., & Umbeck, J. (1983). Compensating stress-induced disability: Incentive problems. In J. D. Worrall (Ed.), *Safety and the workforce: Incentives and disincentives in workers' compensation* (pp. 103–127). Ithaca, NY: ILR Press, Cornell University.

Subcommittee on Social Security, (1976). *Disability Insurance: Legislative issue paper* (WMCP Report No. 94-132). Washington, DC: U.S. Government Printing Office.

Texas Rehabilitation Commission. (1978). *Rehabilitation proposals for legislation concerning SSDI and SSI.* Austin, TX: Department of Vocational Rehabilitation.

Walls, R. T. (1982). Disincentives in vocational rehabilitation: Cash and in-kind benefits from other programs. *Rehabilitation Counseling Bulletin, 26,* 37–46.

Walls, R. T., Masson, C., & Werner, T. J. (1977). Negative incentives to vocational rehabilitation. *Rehabilitation Literature, 38,* 143–150.

Walls, R. T., Moriarty, J. B., McLaughlin, D. E., & Dowler, D. L. (1984). *Key operating indicators of vocational rehabilitation: State, regional, national.* Dunbar, WV: West Virginia Rehabilitation Research and Training Center.

Wesolowski, M. D., & Zawlocki, R. J. (1980). The Job Club in VR agencies: The effects of attendance and disincentives. *International Journal of Rehabilitation Research, 3,* 531–532.

Wise, E. H. (1974). The right to work versus social security disability benefits. *Rehabilitation Literature, 35,* 79–80, 95.

Worrall, J. D. (1983). Compensation costs, injury rates, and the labor market. In J. D. Worrall (Ed.), *Safety and the work force: Incentives and disincentives in workers' compensation* (pp. 1–17). Ithaca, NY: ILR Press, Cornell University.

Worrall, J. D., & Appel, D. (1982). The wage and replacement rate and benefit utilization in workers' compensation insurance. *The Journal of Risk and Insurance, 49,* 361–371.

Chapter 24

Quality of Life
Does Competitive Employment Make a Difference?

Johnny L. Matson and Frank R. Rusch

COMPETITIVE EMPLOYMENT FOR persons with handicaps is foremost among the major growth areas in special education today. Until recently, services for adults with handicaps were restricted almost exclusively to segregated day programming (see Chapter 20 for an overview of these alternatives), if available. Fortunately, individuals who previously received little vocational attention and/or were provided meaningless prevocational training are now beginning to enjoy improved services. To a large degree, work defines the worth we ascribe to persons and their status among peers. As a result of focusing on the competitive employment potential of persons with handicaps, therefore, our perception and hence our definition of these individuals is changing. The following information addresses several of these changes, their origin, and impact.

EMERGENCE OF COMPETITIVE EMPLOYMENT

Before 1980, habilitation of adults with handicaps received little emphasis in both the fields of education and psychology, particularly with respect to vocational training. For example, applied behavioral analysis and, to a lesser degree, classical conditioning were not yet part of the educational programming and training of these persons. Thus, a custodial approach prevailed. As a result, thousands of persons with mental retardation, emotional disturbances, and other handicaps resided in institutional settings, or were considered helpless and,

therefore, sheltered by their parents and other relatives.

Habilitation and vocational training of persons with handicaps have received great impetus from general social changes as well as more specific technological and educational advances.

Social Change

This most fundamental influence on the habilitation of persons with handicaps may be traced to three major events: 1) Civil Rights Act of 1964, 2) the *Wyatt v. Stickney* right-to-treatment court case in Alabama in 1972, and 3) the emphasis on normalization. As a result of these historic events, which are interrelated, many persons previously institutionalized now have the opportunity to enjoy integrated service options in the community. Additionally, vocations have come to the forefront, fitting well into the concept of right to participation and community integration.

Technological Developments

The application of technologies to teach various skills to persons with handicaps has led to a great deal of optimism regarding the outcome of habilitation. For example, many persons were considered untrainable until researchers such as Azrin and his colleagues demonstrated that chronically hospitalized persons could learn to eat and use the toilet independently (Azrin & Armstrong, 1973; Azrin & Foxx, 1972). Similarly, Bijou and his colleagues (Bijou, 1958; Bijou & Baer, 1978) proved the success of behavioral procedures with children who were mentally retarded. Furthermore, the behavior-change literature has shown that many adaptive behaviors can be taught by reducing stereotypes (Foxx & Azrin, 1973; Ollendick & Matson, 1978) and self-injury (Baumeister & Baumeister, 1978; Luckey, Watson, & Musick, 1968; Jones, Simmons, & Frankel, 1974). Finally, a wide range of persons with handicaps have learned social skills (Matson & Andrasik, 1982; Matson & Senatore, 1981), showering (Matson, DiLorenzo, & Esveldt-Dawson, 1981), pedestrian skills (Matson, 1980), dining skills (Matson, Ollendick, & Adkins, 1980), clothes mending (Cronin & Cuvo, 1979), and work behavior.

Role of Special Education

Many special educators are beginning to realize that although education during the school years is important, it is not the only area to which they must attend (Rusch & Mithaug, 1985). With medical advances resulting in greater longevity and increasing emphasis on normalization and community placement, work potential has become a central area of consideration. Not only does work consume a large percentage of the day for most adults—indeed, employment structures our daily activities—it is important for establishing self-worth. Social status in a community is largely determined by one's employment, hence enhancing opportunities for competitive employment enhances social status.

Special educators, in particular, have recognized the benefits of recently formed social attitudes and technological advances. Thus, the research and training reported in this book point to the many innovative special education efforts in recent years and address the potential for further development in years to come. A new field within special education is being defined, and emerging federal funds will result in additional future gains.

QUALITY OF LIFE

Quality of life has been recognized only recently as an important component of program development for individuals with handicaps. This goal has become an essential issue, since all educational and habilitative efforts are framed around the goal of providing the most fulfilling experiences for the individual. The *Wyatt v. Stickney* case, which began in 1972, represents the first effort to combine social policy and law to enhance the quality of life for persons with handicaps. Much of what has been established as a result of this case harkens back to the Constitution—the concept that everyone deserves equal treatment under the law. Specifically, attention has been focused on everyone's right to: 1) live where they choose, preferably in a setting where they are integrated into the community; 2) equal access to services, such as medical and mental health care; and 3) the opportunity to attend community schools and engage in other normalized activities, such as working in competitive settings.

Edgerton (1979) discussed the concept of work as a normalized aspect of life in our society, voicing the sentiment of most professionals in the field when he noted that "work is an essential step toward becoming normal" (p. 94). Until recently, no systematic efforts were made to provide fulfilling and productive jobs for persons with handicaps. Today, however, the range of work options appears to be limited only by the ingenuity and enterprising nature of professionals. Tremendous strides have been made both in the type and complexity of tasks that persons with handicaps can perform. From formerly sorting bolts and assembling bicycle parts, persons with handicaps have now progressed to jobs as dishwashers in food service settings, janitors in a variety of integrated settings, and technicians in electronic manufacturing. With the assistance and cooperation of business and industry, such advances can be extended even further. Often, such efforts are most successful when geared specifically to a particular community, that is, when they are community referenced and community based.

In Chapter 2, Wehman discusses the move toward community-based training as exemplified in his supported work model aimed at providing training in integrated employment settings. According to this model, daily training and advocacy are provided by professional staff until the client demonstrates the ability to perform the designated tasks with little or no assistance (e.g., fading procedures are used to gradually decrease prompts and cues). Competitive employment involves complex applications of learning principles, which in turn result in demonstrations of work competence that are new. Wehman and his colleagues have contributed to an enhancement of quality of life through a demonstration of competence.

The strategies for teaching competitive work tasks in naturalistic settings outlined by Wacker, Berg, and others in this text deserve serious consideration. However, since the proposed competitive employment approach alters many of the ways in which we have typically provided services, we must rethink traditional approaches to service delivery. For example, Wehman, Rusch, and others suggest that 40–80 hours of one-to-one job-site follow-up after placement places the rehabilitation counselor or other professional in a dilemma of viewing the potential employee as handicapped. Co-workers and supervisors may form lowered opinions of potential co-workers when these potential co-workers require intense, long-term training. Traditional approaches to preparing individuals with handicaps for employment have included various forms of long-term prevocational preparation in workshop or classroom settings. The client is taught work readiness skills and behavior with the goal being to eventually place the better prepared client in a job. Conceptually, this prevocational training is believed to be necessary because it prepares a potential employee for work. Unfortunately, prevocational training usually does not help the client get a job in the community. In part, opinions formed during training in the sheltered workshop have been shown to interact positively with placement, i.e., lowered expectations result in fewer placements. This same dilemma also exists outside the workshop in competitive employment. Consequently, these opinions must become the focus of interventions.

The focus of competitive employment training also deserves serious consideration. For example, Rusch points out in Chapter 1 that social skills, which have received considerable attention (Andrasik & Matson, 1985; Matson, 1984; Matson & DiLorenzo, in press), and slow production rates are often problems that markedly limit success in competitive employment. In addition, competitive employment outcomes have suffered from: 1) lack of functional assessment instruments (Matson & McCartney, 1981; Menchetti, Rusch, & Owens, 1983), 2) poor training procedures that have been vaguely defined and applied, 3) insufficient generalization and maintenance data, and 4) lack of adequate job sites. To maintain and increase the growing support for community-based educational and rehabilitation services, issues such as these must be resolved.

Independence is another major consideration in efforts to enhance quality of life. For many years, adults with handicaps were viewed as helpless, hence perpetuating the myth that they were incapable of dealing with everyday problems and interactions. In fact, persons with handicaps can achieve much more. Edgerton (1979) noted:

> Many retarded adults gladly accept the dependent role they have occupied for so long. They are more than happy to accept small loans, transportation, advice about dealing with bureaucracies, help in medical or dental appointments, shopping, handling money, reading and the like. It is obvious that many retarded people can learn to do without help in most of these matters, but it is sometimes easier for them not to learn. Retarded adults who are learning to adapt to community living need more opportunity to learn for themselves. Clinically retarded individuals who are attempting to live normal lives may always need access to medical services. A system for providing that help and those services must continue to be a social priority. (p. 98)

Social acceptability, personal independence, and responsibility require proper social networks and support systems in the community. In addition to ensuring that comprehensive competitive employment training facilities are available, therefore, we must obtain the cooperation of local mental health/mental retardation centers, schools, businesses, and city agencies that govern public transportation and other integral services.

Self-esteem and self-worth also determine quality of life. Although these issues have infrequently been addressed directly from an empirical point of view, work has been found to be a critical variable in the way we feel about ourselves. Thus, improved self-worth is another important way in which vocational education and placement can markedly change people's lives in a positive direction.

Work can also enhance quality of life by influencing the way in which individuals with handicaps are perceived by others. Thus, by demonstrating that they are productive and integral parts of society by working in integrated work settings, people with handicaps greatly increase the likelihood of being accepted by the nonhandicapped community (Gold, 1973; Sternberg & Adams, 1982; Turkel, 1972).

Expanded opportunities for competitive employment may also help decrease the stigma associated with handicaps. In addition to a general low perception of the worth of persons with handicaps on the part of nonhandicapped persons, other stigmas include inappropriate restrictions imposed on handicapped individuals (e.g., requiring longer than necessary prevocational training periods and extensive evaluations) deterring normalized roles, treating adults with handicaps in a childlike way, establishing artificial barriers between the person with handicaps and society at large, imitating the limitations of a person with handicaps, open ridicule, and denying persons with handicaps an opportunity to present their views (Dudley, 1983). As mentioned, one of the most pervasive of these stereotypes is that the individual with handicaps is helpless. Again, by demonstrating their ability to be productive and independent or semi-independent members of the work force, persons with handicaps will greatly reduce traditional stereotypical perceptions.

As noted, self-esteem and self-worth are very important in influencing quality of life. Describing how encounters with the general public can be degrading for persons with handicaps, Dudley (1983) gave the following example of a mentally retarded woman's bus experience:

> A passenger sat next to Helen, noticed her, and then moved to sit somewhere else, resulting in Helen's expressing awareness of what had happened, and the way that she chose to handle it was to get off the bus and walk the rest of the way home alone. Many of the participants, when asked how they felt about such encounters, said something like, 'I don't want to think about it', or 'I don't let it upset me.' Yet it was evident, in most of these cases, that the experiences were painful for the participants; the pain simply was difficult to express. (pp. 64–65)

Painful encounters such as these have a tremendous impact on individuals with handicaps. The ability to work independently involves more than being able to handle the job situation itself. Thus, enhancing skills in coping with the overall employment experience, including situations such as the one encountered by Helen, must be an integral part of competitive employment training. Similarly, good dressing and hygiene skills paired with community awareness are important for overall adjustment and community integration. Several strategies are valuable for achieving these goals. One such strategy, ecological and social validity, is briefly reviewed.

ECOLOGICAL AND SOCIAL VALIDITY

Until recently, most research applied to persons with handicaps has been analogous in nature with no applied value; thus, professionals and advocates have expressed concern that our research efforts often attend to problems that are more realized than real. Ecological and social validity criteria have been offered as a response to the demand for a more practical research focus. To date, much research has incorporated the new criteria, and nowhere is this trend more evident than in the area of competitive employment. Factors such as the type of work that can be performed, social behaviors necessary to ensure proper adjustment in the work place, and many related issues have been found particularly amenable to novel applications of ecological and social validity.

For example, social validation has been used to establish the acceptability of instructional goals (Rusch, Weithers, Menchetti, & Schutz, 1980), instructional procedures (Schutz, Rusch, & Lamson, 1979), and the effectiveness of these instructional programs (Schutz, Jostes, Rusch, & Lamson, 1980). This approach is especially important since community placement involves identifying and training the types of skills that are likely to be the most crucial to overall adjustment in addition to specific job requirements.

White and Rusch (1983) provided a good model for future application of social and ecological validity criteria. In their study, five males and five females, ranging in IQ from 42 to 80 and from 20 to 41 years in age, were competitively employed in one of five cafeterias within large university food service settings. Over a 3-year period, five supervisors who worked with these clients evaluated each person every 60 days on a 26-item Work Performance Evaluation Form (see Chapters 13 and 15 for samples). Characteristics reviewed included job skills and work quality, level of responsibility, relationship to supervisors and co-workers, and ability to manage time. The ratings of co-workers and handicapped employees were also evaluated. Supervisors consistently rated performance lower than did co-workers, followed by the handicapped employees. Job and social skills proved to be highly interrelated, suggesting that social skills may be closely related to nonsocial skills in ascribing success to the individual placed. Another issue pertains to the role of co-workers in such ratings. Peer ratings are the best measure of children's social skills. It is likely, therefore, that they should receive greater emphasis also in competitive employment situations. At least, this type of assessment should be considered another important source of information. As a research tool, social validation must become an indispensable method of better understanding the means by which competitive employment can most efficiently be achieved

and utilized for the long-range self-fulfillment of employees.

FUNDING

One major problem encountered by competitive employment programs in this country is that the emerging emphasis on community integration is not being considered from the perspectives of multiple agencies serving persons with handicaps. For example, entitlement programs, such as Title XIX and Title XX, are based on the assumption that persons with handicaps cannot benefit from services that lead to competitive employment (Rusch, Chadsey-Rusch, White, & Gifford, 1985). Furthermore, policies have not kept pace with rapidly advancing teaching technologies that have greatly expanded what we considered the limits of employability. Thus, the disincentives outlined by Walls and his colleagues (Chapter 24) suggest that we have been successful in advancing our knowledge, but that we must now advocate for changes in funding policies to catch up with empirically documented trends in education and other services.

Funding problems are further compounded by a general incompatibility between funding programs and the results of state-of-the-art competitive employment practices. For example, as Rusch and his colleagues (1985) pointed out, work activity programs require that individuals, to be eligible for income maintenance (SSI), simultaneously must be shown to be incapable of competitive employment. As a result of this catch-22 situation, competitive employment and increased earnings may decrease overall income. Existing efforts to modify SSI eligibility based upon income is a positive step toward what appears to warrant a competitive employment large-scale evaluation.

PUBLIC RELATIONS

The public relations aspects of competitive employment also deserve attention. Since the ultimate goal is community integration, improved community relations are highly desirable. To this end, research is required to determine: 1) how persons with handicaps can most effectively be mainstreamed into the world of work, and 2) how public relations may best be advanced. Social validation studies and efforts to systematically identify and enhance business people's awareness of the needs of persons with handicaps through public relations in the community and talks to business majors in colleges and universities represent a viable approach.

SUMMARY AND CONCLUSIONS

Competitive employment of handicapped persons has undergone major developments in recent years. Through the contributions of many of the outstanding researchers in the field, the comprehensive overview of current research presented in preceding chapters makes the present volume a state-of-the-art review of competitive employment.

All efforts should be directed toward providing the necessary services and enhancing those skills that will result in a happier and more meaningful existence for persons with handicaps. In this concluding chapter, we delineate what some of these quality-of-life issues are, and how competitive employment plays a most significant role in promoting self-esteem, self-worth, and independence.

Special educators have served as leaders in enhancing the quality of life for persons with handicaps and have generally been at the forefront in habilitative efforts with adults. A greater multidisciplinary effort (involving psychologists, social workers, psychiatrists, local businessmen, and others who have an interest in enhancing competitive employment) is required to further capitalize on the current impact of social change. As noted, many related skills, such as dressing, using transportation, and so forth, must be trained in addition to specific job requirements. Therefore, a total community effort is required. Advances in competitive employment are among the best successes in the habilitation of persons with handicaps in recent years. Accomplishments to date, however, seem to have only scratched the surface, as pointed out by the contributors of this text.

REFERENCES

Andrasik, F., & Matson, J. L. (1985). Social skills with the mentally retarded. In M. A. Milan & L. L'Abate (Eds.), *Handbook of social skills training and research*. New York: John Wiley & Sons.

Azrin, N., & Armstrong, P. M. (1973). The "mini-meal"—A method for teaching eating skills to the profoundly retarded. *Mental Retardation, 11,* 9–13.

Azrin, N., & Foxx, R. (1972). A rapid method of toilet training the institutionalized retarded. *Journal of Applied Behavior Analysis, 4,* 89–99.

Baumeister, A. A., & Baumeister, A. A., Jr. (1978). Suppression of repetitive self-injurious behavior by contingent inhalation of aromatic ammonia. *Journal of Autism and Childhood Schizophrenia, 8,* 71–77.

Bijou, S. W. (1958). Operant extinction after fixed-interval schedules with young children. *Journal of the Experimental Analysis of Behavior, 1,* 25–29.

Bijou, S. W., & Baer, D. M. (1978). *Behavior analysis of child development*. Englewood Cliffs, NJ: Prentice-Hall.

Cronin, K., & Cuvo, A. J. (1979). Teaching mending skills to mentally retarded adolescents. *Journal of Applied Behavior Analysis, 12,* 401–406.

Dudley, J. R. (1983). *Living with stigma: The plight of the people who are labeled mentally retarded*. Springfield, IL: Charles C Thomas.

Edgerton, R. B. (1979). *Mental retardation: The developing child*. Cambridge, MA: Harvard University Press.

Foxx, R. M., & Azrin, N. H. (1973). The elimination of self-stimulatory behavior by overcorrection. *Journal of Applied Behavior Analysis, 6,* 1–14.

Gold, M. (1973). Research on the vocational habilitation of the retarded: The present, the future. In N. R. Ellis (Ed.), *International review of research in mental retardation* (Vol. 6, pp. 97–141). New York: Academic Press.

Jones, F. H., Simmons, J. G., & Frankel, F. (1974). Case study: An extinction procedure for eliminating self-destructive behavior in a 9-year-old autistic girl. *Journal of Autism and Childhood Schizophrenia, 4,* 241–250.

Luckey, R. E., Watson, C., & Musick, C. (1968). Aversive conditioning as a means of inhibiting vomiting, and rumination. *American Journal of Mental Deficiency, 73,* 139–147.

Matson, J. L. (1980). A control group study of pedestrian skills training for the mentally retarded. *Behaviour Research and Therapy, 18,* 99–106.

Matson, J. L. (1984). Social competence in developmentally disabled children. *National Academy of Education Monographs* (Vol. 1). Pittsburgh, PA: National Academy of Education.

Matson, J. L., & Andrasik, F. (1982). Training leisure time social interaction skills to mildly mentally retarded adults. *American Journal of Mental Deficiency, 86,* 533–542.

Matson, J. L., & DiLorenzo, T. (in press). Mental handicap and organic impairment. In C. R. Hollin & P. Trower (Eds.), *Handbook of social skills training.* Oxford, England: Pergamon Press.

Matson, J. L., DiLorenzo, T. M., & Esveldt-Dawson, K. (1981). Independence training of the severely retarded. *Journal of Mental Deficiency Research, 23,* 9–16.

Matson, J. L., & McCartney, J. R. (1981). *Handbook of behavior modification with the mentally retarded.* New York: Plenum.

Matson, J. L., Ollendick, T. H., & Adkins, J. (1980). A comprehensive dining program for mentally retarded adults. *Behavior Research and Therapy, 18,* 107–112.

Matson, J. L., & Senatore, V. (1981). A comparison of traditional psychotherapy and social skills training for improving interpersonal functioning of mentally retarded adults. *Behavior Therapy, 12,* 369–382.

Menchetti, B. M., Rusch, F. R., & Owens, D. (1983). Assessing the vocational needs of mentally retarded adolescents and adults. In J. L. Matson & S. E. Breuning (Eds.), *Assessing the mentally retarded* (pp. 247–284). New York: Grune & Stratton.

Neff, W. S. (1970). Work and rehabilitation. *Journal of Rehabilitation,* September-October, 16–22.

Ollendick, T., & Matson, J. L. (1978). Effectiveness of hand overcorrection for topographically similar and dissimilar self-stimulatory behavior. *Journal of Experimental Child Psychology, 25,* 396–403.

Rusch, F. R., Chadsey-Rusch, J., White, D. M., & Gifford, J. L. (1985). Programs for severely mentally retarded adults: Perspectives and methodologies. In D. Bricker & J. Filler (Eds.), *The severely mentally retarded: From research to practice* (pp. 119–140). Reston, VA: Council for Exceptional Children.

Rusch, F. R., & Mithaug, D. E. (1985). Competitive employment education: A systems-analytic approach to transitional programming for the student with severe handicaps. In K. C. Lakin & R. H. Bruininks (Eds.), *Strategies for achieving community integration of developmentally disabled citizens* (pp. 177–192). Baltimore: Paul H. Brookes.

Rusch, F. R., Weithers, J. A., Menchetti, B. M., & Schutz, R. P. (1980). Social validation of a program to reduce topic repetition in a non-sheltered setting. *Education and Training of the Mentally Retarded, 15,* 208–215.

Schutz, R. P., Jostes, K. F., Rusch, F. R., & Lamson, D. S. (1980). The use of contingent pre-instruction and social validation in the acquisition, generalization, and maintenance of sweeping and mopping responses. *Education and Training of the Mentally Retarded, 15,* 306–311.

Schutz, R. P., Rusch, F. R., & Lamson, D. C. (1979). Evaluation of an employer's procedure to eliminate unacceptable behavior on the job. *Community Services Forum, 1,* 4–5.

Sternberg, L., & Adams, G. L. (1982). *Educating severely and profoundly handicapped students.* Rockville, MD: Aspen.

Turkel, S. (1972). *Working.* New York: Pantheon.

White, D. M., & Rusch, F. R. (1983). Social validation in competitive employment: Evaluating work performance. *Applied Research in Mental Retardation, 4,* 343–354.

Epilogue

On Integrated Work
An Interview with Lou Brown

Frank R. Rusch

Professor Lou Brown is past president of The Association for Persons with Severe Handicaps. Brown has published several texts, chapters, and articles on topics related to curriculum development, instructional strategies, and vocational training. Recognized as one of the leading authorities on these topics, he has traveled extensively in the United States and internationally as a lecturer and consultant. Although well known for his research and teaching, he is best known for his advocacy and support of people with severe disabilities and their families, as well as young professionals in the field.

Q: Our society stresses the importance of employment. Should everyone, including persons with severe intellectual disabilities, work?

A: Yes. I am very American on that issue. I believe that the goal of our social service programs is to enculturate people. In this culture, people who do not work are not highly regarded. People who are severely intellectually disabled deserve to be respected and appreciated.

I believe we have to answer three basic questions in ways that allow people with severe intellectual disabilities to achieve and produce as best they can. The first question is, "*Who* should a person with severe intellectual disabilities be next to?" In the past, we said they should be next to people who are paid to serve them and other people with severe disabilities. Residents and professionals in institutional settings are obvious examples. This custodial orientation has not worked. People with severe intellectual disabilities must experience decent and enhancing social environments. They do best when in the physical presence of large numbers of nondisabled people. In sum, the more disabled you are, the more you need to be next to nondisabled people who are not paid to be near you.

The second question is, "*Where* are the most effective, creative, adjusted, and productive nondisabled people in our society during the day?" They are in real work places, the stores, factories, and offices of our nation. That is where people with severe intellectual disabilities should be.

The third question is, "*What* should people with severe intellectual disabilities be doing in real work environments next to nondisabled people?" They should not be squeezing a squeeze toy, looking at a mobile, or rocking in a chair with their foster grandparent. They should be doing what others around them are doing. They should be at least partially participating in work routines that will allow them to be absorbed into the social system. In the past, it has been too easy to excuse people from the responsibility of employment because they were intellectually disabled. Cultural disrespect, a segregated life space, and an outrageous bill for the taxpayer are too high a price.

Q: I agree with your point about work, especially where people should be working and what they should be doing. I believe, however, that there are people who will read this text who will say that there are people who are so significantly handicapped that their needs pose real, complicated questions with regard to employment options that ought to be available. Do we have good answers for these people with regard to work?

A: Well, I believe we have two rich sources of data to guide us when we address questions related to who should be working. We have what has happened to such people in the past, and we have our existing ideology. In one of your recent chapters (Rusch, Chadsey-Rusch, White, & Gifford, 1985), you offered that the environments in which people are placed and the demands and expectations these environments make are absolutely critical for decent human growth. In the past, most people believed that societal demands were too high for people with severe intellectual disabilities, and so sheltered workshops and activity centers proliferated. This was a terrible error. What did we do with or for them in the sheltered workshops? Generally not much and not enough at best.

Sheltered workshops and activity centers keep people with severe intellectual disabilities in custody. My ideology is that custodial models that pay people to *watch* other people act, usually in ways that are inappropriate, are unacceptable. We need integrated options that put pressure on the entire social system to consider a series of interventions that produce equitable and enhancing outcomes. For example, many years ago, the Madison school district operated a segregated school that served many students with behavior problems. As adults, those students are in sheltered workshops, which are logical and empirical extensions of segregated schools. They still have behavior problems. Now our students with severe intellectual disabilities attend integrated, chronological age-appropriate schools and express substantially fewer behavior problems. For the past 2 years, our school system has placed 100% of its 18 graduates in integrated employment environments. Some of these same people were smearing feces, biting

the backs of their hands, and punching people when they were in segregated settings as young children. The same can be said about people with severe physical and cognitive disabilities. I do not accept the position that we should maintain segregated settings so as to manage or tolerate deviance. I think that we have moral, programmatic, and economic responsibilities to provide opportunities for all who are disabled to function in the real world as you and I know it. That requires doing away with segregated developmental experiences and the ideologies that nurture them.

Q: Why is it considered feasible to place and maintain people with severe intellectual disabilities in integrated jobs now, when it did not appear even remotely possible in the recent past?

A: First, our predecessors chose segregated service models. We put millions of dollars, many years, thousands of careers, and many other resources into these services. We tried but we could not make them work for an acceptable proportion at a reasonable cost.

Second, our general cultural tolerance of related segregation has changed for the better. Race, gender, and religion are a few examples. Segregation on the basis of intellect is now being rejected.

Third, our attitude toward the achievement potential of all people with disabilities has changed. Initially we thought they could not make a contribution to the enterprise system. We were wrong. Then we thought they could produce, but only in a sheltered and highly subsidized environment. Wrong again. Then we thought that people without disabilities would not work next to them. Wrong again. We should be getting tired of being protectionist, custodial, negative, and wrong. It is time to be affirmative and right.

Fourth, the parents of today want integrated schools, decently preparatory educational curricula, and personal relationships with nondisabled people. They are not abandoning the quest for an integrated life space when their children reach age 21.

Fifth, the ways we organize our thoughts are

different. We used to think "all or nothing," independence, and "competition." Now we think part-time, subminimum, and support.

Sixth, out instructional technology is better. Specifically, we are better at teaching people to do real things in the real world and at devising adaptations that allow at least partial participation.

Seventh, more and more talented, creative, and ideologically sound young people are devoting their energies and careers to the enhancement of people with severe intellectual disabilities. This is particularly gratifying to me because I am a recruiter and trainer of young talent. Twenty years ago, it was extremely difficult to get the best and the brightest to work with the lowest intellectually functioning people in our society. Not so now.

In sum, major positive changes have been made in every other human endeavor, and it should not be shocking to anyone when we experience growth in our field. Arranging for historically excluded people to perform real work in the real world for real pay is exciting, challenging, meaningful, and fun. It is hard to stay excited about contributing to the "Great American ceramic glut" and other such nonsense too often experienced in segregated workshops and activity centers.

Q: Our preliminary research findings indicate that people with disabilities do behave more normally once they have been placed on jobs in excess of a few weeks, supporting one of your arguments. Lou, what about choice? Should our youth with handicaps have a choice between employment and unemployment?

A: I do not mind people choosing unemployment. But don't ask taxpayers to give them money to buy clothes, go to the movies, and have a great place to live. I think it's wonderful that some choose to live alone on a mountain, to spend their lives on a private island, or to live off the land. Fortunately, there are still some places in our country where you can do just those things. But don't ask the coal miner, the truck driver, the mail clerk, or any other hard-working citizen to pay for their dental bills, their telephone, or a video cassette

recorder. If you are unable to work, so be it. We will all pitch in and help. If you are able to work, but choose not to, good luck.

Additionally, I believe that people should have the opportunity to make experientially based choices. Thus, schools should develop systems that allow students to function in many actual job environments before they graduate. If they did, we would then have more meaningful information to arrange for and support informed vocational choices.

Q: Do you believe that a major goal of employment is meaningful integration?

A: Yes. We have just finished a survey based upon direct observations of people with severe intellectual disabilities who once were in our school system. Our data indicate that these people are too often alone after work and on weekends and holidays. For many, the only integrated experience they have is at work.

Q: Some argue that people who work in segregated facilities make money and can buy integration after work, and on weekends and holidays. Does money buy integration for people with severe intellectual disabilities?

A: No. Two major points are in order. First, in 1984 and 1985, the Madison Metropolitan School District graduated 18 people with severe intellectual disabilities. At this writing, 15 are being paid, 7 are earning minimum wages or above, and 8 earn below the minimum wage. If you can make money in a sheltered facility, you can make money in the real world.

Second, people who are severely intellectually disabled need longitudinal, consistent, and intensive interactions and relationships with people who are not disabled. Shopping and going to real movie theaters and restaurants are wonderful integrated experiences, but they do not allow for the building of many longitudinal relationships. If you work in the real world, you can have both.

Q: Tom Bellamy and his colleagues at the University of Oregon recently introduced the supported employment model, whereby the individual enjoys all the advantages of integrated employment, including the presence of nonhandicapped co-workers. They also receive wages for the work they provide. However, they are usually paid below minimum wage. You have advocated recently the consideration of no wages. How important is money in the development of one's career?

A: Money is important and all should be paid for work performed. However, assume that initially a person cannot work at a level that is acceptable for pay in the judgment of an employer. He or she still should be placed in that real work environment where he or she can receive relevant and meaningful instruction. Once that person demonstrates that he or she can be productive, he or she should be paid accordingly. Why? Because being in the presence of nondisabled people and doing meaningful work is critical to a decent life. Our dream is that one day in Wisconsin every single person with severe intellectual disabilities will do real work in the real world for real money. Some will require many, many years of training. Almost all, however, if provided adequate instruction and support, can learn to work adequately for direct pay in less than 1 year.

Before we leave this concept of supported work, it is important to communicate that in my view the word *supported* is a synonym for the word *integrated*. If supported does not mean integrated, I reject it.

Q: Lou, are you suggesting that all persons who are handicapped should be allowed to volunteer if volunteering leads to a job?

A: All citizens of the United States have the legal right to volunteer. Americans with severe intellectual disabilities are now recognized as citizens. All Americans who have severe intellectual disabilities have the legal right to volunteer.

The concept of "volunteering," however, usually means making a volitional decision to forego direct pay for the performance of meaningful work. When discussing people with severe intellectual disabilities, I try to separate the *volitional* foregoing of direct pay, volunteering, from other important concepts. Why? Because I have never met a person with severe intellectual disabilities who would get up in the morning, look out the window, determine it

was not a good day for golf or to get a haircut and, consequently, decide to volunteer time and talent to a worthy cause. The alternative I am currently comfortable with is the "extended training option." That is, all people who have severe intellectual disabilities have a right to learn to perform real work in the real world for direct pay. Some can learn to do so in 13 weeks, 1 year, or 1 month; others need longer. Those who need more time and training should have access to them. They should not be locked up in a sheltered facility for the rest of their lives if they cannot reach a certain production level at an arbitrary point in time.

Please realize that I live in Wisconsin. When Vince Lombardi was the coach of the Green Bay Packers, we never lost an exhibition or a regular season game. However, every once in a while, time would run out before the task was accomplished. Time should not be allowed to run out on any citizen's opportunity to learn to do real work in the real world for direct pay.

Q: Are you really saying that *one* strategy that you use to get people into integrated settings is not demanding a wage from the employer *before* the person enters the work environment?

A: Exactly. If an employer is willing to pay from the beginning, wonderful. Generally, however, you must first place a person with severe intellectual disabilities into a real job environment. *Then,* you must teach them to perform to meet the expectations of the employer. *Then,* direct pay will be dispensed contingently and proportionately.

The strategy of providing training in school buildings and in sheltered workshops and then moving to the real world has been a monumental failure. Segregated training clearly results in segregation. You once pointed out that around 1950 there were about six sheltered workshops in the United States. Now there are almost 5,000. Obviously, people with severe intellectual disabilities have been placed into sheltered workshops and activity centers and they have not been provided the instruction so necessary for performing real work in the real world for real money. That is, you cannot teach people who do not transfer training or generalize well in a segregated environment, and then expect them to function acceptably in a real job. That is why they stay locked up for life. You must teach in the real world.

Q: Lou, you have had a chance to read this text. What are some of its strengths?

A: First, before reading this book, readers will have a perception of what is attainable, what makes sense in their community, and what they think can be done for and with people who are severely intellectually disabled. This book challenges current understandings and assumptions about real-world employment. Specifically, this text will challenge us all to think about new, different, better, and more community-oriented day-to-day approaches to training for employment. Second, this book questions the goals that have traditionally guided our service options—goals that were established for people with disabilities 50 years ago. Children born in the 1980s must grow up and be prepared for environments that will be equitable and meaningful in the year 2000. They must experience methods and curricula that are much more effective than those that directed education and training for people who grew up in the past. This text contains technological innovations that will allow people to meet goals that the professional community would never have dreamed of even 10 years ago. Thus, this book is another nail in the coffin of segregation. It is an inspiration for both young people coming into our field and for people who work in segregated settings. After reading this book they can say, "If that is what is going on in Illinois, Vermont, Virginia, Oregon, and Wisconsin, why can't it happen here?" Finally, one of the biggest accomplishments of this book is that you have collected a group of people who have something to say to parents.

Q: Do you believe that parents will read this book?

A: Some will. All should. We can now deliver outcomes that most parents never thought possible. The problem is that not all parents have access to the best services or the best information regarding real work in the real world for their children. The only local options

most parents have are to place their children in sheltered workshops and activity centers or to keep them at home. Tragically, this extremely constricted option range controls their dreams, thoughts, and decisions. Now, if you live in the State of Washington, that is not the case. If you live in Madison, Wisconsin, that is not the case. In more and more places across this country, the stay-at-home or go-to-a-segregated-facility options are being challenged and rejected as untenable.

Q: What changes need to occur to promote wider adoption of new employment options?

A: I believe many existing rules and regulations that guide our services need to change. Unfortunately, rules and regulations that were designed decades ago are impeding progress. Technology, education, and philosophy have changed and so must our rules and regulations. Too much legislation and too many regulations have been designed by protectionists and segregationists. For example, we want to arrange for a student who is severely intellectually disabled to work at a local brokerage house. They ask us if this person can really do a job and we say yes, but maybe not at minimum wage just yet. They will pay for work performed. Let's say he or she can perform at 15% of the minimum wage. The bureaucratic problem is that in order to pay someone less than 25% of the minimum wage, the business must be licensed as or affiliated with an activity center. This company is not particularly interested in becoming an activity center. Nevertheless, such environments provide integrated work options and offer tasks that can be performed by people with severe intellectual disabilities. Running electric staplers and laminating machines, and collating and opening mail are a few examples. This regulation deprives people of the chance to work in the real world and it must be adapted or rejected.

A second example is what we call the "retarded contract paradox." With good intentions, government officials give a company a contract *only* if, for example, 75% of its work force consists of people who are disabled. Obviously, this is another practice that must be changed because it results in segregation. If someone can do meaningful work, he or she should be able to do it next to nondisabled workers. Let's give employers bonuses and contracts for hiring people with disabilities. Let's give unions bonuses for recognizing workers who assume supervisory and instructional responsibilities for employees with severe intellectual disabilities. Let's change and expand our dreams and practices.

Q: Can we expect some dramatic changes in the way we deliver services in the next 5–10 years?

A: Definitely. Look at the changes that are occurring in public school systems. The rapid movement from segregated to integrated service models, from school-only instruction to direct teaching in real community environments, from blatant curricular irrelevance to systematic preparation for functioning in the real world at age 21, and from custodial care and buck-passing to the assumption of responsibility for postschool functioning are but a few examples. Segregated services will pass. Do you really think a mother and father will work for years to get their child into a regular school and then allow him or her to be confined to a sheltered facilty for life? Of course not.

Q: When you refer to the people who are fostering segregation, are you talking about those operating rehabilitation facilities?

A: Yes. Many are standing in the way of real employment as we know it in our culture. Many who administer segregated facilities are understandably defending their segregationist practices. They must change or step aside. Many do not believe that people with severe intellectual and physical disabilities can learn to perform real work in integrated settings, and they do not know how to make it happen. My view is that the technology is available. If they believed it could happen, they could arrange it. Some now believe and changes are being made.

Most of the operators of these facilities have been delivering services in the same way for 25–30 years. They have tried the traditional approaches to community placement that you discuss in Chapter 1, and they have failed. They also have a stratified view of the value of

people—the more intelligent the person, the more value is ascribed. Thus, the lowest functioning people are kept locked up. Integrated community functioning values do not coexist well with sheltered facilities.

Q: Do you predict that parent attitudes toward sheltered facilities will change?

A: Yes. Public schools have been where most of the intense parent advocacy efforts in our field have been directed. Most of these informed and experienced parents have not yet been exposed to the existing adult service delivery systems. Ready or not, here they come.

In fact, let me give you a good example. There is a wonderful woman in Illinois. Her son aged out of the public high school and was evaluated by local workshop professionals who, of course, concluded that he should spend the rest of his life in their workshop. No conflict of interests there, right? She said, "No, I do not want that. What are my options?" Well, he could stay at home and do nothing. She shopped for and tried several other programs. Finally, she decided to do it herself. She gathered and organized other parents, and they actually arranged for jobs in the real world. But then their efforts fell short, because they did not have the skills and the time for the instruction and maintenance so necessary for long-term success. Specifically, they could not solve behavior, attitude, and adaptation problems. Nevertheless, they still did not want their children to stay at home and do nothing, nor would they tolerate the local workshop. They then went to the Illinois State Department of Rehabilitation Services. Ms. Susan Suter, the director, and her staff came through for them. As far as I know, they now have the first parent-operated, integrated employment program for people with severe intellectual disabilities in the United States. Their program will work because they have hired competent professionals to address the problems they could not resolve acceptably.

When other parents learn about this, local competition will develop all over. More and more of these parents with higher expectations and with the guts to challenge the sheltered monopoly will leave school systems, meet face-to-face with the adult service personnel, and say, "Change or get out of the way. We will do it ourselves. We did it before when you professionals said our children could not go to public schools and we will do it now."

These parents are spoiled in a sense because when they went through the public school system they were legally entitled to a service. Money was not an issue. Public schools cannot say, "We ran out of money to hire teachers, so your child stays home this year." Everybody in the United States is entitled to a free public education.

As more and more public school students turn 21 and are put on waiting lists for services, more and more parents will become irate and intolerant. They did not tolerate being told that their children were too handicapped for school and they will not tolerate being told they are too handicapped for the real world of work.

Q: Almost 40 programs were funded in 1985 in the state of Illinois to establish supported work models. Do you see this as a national phenomenon?

A: The integrated work model is spreading rapidly. Many young professionals are establishing private not-for-profit corporations. This is wonderful. It is vital that we get new, young talent into our field. This will result in competition, more individualization, more cost efficiency, and higher quality services. People with severe disabilities will have meaningful choices after never having had them before.

Q: Lou, do we have the personnel so necessary for the success of these changes? Is there a significant personnel shortage in the field right now?

A: No, and no doubt. I receive five phone calls a day for people who have some experience in integrated job development, placement, training, and follow-up. They are simply not available. Madeleine Will and Joan Standlee of the Office of Special Education and Rehabilitative Services in Washington are aware of this and I am sure corrective action is already being taken.

Q: Sounds like we have the seeds sown for a major revolution in secondary-level and adult special education.

A: Historically, curricula do not even come close to preparing people with severe intellectual disabilities to live, work, and play in the real world at age 21. We educators are getting great pressure from many good sources to radically change secondary and adult special education. Education is a means, not an end. The end is not life in a segregated facility. More and more people are asking, "What are you teaching my child? You spent all this money for 21 years and what do we have? Why didn't you teach something important?" Even though our field is in its infancy, we can still look back at some of the horrendous things we did under the guise of education and can only feel embarrassed. When I see people in my community whom I taught to touch red and blue blocks and to count four marbles during their last year in school, I feel terrible. I could have taught them to cross streets, ride buses, eat at public restaurants, and do real work in the real world.

Q: What is your view on relationships between work and other aspects of a person's life?

A: My dream is that some day all people with disabilities will live in decent homes, will perform real work in the real world for real money, will enjoy rich and varied recreation and leisure environments and activities, and will avail themselves of all relevant community environments. To have a decent job and have to live on an institution ward or in a group home with six other people with disabilities is unacceptable. All aspects of someone's life should be complementary, enhancing, and humane.

Q: Finally, are you saying that sheltered facilties must drop by the wayside?

A: Segregated services must go. All people need access to meaningful choices and opportunities. We can no longer put hard-earned tax dollars behind bad models. Local competition is wonderful. Monopolies and cartels must be rejected. Like "institutions for the retarded," these facilities were built by well-meaning people, but on foundations of sand. The strength and meaning of America are in our streets, factories, offices, parks, and neighborhoods. People with severe intellectual disabilities must be allowed access.

My response to your question is yes.

REFERENCE

Rusch, F. R., Chadsey-Rusch, J., White, D. M., & Gifford, J. (1985). Programs for severely mentally retarded adults: Perspectives and methodologies. In D. Bricker & J. Filler (Eds.), *Severe mental retardation: From theory to practice* (pp. 119–140). Reston, VA: Council for Exceptional Children.

Author Index

Subject Index

Pages in italics indicate table or figure